BASIC PRINCIPLES and TECHNIQUES in
Short-term Dynamic Psychotherapy

BASIC PRINCIPLES and TECHNIQUES in Short-term Dynamic Psychotherapy

Edited by
HABIB DAVANLOO, M.D.
*McGill University and
The Montreal General Hospital*

JASON ARONSON INC.
*Northvale, New Jersey
London*

THE MASTER WORK SERIES

First softcover edition 1994

Copyright © 1978 by Spectrum Publications Inc.

All rights reserved. Printed in the United States of America. No part of this book may be used or reproduced in any manner whatsoever without written permission from Jason Aronson Inc. except in the case of brief quotations in reviews for inclusion in a magazine, newspaper, or broadcast.

ISBN: 1-56821-354-9
Library of Congress Catalog Card Number: 94-72557

Manufactured in the United States of America. Jason Aronson Inc. offers books and cassettes. For information and catalog write to Jason Aronson Inc., 230 Livingston Street, Northvale, New Jersey 07647.

Contributors

H. DAVANLOO, M.D.
  Associate Professor of Psychiatry,
    McGill University
  Senior Psychiatrist and Director,
    External Services in Psychiatry
  Director,
    Institute for Teaching & Research of
    Short-Term Dynamic Psychotherapy
  Director and Coordinator,
    Psychotherapy Program
    The Montreal General Hospital
    Montreal, Canada

C. GOLDEN, M.D.
  Lecturer in Psychiatry,
    McGill University
  Director, Adolescent Unit
  Associate Director,
    External Services in Psychiatry
    The Montreal General Hospital
    Montreal, Canada

D.H. MALAN, M.D.
  Consultant,
    Travistock Clinic
    London, England
  Visiting Professor of Psychiatry,
    McGill University
    Montreal, Canada

J. MARMOR, M.D.
  Franz Alexander Professor of Psychiatry,
    University of Southern California
    School of Medicine
    Los Angeles, California
  Visiting Professor of Psychiatry,
    McGill University
    Montreal, Canada

P.E. SIFNEOS, M.D.
  Professor of Psychiatry,
    Harvard Medical School
  Associate Director,
    Department of Psychiatry,
    Beth Israel Hospital
    Boston, Massachusetts
  Visiting Professor of Psychiatry,
    McGill University
    Montreal, Canada

CONTRIBUTORS

M. STRAKER, M.D.
  Professor of Psychiatry,
    University of California
    Los Angeles, California
  Chief of Psychiatric Services,
    Brentwood Hospital
    Los Angeles, California

H. STRUPP, Ph.D.
  Distinguished Professor of Psychology
    Vanderbilt University
    Nashville, Tennessee

C. YUNG, M.D.
  Assistant Professor of Psychiatry,
    Texas Tech University
    School of Medicine
  R.E. Thomason General Hospital
    El Paso, Texas

Preface

One of my earliest observations when I was a psychiatric resident at the Massachusetts General Hospital was that a small percentage of the patients was in long-term psychoanalytically oriented psychotherapy, and a large percentage of cases was on the waiting list. All residents were in psychoanalysis, and almost every social worker was in controlled analysis. Most of our time was spent with patients in long-term psychoanalytic psychotherapy, and many of them for 2-3 sessions per week. This has been a common phenomenon in many psychiatric services.

In the early 1960's some of my observations in the outpatient psychiatric clinic of The Montreal General Hospital were that there was a very long waiting list, a small number of clinic patients were in long-term psychotherapy, and generally speaking, the number of patients treated with long-term psychotherapy was extremely limited compared to the number of patients seeking treatment. At the same time, a large number of patients were seen for from 5-10 minutes on a weekly or bi-weekly basis, without any clear understanding of their pathology or the goal of their therapy. There were patients who had been transferred from one resident psychiatrist to another, from one medical student to another, when their assignment to the outpatient psychiatric service had come to an end. The problem with this group of patients was enormous since they had developed institutional transference neurosis.

In 1961 and 1962, Manuel Straker and I undertook the study and careful appraisal of the clinic's strengths and weaknesses. We hoped to understand more clearly those factors responsible for the situation. Problems were evidenced by the high drop-out rate, lack of clear-cut goals in therapy, fragmented psychotherapeutic contact, and sloppy, inadequate assessment. A large percentage of the professional's time was taken up by the long-term psychotherapy program. At the same time, these patients were universally transferred from one resident psychiatrist to another. All these had "clogged" the work of the clinic. Our findings further indicated that in our setting, similar to other psychiatric facilities, the severity of the patient's complaint had always played a determining role in the decision to offer him long-term psychotherapy.

In 1962 we set-up a psychotherapeutic program of short-term duration, and I started to conduct a weekly seminar on this subject for the residents and medical students. During that year I treated a few patients, mainly for teaching purposes, but the force of tradition was not easy to overcome. A majority of the psychiatrists considered long-term psychotherapy the treatment of choice for psychoneurotic disorders. But in spite of the difficulties, in 1963 I began systematic research in a special kind of short-term psychoanalytic psychotherapy. My conviction was that some shorter form of psychotherapeutic technique could be the treatment of choice, and could be tailored to the needs of a selected group of patients suffering from psychoneurotic disorders. I then found myself in a difficult position. My basic intention had been to return to Boston, but I was very much encouraged by Bert Moll, who was then Psychiatrist-in-Chief, and decided to continue my work in his Department.

From 1963 to 1974 I had an opportunity to evaluate 575 patients, 130 of whom fulfilled the criteria for short-term psychoanalytic psychotherapy. These criteria were originally set-up in 1963 and were rather rigid. They were revised in 1965 after I had completed the treatment of 30 patients. Of the 130 patients who fulfilled our criteria for short-term dynamic psychotherapy, 115 were successfully treated within an average of 20 sessions. By 1974, when we had completed this phase of our research, we had documented a 2-7 years' follow-up on almost 40 percent of these patients. In all of our research projects the initial evaluation, psychotherapeutic process, and outcome have been audiovisually recorded.

Up to 1973 I was not acquainted with the work of Peter Sifneos in short-term psychotherapy. It was a coincidence that in 1973 while attending the 9th International Congress of Psychotherapy I became aware that this was one of his major interests. We discussed our common interest, and I invited him to collaborate with me on the faculty for a symposium in Montreal. In March 1974 he collaborated with me in a Montreal symposium on short-term dynamic psychotherapy, with the participation of more than 200 psychiatrists, mostly from Canada and the United States. This was the first time that we had ever seen each other in action.

During a discussion with Dr. Sifneos, he indicated to me that David Malan at Tavistock had been working along similar lines. In early September of 1974, I visited David Malan, and had the privilege of attending one of his workshops. This coming together of the three of us had a great impact on the future of short-term dynamic psychotherapy.

I became very interested in setting up the First International Symposium and Workshops on Short-Term Dynamic Psychotherapy, which was held in Montreal in March of 1975. It was an audiovisual symposium with Sifneos, Malan, Manny Straker, Hans Strupp, Maurice Dongier, Alan Mann and Bert Moll participating. Six hundred mental-health professionals, most of whom were psychiatrists and psychoanalysts, attended from various parts of the world. The overwhelming enthusiasm generated by the First International Symposium was the major motivating factor for my setting up the Second International Symposium in Montreal in March of 1976. Similar to the First, it was an audiovisual symposium and was co-sponsored by our Short-Term Psychotherapy Unit and the Department of Psychiatry of McGill University and the Psychiatric Service of Beth Israel Hospital of Harvard Medical School. Similar to the First International Symposium, the Second International Symposium focused primarily on the work of Malan, Sifneos, and myself, and generated a great deal of discussion centered around the similarities and differences in our conceptual frames of reference, our criteria for the selection of patients, the types of patients we treat, and techniques and outcomes. Seven hundred psychiatrists, psychoanalysts, and other mental-health professionals attended. The faculty had expanded. We had Judd Marmor, John Nemiah, Frederick Lowy, Samuel Eisenstein, and Saul Brown—some of them early collaborators with Franz Alexander. These two major international gatherings brought into focus the fact that the analytic psychotherapeutic community was ready for change.

The search that Franz Alexander and his colleagues conducted in the 1940's for ways to shorten the lengthy psychoanalytic process met with great resistance. The endeavors of Franz Alexander and his associates were a turning point in the search for a briefer psychoanalytic psychotherapy. It seems that the psychoanalytic community of three decades ago was not ready for this change. At a press conference which Judd Marmor and I attended during the Second International Symposium, he said, "The psychoanalytic community in the 1940's was not ready for change, and it was considered that the work of the Alexander group was muddying the pristine waters of psychoanalysis. Alexander was subjected to many abuses." But as Marmor indicates, the studies done at the Chicago Institute of Psychoanalysis opened the door to a more fluid and flexible approach. With these studies we saw the introduction of the concept of flexibility, experimentation, the setting of time limits, and different ways of dealing with transference phenomena.

The two International Symposia were catalytic agents which served to bring together the experiences and views of many hundreds of psychiatrists and psychoanalysts, most of them teachers. There was a convergence of three systematic research projects which were carried out independently at Harvard, at the Tavistock Clinic, and at McGill.

This volume contains the substance of the audiovisually recorded clinical presentations of the two International Symposia. The psychotherapeutic work which is described in detail was conducted predominantly by Peter Sifneos, David Malan, and myself. In view of the fact that the short-term dynamic psychotherapy practiced by each of us differs in scope and technique, this multi-authored book is intended to augment the knowledge of those who are involved in the teaching and the practice of short-term psychotherapy based on psychoanalytic principles.

In Chapter 3, Peter Sifneos very clearly describes his basic conceptual frame of reference on a specific kind of short-term dynamic psychotherapy which he calls "short-term anxiety-provoking psychotherapy." In Chapter 5, David Malan, as completely as brevity permits, describes his conceptual frame of reference of short-term dynamic psychotherapy as practiced at the Tavistock Clinic. The short-term dynamic psychotherapy which I have developed, and which I call "broad-focused short-term dynamic psychotherapy," is discussed in various chapters of this book. It is the culmination of systematic research since 1963, and throws light on the great confusion which existed and still exists about the role of short-term dynamic psychotherapy. I have never been convinced that short-term dynamic psychotherapy has a limited application and is a psychotherapeutic technique useful only in the treatment of mild neurotic cases. Nor have I ever agreed with those who see short-term dynamic psychotherapy as a technique which offers help best to those patients who are unable to deal with their emotional crisis and develop circumscribed neurotic conditions. Such therapy is of great value for this group of patients, but it has always been my conviction that it can be the psychotherapy of choice for patients suffering more severe psychoneurotic disorders of many years' duration, which have paralyzed their lives. Further, it has been my position that short-term dynamic psychotherapy, properly conducted, can bring about massive characterological change in a carefully selected group of patients by utilizing a specific psychotherapeutic technique. Our systematic audiovisually recorded research studies have validated these convictions, and in Part IV of this book I have attempted to demonstrate the short-term psychotherapy of this "sicker" group of patients.

All of the initial interviews presented in Part II, which were conducted by Sifneos, Malan, and myself, are patients from my private practice or from the Short-Term Psychotherapy Unit of The Montreal General Hospital. In Part IV, which describes techniques in detail, "The Case of the Man with the Façade," and "The Case of the Woman with a Prostitution Fantasy," come from the library of Peter Sifneos and the Psychiatric Service of Beth Israel Hospital. "The Case of the Woman in Mourning" comes from the short-term psychotherapy unit of Tavistock Clinic. I want to take this opportunity to express our thanks to all these patients for their cooperation; they have greatly contributed to our work. But I want also to reassure them and our readers that all of us have made sufficient changes to protect their confidentiality and at the same time have not made changes in the basic facts.

I want to express my gratitude to my teachers. It was my good fortune to be in training with the late Erich Lindemann and Elizabeth Zetzel, who greatly influenced my psychiatric thinking, and also to John Nemiah, who was not only a great teacher and admired friend, but who also made an effort to correct my errors in the English language whenever he reviewed my case histories. To my wife, Doris, for her continuing support and her invaluable work in both the organization of the Symposia and the preparation of this manuscript, I extend my deepest appreciation.

My gratitude, also, goes to Maurice Dongier, Professor and Chairman of the Department of Psychiatry at McGill, for his continued interest in and support of these projects. I also express my thanks to Alan Mann, Psychiatrist-in-Chief of The Montreal General Hospital, who has always encouraged us, for his continued interest in our work. I should like to thank Peter Kerby, our Media Director, who has so devotedly worked for the two Symposia, and to express my grateful thanks to Dawn Smith, Claire Messier, and Jacqueline Pichette, who did so much for the Symposia, and who did the typing and preparation of this manuscript.

H. Davanloo, M.D.
Montreal
February, 1978

Introduction

One can expect psychiatry to remain in the forefront of controversies in social medicine for the next few years. And among many topics in psychiatry, one can expect psychotherapies and psychotherapists to remain in the forefront of these controversies.

The critical questions most often faced are "What makes the difference between psychoanalysis and briefer forms of psychotherapy?" "Do we have evidence that brief psychotherapy results are generally more limited than those of psychoanalysis?" "Do we have good reasons to believe that psychoanalytically trained therapists do a better job than others in the field of briefer psychotherapies?" "Is psychotherapy going to remain eternally a matter of faith?" Jungian, Adlerian, Neo-Freudian, Kleinian, Orthodox Freudian schools of psychoanalysis, Gestalt Therapy, Reality Therapy, etc.—all lie side by side in the most widely read and comprehensive textbooks of psychiatry, unembellished by any convincing argument that one method is more indicated than another in a specific case. Far from producing a progressive selection of the best methods and of their indications, the past decade has yielded an increase in the variety of therapeutic approaches. "New Psychotherapies" flourish one after the other in the course of years like religions in the course of centuries, with as little scientific evidence of the superiority of one over another.

There have been some attempts to bring order out of chaos. A mammoth effort to analyze and synthetize the data was carried out by Bergin and Strupp (1) with the support of the National Institute of Mental Health. The outcome was not very encouraging to say the least. A few years later, Bergin and Strupp wrote their excellent follow-up book: *Changing Frontiers in the Science of Psychotherapy* (2). They canvassed most of the U.S. experts in the field, and pointed to two outstanding features of psychotherapy research: the despair about research expressed by leading workers in the field, and the lack of impact of research on clinical practice. A majority of the contributors seemed rather pessimistic about the future.

After the pioneering effort of Alexander in the early Fifties, however, a handful of keen clinician-researchers such as Drs. David Malan (3,4), Sifneos (5) and Davanloo are illuminating very important developments in brief psychotherapy. For fifteen years now, Dr. Davanloo has been developing the short-term psychotherapy unit of The Montreal General Hospital, accumulating experience and collecting follow-up data on more than 130 patients. And for three years he has had the courage and perseverance to bring together in Montreal some of the leading experts in dynamic short-term psychotherapy—experts in the field of systematic evaluation of outcome of this very important therapeutic modality.

These symposia have had a remarkable impact on the psychiatric community, attracting hundreds of psychiatrists and other mental health professionals from numerous countries. They have been able to discuss criteria for patients' selection, indications, details of techniques, research strategies, based not only on case histories and statistics, but on the live material provided by videotapes.

The present book is a summary of the proceedings of the First and Second International Symposiums (1975 and 1976). It is primarily clinical and contains selected presentations to these two symposiums. Both for those who could attend and discuss the present book and for those who could not, this volume will be an invaluable source of reference and a report of further progress in their work.

MAURICE DONGIER, M.D.
Professor and Chairman
Department of Psychiatry
McGill University
Director
Allan Memorial Institute
Montreal, Canada

REFERENCES

1. Bergin, A.E., and H.H. Strupp. *Research in Individual Psychotherapy: A Bibliography.* Washington, D.C.: National Institute of Mental Health. 1969.
2. Bergin, A.E. and H.H. Strupp. *Changing Frontiers in the Science of Psychotherapy.* Chicago, Ill.: Aldine, Atherton, Inc., 1972.
3. Malan, D.H. *A Study of Brief Psychotherapy.* New York: Plenum, 1963; Rosetta Editon, 1975.
4. Malan, D.H. *The Frontiers of Brief Psychotherapy. An Example of the Convergence of Research and Clinical Practice.* New York: Plenum Medical Book Co., 1976.
5. Sifneos, P.E. *Short-Term Psychotherapy and Emotional Crisis.* Cambridge, Mass.: Harvard University Press, 1972.

CONTENTS

Preface, *by H. Davanloo*

Introduction, *by M. Dongier*

PART I

Chapter 1
Current Trends in Psychotherapy, *by J. Marmor* 1

Chapter 2
Evaluation, Criteria for Selection of Patients for Short-Term Dynamic Psychotherapy: A Metapsychological Approach, *by H. Davanloo* 9

Chapter 3
Short-Term Anxiety-Provoking Psychotherapy, *by P.E. Sifneos* 35

Chapter 4
Exploring the Limits of Brief Psychotherapy, *by D.H. Malan* 43

PART II
EVALUATION, CRITERIA FOR SELECTION OF PATIENTS FOR SHORT-TERM DYNAMIC PSYCHOTHERAPY

Chapter 5

Short-Term Dynamic Psychotherapies
Introduction, *by A.M. Mann* **71**

    Continuum of Psychotherapeutic Possibilities
    and Basic Psychotherapeutic Techniques,
    by H. Davanloo **74**

    Evaluation, Criteria for Selection of Patients,
    by P.E. Sifneos **81**

    Evaluation, Criteria for Selection of Patients,
    by D.H. Malan **85**

Chapter 6

"The Case of the Italian Housewife", *by P.E. Sifneos* **99**

Chapter 7

"The Case of the Secretary with the Violent Father",
by D.H. Malan **129**

Chapter 8

"The Case of the College Student", *by P.E. Sifneos* **149**

Chapter 9

"The Case of the Teeth-Grinding Woman",
by H. Davanloo **171**

Chapter 10

"The Case of the Secretary with the Temper Tantrums",
by D.H. Malan **201**

Chapter 11

"The Case of the Woman in the Tower of London",
by P.E. Sifneos **225**

Chapter 12

"The Case of the Angry, Childlike Woman",
by H. Davanloo 247

PART III
THE BORDERLINE BETWEEN EVALUATION AND THERAPY

Chapter 13

Implications of the Interviewer's Technique on
Selection Criteria, by C. Golden 269

    "The Case of the Submissive Woman" 275
    "The Case of the Man With a Headache" 277

Chapter 14

Where Does Evaluation End and Therapy Begin?
by C. Yung and H. Davanloo 291

    "The Case of the Man with an Impulse
    to Murder his Stepfather" 293

    "The Case of the Masochistic Statistican" 299

Chapter 15

Short-Term Dynamic Psychotherapy of One to Two
Sessions' Duration, H. Davanloo 307

    "The Case of the Woman with the Fear of
    Losing Her Husband" 308

PART IV
TECHNIQUES OF SHORT-TERM DYNAMIC PSYCHOTHERAPY

Chapter 16

Principles of Technique in Short-Term Anxiety-Provoking
Psychotherapy, by P.E. Sifneos 329
             by D.H. Malan 332

Chapter 17

Basic Methodology and Technique of Short-Term
Dynamic Psychotherapy, *by H. Davanloo* **343**

    "The Case of the Cement-Mixer Man" **345**

    The Patient as the Evaluator of the Psychotherapeutic
    Process and Outcome **381**

    Psychodynamic Criteria For Evaluation of Treatment
    Outcome of This Patient **387**

Chapter 18

Techniques of Short-Term Anxiety-Provoking
Psychotherapy (1), *by P.E. Sifneos* **389**

    "The Case of the Man with the Facade" **390**

Chapter 19

Techniques of Short-Term Anxiety-Provoking
Psychotherapy (II), *by P.E. Sifneos* **433**

    "The Case of the Woman with a Prostitution Fantasy" **433**

Chapter 20

Techniques of Short-Term Dynamic Psychotherapy (I),
by D.H. Malan **455**

    "The Case of the Woman in Mourning" **455**

Chapter 21

Techniques of Short-Term Dynamic Psychotherapy (II),
by H. Davanloo **469**

    "The Case of the Man Obsessed with the
    Small Size of His Genitals" **469**

PART V

Chapter 22

Teaching and Supervision of STAPP, *by P.E. Sifneos* **491**

Chapter 23

The Challenge of Short-Term Dynamic Psychotherapy,
by H.H. Strupp 501

Chapter 24

Short-Term Dynamic Psychotherapy: A Retrospective
and Perspective View, by M. Straker 515

Chapter 25

Research Strategies in Short-Term Dynamic Psychotherapy,
by C. Yung 527

INDEX 551

BASIC PRINCIPLES and TECHNIQUES in Short-term Dynamic Psychotherapy

Part I

Chapter 1
Current Trends in Psychotherapy

J. MARMOR

The past twenty-five years have witnessed an explosive profusion of psychotherapeutic techniques. Any effort to classify or organize these must of necessity be somewhat arbitrary, since there is a tremendous amount of overlapping between the various techniques. However, it seems possible to discern three major trends in contemporary psychotherapy, together with a multitude of minor ones—the latter not necessarily minor in terms of the number of their adherents, but rather in terms of the degree of their acceptance in scientific and academic circles as compared with the major trends.

The major trends that can be delineated are those of dynamic psychotherapy, behavior therapy and group therapy. These are by no means discrete entities, however. Dynamic psychotherapy may be individual- or group-oriented, as may behavior therapy. Similarly, group therapy may be either psychodynamically or behaviorally oriented, or may utilize still other frames of reference, as we shall see.

THE DYNAMIC PSYCHOTHERAPIES

For most of this century, and certainly throughout the 1930's, 1940's and 1950's, the dynamic psychotherapies were clearly the dominant model in American psychiatry. To a certain extent they remain so. These therapies rest primarily on the psychoanalytic framework developed by Sigmund Freud, but also include a wide range of modifications proposed by other analytic schools. From its earliest inception, however, the length and expense of the original psychoanalytic model have caused some concern, even among the pioneers in psychoanalysis. Efforts to find shorter, more efficient methods within the analytic framework go back to the earliest work of Ferenczi and Rank, who were the first psychoanalysts to experiment consciously and deliberately with more active techniques.

Their work was premature, since the psychoanalytic model was still in the process of developing, and the early psychoanalytic community was not yet ready to consider such technical innovations. Then, beginning in the early 1940's, the Chicago Psychoanalytic Institute, under the leadership of Alexander and French, began to hold a series of symposiums and workshops on brief psychotherapy. Out of the studies of the Chicago group the classic book entitled *Psychoanalytic Therapy* emerged in 1946. Initially greeted with hostility in the analytic world, its eventual impact was tremendous. It presented for the first time a well considered psychoanalytically oriented framework for short-term flexible alternatives to the classic psychoanalytic model for some patients. It stimulated considerable clinical experimentation, particularly in the length of interviews, the frequency of interviews and even their regularity. It transformed the dynamic psychotherapist from a passive listener into an active participant observer, and went so far as to suggest that it was possible to control and manipulate the development of transference, depending on the psychodynamic needs of the patient. Out of this seminal work eventually emerged the basis for crisis therapies and other short-term dynamic psychotherapies. What is of paramount importance in this work of Alexander and French is their demonstration that it is possible to achieve not only symptomatic change, but even characterological change by less intensive, short-term techniques, at least with selected patients.

These changes also led to a greater focus within the dynamic psychotherapy field on the *process* of psychotherapy, on the recognition that the psychotherapeutic process was transactional, taking place *between* patient and therapist rather than imposed by the therapist. The therapeutic process began to be recognized as a learning process, which led to a renewed interest in theories of learning. In addition, through the later work of Jerome Frank, there developed a greater recognition and respect for the influence of motivation, faith and trust on the part of the patient in the therapeutic outcome. Although transference had always been a major area of interest in psychoanalytically oriented therapy, there now developed a new interest in countertransference, as well as a heightened appreciation of the reality factors that play a part both in the therapeutic process and in the outcome. Finally, the focus on process led to a growing realization that inasmuch as patients were able to be helped by therapists of different theoretical persuasions, the theoretical orientation in itself could not be the *specific* determinant of therapeutic change and there had to be certain basic common denominators in the therapeutic process that cut across these diverse theoretical frames of reference.

THE BEHAVIOR THERAPIES

Although the behavior therapies have come into prominence only in the past twenty years or so, their earliest origins, as Isaac Marks has pointed out in a recent review article, probably go back many centuries to the recognition that fears could be "desensitized" by a gradual exposure to the phobic object. Freud himself arrived at a kind of behavioral conclusion in the psychoanalytic treatment of phobias when he recognized that there came a point where it was imperative to expose the patient to the phobic situation in order to enable him to overcome it. Modern behavioral therapies are strongly rooted in academic psychology and based on theories of learning and conditioning, notably those of Pavlov, Hull and Skinner. One of the earliest and best-known of these techniques was that of reciprocal inhibition, introduced by Joseph Wolpe, based on the assumption that if an individual could fantasy a graded hierarchy of his fears while in a state of relaxation the fears would become progressively desensitized. More recently, techniques of operant conditioning, based on reward-punishment techniques, have come increasingly to the fore, together with a wide variety of other techniques such as desensitization, flooding or implosion, rehearsal, and exposure to anxiety-provoking situations, either in fantasy or *in vivo*. Although behavioral therapists initially claimed a wide area of indications for their approach, it is becoming clear that behavioral techniques are the primary methods of choice particularly in phobic disorders, certain social anxieties, some obsessive-compulsive rituals and certain sexual dysfunctions. In these areas they have made a major contribution and have often cut down considerably the length of time needed to achieve a reversal of clinical symptomatology. Isaac Marks estimates that behavioral therapies are primarily indicated in only about 10 percent of all adult psychiatric disorders, although they may be useful as adjunctive therapies in a wide variety of others. In general, they seem to be more useful in symptom neuroses than they are in character disorders. In the latter, dynamic psychotherapy still, as a rule, seems to be more effective.

GROUP THERAPIES

Group therapies as a new modality first came into prominence in the 1930's, but their influence did not begin to spread until the 1940's. The earliest group therapies were all analytically oriented. Originally, the approaches seemed simply a transfer of one-to-one techniques within a group situation, but as systems theory became better understood the multiple transference and transactional relationships within groups began to be more clearly recognized and utilized therapeutically. More recently, a group of English group therapists, mainly Kleinian, have emphasized certain integral characteristics of the group itself, and tend to make interpretations involving the dynamics of the group as a whole.

Psychodynamic group therapies can be oriented either toward Freudian theory, neo-Freudian theory or Kleinian theory. Other group therapies, however, abjure the psychoanalytic framework and place emphasis instead on various behavioral techniques or on techniques designed to bring out emotional abreactions or various types of sensate stimulation designed to break down inhibitions. In recent years many special types of groups have emerged—groups for married people, for single people, for divorced people, for homosexuals, for criminals, for multiple families, and so on. A special type, or subtype, of group therapy is conjoint marital therapy, which treats husband and wife in a marriage unit as a small group and attempts to understand their transactional relationship to one another rather than analyzing each of them individually. Perhaps the most important subtype under group therapy that has emerged in recent years, however, is family therapy, which makes an effort to treat the entire family as a dynamic group or small system. Family therapy is showing its greatest application in the treatment of children and adolescents, but it has a unique place in the group therapies because the family is the only group which has a continuity that goes beyond the therapeutic situation and extends into the total daily life of the individuals involved. Thus its potentials for therapeutic change are undoubtedly very great, although the field of family therapy is still in its infancy.

OTHER THERAPIES

We now move over to the large and disparate group of "other" therapies, which I have designated as "minor" ones. Perhaps the largest of these is a group of therapies which I would designate as *sensate-emotive*, essentially designed to encourage emotional abreaction and utilizing sensate stimulation of various kinds in an effort to facilitate such abreaction and break down emotional inhibitions. These therapies are usually conducted in groups. Some of them take the form of marathons, nude or otherwise. Others are described as T-groups or sensitivity groups. Others place a great deal of emphasis on various sensual arousal techniques, such as the touching-feeling types of therapy that became so prominent at Esalen in northern California and are sometimes irreverently referred to as "group-gropes." Many of these techniques utilize various types of physical massage and manipulation in an individual or group context. Many carry exotic names like Arica, Lifespring, Mind-Control, etc. Gestalt therapy, so-called, is a combination of sensate-emotive techniques that also makes use of various aspects of dynamic and behavioral therapy but places its primary emphasis on emotional expressiveness rather than on cognitive awareness. Another subvariant of the sensate-emotive therapies is primal scream therapy, which rests on the improbable assumption that therapeutic progress depends on the ability to recall the earliest infantile memories going back to birth itself, accompanied by loud and violent expressions of emotion. A somewhat related approach is that of scientology, which first appeared in the 1940's under the name "dianetics." This began as a science-fiction fantasy, but its author capitalized on it when he discovered that some people were taking it seriously. After a brief flurry of popularity, it came into disfavor, but in recent years has had a renaissance under the religious cloak of the "Church of Scientology." One of the assumptions involved in this approach is that the patient must be able to recall not merely the moment of birth, but even experiences within the uterus!

Another large group of therapies fall into what might be called the religio-inspirational therapies. These rest heavily on Eastern religions and Eastern philosophies, and are led by various charismatic individuals, usually of Eastern origin. Variants include techniques of yoga, Zen and transcendental meditation, the success of the last presumably depending on a uniquely chosen "mantra" for each individual. The existential therapies rest heavily on psychodynamic orientations, but some of them also have ties to the religio-inspirational group.

A therapeutic approach that enjoyed some prominence about a decade ago was the so-called "reality therapy" of William Glasser, which treats all psychopathology as though it is essentially a matter of personal responsibility on the part of the patient. Although this approach has some credibility in the treatment of the delinquent youths for whom it was originally intended, it becomes a rather simplistic model when applied to more severe types of psychopathology, including psychosis. Its chief methodological approach consists of the therapist talking to patients like a "Dutch uncle," and it seems to be a throwback to the exhortative techniques used in the nineteenth century before the advent of psychoanalysis.

More recently, a remarkable phenomenon known as "EST" (for Erhardt Seminar Training) has developed on the West Coast and is rapidly spreading to other parts of the country. This is a technique which borrows cleverly from a variety of approaches including dynamic, behavioral and sensate-emotive approaches in large group settings, utilizing marathon sessions and modern techniques of mass merchandising.

Still other approaches include the hypno-therapies, which may be partly behavioral, partly analytic; various self-help groups such as Alcoholics Anonymous, and others for tall people, for obese people, for ex-convicts, for drug addicts, etc.; techniques leaning heavily on technological devices, such as biofeedback, audiovisual techniques utilizing televised sessions as a feedback experience to patients, and efforts to develop computer techniques of therapy. There are many other types of approaches, too numerous to mention, that are variations on these themes.

What can we make of this confusing array of therapies? Are there any underlying organizing principles that explain what has been going on in the psychotherapies in the past two decades? I believe there are three major cultural currents that shed some light on what has been happening. The first of these is the strong counterculture movement that developed out of the disillusionment of the post–World War II generation, with a technology that threatens human existence with nuclear annihilation and the exhaustion of our natural resources. This movement is antiintellectual, antiscientific and antitechnological, and consequently it looks for answers outside of the scientific-intellectual paradigms. This current is responsible for the strong trend toward the sensate-emotive therapies and the religio-inspirational therapies that occupy such an important area on the current psychotherapeutic scene, as well as, incidentally, in the renascent widespread interest in the supernatural, mysticism, astrology and the like that we are witnessing.

The second major trend is in direct contrast to the first, namely, an emphasis on technological factors. Out of this trend come the techniques that make use of biofeedback, audiovisual assists, computers and the adjuvant use of psychopharmacological medication.

The third cultural current, and in some ways perhaps the most important one affecting the contemporary psychotherapeutic scene, is the socioeconomic transition that has been taking place in this country since World War II. Combined with a growing acceptance of the relevance of psychotherapy in the treatment of emotional distress, there has been a growing emphasis on the right to treatment and a growing demand for access to treatment by people of all economic levels. This has put great pressure on the psychiatric profession and on mental health professionals in general to develop more efficient and economical techniques of therapy. The expanding emphasis on short-term techniques and on group therapies is in large part a response to these cultural pressures. It seems fair to predict that with the ultimate development of some form of national health insurance and the continued impact of third-party payers this trend will accelerate in the years ahead. We can also anticipate that there will be increasing pressure on psychotherapists to justify what they are doing and to be accountable to the third-party payers with regard to the length and expense of the therapeutic procedures involved.

We are left still with a final question. Given this tremendous profusion of psychotherapies, how can we find our way through the confusing maze of differing techniques? My own conviction is that there is no substitute for a psychodynamic understanding as the basic framework upon which any variations in technique must rest. This presupposes a sound knowledge of psychodynamic principles, an understanding of the genetic (historical) roots of the patient's problems and an ability to evaluate the factors involved in the presenting psychopathology. Obviously, the more psychiatrists possess such competence, the better they are able to make a rational decision about what psychotherapeutic technique or combination of techniques is most likely to be helpful to any particular patient. It is precisely this competence that distinguishes the clinical approach of the well-trained psychotherapist from the indiscriminate merchandiser of one or another form of psychotherapeutic gimmickry.

Chapter 2

Evaluation, Criteria for Selection of Patients for Short-Term Dynamic Psychotherapy: A Metapsychological Approach

H. DAVANLOO

Freud opened a new horizon to the science of human behavior. His contribution to the understanding of human behavior from a psychodynamic point of view implied that the psychological process underlying the symptoms should be investigated and studied. With this contribution psychiatry saw a radical change in the static nosology, which then was replaced by a fluid and dynamic method.

It was nearly ninety years ago, about 1888, when Freud started using the cathartic method; within a span of twenty years he arrived at a technical procedure which is now known as the classical psychoanalytic technique. Psychoanalysis has traditionally been considered a method of investigation of unconscious mental processes, Freud's greatest contribution: a theory of human personality, and a technique of therapy. I have no intention here of elaborating further on these issues, but one might say that Freud's formulation is more or less accepted as the basis of present-day classical psychoanalysis—the use of the method of free association, the development of a regressive transference neurosis, and the resolution thereof by the exclusive technique of interpretation.

By 1905, Freud had set down in his paper "On Psychotherapy" the standards for undergoing psychoanalysis. He outlined four major criteria: the patient must (1) suffer from a chronic neurotic syndrome (which came to be called "transference neurosis"); (2) have passed adolescence but not yet reached fifty years of age; (3) possess "a good intelligence"; and (4) show "a reliable character." These criteria were easy to use up to the time patients were classified into "analyzable transference neuroses" and "untreatable narcissistic neuroses." But the problems started when psychoanalysis came to be used in a wide range of character problems.

With the birth of psychoanalytic ego psychology in the past few decades, we have seen the development of a wide range of dynamically oriented psychotherapeutic methods. Freud's publication of *The Ego and the Id* in 1923 might be considered the birth of ego psychology. We also see further emphasis on ego psychology in his 1926 paper, "The Problem of Anxiety." Then came the publication of Anna Freud's *The Ego and the Mechanism of Defense*.

Psychoanalysis and clinical psychiatry subsequently saw a shift from an id-oriented psychology to an ego-oriented psychology, initiated by Freud in 1923 and carried forward by Anna Freud, Heinz Hartmann, and many others, which was followed by the introduction of cultural orientation from Horney and Erikson, and the development of the interpersonal framework of Sullivan and the adaptational framework of Rado.

In the past few decades, as a result of the many changes in the theoretical and therapeutic concepts of classical psychoanalysis, as well as elaboration in the theoretical concept of psychoanalytic ego psychology and its practical application to psychotherapy, we have seen the development of a wide range of dynamically oriented psychotherapeutic methods. Still, despite this development, we have been witnessing the fate of patients who are forced to accept the only standard prescription of treatment in vogue in a specific psychiatric setting, with no relevance to individual needs. In my opinion, what is urgently needed in the clinical practice of psychiatry is a refined set of criteria for selection of patients for a specific psychotherapeutic method.

It is the hope of this volume that in the area of short-term dynamic psychotherapy we will be able to outline the specific steps that must be taken in order to establish the criteria for selection, the technique, and the process in this specific kind of psychotherapy. Obviously, we are not able to draw a clear line between evaluation of patients, criteria for selection, technique, and psychotherapeutic process and outcome. The personality of the evaluator, and his style and technique, affect to a great extent the evaluation process, which influences the type of patient he selects and the psychotherapeutic technique he uses. Finally, all of these influence the therapeutic results. In this paper I will focus primarily on the process of evaluation and then elaborate on the criteria for selection of patients for short-term dynamic psychotherapy.

The suitability of a patient for a particular type of psychotherapeutic method requires a clinical evaluation that is not based simply on a clinical diagnosis. Psychotherapeutic treatment cannot be carried out rationally unless the therapist has a clear idea of the central dynamic structure of the patient's problem and determines what it is that he wants to correct. This should be done in the first or second diagnostic interview. Every clinician must develop to a sufficient degree the clinical skill to understand and describe his patient in the light of his developmental history, the genetics of his disturbances, his intrapsychic conflicts, the strength of his id and ego forces, his character structure, and his adaptation to and interaction with his environment. The clinician's ability to think in dynamic, genetic, economic, structural, and adaptive terms is central to sound evaluation and therapeutic planning.

Maurice Levine has described in excellent fashion an outline of dynamic criteria for treatment choice. The essential tasks of a therapist are as follows:

 I. Formulation of a clinical diagnosis
 II. Formulation of a dynamic diagnosis
 III. Formulation of a genetic diagnosis
 IV. Formulation of psychotherapeutic possibilities
 V. Transference, countertransference evaluation

I. FORMULATION OF A CLINICAL DIAGNOSIS

The present state of clinical diagnostic formulation is unsatisfactory. It is obvious that external adjustment does not necessarily mean intrapsychic stability and mature achievement. The same applies to psychopathology; one cannot measure psychopathology in terms of immediate symptomatology. In general, a patient's distress and symptomatology should be understood and evaluated in the light of their developmental implications. Descriptive diagnosis gives us limited information with respect to the choice of psychotherapeutic methods.

In the past few decades the rapid integration of psychiatry with the rest of medicine has been helpful in creating the need to have psychiatric nomenclature and classification closely integrated with those of other medical specialties. There has been increasing success on the part of the World Health Organization in promoting a uniform international classification. D.S.M. and its latest edition have no doubt been of high value in general hospital psychiatry, community mental health centers, mental hospitals, and office practices.

But there is still considerable confusion in that the present diagnostic classification is not a guideline to treatment. It is a clinical fact that patients who belong to a similar clinical diagnosis may vary considerably from the point of view of their individual psychodynamics, character structure, and suitability for a particular psychotherapeutic method. The therapeutic potential of a patient cannot be determined by the clinical diagnosis of that patient.

II. FORMULATION OF A DYNAMIC DIAGNOSIS: PSYCHODYNAMIC FORMULATION

Dynamic formulation refers to the evaluation and understanding of the forces that, in the current life of the patient, are operative in producing the patient's difficulties and problems, the external and internal forces that account for the patient's symptoms. Psychodynamic evaluation refers to the evaluation of conscious and unconscious forces and conflicts, social and environmental forces that are influencing the patient and playing a major role in his illness. The evaluator should determine how much of the patient's problem is internal and how much is reactive to his environment, the nature of the patient's underlying conflicts, the strength of his ego-adaptive capacities in relation to his life stresses. It is based on the psychoanalytic theory of psychopathology that neurotic symptoms are the result of an unconscious attempt at a compromise solution of an unconscious, painful intrapsychic conflict or an unconscious conflict within the person related to his external environment. Psychic symptoms are regressive phenomena with an unconscious meaning; they are a compromise formation between the repressed and the repressive forces of the ego, between ego defense and instinctual impulses that are not accepted by the superego.

The major tasks of the evaluator can be summarized as follows:

> Formulation of the way in which an external force, an interpersonal conflict, gives rise to an intrapsychic conflict and anxiety, and of the way in which the defensive operation of the ego attempts to lessen the anxiety.

> Dynamic assessment of the various structural components of the patient's personality; evaluation of an overall ego function in the maintenance of adaptation; evaluation of the patient's intrapsychic equilibrium and his external environment.

Evaluation and identification of the presence of a crisis. (Freud originally stated that an adult neurosis breaks out when a contemporary life situation repeats a traumatic infantile situation.)

It is a well-documented clinical fact that the optimal opportunity for successful intervention is at the time of crisis. This is the time of greatest fluidity within the defensive structure, and the patient might show the greatest potential for change. It is the time when our psychic apparatus, faced with external and internal challenges and changes, is capable of progressive and regressive responses, as shown in the work of Eric Lindemann and Gerald Kaplan.

Regression in a crisis situation is not exclusively pathological. This is well shown by Ernst Kris and others who consider regression an essential concomitant of learning and of the creative process. We all know that in the course of psychoanalytic treatment regression is an essential concomitant of genuine insight. A crisis may be associated with regression which is characterized by symptom formation, and this in a potentially healthy person might bring about the resolution of previously unresolved conflicts and ultimately increase emotional maturity.

Maturational crisis should be taken into consideration; adolescence, with the onset of sexual maturity, might revive unresolved early conflicts and lead to manifest symptom formation. Early adult life, with the demand to choose a profession or a life partner, might lead to symptom formation; parenthood, with the revival of passive-dependent wishes at a time of added responsibility, might be associated with symptom formation.

It is important to make a clinical distinction between (1) instinctual regression limited to neurotic symptom formation; (2) more serious regression, including impairment of the basic ego function, with respect to which the clinician must determine whether it is in a setting of crisis; and (3) insidious regression, which characterizes certain types of psychoses. It is the clinical task to differentiate regression from developmental failure, e.g., in a patient who comes from a very emotionally deprived background, who has never experienced a genuine triangular conflict.

III. FORMULATION OF A GENETIC DIAGNOSIS

Genetic diagnosis refers to the evaluation and understanding of the dynamic forces that molded character structure and the genesis of the patient's current conflict. The evaluator should determine the external forces that affected the patient's early life and his reaction to these forces.

In formulating the genetic diagnosis, the following are required:

Early human relationships; important people in the life orbit of the patient.

A general overview of the patient's life: unusual traumatic events, to determine what past experiences have exposed the patient to psychological illness; the old conflicts that have been reactivated by current crises in the patient's life. An attempt should be made to reconstruct the historical determinant of the patient's current conflict.

To evaluate the relative importance of regression and fixation, it is essential that the evaluator differentiate between characteristics of predisposed individuals which suggest developmental failure and those which suggest significant regression during the course of a psychological illness.

A genetic diagnosis indicating that fixation is predominant calls for a much more protracted therapy.

IV. FORMULATION OF PSYCHOTHERAPEUTIC POSSIBILITIES: PSYCHOTHERAPEUTIC DIAGNOSIS

A clinician, in order to fulfill his function as a psychotherapist, must have the clinical skill, ability, and flexibility to choose the psychotherapeutic method which will most effectively alter the patient's neurotic pattern of adaptation. The choice of the psychotherapeutic method, the determination of the indication or contraindication for a specific psychotherapy, must be based on the evaluation of a set of criteria in order to determine what specific psychotherapeutic method might be of benefit to the patient. For the sake of simplicity, these criteria can be grouped into four areas:
    A. Evaluation of ego function (of primary importance in psychotherapeutic work)
    B. Evaluation of the structure and function of the id
    C. Evaluation of the structure and function of the superego
    D. Establishment of a psychotherapeutic focus

A. Evaluation of Ego Function

Such an evaluation should include determination of the following:

    1. The quality of human relationships

2. The affective function of the ego
3. Motivation
4. Psychological-mindedness
5. Response to interpretation
6. Intelligence
7. The ego's defensive psychological organization

I will attempt to elaborate on each of these items, as they are the basis of the criteria for selection of patients for short-term dynamic psychotherapy as we developed them in the early 1960's.

1. *The Quality of Human Relationships.* The evaluator should determine the ability of the patient to involve himself in emotional interaction with the therapist, to confide his most personal thoughts and feelings. The extent to which the patient reaches out for the therapist is an essential factor in the development of the therapeutic alliance. One should determine if the patient has had previous emotional ties with other people. Such patients are more likely to invest in a psychotherapeutic relationship. Clinical observation indicates that the patient's style of human relationship will be clear in the very first interview by the way in which he interacts with the evaluator. Sifneos has emphasized the presence of "one" *meaningful* relationship in the patient's life orbit, and his criteria for selection of patients includes the presence of an altrustic relationship, that is, a give-and-take relationship.

Psychoanalytic observation from its earliest phase emphasizes the relationship of the libidinal development to ego and object cathexis. Abraham's early contribution was an attempt to correlate different levels of libidinal development with the characteristic types of object relationships. Current psychoanalytic thinking indicates that failure of the establishment and maintenance of a positive ego identification, which is based on good object relations may substantially impair ego and superego development. Further psychoanalytic observation has indicated that previous capacity to establish and maintain emotionally significant ties with other people will positively influence the patient's ability to establish and maintain a therapeutic alliance. Based on these observations and clinical experience, the quality of human relationships has been one of our major criteria for selection, to which I shall refer later on.

I should like to emphasize, however, that the evaluator should determine to what extent regressive changes in the ego have brought about impairment of the ego's capacity for object relationships. For example, in a depressive state regressive changes in the ego may bring about regressive demands for attention, reassurance, and support. Through a careful evaluation one should determine the developmental failure which limits the capacity for positive object relations.

2. *The Affective Function of the Ego.* The degree, accessibility and tolerance of affect are of great importance. Freud, in *New Introductory Lectures* (1933), distinguishes between two types of anxiety. To one he gives the name "primary traumatic anxiety" and states that it is brought about directly by helplessness in the face of overwhelming instinctual excitation. By contrast, he defines the second type of anxiety as a defensive reaction brought about in the face of an "internal danger situation." He further states, "I can see no objection to there being a two-fold origin of anxiety; one as a direct consequence of a traumatic moment, and the other as a signal threatening a repetition of such a moment." Subsequently, in *Inhibition Symptom and Anxiety*, he emphasizes the signal anxiety, which threatens repetition and is the basis of the defense mechanism.

The clinician should differentiate between a primitive form of externally directed separation anxiety and the anxiety which arises as a signal of internal danger. The second form of anxiety is associated with a higher form of ego organization.

In evaluating the capacity of the ego to experience and tolerate anxiety, the clinician should differentiate between anxiety as a stimulating and as an inhibiting factor. In secondary anxiety the individual experiences some uncomfortable physical sensations but maintains his usual mental alertness, with the ability to use his resources to their fullest. Here anxiety acts as an ally. The opposite side of the picture is the individual who is not able to tolerate anxiety, who shows helplessness, a manifestation of the infant confronted with a situation with which he cannot cope. His mind goes blank; he becomes tremulous, and there is an inability to use his resources in a purposive way. At this point we see the emergence of what is called primary anxiety. Primary anxiety has its roots in the earliest period of life. The capacity to experience, tolerate, and master secondary anxiety depends on considerable ego development and mature psychic apparatus. Zetzel has indicated that the presence of anxiety, both in childhood and in adult life, is often associated with a good prognosis and that if, during the course of his development, the individual has been capable of tolerating a great amount of anxiety, he is on the whole less liable to develop irreversible neurotic reactions.

We know that in psychoanalysis the clinical criteria emphasize that the ability to tolerate anxiety is of great importance for the resolution of an analyzable transference neurosis.

In evaluating the affective function of the ego one should also evaluate the patient's capacity to experience and to tolerate guilt and depression.

Edward Bibring, in *The Mechanism of Depression* (1953), an ego psychological approach to depression, proposed that both anxiety and depression are basic ego states. Depression, like anxiety, represents an ego response to internal or external events. Distinction should be made between depression as an affective experience of general psychological significance and as an illness representing a complex regressive syndrome. Zetzel emphasizes that the capacity to recognize and tolerate "the existence of an internal unconsciously determined danger situation is very closely linked with the problem of psychological insight." She further states that "the experience of depression is a pre-requisite for optimal maturation."

To summarize: the evaluator should determine the extent to which the patient's emotional life is close to conscious awareness; the patient's capacity to experience and tolerate the anxiety, guilt, and depression which will be mobilized during the interview; his responses to mobilization of the affect which is latent under the surface. Attempting to mobilize latent affect and evaluate the patient's ability to respond affectively is a crucial part of the assessment process. Evaluation of the patient's capacity to experience and tolerate anxiety, guilt, and depression is an essential task of the evaluator.

3. *Motivation*. Motivation is considered a major ego function of primary importance in psychotherapeutic work and very closely related to the psychotherapeutic choice. Both conscious motivation, which is what the patient consciously verbalizes, and unconscious, nonverbalized, implied motivation, which is based on the patient's unconscious attitude, should be evaluated. The patient's unconscious attitudes and expectations are very important in the evaluation of motivation. One should differentiate between a neurotic type of motivation, e.g., motivation to enter into a treatment situation is based on satisfying an infantile need, and the kind of motivation that is based on a genuine conscious and unconscious desire for change. Sifneos has done a great deal of work in this area and has designed a number of subcriteria for evaluating the patient's motivation for short-term anxiety-provoking psychotherapy (see Chapter 3).

4. *Psychological-Mindedness*. Psychological-mindedness, the capacity for introspection, is another significant ego function. It involves the degree of and capacity for verbal communication of one's thoughts,

feelings, fantasies, and inner psychic life, as well as the awareness of one's inner emotional reactions and the ability to see how these psychic processes are integrated and related to past experiences. The evaluator should take into consideration that in the first interview some patients show inhibitions in the communication of their inner emotional experiences and by the second or the third interview resolve these inhibitions.

The evaluator should also keep in mind that in some patients an extreme degree of introspection may be a manifestation of resistance. We all know patients who ruminate excessively on inner fantasies, feelings, and thoughts while completely ignoring the realities of external life.

5. *Response to Interpretation.* We consider this to be the most crucial. Here the evaluator should note the ability of the patient to respond to interpretation. Does he elaborate on it? Is he receptive to it? Does he avoid and disregard the evaluator's interpretation? The depth, degree, and type of interpretation basically depend upon the clinical situation, and one is not necessarily able to use these criteria in every first evaluation interview. One might use a focus interpretation. Here the evaluator might give an interpretation of what he perceives as a central focus, then listen to the patient's response to this intervention.

6. *Intelligence.* This is an ego function with some specific relationship to the choice of psychotherapeutic approach. In assessing intelligence one should keep in mind that intellectual deficiencies might be secondary to anxiety. Above-average intelligence is one of the criteria, keeping in mind that there are patients with superior intelligence who are poor candidates for any analytically oriented psychotherapy. I refer particularly to those patients who possess superior intelligence and use it in the service of resistance.

7. *The Ego's Defensive Psychological Organization.* To evaluate the model mode of the ego function, the evaluator should determine the number of ego defense mechanisms available to the patient: the greater the *flexibility* of the ego's defensive psychological organization, the greater the number of mechanisms available, and the less the ego is dependent upon any specific defense mechanism to maintain adaptation. The ability of the patient to call upon all kinds of defense mechanisms is an indication that the patient is making an effort to see which appropriate combination of reactions is best suited to deal with the particular emotional problem. One might say that the more able the patient is to utilize a variety of mechanisms in facing different situations, the more he is a candidate for any form of dynamic psychotherapy.

In research over the period 1963–74 we evaluated 575 neurotic patients. We rejected some of these patients, and one of the reasons for rejection was due to the finding that these patients were using primitive defense mechanisms. We came to learn that one should not be alarmed if a patient uses a primitive defense mechanism such as projection, if the patient has the flexibility to shift to other defense mechanisms. Our observation is that the patient's ability to use defense mechanisms flexibly is a positive criterion, irrespective of his pathology. Of 575 patients evaluated, 130 were treated in short-term dynamic psychotherapy, and a sizable number of the rejected patients were accepted in supportive psychotherapy of one form or another. Our findings indicate that the following combination of defense mechanisms were predominantly used by those patients who were taken into support therapy:

—intense reliance on projection
—massive denial
—major reliance on acting out in dealing with conflicts
—acting out combined with projection
—a few rigid persistently used ego defense mechanisms

B. Evaluation of the Structure and Function of the Id

As I mentioned previously, evaluation of the level of psychosexual adjustment and drive organization is very important as compared to pre-oedipal, oral, and anal drive organization in terms of choice of psychotherapies. Although the components of both are present in all individuals, it is necessary to determine the degree and intensity of fixation at the pregenital developmental period. Evaluation of the intensity of the genital drive organization as compared to the pregenital has a prognostic therapeutic value. In addition, it determines the type of therapy. If the major area of the patient's conflict is at the oedipal genital level, for example, the overall therapeutic prognosis is good. Yet one should also differentiate between regression and fixation; e.g., in a person whose major area of conflict is at the oedipal genital level and shows regression to the pregenital stage, one is dealing with a situation which has a much better therapeutic prognosis. In general, the more the central core of the patient's conflict is at the oedipal level, the better the prognosis despite the fact that in every neurosis there is usually some regression from genital to pregenital. In contrast, the more the central core of the patient's conflict is fixated at the pregenital level, the more problematic is the therapeutic course.

C. Evaluation of the Structure and Function of the Superego

The superego should be explored—the state of shame and guilt, the level of aggression and the way the patient deals with it—to evaluate the presence of self-destructive impulses, behavior and suicidal risk, to take into consideration that there are individuals who have never internalized a set of usable moral values. There are those in whom the superego function is externalized and is not involved in the intrapsychic conflict.

D. Establishment of a Psychotherapeutic Focus

During the process of evaluation a conclusion must be reached with respect to the problem or problems needing treatment. This is not based entirely on what the patient himself says nor is it based entirely on the point of view of the evaluator. It is a function of the evaluation process that both patient and evaluator come to the conclusion that a specific problem at the time of the evaluation is the focus of the treatment. In the evaluation of patients for short-term dynamic psychotherapy the establishment of the psychotherapeutic focus is of major importance. The identification and understanding of the psychodynamics and psychological processes underlying the patient's psychological problems is the key issue in the evaluation proccess. The evaluator makes an attempt to explore and to explain the patient's emotional difficulties and their repetitive, self-punishing, self-defeating pattern.

In summary, the establishment of the psychotherapeutic focus is the function of the evaluation process, and both therapist and patient must agree on the focus. In such an evaluation the central structure of the patient's conflict must be determined in order to focus on what French called the "focal conflict," hopefully the "nuclear" conflict, which might be oedipal or non-oedipal.

At this point I would like to elaborate somewhat on this issue. In Chapter 19, "The Case of the Man Obsessed with the Small Size of His Genitals," the psychotherapeutic focus can be outlined as follows:

(a) Disturbances in the area of interpersonal relationships. A self-denying, self-punishing, self-defeating pattern of behavior. Conflict in the area of success. He indicated that he could have become a professional person, but he managed to "mess it up" and left college during the second year. He would set up competitive situations and then contrive to be the loser.

(b) Problems in his marriage from the beginning. He lost affection

EVALUATION, CRITERIA FOR SELECTION OF PATIENTS

for his wife, became brutal with her, and finally pushed her to another man. Then he suddenly developed a panic attack, which brought him to treatment.

(c) In the initial evaluative interview the psychodynamic formulation to explain the aforementioned difficulties was an unresolved triangular Oedipal conflict. The hostility that he had felt in the past toward his mother was displaced onto his wife the moment she assumed the same name as his mother.

A hostile, negative relationship with his father, as well as castration anxiety, was brought into focus. At the same time there was a positive feeling for his father—he was envious of his younger brother, who enjoyed a very good relationship with his father.

Thus we emphasize that the therapist and patient should agree on the psychotherapeutic focus. This is the function of the evaluation process. It is also essential to emphasize the correlation between two important variables—the psychotherapeutic focus and the patient's motivation.

To give an example from our research data: In "The Case of the Journalist" the patient was first seen when she was twenty-eight years old. She suffered from a severe depression of approximately six months' duration, which was interfering with her job. She was very happy with her job, and her work record was excellent. She indicated that the onset of her depression had been gradual and that she had no clear idea as to what had caused it.

Since age twenty-three she had lived with another girl three years younger than herself. She had always enjoyed this relationship, which was a homosexual one. She was seen by two different psychiatrists, two sessions with one and three sessions with the other, with no change. Both had recommended long-term intensive psychotherapy, and both had indicated that her motivation was questionable. By the third session the second psychiatrist had put her on an antidepressant.

In my first interview with this patient it became evident that she dreamed a lot. Her dreams centered around her mother, and some of them were vivid. This recurrent dream started a few months prior, which to me was supportive of the central dynamic structure of the patient's conflict.

Her background history showed that she was an only child and that her father left her mother when she was three years old. When she was five, her mother died from metastatic cancer of the breast. She was brought up by her mother's sister, an older woman with whom she had a very good relationship. When she was fourteen, her aunt died suddenly. She then boarded with a family, doing baby-sitting, and worked through high school and college, finally obtaining a responsible position as a journalist.

While she was boarding with the family, she developed a close relationship with a neighbor, an older woman. This relationship continued, and she saw the woman once a week. She bought her gifts and groceries, and the woman cooked for her. She always looked forward to these visits. A year before she came to us, the woman was told she had cancer and that her life expectancy was short.

The central dynamic force underlying this patient's depression was then brought into focus in the first evaluation. There was a revival of old memories and conflicts related to her mother, and an active mourning process was in operation. The motivation score was high, and the psychotherapeutic focus centered around the process of mourning.

E. Transference, Countertransference Evaluation

A specific psychotherapeutic decision should be based on the observation and evaluation of the transference situation. Usually, transference begins when the patient makes the appointment. There is a mobilization of infantile fears and wishes at the first thought or suggestion of seeing a psychiatrist. The patient's conscious and unconscious attitudes toward the therapist usually manifest themselves from the very beginning of the interview. There is a close interrelationship between the capacity for the development of transference relationships and the capacity for object relationships. The greater the patient's capacity for a meaningful human relationship, the greater is his potential for the development of a transference relationship. At the same time, one should keep in mind that in some patients there is excessive readiness for transference, which might be the sign of a disturbed object relationship. Among the many variables in the evaluation process are those of the patient himself—his discomfort, his maladaptive neurotic pattern of behavior, his hopes, faith, expectancy, and motivation. The patient's negative or positive reaction toward the evaluator might be a transference reaction or might be a realistic reaction to the negative or positive attributes of the evaluator. The evaluator's variables—his social and professional standing, his objectivity, his value system, his integrity, his clinical maturity, his empathic capacity, his conscious and unconscious needs—greatly influence the process of evaluation and selection. We should take into consideration the impact of countertransference feelings in evaluation and selection criteria. In the process of evaluation, countertransference feelings might affect the evaluation of the patient's motivation.

Our clinical data indicate that to some extent there is a direct correlation between the patient's motivation and the focal points of the patient's problems. If the evaluator is focusing on the central core of the patient's problem, this might increase the patient's motivation, but if, due to countertransference reaction, the evaluator moves away from the focal point, this might decrease the patient's motivation for therapy. Included in these data are so-called "dropouts," patients who left therapy prematurely. Countertransference, then, is one of the variables which is continually in operation and affects the decision whether or not the patient will be accepted into treatment.

Having completed the psychodynamic evaluation with the formulation of the genetic diagnosis and the psychotherapeutic evaluation, the therapist is in a position to tailor a specific psychotherapeutic method to the patient's needs. It is a fundamental principle in the field of psychiatry that the treatment should be individualized. Human beings, in their character structure, pattern of interpersonal relationships, and emotional life are so different from one another that individualization of treatment adds immensely to the effectiveness of therapy.

If for the sake of simplicity we conceptualize the spectrum of psychotherapies in the continuum as outlined on the following chart, the choice of a psychotherapeutic method requires a refined set of criteria for the selection of the patient for a specific psychotherapy. On the right-hand side of the continuum there is a wide range of dynamic psychotherapies, and somewhere on the right-hand side we have short-term dynamic psychotherapies. For example, the short-term anxiety-provoking psychotherapy described by Peter Sifneos, the short-term dynamic psychotherapy described by David Malan, as well as the kind of short-term dynamic psychotherapy that I have developed since the early 1960's, and the short-term dynamic psychotherapies described by other workers in this field. In each of these short-term psychotherapies, there is a specific set of criteria for selection of patients.

At this point I would like to focus primarily on Broad-Focused Short-Term Dynamic Psychotherapy. It is a specific kind of dynamic psychotherapy with the aim of replacing the patient's neurotic pattern of behavior. It is based on psychoanalytic principles, using a special kind of focus interview. One focuses on the exploration of genetic material with the technique of confrontation, clarification, and exploration into conscious, pre-conscious, and the derivative of unconscious material.

CHART 1
The Continuum of Psychotherapeutic Possibilities

Client-Centered Therapy

Focuses on patient's immediate experience

Integration through self-exploration

Therapist provides empathy, respect, authenticity

Psychoanalysis

Techniques which analyze transference and resistance back to their genetic, dynamic roots

Behavior Therapy

Learning principles define therapy conditions

Target symptom defines procedure

Response facilitation/extinction almost independent of therapist

Supportive Therapy

The technique which uses predominantly suggestion, abreaction; therapeutic weight is primarily in favor of control over impulses and strengthening impulses

Dynamic Psychotherapies

The technique which recognizes the transferences and resistances and rationally utilizes their recognition in the therapy

Dream interpretation and the analysis of transference reaction are used in varying degrees with an active attempt to avoid the development of transference neurosis.

The criteria for selection of patients that we have developed and used in one of our research projects for the period from September 1963 to March 1974 are outlined in the next few pages. In this project we evaluated 575 patients. Of these, 130 patients fulfilled our criteria, scoring from "fair" to "excellent"; that is, of 575 randomly evaluated neurotic patients, almost 23 percent were selected for short-term dynamic psychotherapy. One hundred fifteen were treated successfully, with a two- to seven-year follow-up. Successful outcome in this research applies to those patients who fulfilled our outcome criteria for psychodynamic change: a disappearance of the symptoms and a definite change in the pattern of defense mechanisms and mode of ego function. The patient has insight into his emotional conflicts and understands his symptoms in dynamic terms.

For criterion VI, our data indicate that there is a significantly positive correlation between the subcriterion pertaining to the ability of the patient to get into interaction with the evaluator and a successful outcome. But when it comes to the subcriterion pertaining to meaningful relationship, we cannot make any definite statement due to the fact that there was a high percentage of patients who were questionable as to whether or not they had had such a relationship. In terms of the subcriterion pertaining to consistent versus promiscuous pattern of relationship, our findings indicate a correlation between a promiscuous pattern and an extended length of therapy.

For Criterion VII, which is related to the extent to which the patient's emotional life is close to conscious awareness, as well as to the degree and capacity to experience and tolerate anxiety, guilt, and depression, again there is a statistically significant correlation between patients with a high score and successful therapeutic outcome. This is also true of Criterion VIII, having to do with motivation for change.

Regarding Criterion IX, we find no correlation between above-average intelligence and successful psychotherapeutic outcome.

Criterion XII was one of our major criteria. From the beginning of our research project we used partial or total interpretation in our initial interview. For many years we have used the subcriterion of the past-present transference link in the evaluation and selection of patients for dynamic psychotherapy to determine whether the patient has the ability to recognize the connection that the evaluator makes and whether he elaborates on it. Alexander refers to this kind of interpretation in his book *The Technique of Psychotherapy* (1957): "Interpretation which

FORM B

CRITERIA FOR SELECTION OF PATIENTS
FOR
SHORT-TERM DYNAMIC PSYCHOTHERAPY

NAME: _____

ADDRESS: _____

TELEPHONE: _____

AGE: _____ SEX: F _____ MARITAL STATUS: S _____ M _____ SEP _____
                 M _____   D _____ W _____

OCCUPATION: _____

EDUCATION: _____

INTERVIEWER: _____

DATE OF INTERVIEW: _____

I. DESCRIBE PATIENT'S SPECIFIC CHIEF COMPLAINTS AND DIFFICULTIES.

_____
_____
_____
_____
_____
_____
_____
_____

Criteria for Selection Form (Cont'd)

    A) Is patient's problem a
       circumscribed one?   YES _____ NO _____

    B) To which one of the following
       categories does the clinical
       diagnosis belong?   ANXIETY _____   DEPRESSION _____
                                      CONVERSION _____   OBSESSIONAL _____
                                        PHOBIA _____   SOMATIZATION _____

II. IS A CRISIS PRESENT?   YES _____ NO _____

III. HAS A PSYCHOTHERAPEUTIC
     FOCUS BEEN ESTABLISHED?   YES _____ NO _____

    Do the evaluator and the patient
    agree on the psychotherapeutic focus
    which has been established?   YES _____ NO _____

IV. IS THE PSYCHOTHERAPEUTIC FOCUS
     RELATED TO A DISTURBANCE IN
     INTERPERSONAL RELATIONSHIPS?   YES _____ NO _____

V. CAN YOU PROVIDE A PSYCHODYNAMIC
   FORMULATION FOR THE PATIENT'S
   PROBLEM?   YES _____ NO _____

   Brief Description: _____

_____

_____

_____

_____

_____

VI. HUMAN RELATIONSHIPS.

    A) Ability to get involved in
       emotional interaction with
       the evaluator.   1   2   3   4   5

Criteria for Selection Form (Cont'd)

    B. Is there a history of a give-and-take relationship with a significant person in the patient's life orbit?   1   2   3   4   5

    C) Heterosexual Relationships.

        Consistent _____
        Promiscuous _____
        None _____

VII. AFFECT.

    A) The extent to which patient's emotional life is close to conscious awareness.   1   2   3   4   5

    B) Degree and capacity to experience and tolerate anxiety, guilt, and depression.   1   2   3   4   5

    C) Did you mobilize some latent affect during the interview?   YES _____ NO _____

    D) If yes, did the patient respond affectively?   YES _____ NO _____

VIII. MOTIVATION FOR CHANGE.   1   2   3   4   5

IX. IS THE PATIENT OF ABOVE-AVERAGE INTELLIGENCE?   1   2   3   4   5

X. PSYCHOLOGICAL MINDEDNESS.

    A) Capacity for introspection.   1   2   3   4   5

    B) Ability for verbal communication of thoughts, feelings, fantasies, and his inner psychic life.   1   2   3   4   5

    C) Patient's ability to see how these psychic processes are integrated and related to his past experiences.   1   2   3   4   5

Criteria for Selection Form (Cont'd)

XI. DID YOU GIVE ANY INTERPRETATION
DURING THIS INTERVIEW?   YES _____   NO _____

XII. PATIENT'S ABILITY TO RESPOND
TO INTERPRETATION.   1   2   3   4   5

　A) Is he able to respond to
　transference confrontation
　or interpretation?   1   2   3   4   5

　Give an Example: _____

_____

_____

_____

_____

　B) Is patient able to respond
　to past-present transference
　link that the evaluator was
　able to make? (P.P.T. Link)   1   2   3   4   5

The scoring is based on:

(1) EXCELLENT   (2) GOOD   (3) FAIR (4) LOW (5) POOR

Do you consider this patient a
candidate for Broad-Focused
Short-Term Dynamic Psychotherapy?   YES _____   NO _____

Scoring: 1   2   3   4   5

Please indicate the number of sessions
you estimate to be required.   2 - 5 _____   6 - 15 _____
                                     16 - 25 _____ 26 - 40 _____

If no, what other modality of therapy would you recommend?

_____

_____

APPENDIX TO FORM B

If you cannot make a decision, do you
consider a second interview to be
necessary in order to decide if this
patient is a candidate for Broad-Focused
Short-Term Dynamic Psychotherapy?   YES _____   NO _____

If yes, the date of next interview: _____

When the first evaluator decides on a second interview, before he refers the patient to an independent evaluator, he must still fill out the Criteria for Selection Form (Form B) at the end of the first interview. Another Form B is to be filled out at the end of the second interview.

---

connects the *actual life situation* with *past experience* and with the *transference situation*—since the latter is always the axis around which such connection can best be made—is called total interpretation." He further states, "The more that interpretation approximates this principle of totality, the more it fulfills its double purpose; it accelerates the assimilation of new material by the ego and mobilizes further unconscious material."

In the early part of an assessment interview, data are usually obtained with respect to the patient's pattern of behavior with significant persons in his life at the present time. Further exploration will bring data regarding the vertical or genetic pattern of his behavior with a significant person in the very early part of his life. The pattern of the patient's behavior during the interview, that is, the transference situation, is also clear. At this time, the evaluator has the opportunity to link the three dimensions, namely, the past pattern of behavior to the contemporary pattern of behavior, to the transference situation. Our clinical data indicate a very high positive correlation between response to interpretation and successful therapeutic outcome, and more so if the impulse component of the link is also interpreted. I have found that this linking of the three patterns of the patient's behavior is an excellent technique in dealing with resistances in the first interview and that it increases the patient's spontaneity and motivation for further psychotherapeutic work.

Finally, as I have indicated, we have found a significant positive correlation between motivation and a psychotherapeutic focus. The interaction between being able to see a psychotherapeutic focus and the patient's motivation to work with this focus and the outcome of the psychotherapeutic work are interrelated. We came to learn that motivation may not have been scored high in the first interview but had developed solidly by the second or third interview as the individual became more aware of the nature and core of his problem. At the same time, we learned that when interpretation of the kind I have just described brought about a positive response, the patient's motivation was increased. We have been concerned about the subject of motivation and the theoretical orientation of the evaluator. Some of the work done by medical students in the early phase of our research indicates that the evaluation process and motivation are definitely much less dependent upon the theoretical orientation of the evaluator than they are upon the personality characteristics of the evaluator and his empathic capacity.

In March 1974 Sifneos and I conducted a workshop on short-term dynamic psychotherapy called "Evaluation, Criteria for Selection." It was during this time that I became acquainted with Sifneos' contribution in the area of motivation and learned that he uses seven subcriteria in evaluating motivation. We then set up a small research project involving the treatment of twenty-five patients and incorporated his seven subcriteria on motivation. The last patient was taken into treatment in this project in November 1976. We hope to be able to publish our findings on these twenty-five patients in the near future.

In summary, I have attempted to elaborate on the evaluation of patients using a metapsychological approach and have indicated that the clinician's ability to think in dynamic, genetic, economic, structural, and adaptive terms is central to sound evaluation and therapeutic planning. I have outlined the criteria for selection of patients for short-term dynamic psychotherapy which I used in the evaluation of 575 patients. Based on successful treatment of 115 patients with a two- to seven-year follow-up, I have discussed some of those criteria which very significantly correlated with outcome. I have further emphasized the diagnostic and prognostic value of response to interpretation as one of the major criteria for selection of patients for short-term dynamic psychotherapy.

REFERENCES

Alexander, F. A Metapsychological Description of the Process of Cure. *Int. J. Psycho-Anal.*, 6, 1925.

Alexander, F. Analysis of the Therapeutic Factors in Psychoanalytic Treatment. *Psychoanal. Quart.*, 19, 1950.

Alexander, F. and H. Ross. *Dynamic Psychiatry*. University of Chicago Press, 1952.

Alexander, F. Principles & Techniques of Brief Psychotherapeutic Procedures. *Proc. Assoc. for Res. Nerv. & Ment. Dis.*, 31:16, 1951.

Balint, M. *The Doctor, His Patient and the Illness*. N.Y.: Pitman Publ. Corp., 1973, Second Edition.

Balint, M. *Psychotherapeutic Techniques in Medicine*. London: Tavistock Publ., 1961.

Balint, M. et al. *Focal Psychotherapy: An Example of Applied Psychoanalysis*. London: Tavistock Publ., 1972.

Barten, H.H. *Brief Therapies*. N.Y.: Behavioral Publ. Inc., 1971.

Bellak, L. and L. Small *Emergency Psychotherapy and Brief Psychotherapy*. N.Y.: Grune and Stratton, 1965.

Berliner, B. Short Psychoanalytic Psychotherapy: Its Possibilities and Its Limitations, *Bull. Menninger Clins.*, 5:204, 1941.

Bibring, E. Contribution to the Symposium on the Theory of the Therapeutic Results of Psycho-Analysis, *Int. J. Psycho-Anal.*, 18, 1937.

Bibring, E. *The Mechanism of Depression In Affective Disorders*. Edited by P. Greenacre, New York: International Universities Press, 1953.

Bibring, E. Psychoanalysis and the Dynamic Psychotherapies, *J. Amer. Psychoanalysis* 2:745–769.

Blaine, Jr., G. Short-Term Psychotherapy with College Students, *New England J. of Medicine*, 256:208–211, 1957.

Boileau, V. New Techniques in Brief Psychotherapy. *Psychol. Rep.*, 4:627–645, 1958.

Bulletin of the Menninger Clinic. Final Report of the Menninger Foundations Psychotherapy Research Project, 36:1/2, 1972.

Davanloo, H. Evaluation, Criteria for Selection of Patients for Broad-Focused Short-Term Dynamic Psychotherapy. Presented at the World Congress of Psychotherapy, Paris: 1976. Published in *Psychotherapy and Psychosomatics*. Basel: S. Karger Publ.

Doeff, et al. Brief Psychotherapy in a Community Mental Health. *Pennsylvania Psychiat. Quart.*, 6:62–64, 1966.

Ferenzi, S. (1920). *The Further Development of an Active Therapy in Psychoanalysis; In Further Contribution to the Therapy and Technique of Psychoanalysis*. New York: Basic Book, 1951.

Ferenzi, S. and O. Rank. Development of Psychoanalysis: C. Newton, Trans. *Nervous & Mental Disease Monographs*, 40, 1925.

French, T. and F. Alexander. *Psychoanalytic Theory*. New York: Ronald Press, 145–164, 1946.

Freud, A. (1936). *The Ego and the Mechanisms of Defense.* London: Hogarth Press, 1937; New York: Int. Univ. Press, 1946.
Freud, S. *On Psychotherapy.* Standard Edition, 7, 1905a.
Freud, S. *Mourning and Melancholia.* Standard Edition, 14, 1917.
Freud, S. (1901). *Fragment of an Analysis of a Case of Hysteria.* In J. Strachey, ed., Standard Edition, Vol. 7, London: Hogarth, 1953.
Freud, S. (1909). Notes Upon a Case of Obsessional Neurosis. In *The Complete Psychological Works of S. Freud,* Vol. 10, London: Hogarth, 1955.
Freud, S. (1918). *From the History of an Infantile Neurosis.* in J. Strachey, ed., Standard Edition, Vol. 17, London: Hogarth, 1955.
Garner, H.H. Brief Psychotherapy. *Int. J. Neuropsychiat.,* 1:616–622, 1965.
Grinker, R. Brief Psychotherapy in War Neuroses. *Brief Psychotherapy Council Proceedings,* 2:6–19, 1944.
Gutheil, E. Psychoanalysis and Brief Psychotherapy. *J. Clin. Psychopath. Psychother.,* 6:207–230, 1944–45.
Hartmann, H. (1939). *Ego Psychology and the Problem of Adaptation.* New York: International Universities Press, 1958.
Knapp, P.H., S. Levin, R.H. McCarter, H. Wermer, & E. Zetzel. Suitability for Psychoanalysis: A review of One Hundred Supervised Analytic Cases. *Psychoanal. Quart.,* 29, 1960.
Knight, R.P. Applications of Psychoanalytic Concepts in Psychotherapy: Report of Clinical Trials in a Mental Hygiene Service. *Bull. Menninger Clinic.,* 1:99–109, 1936–37.
Lindemann, E. Symptomatology and Management of Acute Grief. *Am. J. of Psy.* 101:141–148, 1944.
Mann, J. *Time-Limited Psychotherapy.* Cambridge: Harvard Univ. Press, 1973.
Marmor, J. Changing Trends in Psychotherapy. In Usdin, G. (Ed.), *Psychiatry: Education and Image.* New York: Brunner/Mazel, Inc., 84–104, 1973. (Presented at teaching symposium, Am. College of Psychiatrists, New Orleans, La., 1/1973).
Marmor, J. Frigidity, Dyspareunia, and Vaginismus. In Sadock, B., Kaplan, H., and A. Freedman (Eds.), *Comprehensive Textbook of Psychiatry* (Second Edition). Baltimore: Williams & Wilkins, 1520–1523, 1975.
Marmor, J. The Future of Psychoanalytic Therapy. *Am. J. Psychiat.* 130: 11, 1197–1202, 1973. (Presented at 18th Annual Meeting, American Academy of Psychoanalysis, Honolulu, Hawaii, 5/73).
Marmor, J. Impotence and Ejaculatory Disturbances. In *Comprehensive Textbook of Psychiatry* (Second Edition). Baltimore: Williams and Wilkins, 1524–1528, 1975.
Marmor, J. (Ed.) *Modern Psychoanalysis: New Directions and Perspectives.* New York: Basic Books, 1968.
Marmor, J. The Nature of the Psychotherapeutic Process Revisited *Canadian Psychiatric Assn. J.,* 20: 8, 557–565, 1975.
Marmor, J. New Directions in Psychoanalytic Theory and Therapy. In Marmor, J. (Ed.), *Modern Psychoanalysis: New Directions and Perspectives.* New York: Basic Books, 3–15, 1968.

Marmor, J. Some Considerations Concerning Orgasm in the Female. *Psychosom. Med.* 16: 3, 240–245, 1954.

Rosenbaum, C.P. Events of Early Therapy and Brief Therapy. *Arch. Gen. Psychiat.*, 10:506–512, 1964.

Rothenberg, S. Brief Psychodynamically Oriented Therapy. *Psychosom. Med.*, 17:455–457, 1955.

Semrad, E. et al. Brief Psychotherapy. *Amer. J. Psychiat.*, 20:576–599, 1966.

Sifneos, P. *Short-Term Psychotherapy & Emotional Crisis*. Cambridge: Harvard University Press, 1972.

Small, L. *The Briefer Psychotherapies*. New York: Brunner/Mazel Publ., 1971.

Straker, M., H. Davanloo, and A.E. Moll. Chronic Psychiatric Out-Patient in a General Hospital Setting. *The Canadian Psy. Assoc. J.*, II:5, 1966.

Strupp, H.A. Multidimensional Analysis of Techniques in Brief Psychotherapy. *Psychiatry* 20: 387–397, 1957.

Strupp, H. Psychoanalysis, 'Focal Psychotherapy' and the Nature of the Therapeutic Influence. *Arch. Gen. Psychiatry*, 32: 127–135, 1975.

Visher, J. Brief Psychotherapy in a Mental Hygiene Clinic. *Amer. J. Psychotherapy*, 13:331–342, 1959.

Wayne, G. and R. Koegler. *Emergency Psychiatry and Brief Therapy*. Boston: Little Brown & Co., 1966.

Whittington, H.G. Transference in Brief Psychotherapy: Experience in a College Psychiatric Clinic. *Psychiat. Quart.*, 36:503–518, 1962.

Wolberg, L. *The Technique of Psychotherapy*. New York: Grune and Stratton, 1965.

Zetzel, E. and W.W. Miessner. *Basic Concepts of of Psychoanalytic Psychiatry*. New York: Basic Books Inc., 1973.

Zetzel, E.R. *The Capacity for Emotional Growth*. New York: International Universities Press, Inc., 1970.

Chapter 3

Short-Term Anxiety-Provoking Psychotherapy

P. E. SIFNEOS

In this chapter I shall not recapitulate the historical development of short-term anxiety-provoking psychotherapy (STAP) at Massachusetts General Hospital and Beth Israel Hospital in Boston, since it has been described extensively by Dr. Davanloo. Rather, I shall describe in detail what STAP is all about, placing the main emphasis on criteria for selection of patients, techniques, and results (1).

Both Massachusetts General and Beth Israel are private teaching hospitals of the Harvard Medical School. The patient population served by both hospitals is large and diversified, and they have no catchment area (2). Furthermore, the psychiatric clinic population is not representative of the general population. Patients of all ages qualify equally as candidates for this kind of treatment, but because of the many educational institutions in the Greater Boston area, because of the psychiatric sophistication prevailing, and because of the popularity of psychoanalytic psychotherapy among the students, the clinic population has been composed primarily of younger patients. In a recent survey of the psychiatric clinic population of Beth Israel Hospital, women outnumbered men by a ratio of 2 to 1. The age distribution, by and large, was between 20 and 30 years, and more than half of these patients were full-time students. Moreover, 47 of a total of 182 patients, surveyed over a period of six months, fulfilled all our criteria for selection for STAP and had good-to-excellent motivation for psychotherapy. A large percentage of young people who have psychological difficulties were found, on the basis of our selection criteria, to be good candidates for STAP. These criteria will now be presented in more detail.

THE EVALUATION PROCESS (CRITERIA FOR SELECTION)

There is always a problem inherent in any discussion of criteria for selection of appropriate patients: oversimplification of complicated parameters having to do with the choice from a myriad of important character traits encountered in each patient, from the ones which are shared by most and which are important in helping differentiate them from other patients with similar difficulties. Furthermore, even if one was able to think abstractly or even to know which might be theoretically the ideal dimensions to look for in the evaluation of all the patients, clinically one has great difficulty in achieving such a perfect result. Therefore, we arrived at our criteria for selection on a practical trial-and-error basis, adding some and eliminating others until finally we settled on the following:

(1) A circumscribed chief complaint
(2) A history of a "meaningful" relationship with another person during his early life
(3) An ability to interact flexibly with the evaluator and have access to his feelings during the evaluation interview
(4) An above-average psychological sophistication and intelligence
(5) A motivation for change

Looking closer at these criteria may help give the reader a clearer picture as to why we decided to pick those and not others, and as to the ways in which these five help us to be doubly sure that the patients chosen according to them possess the necessary strength of character to deal with a psychotherapeutic process which tends to exert a great deal of pressure but which, despite its anxiety-provoking components, enables them to do the necessary work and helps them overcome their difficulties.

A *circumscribed chief complaint* usually denotes the ability to choose and as such is indicative of strength of character. A patient who is experiencing a variety of difficulties and who is asked to pick the difficulty that bothers him most faces a dilemma. By agreeing to such a limitation, he leaves himself open to the unpleasant realization that all his problems will not disappear. As a result of treatment he may be able to solve one of these problems, but he will be left with others which he must face alone.

Circumscribing the chief complaint, however, is not enough. The patient must become aware of the psychological conflicts underlying his difficulty. These conflicts, of which he is only vaguely aware, must be clarified since they will become the basis of the therapeutic focus upon which the whole treatment will be concentrated.

As far as the second criterion is concerned, the nature of the *"meaningful" relationship* must be examined. The word "meaningful" is used to imply trust, give-and-take and altruism. Such a relationship, if it has existed, should have more or less constituted the prototype on which all future interactions with people have been patterned. It is important, therefore, that the evaluator scrutinize very carefully the nature of such an important interpersonal relationship in the patient's early life so as to make sure that it was indeed meaningful. It usually involves one of the parents or a parent surrogate. On occasion, however, if one is unable to discover immediately the existence of such a relationship, he must inquire closely about the presence of individuals in the patient's early life who may have left or have died while he was young and who, as a result of the painful feelings which have been aroused at that time, may have been forgotten. One should not confuse a series of superficial friendships with meaningful relationships unless it can be demonstrated conclusively that they involved a willingness on the part of the patient to make a tangible sacrifice for another person. A masochistic tendency for self-sacrifice, however, is not to be confused with genuine altruism.

The *ability to interact* with the evaluator during the interview can be seen as a test for the second criterion. Although the evaluation interview is stressful for the patient, his ability to interact with the evaluator flexibly and with appropriate expression of feeling will denote that he has experienced similar feeling for another person in the past. Furthermore, a meaningful interaction with the evaluator will foreshadow the nature of the transference feelings which will appear during the course of the therapy, the proper use of which is a cardinal technical point of STAP.

The fourth criterion appears simple at first glance, yet while helping to develop a STAP research project at the Psykiatrisk Klinikk of the University of Oslo, Norway, we had lengthy discussions about the meaning of *above-average psychiatric sophistication and intelligence* and how one should go about evaluating them. Aside from IQ, this criterion involves the ability of the patient to make connections between seemingly unrelated situations, to inquire into the meaning of paradoxical occurrences, and to scrutinize difficult and painful interactions. This aspect of the patient's personality is not related to his education or his social status; rather, it is an integral part of his character structure.

The patient's *motivation for change,* as opposed to symptom relief, is probably the most important selection criterion. In addition to its prognostic value, it is correlated directly with a successful therapeutic outcome. We decided, therefore, to look more closely into the question of motivation. During the early years, while we were in the process of developing STAP at Massachusetts General Hospital, we devoted a special interview to the assessment of the patient's motivation. As a result of this special interview, we were able to develop additional criteria specifically for motivation which needed to be assessed during the evaluation interview.

—Ability to recognize that the symptoms are due to psychological and not physical difficulties
—Tendency to be introspective and to give an honest and truthful account of these difficulties
—Eagerness to participate actively with the therapist during the treatment process
—Curiosity and willingness to make an effort to understand himself.
—Willingness to change, explore, and experiment
—Realistic expectations about the therapeutic outcome.

Willingness and ability to make reasonable and tangible sacrifices—in terms of money or time, for example—in order to achieve the goals of treatment.

Patients who fulfill these seven criteria are considered to have excellent motivation, while those who fulfill as few as three are considered to be unmotivated. A recent study of forty-two patients evaluated over eight therapeutic interviews showed that high motivation in thirty-three patients had increased or remained unchanged. Only in nine did it decrease. Thus using motivation as a prognostic criterion for achieving successful therapeutic results, one could safely predict that approximately 75 percent of the patients in this sample were likely to improve.

THE THERAPEUTIC FOCUS

After he has selected a suitable patient for STAP, the evaluator must perform an additional task involving the establishment of a therapeutic focus. In other words, he must make a formulation of the patient's psychological problem in psychodynamic terms. The solution of this problem will depend on the therapeutic focus, which becomes the basis of the treatment. The evaluator must not only make a correct dynamic formulation; he must also present it to the patient and obtain his agreement. The cooperation of both therapist and patient in this area is a vital ingredient of success.

The psychological problems usually underlying the difficulties encountered in STAP candidates have to do with triangular, or oedipal issues. Although we have accepted patients who complained of reactive depressions following the loss of a loved one, in which case the therapeutic focus involved the clarification of the underlying grief reactions, the majority of failures of STAP occurred with individuals in this group. Assessment of the ambivalent feelings that predominated for the lost person were not difficult to ascertain. Those ambivalent feelings representing a regressive pattern from oedipal triangles were easy to deal with during therapy, and there was no difficulty in helping the patient come to grips with such feelings, understand the behavioral patterns they elicit, and eventually overcome them. If, on the other hand, the ambivalent feelings represented a more basic character deficit, and particularly if passive traits tended to predominate, when the therapist approached the issue of termination of treatment these primitive traits became aroused, the patient regressed, and an impasse was reached. Under these circumstances a more prolonged, supportive kind of psychotherapy was indicated.

THE TECHNIQUE OF STAP

It should be made explicitly clear that, unlike others who offer short-term psychotherapy, we do not set a time limit for STAP (3,4). We believe that the patient should have the option to resolve his difficulties on his own short-term basis. Thus, although it is made clear to our patients at the time of the evaluation that the psychotherapy is expected to last only a few months, no rigid number of sessions is specified. The only stipulations are that the interviews will be face to face, will be held weekly, and will last forty-five minutes.

As far as STAP technique is concerned, first the therapist attempts to establish a good rapport with the patient in order to create a therapeutic alliance conducive to the problem-solving task at hand. Second, the patient's transference feelings for the therapist, which are usually positive, are utilized extensively in order to strengthen the therapeutic alliance and help create a joint venture where understanding and learning can take place, both of which are basic prerequisites for the solution of the patient's problem.

Also, while concentrating on the therapeutic focus which has been outlined, the therapist uses these transference feelings to make the necessary connections with earlier feelings felt by the patient toward his parents. This parent-transference link was found by Malan to be the most important therapeutic tool in short-term dynamic psychotherapy and is primarily responsible for its successful outcome.

Third, while the patient is encouraged to pursue his investigation of the painful conflicts underlying his difficulties, the therapist uses anxiety-provoking questions, confrontations, and clarifications to help him concentrate and provide information about his early life situations and to experience the anxiety which has motivated him to forget, deny, repress, displace, and project.

Fourth, in contrast to the emphasis on the therapeutic task which has been described, the STAP therapist must be on the alert to by-pass the discussion of certain character traits of the patient, such as passivity, dependence, and acting out, which are regressive in nature and tend not only to prolong therapy by deviating from its focus but also to complicate it to such a degree that they interfere with its termination.

Fifth, the early termination of STAP depends on the therapist's assessment of the progress of the treatment, his recognition that the main task has been accomplished, and the evidence that the underlying conflicts of the therapeutic focus have been resolved. We have always insisted that throughout this kind of treatment the therapist must have enough evidence to justify his clarifications and interpretations, and the same factors should apply when he is ready to end it. Usually, the patient provides him with such evidence. For example, in about 50 percent of the cases the patients claimed they felt much better and were aware that the psychological problems that had been identified were about to be or had actually been resolved. Furthermore, they were able to give tangible examples to support their assertions. In the rest of the cases it was the therapist who had to confront the patients with the possibility of termination and give them an overview of the progress that had taken place. The patients, despite their initial reluctance to accept the possibility of ending the therapeutic process, usually tended to agree with the therapist.

The description of any psychotherapeutic technique must specify what outcome should be achieved. As in the case of selection, criteria for a successful outcome must be established to determine whether or not the patient fulfills them. Since 1961 we have investigated the results of STAP as systematically as possible in four different studies (5,6). Originally, and even since, we were struck by the learning component of the patients' achievements. They talked about "new ways in which they have learned to look at themselves," "overcoming the critical problems which have brought them to therapy by understanding better the hidden components of their conflicts," "educating themselves," "solving their problem by learning a technique of self-inquiry," and so on. On the other hand, the symptomatic improvement of our patients was not striking. What was emphasized in reference to their symptoms, however, was that they had developed a new attitude toward them. Learning to live with them, discovering their causes or paying less attention to them, played an important role.

As we looked more closely into the results of STAP, we were impressed by the fact that the patients' improvement was due to a basic increase in their self-esteem as a result of having found new understanding of themselves which helped them relate better to key people in their environment. This improvement stimulated them to continue to investigate the causes of their actions in the past and to search for novel approaches to understanding their behavior.

We used the following criteria to assess the psychotherapeutic outcome:

(1) Symptomatic improvement in physical and/or psychological areas.
(2) Increase in self-esteem.
(3) Improved relations with key persons in the patient's environment.
(4) Development of new, more adaptive attitudes
(5) New learning
(6) Problem solving
(7) Self-understanding
(8) Positive feelings for the therapist
(9) Dynamic change in the therapeutic focus of the treatment or in the patient's specific internal predisposition (SIP) which was considered to be responsible for his special vulnerabilities.

Generally speaking, we have seen improvements in all these parameters, indicating that a limited psychodynamic change had taken place as evidenced by replacement of maladaptive defense mechanisms with more adaptive ones.

From all the above, it should be apparent that STAP is both an exacting and difficult treatment. It is obvious, therefore, that it should be taught systematically under intensive individual supervision. In Chapter 22 I shall discuss the teaching of STAP as it has been offered over the years at Massachusetts General Hospital and presently at Beth Israel Hospital.

SUMMARY

Short-term anxiety-provoking psychotherapy STAP has been described in reference to the criteria for selection of appropriate patients, the technical requirements which must be met, and the criteria for evaluation of its therapeutic outcome. It is my firm conviction that STAP is the treatment of choice for mildly neurotic patients with circumscribed complaints.

REFERENCES

1. Sifneos, P.E.,: *Short-Term Psychotherapy and Emotional Crisis*. Cambridge, Mass.: Harvard University Press, 1972.
2. Sifneos, P.E.: An overview of a Psychiatric Clinic Population. *American Journal of Psychiatry*, 130/9: 1033–36.
3. Mann, J.: *Time Limited Psychotherapy*. Cambridge, Mass.: Harvard University Press, 1973.
4. Malan, D.H.: *A Study of Brief Psychotherapy*. Tavistock Publications, 1963.
5. Sifneos, P.E.: Seven Years' Experience with Short-Term Psychotherapy. 6th International Congress of Psychotherapy. In *Selected Lectures*, Basel/New York: S. Karger, 1968, pp. 127–38.
6. Sifneos, P.E.: Learning to solve emotional problems. In R. Porter ed., *The Role of Learning in Psychotherapy*, J.&A. Churchill Ltd., Ciba Foundation Publications, 1968, pp. 87–96.

Chapter 4

Exploring the Limits of Brief Psychotherapy

D. H. MALAN

The history of psychoanalysis and psychoanalytic therapy provides some fascinating examples of how clinical impressions can lead to vast areas of empirical knowledge that for many years have remained undiscovered. The following is one kind of composite experience known to generations of analysts: In the early stages of therapy many patients feel better. Some of these may nevertheless decide to stay in treatment, in which case they usually later relapse; others may leave treatment, but again they often relapse and return. The definitive improvement occurs only after prolonged working-through of the transference relationship. Thus is born the generalization that patients can show permanent and real improvement only after long-term treatment.

At the same time, however, generations of therapists have had the following kind of sporadic experience: A patient complains of symptoms of acute and recent onset. During the interview it becomes very clear that these are the result of a current identifiable conflict. When this is interpreted, there is a dramatic improvement. Robert Knight (4) quotes a typical example: The patient, a farmer, suffered from a recent paralysis of his right arm, which was clearly a conversion symptom designed to prevent him from hitting certain people with whom he was currently quarreling. Knight interpreted this to the patient, and the symptom disappeared. Does such an experience contradict the conclusion reached above? The answer is, Not really. This type of result is regarded as a purely symptomatic improvement in no way comparable with the results of long-term treatment. There is then born another generalization, put very clearly by Knight:

> Short therapy of this kind, based on analytical understanding, is valuable in relatively acute but not too severely sick cases in which quick help is needed and in which more prolonged, orthodox psychotherapy is inexpedient. It should be understood that such treatment is more or less symptomatic and palliative, tends merely to relieve the distressing symptom and does not alter to any great extent the underlying personality. It may be, however, that the insight gained by the patient from such psychotherapy may enable him to understand himself better and thus strengthen him against breaking down under the stress of similar situations in the future.

It is worth noting that in the last sentence Knight does envisage the possibility that some permanent inner change may result from this kind of treatment. An exactly similar opinion of *psychotherapy in general* (as opposed to *analysis*), though initially expressed in rather more contemptuous terms, is given by Eissler (quoted by Murphy [9]):

> Psychoanalytic scrutiny will disclose that the majority of cures by psychotherapy have been based on elaborate rationalizations which depend for their effectiveness on what is dynamically a repression of the basic conflict after some partial solutions of derivative conflicts have been attained and accepted as a compromise. In this sense psychotherapy has simply effected a change in the content of the neurosis or a re-channelization of libidinal energy based on displacement, or has led to new repression, or an exchange of illusions, the building up of magic beliefs or the development of an imitation of health.... Of course all such cures may be extremely worth while, lasting in effect and economically more feasible than results obtained in analysis.

Both Knight and Eissler worked mainly in settings where it was usually possible to offer analysis if this was regarded as the treatment of choice. What happens where this is not so, in busy outpatient clinics or the student health services of universities? While some such centers attempt to solve their problems by the use of long-term groups, others do so by offering some kind of relatively brief intervention as a routine. Here the majority of patients may be those suffering from some current situational crisis, and again the nature of the conflict may be brought out and the immediate crisis relieved. Casual follow-up may even reveal that such interventions sometimes lead to important permanent improvements, which produces another kind of generalization.

Speers (13), in connection with the brief psychotherapy of women students, writes:

> If the conflict is the result of a current situation, or the result of normal active adjustment reaction, brief psychotherapy can be effective.... Students then seem to be able to resume growth towards their ultimate potential.

Bellak and Small (2) write:

> The goal of brief psychotherapy is limited to the removal or amelioration of specific symptoms; it does not attempt the reconstitution of personality except that any dynamic interaction may secondarily, and to a certain extent, autonomously lead to some restructuration.... but at the same time we would stress that for many people limited psychotherapy may in itself be sufficient to help them achieve a point from which they continue autonomous improvement.

As I have stated many times, the investigation of any form of therapy must involve the consideration of three aspects—selection, technique, and outcome—which are inextricably intertwined in a way that often makes it impossible to consider one without the others. This is illustrated by most of the above quotations, which, though intended as illustrations of opinions about *outcome*, contain clear statements about *selection criteria* as well. The implication here is that this kind of psychotherapy is suitable only for *current crisis situations*, or *symptoms of recent onset*, in people with *essentially healthy personalities*.

What, then, about technique? The psychoanalytic technique contains a whole range of therapeutic devices and factors, including insight of all kinds given through interpretation, the interpretation of resistance and dreams, the development of transference and its interpretation and working-through, the transference neurosis, the link between transference and childhood, and what Alexander (1) calls the "corrective emotional experience"—the reexperiencing of an old relationship but with a new ending. Which of all these elements are relevant to brief psychotherapy?

Here again, experience seems to lead to clear-cut answers. Where the illness is of recent onset, or is due to a current crisis, it is often sufficient to give the patient insight into the conflicts involved, and thus many of the above elements in technique are found to be unnecessary. Moreover, since these elements are a feature of long-term therapy, it is reasonable to conclude that their use is likely to lead to long-term therapy and that therefore they should be avoided. The result is generalizations, of which the following are typical examples:

Finesinger (3):

> When used in relatively brief psychotherapy, it [insight therapy] seldom exposes the fantasies and memories that are most deeply repressed.... Dream or fantasy material is seldom used for interpretation excepting when a more extensive therapy is undertaken.

Pumpian-Mindlin (10):

> Interpretations ... are couched in more general terms and not related to necessarily specific historical conflicts and difficulties in the patient. In addition, the interpretations are usually made not in terms of unconscious underlying impulses but in terms of the more readily available preconscious material. One works primarily with the reverberations of earlier conflicts as they are reflected in adult and adolescent behavior and attitudes rather than attempting to uncover the genetic childhood conflicts *per se*.
> In short-term therapy there is a general tendency to avoid an intense transference and to take measures to diminish the transference phenomena which inevitably appear. Mechanically this is accomplished by means of less frequent visits and by implicitly or explicitly structuring therapy in terms of the circumscribed presenting problem only.

Bellak and Small (2):

> ... in brief psychotherapy positive transference is sought and maintained from the beginning to the end.... The emergence of negative transference is avoided as much as possible and referred to only on rare occasions when it can, in a helpful way, be related to other manifestations or when it stands in the way of therapeutic progress.

Straker (14):

> In essence, the aims of brief psychotherapy are to provide ego support and some gratification of oral needs while there is concurrent exploration of current interpersonal, family, and intrapsychic conflicts. The main problems are clarified, together with the patient's characteristic defenses and methods of problem solving. Transference interpretation is avoided where possible.

Now let us make a sudden leap to the following quotations:

(1) The patient was a young man of nineteen, complaining of depression, whose mother had died of burns when he was three and who was treated by a woman therapist with thirty-five 20-minute sessions over a few months.

> [Therapist:] "I feel you have been repressing not only your angry feelings for your mother, but also perhaps, the fact that you and she loved each other. . . . " Suddenly tears welled up, and the patient threw himself sobbing on the couch. After ten minutes he grew calm and said, with great feeling, "Silly, but I feel as if my own mother were all around me here. It's something so familiar."
>
> The emotional change in the patient was dramatic, he was ecstatically moved. Turning his attention to the therapist. he ordered her, "Tell me about *your* standards. I will accept them. Tell me what is right about sex, possessions, religion. Talk to me as you would to an adolescent. . . ." At the end of the interview, he said, "I know who I've been talking to—my mother! And I feel wonderful!"

(2) The patient was a young doctor of twenty-four complaining of bronchial asthma severe enough to make it impossible for him to practice. He was seen once a week by a woman therapist for nine months (i.e., about forty sessions). The quotation is from the first session after the therapist had been away for a holiday:

> When the patient came to the office, he was in the midst of a severe asthma attack. . . . It occurred to the therapist that he was probably angry with her for going away with her husband, so she mentioned that when he had found that his girl was still somewhat attached to a former suitor, he had dropped her immediately. The patient understood the allusion. "Oh yes," he said, "and this probably brings up your husband whom we were discussing as a rival before you left." Suddenly the asthma stopped completely. The patient began to laugh and said that . . . not even adrenalin had ever ended an attack so suddenly. He was at last convinced that he had been inhibiting feelings towards the therapist and he now confessed erotic impulses to her.

Here it should be added that the patient's stepmother was very young and openly seductive, and he had consciously had sexual feelings toward her; also, in the above exchanges he clearly understood references to the past.

(3) The patient was a man of thirty-one whose lifelong pattern was to suppress his own feelings and conform to what others required of him. He was seen for fourteen sessions by a male therapist. The following are quotations taken from throughout the course of therapy:

> (Session 7) I made the interpretation that always he must keep angry feelings out—that he deals with me in the same way as he deals with his boss, swallowing his resentment at the injustice of what is expected of him; this originating in his relation with his father, who, like me, was really felt to be of little use, but towards whom no resentment or anger or criticism could be acknowledged.
>
> (Session 11) The patient says that these talks must have made him become aware of feelings that he hadn't understood—of resentment—and he finds he is becoming increasingly indulgent towards himself and increasingly able to be angry when unreasonable demands are made on him. This is demonstrated in his relationships at work where he has been spontaneously angry and has found that it achieves good results. . . . it just seems to happen and only in retrospect does he see what he is doing.
>
> (Session 11, later) I interpreted the similarity between his description of his marriage and his description of his childhood feelings—that he must be grateful for what he has got, be uncomplaining, cut his losses, and look elsewhere for something to fill the gaps—that the same is happening here in therapy, he must be grateful for what he has got from me, and be uncomplaining about the very real dissatisfactions that still remain—he must cut his losses and retreat for fear that his demands, if they were to be expressed, would represent an aggressive, destructive, soiling attack upon the person to whom he also feels gratitude.

In session 12 the patient described a quarrel with his wife over her not allowing him sex as often as he would wish.

> Nothing more was said for a couple of days, but then to his surprise, his wife initiated love-making and it was entirely satisfactory to both sides.

(4) The patient was a man of fifty-four who had been on the waiting list for psychoanalysis for fifteen years and whose main problem was a lifelong inability to value himself as a man or to behave like one in any situation. He was seen by a male therapist for fourteen sessions.

(Session 14) He went on with a story about his father coming back from the War, with gifts for the family. It was a tragicomedy, for all these gifts were no good—a watch which fell to pieces for the daughter, some silver thing that almost broke in your hand for the son, etc. I interpreted this in the transference, how he appreciated my goodwill but thought little of what I had given him, and I pointed out how his father, impotent and unable to be anything but laughable, was his view of all men including himself and me. He went on to say that of course he hadn't known his father much—when he was near puberty his father had gone away to the War. The hint here was that his father had not helped him with his sexual problem as I had not, and I took this up. He repeated that he had been independent from an early age. I pointed out that he was now being "independent," and that on three occasions when the prospect of ending the treatment had occurred he had become independent and threatened to leave—rather than be deserted he was doing the deserting, to avoid having feelings of disappointment, longing and dependency on a man. I pointed out his loneliness all his life, his need for men, and this really shook him. He paused, sat back in his chair and thought, and said, "I have always felt my independence to be virtuous and never allowed myself to be owned by anybody." I pointed out that his ancestors included men as well as women, and contrasted his view of women as being people who had sexual tensions that "needed relief" with his view of men who brought home broken toys and gifts. I pointed out how he castrated his father regularly and denounced his potency in order to have his mother for himself. He again took this soberly and said, "Like Moses, like the Virgin Birth," and went on with a dawning realization that he had never allowed himself to have a father.

(5) The patient was a young man of twenty-eight who initially appeared to be suffering from a typical Oedipal syndrome but was quickly revealed in his thirty-three session therapy to be a paranoid personality, full of the kinds of fantasies that appear in schizophrenics as delusions. The following extracts are taken from session 18, immediately before a holiday break in treatment:

> I asked how much of his feelings of anger came out at me, since we had recognized that it was easier for him to talk about anger towards his parents than towards me right here. He said, "I feel despair. I still have feelings of being isolated and used. This feeling of being used brings rage and a feeling of being abandoned brings with it a sense of isolation."

I picked up the feeling of being used and abandoned right here. He said, "I do feel I've been put in a pigeon-hole of psychiatric bureaucracy. I wouldn't like to make you angry, though, for then I would be the loser." I brought out his fear that I could not view anger as part of a helping interchange in a good relationship between two people.

Later he started talking about how at work he was having to deal with some idiotic bosses. He then brought out anger towards a therapist who had said to him 4 years ago that he could never hold down a job or get a better job. "I feel small, ugly, and repulsive. It's a mood like I had in childhood." I mentioned that this must be the child part of him feeling used, and being angry at being abandoned. Probably he was afraid that this anger would spoil that which has been good. . . . He went on to say that he had a stomach ache over the week-end and it was coming up here right now. It must be with rage and despair. In fact this stomach pain must be rage. ". . . I felt we left this final session before the holiday emotionally closer to a working relationship.

(The fact that all the patients were men is neither here nor there—we have plenty of examples of similar occurrences with women patients, but the examples happen not to be sufficiently clear or suitable to be used as illustrations.)

It needs to be said at once that all these patients—with the possible exception of the last, for whom we have only a short follow-up—showed permanent major changes in long-standing behavior patterns, some of them clearly of the kind that would be called "character changes" if treatment had been long-term.

The first two examples were taken from Alexander and French's classical book *Psychoanalytic Therapy* (1946); the third and fourth, from patients treated at the Tavistock Clinic under the leadership of Michael Balint (see Malan [5,6]); the last, from a trainee's treatment of a patient in my Brief Therapy Unit in 1973 (see Malan [6]).

What is happening here? How can these examples be reconciled with all the statements quoted above: that insight therapy seldom exposes the fantasies that are most deeply repressed; that interpretations should not be related to historical difficulties; that the emergence of negative transference is avoided wherever possible; that suitable patients are those who are basically healthy and are suffering from recent symptoms of acute onset; that the results are essentially symptomatic and palliative; and finally that implicitly any attempt to go further will lead inevitably to long-term treatment?

The answer is very simple. The statements quoted above are

incorrect only if they are regarded as *exclusive* generalizations, that is, if they describe a single kind of brief therapy and imply that no other kind exists. If they are *inclusive* rather than exclusive, merely showing that this is a kind of brief therapy that does exist, then they are perfectly correct.

Now, clinicians may scoff at "scientific" attempts to investigate psychotherapy, and often their contempt may be justified, but much of science consists of no more than systematic common sense—trying to make sure that, if one has made a particular phenomenon into a generalization, there are not other phenomena that make the generalization invalid. The phenomena of nature are often so complex and unforeseeable that this procedure is very necessary, to whatever extent the observation fits in with what is expected. In this particular case the basic observations are that superficial (though useful) results may follow brief and superficial therapy in healthy individuals and that deeper results follow longer and deeper therapy in less healthy individuals, and it is very natural to conclude that these are the only phenomena to occur—especially as they fit in so well with expectation. This is the way in which highly plausible conclusions are reached from clinical impressions. Surely, it is merely being obsessional to investigate other possible combinations which seem on the face of it so improbable. For instance, can deep results follow brief and superficial therapy? Obviously not: this is a contradiction in terms and in any case would be very close to spontaneous remission, which does not exist. Can therapy be deep but remain brief? Obviously not: deep therapy inevitably leads to the transference neurosis, the resolution of which is uniformly time-consuming. Can brief therapy be effective in severe and long-standing illnesses? Again obviously not: a pattern established for years will take years to correct. And so on. Yet the truth is that anyone who attempts to carry out brief psychotherapy does sporadically meet observations that seem to contradict these apparently obvious conclusions. The case histories in Alexander and French, two of which were quoted above, are clear examples. Here are three general statements that speak of the same kind of observation:

Pumpian-Mindlin (10):

> First, I should like to point out an important negative finding for this type of therapy, namely, that short-term treatment is not dependent upon the amount or seeming severity of the psychopathology present in the patient nor upon the severity of the earlier traumata suffered by the patient. Our case material included cases

of transvestitism, frigidity, colitis, pedophilia, depression, paranoia, impotence, and various character disorders. The mere presence of severe psychopathology is no contra-indication to short-term therapy.

Wolberg (15):

> It is essential here to qualify the finding that acute problems are best suited for short-term approaches.... I have personally treated chronic cases with short-term methods, including obsessive-compulsive neurosis and borderline schizophrenia and I have observed many gratifying results.... The best strategy, in my opinion, is to assume that every patient, irrespective of diagnosis, will respond to short-term treatment unless he proves himself refractory to it.

Mann (8):

> The selection of patients for this kind of time-restricted psychotherapy remains to be satisfactorily defined.... My present experience indicates that it can be useful to any patient in whom a fairly clear central present issue can be defined.

It is clear that there are two entirely different views of brief psychotherapy represented here, which—by analogy with terms used in surgery and not, be it said, in politics—I have called the "conservative" and "radical" views, respectively. According to the conservative view, only mild illnesses of recent onset can be relieved, the technique should be superficial and should avoid the use of transference, and the results can be no more than palliative. According to the radical view, severe and long-standing illnesses can be altered at depth by a technique freely employing transference and the link with the past, and, in fact, containing most of the elements thought to be essential to psychoanalysis itself. The conservative view fits in well with the preconceptions derived from long-term therapy, while many authors seem to have made observations that *in certain cases* fit in with the radical view. What is not clear is whether these latter cases represent any appreciable proportion of those suitable for brief therapy; indeed, perhaps they are very exceptional, and the conservative view is basically correct. Obviously, only systematic investigation will settle the question.

The above anticipates both later thinking and later results; the problem could not be put so clearly twenty years ago. When Balint decided to investigate brief therapy at the Tavistock Clinic in 1955, the situation was somewhat different. In 1946 Alexander and French had published their book, based on the systematic study of brief therapy in Chicago over a number of years (they said their material numbered over 500 cases). But something had gone seriously wrong. Not only was their claim of far-reaching therapeutic results with brief therapy a challenge to orthodox psychoanalytic opinion; in addition, they had experimented with various modifications to the standard analytic technique, such as varying the frequency of sessions or role-playing in order to highlight transference attitudes, and, worst of all, they seemed to be advocating changes in analytic technique rather than a method of brief therapy based on analysis. The result was that their work brought a storm of hostility, with no one apparently capable of realizing that these authors' case histories represented empirical observations that needed to be taken seriously. Even Balint himself dismissed me somewhat abruptly when I pointed out parallels between cases of theirs and cases that we were about to take on, with the intention of suggesting ways in which we might ourselves proceed.

What was most important, however, was Balint's realization that if psychoanalytic methods were ever to make any contribution to the routine treatment of patients in psychotherapeutic clinics, this had to be through the development of shortened methods and hence that the whole question of psychoanalytic brief therapy needed to be reinvestigated.

From a scientific point of view, our method of working was crude in the extreme: to take on patients thought to be appropriate and to see what therapeutic results ensued. Since every one of us started with essentially conservative preconceptions, this amounted to taking on relatively healthy patients with acute and recent illnesses, employing a nontransference technique for a maximum of about a dozen sessions, and seeing what happened.

Crude though it was, there are many tentative conclusions that it could have prompted: if, for example, even with these apparently suitable patients improvements were never anything more than palliative and short-lived, or if whenever strong transference feelings arose therapy got into serious difficulties, or if results had been spectacularly good, in which case further exploration of the limits of brief therapy would have been clearly indicated.

On the other hand, such a design does have serious drawbacks, most of which arise from the elementary scientific principle that a study of this kind can only be meaningful if it involves the possibility of *comparison*. Thus if *all* patients were suffering from illnesses of recent onset it would not be possible to study the effect on outcome of *duration of complaints*; if all patients were given nontransference therapies it would not be possible to study the effect of transference interpretation;

since all patients were to be given *treatment*, it would not be possible to check on the kinds of change that might occur without treatment; and so on.

As I said at the outset, the history of psychoanalysis provides fascinating examples of empirical observations going undiscovered. The history of Balint's research now gave a fascinating example of the operation of chance in scientific discovery. What happened was twofold. First, patients with mild illnesses of recent onset were not as common in the population referred to the Tavistock Clinic as we could have wished, with the result that we took on many patients who did not fulfill our criteria. Second, as well-trained analysts we were quite incapable of using either a superficial or a nontransference technique, with the result that we both provided a sample far more suitable for scientific scrutiny than we had originally intended and at the same time began the process of exploring the limits of brief psychotherapy—a process which has continued ever since and is not yet by any means complete.

Following is an example of how we got drawn into much deeper therapy than we had planned:

One of our first patients was a man of thirty, the Lighterman (i.e., a barge pilot), who had begun to suffer from severe anxiety attacks after a minor head injury two months before. He was clearly a man with a good personality and a good marriage, but behind the acute symptoms lay a relatively severe compulsive and hypochondriacal personality—illustrating at once how acute symptoms often cannot be separated from long-standing personality disorders. He was referred to us by a psychiatrist, and his first contact with us was for projection testing (ORT, a psychoanalytically based version of the TAT). Extracts from the psychologist's report are as follows:

> ...vainly fighting off hostile forces coming at him from all sides... fairly strong obsessional defensive tactics...anxiety and lack of spontaneity in his relations with women...wish to regress and return to a primitive nursing situation...must control his aggression at all costs...destructive wishes towards a mother-figure are shown quite transparently with extreme guilt...fear that his ego will be overwhelmed by hostile forces within himself...unconscious aggressive feelings, especially towards women, are controlled by compulsive reparative activities...his feeling of tremendous demands made on him must reflect his own primitive demands for support and satisfaction....

Thus, though the patient's presenting symptom was certainly of acute and recent onset, the underlying pathology seemed very different from the kind that we had imagined we were likely to be able to deal with.

This did not deter us in the least. The patient was seen by the therapist immediately after his projection testing, and now there seemed to emerge first the theme of guilt about being *selfish*, which the therapist pointed out, and later a story about a woman living upstairs in their house whose husband had come down to complain about the patient's children making a noise and how a fight had nearly developed.

The patient was seen again the next day. When he was asked what he remembered from the previous session, he said, "I seem to remember you told me I was selfish."

In the discussion on this, one of the workshop members, Mr. Phillipson, pointed out that surely the basic interpretation of this material involved both transference and the link between transference and the relation to parents: the patient was afraid that the therapist, representing his father, might criticize him for being a nuisance to his mother.

At the next session (no. 3) the therapist gave the patient this interpretation, which had the most extraordinary effect. The patient was precipitated into a confusional state, and there emerged a story about a road accident involving a little girl that the patient had witnessed about a year before. This incident proved to be a focal point of therapy. The patient revealed (1) that he felt his recent anxiety had started from that point and that the head injury had only been a further exacerbating factor; (2) that he had then forgotten it but had been reminded of it by one of the cards of the ORT; (3) that this had resulted in his arriving at the first therapeutic session in an anxious and confused state; but finally (4) that from then he had begun to feel better. The incident led into his whole childhood relation with his mother, who had always been overanxious about his playing in the road, was compulsive like the patient, had recently told the patient he was an unwanted child, had suffered what appeared to be a paranoid-depressive breakdown when the patient was three and had apparently been shocked out of this by the death of the patient's sister when he was eight, had remarked that she wished it had been the patient who had died rather than his sister, had required the patient to help in the house instead of allowing him to go out and play, and had used the threat of suicide if the patient did not behave himself.

The patient, a working-class man with little education but a great capacity for insight, was able to see intuitively the connection between his mother's overanxiousness and her wish to get rid of him, to accept interpretations about the link between his anger against his employers, who expected too much of him, his anger with his mother, and his overcompensating inability to refuse extra work when it was thrust on him, and finally to work with interpretations about his anger with the therapist for not looking after him properly and to see the link between this and his relation with his mother. Therapy was terminated after seventeen sessions.

It is now clear that the therapeutic result was only partial. The patient retained a phobia of going out in the open river (the parallel with going out into the street was pointed out to him but did not help) and remained fairly strongly hypochondriacal. On the other hand, he lost his acute anxiety and apparently to a large extent his long-standing compulsiveness, and he seems, within the above limits, to have made a relatively satisfactory adjustment to life. Direct follow-up by interview was one year seven months; indirect follow-up through the G.P. was nearly twelve years.

This is obviously not an ideal example since the therapeutic result was equivocal. This was one of our earliest therapies, however, and it illustrates that the work into which we became drawn was by no means superficial; that the interpretation of the transference apparently resulted in a dramatic penetration of early resistance; that this interpretation involved the *link with his parents;* and finally that in the later stages of therapy the interpretation of negative transference and dependence together (once more) with the link with his parents apparently played a crucial part. In other words, this was a therapy that seemed to contradict every aspect of the conservative view of brief psychotherapy.

During the second year of operation of Balint's workshop we were joined by therapists from the Cassel Hospital. By this time most inhibitions about severe and chronic conditions, and all inhibitions about the use of transference, had been swept aside, and among the results was the above-mentioned therapy of a man of fifty-four who had been on the waiting list for fifteen years. This patient, after fourteen sessions, became capable of functioning as a man in a way that had never been possible for him before.

It is worthwhile telling the story of how this apparently totally unsuitable patient came to be taken on. At that time one of my functions in the workshop was to screen the applications for treatment coming into the clinic, and while doing this I happened upon a letter from this patient. He had been locked for many years in a hopeless marriage with an exceedingly neurotic woman who had finally been admitted to a hospital for one of her psychosomatic illnesses, at which point a change had come over him. The following is a condensed quotation from his letter of application:

> An urge has come over me to throw away what is useless in the house, to let the air and light in. This urge must be complementary to my wish to clean up the dark corners of my own soul. I am stressing, perhaps overstressing, the hopefulness of this moment, but I cannot overstate the case for the urgency.

I read this letter out loud in the workshop, and one of the Cassel therapists volunteered to take him on. At the initial assessment the only feature in his favor was the letter, from which two factors may be extracted: *capacity for insight* and *motivation*.

The conclusion to be drawn from these cases and those quoted from the literature is that *sometimes* relatively severe and longstanding illnesses can be changed radically and that *sometimes* it is not harmful to use transference and make the link with childhood. But this is the kind of basis on which conclusions are reached by clinical impression, which is inadequate to say the least. What is needed is a systematic study of the factors associated with favorable and unfavorable outcome in all the cases treated, taking into account the characteristics of the population from which the cases were drawn.

A detailed account of this work, which has spanned nearly twenty years, is given in three publications: *A Study of Brief Psychotherapy, Toward the Validation of Dynamic Psychotherapy, The Frontier of Brief Psychotherapy* (Malan [5,6,7]). Here I shall do no more than summarize the conclusions.

First of all, the following statements need to be made: (1) As described above, the conservative view of brief psychotherapy is that suitable patients are those with mild illnesses of recent onset, that the technique used should avoid transference, and that the results, though sometimes valuable and long-lasting, are essentially superficial. (2) The number of clear-cut exceptions I have quoted above may well be extremely rare, with the result that the conservative view is still *statistically* correct and for all practical purposes should continue to be used.

It should be said at once that the latter statement is invalid. In the first study, which was of eighteen patients, the conservative view was contradicted in every detail. This, however, might possibly be no more than a chance result, produced by the characteristics of the sample that we happened to have been given. On the other hand, if the result were to be repeated on a second sample, it would approach the status of a scientific conclusion. This is in fact what happened. In both samples neither *severity of pathology* nor *recent onset* bore any relation to outcome; the best results were those in which *transference* was not only extensively interpreted but was *related to childhood;* and the improvements were clearly *deep-seated* and often survived a follow-up of more than five years.

Of course, this does not mean that patients with mild and recent illnesses are *unsuitable* for brief psychotherapy; it simply means that they are not the *only* patients suitable. Yet what our results do indicate is that there are many patients with such illnesses who *are* unsuitable and that, on the other hand, there are many patients who do *not* fit into this category but who *are* suitable. The result is that these criteria pertaining to severity and duration are relatively useless.

But they are not entirely useless. They serve a major purpose, namely, to exclude obviously unsuitable patients at the beginning.

There are certain categories of patients who should never be considered. The following is a list of features adapted from H. P. Hildebrand (unpublished) and used for many years as excluding factors at the London Clinic of Psycho-Analysis: serious suicidal attempts, gross destructive or self-destructive acting out, serious drug addiction or alcoholism, long-term hospitalization, several courses of ECT, and incapacitating chronic obsessional or phobic symptoms.

Once such patients have been excluded, the criteria arise from three processes: first, taking the patient's history; second, the interaction between patient and therapist in the initial assessment period; third, the way in which findings from these two processes can be used to forecast events in therapy.

During the initial assessment as many as possible of the following conditions should be sought:

(1) **The focus**
   (a) *The current conflict.* There is a precipitating factor that gives a clue to the current conflict.

   (b) *The "nuclear" conflict.* There are (i) previous precipitating events, (ii) early traumatic experiences, (iii) family constellations, or (iv) repetitive patterns, that give a clue to the "nuclear" conflict.

   (c) *Congruence between current and nuclear conflicts.* The current conflict and the "nuclear" conflict can be seen to be essentially the same.

It is when these factors are present that the therapist is most likely to be able to formulate a basic circumscribed theme for his interpretations, which we call the *focus*. Thus the first main selection criterion is concerned with the *therapist* and may be stated as ability to *formulate a focus*. But the therapist must also make sure that the focus is acceptable to the *patient*. For this the following criteria must be met:

(2) *Response to interpretation*
During the assessment period the patient has been given partial interpretations relevant to the focus and has responded to them in a way that convincingly confirms them.

(3) *Motivation for insight*
It goes without saying that the patient must be able to talk about feelings and to recognize that his problems are psychological. Besides this, however, he must show adequate *motivation* to attempt to solve his problems by *achieving insight*. This is an additional—and equally important—reason for giving interpretations during the assessment period; since in this way the patient has been provided with a foretaste of the kind of therapy he will be offered. It is not necessary for his motivation to *start* high as long as it increases during his exposure to the clinical situation; correspondingly, decreasing motivation is a poor prognostic sign.

Finally, we must add the following crucial criterion:

(4) *Dangers*
The therapist must project himself into the future and try to forecast the types of events that are likely to occur if the patient is taken into interpretative therapy. Here there are a number of *dangers* that need to be foreseen and may be thought to be so probable as to cause the patient to be rejected. The most important of these are (a) the prediction that issues will become involved that are too complex and deep-seated to be resolved in a short time; (b) severe dependence and other forms of unfavorable transference; (c) the danger of decompensation, depressive or psychotic; (d) suicide; and (e) uncontrollable acting out. If any of these dangers are forecast, the therapist must be able to state firmly that he believes they can be avoided. Put in a more positive way, the therapist must believe that the patient has the strength to manage on his own both in-between sessions and after termination.

These criteria can be summarized as follows:
After obviously unsuitable patients have been eliminated,
(1) a circumscribed focus can be formulated;
(2) the patient has responded to interpretations based on this focus;
(3) the patient has the motivation to work in therapy based on this focus;
(4) the possible dangers of uncovering psychotherapy in this particular patient have been considered and are thought to be avoidable.

TECHNIQUE

The first important characteristic of technique is that it is "focal," i.e., the therapist tries to concentrate on a single basic theme, planned in advance. In *The Frontier of Brief Psychotherapy* (6) I have written that I am often asked how this is possible—after all, what the therapist can interpret depends essentially on what the patient says, which is not under the therapist's control—and in the past have found this question difficult to answer. The reason it is difficult has not so much to do with technique as it does with *selection*. If the patient has the characteristics of the focal patient described above, i.e., if the current conflict and the "nuclear" conflict can both be identified and are seen to be the same, then this conflict will be the inevitable theme of his communications and—with a therapist who is reasonably skilled—therapy *cannot help* being focal. In addition to this, of course, the therapist can exercise further control by always choosing those interpretations that are relevant to the focus and carefully avoiding those that are not. This is what is meant by *selective attention* and *selective neglect*.

Put another way, the technique is *active* in pursuit of the focus, but otherwise the interpretations used differ in no way from those used in any form of psychoanalytic therapy, that is, interpretations of resistance, fantasies, and, above all, forms of transference.

The importance of transference needs to be very carefully demarcated. We have shown empirically, in two separate studies, that *statistically* the therapies that have been most successful are those in which the transference has been not only extensively interpreted but *linked with childhood* (this entails what I call the transference/parent or T/P link). Yet this should not be overvalued and elevated into a fundamental principle—a common error when some important new observation has been made. We have in our case material successful therapies in which the T/P link was never made and others in which even the transference was never interpreted at all. Here we would say that if transference arises it should be interpreted, and if the link with childhood becomes clear—and obviously only then—it should be made.

NUMBER OF SESSIONS, TIME LIMITS, AND TERMINATION

The word "brief" is relative, and our own form of brief therapy probably has an upper limit longer than would be allowed by many other workers. In our own two series combined (forty-seven patients successfully followed up) there were outstandingly successful therapies with eleven, twelve, fourteen, twenty-nine, thirty, and forty sessions, respectively.

In our early work we made it clear to the patient at the outset that the work was not intended to last more than a few months, but we left the actual number of sessions indefinite. As we grew in confidence we began to feel that it was possible to set a time limit from the start. This has considerable advantages, since it gives the work a definite beginning, middle and end, and the issue of termination enters naturally. It is now standard practice to use a time limit of twenty sessions for an experienced therapist and thirty for a trainee. If dependence is likely to become a major issue, thirty sessions even for an experienced therapist is probably better. I find thirty sessions a convenient number because it provides time for a good deal of working through and makes it possible to deal with more than one major issue.

In our later work—in agreement with James Mann—we have found it much better to set a time limit in terms of a definite *date* rather than a *number of sessions*. This eliminates at a stroke the necessity for keeping count and also the problem of what to do about sessions that the patient misses and the question of whether this was due to reality or acting out.

As I have implied above, a certain degree of dependence on the therapist (obviously not too much) is entirely acceptable in our form of brief therapy and indeed is welcomed, as are almost all forms of involvement in transference. This means that interpretations about anger and feelings of loss at termination are standard practice. The therapist should always be on the lookout for such interpretations, and often the last quarter of therapy should deal with this as a major issue. On the other hand, of course, there are therapies in which this does not even become an issue.

Providing it is practically possible, we always make it clear to the patient that we wish to keep in touch with him and that if he has a crisis or anything at all that he wants to talk over after the termination of regular sessions he may come back from time to time. It is our experience—here in disagreement with Mann—that this in no way softens feelings about termination, which is still felt by the patient as if it were absolute.

Just as the main transference during therapy will repeat relationships from the past which need to be interpreted where possible, the transference at the end of therapy will repeat feelings about losses in the past which also need to be interpreted. If the main transference also involves loss, which it often does, then there is no discontinuity whatsoever.

Once more, it must be emphasized that dealing with termination should not be overvalued and elevated into a fundamental principle. There are many patients who never become dependent; they get what they want from therapy and feel ready to terminate and go their own way. In our two series, work on termination always correlated positively with favorable outcome, but in the second series this correlation was far from significant and—as mentioned above—there were a number of highly successful therapies in which termination never became an issue at all.

OUTCOME

In the second series of thirty patients followed up, there were twenty-two who had fewer than forty sessions, and of these, nine were judged on strict psychodynamic criteria to be at least "improved." In these nine, the length of follow-up ranged from three years four months to seven years four months, with a mean of just over five years. Details of these patients are shown in the following table.

Although the limited information included in such a table cannot convey the full quality of the improvements, enough is given to show that these included changes in longstanding neurotic behavior patterns. Full details will be found in *The Frontier of Brief Psychotherapy* and *Toward the Validation of Dynamic Psychotherapy* (6,7).

CONCLUSION

The comparision of three somewhat different forms of brief psychotherapy has led to some very important observations which need emphasis and which have both practical and theoretical consequences.

The first is as follows: In the past I have always been struck by the remarkable convergence between my conclusions and those of Dr.

Sifneos, reached in very different ways, and did not think there were any major differences between us. As I now realize, this is not entirely true. Apart from patients suffering from acute grief reactions, Dr. Sifneos largely confines his selection for brief therapy to patients (of either sex) suffering from oedipal problems. This is clearly a consequence of the conditions under which he has worked, in the sense that patients suitable for brief therapy have been relatively plentiful and therefore he has tended to confine his approach to those patients who, it would seem, are most likely to be helped by brief methods. But this is, again, one of the consequences of operating in a clinical setting with preconceptions that are never tested out. As I have outlined above, we started with similar preconceptions but, because of the dearth of patients suitable for brief therapy according to our ideas, by chance took on a number of patients with different and "deeper" kinds of problems and in some of them obtained good results. Here it must be said that Dr. Sifneos tries to keep his therapies to about fifteen sessions, whereas at the Tavistock Clinic we use a standard therapy of thirty sessions, which may account for some of the differences between us. Nevertheless, an extremely important point that I wish to make in this chapter is that while of course I do not differ from Dr. Sifneos in believing that patients suitable for brief therapy are largely made up of those with oedipal problems, I do disagree very strongly with the view that they are the *only* patients who are suitable. Again I would like to emphasize that if one has the courage either to take on patients with deeper problems or —as has happened to us—to persist with brief therapy when a patient has been wrongly assessed and turns out to be much more ill than originally supposed, then one may be very favorably surprised by the kinds of result that can sometimes be obtained.

This can be immediately demonstrated by one of Dr. Davanloo's cases, presented in "The Case of the Cement-Mixer, Man," Chapter 17 of this volume. The patient was a man with a severely obsessive/compulsive character who also showed a preoccupation with women's breasts which could only label his relation to women as one to "part objects." In addition, he showed a lifelong pattern of passivity and compliance. He would never have been considered suitable for brief therapy by either Dr. Sifneos or myself. Yet Dr. Davanloo, by using a highly confrontative technique, with frequent transference interpretation, achieved an outstanding therapeutic result within about forty sessions.

It is significant that in this particular case the focus used by Dr. Davanloo was entirely oedipal. This leads to a second important point. As mentioned above, Dr. Sifneos confines himself largely to oedipal foci. In addition, he employs two aspects of technique that differ from

Details of Successful Brief Therapies

Patient	Age	Initial State (duration)	Final State	No. of Sessions	Follow-up (since termination)
Stationery Manufacturer	45	Severe "jealousy paranoia" (7 mos.)	Apparently recovered; fully effective in all areas of life	28	3 yrs. 4 mos.
Indian Scientist	29	Premature ejaculation (6 yrs); inability to commit himself to a woman; working below potential; strained relations with work (all for many years)	Highly satisfactory marriage; fully potent; leader in his field; gets on well with men	12	7 yrs. 4 mos.
Almoner	22	Depression (a few months); character defense of keeping everything "nice"	Recovered from depression; emotional freedom; satisfactory marriage	11	5 yrs. 8 mos.
Maintenance Man	39	Acute anxiety (5 wks); inability to be effective with very difficult wife (many years)	Anxiety recovered; effective with wife within limits of situation	30	4 yrs. 9 mos.
Gibson Girl	18	Agoraphobia (5 mos.); sexual anxieties	Recovered; satisfactory marriage	28	5 yrs. 8 mos.
Buyer	27	Blackout in response to crisis situation with fiancée and her father (2 days)	Moderately satisfactory marriage; more effective in work	18	7 yrs. 3 mos.

Details of Successful Brief Therapies *(continued)*

Patient	Age	Initial State (duration)	Final State	No. of Sessions	Follow-up (since termination)
Zoologist	22	Depression (2 yrs.); pattern of self-destructive anger (abandoned studies); internal "barrier" preventing contact with girls	Depression recovered; successful as zoologist; satisfactory marriage; some residue of self-destructive anger but much improved	32	3 yrs. 5 mos.
Pesticide Chemist	31	Obsessional rumination; inability to assert himself at work; lack of emotional freedom with wife (all for many years)	Obsessional rumination recovered; able to assert himself; limited improvement in relation with wife	14	3 yrs. 10 mos.
Mrs. Morley	60	Extremely possessive relation with grown-up daughter (many years)	Daughter allowed freedom	9	5 yrs. 4 mos.

those used by us, namely, (1) continuing to interpret his focus even when the patient is manifestly in resistance and (2) ignoring manifestations of dependence. It is quite clear both that this can lead to successful therapy and that it tends to *prevent the development of dependence as a major issue.* The patient feels that he is doing his own work and, having solved his problem within about fifteen sessions, feels ready to manage on his own. This demonstrates the important influence that our technique can have on the course of therapy and is something from which we all can learn.

It is also evident, however, that *it is not always necessary to prevent the development of dependence,* and that dependence can be allowed to become a major issue and can even be used as the main focus of therapy—though it may well be true, of course, that therapy will tend to be somewhat longer. Here "The Case of the Woman in Mourning," (Chapter 20), is highly relevant. For this patient the whole issue of therapy was her need for human closeness and her depression when this was disappointed, and this clearly arose from a severe loss she had suffered at the age of five, which in turn became a major issue of her therapy especially in the transference at termination.

It thus becomes obvious that although each of us has formulated certain principles concerned with selection criteria and technique which work in practice, we have not by any means exhausted the possibilities. Dependence may be avoided by the use of a certain kind of technique, but equally it can be made the main issue of therapy; improbable patients may be made into good patients by means of aggressive and confronting interpretations; and, as described at the beginning of this chapter, certain severely disturbed personalities may benefit if the therapist fearlessly interprets some of their deepest mechanisms. So, if there is one message that I would wish to convey, it is to stress the need for further exploration of the limits of brief psychotherapy so that we can make a true estimate of its potential contribution to mental health.

REFERENCES

1. Alexander, F. and T.M. French. *Psychoanalytic Therapy.* New York: Ronald Press Co., 1946.
2. Bellak, L. and L. Small. *Emergency Therapy and Brief Psychotherapy.* New York: Grune & Stratton, 1965.
3. Finesinger, J.E. Psychiatric Interviewing. I. Some Principles and Procedures in Insight Therapy. *Amer. J. Psychiat.,* 105:187, 1948.
4. Knight, R.P. Application of Psychoanalytic Concepts in Psychotherapy. *Bull. Menninger Clin.,* 1:99, 1937.

5. Malan, D.H. *A Study of Brief Psychotherapy.* London: Tavistock; Philadelphia: Lippincott, 1963. (To be republished by Plenum Press, New York.)
6. Malan, D.H. *The Frontier of Brief Psychotherapy.* New York: Plenum Press, 1976) (Republished by Plenum Press, New York, 1975).
7. Malan, D.H. *Toward the Validation of Dynamic Psychotherapy.* New York: Plenum Press, 1976.
8. Mann, J. The Specific Limitation of Time in Psychotherapy. *Seminars in Psychiatry,* 1:375, 1969.
9. Murphy, W.F. A Comparison of Psychoanalysis with Dynamic Psychotherapies. *J. Nerv. Ment. Dis.,* 126:441, 1958.
10. Pumpian-Mindlin, E. Considerations in the Selection of Patients for Short-Term Therapy. *Amer. J. Psychother.,* 7:641, 1953.
11. Sifneos, P.E. *Short-Term Psychotherapy and Emotional Crisis.* Cambridge, Mass.: Harvard University Press, 1972.
12. Sifneos, P.E. An Overview of a Psychiatric Clinic Population. *Amer. J. Psychiat.* 130:1033, 1973.
13. Speers, R.W. Brief Psychotherapy with College Women. *Amer. J. Orthopsychiat.,* 32:434, 1962.
14. Straker, M. Brief Psychothrapy in an Outpatient Clinic: Evolution and Evaluation. *Amer. J. Psychiat.,* 124:1219, 1968.
15. Wolberg, L.R. (ed). *Short-Term Psychotherapy.* New York: Grune & Stratton, 1965.

Part II

EVALUATION, CRITERIA FOR SELECTION OF PATIENTS FOR SHORT-TERM DYNAMIC PSYCHOTHERAPY

This section presents three papers (Chapt. 5) read by H. Davanloo, P.E. Sifneos and D.H. Malan at the First and Second International Symposium with the introduction by A.M. Mann and A.E. Moll and subsequent discussions. The remaining seven chapters of the section present edited audiovisual transcripts of interviews with patients, each followed by discussion as to whether the interviewees were candidates for short-term dynamic psychotherapy:

Chapter 6: "The Case of the Italian Housewife," initial interview by P.E. Sifneos

Chapter 7: "The Case of the Secretary with the Violent Father," interview by D.H. Malan

Chapter 8: "The Case of the College Student," interview by P.E. Sifneos

Chapter 9: "The Case of the Teeth-Grinding Woman," initial interview by H. Davanloo with vignettes of the psychotherapeutic process presented during discussion

Chapter 10: "The Case of the Secretary with Temper Tantrums," initial interview by D.H. Malan

Chapter 11: "The Case of the Woman in the Tower of London," initial interview by P.E. Sifneos

Chapter 12: "The Case of the Angry, Childlike Woman," initial interview by H. Davanloo

Chapter 5
Short-Term Dynamic Psychotherapies

1. Introduction

Dr. A. M. Mann:

The two International Symposiums have brought together psychiatrists from many parts of the world, mental-health professionals with diverse backgrounds, viewpoints and origins. Dr. Davanloo, the major dynamic force behind these events, has provided a situation in which we can meet and exchange ideas and learn from one another. Here Ghandi's classic exposition of his basic philosophy—"La véritable éducation consiste à tirer le meilleur de soi-même. Quel meilleur livre peut-il exister que le livre de l'humanité?"—serves as our working motto. The chief protagonists—in alphabetical order, Drs. Davanloo, Malan and Sifneos—are not here merely to bask in the fleeting glow of the psychological spotlight. Their presence serves as a focus for discussion; they are here to lead the way, to share with us their guidelines and, most of all, to serve as role models.

These symposiums are not merely theoretical exercises nor hackneyed anecdotal accounts of certain psychotherapeutic endeavors. Far from it. The people involved take on the task many consider to be *the* most challenging in our field; they put themselves *on the line*. They demonstrate their techniques, expose their weak points and strong points, their successes and failures, to the scrutiny, criticism and commentary of their peers. This in my opinion is a determined step in the search for truth. Perhaps the truth will not be found; perhaps there are several truths and not just one. But I do feel confident that we will have here an opportunity to scrutinize with the most rigorous and comprehensive methodology we have yet seen the way in which one person can explore the thoughts, feelings, intimacies, conflicts, joys and sorrows of another person's life.

We are here searching for better ways to ease the tremendous burden of human suffering that emotional conflict carries. If from our sessions comes a better understanding of the mechanisms of human behavior, each of us will have gained something personally.

We will probably see that there is no "magic," but I think also we will find ourselves at least at the starting point of devising a technically sound approach to certain kinds of emotional illness—illness that can be absolutely disabling and have a devastating impact on human dignity and interaction.

The topic, short-term dynamic psychotherapy, is by no means a neonate or even a fledgling. It is already a youngster brimming with enthusiasm, a youngster already recognized as showing strength and inventiveness, and promising great hopes for the future.

The development of the Short-Term Psychotherapy Unit at Montreal General Hospital dates back to 1963, when Dr. Davanloo organized what was then called the "Short-Term Psychotherapy Program." From 1963 through 1974, 130 patients were treated by this method, and the unit has by now three- to seven-year follow-ups on at least 40 percent of these patients.

From the historical point of view, it is an interesting observation that Drs. Davanloo, Malan and Sifneos were mutually unaware of one another's work in short-term psychotherapy until 1973. It was then that they came together, which led ultimately to the Montreal Symposium on Short-Term Dynamic Psychotherapy, then to the First International Symposium in 1975, and finally to our assembly here today.

I realize that because of our diversities of background, our experiential differences, our disparate theoretical orientations, we will not all agree on what is "right" during this symposium. Let us not be afraid of honest difference of opinion; let us not hesitate to voice our doubts, to bring our concerns into the open. Frank and full discussion of how each and every one of us feels about the human condition is expected—indeed, absolutely necessary—during the next few days.

After all, this is an educational process, and as the famed revolutionist Danton said, "Après le pain, l'éducation est le premier besoin d'un peuple."

As to our differences, let's emphasize the *positive*. The poet Paul Valéry put it best when he said, "Enrichissons-nous de nos différences mutuelles." What could be more suitable for this symposium?

Dr. A. E. Moll:

The bridging between the classical teaching and training in psychoanalysis that a patient can only really be helped by full analysis lasting anywhere from two to five or more years, and the more modern if not radical view that the patient can be successfully treated not only symptomatically, but with lasting improvement and changes in his neurotic pattern by short-term psychoanalytically oriented psychotherapy of, say, ten full sessions, can be a source of conflict if not of utter confusion.

I shall never forget the endless discussions, arguments, rationalizations and hostilities engendered by Alexander and French when they dared to challenge the then-sacred tenets of classical psychoanalysis. Let's face it: the risk is still present and, I surmise, may always be present so long as any new technique or approach to psychotherapy is purported to be modified psychoanalysis—spelled with a capital *P*—instead of a new technique of brief psychotherapy founded on, and making use of, some of the tenets of orthodox psychoanalysis. Curiously enough, even the above tentative explanation does not fully satisfy me, nor does it remove the dichotomy still present in me. Notwithstanding my conscious sincere claim to eclecticism, it is quite possible that some may feel the same tensions. What we do not doubt is a great need for effective short-term psychotherapy, and the achievements in this area by Drs. Sifneos, Malan and Davanloo, and their co-workers, are examples of excellence.

As chief psychiatrist and chairman of the Department of Psychiatry of The Montreal General Hospital from its inception up to my retirement from administrative duties just three years ago, I was witness to an ever-decreasing interest in the specialization of interview psychotherapy, with more and more time and energy being oriented and directed to the teaching and training of organically centered psychiatry, with money for research being specifically directed toward pharmacotherapy and allied sciences. In Canada, the advent of Medicare has given a further push in this direction, and in my opinion is not entirely promising for the future of psychiatry. More recently I have noticed, especially among the students, both undergraduate and postgraduate, a resurgence of interest in psychodynamic psychiatry, with insistent requests that more time be allotted to the teaching and training of psychotherapy.

2. Continuum of Psychotherapeutic Possibilities and Basic Psychotherapeutic Techniques

H. Davanloo

In about 1888 Freud began to employ the cathartic method. In a publication by Nunberg and Federn in 1962, from the minutes of the Vienna Psychoanalytic Society, it becomes clear that it was during the analysis of the "Rat-Man" in 1907–1908 that the patient's associations were allowed to be free for the first time. Thus within two decades Freud arrived at what is now known as the classical psychoanalytic technique. By 1905 he had set down the criteria that were necessary for undergoing analysis. The patient must:

1. Suffer from a chronic neurotic syndrome ("transference neurosis").
2. Be a young adult, past adolescence, but still in the prime of adulthood.
3. Have good intelligence.
4. Have a reliable character.

The implication at this time was that the psychoanalyst did not have much to offer except to those patients suited to the classic psychoanalytic method.

Now the emphasis is changing, as Dr. Marmor puts it, "from one in which the therapist does something to the patient by analyzing him to an examination of the nature of the reciprocal interaction beween the therapist and the patient." The therapist is viewed not as a neutral, impersonal conveyor of interpretation, but rather as an active human participant in a verbal and nonverbal, affective as well as cognitive, reciprocal interaction.

We have witnessed the development of a wide range of analytically oriented psychotherapeutic methods. Among these, there has been high interest over the last two decades in analytically oriented short-term psychotherapy. Franz Alexander at the Chicago Psychoanalytic Institute described how psychoanalytic principles can be applied to short-term psychoanalytic technique. Then came the work of Balint, Sifneos, Malan, our own work at McGill, and that of many others.

The purpose here is to outline evaluation, criteria for selection, technique and outcome for a specific method which we call short-term dynamic psychotherapy.

As I have mentioned previously, it is obvious that the clinician's ability to think in dynamic, genetic, economic, structural and adaptive terms is central to sound evaluation and therapeutic planning. In our work we evaluate the patient in five major areas:

(1) *Formulation of a clinical diagnosis*

(2) *Formulation of a dynamic diagnosis,* which refers to conscious and unconscious forces and conflicts, social and environmental forces which are influencing the patient and playing a major role in his illness, in order to evaluate and identify the presence of crisis.

(3) *Formulation of a genetic diagnosis,* which includes a general overview of the patient's life and a determination of those past experiences that have exposed the patient to psychological illness.

(4) *Formulation of psychotherapeutic possibilities,* which includes evaluation of those ego functions of primary importance in psychotherapeutic work, as of the quality of human relationships, affective function of the patient's ego, evaluation of the patient's motivation, the extent to which the patient is psychologically-minded, intelligence, as well as evaluation of the ego's defensive psychological organization and of the structure and function of the id and the superego.

(5) *Transference-countertransference evaluation.* Having completed such an evaluation, the therapist is then in a position to tailor a specific psychotherapeutic method to the patient's needs. If, for the sake of simplicity, we conceptualize all psychotherapies in a continuum, we place behavior therapy on the extreme left, psychoanalysis on the extreme right, and other kinds of psychotherapies such as client-centered therapy, supportive psychotherapy, and dynamic psychotherapies in the middle (see the table below).

In *behavior therapy* learning principles define therapy conditions, target symptoms define procedure, and there is response facilitation/extinction almost independent of the therapist.

In *client-centered* therapy the focus is on the patient's immediate experience, there is integration through self-exploration, and the therapist provides empathy, respect, and authenticity.

In *supportive therapy* the goal is limited and the focus is on symptom relief and behavioral changes. The therapist focuses carefully on the patient's current conscious conflict. No attempt is made to bring under-

The Continuum of Psychotherapeutic Possibilities

Behavior Therapy	Client-Centered Therapy	Supportive Psychotherapy	Dynamic Psychotherapies	Psychoanalysis
Learning principles define therapy conditions	Focus on patient's immediate experience	Uses predominantly suggesion, abreaction. Therapeutic weight is primarily in favor of control over and strengthening of impulses	Recognize and rationally utilizes transference and resistance in therapy	Analyzes transference and resistance back to their genetic, dynamic roots
Target symptoms define procedure	Integration through self-exploration			
Response facilitation/extinction almost independent of therapist	Therapist provides empathy, respect, authenticity			

lying unconscious psychological conflicts into conscious awareness or to modify the patient's character structure. The aim is restoration of the patient's defenses. Positive transference is encouraged, transference neurosis is avoided, and from a technical point of view suggestive technique, emotional catharsis, clarification, and environmental manipulation are used. The reason for not making an attempt to bring the underlying unconscious psychological conflicts into conscious awareness is that our evaluation indicates a weak ego and the inability to do such introspective work as can be done in dynamic psychotherapy.

Dynamic psychotherapies recognize and rationally utilize transference and resistance. The basic ingredients referred to in the definition of classical psychoanalysis appear in dynamic psychotherapies, such as the recognition and use of transference, references to the past, the use of interpretation, and the working through of resistance.

Psychoanalysis analyzes transference and resistance back to their genetic, dynamic roots.

The right-hand side of the continuum shows a wide range of psychoanalytically oriented psychotherapies, as well as short-term dynamic psychotherapies—for example, short-term anxiety-provoking psychotherapy as practiced by Dr. Sifneos and the Harvard group, the short-term dynamic psychotherapy practiced by Dr. Malan and the Tavistock group which lasts from two to twenty-five or thirty sessions, the short-term dynamic psychotherapy that we have developed in the psychiatric clinic at The Montreal General Hospital, and other types of short-term dynamic psychotherapy practiced by other workers in this field.

There is a specific set of criteria for the selection of patients for this specific kind of psychotherapy. These criteria have already been presented, but I will briefly elaborate on two of them: motivation and response to interpretation, between which our findings indicate a positive correlation. We have used interpretation in the first interview with patients who show a low score in motivation. Then we have conducted a second interview. We have collected a sizable number of audiovisually recorded interviews showing a low motivation score during the early part of the interview but a marked increase in motivation after an interpretation.

Our research data show that there is a high positive correlation between the patient's response to interpretation and the psychotherapeutic outcome. According to the clinical situation, one might evaluate the patient's response to interpretation as being related to defense or impulse, but most specifically we are interested in evaluating the patient's response to what we call the past-present transference link. The evaluator links the patient's contemporary pattern of behavior in relation to significant people in his life orbit with his vertical or genetic pattern of behavior in relation to a significant person in his past (parent or parent substitute) and then with his transference pattern of behavior.

What I would like to emphasize is that these criteria, e.g., patient's motivation and patient's ability to respond to interpretation, reflect what has gone on in the initial interview and depend upon two sets of variables, those of the therapist and those of the patient. At the evaluation level we have an immediate interaction between both sets of variables, and hence the entire evaluation process involves an interaction between the patient and the therapist.

In terms of psychotherapeutic technique, there is no adequate terminology available to describe psychotherapeutic process and technique. Bibring, in his contribution to a 1954 symposium in Boston, categorized the range of psychotherapies in terms of their differential development into five basic areas of technique. He then described four major types of activities interwoven into the total course of psychotherapeutic processes.

(1) The process of the production of material.
(2) The process of the utilization of the produced material, as a rule by the therapist.
(3) The process of assimilation by the patient of the result of this utilization.
(4) The process of reorientation and readjustment.

Bibring defined technique as "any purposive, more or less typified, verbal or non-verbal intent to affect the patient in the direction of the goal of the treatment."

The five major psychotherapeutic techniques may be described as follows:

1. Suggestive technique.
2. Abreactive technique.
3. Manipulative technique.
4. Technique of clarification.
5. Technique of interpretation.

What distinguishes the various methods of dynamically based psychotherapies from one another is their particular selection and combination of basic psychotherapeutic techniques.

The *suggestive technique* is the induction of ideas, emotions, and actions in the patient by the therapist. Within the continuum of dynamic psychotherapies, suggestive technique is predominantly placed to the left, namely, under supportive psychotherapy. Therapeutic suggestion aims at a symptomatic change ("transference cure").

The *abreactive technique* brings relief from acute tension through emotional discharge. Abreaction is a technical tool in the process of acquiring "insight" through interpretation ("emotional insight"). The abreactive technique as a curative agent is used in acute emotional conditions and acute traumatic neuroses, especially those associated with amnesia due to acute repression. In addition to the therapeutic function in traumatic neurosis, abreaction has a preventive function. In verbalizing one's feelings, thoughts and conflicts one is able to see them more objectively when associated with the discharge of emotional tension.

In psychoanalysis abreaction does not play a significant curative role, but the patient gets relief from the discharge of emotional tension.

The *manipulative technique* is "learning from experience." Advice, guidance, or manipulating the patient's environment are not involved here. Technical manipulation may be employed in a positive form, e.g., to produce in a patient a favorable attitude toward treatment. There might be redirection of the emotional system existing in a patient, such as a change from submissiveness to independence.

Bibring has used the term "experiential manipulation" to indicate cases in which the therapist offers freedom of choice to a patient who resentfully believes he will be forced or in which the therapist does not accept submissiveness, expecting the patient to assume self-responsibility. For example, the therapist might say, "You should not accept the interpretation that I give you until you are convinced of its validity." The statement neutralizes the patient's anxiety of being forced into submission. Another example would be the acceptance by the therapist of the patient's need for independence.

The term *technique of clarification* was introduced by Carl Rogers. This technique helps the patient to see much more clearly, to achieve "clear differentiation of the meaning of things to him," which produces insight. Clarification refers not to unconscious, repressed material but to conscious or preconscious processes of which the patient is not sufficiently aware, yet of which awareness is possible, and involves elaborating on the patient's pattern of conduct, separating objective reality from his subjective, distorted conception. Since the introduction of the ego-psychological approach, clarification has become an important part of the psychoanalytic technique.

The *technique of interpretation* produces insight, "insight through interpretation." Interpretation refers to unconscious warded-off, instinctual impulses, and the unconscious operation of the ego. Insight through interpretation is dynamically different from insight through clarification, but the two processes are closely knit. In classical psychoanalysis interpretation is the supreme therapeutic agent, and all other techniques are used with the aim of making interpretation possible.

The various methods of dynamically based psychotherapy, from supportive psychotherapy to the other types of dynamic psychotherapies, e.g., short-term psychoanalytic psychotherapy and other types of insight psychotherapy, are characterized by particular selection and combinations of basic psychotherapeutic techniques and curative agents.

In other words, to the left of the continuum the methods are primarily supportive and to the right they are primarily exploratory; in between we have all grades of dynamic psychotherapies whose goals are intermediate between symptom resolution to one side and character changes to the other.

In classical psychoanalysis the objective is exploration of the unconscious, using the technique of free association. There is mobilization of the previously repressed libidinal cathexis; repressed ideas, emotions, and fantasies are involved in transference and displaced from the original object to the therapist. The task here is to analyze the transference and resistance so as to reconstruct the infantile conflict. The old conflict is reactivated and the ego reexposed to it in order to find a new solution.

In classic psychoanalytic technique the essence of the therapeutic work is based on the development of a regressive transference neurosis and its resolution by the exclusive technique of interpretation. Reproduction of the infantile neurosis in the transference (transference neurosis), is the essential element of psychoanalysis.

In short-term dynamic psychotherapies the aim is to replace the patient's neurotic patterns. One focuses on the genetic material, using the techniques of confrontation, clarification, and exploration into the conscious, preconscious, and the derivatives of unconscious material. The psychoanalytic method is used, consisting of analysis of defense and transference reactions and exploration into the part of the libido structure involved in the patient's actual conflict. Interpretation is used, but the therapist should keep this on a level that is understandable to the patient. Transference reactions are frequently interpreted, and transference clarification and confrontation are used extensively. Interpretation of negative transference is highly essential, and the emphasis is on early and repeated interpretation of resistance. Basically, there is an avoidance of characterological issues and of the development of regressive transference neurosis.

Where do we stand with respect to psychoanalysis and the dynamic psychotherapies? It seems that two general trends continue to exist within the American Psychoanalytic Association in regard to psychoanalysis and the dynamic psychotherapies. There are those who place all the dynamic psychotherapies within a continuum, with no practical line of demarcation between the two disciplines. Since 1930 the classic psychoanalytic model has undergone a number of modifications, and the line of demarcation between psychoanalytic treatment and other forms of dynamic psychotherapies has become increasingly blurred. Quoting Alexander, "All treatments utilizing the basic psychoanalytic psychodynamic concepts in an uncovering insight type of psychotherapy should be considered psychoanalytic therapy."

The other point of view is that the two are distinct entities and procedures, and that the two disciplines are qualitatively different from each other. Of interest is the report of the Committee of Evaluation of Psychoanalytic Therapy which appeared in the Bulletin of the American Psychoanalytic Association in 1952. This committee, after four years' effort, was unable to arrive at any clear-cut criteria for differentiating between psychoanalysis and psychoanalytic psychotherapy. At the same time, experience shows that it is very difficult to set up polar opposites, and that the technique and procedure in psychoanalysis and other forms of psychoanalytically oriented psychotherapy are not at opposite ends of a spectrum. We have rich clinical data to indicate that brief psychoanalytic psychotherapy, properly conducted, can bring important changes and can exert an influence which can permeate character structure.

3. Evaluation, Criteria for Selection of Patients
Dr. P. E. Sifneos

On August 15, 1956, I was informed of a patient who had arrived at the psychiatric clinic of the Massachusetts General Hospital complaining of an acute onset of phobia of trains and cars—enclosures of all kinds—and was demanding to be cured by November 15 (he felt he had the potential) so he could get married. The note I read said this patient would require at least three years or more of psychotherapy. Since I happened at that time to see all patients who were referred to the clinic for a study of my own, I was told, "You can do whatever you want with him; he is not recommended for treatment." I was inclined to agree but I thought perhaps it was important to see this patient. What I saw was a twenty-three-year old, bright, intelligent individual who said that indeed he had had some phobias in the past. The onset of this particular one was quite acute. It was associated with his decision to get married, and although this was a major complaint and he was worried about how he could make it through the wedding ceremony, there was a more basic problem that bothered him: his general relationship with women. Was it possible for him to try to get some perspective on his difficulties and possibly to meet the fixed wedding date of November 15?

This presented an interesting question. We decided to take him on in therapy without really knowing exactly what to do—to give him a smattering, I suppose, of psychodynamic psychotherapy and see what would happen by the deadline. The fact was that in the last interview before November 15 he was still quite anxious but felt better about himself and intended to go through with the wedding ceremony. He was seen in a two-week follow-up after he got married, and he told us that he had made it through the wedding and gone on a honeymoon to New York. He felt that he was exceedingly happy, and he said that the time he did not spend with his wife, which was considerable, he "spent riding the New York subways, and indeed they are formidable compared with our measly Boston ones."

This case was presented to our staff, and we were told that we had "*a flight into health.*' Someone disagreed and said, "No, that was a *transference cure.*" Someone else said that this was a *symptom substitution* and that there was a good chance this fellow was going to relapse. We have a follow-up of three and a half years for him. He still had some occasional twinges of anxiety when he entered closed spaces, but he said, "I know what these things mean, and they don't bother me so much. I have learned to live with them. I am happily married and I have two children."

Now, this was our first case. What kind of person was he? Was it worth finding out what idiosyncratic aspects made this patient different from other people? Could we go about finding similar people with similar problems and give them a similar kind of therapy which we had to develop for ourselves?

What we did was to use a lot of transference feelings and a variety of other techniques—clarifications, some form of interpretation, and so forth—to be able to reduplicate this finding as well as to see such patients in longer-term follow-up—indeed, to make certain that whatever changes had taken place did indeed last over a long period of time and that there were no symptom substitutions.

Within the next four years we managed to collect fifty patients. Our criteria for selection were very stringent—so stringent that out of a population of about 2,000 new patients per year we were able to find only these fifty. Nevertheless, we felt there were certain things these patients had to tell us, that they were worth presenting somewhat systematically, and I submitted a paper to the American Psychiatric Association meeting in Atlantic City in 1960. The paper was accepted and Dr. Franz Alexander, a pioneer in short-term psychotherapy, was scheduled to be the discussant. When he saw the case material, Dr. Alexander felt that these patients were suffering from serious problems in their lives, incapacitating to a great degree, although they were still capable of loving and working. This was a crucial time for us as far as our development in short-term psychotherapy was concerned, since both he and Dr. Elizabeth Zetzel in Boston were exceedingly encouraging.

We went on to relax our criteria, and we systematically attempted to select individuals out of our large clinic population.

What are these criteria? Upon reading Freud's initial criteria, I was quite impressed in many ways, but I had not picked up his feeling that intelligence was of importance. One of our criteria was above-average intelligence, but that has since been modified. We do not mean an IQ of 200 or 180 or whatever, but rather a psychological sophistication, an ability to see paradoxical situations, to ask questions that would have been much easier left alone. Thus, one of our criteria is above-average intelligence in the sense of an interest within oneself to understand complex processes.

The first criterion is *the ability to circumscribe a chief complaint*, to select out of a variety of problems the one that is of top priority. Therefore, it is part of our effort to help the patient circumscribe his problem and to select, if he must make a choice, one out of many problems with which he wants assistance. Remember that the patient who had an onset of acute phobias of trains and enclosures added that the bigger problem as far as he was concerned was his relationship with women in general. The question was "If I could help you in solving one of these two problems, assuming these two problems were not interrelated, which one would you settle for—namely, would you choose the problem that you have in your relationship with women even if you had to go on being afraid of cars and trains and so forth, or not?" The answer to that was a categorical "My problems with women are of the greatest importance to me, and this is what I would like, and if necessary I may have to walk to work without taking the subway." Here was a definite choice, an ability to take one problem over others and work on that.

The second criterion is the ability to demonstrate by history one meaningful relationship. What is meant by the word "meaningful" is give-and-take, altruistic to a certain degree, showing a willingness to sacrifice part of oneself for another person, not viewing the world as a source of individual gratification. If a person has passed this vitally crucial test to relate to other human beings, then I think he is immune to having serious psychotic or psychological difficulties for the rest of his life, although he may indeed have problems in these various relationships. Thus we scrutinize extensively this ability of the patient to have one meaningful relationship with another person, particularly during his early life.

The third criterion is a test of the second. If the patient has had a meaningful relationship with another person, can this capacity be tested right here and now—namely, in the way he relates to the interviewer? Therefore, we utilize the therapeutic evaluation of the patient's interaction during that interview as a test of how flexible he is, how open-minded he is, how willing he is to look at himself and understand himself.

The fourth criterion, as I mentioned before, is above-average intelligence, meaning psychological sophistication.

The fifth criterion is motivation. In our experience this was of such importance that during our initial series I had a special interview with the patient just to assess motivation as such. We found that patients who appeared to be highly motivated, even if they were quite disturbed (and I'm speaking not only of patients for short-term psychotherapy but also of patients receiving other kinds of treatment), tended to do much better than patients who might have been superficially healthier but who were not particularly motivated.

We have devised seven subcriteria for motivation: a person who has a score of seven is considered to have excellent motivation; six, good; five, fair; four, questionable; below four, not motivated and not taken for our research for short-term psychotherapy. These subcriteria involve the patient's ability to recognize that his symptoms are psychological in nature (not saying, for example, "I have a pain in my stomach and I think it's a tumor and the intern has sent me here to see you, and all this psychological stuff—I don't know, but I still think it's a tumor or something like that"); a willingness to experiment with new situations; an active curiosity about himself, a kind of raising questions, such as, "Why am I the way I am? Is it possible that I can look back in my life to try to understand?"; a willingness to change, that is, a dissatisfaction with one's own life patterns and a feeling that "This is an opportunity now that I have"; realistic expectations of the result of psychotherapy and not expectations of some kind of magic; and finally a willingness to make a tangible sacrifice, to go out of his way to receive the psychotherapy.

These criteria are more or less guidelines and do not have to be followed strictly all along the way. With a thorough history-taking that has given a picture of what the patient is like, one usually arrives at a contract with the patient at the end of the evaluation—namely, that both should agree that there is a problem worth investigating together over the process of the psychotherapy, which will be of short duration. We—and here our center differs from others—do not set up a standard number of visits. In a sense the duration is tailored to how long the patient requires, with the assistance of his therapist, to sort out his emotional problems. Some take nine interviews. The majority take from between thirteen and sixteen, with some taking up to twenty, and we have also had some, though very few, who have taken only one.

4. Evaluation, Criteria for Selection of Patients
Dr. D. H. Malan

What seems to be emerging is the phenomenon of convergence of thinking. What Dr. Davanloo states on the classification of the various forms of psychotherapeutic intervention summarizes almost exactly what I have to say. Dr. Sifneos and I had an extraordinary experience in this same sense. I started work on brief psychotherapy as a member of Michael Balint's team in 1955. The patient that Dr. Sifneos talked about was seen in 1956. We somehow failed to come across each other's writings—or each other—until 1964, when we met at the Psychotherapy Congress in London and discovered that each of us was interested in short-term psychotherapy. I brought up that our team had done some work on selection of criteria for brief psychotherapy and that the factor that seemed to come out in our work as being more important than others was motivation. It was amazing to me that Dr. Sifneos had in fact been working on this and had come to exactly the same conclusion in his clinical experience with a very much larger number of patients than I'd ever had the chance to study. I am convinced that we who are dealing with the investigation of short-term psychoanalytic psychotherapy are all working toward a truth, and that if we investigate with an open mind we are likely to come essentially to the same conclusion.

Our selection criteria for this form of psychotherapy are worded entirely differently because of the way we have developed them.

All of us who have worked in this field were brought up in the psychoanalytic tradition, and just as Dr. Sifneos describes his own experience—having to stumble on something almost in spite of himself—we had to make our own discoveries, each in our own way. We all came to this work with an open mind. Dr. Sifneos mentions Alexander, who had worked on the problems of short-term dynamic psychotherapy for about twenty years. Yet Alexander and French's book somehow got under the psychoanalysts' skin, whether because of the way it was presented or because of something in psychoanalysts. It met with intense hostility, an example of which can be found in Ernest Jones's review in the *International Journal of Psychoanalysis* around 1946.

Thus all of us were presented with an historical problem when we started to examine this subject: mainly that someone had once tried to investigate short-term dynamic psychotherapy, had come up with a number of exceedingly interesting results, and had, so to speak, burned his fingers. The whole subject was under a cloud, and we had to start over from the beginning.

We began with the view that the only type of patient who would be suitable for this kind of therapy would be a very healthy patient who was suffering a very recent illness. So we set about investigating short-term psychotherapy at the Tavistock Clinic. Very healthy patients who have very acute illnesses are very few and far between at the clinic. In fact, we found none. We were then forced—and this is one of the fascinating chances of our history—to take on any type of patient that came for treatment. At the same time, we came into this with the prejudice that one had to be superficial in his interpretations, that one couldn't use transference or he would get himself into terrible trouble. Thus we set about trying to use a nontransference technique with these patients.

Since we were well-trained analysts, however, the moment the patient produced transference material an absolutely conditioned response appeared in us, which was to interpret the transference. If we saw a relation between the transference and the past, the genetic component of the transference, then we interpreted that as well. The end result was that we stumbled on a finding that was totally unexpected by any of us, namely, that it wasn't only very healthy patients with very acute illnesses who were suitable and that one didn't have to use the superficial technique; one could use as deep a technique as he felt appropriate. We were experienced therapists and didn't go deeper than we felt the patient could bear, and contrary to the preconceptions of so many analysts, including ourselves, the results could be deep and lasting.

Now, about the criteria that eventually came out of our work and the patients that one does *not* take on for this type of treatment. The list of contraindications would include serious suicidal attempts, drug addiction, convinced homosexuality, long-term hospitalization, more than one course of electroshock treatment, chronic alcoholism, incapacitating chronic obsessional state, incapacitating chronic phobic state, gross destructive acting out and gross self-destructive acting out. Of course, no such statement is absolute, but it seems highly improbable that I would accept a patient from this list.

Having eliminated patients with the above contraindications, we selected patients who had what one might call a "prima facie case" for being suitable for brief psychotherapy: a discernible simplicity somewhere, either a simplicity of complaints or a perceptible simplicity of pathology. We would then discuss these patients and, on the basis of our evaluation, project ourselves into an imaginary uncovering therapy for them in order to forecast some of the events and dangers inherent in the therapy.

Following are two examples. One involved a woman in her thirties who was complaining of a travel phobia which she had had for two months. When an interpretation was made to her about her need to control herself, she made a marked response.. So far everything was favorable. We had acute and recent onset, which must have meant some current problem that we ought to be able to get at, and the patient's response to interpretation met one of our crucial selection criteria. But we then observed various other phenomena. She seemed to be markedly dependent. She was being seen by a woman G.P. upon whom she was extremely dependent. We felt that this probably had a homosexual basis. The patient went into resistance the moment it was suggested to her that she might receive treatment from us, and we felt that the reason for this was her fear of losing her relation with the G.P. who was treating her. Although she had responded to the interpretation of her need for self-control, it was not at all clear to us what impulses she had to control and the projection test didn't help in this respect. Here was a patient whom we rejected. Since she went into resistance the moment treatment was suggested, her motivation for being evaluated was not high. We could not see what the positive therapy was, and self-control was too vague. We thought we might well get involved in problems of deep dependence if we tried uncovering therapy with this patient.

The second example involved a young man who came complaining of premature ejaculation. He was an Indian, married for eleven months, and he had only just discovered his problem. Thus, in a sense, there was a current crisis. He made quite good contact at the interview and communicated some things about difficulties with his father. Again everything seemed fine up to this point. At the second appointment, however, the projection test suggested that he had a marked impoverishment of relationships. He seemed to have no interest in having a sexual relationship with a woman. His basic attitude was that women demanded it of him and that he had to comply. Therefore, he did not meet the criterion of a meaningful human relationship, and we did not take him into treatment.

It is extremely important not to make any implication of omnipotence. There are many, many patients whom one sees and for whom one can forecast all sorts of dangers and problems in therapy; one does not take these patients into treatment.

Both the above patients showed some of the positive criteria but not others, which is why we rejected them. We have basically four essential criteria. What Dr. Davanloo says on the subject of making psychodynamic diagnoses—and the rest of his statement, in fact—fits in very well with our view. And in the same way, although the wording is different, what Dr. Sifneos says about his criteria shows them to be almost identical with ours. The criteria are all at least partly based on an imaginary therapy with a patient and/or the direct evidence that one has gained from the patient about how he has already responded and therefore how he is likely to respond in any therapy that is offered.

Our first criterion concerns the feeling that there is a circumscribed problem which would be useful to the patient to work through. This is entirely from the point of view of a potential therapist or of the evaluator rather than from exactly what the patient himself is saying. So we again project ourselves into an imaginary therapy and say, for example, "I think it might be valuable to work through this patient's latent hostility to his father. This might help him overcome the problems he's presently bringing to us." Thus the first criterion is a conceivable focus that we think we can "dissect out"—a term borrowed from Maguire, who has thought a lot about these problems as well—from the overall pathology that the patient brings into the treatment.

The second criterion, which involves the patient's point of view, is concerned with the interaction between the evaluator and the patient. We feel that it is essential to give partial interpretations to the patient at the initial interview. These interpretations are based on the focus which is beginning to emerge, and we regard it as an important factor for acceptance for our kind of psychotherapy that the patient should have responded to interpretation of this focus.

Our third criterion is motivation. Although it is not my style to lay down specific detailed criteria on any of these issues, I agree entirely with Dr. Sifneos' seven criteria by which to judge motivation. What I myself do is put the patient's behavior and responses through an unconscious computer and come up with a judgment about his motivation. I'm sure that many of the variables are identical with the ones used by Dr. Sifneos.

Finally, one must project himself forward into an imaginary therapy and think of the possible dangers that may arise if the patient is taken into interpretative psychotherapy. There are patients who may be potentially very depressed, and one may feel that they might be precipitated into a suicidal attempt. There may be patients who, although functioning quite adequately, one feels are latently psychotic, and again injudicious interpretation may well precipitate them into a psychotic breakdown; on the whole, we avoid such patients, but when we don't, we make very certain that we have forseen the danger and go carefully in order to avoid it. And there are other factors: rigid defenses that we can't penetrate, not enough motivation, complex transference situations, potential extreme dependence, and so on. Although these dangers may be present, if we are forewarned and feel that we can avoid them, and if the other criteria are favorable, then I would agree to recommending treatment.

The question that must be asked is: "How brief is brief?" This is very much a matter of the therapist's choice and definition. There are unquestionably some patients who benefit markedly from a single interview. We've picked these up almost by mistake, in fact, in an attempt to study what we call untreated patients, but this is a special category which I'll omit here.

There are many psychiatrists working in busy psychiatric clinics who think that "brief" precludes more than five or six sessions. James Mann of course, uses a strict time limit of twelve sessions, set down from the beginning. Dr. Sifneos uses about fifteen sessions, not adhered to exactly. When I personally do brief psychotherapy, I try to set a limit of twenty sessions from the beginning. When I'm supervising a trainee, I use a limit of thirty sessions, and I use an upper limit of forty sessions for the definition of brief psychotherapy. Dr. Davanloo is in much the same range.

We have a second series of brief-therapy patients treated at the Tavistock Clinic. The median length of therapy in those thirty patients was 19.5. This is to give you an idea of the relative number of sessions that we're speaking about. Now, of course, brief psychotherapy has been known from the beginning of psychotherapy. It certainly goes back to Freud, and many clinicians in the 1930's and 1940's have said repeatedly that the patients who were suitable for brief psychotherapy were patients whose illnesses were of acute and recent onset. Another way of putting this is to say the patient is in a crisis. There is absolutely no question that such patients may often be suitable for brief psychotherapy, but the observation has always existed that apparently some patients who do not fit this criterion are still suitable for such therapy. There are a number of quotations from the literature which give evidence of therapists having come across this other type of patient, but no one knows—or knew, at any rate—what proportion of the population these patients might represent or how to recognize them.

What has been needed above all is a systematic study of patients of this kind in order to find out the truth about brief psychotherapy and to whom it may be applied. In my experience, whenever one investigates any scientific subject at all, one is in for surprises. As I mentioned previously, Michael Balint's team had the fantasy that the only patients suitable would be those of illnesses of acute and recent onset. In fact, what happened was that, since such patients were not as common as we wished, in our enthusiasm we took on many patients to whom this criterion didn't apply at all and to our astonishment we got very dramatic and excellent therapeutic results with some of them in under forty sessions.

This was published in 1963, but I don't think the message has ever really gotten across that there's something wrong with this acute and recent onset type of criterion, although it certainly got across to people like Drs. Sifneos and Davanloo. In the 1960's another fantasy came into being which one can call the student health fantasy. This has been promulgated by people who work in busy student health centers which by now appear to exist in practically every university in the States, and it goes something like this: "Yes, it's the patient in crisis who is suitable for brief psychotherapy, but..." The "but" is that "...this may enable the patient to grow beyond the point which he'd reached when he came to you in crisis." Most of the previous fantasies about the outcome of this kind of psychotherapy have been, "Well, all right. It's a symptom cure. You return the patient to exactly the same position he held before he came to you in crisis. Nothing else occurs." In the student health view, however, the statement appears again and again in the literature: "Yes. You deal with the crisis, but something else happens as well." Now, as we all know, whenever you meet a patient in crisis it is very rare that only the recent crisis has caused him to be ill. What has happened is that he has been sensitized by previous experiences to the particular crisis that he's had to go through, and it is this that causes him to break down and come to you. If you're going to do proper therapy on him, it's simply no use trying to concentrate only on the present crisis. You've got to relate the present crisis to antecedent events.

The moment you start doing this, you're dealing with the patient's life problem, and therefore it's not too surprising that you get the statement that not only do you help the patient with his current crisis, but something else happens as well—that certain permanent major changes may occur as well. If you can deal with a life problem in a patient in a current crisis, you can continue this spectrum further. Why does he have to be in a current crisis if you can deal with life problems; can't you deal with them in a patient who is not in crisis? The answer is "Yes, you can," and this is the major finding of anybody who starts investigating brief psychotherapy systematically. Then, of course, you often get a previous crisis, or, if the patient doesn't come to you actually in his crisis, you get what are called precipitating events or precipitating factors. In your therapy of the patient, and indeed in your initial evaluation of the patient, these precipitating events are of enormous importance in your understanding of the case, and you are constantly focusing on them in your treatment.

You can then continue that spectrum to the limit. The patients haven't had any precipitating factors that you can understand. Yet, at the same time, you can understand what their life problem is. They fulfill the kind of criteria that Drs. Sifneos and Davanloo outline, and in trying to deal with their life problem in brief psychotherapy—again perhaps surprisingly—with some of these patients you can in fact accomplish an enormous amount. What I want to emphasize is that once you start talking in terms of dealing not only with the immediate crisis but with the patient's life problem and its antecedents, you are really on the road, on the logical road, to doing brief therapy in regard to the patient's life problem whether he is in a crisis or whether there was an acute onset a few years before.

The next problem, and this is a major one, is how to recognize these patients in advance. My response to this is a sort of "yes and no" answer. I think that Drs. Davanloo, Sifneos and I, and a number of other workers, have succeeded in delineating a particular set of criteria by which one can recognize some of these patients. But I would emphasize that these criteria are provisional and inadequate, in that there is no question that there are patients who don't fulfill them but nevertheless do well. This is a factor that urgently needs investigation.

When one sees a patient, there is first of all a current conflict that can be identified. Often there is a precipitating factor that gives a clue to the nature of the kind of conflict. Then there is also the patient's life problem, or what French has called the "nuclear conflict," which can often be recognized by seeing previous precipitating events or early traumatic experiences or family constellations or repetitive patterns in the patient's life. It is desirable to be able to see the current conflict as an aspect of the nuclear conflict—as an example of it.

In the initial evaluation period—which for me is usually a single interview but which lasts about two hours—one has been able to identify those kinds of things about the patient's pathology which I have just mentioned. Next, one has formulated some sort of focus and has given the patient an interpretation based on it, probably a partial interpretation, and the patient has responded.

With respect to the criterion of motivation, I don't agree with the concept of "motivation for change." What I seek is motivation for what the patient is going to be offered, which is insight and interaction with the therapist.

Regarding transference, it is not my usual method to make transference interpretations in the initial interview, although I sometimes find it necessary. It is an advantage for the prognosis in brief therapy if the conflict that has been identified is likely to be one that will manifest itself in the transference in such a way that you can deal with it in the clearest possible manner.

That a proper psychiatric history be taken in the initial evaluation interview is of the utmost importance. One cannot formulate a realistic therapeutic plan if one does not know, for instance, that the patient had a post-partum psychosis when she had her first baby, or that the patient has made two previous attempts at suicide in which his life was actually in danger.

Dr. Lowy:

It seems to me that this is indeed an exciting time to be in psychiatry—and particularly in the field of psychotherapy. The excitement in psychiatry is generated by advances in a variety of fields, in biological psychiatry, and in the development and the specificity of behavioral approaches, etc., but most particularly, I think, because perhaps we are finally coming of age.

There appears to be recognition pretty well across the spectrum of psychiatrists that there is a great need, as Dr. Marmor puts it, to suit the treatment to the patient's needs rather than to cram the patient into whatever pigeonhole we happen to be espousing at any given time. It is a question not of offering, let us say, a size 40 or 42 suit in a particular haberdashery because that happens to be one of the averages, but of trying to tailor the cloth to the patient—not just to the patient's needs, but also to what offers a favorable prognosis. Here is where such things as specificity of criteria and outcome measure come into play because obviously what is needed is more work of the kind where there is some attempt to produce a servomechanism by which the results achieved with given patients can be measured, then feedback to determine the selection of treatments for patients. I think this cuts across schools of psychiatry, although probably most of the people here are committed to a psychodynamic approach under certain circumstances when the patient is suitable for such an approach. What is remarkable about this meeting is the absence of a school of thought. It has been pointed out a number of times that schools are for minnows and fish and not for scientists, and it is really quite refreshing to have an absence of "this school versus that school."

Nevertheless, one cannot entirely avoid the question of specificity of approach in line with a certain theoretic position at one end of a spectrum and at the other end a "you know everything goes and everybody can do it" position. Clearly, if everything goes and people in a wide variety of training bases and theoretical bases can do it, then there is nothing at all specific. I think the solution, to the extent that it is possible, is the kind of operational definition of what is being done, which is in evidence in the work of the people who have spoken here today.

With respect to clinical diagnosis, I would like to underscore what Dr. Malan said about a proper psychiatric evaluation. The fact is that clinical psychiatric diagnosis is becoming more specific, and where specificity is possible and appears fruitful, it is perhaps one of the most important things that can be done for the patient. For example, nowadays it's almost negligent not to recognize that someone has a primary affective disorder which has the strong promise of being treated successfully by biological means—by, for example, lithium and antidepressants or phenothiazine drugs, etc. In the area of, say, phobic neuroses, it seems highly likely that the patient is benefited by the identification of those phobias which can be very rapidly treated by behavioral techniques, etc., and perhaps what the speakers are coming to now is a consensus on the kinds of criteria for brief intensive dynamic psychotherapy which may offer the same kind of specificity—and which may, indeed, influence diagnosis or subdiagnosis chiefly of the neurotic and characterological disorders.

I suppose the field of short-term psychotherapy, however ancient its roots, is still in our times sufficiently new that most speakers define it in terms of what it isn't, namely, psychoanalytic therapy of three to eight years, or whatever. In fact, as the criteria are extended, at least with respect to timing, given both Dr. Davanloo's and Dr. Malan's upper limit of forty sessions, and taking into account Christmas and a few other holidays, we're talking about a year's treatment on a once-a-week basis. This happens to coincide remarkably with the training period of many therapists as they go through their rotation. Now, this may be fortuitous. In any event, it underlines the point that it ought to be possible not just for therapists in training but for everybody to achieve certain results in a given time or the treatment has to be rethought.

Personally, I have become convinced by the work of people such as the three speakers. I have come to the position where, unless a patient referred to me is extremely well evaluated by someone else whose judgment I am particularly sure of, I will in fact offer a trial of short-term psychotherapy with both the patient and myself keeping in mind the possibility that the treatment may be revised and that I might perhaps go on to more intensive, more long-term psychotherapy or psychoanalysis. But I do believe that nowadays we have come so far that it may be quite justified in every instance to think first of a short-term treatment, regardless of the indications. If you look at the criteria of Drs. Sifneos and Davanloo, you would probably say that the patients who met these criteria would be ideally suited to virtually every dynamic psychotherapy. Indeed, Dr. Sifneos' point of departure in Boston was in 1956. The fact is that these are good analytic candidates and good candidates for a good many other therapies. That being the case, and, as is being shown now quite clearly, if these patients can frequently make substantial gains which are self-respecting successes of therapy, then why not aim at that to begin with?

I say this in all humility. I am a psychoanalyst. I am quite committed to the advances which psychoanalysis has brought. But in my view the strength of the contribution of psychoanalysis does not rest with exclusivity or the notion that it is best for everyone, that it is the most efficient treatment.

A point that should be underscored is the value of spontaneously reported dreams and even those reported at the first interview as a response to a casual request, because it sems to me that in addition to transference interpretation a simple comment by a therapist about a dream brought up by a patient very rapidly establishes several things: the degree of empathic communication which will facilitate the relationship, a channel of communication where the therapist says, "I am interested not only in your here-and-now problem, but also in what is going on inside you," and, of course, if the comment is at all relevant to the situation, the statement "I have some hope of understanding you."

With regard to motivation, in my view this is not a static phenomenon; it can change, and you find so often that after the first or second session it increases dramatically. The response to interpretation, particularly a good one, is in fact an increase in motivation. Dr. Davanloo has emphasized the patient's response to interpretation as one of his major criteria.

Dr. Straker:

Rather than attempting to summarize all the foregoing papers, I'll just mention a couple of points that caught my special interest. Dr. Davanloo commented that very often the only treatment prescribed for patients is the treatment used in that setting whether it is relevant or not to the patient's needs. I know how true that is from my own clinical experience in different settings.

In criteria for selection, Dr. Davanloo mentioned intelligence, motivation, psychological-mindedness of the patient, the capacity for human relationship, the assessment of personality, getting some feeling about superego functions, noticing the way the patient relates in therapy, and so on. All of these issues certainly go into the decision-making process in selecting patients for short-term psychotherapy. I would like to underline the presence of a crisis. It is at the time of acute emotional decompensation, either threatening or already begun, that the short-term psychotherapies really have their moment not only of greatest expectations but also of greatest potential. Dr. Sifneos also emphasizes that the greatest potential for change is during the period of crisis.

I think it might also be helpful to look at who is doing the treatment. We all have different capacities, different preferences, skills and qualities to function in a variety of settings, which certainly influences the total interaction between the therapist and the patient.

In his selection criteria, Dr. Sifneos described the ability to focus on priority or to establish or identify priority problems, to demonstrate the capacity for meaningful human relationships, to show some psychological sophistication, which he equates with intelligence, and to show motivation, which he describes under a series of headings including the capacity to make some sacrifices, to have realistic expectations, to show a willingness for change, a willingness to experiment, and so on. I would like to underline the impact of external and environmental forces which have to be somehow included in the decision-making process.

Dr. Sifneos mentioned a patient who was given a choice of two symptoms to select from for treatment—his phobia in trains or his fear of women. To me, it appears that these two symptoms were part of the same pathology: the fear of being closed in. Perhaps from the patient's point of view it might have been two separate symptoms, but from the therapist's point of view they would be one and the same.

Dr. Sifneos:

I agree with you. One could conceive of two symptoms that are not related to each other, but I think as you do that these were related. Part of the task of establishing contact with the patient, as well as the focus, is to show him that his difficulties about closed spaces had something to do with his relationship with his father and mother, and that the whole psychotherapy would be focused on those two issues. In my opinion, symptoms can be represented as tips of an iceberg, and underneath the ocean surface, in the main part of the iceberg, lies the basic triangular problem which he had with his father and mother, and, after his father died, with his brother and mother.

Dr. Marmor (*in answer to a question addressed to him regarding the term "psychodynamic" and whether the term includes a firm belief in the "dynamic unconscious"*):

Let me say primarily what I had in mind. It does include the dynamic unconscious. Basically what I am referring to is an ability to evaluate both the inner and the outer forces—that is where the dynamic concept comes in—which are determining the patient's psychopathology. There are things going on internally, within the patient, and there are things going on externally, within the patient's life. Only by adequately evaluating the balance of these forces can one determine what kind of approach is indicated. There are times when practically no psychotherapy is indicated. Sometimes the simplest way of resolving the patient's difficulty is to remove some problem in the patient's reality situation, and no psychotherapy in the formal uncovering, interpretive sense is necessary. There are other times when the required approach is more a simple education or helping the patient in certain social skills if the forces have been adequately evaluated. Therefore, when I speak of a dynamic diagnosis, I am referring to that kind of evaluation of the forces, and I think the concept of repression and many other defense mechanisms are part of the total evaluation. I do believe in defense mechanisms. I think some operate positively; not all defense mechanisms are bad. Some of them enable us to live, and that's part of our dynamic evaluation, too. But what we are talking about here is short-term dynamic psychotherapy, not short-term psychotherapy. Fundamentally, we are talking within a psychoanalytic framework, and our premise and the premise upon which many of these criteria are dependent is the ability of the patient to work with us within a psychodynamic framework. Now, it is possible—and it is only fair to state this, although I myself am most comfortable working within a psychodynamic framework—to work psychotherapeutically with patients on a short-term basis without using dynamic concepts of interpretation and insight-giving. Patients can respond to emotive reactions or comments on the part of the therapist. They respond to persuasion and to suggestion. They respond to inspirational approaches. Perhaps later on we will be able to define what differences there are, but it is only fair to say that the capacity to be verbal, to be psychologically sophisticated, to have the kind of intelligence to which we are referring here, is dependent on this particular dynamic framework in which we are choosing to do this kind of therapy. We should not generalize it to all forms of psychotherapy.

Dr. Sifneos (*in answer to a question raised as to whether or not there is a contraindication to treating a suicidal patient with short-term psychotherapy*):

Indeed, potential suicide is very important for the psychiatrist to evaluate but not necessarily to treat with short-term psychotherapy. The criteria which we have presented are specific for short-term dynamic psychotherapy and not for all kinds of psychotherapy.

In general, there are many patients who make manipulative suicide attempts. A patient tries to put his life at stake in order to get, by force if you like, what he wants from another person. This kind of patient, in my experience, suffers from a severe characterological problem and has a very serious psychopathology. You can see that such a case could not be touched by the kind of psychotherapy that we are talking about.

Dr. Davanloo:

In our research of 575 patients, we treated a group of patients who did not fulfill our criteria for selection but whom we accepted for the purpose of exploring the limits of short-term dynamic psychotherapy. Some of these patients were depressed with suicidal ideation, and the outcome of the treatment of some of them was excellent. Later, I shall discuss in detail "The Case of the Teeth-Grinding Woman," who was suicidal and was treated with short-term dynamic psychotherapy with excellent results in thirty-two sessions. But suicidal patients with severe psychopathology are definitely not candidates for short-term dynamic psychotherapy. In our work, we treat them with crisis intervention short-term supportive psychotherapy or other modalities of treatment.

Chapter 6

"The Case of the Italian Housewife"

P. E. SIFNEOS

The patient is a twenty-nine-year old housewife and mother of two children, a daughter nine and a son seven years old. She had a poor relationship with her own mother but a fairly good relationship with her maternal grandmother, who died when the patient was four or five years old. She had been seen in our clinic with a number of problems. She described her difficulties as fear of emotional closeness, general problems in interpersonal relationships and problems in her marriage, which she described as a masochistic pattern of relationship with her husband. Both she and her husband have had extramarital relationships, and the precipitating factor that brought her to the clinic was her decision to get a divorce and also her relationship with the man that she loves.

Pt: It wasn't really me. I could just picture another person when I did it.
Th: So you're saying, then, that you do that just to please the other person or is it that you expect something from your husband?
Pt: No, I just do it to please the other person.
Th: Why do you feel that you have to please somebody so much?

Pt: To make them happy.
Th: Why is that important?
Pt.: Well, for him it was. He was always unhappy.
Th: But since he doesn't give you any pleasure, why would you have to sacrifice? And that's what it amounts to.
Pt. To make him happy.
Th: Yes, all right. But that is a problem and that is why you're here. Is that correct? Can you tell me something about what it is like to be unhappy? What kind of thoughts do you have?
Pt: I just want to run away from everything, just leave the city and go away by myself.
Th: Can you give me a recent example of this particular problem?
Pt: Well, I left at Easter because I wasn't happy with him, so I just took my kids and I left. I went out of town. I sorted out all my thoughts.
Th: What, for example, did you think about?
Pt: Him and the marriage, and if I'd go back, would we stay together and everything.
Th: So then your marriage is also a problem?
Pt: Yes.
Th: And is it as a result of this problem that you have just told me about that you want to do things for your husband that you don't like to do?
Pt: No. I think I've always been that way. Since I was a child.
Th: You always were?
Pt: Yes, I wasn't happy. I was always trying to run away from something. From my parents, just from everything.
Th: Running away. Now, does that solve anything?
Pt: It does for me for a while.
Th: All right. For instance, this time you said that you did some thinking, so you went back and you felt happier. Do you have to run away? Can't you do the thinking while you are there?
Pt: No, because I'm always in the same place. Like I'm in the same city and it's always revolving around the problems, so I have to leave the city to settle that much.
Th: You want some distance?
Pt: Right.
Th: What do you feel like when you're unhappy? What is it like?

Pt: It's terrible.
Th: Really. Can you describe it?
Pt: I start drinking, crying.
Th: What thoughts do you have? What are you preoccupied with?
Pt: Well, what went wrong? How come I landed in such a predicament? Why did I go that way? I don't know; I just went the wrong way. Things just didn't turn out right for me.
Th: I can't see that running away tends to solve it, as you said. I have some questions whether it does or it doesn't, but what I'm really interested in is what is the problem from which you are running away. You told me something about wanting to please the other person at the expense of your own pleasure. That's where we are now. But what makes you do that is what I'm not clear on. Why do you want to do that since you know it's going to create problems?
Pt: I don't know; I just do it.
Th: I know that, but since you know that it's going to create problems, since you know that you have a tendency to run away, since you know that you would feel unhappy, what is it that motivate you to do it in the first place? You see what I mean?
Pt: It's something inside me.
Th: All right, that's what we're interested in, what we are **trying to** find out. What is this something inside you? I mean, do you have any thoughts or any urges?
Pt: I don't know.
Th: Do you feel suddenly like that?
Pt: Let's say I date this certain fellow but I wouldn't like him, but I'd make love to him. I don't even know why I do it. I just **do it**, and I just can't see why I do things like that.
Th: Can you give me an example of that? For instance, what **makes** you go out with that particular fellow?
Pt: A change from what I was married to; to see if he's any **different**: to see if I get along with him or to get the attention I never got from my husband.
Th: Wait a minute, now; that is the running away, isn't it? If you're unhappy with your husband and you go out with someone else to see whether you are happier with this other person, that is running away from the problem, right? What makes you sleep with the other person? Also a part of experimentation or what?

Pt: Probably. I never give it a thought. I just do it. I don't think before I do it. I just do it, and after it's done, I say: "Well, I shouldn't have done it."

Th: Yes, so that is a problem, isn't it? Not thinking about but doing things, impulsively.

Pt: Yes. I'm very impulsive.

Th: Okay, and then you feel bad about it?

Pt: Yes.

Th: And when you feel bad, what is that like? I mean what kind of thoughts do you have? Or when you start feeling bad, do you feel the impulse to do something else again? Is that right?

Pt: No, I just think that, like I might hit my child and feel awfully bad after and I'll wonder why I did it and I won't want to do it again. I'll just try to the next time, if I bring him to bed and I smack him for not doing something, then I'll probably go over after; I will feel bad and I'll apologize, and I'll say: "The reason why I hit you was because you weren't listening and I really think if you would have listened when I spoke to you . . ." Like it will really hurt me, but I have that problem with my children that I just can't go up to them and kiss them and hug them. It's just something in me. My own kids; it's something that I just can't do. My husband is the same way. If I get too near him, he'll just step all over me, and I think my kids are like that, too. So I just can't lower myself down to that affection level with them.

Th: All right. Let's change the subject just for a minute to get a picture of your life. How old are you?

(*Here the therapist obtains some data re personal history.*)

Th: What is the earliest experience that you remember as way back as you can go? The earliest thing that you remember about life?

Pt: My grandmother.

Th: What comes to mind?

Pt: She spoiled me a lot. She loved me.

Th: What do you mean spoiled you?

Pt: Everything I wanted, she used to give me. It was always a threat to my parents, and her, like, she'd wake me up when the neighbors would come; my parents wouldn't want that. I was really close to her.

Th: Was she your father's or your mother's mother?

Pt: My mother's mother.
Th: Is she alive?
Pt: She's dead.
Th: When did she die?
Pt: When I was four or five. She died of breast cancer.
Th: Do you remember?
Pt: Yes.
Th: Do you remember the death also?
Pt: Yes. I remember she was on the couch and she died.
Th: I see. What do you remember?
Pt: I remember when she was just about to die; then I saw her in a coffin in the funeral parlor. That's all I remember.
Th: But you remember her alive also? Right?
Pt: Yes.
Th: Do you remember what your feelings were like, having lost somebody who was important to you?
Pt: No, not really. I liked... I loved her a lot.
Th: When you say not really, what do you mean? Is it that you don't want to think about it, or is it that you don't understand?
Pt: I've always been afraid of that woman, even today. If I see her picture in my grandfather's room, I'll just be really afraid of her, and if I'm home alone at nights like I was this week, I thought of her and it really scared me because I believe in witchcraft and things like that, and I always think that she'll appear or something. I always feel, like when my mother's home, if I go up on the roof... My grandfather sleeps downstairs in the basement; he's got a room there. Even when I was thirteen or fourteen, if I used to just go by the room, I used to always think that she was in his bedroom. I just felt her presence in the room.
Th: But would that be bad?
Pt: That scares me.
Th: Why?
Pt: I don't know, it just scares me.
Th: If she was such a nice person who gave you everything...
Pt: It just scares me.
Th: Why does it scare you?
Pt: She just... she really frightens me.

Th: Yes. That's what I want to know. Why?
Pt: I don't know.
Th: What comes to mind? Obviously, you don't know, but if she was such a nice person . . . She spoiled you, as you put it. Spoiling is an interesting word; spoiling means doing something bad?
Pt: No, not really. Just getting everything I wanted. Toys and things like that.
Th: Yes, but you said, She made me happy, she spoiled me.
Pt: Oh, I always use that word.
Th: But we're interested to know why.
Pt: Well, I think the reason why I'm afraid of her is because she caused my mother a lot of trouble. My mother used to live with her, like they were all one big happy family, and she put her through a lot of trouble.
Th: For instance?
Pt: They wouldn't let her go out or anything. Her father was the same way. I don't know.
Th: Now, as far as your parents are concerned, who were you closer to, your mother or your father?
Pt: My father.
Th: Your father?
Pt: Yes, I don't know why, because my mother was always home and my father had a hardware store and he just wasn't home all the time.
Th: Now, what was your relationship—we'll come back to your father— but what was your relationship to your mother?
Pt: Terrible. We were always fighting.
Th: About what?
Pt: My husband; my first boyfriend.
Th: Now, that's a bit too old. When you were a little girl?
Pt: When I was a little girl? I don't remember.
Th: Are you saying, then, that you fought with your mother and you had a good relationship with your grandmother? Do you split those two people?
Pt: I can't remember my younger days with my mother, like when I was five or six; I don't remember anything, not a thing.
Th: But you remember your father?
Pt: I remember my uncle, because he used to be around me more

than my dad was when I was a little girl. He took me everywhere, but my dad never did that. It's always my uncle that did.
Th: Yet you were closer to your father, you said.
Pt: Yes.
Th: What did you and your father do together?
Pt: Went for rides once in a while.
Th: Do you remember that as a pleasant experience?
Pt: Yes.
Th: Only the two of you?
Pt: Yes. He used to wash his car, or when he used to go somewhere he used to ask me if I wanted to come. I used to go with him.
Th: Now, when your brother was at home, did all three of you go?
Pt: No. He was never that close to Dad.
Th: Who was he close to?
Pt: I don't know. My mother, I guess.
Th: You're smiling. Why do you smile?
Pt: I didn't really ever pay attention to my brother.
Th: You didn't? Why not?
Pt: I don't know. I never did. I was always in my own little world all the time.
Th: Then what?
Pt: I used to go upstairs and listen to music and just think of things. That's how I... Even today I do that. If I want to think, I just listen to music. I don't know if that's being immature; I don't know, but I just close the door and I'm complete.
Th: Well, it's not right to judge things or call them immature or anything. What we're doing is trying to understand. Let's come back to your brother. What was the problem between you?
Pt: I think that... I don't know, my family was never close. It was never a close family.
Th: But, you were closer to your father, you said.
Pt: I don't know why. I still am today. I don't know why. My mother used to pound on this thing that you have to have respect for your father. And it's always that thing, you know.
Th: But now, wait a minute. Are you saying that it was because your mother pounded that into you, or is it because you really enjoyed washing the car or doing this and that?
Pt: Oh, no. I loved doing that. It used to make him happy. I just

loved seeing my father happy.

Th: It made your father happy, and sometimes maybe you were not so happy yourself?

Pt: No. I used to be happy when I used to do it.

Th: Yes, but at other times?

Pt: Make me unhappy?

Th: Yes.

Pt: No.

Th: Never?

Pt: Today it does, because if you're a woman you have to act like I was not married or still his little girl, and I just can't act that way today.

Th: He wants you to act as if you were unmarried? Isn't that interesting. What do you mean by that?

Pt: Well, when I went on vacation in the spring, he didn't like that. He wanted me to stay with him for Easter. Well, he didn't say directly, but my mother told me that he didn't like the idea too much.

Th: So your father still views you as his little girl?

Pt: He's always done that.

Th: He always did?

Pt: Yes.

(*The therapist explores the patient's grade school: as a child she did not have many friends, didn't like the teachers and preferred to stay at home.*)

Th: Come now, you never gave it a thought? You just told me how important it was for him, at least how, to some degree, it was important to you. Yet you say that you never gave it a thought. You had no friends at school. You didn't get along so well with the teachers who were picking on you. You didn't get along so well with your mother. You didn't get along so well with your brother. Your grandmother, who gave you everything, was dead. Well, it's quite clear, at least in my opinion, that your father must have been a very important person.

Pt: No. Well, I didn't like going to school because the teachers were all picking on me, so I had to stay home, just away from the problem.

Th: But could it be also that maybe you did something to make the teachers pick on you so that you could run home?
Pt: No. It never upset me long. I used to face it quite often. I just hated school.
Th: Now, what happened then? What did your father do? I mean, what was his job?
Pt: He used to run a hardware store, so he was never home.
Th: He was never home?
Pt: Well...
Th: Did you ever go to the store? You did? What happened then?
Pt: I used to help him out.
Th: Yes? What did you do?
Pt: I used to work as cashier or put things on the shelves or...
Th: I see. Then you were how old?
Pt: Twelve.

(The therapist explores the patient's first period and her reaction to it, and she expresses resentment that she was unprepared, that her mother did not tell her anything about it.)

Th: How did your father feel, you now being a woman rather than a child?
Pt: I don't know; I never asked.
Th: What did you think?
Pt: I didn't think of anything.
Th: You know, I think you're running away from my question.
Pt: Yes.
Th: So, why is it that when I ask you some questions, you don't know?
Pt: Because I just never had the time.
Th: Well, it's just as good a time to do it right now, since you are capable of thinking. What about that? What do you think? Did you see any change in your father's attitude, for instance, when you were twelve or thirteen?
Pt: No. I don't remember.
Th: You don't remember?
Pt: No, I really don't.
Th: For instance, at the store?
Pt: I don't remember.

Th: You don't remember meaning that you didn't remember any change, is that it?
Pt: No, I don't.
Th: Or you don't want to remember?
Pt: I never probably observed any change in my dad, except when I got pregnant with my daugher. Then I observed some change. I was really embarrassed.
Th: I see. We'll go into that later. How was high school?

(*The therapist explores the patient's high school, which she didn't like; she had two or three friends. Her husband was her first boyfriend. She became pregnant before marriage.*)

Th: You were pregnant? Now tell me about your father's attitude that changed.
Pt: He didn't like the idea of me... he was going to have me put away and everything or shipped back to Italy or... I was always embarrassed when I was pregnant in front of my dad, like I was always in when he wasn't because I had to live with my parents. I don't think he liked that idea very much.
Th: I get the message. What about your mother?
Pt: I don't know. It didn't bother me that much if it upset her or not. It did, but not as much as it did my father.
Th: Was she upset?
Pt: Oh, yes. She wanted to let me have an abortion; just have me carried away one night and have an abortion.
Th: What happened? How did you become pregnant?
Pt: Well, I came back from vacation with my whole family and I met this young fellow back there that I really liked a lot.
Th: That was your husband?
Pt: No, that was another one.
Th: I see. I thought you told me your husband was the only one.
Pt: I never made love to this fellow. He was two years younger than I was. I was still a virgin and he couldn't touch me. So I came home and I became pregnant.
Th: And this was the first time you had intercourse?
Pt: Oh, no.
Th: What about that?
Pt: I didn't want to do it and he made me. He said: "If you don't make

love to me, I'll drop you," and that scared me so I just wanted someone to give me affection and I was getting it from someone and that's why I kept him.

Th: But you had your father's affection, didn't you?
Pt: No.
Th: No? What happened?
Pt: I don't remember my father ever hugging or kissing me. Oh, a few times he used to put his arm around me in public or even as a kid, but never . . .
Th: You mean to say that you wanted some affection from your father and you didn't get it?
Pt: No, not really.
Th: Even at the store?
Pt: No.
Th: No?
Pt: He never used to make smart remarks. I don't know; people would see us on the street or in public and they'd just sense that I was really close to my dad. They'd say it right in front of him, too.
Th: But you see, that's what I'm impressed by. You tell me you were attached to your father. He was attached to you. There were always things that you did together, the grocery store, etc., but somehow or other you tell me that you lacked affection.
Pt: My kids are the same way. There is an understanding like what my father and I had.
Th: Yes, but let's get back to you. What about that?
Pt: I don't know. That's why I can't seem to kiss my kids. I'll do it, but . . .
Th: Are you saying that the first time that you had intercourse with this boy who somehow or other threatened you for love, you were going to lose affection or something?
Pt: Yes.
Th: That is the same pattern that we know, that you do something for someone else because you're afraid that you're not going to get affection.
Pt: Probably.
Th: What happened? What was your reaction to having sexual intercourse?
Pt: Well, I was really afraid.

Th: Yes, and?
Pt: Well, I still did it.
Th: Yes? Did you enjoy it?
Pt: Not the first time.
Th: All right, then, Did you go out with other fellows?
Pt: No, just him; he was the only one.
Th: All right. So I interrupted you when you told me that you went on vacation, and you came back from vacation and there was a boy who was younger than you.
Pt: Yes. He was really nice.
Th: Yes. What about him?
Pt: Well, when I went back home he wrote letters saying he wanted to marry me. The day I got married he wrote me that he still wanted to marry me, but since I was married to my husband...
Th: Now, before you married. We arrive at the time that you had intercourse with your husband and you became pregnant, yet you were talking to me about this other fellow.
Pt: I used to like him.
Th: Yes. Why did you decide to go with your husband?
Pt: He had made love to me and that really tied me down; just that one thing really touched me.
Th: When, now? In reference to that vacation?
Pt: No, from the first time we made love I really got attached to him.
Th: When did you meet him?
Pt: I knew him when I was twelve, but I didn't go out with him until I was fifteen.
Th: So then, what about the other fellow with whom you had intercourse?
Pt: He was from New York, so when I came back home here I didn't see him.
Th: So your husband was the only person around you, and you were going together off and on for two years. Then you more or less liked the other fellow who was younger?
Pt: I've always liked him. Even today I think of him.
Th: How long have you known him?
Pt: Since I was seventeen. But I got married in September and this fellow came up to see me in February and I had my daughter and he didn't even know I had a baby, and he was shocked when he saw her.

Th: What was the attachment, then, that you had to your husband, since there was somebody else?
Pt: Sex. That's all it was.
Th: Was it satisfactory at that time? Okay, then you became pregnant and your response to the family was what?
Pt: We used to have discussions at three or four in the morning, arguing about it, ridiculous things. Like nothing could be done; I was already pregnant. They were still arguing that they were going to put me away and they got really violent.
Th: Who, your father?
Pt: Yes. He even does it today.
Th: You mean your husband and your father don't get along?
Pt: No, my father never liked him from the beginning.
Th: Why?
Pt: Because he wasn't the type of person for me. His character was the complete opposite of mine, I don't know; he used to beat me up, and like they knew that I was smarter than that but I just accepted it. I didn't fight back, because if I did, I would never see him again.
Th: Are you saying that you married your husband only because of sex and because you were pregnant? All right. Why didn't you tell me that from the beginning? Now, there were problems? Did you feel that your father's reaction, which was pretty violent, meant that he was interested in you, that he was sorry you were making a mistake? Didn't that show to you that your father loved you, that he had such a reaction, and that you created such a reaction in him?
Pt: Right.
Th: You did? So that was of importance to him? Was it because he was losing his daughter?
PT: I think my father is very possessive, more than my mother. I don't know; I think he is.
Th: What does your father look like?
Pt: He's got dark hair. He's five feet five inches tall. Others tell me he's really good-looking. I think he's all right.
Th: I don't care what others tell you. Now what did he look like?
Pt: He's got dark hair, He's of medium build.
Th: And do you think he's good-looking?
Pt: Yes, but he's domineering and possessive. I think the reason

why he's behaving the way he's behaving today is because his mother was too domineering and possessive also, because he's running around behind my mother's back. I know he is because the way he acts around home is the way my husband acted with me when he was running around. I see right through that man and he knows I do. I just look at him and he knows when I look at him what I mean. I just sense a lot of things in people like that, you know?

Th: How does that make you feel?

Pt: Terrible.

Th: Why?

Pt: Because of my mother. She knows; she has a feeling that something is going on. She doesn't have proof or things like that, but I know. He's going around buying Barry White tapes and the sort of thing that we play. A man his age doesn't buy records like that unless he's got a young girl.

Th: Oh, a young girl?

Pt: Yes.

Th: What age?

Pt: My aunt saw her, but I don't know how old she is. She saw her at a restaurant where she works. Maybe thirty. I didn't see her. She's brunette, that's all I know.

Th: And so you're upset because of your mother?

Pt: Yes, because, you know, like I know what she's going through. It's the same thing I was going through last year at this time. Depression, except I took it really bad. She'd take it worse.

Th: In what way? In what way are they the same problems that you were going through last year?

Pt: Well, he runs around the way my husband did.

Th: Your husband does, too?

Pt: He was. It was terrible.

Th: I see.

Pt: I used to follow him in the streets with the car with his girl friends and I wanted to smash his car. I didn't do anything violent, but I felt like doing something really bad to both of them.

Th: Now your husband and your father are having affairs?

Pt: My husband stopped, I think, since we got back together in July. That's what I think, but I can't trust him any more. Like, I've met one fellow that I can really trust and I don't want to see any other man.

"THE CASE OF THE ITALIAN HOUSEWIFE" 113

Th: Who is this other man?
Pt: The one I went to see at Easter in Winnipeg.

(*Some exploration into the patient's family life and early part of marriage—her husband beating her up—and a confrontation that she married to get affection but got beatings, indicating a self-punishing pattern.*)

Th: Just think, does it have something to do with your mother?
Pt: The beating up?
Th: No. Your reaction to being a victim.
Pt: Yes.
Th: In what way?
Pt: Because she took a lot of ... He did beat her once. He just hit her on the arm, but like all the trouble she's been through in her life, she just stood back and took them all.
Th: Like you?
Pt: That's why I left, because I don't see myself going through the same cycles as my mom and my husband's mother went through.
Th: But if you wanted to do so much, this same bit that your mother did, why were you doing that? To please your father?
Pt: Why was I doing what to please my father?
Th: Being like your mother.
Pt: Because that's the way she brought me up, to respect my father. Well, that's what I think; I don't know.
Th: That's what you think, but my question is not that. My question is straight to you now.
Pt: Why did I do it?
Th: Yes. Why are you like your mother? Why are you getting the beatings in the same way she did, maybe not as many?
Pt: She just got it once.
Th: I understand that, that she got it once. She is married to somebody who has affairs, like you. You are exactly like your mother.
Pt: I know.
Th: My question is, Why did you do that?
Pt: Why did I take all those things?
Th: Yes, from your mother. Why did you become like your mother? *Was it to please your father?*
Pt: *Yes.*

Th: Have you thought of it that way?
Pt: Yes, a few times.
Th: Okay. Can you tell me about it? Because it's important. You can do that thinking now by yourself, if you really want to get out of this. That's why you're here and that's what we're trying to do.
Pt: No. I'm not trying to hide anything. I just want to say that I don't know; I really don't know.
Th: I know you really don't know, but you have to think, and if you're going to get this treatment here it will be something like what we are doing now. Obviously, I don't know anything, like I said before, but a person like me, your therapist is someone to help you out. You know, some things but you're not sure. Now, let's get back to pleasing your father.
Pt: Well, he thinks a lot of my mother. He thinks very highly of her.
Th: So if your father thinks very highly of your mother, and if you are like your mother, then he thinks very highly of you?
Pt: Right. Yes, he does. I know he does.
Th: Of course, I was convinced of that a long time ago, but now I'm glad to hear it from you. Now, okay, is he jealous?
Pt. Yes. He's very possessive.
Th: What does that mean, possessive of you now?
Pt: Well, I'm his daughter and he doesn't want anybody to hurt me because I guess he loves me.
Th: Of course. I understand that, but does it mean more than that?
Pt: I don't know.
Th: No. We cannot have "I don't know." What, for instance?
Pt: I am his daughter and I guess he doesn't want anybody else to just probably share me, or he always wants to spend all his time with me, I guess. Whenever I go to visit him, he just goes crazy.

(*At this point, the therapist makes further exploration, and it becomes clear that the patient's father gives her a lot of affection, which disturbs her greatly. The patient verbalizes much negative feeling about the character of her husband. The therapist then explores the patient's relationship with her two children, and she indicates that she loves them both. Then she talks about her relationship with her husband; he is very jealous and does not know about her affairs with other men, and if he knew he would kill her. She says she is also jealous.*)

Th: You are really still attracted to your husband?
Pt: No, I'm not as I was before. The one in Winnipeg attracts me more than any other kind of man.
Th: Yes. Now, what about the one in Winnipeg?
Pt: Oh, I love that guy.
Th: How long has this been going on?
Pt: Two years, but I haven't seen him since last—well, I haven't seen him for eighteen months and I saw him for the first time after eighteen months.
Th: And?
Pt: Well, it was nice to see him. You know, he came down to my doorstep.
Th: How did it go? Did you tell your husband about this?
Pt: No. I told him I was going to a singles' Sara Coventry party on Friday night. So we went for supper together; we went to the mountain, and then he drove me home. There was no sex or anything.
Th: So with this man from Winnipeg there was no sex?
Pt: No, there wasn't at the time. After eighteen months of not seeing him, I didn't do anything then, but when I went up to see him at his country place, I went for the weekend, and it was just, you know, a friendly weekend. But then I went back this month for nine days and he fell in love with me.
Th: How do you feel about that?
Pt: How do I feel about that?
Th: Yes.
Pt: That's what I'm worried about.
Th: So are you going to get a divorce?
Pt: Oh, yes.
Th: You are?
Pt: Definitely, but not because of this fellow, it's because I want a divorce. I spoke to this man; I spoke to him on the phone three days ago and I told him, and he said, "Why don't you come up here and live with me," and all that. I said to myself, "Well, I can't get into something that fast now because I want to be alone for a couple of years." So when he heard that I had gotten beaten up, he just changed his mind and he said he wouldn't come up to see me and live here.

Th: Why not?
Pt: Because he doesn't want to be part of my troubles, because I'm with the children and if he lives with me . . .
Th: So, is your husband willing to give you the divorce?
Pt: I don't know. I spoke to him this week, and he just threatened me on the phone and I just slammed the phone down.
Th: You don't live together now?
Pt: Oh, no.
Th: How long have you been separated?
Pt: We moved this summer, and in November I just packed his bags in his car and locked the door behind him. He went out for a while and I left a note saying I was going out of town, and I was gone for nine days and I came back and he walked in the door. I didn't even see him come in. I just held on to the wall; I don't know if he punched me or hit me. He came for his hi-fi and things like that. You see, he's very possessive as far as belongings go. He's more materialistic than I am.
Th: Let me ask you this. What prompted you to come here?
Pt: I just wondered what made me do things I don't like doing.
Th: Yes, but you've been doing these things for a long time.
Pt: Yes.
Th: What made you come here this time? Is it because of this beating or this difficulty with your husband just now?
Pt: It's just everything in general.
Th: Yes, but what made you call to make an appointment to come here?
Pt: I called way back in the beginning of November, because I was really confused then. I don't know.
Th: What?
Pt: I didn't know where to go any more.
Th: Why were you confused then? What was the problem? Was it the other man in Winnipeg?
Pt: No. It was my husband. It was just that I thought I ought to get some professional help instead of speaking to my girl friend all the time about it.
Th: Let me ask you this. What do you think is the key problem that you have in terms of relationships? Is it your father?
Pt: I just want the perfect man, perfect in what I see.
Th: Is it your father?
Pt: I don't know.

Th: What do you think?
Pt: My father isn't the perfect man.
Th: Does he come close to being perfect?
Pt: I don't really compare the fellows I go out with with my dad. Never.
Th: Maybe you should. But tell me, is he close to being a perfect man?
Pt: I don't know. I don't live with him.
Th: That's no answer. What do you think?
Pt: I don't know.
Th: What do you think? I know you don't know, but what do you think?
Pt: Well, nobody's perfect.
Th: I know that, too.
Pt: But I want the kind of man I imagine, and that's the kind I can't get.
Th: So, is he the closest to that?
Pt: My father?
Th: Yes.
Pt: I don't know.
Th: His possessiveness, his attractiveness, his affairs...
Pt: I never think that way.
Th: All right, probably I'll accept this. I think this is something you're going to have to do something about. You're not going to get out of your problems unless you do some thinking about them, and unless you do the thinking with somebody else. You cannot somehow run away from it. I think you know by now that it doesn't work, and you can carry on with twenty other people looking for somebody and always finding problems unless you get down to brass tacks as to what your difficulties are. We touched on some. We have a pretty good idea now as to what they may be, and you now have to pursue that in a pretty systematic way. But it's up to you if you want to do that. Do you think you might?
Pt: If I really can, I might.
Th: Okay, that's fine. I think that's about all our time.

Question from the floor:

I felt that this was an interview with a predetermined course. The course was set very early in the interview, and it was a Freudian course with a very strong oedipal bias. The interviewer, I thought, got interested and excited at anything that smacked of Oedipus and not much else, and I felt that this was unfair to the patient, who obviously has some crucial problems that I don't think got clarified for her. I can list a number of them. I thought the central one was that of closeness, her need for closeness, her fear of closeness. This is particularly true in terms of the husband and the children, and the man with whom she was having an affair. I have a feeling that if that had been touched on, the interview would have taken quite a different course.

Dr. Sifneos:

I think it's very possible that what you're saying is true. I'm also a psychoanalyst, and I believe in Freud and Socrates. There is some evidence that this particular patient talked about her father and used terms that I did not give to her but that she gave to me. She talked about possessiveness in relation to her father. She told of the identical aspects that her father had in his affairs and her own identification with her mother to please her father. I may have brainwashed her, or whatever you may call it. The fact is that these are the things she had to say, unless you view her as an absolute weakling who is indeed so suggestible that you cannot do anything about it. I don't think this is the case, because many times she disagreed with me. I would say that it remains to be seen whether a different emphasis may have been more fruitful. You may be absolutely right.

Question from the floor:

I was struck by the intensity of the interview, and I'm wondering if we could get away with this type of style if the patient were not a lovely one and a tough one.

Dr. Sifneos:

It's a difficult question to answer. What I would say is that one interacts with the patient on the basis of the information given by the patient. So the intensity of this particular interview possibly would not have been the same with another patient. I would say that for the type of patient we select for this kind of short-term psychotherapy, keeping the criteria that I mentioned in mind, this type of interview is much more appropriate. With other patients I might not be able to touch any of these issues, and, even if the patient were to bring them up, I may change the subject or avoid or try to suppress the anxieties that may be coming up.

"THE CASE OF THE ITALIAN HOUSEWIFE"

Question from the floor:

In the interview, there are a number of things that she started and never completed, such as her high school and her marriage. I wonder how that relates to what you might predict for success in psychotherapy?

Dr. Sifneos:

One has to choose how much material to pursue. There are many things that I did not touch on. I did not go into her medical history, for example, which could possibly be of some importance. I have not gone into more specific aspects of her intellectual development, but again I think this is the kind of assessment that keeps on giving us the information that maybe we should pursue one aspect and not something else. Was there a preconceived idea? Yes, I do believe in the psychodynamic principal of the functioning of the human mind, and therefore if this is a preconception I do have it, but I think I would draw the same parallel with the surgeon who has a preconceived idea about the anatomy of the abdomen. He must know something, and, indeed, for the 99 percent of the patients that he operates on for appendicitis, he's going to find that the appendix is inflamed and that it is located at the right lower quarter of the abdomen. Well, it might be that sometimes, when the oedipal issues might not be present, one has to proceed in the same way as the surgeon, trying to find out where the oedipal issues are?

Question from the floor:

I think I agree with that. What I'm saying is that there are particular indications in the past history that you haven't completed in order to do this kind of therapy. I was wondering what kind of prognostic motivations there are.

Dr. Sifneos:

I would not say that this is a full interview and that I would be satisfied to accept her for short-term psychotherapy. There are some questions about the earlier relationships in terms of the criteria that we have, particularly about the motivation.

Question from the floor:

I had mixed feelings about this interview. I appreciate the fact that you took a very active part in the interview, with very confronting-type questions, but I am concerned about the fact that you seemed not to focus. In other words, many times when you had opportunities you kept picking up the ball and dropping it. I was curious as to why you didn't focus and go in more with your questions at different points on things that she would bring up. Instead, you would change the theme. You said it was because of her anxiety, and I wondered if it might have something to do with your own anxiety.

Dr. Sifneos:

No, you misunderstood me. I didn't say that I changed the focus when she was anxious. Far from it. I think I asked her some anxiety-provoking questions. Therefore, I was not letting her go. Concerning the decision as to where to shift, one is presented with the problem in an evaluation of having a complete history and at the same time of arriving at a focus on which the therapy will be concentrated. Thus, keeping those two balls up in the air is a bit of a problem. Sometimes one feels that if he pursues the issue which appears to be a meaningful focus, he may not get enough information about some key relationships in the past. Now, why I would shift at certain times and not at others is hard to say, but I could state one thing. I felt very comfortable with this lady, and I wasn't anxious and excited. My own anxiety was not a factor. One may be anxious with other patients, but certainly not with her.

Question from the floor:

In other words, you don't know why you actually shifted when you changed focus?

Dr. Sifneos:

I shifted because at the time I thought some specific information was necessary and that we had covered enough of a particular subject. It was possibly of importance to bring new information into the picture.

Dr. Mann:

As we all know, this was a patient who was presented to the interviewer without any prior knowledge of her history, and if he had had a fully detailed case history perhaps things would have been conducted differently. I was also particularly struck by the intuitive nature of Dr. Sifneos' interventions, or, in fact, his noninterventions, and I think this is the factor that we really can never measure; what you might have done or what I might have done might not have been quite the same at quite the same time. Clearly, something clicked with you, Dr. Sifneos, to say. "Well, I will focus more here," or "I will ask this other question."

Dr. Malan:

I think that Dr. Sifneos and I differ very little in most of our views about brief psychotherapy. Yet we differ on how one should do an initial evaluation. I have some uneasiness about this initial interview, which is not to deprecate the great skill that was used to conduct it. I think that what Dr. Sifneos did with this lady was to go for a particular focus—and one of the first questioners made this point—to the exclusion of exploring what the other areas of disturbance are in this patient.

Now, this is legitimate, but it isn't what I would do. There are many, many issues here. One of the things Dr. Sifneos had talked about is how long one spends on the initial interview with the patient. He says he spends about forty-five minutes with the patient and he trains his residents to do the same. I spend two hours with a patient, if necessary, and I don't leave any stone unturned. If a patient gives me clues, I follow them up; I don't ignore them, or, if I do, it is because I feel this is an area which shouldn't be touched on at this time. What I want to do with a patient is to make an overall and as thorough a survey of what the disturbances in him are, and to pick up a focus from that.

What Dr. Sifneos has done with this interview is to pick a focus during the interview and to go for it. I'm not necessarily convinced that the focus he chose was the correct one for this particular patient. I don't like to say this, but there was a point at which Dr. Sifneos actually distorted what the patient said in the interest of making an oedipal focus. He said something like, and I hope I quote correctly: "Your father beat your mother up even more than your husband beat you up." Now, this wasn't true, but you said this to her, didn't you, Dr. Sifneos? It wasn't true. The father had beaten up the mother once, whereas the husband had beaten up the patient on, apparently, a number of occasions. Dr. Sifneos was so excited about his focus with this patient that he was prepared to distort the evidence in the interests of it. I'm not entirely happy about this. I also am not happy about the degree of direct suggestion he used on this patient; that he pinned her down and pinned her down until she agreed with him. I wouldn't do this with a patient. I would say something gentle to her. If she didn't like it, I'd go on to something else. I feel that one is in terrible danger of imposing a fantasy on the patient, where, in fact, it might be one's own fantasy and not the patient's, although I doubt this is so in this patient's case. I'm sure that what Dr. Sifneos brought out in this patient is, in fact, part of her pathology.

There are other parts in her pathology that I'd want to know about before I finally picked this patient for any form of psychotherapy. At one point she said: "I let people step all over me." Now, what does that mean? That wasn't gone into—or perhaps it was, because Dr. Sifneos is a very skilled interviewer and if she gives a clue like this one may find an answer to it in another part of the interview. However, I would have wanted to know more about her pattern of allowing people to step all over her, and in what circumstances she did this.

We got something later on about a pattern of having to give to people in case she lost them or something of this kind. I would have wanted to go into that in far more detail and try to understand what it was all about. Somebody from the floor mentioned this problem of closeness, with which I agree because she says something terribly significant at one point about how she couldn't kiss her children. Is this right? I would have said to her immediately: "Why can't you kiss your children? What goes wrong? What are you afraid of? What is it?" I would try to get at that problem. This is a problem of human closeness, as was said from the floor. Now, that lady doesn't look to me like someone with pre-oedipal problems and deep dependence and all the rest. At the same time, I would have wanted to know what her problem of closeness is about because it's not the same as her problem with her father since it is manifested with both her children, one of whom is female. It can't be anything to do with her father. So, what's that all about? I would want to know in order to be able to get a thorough overall assessment of this patient.

I feel this is a disadvantage of having to cram your interview into forty-five minutes. There are other questions that were not asked. Nobody mentioned how depressed she got when she was depressed. Now, this doesn't look like a severely depressed lady to me. She doesn't look like a patient who is subject to severe depression, yet one wants to know. I would have devoted five minutes to saying to her: "What happens when you get depressed? What is the worst you've ever been depressed in your life? Have you ever felt like suicide?" For all we know, this patient may have made a suicidal attempt at the age of seventeen which she never told us about, but which we must know if we're going to take her into therapy. I have a lot of feelings about this interview. All I can say is that it isn't the way I would do it.

Dr. Moll:

When we are talking about brief psychotherapy based on psychoanalysis and so on, perhaps the tendency might be to push things too much. Certainly, if we're thinking of the term "free association," there wasn't very much chance in this session of showing any free association, because really the patient was pounded with one question after another and some of the questions were left in midair. It was very skillfully done, and I think that, in a session of forty-five minutes, to be able to reach out for the resolve-electra, or what have you, is really an achievement. In other words, what I'm coming to is that we all have our own way of dealing with a patient; it doesn't matter what school of analysis you belong to or what institute you've been certified from. Everybody has an individual way of dealing with the patient, and I'm pretty sure that if Dr. Sifneos had watched this session and instead of seeing himself had seen someone else, he might have had a lot of thoughts or second thoughts about the interpretations given to the patient. I feel that with such a subjective relationship existing between the patient and the therapist, there are a lot of things that happen in that relationship, a so-called rapport. Someone suggested that there was too much intensity. Well, that remains to be seen. Maybe too much intensity on the part of one individual might not be too much intensity on the part of another. This is what produces a certain amount of consternation within me when we see different parameters of a similar situation.

For instance, I was quite impressed by this patient when she mentioned something about trying to get away, and Dr. Sifneos mentioned, "Well, what was she trying to get away from?" Well, I think she gave us a pretty good lead. The moment she felt close to anybody, she felt that she was going to be stepped all over. In other words, she was getting away from intimacy. She was afraid of allowing herself to get too close to whatever the relationship might be, and I thought there was an association there. For example, the death of the grandmother whom she loved so dearly and who disappeared. Now, this might be my own fantasy, like saying: "Well, you can't love anybody because if you love somebody, either because of your ambivalence and you've killed that somebody and that somebody's disappeared, or because of other circumstances that somebody dies and so, you're just left with a big hurt."

I therefore want to conclude by saying that we ought to be extremely careful in judging or criticizing sessions and interviews in which we ourselves have not participated, and that it would be quite possible, incidentally, for the patient to improve even if the material brought forth by the patient is entirely different from the material that was brought out in this session.

Dr. Naiman:

I would like to mention a couple of points. One is that it seems to me that from the variety of comments that have been made about the clinical material, notwithstanding the fact that Dr. Sifneos asked more quesions and guided the patient perhaps more than any one of us would do, the data came out anyway. I think the patient provided us with a great deal of information and in that short period of time there is pretty good evidence that she was not, so to speak, overwhelmed by the interviewer into providing only the kind of data that he wanted to hear. I think that's pretty clear from the interview itself.

I have two questions for Dr. Sifneos. First, I was a little surprised about your comment on the question of her identification with her mother, that she had identified with her mother in order to please her father. I would think that identification with the mother is a normal process of development for a young woman, and I would not attach any particular significance to it.

My second question is related to the paper that Dr. Zetzel wrote a number of years ago. I wonder if you accept her classification, and if you do, where do you place this patient by focusing entirely on the oedipal situation? I had the impression that you were categorizing her in category 1. My own impression, linked to some of the other comments that were made in terms of her difficulty in being affectionate with her children, her tendency to break off the things that she starts, is that she may be perhaps closer to category 3 than to category 1, and this would perhaps make a difference to any form of psychotherapy that one would be prepared to offer her. I'm not saying that I'm convinced that she is category 3, but I have some reservations about whether she is category 1, and I'd like to hear your comments.

Dr. Sifneos:

Very briefly, I would like to say that there are several points that have been brought up with which I am completely in agreement. I would prefer to use the time element to get as much information as I can from my patients, and we teach this actively to our residents.

It does not mean that in one interview we will decide whether this patient is going to be accepted or not. We have to take into consideration the differences in different settings. In our clinic a patient may be seen by three or four different evaluators who are doing exactly the same type of interview. The setting at The Montreal General Hospital is more or less similar to ours, but the setting at Tavistock is different.

I had no information about this patient. What I meant to emphasize is that I would like to focus in a specific area as quickly as I can, and, as you all witnessed, I tried to do just basically that. If, indeed, there were some serious questions in the back of my mind about her pathology, even if there was a 5 percent possibility, I would have had a second interview to explore some of those questions. I would say that we can by-pass the pregenital characterological issues even if they are present to some small degree. They are not going to flood her personality or the therapy and will not create difficulties during its course. We focus very systematically on one and only one area that appears in the mind of the evaluator as well as the patient; that is the most important area on which to concentrate.

I'm talking now about technical issues that we're really, at this point, unprepared to answer. As to the degree of serious pathology that may have existed in this woman, I can categorically state that it is not significant on the basis of this interview. I would not worry about suicidal attempts. I would not worry about oral deprivations or things of that kind. All of us have a certain degree of dependence and a certain degree of passivity, and in my opinion these are of secondary importance, as far as this patient is concerned, compared to this crucial oedipal aspect, which personally I feel satisfied plays a key role. Now, the reference to her identification with her mother, I think, is very well taken. It was only trying to reinforce the possibility to her by emphasizing that she was a masochist as her mother was. I also have an unconscious, and I guess it was running a bit too fast when I was thinking her mother had more punishment than she herself did. Yes, I got a bit too excited. If, indeed, I get excited about discovering a nonexistent Oedipus complex, the evidence would appear after, let us say, sixteen interviews. The patient would be unchanged, no different than she was at the outset. I hope that later we can give you some typical evidence as to what the findings are about this kind of psychotherapy.

As far as the question about being an oral hysteric is concerned, I think this is a very good point. The distinctions that Dr. Zetzel has made in reference to hysteria are absolutely outstanding. I am not sure that she is category 1, namely, a good patient with a basically oedipal problem. I would like some more information on that, although again I would be inclined to say that if I have to weigh these two, I would have to put her more in category 1 than in category 3.

Question from the floor:

It seems to me that most of the comments so far have been just on the style of the interview, and perhaps on the dynamic formulation or dynamic diagnosis. Admittedly, there is not a dichotomy that you can draw in terms of, as was pointed out in earlier discussions, the therapist's input relative to developing criteria for selection for short-term dynamic psychotherapy. But aren't we putting the cart before the horse by focusing so much on this? I'd like to hear more discussion on whether or not this woman does or doesn't—and the reasons why she does or doesn't—get into the criteria for short-term dynamic psychotherapy as were developed earlier. I'd particularly like to hear Dr. Sifneos' feelings about this. I gather you said that you were not quite sure. I was struck by the difference in this woman. The first half of the interview contrasted with the second half of the interview and this may get us back somewhat to the style issue, because I think there was something about the way you were focusing on her relationship with her father which tended to make her demonstrate more affect, perhaps more motivation, more interest, but I was very skeptical about whether or not she was a good candidate.

Dr. Sifneos:

The question was about the criteria for short-term anxiety-provoking psychotherapy that I have outlined briefly before. I would certainly say that she seems to have a circumscribed chief complaint. What happened during the first minute of her interview, which you did not hear, was an explanation to her of the fact that I did not know anything about her history and that I wanted her to tell me her problems. She said she had a tendency to run away at times when she felt that she was being stepped all over by her husband. I would say that in terms of a meaningful relationship, although I would want more information, I think she did pass this criterion. Certainly in terms of her relationship to me, which is the third criterion, she had a very flexible, emotional interaction. As far as her intelligence and her psychological sophistication are concerned, she seemed to be above average. You heard that she, herself, seemed to be quite interested in pursuing this very specific area which we focused upon and which we have outlined. I would consider her possibly as having a motivation of five or six, which is "fair" to "good." I would be inclined to therefore accept her for short-term anxiety-provoking psychotherapy.

Dr. Straker:

The style and procedure of the interview involved a very early focusing on specific problems. There was a lot of leading and a very active participation by the interviewer. There were suggestions and confronting interpretations and an avoidance of some issues, in that some of the comments made by the patient were dropped or not pursued. I would describe this as the interviewer going for the jugular vein, in a sense. I might say that the patient's anxiety in the session appeared to me to be masterfully handled. There was sufficient probing, and sufficient interference with the patient's willingness to back off at certain times, so that Dr. Sifneos persisted with a particular line of questions by which he was able to read or respond to the patient's anxiety level in such a way as to not have her become overwhelmed.

The question that concerns me is at what point does one make a decision as to what the important problems are. If one makes such a decision, then to some extent one establishes a prophecy which can be self-fulfilling. If one decides what the problems are, it's not too difficult to lead the patient to focus on this particular problem, especially if one excludes other issues or fails to respond to them. We might say that it's not only the therapist's style in interviewing which is at work, but also the patient's response—her style, too. This patient's style, as we learned right from the beginning of the interview, is to get stepped on, and she has a desire to please everybody. That is a characterological issue which has been present all her life, and I'm sure was equally expressed during the interview.

Some of us can make decisions about where the appropriate focal material really lies, relevant to the presenting problem, more quickly than others. Dr. Malan indicated that he might have been inclined to delay a little more before making his decision, and I must confess that would probably be my own style as well. This is not to criticize the correctness of the choice. It only leaves open the question: "What about the patient's participation in the choice?" The doctor in this situation makes the choice very early, very clearly, very forcefully, and limits, in a sense, further data collection by excluding or not following up other leads. This satisfies the therapist, but again I raise the question: "What about the patient?" Coming from the West Coast, where this is a very lively issue, I have this recurrently in my own thoughts. What about the degree of participation of the patient in deciding which way the therapy goes?

Chapter 7

"The Case of the Secretary with the Violent Father"

D. H. MALAN

The patient is a twenty-seven-year old single secretary who came to the psychiatric clinic subsequent to a crisis. Her boyfriend had attempted suicide and was admitted to the psychiatric service of a hospital. She complained of having been depressed since age thirteen and also of problems in interpersonal relationships. She felt that her depressions were caused by the fact that she led a very restricted life at home and that this had been imposed on her by her father. As a child, she would sit at the window and watch the other children going out and enjoying themselves while she could not. She talked about her father being a rather strange man who drank heavily and who had frequent violent behavior. She indicated that her depressions tend to get worse in February and March. She said there were a lot of things to do in the summer but she didn't find things to do in the winter, and this caused her depression. Exploration was made into what she meant by "depression." She said she had a feeling of futility, and she also used the word "demotivation" to describe her depression. But her depression has never incapacitated her to the level at which she would have to take off time from work.

Th: I notice you don't mention the thing that has apparently precipitated your coming here, which is something to do with your boyfriend having attempted suicide. Now, where does that fit into this story?

Pt: Well, it was the last straw. It's what made me decide to stop wasting time and go talk to somebody. I think I would have eventually done it. I think that this has caused me to do it at this particular time. Also, it's a very bad time for me to be depressed because I don't think that's what he needs right now, to see me depressed. I think if he realized that I am depressed, it would make him a lot worse because he would be seeing himself as the cause.

Th: You've managed to keep this from him, have you?

Pt: Yes, although I've told him that I was seeing a psychiatrist because I would like to talk to somebody and that I'm not feeling that great. But he doesn't understand that I felt this way before and that I get depressed. I didn't feel that this was the time to talk to him about it.

Th: All right. Can we talk a little bit about the relation with him, then? Let's start with how long ago you met him.

Pt: Almost two years ago.

Th: Can you tell me how your relation developed?

Pt: Yes. It was very sudden. We met, and it took us about a week to establish the fact that we liked each other, and we were not separated very much after that. He stayed at my place all the time and went home for extra shirts. We've been very close and we're now living together. He's been really good for me because he's mature, very logical and steady-headed. He doesn't express his emotions very much, but he's been much more open as we've gotten to know each other. What I really liked about him was his stability. That's very unusual, I think, for people not to have a hang-up somewhere. It was very confusing when he got depressed like that.

Th: Yes, I can imagine so. What do you think happened?

Pt: He doesn't know what's in his head, and he doesn't know what he's depressed about except that he's also demotivated and nothing interests him. He really wanted to kill himself a few times.

Th: Are you saying that this is something that has happened before? And does he have attacks of depression the same way you have attacks of depression?

Pt: Not that I know of, although I have heard that a few years ago, maybe seven years ago, he was slightly suicidal but not in any way like he is now.

Th: So, this is something that came out of the blue for you. How long ago did it start?

Pt: It really got thrown in front of me about two months ago, when he broke down and told me that he wanted to kill himself. He had just come home, and he had been drinking and he got really depressed and he was thinking of smashing up the car, of "having an accident because it was the perfect evening for it." He ended up not doing it and coming home crying and getting all emotional about it. I guess part of him doesn't want to do it.

Th: The way you're telling me this, you're hiding the fact that it must affect you a lot.

Pt: To him, yes.

Th: But you're hiding from me how much it must affect you. You're telling me that the boy you live with suddenly gets depressed out of the blue, saying he wants to kill himself and finally making a suicidal attempt. You're telling me as if it were just a tea-party conversation.

Pt: No, definitely, it affected me very much. It's still affecting me because he's in the hospital.

Th: This must be a shock to you.

Pt: Yes, because he's a completely different person.

Th: Exactly. Had you no warning that this was going to happen? I mean, was it really the first time you noticed anything was wrong, when he came home one evening after going to a party?

Pt: That's right. In fact, I didn't even take him seriously at that time because he had been drinking, and sometimes he gets emotional when he's been drinking. So I just thought it would be over in the morning, and he was very sober and he was still feeling the same way, and that's when it struck me that the guy was serious.

Th: What has this made you feel?

Pt: Well, I feel like I've lost a friend because I don't seem to be talking to the same person. I really feel like I've lost a guy. He's just like black and white, completely different.

Th: He's not the same person at all?

Pt: No, although the last couple of days that I've seen him he's been looking a lot better. So I hope that he'll come out of it and stay out of it. I guess I'll feel better when he's feeling better.

Th: What do you think it's due to? The fact that he got into this state afterwards.

Pt: In his case, I think one idea that came to mind was that he was not meeting his own expectations about himself, and also his father's expectations. He will never agree with that, but that, I think, accounts for a lot of what is getting him down.

Th: What about the relation with you? Do you think there was anything there that might have brought this on?

Pt: I doubt it very much.

Th: How have things been going between you?

Pt: Just great.

Th: What have you thought about your future together?

Pt: Well, right now I'm confused.

Th: Yes, obviously you're confused now, but before this happened what had you thought?

Pt: We were thinking of getting married.

Th: I can see that this has altered the situation altogether.

Pt: Yes, until I find out what's going to happen. I think if he's going to continue going into these cycles it's going to be impossible for us to do that. We'll be getting each other down.

Th: I take it he wasn't your first important boyfriend. Or perhaps he was. I don't know.

Pt: Well, he's the first one that I've really enjoyed. I had a boyfriend for two years just before him, but I think it was more of a companionship rather than anything I'd get excited about. This boyfriend is the first one that I've really been interested in.

Th: One of the things you've said to me is that you tend to get depressed toward the end of the winter when somehow there isn't enough to do. This implies to me that in some way you feel cut off from people and you can't really make use of your relations with people nor compensate for activities which are no longer there. Would this be right?

Pt: I think so.

Th: You've described yourself as sitting in the window and seeing the other children enjoying themselves. Have you felt, in some way, outside life and you couldn't quite get into it? It seems to me that you must be saying something like this to me. Is this right?

Pt: Yes.

Th: Does that mean that you've had some difficulty in making close relationships with men until perhaps these past two years?
Pt: No, I haven't had any difficulty. A person like me always has a lot of friends because I've always been a good listener. I'm the type that will go to the back of a bus and sit in a corner and watch everybody. So, I watch people. At a party, I'll sit there as opposed to going in there and being in the party. I'm also a good listener, and therefore people usually like me because I'm somebody they can talk to and people like to talk. I never had any problem with relationships. Most men I met I wasn't interested in simply because they ended up telling me their problems and I didn't want to start with anybody who had all these problems. It's great to listen to them, but, you know, you don't hold your breath until the next phone call.
Th: So, what was different?

(The therapist explores the characteristics of the patient's present boyfriend. The patient indicates he had gone through a rough childhood himself and emphasizes he was very mature, responsible and intelligent. Then she goes on to say that she has always had difficulty in talking about herself to others and that this boyfriend was the only one she felt close to. Sexual relationship was good. Then the therapist explores her previous sexual experiences, and she says she did not get anything out of it personally. The patient elaborates that her present boyfriend was the first person she ever cared for. She met him two years ago, in November.)

Th: I'm interested in something which I find just a little strange here. You've suffered from these attacks of depression more or less every winter since you were thirteen, which is a long time, and you had difficulty remembering whether or not you had an attack. You would have thought that it was marvelous, that it's gone away at last. Yet somehow you haven't felt that because you couldn't remember whether it was there or not.
Pt: The reason for that, I think, is because I never sat down and thought about the fact that it happens every winter. It's only very recently that I've tried to analyze why I'm getting depressed. It's never occurred to me whether I've been depressed before. It's only occurred to me that I'm depressed now. Why am I depressed now? So, it's just very recently that I've thought

about my past depressions. It never occurred to me to link them up.

Th: How do you feel about being by yourself? Is that something you feel able to cope with?

Pt: Yes. I have lived by myself for quite some time because I've been away from home. It doesn't bother me. I'm pretty active on the whole, so it doesn't bother me.

Th: I get the feeling that you're the sort of person who needs to keep active. If you don't keep active, then something goes wrong. Is that true?

Pt: Yes.

Th: I get a second feeling about you and that is that you must, underneath all this, have an awful lot of very strong and upsetting feelings. Somehow they're there but you aren't really quite in touch with them. Isn't this right? I feel you've been like that as long as you can remember.

Pt: For quite a few years, whenever I really sat down and thought about it I got depressed, so I tried not to think about it.

Th: You see, you've established a pattern, haven't you? You're even like that here with me, because in spite of the fact that you're in some trouble and you feel that the bottom is falling out of your world, the way you're telling me this is just as if there wasn't anything wrong.

Pt: I'm so used to not telling anybody anything. When you don't tell people, then you can't go around looking grim. I guess you just go around with a permanent smile, and I know I have a nervous giggle, too.

Th: What's the present position between you and your boyfriend? He's still in the hospital, is he? Is he beginning to come out of his state of depression?

Pt: Well, he's looking better. I don't know if he's coming out of it. What worries me is that I hope that he can come out of it and stay out of it. He's looking quite a bit better in the last few days.

Th: What have you said to each other about your future?

Pt: I didn't want to lay any heavy conversation on him unless he brought it up. We sit around and talk about the institution and what happened that day. We keep it on that level. He's been feeling better, so I try not to have any depressing conversations.

Th: Have you been given some doubts about what's going to happen between you? He's going to come out of the hospital. You're going to go back to living together, and then you're going to have this hanging over you—when is it going to happen again? You also have suddenly realized that he isn't entirely the person that you thought he was, isn't this right? What does that make you feel?

Pt: I really feel that I've lost somebody unless it's very possible that its not going to be a recurring thing. It's very possible that there's something particular that he can point a finger at eventually and say: "This is what gets me depressed." Then the problem will be solved. Right now he doesn't know what it is that's depressing him. We're very, very similar, and this is something that amazed both of us when we first met and still does, even now. Of course, we didn't realize we were that similar. It would be good if we could work it out.

Th: Are you afraid you can't?

Pt: Yes, I would be.

Th: What do you mean?

Pt: Just about him, because my depressions aren't as bad. I get depressed. He gets suicidal and I get depressed because I worry about him. There was a time when I was going to work and I really wondered what he was going to do with himself at home. I would open the door and wonder what I was going to see. I'd check every room the minute I'd walk in the house.

Th: Can I say to you that you still tell me now with a smile, and yet you must have gone through hell?

Pt: I don't think that's a smile.

Th: You don't think so. Well, it's some sort of a smile. It appears to me as a smile, but you must have gone through absolute agony. Can you tell me something about that?

Pt: He'd get so depressed that he wouldn't want to go to work. I was worried about him being suicidal, but I would have to go to work anyway. I would sit there all day worrying about him, phoning him, making sure that he was okay. Once, in particular, he had taken a bottle of pills that would have killed him. He started throwing up. I don't know whether he induced it. He probably did, although he didn't say he did. After that, I was afraid to leave him alone, so that when he got into this kind of shape I would stay with him.

Th: So, you had to stay away from work?

Pt: Yes, or I'd go into work later. Just shortly before he went into the hospital he was like that one day. I stayed at home with him.

I took him out to lunch so he'd get dressed and have to go somewhere. Once he's out and walking around, he's okay. But when he's lying in bed and has all the time to think about it, he gets worse. So I was able to go to work that afternoon.

Th: So, what did you do in the end, when you took him to the hospital?

Pt: He started having strong suicidal feelings. He wanted to jump off a building this time. The feelings were really upsetting him. He was crying and he wanted to, but I guess he didn't want to because he came back.

Th: Were you with him?

Pt: No, I wasn't. In fact, I was starting to get worried about him because he came home at 8:00 in the morning. He had been drinking, and he said he drove his car with the plan to commit suicide. He fell asleep in his car while he was thinking about it. He came home that morning crying and looking pretty upset. He went to bed, and when he woke up he was still in the same shape. He started crying, and I thought he would get it out of his system. But he cried for about two hours, and then he started to get almost hysterical. He was trembling and crying to the point where he had a hard time to sort of gasp for breath. So I called his doctor, and we got him admitted to a hospital.

Th: So, he didn't actually make a suicide attempt. It was the thought of suicide.

(*The therapist explores some of the patient's childhood experiences. She is an only child. The patient says her father was "really hard to believe," a disciplinarian who was violent at the same time—especially when drunk. He was mostly violent with the patient. The patient indicates he was violent for no reason. He drinks heavily. She has memories of his coming home, waking up her and her mother, and slapping her as far back as she can remember. The father came to Canada from Europe after she was born. He joined her and her mother when she was five. Her parents were married at that time.*)

Pt: The first time I met him, my mother was pointing him out to me and I just couldn't see him. There were so many people—we were at the airport when his plane landed. I still remember that I was excited that I was going to meet my father because this was "cool." Everybody had a father and now I was going to have one. We got close enough to him that my mother said, "That's your father over there." But she was pointing at two guys that were standing together. One was my father. I was hoping it was the other one. I remember that because it wasn't until I got right up to the both of them and one of them picked me up and I realized it was my father. I thought, "Oh, shucks," because I thought the other guy looked like a really nice guy.

Th: You've said really only unfavorable things about him. Were there any favorable things? Or perhaps there weren't.

Pt: I think there might have been. He had a chance to be a nice guy. The qualities never came out in him. I think my mother was swirled all over all of her life, even though they were poor. She had five brothers to protect her all the time and take care of her. She was doing the cooking and stuff, but she never really had a problem. To meet a man like this, I think she didn't know how to handle him, and she still, to this day, doesn't know how to solve the problem. He was a guy who very much needed admiration, to be told that he's a good guy and stuff like that, and he never got it from anybody. I think had he married or somehow had a friend that would help him along, he would have turned out quite a bit better. As it was, he was always depressed and angry that he wasn't doing better.

Th: Angry that he wasn't doing better? Was that an important issue in his life?

Pt: I don't know if he would say so, but I would say so, very definitely. He expected to come over here and do rather well and maybe be someone fairly well known with a nice house and a charming wife and all that sort of thing. I think he got to an age where he realized that he wasn't getting any of those things and was never going to get them. I think that's when he really started to go downhill.

Th: Can you remember any good moments with him at all?

Pt: Not really.

Th: Would he play with you when you were small and take you for walks and cuddle you or anything?

Pt; No, he would but then he'd get mad. It never was consistent, so you're always on the edge of your seat because you know if you get really friendly with him he's going to get mad about something and you're going to be right there really close to him where you can really get it the worst. I would stay away from him. He got pretty upset about everything. I remember we went out once. We were at the shoemaker's and I was six years old. The man wanted to be nice and he said, "Oh, hi. Come here."

I was a little kid and he said, "How old are you," and I didn't know. My father got really upset. He dragged me home and he really got emotional and violent about the fact that I didn't know my age—what a dumb kid I have here. But he never told me my age. He never thought about it before and that's the sort of thing he would get upset about. Anything. It really upset him that he didn't have an extremely bright kid.

Th: What about your feelings about your mother?

Pt: It was kind of confusing, because I didn't know whether to trust her or not because sometimes she'd be making me feel better about my father and talking to me so that I wouldn't be so upset and I'd like her. Sometimes it was difficult to understand why she would leave me with this man when she must see what he's like. So it was confusing. As I got older, I started to resent it more that she wasn't doing anything about it, because he's sufficiently afraid to be alone that if she gave him an ultimatum then he would be a good boy, at least most of the time. Now he's really finished. He's an alcoholic. He's got to have a case of beer for breakfast. He's got a capacity like an elephant. It's really remarkable. I'm sure that most doctors wouldn't believe how much he drank. He doesn't leave without a case of beer and goes walking straight as an arrow to work. Then he really gets sick on vodka and changes to wine. He blames it on the beer instead of on the fact that he's been drinking for so many years.

Th: Can you tell me something about sexual feelings earlier? We have talked about your sexual relation with your boyfriend and your relation with the boy before that. How long before that do you remember sexual feelings?

Pt: When I was very young, I must have been around nine, I remember feeling curious about myself. As I got older, I didn't even think about it.

Th: No? So, when did it come back again?

Pt: I guess since I've been going out with my boyfriend. Before, I didn't even consider it in any way because I could always take it or leave it.

Th: What about masturbation?

Pt: Only when I was around nine.

Th: Only when you were around nine, but not since? What about sexual fantasies? Things that you imagine?

Pt: I wouldn't say that I have any.

Th: Or have had any in the past?
Pt: Whenever I had any fantasies, it was about a man that I could be with, and maybe we'd be hugging or something but we'd never be having sex. It was never more than hugging and stuff, and being with somebody that's masculine.
Th: What about dreams? In your dreams some of your inner sexual feelings may be expressed. Do you remember sexual dreams?
Pt: The only ones that I considered sexual were when we actually were holding hands or something. I considered that sexual because I enjoyed it, but never sex. The kind of men that I usually—you know, you have heroes when you get to a certain age—my heroes were not the type that other girls had. It wasn't the Beatles or Elvis Presley or anything. It was Danny Kaye.
Th: All right. Now why? What's important? What did you like about him?
Pt: Because he was funny and people liked him and he seemed understanding. Maybe I found him fatherly, but I don't really think so. I just found him interesting.
Th: I wouldn't have said he was fatherly, but one thing about him is that he's got a lot of tenderness in him. It may not be appropriate to you.
Pt: Yes, I would agree. Well, he's still my all-time hero, I think. For years, ever since the Danny Kaye show . . . I don't know how far back that was but it's been quite some time since he's had his own show . . . and I'd make sure I saw him, all his movies, many times. He's my hero.
Th: I think I've asked you most of the questions I want to know about you, but I've got to ask you a lot of routine questions. You mentioned something about feeling suicidal yourself. Now, how far back does this go? How often does it happen, and how bad is it?
Pt: I haven't had it since adolescence, really.
Th: What's the worst it's ever been?
Pt: When I was in high school, probably around fourteen years of age. I was really reading about it, trying to find out more about how I could do it. I was trying to pick up literature anywhere on suicide in order to find out how people had done it so I could figure out how to go about doing it without causing myself any pain.
Th: What conclusion did you come to?
Pt: I really pursued the idea of pills because that seemed to be the

least painful way, but at the time I couldn't get my hands on any literature telling me which pills will do it. It doesn't tell you which pills will do it and how many.

Th: Have you ever actually been in a state in which you were really looking for an opportunity to commit suicide?

Pt: Yes, I remember one time standing in front of a railroad track hoping to get the guts to do it because I hate pain. So that was the only thing that stopped me, the fact that I might feel pain.

Th: At what age was that?

(*Here the therapist explores the question of suicide. The patient remembers at one time being so depressed that she had suicidal ideas, and she ties it in with the difficult relation with her father. The father made big scenes around the time of report cards. It becomes clear that the patient came for help on her own.*)

Th: Something which I felt rather strange about, knowing something of the story, you know, that your boyfriend had got near to suicide and had to be admitted to the hospital . . . I expected you to come saying that you're desperately depressed because of what's happened to him. But you've never really said that. You've said that you've been depressed since the age of thirteen and it happens every February and March and, of course, we're in February and March now. Do you feel that this is what you're asking for help for?

Pt: I'd like to get motivated again so I can go about helping myself. I'd like to be able to enjoy living.

Th: But then as the summer comes it will go away, won't it?

Pt: Yes, it will, until next winter. What I'm worried about now is that as I'm getting older and my job becomes more important, because I'm on my own and I have to support myself, if I get demotivated now I'm afraid that I'll get into worse shape by losing my job and then getting further demotivated and becoming a loser all around just because I was depressed. Certainly, this is, I think, what started my father off, although he's a much worse case than I am.

Th: How do you hope to get help? What do you feel anybody might do or what do you feel you might do?

Pt: It would help me very much to know either what gets me depressed or what will get me out of it, and I think that it takes somebody who is not involved to help me find that out.

"THE CASE OF THE SECRETARY WITH THE VIOLENT FATHER"

Dr. Naiman:

First, I would like to get one or two points out of the way. In terms of these recurrent depressions, which occur every year, it would seem to me from the standpoint of clinical psychiatry that the possibility of recurrent endogenous depressions should be considered. I think Dr. Malan went after that in terms of the early-morning awakening which she denied; she has hypersomnia rather than insomnia, but I don't think that necessarily rules it out. I think perhaps one might have wanted to know a little bit about whether there is a family history of manic-depressive illness in this patient or if there were any suicides among grandfathers, uncles, father's uncles, and so on. Now, this having been said, I'll then assume that this is not a case of recurrent endogenous depression and go on with commenting about the interview and what would appear to me to be the psychodynamics.

In terms of the interview technique, Dr. Malan seems in the first part of the interview to point out repeatedly the somewhat shallow affect. I don't think it's shallow in the schizophrenic sense. She was not showing as much affect as one might have reasonably expected under the circumstances, and Dr. Malan pointed that out to her repeatedly.

It is a fairly nondirective interview in which the patient had a chance to express what she felt. I feel it might have been helpful to know a little more about what happened during the first five years when she was alone with her mother. From what was presented here, I got a better picture of what the father was like than of what the mother was like.

Concerning what she is depressed about, which was the question in the end, it would seem to me we have a number of clues. One is—and I think Dr. Malan actively interpreted this in the early part of the interview—that she had looked for a rather ideal male. She had believed that she had found such a person. Here was this person who was strong, reliable, steady and quite different from her father, and then, lo and behold, the giant turns out to have feet of clay. It turns out that he's an alcoholic like her father or, at least, he has a drinking problem. The patient's fantasy collapses, and I would think this certainly contributed to her feeling depressed. She does not really have what Freud would probably have called an anaclitic object relationship with somebody that she could lean on.

As to what came out, it would seem that her difficulty in having an anaclitic object relationship is both internal and external. The character structure that emerged was that she is the kind of person that other people tell their troubles to rather than her finding it easy to confide in someone else.

Regarding the object choice that she made in which we are told that the father was very demanding, there were a lot of things to do with report cards and so on, the boyfriend seems to have had a somewhat similar father and also seems to have had difficulty living up to very high aspirations. In a way, it would seem that, rather than finding an idealized father, she ended up with someone who is perhaps rather like herself and who has difficulties with his father somewhat similar to the difficulties she had with her father.

The oedipal situation that she described is rather interesting in that she is critical of her mother on two counts. One is that she seems to be blaming some of her father's difficulties on her mother. She is saying that if her mother had been a different kind of person then her father would have had a happier life and then maybe things would have turned out better for him. Now, I would think this would lead into the fantasy that she could be this woman who could have saved her father, and that if her father had her as his woman then things would have been a great deal better. I would suspect that on this basis there would be a fair bit of rivalry with her mother and, at the same time, a fair bit of guilt toward her mother.

The other criticism she has against her mother is more or less opposite. She is saying, Why didn't Mother protect me against my father? Why did Mother put up with this? She really feels that her mother should have been more self-assertive and taken a stronger stand with her father to prevent him from abusing both the patient and her mother. Therefore I would think this is a fairly complex situation with which she would need some help.

Dr. Sifneos:

I would like to make three comments in the area of the nature of the interview, the psychodynamics, and, at the end, to review our criteria for short-term anxiety-provoking psychotherapy to see whether this particular patient would fit them.

I was struck by the careful approach which Dr. Malan used, and by his supportive, gentle and sympathetic way of handling this particular patient. Obviously, he was hit by the fragility that comes across, and despite the fact that there is indeed a certain lack of affect, I was particularly impressed by the way he communicated to her his personal impressions about it, and about her smile, or commented on his own ideas about her. I think this was a very thorough interview.

Now, as far as the depression goes, the crucial question appears to be the periodic depressions every year and not what one may call an almost normal reactive depression of a girl whose boyfriend to

"THE CASE OF THE SECRETARY WITH THE VIOLENT FATHER" 143

whom she was so attached has suddenly become seriously depressed and considers suicide. I don't think one has a clear-cut link here. There are indications that this is a disappointment she had in her own father and that the relationship with the boyfriend was a way out; yet she fell right back into a trap of relating to somebody who was seriously sick.

The question is, as Dr. Naiman pointed out, why this girl was looking to this idealized father and even associating her own serious thoughts of suicide at the railroad, and so on, with her own father. Is it that she was disappointed in her own mother? Indeed, we have no information in this crucial area. I agree with Dr. Naiman that this is a vital question, since if these depressions, which are periodic and associated superficially with her relationship with her father, are because of the basic lack of trust or interaction in the early relationship with her own mother, this, of course, would give us a very different picture.

Finally, in terms of the criteria that we have for short-term anxiety-provoking psychotherapy, the chief complaint is indeed circumscribed. She does not pass the second criterion, which is that of having a meaningful relationship. I am not at all sure whether she had a meaningful relationship with her mother, and she certainly had none with her father. Her relationship with her boyfriend is also questionable. You remember she could not even give, although Dr. Malan repeatedly asked her, one favorable impression of her father, and she went more and more into describing the negative aspects.

There is a question in my mind about how we would rate her in respect to the third criterion, namely, interaction with the evaluator. As I pointed out before, the evaluator was very capable and very gentle with her. She expected a lot from him, but how much she gave in return is questionable.

I think she passes the fourth criterion, which is that of intelligence.

One then gets into the area of motivation, which in my opinion is of the utmost importance. I think she does recognize that her symptoms are psychological. On the subcriteria for motivation, which would be whether she has an interest in actively participating with the interviewer to find out and therefore would have a willingness to change, to experiment, I would not give her any score. I would also want to know what her expectations are from therapy and whether she would be willing to make a tangible sacrifice.

I think her expectations would be more magical. If I am not mistaken, she said at the end that she would like to have somebody do the work for her, an outsider to help her, and she would be looking for support from him rather than using her own resources to solve her problems.

As far as I am concerned, she is not a candidate for short-term anxiety-provoking psychotherapy.

Dr. Naiman

I don't know if she would be a good candidate for short-term dynamic psychotherapy. The point that I think Dr. Sifneos and I both picked up was the issue of the first five years and just how much depression, how much early deprivation, there was.

I think she related to the interviewer. My own impression was a little more favorable than that of Dr. Sifneos. I think she related rather well to Dr. Malan. Actually, I would be curious to know what Dr. Sifneos' criteria are for a meaningful relationship. The relationship that she had with this man was obviously not ideal, but she was quite involved. She lived with the man for two years. I would have thought that she passed the criteria for a meaningful relationship.

The other issue, I think, is that of the object choice. I think she has dynamics, those mentioned earlier, which seem to me reasonably clear evidence that one can work with her. How long it would take is a more doubtful and more difficult question. I think I would treat this patient right now for a period of time because she is asking for treatment, and I think she has neurotic problems which are in a sense treatable. Then, at the end of a few months, one could determine how far one could go with this patient.

Dr. Davanloo:

Regarding Dr. Malan's technique in this interview, I was also impressed with his gentle approach. I will review very briefly our criteria for short-term dynamic psychotherapy to determine if this patient would pass them. Indeed, there are areas where we don't have enough information which I consider crucial in making a decision. We don't know much about her relationship with her mother, especially in the very early phase of her life. She was five when she came to Canada and reacted negatively when she saw her father for the first time. There is some indication that there were incestuous relations with her father. I felt that there was a conscious resistance to latent affects, and I would have wanted to mobilize this by a more confronting technique. I felt she interacted very well with Dr. Malan, but again I felt there were many latent feelings that she fought throughout the interview. Overall, she passed this criterion well.

Regarding the meaningful relationship, it is obvious that her relationships with her father and her mother were not meaningful. Was the relationship with her boyfriend meaningful? I find it very difficult to decide. I also find it very difficult to agree that this woman has a very fragile ego, as I wonder how then she got this far.

I strongly agree with Dr. Naiman's view, and I would take this patient into treatment. But I agree with Dr. Sifneos that she does not fulfill the criteria for ten to fifteen sessions of brief dynamic psychotherapy. As far as the longer form is concerned, namely, thirty to forty sessions, I cannot definitely say. What I can say is that I would take her into treatment immediately and evaluate the picture after two or three months.

Dr. Kravitz:

I, too, was impressed by the gentle way in which Dr. Malan handled the interview. I wonder whether something that struck me came out in the material that was presented or if it was not touched upon. Regarding the February and March recurring depressions, if we say they are not endogenous recurring depressions, I for one would have wanted to know whether this was about the time when they came to Canada. I understand that she came when she was.... As a matter of fact, one of the striking features about this girl was the way in which she used the word "agony." I think this is a very good word. The tremendous anxiety that she was experiencing lends concern to what she was going to find when she got there, which made me think of how much fantasizing there was.

As a matter of fact, she looked to this other man as the father and was terribly disappointed to find that this was the man to whom her mother handed her over. From then on, we hear relatively little about the mother. I think that now she is once again struck by and stuck with that to which she has handed herself over.

Within the framework, putting aside the evaluation criteria with which Drs. Sifneos, Davanloo and Naiman dealt, in my opinion this is a girl who is struggling with a tremendous narcissistic injury, this tremendous disappointment and disillusionment, and who has not come to grips with the great deal of anger she feels both at her mother for handing her over and at the cruelty of her fate. She looks upon fate as her having been imprisoned by this man who became her keeper and jailer and expecter of performance for so many years.

The other thing which, aside from criteria, I was struck by was the absence of masturbation and sexual fantasies from the age of nine; we usually think of this in terms of morbidity, more or less pathology. I wonder if Dr. Malan would say something from his experience with this. Its striking absence would make me think that one would want to go very carefully in dealing with this girl over the subsequent period of time. Perhaps we would be in agreement that she would not be a suitable candidate for short-term dynamic psychotherapy, but beyond that I keep wondering what one would do with this girl and how one would handle her.

Dr. Malan:

When one does an interview, one always sees at the end the things one has left out. The grossest thing I left out, which I see now, is the relation with her mother before she came over to Canada. Somehow I got put off asking about that. I was, I suppose, so interested in this sadistic relation with the father that I forgot about this obviously crucial question. I have no information on it, and it is a serious goof. I didn't ask her for the family history of manic depression. I also didn't ask her whether she had hypomanic attacks, which is a question I usually ask patients; I think I should have asked, but I just didn't feel she was the sort of person who had manic attacks. I didn't feel these were recurrent endogenous depressions. I think she was making it plain that they were reactive to something. I got the impression in the interview that they were reactive to the fact that, as she made very clear, she really couldn't be left alone without having some activities to prevent her from thinking about herself.

One of the things Dr. Sifneos said was that she is suffering from what he called a normal reactive depression to the total situation with her boyfriend. What I would say is that this is just what she is not suffering from, and this is one of the outstanding features of the whole interview. She was brought to us by this crisis with her boyfriend. Time and time again I had to come back to this in order to get some spark of feeling out of her about this current situation. I deliberately asked her every detail of what happened, what their future was, what they said to each other about their future, what the current position was, etc. At no point did I get anything but a very dispassionate account of the fact that he wanted to jump off a building. He was in an alcoholic state, he fell asleep in the car, and all the rest of it. I think that this is the most striking feature of this girl, and I'm not sure what it means.

Dr. Sifneos asked whether she had a meaningful relation with this boy. I don't think anybody can answer this. If she had been deeply involved with this boy, she ought to have been in a state of acute grief, which she wasn't. It makes me suspect that this relation was in some way idealized, and that she didn't really have any meaningful relationship with him at all. If such is the case, then this obviously quite seriously affects our ideas about the prognosis for treatment. The answer to the question of how she related to the interviewer is yes and no, since there was potential to respond. I think the most striking unconscious communication in the interview was when I said to her, "You seem to be the sort of person who somehow stays outside life and can't get involved in it in some way. You really have difficulty with deep relations with people." In response to that she said: "I have no difficulty getting close to people." Then she went on to say." Of course, I sit outside at a party, people come and talk to me, and this is the way I relate. Of course you don't exactly wait for the next phone call when a boyfriend comes and tells you about his problems." So she made a really beautiful unconscious communication to this sort of implied interpretation. I think this is a terribly important factor in considering the prognosis for any form of psychotherapy. This girl can communicate unconsciously.

During the interview I felt terribly sorry for her. I felt she was in a desperate situation, really. Her home family was no use to her, with this paranoid alcoholic father and the mother that couldn't cope. Now she had lost the relation with the only person that meant anything to her in her life. She was alone and lost. You wouldn't know it from the way she spoke, but one certainly felt this about her. There was a lot of warmth there. She called out a great deal of warmth in me, so that I am not too worried about the way she would relate to a potential therapist. I think she can work in therapy. What exactly would happen in therapy is a very different matter. What one wants to know about this girl is the degree of emptiness in her; how deep does her inability to relate in any real way to people go? One doesn't know the answer to this. One's own feeling about her is that she can relate quite well. All the evidence about what had happened between her and her boyfriend seemed to indicate that she wasn't relating. There is a big discrepancy there. She said the sexual relation was perfectly all right. I didn't press her for details about how she felt, and perhaps I should have done so. How real her relations are is a crucial question.

I would have said she is not by any means an ideal candidate for brief psychotherapy. I think this girl needs something like two years of treatment on a once-a-week basis. I would say that is the ideal form of treatment for her. She needs to be carried gently through her denial of feeling and her inability to relate. She needs to be able to grieve in the most desperate way for the things that have happened to her, and to be angry about them.

In fact, the therapeutic plan which Drs. Naiman and Davanloo suggested, namely, that we would treat her for a few months and see what happened and then make a further decision, is exactly what we talked about. I think it is conceivable that she might turn out to be a possible case for brief therapy in the sense that perhaps this denial is not so massive as it appears to be. Perhaps in brief therapy she could be brought face to face with her lifelong denial of feelings and be able to experience some of them and grow from them, and this is the kind of focus I would prefer to work with in brief therapy. However, I think she actually needs a longer period of time.

Chapter 8

"The Case of the College Student"

P. E. SIFNEOS

The patient is a young, single, female college student who was self-referred to a psychiatric clinic. She complained of having been depressed for a long time and of having had problems in the area of interpersonal relationships, especially heterosexual relationships. She stated that she gets involved with men but then has to drop them—gets men interested in her and then pushes them away. She stated, "I make sure I get to the point where I know they really love me and then I just don't want them any more..."

Pt: Well, the reason I came here in the beginning—it was about a month ago—I had been feeling really, really depressed for quite a long time, and I was completely unmotivated to do anything. Like I would wake up in the morning and I didn't feel like doing anything. It was just an effort to get out of bed, you know. I was in school and I couldn't concentrate. I couldn't read or do any of my papers. I was very emotional. I would start crying over very small things. I would get very hyper, you know, and I realized that there were a lot of things bothering me.

(Patient says at this point that she was seen by a counselor-in-training and that she did not get anywhere.)

Th: That was before you became depressed or afterwards?
Pt: Well, it was afterwards. Afterwards, yes. It kind of made it worse.
Th: All right. But now, did this start out of the blue or did something bring it about? Can you pinpoint anything?
Pt: I guess a lot of things. I guess mainly because I really started looking at myself a lot more.
Th: What prompted you to do that? I mean, why?
Pt: I guess I needed it, and also in school I was taking a human relations course. A lot of things came to the surface. About four years ago, the same thing happened to me. I became very depressed but I kind of worked it out myself, but I realized that there was a lot more to it but I kept avoiding it, and like right now I can be very happy but I know that in a second or two I can become very depressed and not be happy.
Th: Can you describe your symptoms a little bit to me? You say "depressed." Now, what is that like? What thoughts do you have, for instance?
Pt: Very negative thoughts. I think a lot about myself.
Th: What kind?
Pt: I guess they are questions. I question what I am doing and then I get very—I just have a very negative attitude about my family, my boyfriend, school, and myself.

(*The therapist explores the symptom of depression and it comes out that the patient has problems sleeping, has a lot of dreams, eats a lot when depressed. The therapist also explores the reasons for her seeking help at this time, then goes into her background. She has a brother six years younger who lives in another city, and her parents are alive and well. She also has an older married sister.*)

Th: And what is the first thing that you remember about yourself as a very young child?
Pt: The first thing I remember? I have brief memories of house scenes, being at home, living with—we lived with my father's mother for a while. I was very young, Should I remember happy things or negative things?
Th: It makes no difference. What would be more in your mind? Happy or unhappy? The first memory that comes to mind.
Pt: Happy feelings. Very happy.

"THE CASE OF THE COLLEGE STUDENT"   151

Th: Yes. Such as what, for instance?
Pt: Well, walking with my father in the park. We spent a lot of time together when I was younger. That's one thing that stands out very clearly with me. (Smiling.)
Th: Yes. Just the two of you?
Pt: Yes. We spent quite a bit of time together.
Th: Could you tell me something about your relationship with your mother?
Pt: With my mother? We didn't really have a relationship. We never really have had a relationship.
Th: What do you mean?
Pt: Well, we have never really talked. You know, there is very little communication. We seem to conflict a lot, conflict a great deal.
Th: Now, not so much now but way back then, when you were a child, was that still the case?
Pt: Yes. I guess it was. As I remember, I was a very demanding child and I needed a lot of attention—or stimulation, maybe—and it just seemed that we could never—there was never time for that. She was always very busy.
Th: But did you have that response from your father?
Pt: More. Yes, more than from her—when he was around, since he worked.
Th: What was his job?
Pt: He was an engineer.
Th: Would you say that you were your father's favorite?
Pt: Yes, definitely.
Th: You smile. And what about your brother? Did your mother have a favorite? Was it the same situation that you were your father's favorite and your brother was your mother's favorite, or was it your sister?
Pt: Yes, I guess it tended to be my brother who was her favorite.
Th: Do you remember his birth?
Pt: My brother's birth? No, I don't.
Th: Not at all?
Pt: Not at all.
Th: Do you remember? What is the first picture that you have of your brother, this small baby?
Pt: That's very interesting. I've never thought about that. My first memory of him?

Th: It's almost as if he didn't exist?
Pt: Yes, that's right.
Th: No questions as to how suddenly there was another baby in the family? All these things didn't cross your mind?
Pt: They didn't cross my mind at all.
Th: They aren't crossing your mind now?
Pt: Well, I am very close to my brother now. I am sure he is very resentful.
Th: Even when he got so much attention from your mother?
Pt: Yes, probably.
Th: How did your parents relate to each other?
Pt: Oh, very negatively. They don't get along very well at all. There is no communication. My father, I suppose he is more interested in different things than my mother is. He likes seeing good programs on television and talking about things, and my mother, she tends to be very limited in a lot of areas. She is kind of just into doing her role at home and she is working now, but that is what it always tended to be like She did the cleaning and the cooking.
Th: Did they ever fight?
Pt: Oh, a lot.
Th: They did? About what?
Pt: Silly things as far as I was concerned. Things that could have been worked out. At that time I wasn't able to do anything.

(*The therapist further explores the negative relationship of the parents, and the patient volunteers that in her relationship with her mother there was a long series of conflicts; her mother often got angry with her.*)

Th: Now, going to school. What about going to school at that time? Early grade school, for instance.
Pt: In my first three years I did very well. I learned how to read and write very quickly, and then in about grade five, something must have happened that year because I don't remember who my teacher was. I can't place her. I can't place where my class was or who my classmates were, whereas with all my other years at school I can, and that particular year I can't remember, but I did very poorly that year, and since then, grade five, I did poorly in school.
Th: What happened? Why would you suddenly not do well? Were

you preoccupied about something? Did something happen at home?
Pt: I've asked my parents and my grandmother and they couldn't remember anything that happened, but I suppose it could have been conflicts between my parents.
Th: But these conflicts existed all along, you said.
Pt: Yes, but maybe it just...
Th: Was there any conflict—that was fifth grade, you said, so you were about eleven, right?
Pt: Maybe younger.
Th: Does anything come to mind?
Pt: Actually, maybe. We used to have a country place and I think that was the summer—maybe it was a year later, I don't remember—but something happened. There was a man that lived there. I am not sure exactly when it was.
Th: That's all right. Go on.
Pt: There was a man who lived in the area and I remember he tried to, well...
Th: To molest you?
Pt: Yeah, and like I remember trying to tell my mother but she wouldn't listen. I couldn't tell her. She wouldn't understand. My father wasn't there at the time.
Th: Were you frightened?
Pt: I liked it and I was frightened, too, at the same time. I guess I really didn't know what I was doing.
Th: Did this happen several times or just once?
Pt: A couple of times.
Th: And how much older was he?
Pt: Oh, he was married with children that were married. He was probably thirty-five or forty-five.
Th: I see. So it may be, then, that a sexual episode that happened at that time could possibly have quite a lot of ramifications in terms of your adjustment afterwards. You were not doing very well at school. You were kind of preoccupied. You tried to communicate with your mother. She didn't understand. And you are caught with that mixed feeling about some pleasure but also of something being somewhat bad.
Pt: Yes, I guess so. Well, that did happen. It could have been something else, but I don't know. I can't seem to remember.
Th: Now, you were living with your grandmother. What was your relationship with her?

(The patient tells the therapist that she had a very close relationship with her grandmother. The therapist asked if she wanted to talk about this episode with her father, and she said she was afraid he would have been angry with her. Then the therapist explores her first period at age thirteen; she knew about it from friends and from reading.)

Th: What was your reaction to becoming a young woman now and things like that? Were you pleased or was there no feeling at all?

Pt: It was kind of an exciting feeling. I remember it was exciting, but then I wasn't really sure whether I wanted it or not, whether or not I was really ready for that. It seemed that all of a sudden I had to change because I had my period and I was a young woman.

Th: Did, by any chance, any thoughts as to how your father would feel about this occur to you then? Because, you see, this is something again that has to do with sexual matters. We know this reaction about this episode with a man. Did you have any thoughts about your father and how he would react to you now that you had become a young woman, anything like that?

Pt: I guess I must have. They don't stand out right now. Yeah.

Th: For instance?

Pt: I guess I think my relationship with my father probably changed after that. I became less close to him. I was less willing to be physical with him, and actually from then, around that age, I always felt in a way repulsed. My father was always very physical with me and I know it's because he loves me and I am his daughter, but sometimes I really don't want him to touch me or to kiss me or anything, and I feel badly about it but I have these negative feelings.

Th: So there is something here about this that reminds you of your father in connection with that episode?

Pt: I guess so.

Th: They were both rather older. So there is something that might have been exciting at the same time, kind of repulsive?

Pt: Yes.

Th: Now, what was high school like? Did you have any close friends, boys or girls? At what time did you start dating? How did you get along with the teachers?

Pt: That's a lot of questions.

Th: Just pick up whatever you think stands out.

Pt: I had a lot of friends and there were a lot of people I didn't get along with as well, but I did have a lot of friends. Teachers— there were very few teachers that I got along with.
Th: Did you have male or female teachers?
Pt: Both.
Th: And that applied to both?
Pt: I used to like having male teachers, but then female teachers were the ones that I seemed to learn the most from. I can remember that. My first boyfriend was when I was seventeen. That's when I started really dating seriously with one boy. We dated for a long time. There wasn't really much physical closeness because it was my fault—because of me. It was a very nice relationship. It was good. We dated for a few years.
Th: And then what happened?
Pt: I just decided that I was too close, I guess. I didn't want to go out with anybody. I felt I was too young to be involved with one person, which really wasn't that good for him. But that tends to be my pattern. I do that with everybody I go out with. I make sure I get to the point where I know they really love me and then I just don't want them any more, which is really negative because I probably hurt a lot of people by doing that.
Th: Which is a little bit like it was with your father, isn't it?
Pt: Yeah, I guess so.
Th: Is that really the prototype? And then there is the pattern that repeats itself. Have you thought of it that way?
Pt: No, I've never thought of it in terms of my father, but I've thought of it in terms of my boyfriends.
Th: You see, when you said that you know that your father loves you and he wants to express himself physically but that there is something that you find repugnant and you withdraw then and you are caught in this situation, I have a little bit of feeling that the same thing happens with that boy, that you know he loves you and you are very close to him, but somehow it is you who wants to put a distance between you.
Pt: Yes, it is me. I really feel that I probably never am going to have a reciprocal relationship with anybody.
Th: Why?
Pt: I don't know. It just seems that I get to a certain point and I really—I get bored or at least that is my excuse and I am not willing to put anything else into it.

Th: Is it possible that because you have an attachment way back to which you are faithful, you don't want to give any new possibilities a chance? Again I am bringing your father into it. You see, that relationship with your father, it impresses me as being a very close one. The two of you walking in the park; you smiled when you remembered it. There is something there very positive, but slowly that becomes a little bit marred, then there is this very interesting episode that we know about, and then slowly there is a kind of withdrawing on your part. It is after you have your period that it becomes different. You established a distance. Your father is perfectly willing to continue in the old relationship. It is you who has mixed feelings about it. It is you who pulls yourself away and then we hear that you have this pattern of pulling away from every relationship from then on. So, is there something there that happens, that interferes?

Pt: Freud would say there is.

Th: You are interpreting Freud, and although Freud may have said that and they have observed these things in general, he could never tell us specifically what happened to you.

Pt: I could be. It's very possible.

Th: But it somehow or other looks a little bit vague. It doesn't touch anything. It doesn't click or anything?

Pt: It doesn't give me any feeling, but I can understand that that could be very possible. It might be.

(The therapist explores the patient's academic performance. She did not do well in high school. She worked at a firm for a few years, then spent a few months traveling and returned to college; the trip to the West was with one of her best friends, and there were no sexual encounters. Then the therapist explores the precipitating factors of her depression four years before, when she was about eighteen.)

Pt: I'm not sure that I want to talk about it right now.

Th: I see, but there was something?

Pt: Yes. There was something.

Th: Was it something similar to—you don't have to talk about it in general terms—but similar to something like that episode that you told me about when you were a child? Something of this nature? Was it something sexual or what?

Pt: Yeah, that was part of it.

Th: Now, the thing that strikes me about that time is that you were obviously honest enough, looking at yourself, to say to yourself that you enjoyed it, enjoyed that experience, yet somehow or other there was also a notion that you had been programmed by society or your parents and so forth to consider that that was not acceptable. Right? Is it something of this kind that happens when you are depressed? There is a part of you that would like certain things and then there is a part of you—you said that you castigate yourself, that you criticize yourself, and that you have these negative thoughts about yourself. Is it something of this kind that happens?

Pt: Often, yes, as a matter of fact.

Th: What is it, then, that you enjoy that you're not supposed to and that now is internalized within your own head? Is it that part of you wants something and part of you somehow or other opposes it?

Pt: I guess sex can be one of them.

Th: Well, can you tell me something about your sexual life? I know there was that boy for several years. Was there anybody else that you were close to?

Pt: At that time, no.

Th: No. After that?

Pt: After that, yes. I had another boyfriend. I met him at the firm a little bit later, about a year or so later. And he was actually the first person that I had sex with.

Th: What was that like? Was it enjoyable or not?

Pt: Actually, no, that's not true. He wasn't the first, but it was the first where I had had a lot of sex. It wasn't something that just happened. I really understood what was going on. I can tell you about that later. We had a very intense sexual relationship. That is mostly what it was.

Th: Was it enjoyable?

Pt: At times it was good and at times I really didn't want it.

Th: So you were caught in this dilemma. You were how old?

Pt: Twenty.

Th: Twenty. That was after having been depressed for the first time?

Pt: No. That happened during it, too.

Th: During? Then what happened to that relationship?

Pt: I did the same thing.

158   SIFNEOS

Th: You pushed him away? And who ended it? You did?
Pt: Yes.
Th: Then what happened after that? You went west. Was there anything in the West?
Pt: What happened was when I was going out with this fellow, then I went to the West and kind of left him and then I came back. I saw him for a little while after that and then I decided that I didn't want to see him again. No nothing happened in the West. I didn't meet any man or anything like that. It was just a very fun time. I went with my best friend.
Th: And when you came back, did you leave home?
Pt: About a month later.
Th: But you said recently you went back home?
Pt: Yes, because I was finding that I couldn't afford it any more, both going to the university and working—I didn't feel like doing it. I wanted to take some time off and maybe have a place to stay where I wouldn't have to be working at the same time.

(*The patient says she is a student in psychology and that up to the beginning of December she was boarding with a family. She was very fond of both husband and wife and the family atmosphere, and she felt very good there. The therapist suggests that she really had to abandon people she felt very close to. In early December, when she returned home she again faced all the problems and restrictions there. She further said that she was afraid to bring friends home, as her mother kept things so perfect and her friends might get things dirty.*)

Th: How does your father feel about you now? About this old physical relationship?
Pt: Well, he is still the same way. He is always approaching me every time he sees me.
Th: Does that have anything to do with some of these things that we have been talking about?
Pt: With my depression? I don't think so. It could have something to do with it, but that's not—that's just one of the things that annoys me. Like I really more or less don't want him touching me.
Th: We certainly surveyed a whole area very quickly, we covered many years of your life. That is really a lot, but in my opinion there are many things that stand out. I can see your depression, although I don't know this episode that you didn't want to talk with me about, which I understand.

Pt: I guess I could be more open, but maybe you should continue.
Th: I am struck by the fact that in both situations there is a kind of precipitating event that throws you into a kind of situation of a depression. I know the first one. The second one is clearly associated with this family, the people that you like, the prospect that you had to leave them and that begins in September and then it becomes an impossibility and you move home. That reminds you of the whole situation that existed in the past. Then the past is getting quite striking to me because it wasn't by any means as bad as that. Your parents were fighting but it was clear that you and your father had a good relationship. Yet what is surprising to me is that somehow or other, there is a loss of that rapport you had with your father, which I can't explain. That comes from within you. It is you who are pushing your father away. You don't want anything to do with him, although you understand that this is it. And this is repeated with these men, that you have positive feelings, sexual interest, and soon it is you who pushes them away. Now, what it is inside you that does this is what I don't know. You somehow or other must be angry. Now, if you are angry at the men, and if you don't always have a man around after you push them away, how much of this anger of yours do you turn against yourself? And it is then you who says to yourself that you are no good. I mean, that is subcritical. I can criticize you and can say that you are no good and this and that and the other, but if you are not there I cannot criticize the chair, for example, so I guess I could say to myself, you see, I wonder if that has something to do with it because self-criticism is a classic aspect of depression, isn't it?
Pt: Yes, it is.
Th: You have negative thoughts?
Pt: It's true what you are saying and also I criticize if I am having a relationship. I usually criticize that person quite a lot, you know. I guess I am just looking for perfection.
Th: Which comes from your mother's perfect home?
Pt: I don't know if that's it.
Th: If one cannot even move anything around, do you think your depression has anything to do with your mother?
Pt: It could.
Th: What do you think? If you were to have a choice, what would be the area that you would like talking about most? Would it be your relationships to men—father or men in general—or would it be your relationship with women?

Pt: That's interesting. I think I probably have more of a problem with women. I have a lot of friends. I have one female friend that I am very close to. The only one that I am very close to. I have a lot of male friends. I seek out a lot of male relationships.

Th: Is it possible that as a result of your problems with women in general, and with your mother in particular, that you have to push men away?

Pt: Do you think you could repeat that, please?

Th: For somebody who is so psychologically minded, why is it that you didn't see what I was talking about? Is it possible that the problems that you have with women in general, as you said, might be more of a problem and your mother as such is really what makes you push men away? Is that really what motivates you to become slowly the one who pushes them away and ends the relationship? Does that mean anything to you?

Pt: That could be.

Th: Men are being discarded by you?

Pt: Yes.

Th: What is it that they have done that is so bad that you have to throw them away?

Pt: Nothing, really.

Th: I know that in reality. But there is obviously something inside you that is angry at them.

Pt: My mother rejects my father a lot. I guess she always has. I shouldn't use them as examples all the time, but it's hard sometimes not to when you see how conditioned we are.

Th: Do you have any thought about what your parents' sexual life was like?

Pt: I've thought about it. I think it was probably very good in the beginning when they were first married, when it was new and exciting. I don't really know. From what I can remember, they haven't slept in the same room for many years, and I can see them as being very unexploring, having very simple sex probably once a week. I can see my mother often rejecting anything from my father...

Th: Then your father is more the initiator?

Pt: I think so, yes.

Th: The fact is that before, when I was asking you about the birth of your brother, you had almost total amnesia. Now, you were six years old when your brother was born. He was a product of

some sexual activity between the parents at that time. Yet that is kind of pushed out, eliminated.
Pt: Yes, it is.
Th: And if it didn't exist, is it something in you possibly that resented it? You rejected him. Do you feel that your mother might have rejected him? Does that ring any bells?
Pt: No, not really.
Th: All right. Now, if you see a male therapist, are you going to like what happens and then reject him also?
Pt: Dr. X asked me the same question.
Th: He did? And how did you answer it?
Pt: Well, I said I would really try and make an effort not to, because for anything else to happen within the therapy, for me to learn anything, I am going to have to not reject that person and be willing to trust him.
Th: Are you willing? Would you like to do that?
Pt: Oh, very much. It took a lot of effort to come here. I decided that if I was going to make that first effort, then I was certainly going to try and make the most of it.
Th: Good. Then I think that is the most important part of the battle. Fifty percent of the battle is the motivation.
Pt: Yes.
Th: Good. Well, thank you for talking to me, and I think someone from our clinic will be getting in touch with you.

Dr. Brown:

It is difficult to proceed so quickly into a discussion of such a vivid experience. I feel a bit like an intruder into the interview. It was beautifully carried through, consistent, and so internally harmonious that almost anything I say would seem to interrupt its own symmetry. As a first discussant, I feel I can only move toward a kind of summarization of what appeared to occur, keeping in mind some of the frames of reference that were beautifully elaborated on earlier by Drs. Davanloo and Sifneos and each of the other presenters.

From the beginning, the patient exhibited a very high level of trust. This provides a first indication of potential transference that I think most of us would want to note. I assume trust was carefully nurtured in her earlier first interview with Dr. Davanloo and presumably by her total experience in that particular clinical environment. There must be something about that clinical setting that evokes a feeling of trust and reinforces the sense of positive expectancy that a young woman might have in coming for help. So she then related to Dr. Sifneos very quickly in a trusting fashion. One thing I would immediately say to myself is "She probably had a pretty good relationship with her father."

I note that Dr. Sifneos did not use any kind of transference commentary in the session. He didn't say anything like "I notice you seem quite comfortable with me and I assume that's a little bit like how you felt with your father—that you find a man, or an older man, easy to talk with," thereby providing a kind of open-ended transference comment and leaving the patient an opportunity to correct or modify it, but also laying the groundwork for later transference commentary.

The nature of the interview, the process of it, was, as we could all see, very structured. I wondered as I listened what it would be like if it were not so fully structured, how another analytic therapist might have entered into a session with this young woman—for example, a more classical analytic stance with a totally open-ended style in which the analyst said no more than "Tell me about yourself" or did no more than give the patient a nod. However, we see quite the opposite from Dr. Sifneos, and I think the effects of his level of activity became self-evident. What did that combination of structure and focused activity from Dr. Sifneos evoke? What did it induce in the patient? What were the ramifications of such a high degree of structure? I think we can see that, with so many questions put to her in a short time, the patient had no opportunity to regress into a lingering depth of affect. While she is clearly a very sensitive and feeling person who shows an intensity of affect, that intensity was within range of what one would like to call normal. While she was reactive and responsive, the nature of the interviewing procedure gave her no opportunity to dip into a regressive level of affect. I assume this is purposeful in Dr. Sifneos' technique. Another therapist might have lingered longer at certain moments, or underlined certain of her phrases so as to encourage the poignancy of her feelings, but I think Dr. Sifneos consciously chose not to let that happen.

The building stones of the interview were marvelously laid out from the first moment. Dr. Sifneos asked her why she wanted to look at herself. He made it clear that cognitive work was to occur, not regression. It is not taken for granted that because she came she wants to look at herself. I think such a question is experienced by the patient as somewhat disjunctive, as if to say, "I came in the door expecting to tell you all my problems and you ask me why I want to look at myself." That is jarring to the patient, but it creates, I think, an expectation that there is work to be done. The realization occurs that psychotherapy is not simply an injection of good feeling. "Why do you come here?" That question was then followed by "What do you remember about your childhood?" Thus a very clear sequential structure to the interview leading to some difficult feelings.

A positive feeling for the father emerged in the first ten minutes of the interview through her memory of her childhood, and quickly we get a picture of a tilted oedipal situation in which Dad was good and Mom was not good. "Tilted," I would say, but seemingly not a profoundly or severely distorted oedipal situation. In its first round, the tilt reflected good feelings with her father.

Dr. Sifneos then underlined the fact that she has such a vague memory of her baby brother. I assume he intends to build on that later. His phrasing—"It's as if baby brother was never there"—provided a very nice beginning for what could be developed later. I note he did not attribute to her a more active attitude, such as "It seems you erased your baby brother."

In this patient, the "good mother" appears to have been in the form of the grandmother. This was significant historical information to be used later. And then came the story of what happened to her and the natural question, "Why didn't you tell your mother?—father?" The allusions to the childhood sexual experimenting have oedipal implications which she herself later characterized with "Freud is in the room with us." So we learn that she understands the oedipal concept at least at a cognitive level.

Dr. Sifneos asked the patient about moving into womanhood and her transition into the adult side of her femininity. She talked with ambivalence about it, again commenting on the absence of a mother to facilitate her movement into womanhood. She erases or has no memory of her mother as a helpful person at the time of entering into her menstrual phase. Dr. Sifneos does some reconstructing and attempts to make a first-phase comment about her attitude toward boys and her attitude relative to her father. The parallel between the closeness and distance with her father and the push-and-pull kind of relating with boys was firmly shown to her. Dr. Sifneos, for the first time in the interview, now gives the patient a long period of silence. I thought this was striking. Up until that time there was his sequence of questions and his steady structuring. Then, suddenly, when he made his first preliminary stab at an interpretive formulation—father, boys, ambivalence, closeness, pushing away—he gave her a lot of time. She thought for a while, but not much that was verbal came out of her.

She then reviewed her distress upon moving back home. She added that since she has moved home she "sees a lot of things," implying that what she sees makes her quite unhappy. Dr. Sifneos didn't seem terribly interested in that and went on to ask her about her earlier depression. He then attempted to help her see something about guilt and the sexual thing and boys and ambivalence. Here he made a jump, and it is here that I would say his approach gets to be what—from a more conservative point of view—would be called "pushing it." He had a theory about the origins of her discomfort. He wanted to get something across to her about guilt, and he moved that theme forward. Then he went back again to her depression, and she told about the couple with whom she felt so happy. She felt taken in by them and yet frightened of being taken in by them. In that context, we have the childhood picture all over again. She began to get depressed, but she herself didn't see the causal connection there, namely, that the reconstructed family situation was more than she could handle.

Then the return to her home and the discomfort there. The perfectionism of her parents, the sterility, the lack of social vitality, and all those things that she appeared to be associating with her mother. Dr. Sifneos made a stab at the notion when he said that perfectionism was like her mother's house, referring to the sterility and the absence of vitality. She doesn't like to be in that house. At one point he asked her a pointed and, in essence, interpretative question: "Do you think your problem with women is what makes you push men away?" She didn't understand that at all and instead attempted to forward her own theory about discarding men in the way she believes her mother does. Again the bad mother. So I won't attempt to go much further with this. More data will follow.

A personal point of departure. Under the other circumstances in which a patient arrives seeking help but still living at home with parents with whom she is terribly disillusioned and in a state of imbalance, I am inclined to determine whether it is possible to arrange an interview with her and her parents—particularly as she is young and realizes that they are very much alive, not just in her mind but in her daily life. They all live together, and it would be of great interest to me to learn about how they live together by seeing them in a group interview. I believe that in such a family group interview I would get some inkling of the nature of the disruption between this young woman and her mother. Is there a possibility of addressing the depression she feels in the context of her not having had a fulfilled experience with her mother? Might we open up some doors to this through direct interpersonal experience? What is in the way between mother and patient? Of course, to suggest a family meeting to this patient who comes so highly motivated right from the beginning might seem an imposition to her. Still, I feel I could say, "Now, we've had a good meeting. What about your parents? Do you think they might want to come for a session? I think it could be productive for all of you to meet here just to see what might come of it." Possibly such a suggestion could be unnecessarily stressing for her, but I throw that in only to make sure you know the banner I'm carrying in this last moment of commentary.

Dr. Eisenstein:

As I understand brief psychotherapy, one of its most important elements is to locate the individual from the beginning—the nuclear conflict or focal conflict, as it is called. We witness in this interview that Dr. Sifneos has localized the conflict, or thinks he has. I assume that, since it was shown, this case was treated, and probably his assumptions, theoretical assumptions, were confirmed later. From the first interview, I'm not so sure. She talks about oedipal problems so nicely, so easily, and Dr. Sifneos goes after these problems all the time, almost to the end, while the patient throws in certain other elements that, had the interview been less structured, maybe could have been revealed in the first interview. Is her problem—the oedipal problem—spurious? What if it's only defensive? What if this woman is depressed because of her relationship to her mother? What if the mother is a real "bitch" and not just a bad mother of the oedipal phase? What if this was a rejecting mother? The patient became depressed when she left a good family, the family she lived with for a while, and Dr. Sifneos, still following the same course, was curious and wanted to know whether she liked the man more than the woman. "No," she said, she just liked the way she was treated—and became depressed. She mentioned a depression a few years ago. I felt that for the sake of getting out of focal conflict, as Dr. Sifneos saw it, the interview was structured all along, and he needed as much information as he could get from her. I don't blame him—that was the purpose of the interview—but there were issues that were left hanging in the air. We cannot get everything out of a first interview, yet there was room there to follow all the leads and her replies to some of the oedipal questions. If you watched her face, you could see she was left indifferent. She either made a joke of it or she wasn't touched.

The patient comes in for the first interview, wants to give us a dream, just to listen to it. I'm not talking about interpretation, just listening to see where she is at that time. Apparently, it's no part of this technique, although I think it does work with dreams, but in my opinion it would have been tremendously valuable information to find out what happens to her in her unconscious life. She also volunteered at one time: "I get very anxious when I think certain things about myself." I wonder why Dr. Sifneos didn't follow it up. I'm certain there must be a reason, since he heard it and surely thought about it. But there seem to be certain demands in this kind of structured interview that make it necessary for important, valuable gems dropped by the patients to roll under the table. Now, I'm sure that anyone could make a psychodynamic rationale. All of us could get up here and do it our way, but I'm still preoccupied with the fact that if it's vital to localize a focal or a nuclear conflict that would cover the entire brief psychotherapy, then it is vital that patients have more leeway to express that conflict. Maybe they are given that in the second or third interview and the whole structure of the therapy is changed. But if the therapy follows strictly the first impression then I raise the question "Are we right in accepting what the patient thinks in the first interview, or is it possible that we may follow our own theoretical views sometimes and not allow the patient to tell us about different areas that could be more important for brief psychotherapy?" One can make plenty of errors in psychoanalysis—forgive me, those of you who are in analysis—but one has time to catch up with them if they're not very serious. Yet if one limits himself to ten, fifteen or let's say even forty interviews, one must be very sure that he is right.

Dr. Malan:

I agree with Dr. Sifneos that the patient has an oedipal problem, but I'm not convinced that it is her only problem—although it may be. I could not make a decision on the basis of this interview. I would have interviewed her quite differently, and the interview would have lasted an hour and a half or two hours. Dr. Sifneos chooses to put himself within this restriction of a forty-five-minute interview, and I feel he pays a penalty for doing so because one can't really get the full information about the patient, although he got a great deal. So I would not be able to say that I was sure I had a focus. Regarding what I said earlier about the precipitating factor being a crucial bit of information in assessing these patients, I am not sure I know why this girl got depressed at the point at which she did. Dr. Sifneos very skillfully brought out—and the patient was not aware of this until that moment—that it was something to do with the fact that she was living with this other family and with the fact that she moved back home. She made a highly significant remark—that she saw a lot of things at home, which I take it she had half seen before and could now see more clearly. Obviously, this has upset her. We don't know what they were. It seems absolutely certain that part of her problem concerns her oedipal relation with her father. I feel that this was definitely established, and her pattern of rejecting men when they get fond of her can only be, it seems to me, something to do with what went on between her and her father. But I'm not clear on exactly why she got depressed. There are a lot of mixed feelings about both the father and the mother because it is the father, apparently, who restricts the patient and has to have the house spick-and-span, and not the mother.

In any case, my first step would be to make a therapeutic plan on the basis of that interview. Now then, does she respond to interpretation? Again I'm not sure. It seems that I'd have to look more carefully through my notes of the interview. I didn't feel she responded very clearly at any point, and there were a number of occasions when she was made to be very thoughtful about something Dr. Sifneos said and yet somehow one wasn't quite certain about what impact it had on her. I think she probably just passes that criterion because she so obviously was a thoughtful girl who could work in this kind of therapy. Her motivation was fine, and as far as the dangers of psychotherapy are concerned I don't think there are any great dangers with her. The only danger is that one might not be able to stave off the problems of dependence, which might be much stronger than we realize. Now, this is another difference between Dr. Sifneos and myself, because it wouldn't worry me necessarily. I think this girl is basically a good candidate for short-term dynamic psychotherapy as we practice it.

Dr. Davanloo:

One of our procedures, when we have the opportunity, involves my doing an initial interview of forty-five minutes and then asking Dr. Sifneos to see the same patient—without his having any knowledge of what went on in my interview—to see to what extent the data we come up with are similar and to what extent they differ, or Dr. Sifneos doing the initial interview with myself doing the second interview after a one-week interval.

I saw this patient three weeks prior to Dr. Sifneos' interview. I would say that between the first interview and this interview there was a sharp increase in the patient's motivation. She entered the first interview with a passive attitude and brought up the question of trust. When we explored this issue, we learned that the patient has problems in interpersonal relationships and the idea of getting close to and then rejecting men came into focus.

The interview subsequently moved into her relationship with her parents, and it came into focus that she left the family with which she was boarding and has had difficulties since her return home. She was rather vague about the difficulties with her father, and then she questioned me as to whether I am Freudian. I pointed out to her: "Let's not bother about being Freudian or not Freudian. Let's focus on your problems." It immediately became evident that whenever her father hugs or kisses her, sexual ideas pop into her head, and there are mental images of her father's genitals.

The episode with the first older man that she talked about very openly with Dr. Sifneos came up in my interview, but this was after I had made a transference interpretation, pointing out to her that she has made all men useless to her and asking if she were not doing the same thing with me, that I had to be the one who searched actively for information. This confrontation of her self-defeating pattern brought a great change in the interview. She volunteered the information about the older man, and it seems to me that this coincided with the time that her parents no longer slept in the same bed.

In terms of criteria, a patient who is a suitable candidate for short-term dynamic psychotherapy does not necessarily have to have only oedipal problems. I do not think that we could resolve this patient's problems within ten or fifteen sessions, but I see her as an excellent candidate for broad-focused short-term dynamic psychotherapy of perhaps twenty-five to thirty-five sessions. She has a circumscribed problem. I would score her very high in her ability to get involved with the evaluator. She would have a high score on her ability and capacity to experience guilt and anxiety. She withstood Dr. Sifneos' interview very well. Motivation is scored high, and she definitely scores high in one of our major criteria, which is the ability to respond to interpretation.

Dr. Lowy:

I also disagree with Dr. Sifneos on the point of requiring that an oedipal problem be present before such a patient is suitable. My experience suggests that other problems, including problems of separation, are quite amenable to short-term treatment if it is possible to focus on them, particularly in the transference toward the end of the short-term treatment. If further interviewing bore out my first impression, I probably would find this patient quite acceptable. She's certainly introspective, even allowing for perhaps a bit of pseudo-sophistication. She is quite prepared to engage with the therapist. I think that were there a bit more anxiety possible in this not so anxiety-provoking interview today, one might have been able to judge better, but nevertheless, what little we did judge, I felt that her response to Dr. Sifneos' comments was likely to be productive and I don't see any reason why one would not attempt short-term psychotherapy with her.

Dr. Sifneos:

In reference to Dr. Eisenstein's comment, I think he made a wonderful case for psychoanalysis, but this was not the purpose of this particular evaluation. The purpose was to determine whether this particular patient would fulfill the criteria for short-term anxiety-provoking psychotherapy. We are in a hospital–residency training type of program. We try to teach our residents to take a history in a concise form, and by the end of the first hour somehow or other to be able to, with the majority of the patients, arrive at a pretty good idea as to what they have to deal with. Only under very special conditions would we want to have a second interview, and this would probably be the case with this particular woman since as far as I am concerned she fulfills most of the criteria that I have outlined. She has a circumscribed chief complaint. She has had meaningful relationships with several people in her past. She interacts well with the evaluator. She has above-average intelligence in terms of psychological sophistication. She has an excellent motivation. She does have the focus of the oedipal issue, which is one of the prerequisites for short-term anxiety-provoking psychotherapy. I am not at all convinced that the depression is an oedipal depression. I suspect that it is but I am not convinced. A second interview may clarify it better.

If indeed we have to have a second interview to find out whether the secret which she did not tell me, and which I did not pursue since this was a videotaped interview, was possibly one that might have given us a very specific clue to the onset of the second depression, we might be able to decide whether this is an oedipal type of problem or not. I have no way of knowing. So, because this information is unavailable, I could not say that this particular patient is a good candidate, even though she tends to fulfill most of the criteria that I have outlined. I would agree with what Dr. Lowy said. She might well be a candidate for short-term dynamic psychotherapy of longer duration, as was pointed out by both Dr. Malan and Dr. Davanloo.

Chapter 9

"The Case of the Teeth-Grinding Woman"

H. DAVANLOO

The patient is a thirty-two-year old married Jewish woman who was referred to the clinic by another psychiatrist. She presented her problem of having been depressed for quite some time, with suicidal ideation and problems in interpersonal relationships characterized by her being passive and submissive, with the need to please the other person. She also presented a serious problem in her marriage, in which she found herself to be an extremely passive and, as she put it, "childlike" partner who was told what to do and could not make any decision without the agreement of her husband.

The patient was evaluated in two interviews, each of sixty minutes' duration. It became evident that in her interpersonal relationships she was masochistic and that there were problems in her relationship with her young daughter, whom she found to be very self-assertive; this relationship was possibly one of the factors that motivated her to seek help. She got angry with her daughter for her self-assertiveness, and the patient told herself, "Here I am at this age, and still I handle myself like a little child."

Th: By whom were you referred to this clinic?
Pt: No one, really. I have a friend who has been seeing a doctor.

I've been very depressed and my friend said, "I think it's time that you got some help," so I called and made the appointment.

Th: A friend of yours?

Pt: Yes. I have been very depressed, so I called and made an appointment.

Th: So you have been discussing your difficulties?

Pt: No, only that I have just been so depressed. I haven't been able to really cope with anything, and she knows this. I have not discussed it with her, and she hasn't asked me.

Th: Do you mean that there are things that you used to be able to cope with and you're not able to cope with now?

Pt: Right. I used to cope very well, and now I don't seem to be able to cope with anything.

Th: There are problems that you were usually able to handle yourself?

Pt: I mean just—it is very difficult to explain, but I find myself getting very angry for no reason, really, and I just cry all the time, also for no reason. You know, there's no immediate reason. I'm just making everybody nervous, my husband, my children, myself, and I'm just upsetting everybody. So I thought I should come in and see if I can help myself some way.

Th: You get angry for no reason and cry for no reason.

Pt: Yes. I've just reached a point where I don't like anything. There's nothing that pleases me, and there's nothing that I want to do. No matter what my husband says, it's wrong, and he says that I'm beginning to argue with him a lot.

Th: He says that?

Pt: Yes. I think I'm beginning to assert myself, which I never did before. He thinks I'm arguing. He may be right, but I'm at the point now where I can't even judge whether what I'm doing is rational or not.

Th: In a way, you are questioning yourself in this regard, that you assert yourself where you never used to assert yourself.

Pt: I don't think I did, no.

Th: What are the situations where you did or did not assert yourself?

Pt: Oh, it's just silly things, you know. He says, "You sit down and I'll do the dishes," and I'll say, "No! I don't want you to do the dishes. I'll do them myself." Then he says, "Why do you argue so much? I'm just trying to help," but I don't feel—that's a poor example, maybe.

Th: But he wants to help you wash the dishes?
Pt: He wants to help me in any way he can, but he doesn't know what to do, and I don't know what to do any more.
Th: It irritates you when he wants to help you, you mean?
Pt: Sometimes. Sometimes he just irritates me, period.
Th: You find yourself irritable?
Pt: Yes, and I was explaining to the doctor that I have been under a lot of stress for a considerable length of time, and I thought that once the immediate cause of this stress is finished then I won't feel so nervous any more, feel so jumpy all the time, but it hasn't gone away.
Th: These stresses. There are a number of stress situations that you have been faced with?
Pt: Yes. A few years ago my husband decided to quit his job and go back to the university to do postgraduate work, and I was completely in agreement with him. I felt if that's what he wanted to do that's what he should do. So he did. The first year went fairly well. I wasn't particularly unhappy, although our way of living changed radically.
Th: In what way did it radically change?
Pt: Well, suddenly there was no income, and we lived on our savings. My husband had been a banker before that, so whenever we went on an assignment we lived in a large house and we had a staff and all that sort of thing.
Th: You mean, you had to give up all that?
Pt: Well, we gave up all that, and I didn't mind because that sort of life didn't particularly appeal to me. I don't need to live in a big house and have servants. Well, we went from there into a tiny apartment in a very poor area of the city, and he went back to school, and, as I say, for the first year things seemed to be fairly good.
Th: But there was quite a drop in your way of life and the conditions of your life?
Pt: Oh, yes! A complete change. He was walking to his classes one day and he was hit by a truck. He was very badly injured. This was in the winter, and he was in the hospital for quite a while and had several operations. In the meantime, in spite of all this, he managed to continue with his classes, and I stayed on with my job and drove him back and forth all the time and everything. Then he was in a cast for almost a year.

Th: This was during the second year?
Pt: Yes, but then he finished his course, and he then got a job here in Montreal and we moved here. I had to do all the moving and everything. All this time, everything had gone very well for me. I was quite capable, and I coped with all these stresses, and it didn't bother me. I managed my schedule so that I could work and everything.
Th: In spite of all this pressure you were able to cope with it?
Pt: Yes. I coped with it in spite of all the pressure, as you say. Then we came here and he got out of his cast in the fall of last year. Of course, he hadn't been able to move his leg in such a long time that he was still on crutches and everything.
Th: Both legs?
Pt: No. It was just one, and it was all the way up to his waist. We went to visit his mother in another city for a weekend, and he collapsed and he had convulsions and seizures, and we rushed him to a hospital there. He was in the hospital there for almost three weeks while they tried to assess the neurological damage and all this, and I managed very well even with that. Then we came back to Montreal in the fall and he had a massive drug reaction on top of everything else. The drugs they had given him for the convulsions had caused this reaction. Then in January my grandfather died, and I'm from a family where my grandfather was the main person.
Th: When was that?
Pt: It was in January, two years ago.
Th: Two years ago he died? This was your grandfather from which side?
Pt: My mother's father. From that time on, I just really haven't been able to cope with anything. I thought it was the winter, and I always get depressed in the winter. I thought when the spring comes it will get better. Then I started doing a lot of volunteer work at a hospital to keep myself busy, because I don't know anyone to be friends with. Then we bought a house and we moved again.
Th: When was that?
Pt: In February.
Th: What happened?
Pt: Nothing happened, but I just don't even want to cope any more. Then I decided—well, last fall I decided that the best thing for me to do would be to go back to school myself.

Th: When did you decide that you would go back to school? Your husband decided to go back to school a few years ago.
Pt: Yes, well, this was just last fall.
Th: This was around the time that your grandfather died?
Pt: No. He died the preceding winter. I got through the winter and I got through the summer, but I decided I just couldn't face another winter living where we were living. We were living in an apartment out in the suburbs, and I hate apartments. I think its the worst possible way to live, and I didn't want to spend any more time there than I had to. So I decided that I would go back to school, and I would prepare myself for some kind of a job because that's really what I want to do. I miss working. I was accepted at a university here, and then we bought the house. If I had known that we would be moving again, I wouldn't have...
Th: Who decided to buy the house?
Pt: My husband decided. Well, he wants to stay for an unspecified period of time here, where I don't want to stay.
Th: So you were not in agreement with him, then?
Pt: I was in agreement with him that if we were going to have to stay in Montreal we should buy a house, because the prices are going up so much and it's silly to wait. If you're going to make that decision, then it's silly to wait and have to pay all that much more money. He said he likes his job and he doesn't want to leave, and he said he certainly didn't want to leave it now. He wants to have at least five years' experience. He doesn't think it's a good idea to change often, and he's right.
Th: How did you feel about his decision to stay?
Pt: Well, I don't want to stay. I really feel that I'm like—it's like a prison, and I have tried to like it, and I have tried to accept it, but sometimes I feel like I can't even breathe. It just depresses me so much, and I don't know why.

(*Here the patient cries heavily.*)

Th: So, this was quite a source of conflict for you in relationship with your husband because he wanted to stay and you tried to like it, but you have not been able to like it.
Pt: Well, everybody tells me that I have no choice.
Th: How did you feel toward your husband? What was the way you

felt about him deciding that this was the best thing and you had to go along with it?

Pt: I don't resent that. I mean, he is trying to the best of his capabilities to take care of his family, and I'm his family, and he wants to take care of me, and he does take care of me. I know he loves me. I don't feel that he's doing anything deliberately.

Th: But I feel that in a way you are very much threatened with the idea of resentment toward your husband. Because, you see, when I was asking you how you felt, you had to really reassure me that you don't have resentment.

Pt: Yes, I probably do because I don't want to be here, and I feel that I wouldn't have to be here if it wasn't for him. I mean, obviously, if I wasn't married to him I wouldn't have to be here. That's right, but I am.

Th: Because also in the back of your mind is the idea that for a number of years you have been sacrificing so that he could go to school, and you have been in a way struggling all along during that time.

Pt: Yes, but it was as much my idea as his, and I don't think I resent that. I don't think I do. I don't know. I don't even know what I think anymore.

Th: But do you usually find it difficult to announce to yourself that you might resent things?

Pt: Yes, I think I probably do, because all my life I've been told that I have certain duties toward certain people and I don't have any choice.

Th: All your life you have been told this?

Pt: Yes.

Th: Would you like to tell me about it?

Pt: I never really got to make any decisions about my life, except that I'm the one who decided to get married. Nobody else did, but my mother told me I had to go to college and she told me which college I had to go to. I went, and I hated every minute of it. I hated it!

Th: Your Mother?

Pt: Not my mother. I hated college. I didn't feel at the time that I resented her because . . .

Th: She was pushing you to go through things that you didn't like?

Pt: I didn't want to, and whenever I said that I didn't want to

she always said, "It's costing us all this money, so you have to do it." So I did it.
Th: So you did it just to please her?
Pt: No. I did it just because she made me feel so obligated that I didn't . . .
Th: In what way did she make you feel obligated?
Pt: She always said that she was sacrificing so much for me to have all these things, which was true. I'm sure there are lots of things that she would like to have had.
Th: She was sacrificing a lot?
Pt: Well, that's what she said.
Th: This is what she was saying, but . . . ?
Pt: I felt that I was the one who was sacrificing because I didn't want to do it.
Th: But in what way was your mother sacrificing?
Pt: Financially. I mean, if you're spending five thousand dollars a year for somebody to go to college, that's five thousand dollars you don't have to spend some other way. My family is not wealthy, and there were lots of other ways that they could have used it.
Th: Do you mean that they were putting themselves under hardship?
Pt: No, but I suppose it's a difference between being comfortable and being reasonably affluent. Maybe that's the difference.
Th: Your mother was always like that? How about your father?
Pt: Well, my parents were divorced when I was ten, I think.
Th: You were ten.
Pt: I was about ten, and my mother remarried fairly soon after she was divorced.
Th: What happened that your parents got divorced?
Pt: I really don't know except that my father never liked me, and he never liked my mother, either. He never liked anything, which is the way I feel that I'm getting.
Th: That you're getting?
Pt: I feel that I'm getting like that, where I don't like anything any more, either.
Th: Like your father, you mean?
Pt: I don't know. I don't think children ever know their parents until they're adult enough or mature enough to see their parents

as human beings. I've never known my father that way. I haven't seen him for many years, so I don't know what he's like as a person. I know that he was always very antagonistic toward me.

Th: In what way was he antagonistic toward you?
Pt: He used to tell me I was stupid and ugly and fat and ridiculous, and I would never amount to anything. He was right.
Th: Do you mean that he was a very critical person? Why did you suddenly say that he was right?
Ph: Because that's just the way I feel. I feel stupid and ugly and dumb and fat and...

(Here the patient again cries heavily.)

Th: How long has it been that you have felt this way about yourself?
Pt: I don't know. I have never had very much self-confidence.
Th: But a while ago you were telling me that in Vancouver under all those difficult situations you coped and kept the family going.
Pt: Yes, I did.
Th: So, how do you put those two things together? Because you did it, but now you...
Pt: I don't know. Maybe I didn't have time to think about it or worry about it, but I do now. I guess I'm the kind of person who only functions well under pressure.
Th: That means you do better when there is pressure on you?
Pt: Yes, and then when there isn't I brood about things.
Th: So you had quite a difficult time with your parents?
Pt: Yes.
Th: Going back to your relationship with your mother, you had to comply with what she thought was the best for you.
Pt: Yes.
Th: Do you feel some parallel of the same phenomenon with your husband?
Pt: Yes. I told him that. I told him that I feel I'm just another child and that I don't have any—that it isn't a situation where what I want is ever considered. And he said, which is true, "What do you want me to do? Do you want me to quit my job and go back with no income again?" and he said, "You won't be any

happier anywhere else because it's just always in yourself," and I know that's true.

Th: Could you tell me about the areas of your life in which you have to give up your ideas in relationship with your husband, areas in which you have to mold yourself to his way of doing things or of thinking?

Pt: Sometimes I think it's in every way.

Th: Could you talk about it?

Pt: He says that isn't true.

Th: But in your own mind could you look at it?

Pt: Well, I'll give you one example, okay? Last, oh, it must be eighteen months ago, you know, we were in Vancouver visiting my brother-in-law and my sister-in-law, and we went into a furniture store because we very badly needed some new furniture, and we saw this very strange-looking furniture. I suppose, as a psychiatrist, you could make interpretations, but it's very soft and squashy, and when you sit in it it molds itself to you. It's very comfortable for reading and relaxing, and I try to make our house so that it is kind of a haven. I feel that my children and my husband should be able to go there and relax and read or whatever they want. Anyway, we saw this furniture, and it was very odd-looking, and we decided that we liked it.

Th: Who do you mean when you say "we"?

Pt: We both did. We decided that we really liked it and that we would try to get it. So we came back to Montreal, and for a long time we couldn't find any furniture store where they had it or where they had even heard about it. We eventually found a store where the man knew about the furniture, and he said he would get it for us. Well, this has been just going on for months and months and months, and at the time...

Th: Why has it been going on for months?

Pt: Well, because we had to find the place, and then the man had to order the furniture, and then it didn't come in for a long time, and then when the furniture did come we didn't have the money then, and he said, "Well, it doesn't matter. I'll keep it for you." So, we were living in this apartment and the furniture would have fit very well. Then we bought this house in February, and we moved in. In the meantime, the furniture store, the building, had been torn down, and he had to put everything in storage. He hadn't opened a new store yet, and all this kind of thing, and we still don't have this new furniture. But in the meantime we bought this house.

Th: What do you think happened that you couldn't get that furniture?

Pt: Well, it just seemed to be a series of coincidences. Every time we had the money, he didn't have the furniture, and then when he had the furniture, we didn't have the money, and oh, it was just such a "schmozzle."

Th: I was getting the idea that in a way you always have been trying to comply with your husband and you were bringing this as an example.

Pt: Yes. Well, I'm going to get to that part. So then we bought this house, and it's an old house. It was built in 1890, and it has bay windows, and it has funny corners, and it has carvings, and that furniture just doesn't apply any more. It won't go with any of our other furniture, and it won't be suitable in this house, and he insists that we still have to get it and I insist that I don't want it.

Th: Did you have a say in the buying of the house, in the style of it?

Pt: Well, I very much like houses like that.

Th: So, you liked it yourself?

Pt: Yes.

Th: But what you don't like is this furniture in that house?

Pt: Well, we haven't got the furniture yet because I still don't want it.

Th: But you don't like it?

Pt: No.

Th: But then he insists?

Pt: Yes.

Th: How do you feel when he insists?

Pt: I feel that he's being unreasonable.

Th: But how do you feel in terms of feelings?

Pt: Well, I feel that if it's going to be my house, and I'm going to be responsible for the house and making it into a home, then I should be able to decide what kind of furniture I have in it.

Th: But I'm talking about your feelings at this point.

Pt: I don't know. You mean am I angry, do I get angry or something? No. I feel hopeless.

Th: But do you think this hopelessness is a way of dealing with your anger? Because somehow, you know, any person in your position in many of these situations would have been angry. This is what you describe all along, the way with your mother. You say that your were molded and you were pushed under the name that this was the best for you, but you find it difficult to announce to yourself that you felt resentment and you felt anger with it. When it comes to the present life situation, you go through telling me so many situations in which your wishes and desires are not counted, and that you have to mold yourself to others, but at the same time you find it difficult to announce that you feel resentment and you feel angry.

Pt: Yes, I do.

Th: It's as if somehow this has become too frightening to you. Do you see what I mean? It's too frightening to you to announce to yourself that this is what you experience.

Pt: You think I'm afraid of telling you that I'm resentful?

Th: That it is a matter of first announcing to yourself that you are experiencing this within yourself.

Pt: I'm not even telling myself this. Why, though?

Th: But you are experiencing this within yourself, aren't you?

Pt: Well, I suppose so, because even my dentist told me that I had to get rid of whatever was bothering me. I said, "Why?" and he said, "Because you're ruining your teeth." He says that I grind my teeth so much that I'm ruining them.

Th: He says that you grind your teeth?

Pt: Apparently all the time.

Th: In a way, then, he's telling you that this is a way of dealing with your anger within yourself?

Pt: He's a very offhand man, and he said, "Why the hell don't you give whatever it is that's bugging you a kick in the ass?" and I said, "But nothing is bugging me," and he said, "Come on! You can't tell me that. Your mouth is a mess, and it's a mess because you're grinding your teeth all the time." It's true, because I wake up in the mornings and my whole mouth is bloody.

Th: What do you think about what the dentist tells you when you give thought to it?

Pt: I just think, Well, I'll be wearing false teeth in a few years.

Th: What do you think he is telling you?

Pt: I think he's right. I think he's telling me that inside my calm, supposedly, exterior I'm just a seething mass of anger, which is probably true. That's what worries me now, because my anger seems to be coming out, and it's unpredictable, and I get so angry for nothing.

Th: In what way does it come out?

Pt: Oh, I get angry at my children, and it isn't their fault.

Th: You feel that you get angry with the children where you shouldn't be angry?

Pt: Well, I shouldn't be angry with the children. It has nothing to do with them, and I do feel and I'm very much afraid that I'm going to warp them in the way that I feel that I have been, and I don't want to do that because they're sensitive, and they're highly intelligent.

Th: How many children do you have?

Pt: Two.

Th: How old are they?

Pt: I have a son who is ten, and I have a daughter who is eight.

Th: And you find yourself irritable with them? With which one?

Pt: With both of them, although I probably get more irritated with my daughter, and I try so hard not to because she's such a loving little creature that I don't want her to have to suffer from things that are really unjustified. It isn't justified when I get cross with her, and I know it isn't, and she probably knows it isn't, too. But I can't ask a child to understand and cope with something that I can't cope with myself.

Th: How long is it since you've found yourself like this with your children, particularly with your daughter?

Pt: Just recently it's been more noticeable, and I've been trying very hard not to be that way.

Th: Do you think there is a relationship between these phenomena, these experiences that you have with your children, and your relationship with your husband? Do you know what I mean? With the children you get angry, but with your husband you try to hold your anger. Do you think there is a relationship between these two? The reason I'm saying this is that sometimes for adults it is easier to be angry with children because you are not going to get retaliation. For example, sometimes it happens that a person is not able to get angry with the boss because he is afraid of being fired, but then it is easy for him to get angry with the children because the children cannot fight back. Do you feel that somehow such a phenomenon is in operation in relationship there and here?

Pt: Yes, it could be. I mean, if I'm not getting angry with my husband when I should be, then I must be getting angry in some other direction, at myself and at the children.

(*The therapist explores her relationship with her daughter. The patient becomes very irritated because her daughter is so self-assertive*).

Th: Because what we know is that with your mother it was the same pattern. You could not allow yourself to experience your negative feelings. The conflict was also that you were always told that this was the best for you.
Pt: She always made me feel so guilty about everything. She really did. She still does. If she says anything, I feel like I have to do it immediately, and that's so silly. That's how I feel.
Th: Could you tell me more about your mother as a person?
Pt: Well, she is very ill right now. She's quite young. She was only nineteen when I was born. She's the unhappiest person I know. I don't think she has ever in her life had anything that has given her even a little bit of enjoyment. She has a miserable marriage with my stepfather. She had a miserable marriage with my father. She doesn't have a very good relationship with my grandmother, who is quite old now, needless to say, and not very well. I don't know. I think sometimes that the whole family is neurotic, and then that makes me feel better because I think, I'm not too bad then if everybody else is like that.
Th: You mean you compare yourself to your mother?
Pt: No, not really. I try to look at the family as a whole, and I see that none of them are happy.
Th: But at any time do you compare yourself to your mother in terms of in which ways you are similar to her or different from her?
Pt: No. The only way I really think about my mother is that, even at my age, I just resent so much the fact that she pushed all this on me that she did.
Th: She pushed all this? What do you mean by "this"?
Pt: Well, going to college, and I worked through college. It was just a liberal arts school. You couldn't really do anything with what you learned there, and she thought that was just the best thing because they teach you to think, because once you can think that's the main thing. What I really needed was some kind of practical direction, because I am a very practical person.

I can cope with things that are practical, as I told you. With all this, with my husband and everything, that was all practical. There was so much that had to be done, and I could plan the ways to do it, and the plan worked out, and it was successful. But this business about teaching me to think, that wasn't what I needed. Then, I think that it's so stupid at my age—why do I even think about it? I don't know.

Th: You mentioned your grandfather who died. You were discussing his death. What happened to him?

Pt: He was eighty when he died, and he died of cancer, which was a blessing. My grandfather was always the really strong person.

Th: In what way?

Pt: Well, everybody depended so much on him. We all thought that he always knew best no matter what it was, and he was a very kind and a very knowledgeable man.

Th: Your relationship with him was different in comparison with the rest of the family?

Pt: Yes.

Th: Could you tell me about your relationship with him? How was it?

Pt: We were very close, and I always felt that he was my really good friend as well as my grandfather. Next to my husband, I guess he was the only man in my life that I've ever really loved. I felt a great loss when he died, a great personal loss.

Th: Did you used to spend a lot of time with him?

Pt: When I was growing up, yes. I was so unhappy with my parents when I was small that I used to spend most of my time with my grandparents. After my mother left my father, then I lived with my grandparents, and even after she remarried I spent all the time that I could with my grandparents, although I loved my grandfather far more than my grandmother. I feel very close to her, and I do love her a lot, but not . . .

Th: But it was different?

Pt: Very different, and everybody always said that I was a lot like him.

Th: Like your grandfather? In what ways?

Pt: We both liked the same things. He used to take me fishing and for long walks in the country, and he'd show me all about plants and animals. He loved animals, so I could always have a cat or a dog or whatever I wanted.

Th: In other words, he was concerned about your interests, and this made him very different from your mother, didn't it?

Pt: From everybody, I guess. When I was so unhappy over this going to college and everything, he said that I didn't have to, that I could do whatever I wanted.

Th: Are you saying that he was the only person in your life who was concerned about your interests? In other words, he wanted you to do what you wanted to do. Am I right, that in a way he was the only person in your life with whom your relationship went like that?

Pt: Everybody else said they were, but I think he's the only person who worried about it. I know he really was concerned about what I did and how I felt about things, and he wanted me to do what I wanted, and he would always say to me, "Look. It's your life. You make your own decisions. Your mother is living her life. Leave her alone. Don't worry about her."

Th: In other words, he wanted you to be the one to make decisions about things.

Pt: But I never could.

Th: With your mother you couldn't?

Pt: No. I always felt like I had to do whatever it was that she wanted me to do because I would disappoint her so much if I didn't. In spite of all that, I never really felt that I'd ever really done anything to please her, in spite of the fact that I tried.

Th: You mean you were trying hard to please her at the same time. So, this was quite a difficult situation for you, a conflicting situation for you, because on one hand you had to constantly comply with her demands and to give up your own self and your own wishes, but then you had also to hold back that anger and try to please her. Are there any other life situations in which you do the same thing? Do you see what I mean, that you are angry but still you are trying to please the other person?

Pt: Well, I'm sure I do that with my husband.

(*The interview moves to some of the realities of the patient's present life. She has enrolled in a university as a graduate student and is very disappointed in the course, in the way they are running it. In the fall she had a bad case of flu.*)

Th: It seems to me that in a way you always look to others to confirm your views.

Pt: I'm sure I do. I never would even have come here except my friend said, "Look. You are really getting bad, and you've got to go and get some help."

Th: You feel that you came because she suggested that you come?
Pt: No. I just came because I knew that it had helped her.
Th: You have had these difficulties, then, for some time?
Pt: Yes.
Th: When did you start to think about getting help for yourself?

(*The patient saw her family doctor, who said stress does funny things to people and that she should do something about it. She also thought it might be physical. Then the therapist questions the patient: "Of the many problems you have, which one would you like to get help for?"*)

Pt: I would like to be able to work out this obsession that I have of not living in Montreal, of disliking it so much, because I think so many other things hinge on that.
Th: You dislike living in Montreal, but your husband is after you to like it. In a way, he is advocating that you should try to like it, but then you dislike it.
Pt: No. He doesn't say that I should like it. He just says that there really isn't anything that we can do about it right now.
Th: From what you told me about your relationship with your mother, you had to comply with your mother, and in a very submissive way you did everything that she wanted you to do. Now, from what you have told me about your relationship with your husband, do you see some sort of parallel between the two?
Pt: Yes. I find myself in a similar pattern of relationship, but I couldn't cope with it when I was sixteen. But I'm not sixteen any more, and I should be able to say, "Look. Let's get on with it," and I just don't.
Th: Do you feel that if you leave Montreal and return to Vancouver everything would be all right?
Pt: No. I don't think everything would be all right. This is what my husband keeps saying to me. It wouldn't be better there, which in some ways it wouldn't be, but in other ways it would be. I have very close friends, and I miss a lot not having anybody, except I have just one friend here in Montreal. I know that it wouldn't be any better, but there would be a lot of small problems, and it's probably just because I don't really want to face the big ones.

Th: In a way, your mind goes toward the trivial things to avoid the larger ones. In what way do you think a psychiatrist would be able to help you to work through some of these difficulties that you experience?

(Interview continues.)

Dr. Marmor:

The discussion will be followed by ten to fifteen minutes of a few vignettes of some of the psychotherapeutic sessions and the outcome of the treatment of this patient.

Dr. Sifneos:

I just want to comment on two areas. One has to do with the masterful way in which Dr. Davanloo was able to help this woman present her real problem. From a teary, so-called depressed, "poor me," helpless individual, she became an angry one, particularly when she attacked him with her sneezing fits. The second concerns the question of whether this particular patient fulfills the criteria which I outlined for short-term anxiety-provoking psychotherapy, which usually lasts somewhere between thirteen and sixteen interviews.

First of all, I see no evidence that she had one meaningful relationship with another person in her early life. Her chief complaint is fairly circumscribed. Her ability to interact with the evaluator, I think, can be left open for discussion. I think she does interact fairly well. I also think she expresses affect quite well, but she constantly wants to return to her attitude of having people feel sorry for her. She is bright. Her motivation for change, on the other hand, is questionable since I think she wants people to take care of her. She has motivation for symptomatic relief, not for change. She wants to get rid of her anger and her depression.

So, in my opinion, she is not a candidate for short-term anxiety-provoking psychotherapy. Whether she would be a good candidate for a longer form of short-term dynamic psychotherapy, such as Drs. Davanloo and Malan are practicing, I don't know. Maybe she is. Also, Dr. Brown might be willing to comment about the usefulness of "couples therapy" for this particular woman. I don't feel that I know enough about this subject to comment intelligently on it.

Dr. Nemiah:

I think this very dramatic and really quite moving interview answers one question for us, and that is that the initial evaluating interview should not be forty-five minutes or a hundred minutes. It ought to be sixty minutes. I agree with a number of Dr. Sifneos' comments about what this patient presents. It seems to me that on the positive side, toward attempting insight therapy with her, are some of the following factors. She is expressive. I felt that she related quite well to Dr. Davanloo; at least, she appeared to trust him, and to be able to pour out her story, to tell a good deal of intimate things. It seemed to me that she was psychologically intelligent. She was able to be perceptive. She responded near the end to his trying to point out to her the similarity between her compliance with her mother and her husband. That seemed to strike her as a new bit of learning. She appeared to be able to encompass that, perhaps make use of it. I'm not so sure whether she has not had a good relationship. When she talked about the grandfather, it struck me that there was something going on there, and I think that before one can make the decision of the lack of any good relationship one would have to know more about that. These to me are on the positive side for her being a person who could be responsive to insight psychotherapy. Now, as to the duration, I would certainly agree with what Dr. Sifneos says; I don't think she would respond to insight with learning in the briefer kinds of therapy of up to fourteen to twenty hours, something of that sort, because from what one sees about the more instinctual side of her it looks as though her basic position is really one of need.

She is a woman who has developed over her life apparently a number of counterdependent defenses that carried her along quite well in the face of several years of what looked to me like massive deprivation; she may exaggerate a little bit, but in reality she's got a lot of pressure on her, which I think has to be taken into account in understanding her breaking down. Behind this, one does see the need and the tremendous problem with anger, which probably refers to or is the anxiety. There is much more separation anxiety than an oedipal type of anxiety, so that I think that if she is going to be in insight psychotherapy it would have to be for a much longer period of time. I would predict that she might respond to a therapeutic encounter rather rapidly with relief from having been able to talk about this, and perhaps in a few interviews she would begin to feel better as far as her depression is concerned, so that symptomatically she would improve. But I would doubt that there would be much, if any, internal characterological or psychological change that would allow her thereafter to solve problems that she's now unable to cope with.

Dr. Marmor:

It seems to me that both Dr. Sifneos' and Dr. Nemiah's comments illustrate one of the difficulties that we have in focusing on the issues here. One of the points that has not been mentioned is the goal of short-term dynamic psychotherapy. Is it the same as that of long-term intensive psychotherapy? Are we aiming at basic modification of personality structure within a period of five or ten visits? I think if that ever happens, it's serendipitous. Most long-term character modification takes a long time. It may not take five times a week on the couch; we may be able to do it once a week or twice a week over a year or two in suitable cases. But what is the goal of short-term dynamic psychotherapy?

Here is a young woman who, although she has certain basic character problems, one of the most obvious being her inability to deal with anger, nevertheless has been a rather effective human being up until about a year ago. She even coped with some very stressful modifications in her life pattern, and then she decompensated at a certain critical point. Now, do we use short-term dynamic psychotherapy, our understanding of the dynamics and of the balance between her character structure and her life situation, to enable her to restore her previous homeostatic capacity to deal with her life, and do we consider this an adequate short-term goal that we can deal with through short-term intensive psychotherapy, or is our goal the modification of this basic personality structure, in which event we have to think in quite different terms? I think we cannot approach the issue of short-term dynamic psychotherapy without including as one of the variables what our therapeutic objectives are.

Dr. Malan:

Look, there are too many prejudices and preconceptions around. Dr. Marmor asked the question, Is the goal of short-term therapy to modify the character? My answer is a categorical yes, and he now says that in order to modify the character you need a couple of years at once a week. That is not true, and it's time that people realized this. I'm not saying it will necessarily work in this patient. I think it might. We have a number of cases that illustrate this. There was a girl with a similar problem. She was only twenty-one. She had never said boo to a goose. She idealized her parents. In the tenth session she had the first row of her life with her parents. She walked out of her home, and three months later her father wrote to the therapist saying, "Thank you for what you have done for my daughter." I can give you many, many other examples of this. The aim of short-term psychotherapy is often similar to the aim of analysis, and if you examine it empirically you will find it's possible.

Dr. Marmor:

Dr. Malan, I don't disagree with you that this result sometimes ensues. Franz Alexander described a case in which a single interview resulted in character modification. When I said it's often serendipitous, I meant it's not always possible to predict it. But in any event I think the goal, the therapeutic objective of the therapist, has to be one of the things to be considered.

Dr. Nemiah:

At this point, after hearing Dr. Malan, I can give only compliant Colonial assent to my British cousin. What I was aiming at was trying to decide whether or not this woman is a candidate for short-term dynamic psychotherapy of fifteen to twenty sessions. My feeling was that this woman probably would not change in that length of time, but that possibly within a year she might. One might be able to deal with her superego and modify that in a manner so that she can deal with issues in the future in a better way, as opposed to the kind of briefer supportive therapy that I think she may respond to, as I indicated when I spoke, within a very few interviews but without change.

Dr. Davanloo:

In response to Dr. Sifneos' comment regarding criteria for selection, that the problem of this patient is not a purely triangular oedipal one, there are other problems as well. In my opinion, there was a meaningful relationship with her grandfather. Many memories emerged, and there was a great deal of grief and mourning, with the patient saying, "He was the only close person I had." One of her earliest memories was that they used to walk in the field together, and she used to pick flowers for him. He always told her, "Don't let your mother run your life. You should do what you think is best for you." She looked upon him as a substitute father, but a father who had a high opinion of her. To me, the structure of the triangular oedipal situation is of a specific kind.

In response to Dr. Nemiah's comment, perhaps there are counterdependent defenses, but I don't think there is any evidence of separation anxiety, and in my opinion there is a more oedipal type of anxiety.

Regarding the questions about evaluation and therapy, in terms of evaluation I think we should do away with the misconception that we evaluate a patient only with respect to short-term dynamic psychotherapy. I agree that this is one of our goals, but our prime responsibility is to evaluate the patient and come to a decision as to what kind of therapy is the treatment of choice for each individual patient.

Regarding the question of style of the interview, one has to decide what are the most important issues in a given interview.

Regarding the choice of marital or family therapy, I would assume family therapy could also be used with this patient, but in this particular patient I was very concerned about her neurotic need to see herself the victim, and about her repeating in her relationship with her husband as well as with the larger circle of family and friends the same pattern she experienced in her early years. She took a masochistic pattern of life similar to that of her mother. To me, this passive, submissive pattern in her interpersonal relationship had spread into the total area of her human relationships. This was with her mother-in-law, brother-in-law, sister-in-law. So, this self-punishing, self-defeating pattern of behavior was evident in many other relationships. My general procedure in such a clinical situation is to not decide on family therapy immediately, and with this specific patient I decided to take her into treatment and to watch and see if her husband was going to accommodate the changes that I expected the therapy might bring. Her daughter, who irritates her very much, is a very assertive girl and maintains a very firm boundary for herself; she does not allow herself to be pushed by her father. The patient expressed the feeling that she was very envious and jealous of her daughter, stated that when she was that age she was passive and compliant, and also said, "Now I am thirty-two years old and still I am a little child" and, with anger, "My eight-year-old daughter handles herself much better than I can."

In terms of her suitability for short-term dynamic psychotherapy, my answer is a categorical yes. A psychotherapeutic focus has been established. She related to me very well, and I scored her high in our criterion number 6, which has to do with human relationships. To me, she had a meaningful relationship with her grandfather. She also fulfilled our criterion number 7, having to do with affect. She is psychologically sophisticated, and she responded well to my interpretations, etc. Her motivation was good, and I thought she would do well in a longer form of short-term dynamic psychotherapy of twenty-five to thirty sessions.

Question from the floor:

I would like to ask Dr. Davanloo if, unlike Dr. Sifneos, he would be prepared to select a focus other than a triangular oedipal conflict for use in short-term dynamic psychotherapy.

Dr. Davanloo:

Definitely so. As I said earlier, our time limit is two to forty sessions. What I can say is that in a period of twelve years of research we have evaluated 575 patients, and 115 were treated successfully. Approximately one-third of them would fall into the category of Dr. Sifneos' clear triangular oedipal conflict, and the average length of treatment for that category of patients was twelve sessions. The rest of the patients in this research were treated in from fifteen to forty sessions. We have many cases with total characterological changes in this group, and an example is "The Case of the Cement-Mixer Man" [Chapter 17].

Question from the floor:

First, I was very impressed with Dr. Davanloo's interview style. I thought he was able to combine being open-ended and at the same time empathic, which facilitated getting a lot of information from the patient. He was flexible and highly confronting. When she says, "I feel stupid, ugly, fat and ridiculous," he says, "And what about your strengths while you faced all these difficult situations in Vancouver?"

To some degree I feel constrained by the fact that I didn't see the other part of the interview, so I am in a sense flying blind, but I would like to make some comments concerning the ability of the patient for short-term dynamic psychotherapy. I had a lot of doubts about this particular patient for short-term dynamic psychotherapy in comparison with "The Case of the Italian Housewife" [Chapter 6] and "The Case of the Secretary with the Violent Father" [Chapter 7], whom I would be much more comfortable taking into this type of therapy.

Although I feel the majority of criteria were satisfied, I have some questions, particularly about motivation. For example, if the particular focal conflict is primarily an issue involving masochism, I wonder if the patient would really be able to move into an exploration of that issue and attempt to change it.

Dr. Nemiah:

I think there is a very great deal of emphasis on assets in the criteria when we are looking at the ego strengths—in other words, the capacity to relate, to tolerate emotions, to get distance on oneself—and these are the kinds of things that determine positively that the patient is a good candidate for therapy. One has to look also at the pathological side of things, particularly in two ways. One, the nature of the patient's defenses. Are the defenses projection or things that imply deeper pathology? Second, whether in these two rather sharply defined terms it's oedipal or pre-oedipal, because these determine how effective a short-term process is going to be. But there is a great deal of emphasis on assets implicit in the criteria.

Dr. Davanloo:

It seems to me that the limits of short-term dynamic psychotherapy have not been explored fully. I thought that by showing you ten to fifteen minutes of vignettes of the psychotherapeutic process of this patient, it might demonstrate that one is able to bring about characterological changes within a limited time. This is a transcript of some of the vignettes of the process of the therapy of the patient that was discussed in detail.

Vignette of the 20th Session

Th: Then you used to talk about your annoyance and disappointment. Now, somehow, today you are talking about your annoyance with the doctor. What sort of ideas come into your mind? Do you know what I mean?

Pt: Yes. It's progression in a transference of my annoyance.

Th: Do you like to talk about this progression in the transference?

Pt: Well, I would be inclined to say that I was transferring my annoyance from my husband to the doctor, but that's not true because I'm annoyed with my husband.

Th: But you don't talk about that?

Pt: That's not today. That was yesterday. Every day I have something different to be annoyed about. No, that's not really true, either. For quite some time I have been feeling so much better. I felt energetic, I felt optimistic, I felt reasonably happy and content, and I felt like my problems are working out. My emotional problems are being worked out.

Th: What specifically have you in mind when you say your emotional problems are working out?

Pt: Well, I told you when I started coming to you last January I was really suicidal. I had no desire to face the next day. Every night when I went to bed, I just hoped I would die quietly during the night and I wouldn't have to wake up and face the next morning.

Th: What you are saying is that in relationship with everybody there was a need to please them, and in a way to comply and go along with them. With every relationship? Are you saying that this happened in every relationship?

Pt: I think so.

Th: Do you think that happened in relationship with me here in any way?

Pt: Well, I don't know. Our relationship is very complicated.

Th: Well, you said you tried to please everybody and you try to comply and . . .

Pt: Well, probably yes. But when I first came to you I was really so desperate. Yes, I think so, because I was so desperate for help, and I thought the more I could do the way you wanted me to do it the faster I would improve, and I never knew what it was you wanted me to do because you never said anything, and I would think, What can I do now? I never knew which direction to go in.

Th: You are saying that you were looking for me to give you direction?

Pt: Yes.

Th: And do you think you got the direction from me?

Pt: Oh, yes.

Th: In what way?

Pt: In very small ways. But for you to say—when I would talk and you would say, "Well, you have to look at this, or you have to examine that." Sometimes it was something that I would never have looked at, and other times I would say such foolish things, and you would immediately—as soon as it was out of my mouth I would know how foolish it was—and you would just sort of look at me, and I would decide, Well, this is silly to try and keep up. I would just natter away. I had to try and find out what it is that I need, and you were obviously here not as a teacher, which was the relationship I expected, but more as a guide, I guess. Somebody to say, "Why don't you try this direction?" so I would try that direction, and sometimes it didn't work out . . .

Th: But did I tell you at any time what direction? You said you expected that I be a teacher, but later on you expected that I would become a guide.

Pt: A guide in the sense of sometimes when I was completely off the track you would say, "Let's look at something you said five minutes ago or last week." Now, that is not taking me by the hand and saying we have to go in this direction, but it's like saying, "Look at this ninety-degree angle," instead of letting me wander around more or less aimlessly. You have given me more of a direction, but not really sort of saying, "Look, we have to go off this way." You have never done that.

Th: So then, in a way you are the one that you...

Pt: Well, I feel generally much more competent in dealing with things that I have to deal with, just my day-to-day life. Before, there have been times when I honestly was not able to go to the supermarket because I knew it would be such a bad experience. I was so convinced that something would happen that I wouldn't be able to deal with, it just upset me even too much to go. Well, that doesn't happen any more, and I can give you an example of the way it was before, as far as not becoming depressed after giving an opinion or taking a stand. It's more taking a stand than giving an opinion, I think. When I say that I feel more competent and more sure of myself, I think what I am actually saying is that I am coming around to accept myself as a good person.

Th: You couldn't look at it, but you were standing by and trying to watch...

Vignette of the 25th Session (1)

Pt: The whole direction is so enormous, and it has so much connotation. There are so many ramifications that it is impossible for me to discuss. Because it is an internal force, and it does have to be directed, and it does have to be channeled, and I feel now that I am beginning to learn a little bit about how to do it, but the whole concept that it's really possible to do is what is so fantastic for me.

Th: You mean the fact that you could master it?

Pt: Yes, and he calls me. He says he's not being possessive. He says he's interested, but I call it possessiveness. Anyway, we used to have lunch together quite often because he wanted to. He would say, "I will meet you at such and such a time for lunch today," and I would go along with it. Well, I don't any more. I just tell him, "No, I don't want to meet you today. I have other things I want to do." So he says, "All right. I'll see you when we get home."
So he is not bugging me about that, and it was a source of great irritation to me. There are things that I wanted to do on my own,

and I didn't necessarily want him involved, and it seemed as though he wouldn't give me the time to do it. Like today he phoned me. My lunch is from 1:00–2:00 P.M., and he phoned me at 12:00, and he said, "I thought it would be nice if we would meet and have a coffee together or something," and I said, "No. I don't want to." He wanted to know what I was going to do, and I said, "Well, I don't know. I might go to Eaton's and I might look at upholstery material. I might stay right here in my office. I don't know what I am going to do."

Vignette of the 25th Session (2)

Th: This is what you did with your mother. She was always in charge of you, and you never took charge of yourself, and this is exactly over and over what you want to do with me. You don't want to take charge of yourself. You want me to be in charge, namely, to tell you what is what, in spite of the fact that you know very well what is what. Do you see what I mean? Let's go back again. In the relationship with your mother you never took charge.
In your relationship with your husband in the past you never took charge. In relationships with your mother-in-law you never took charge. In relationship with your brother-in-law you never took charge. It is in the last few months that from what you have told me you are taking charge. You are taking a stand. You are establishing a boundary, and then you stand firm. So your very early experience was that you always let your mother be in charge, and you repeatedly want to do this with me. Now, for us it is very important here to know why it is, in spite of the fact that you have answered these things, that you prefer that I answer. Because if you come to be the one, as you are, who has answered all these things, we have to terminate; you have taken charge of yourself, and we have to terminate. Isn't that so? Now, the question is how do you feel about that? How do you feel about coming?

(*Session continues.*)

Dr. Marmor:

It is important to ask Dr. Davanloo what he thinks were the therapeutic factors that brought about the changes in this patient.

Dr. Davanloo:

The treatment lasted for thirty-two sessions. She fulfilled all our dynamic criteria for the evaluation of the outcome in terms of self-esteem, in terms of radical changes in her problem of interpersonal relationships, giving up the masochistic pattern of relationships. Her relationship with her husband improved dramatically, and the relationship became a much more meaningful one.

In terms of the therapeutic factors, it is indeed a very difficult task to single out every therapeutic factor, be it specific or nonspecific. There was a rapid development of therapeutic alliance, and the first part of the therapy focused on mourning and grief over the death of her grandfather, and a few sessions focused on a piecemeal review of her memories of her life with her grandfather, which were associated with a great deal of abreaction. The transference remained positive, and the therapist represented her grandfather, who in a way wanted her to value herself highly. It became evident that she resented her mother greatly in the early years. She was her grandfather's favorite, and her mother was very resentful of this. As I mentioned before, there was a great deal of change in a positive direction with her husband, and this also spread into her relations with other people in her life orbit. She got herself a very good job and also started to pay a lot of attention to her clothes, spending money on herself, which she never did before. This temporarily mobilized a certain amount of anxiety in her husband, but I never felt any indication to intervene, and a new equilibrium slowly emerged.

Among the many therapeutic factors, both specific and nonspecific, one that I would consider of high importance is a repeated transference interpretation and linking it repeatedly with significant people in her life, namely, her husband, her mother-in-law, etc., and further linking it with her pattern of behavior with her mother and father, combined with active interpretation of the impulse component of these links, which were used repeatedly in the treatment of this patient.

Dr. Malan:

I would like to make a comment about this patient. In any single case, you can never say what the therapeutic factors were unless there has been some dramatic improvement in response to an identifiable event in the therapy. If you study a large series of cases statistically, you may be able to get an answer to this question. Now, in our two series of brief psychotherapy patients, we have shown that the more transference is related to the relation with important people in the patient's life, the more the patient is likely to get well. You saw an excellent example of this in those last vignettes where Dr. Davanloo said to the patient, "You've been complying with your mother-in-law; you complied with your mother; you complied with your husband, and you have been complying with me. He obviously was able to do this to a considerable degree, and on a number of occasions during the course of that therapy, and was able to work through that link. The statistical evidence suggests very strongly that that is the therapeutic factor in this kind of therapy.

Dr. Marmor:

Curiously enough, I think it takes more skill and more experience to be a good short-term dynamic psychotherapist than a long-term intensive one, and I think one of the reason residents who have been trained in the long-term intensive model don't do well is that they tend to follow the standard psychoanalytic model in their relationship to the patient, and they're quiet and relatively passive and neutral.

One noticeable thing about all the therapists in the audiovisual presentations is that they've all been very actively involved with the patient. Activity is enough itself; it is a very important psychotherapeutic element. Quite apart from its content, and I'm not minimizing its content, it also at an unconscious level constitutes giving. It is a reflection of the interest of the therapist in the patient, of his concern, of his willingness to participate in the changing of the patient. I believe that the interpersonal transaction that goes on between the therapist and the patient, the amount of warmth and empathy and genuineness that exists between them, is probably the most potent psycho-therapeutic factor of all. I don't think a cold, detached, impersonal therapist can be "ipso facto" a good short-term dynamic psychotherapist.

Dr. Eisenstein:

I, too, feel that it takes experience—long experience and skill—to do short-term dynamic psychotherapy, sometimes even more than for long-term therapy. The other aspect of the question is whether those trained in long-term psychotherapy—or I wonder if that's a euphemism for psychoanalysis; often it is—do not make as good therapists for brief psychotherapy. Well, I don't think this is the case. Most of us do short-term psychotherapy; not all our patients are psychoanalytic patients.

We may not see it as such, but we do take patients for a few weeks or a few months, maybe for a year, and I think the merit of this symposium lies in attempting to develop a methodology. Since we all do it, let's see how we can do it better, but at no time do I think this means shortening the training. It's only shortening the therapy of the patients.

Chapter 10

"The Case of the Secretary with Temper Tantrums"

D. H. MALAN

The patient is in her early twenties. She was brought to an emergency service by her boyfriend and was subsequently referred to the psychiatric clinic. She presented her major problems as having been depressed and having had difficulties in interpersonal relationships which were manifest specifically in her relationship with her boyfriend. She has frequent quarrels and temper tantrums with him. She said she is very, very jealous and that there is mobilization of a great deal of anger in her if her boyfriend even looks at another girl. She has a great deal of fear that he would prefer another girl to her. In spite of the fact that she knows this is irrational, she cannot control her temper tantrums. She said that her interpersonal relationship starts to deteriorate as soon as she starts to feel close to a man.

Th: I think you came into Casualty a few days ago. Is that right?
Pt: You mean at the other hospital? Yes, I went to Emergency.
Th: Will you tell me about that? What made that happen?
Pt: Well, the last few months I've been very depressed, and I started to have tantrums because I felt so burdened mentally, and I can't always control my anxieties and my problems. Unfortunately, the one who seems to be suffering the most from this, apart from

myself, is my boyfriend, since I see him most of the time. He's been having quite a bad spell with me, but he's been very patient and good. He brought me to the hospital and everything. I don't think I have the respect or the control. Perhaps if it was another person, just a friend or something, I would never do those types of things. Maybe I kind of take him for granted in a way. I feel that I can do this and get away with it.

Th: When you say "do those types of things," what do you mean?

Pt: I start to yell and throw things around the room. I get really in a fit.

Th: And do you hit him?

Pt: I have. I've hit him, for which he hits me back, and that makes everything stop. That happened a few times. It's always been all my fault, though.

Th: What do you hit him with?

Pt: Just me. I hit him.

Th: With your hands? Have you ever taken a weapon to him?

Pt: No, not a weapon. I feel destructive. For myself. I would feel like destroying me sometimes, too.

Th: I think I should ask you there what you mean by destroying you?

Pt: I feel like hurting myself. Sometimes I punch the wall or something like that. I just get so tense. I have to do something. It's not always like this, but it happened, and it could happen again.

Th: Did you ever hurt yourself badly?

Pt: Well, I've bruised myself or cut myself a little.

Th: On what?

Pt: I hit his car with my fist, and it was all swollen. I had different bruises on my arm and things like that.

Th: Have you ever actually cut yourself?

Pt: Just a little bit, nothing serious.

Th: I'm sorry, I meant deliberately cut yourself—with a razor blade or a knife.

Pt: No. I've threatened to though, but I suppose it's a form of attention-getting. I never did it actually, but I threatened to, so I guess it was just a way of saying, "Look what I'm going to do."

Th: You say you've been depressed. Have you felt like killing yourself?

Pt: Oh, yes. I don't know how far I would go. I guess everybody, even though they say it, is still scared inside to do it. Sometimes I just don't feel there is any more purpose for my being here.

Th: Have you ever made an attempt to kill yourself?
Pt: No, I've just spoken about it.
Th: You answered that as if you were slightly doubtful about it. Have you got somewhere near it?
Pt: No, not really. Do you mean near it as thinking of it or doing it?
Th: I meant near doing something.
Pt: Let's say I've done things like taking out a bottle of pills or taking out a knife or a razor blade, but I never used them. They were there, but I never did it alone. I always made sure there was somebody there to see me, I suppose to stop me.
Th: All right. I see that.
Pt: I told my boyfriend what I said to him before about if it wasn't him, it would be somebody else. It just seems to be that when I get involved with somebody on the outside, as far as the relationship goes just with friends, I appear to be very all right, I'm okay. I'm sociable and everything, but when I get involved I get upset. I'm afraid to lose this person, and I have a physical conflict myself.
Th: What do you mean?
Pt: Well, I'm very small and skinny, and I guess I've been aware of it ever since I was very young. When it comes time to be involved with somebody, I feel inferior mentally and physically toward other people. I demand, I expect too much of myself and I can't, so I can't cope with it, you see? I have goals in my head and try to reach them.
Th: I think you used the word obsession, and you gave me the impression that this kind of thing is on your mind the whole time. Is this right?
Pt: Yes, one thing or another, but always something. I always feel so much pressure in my head. I'm a real worrier and get nervous, and it's very hard for me to go a couple of hours without getting nervous. I'm not ever relaxed. I'm not ever comfortable with myself.
Th: So there is almost always some thought of that kind preoccupying you. Do you have times when you can be taken out of it by something? Do you have times when something good is happening so that you forget about it?
Pt: Yes. I would say when I speak to a friend of mine I always feel relieved somewhat—when I'm alone with my boyfriend, as long as there is nobody else around. When I'm in a situation where I feel I'm jeopardized, I feel that he's the world to me. He couldn't

possibly say anything to offend me. But it's not him, it's me, because I'm always on the defensive.

Th: So when the two of you are together, it's usually better? Is that right? Is it usually a third person who causes trouble?

Pt: No. It's always a third thing that causes trouble.

Th: Such as?

Pt: Such as a comment, a remark.

Th: By him?

Pt: Yes. I'm very, very jealous. I guess it would be normal if you would call it jealous, but I know it's not just jealousy. It's this inferior thing I have toward everybody.

Th: I think we should have some examples. Can you give me an example of such a third thing that would set you off?

Pt: Well, a picture makes me sick. A picture of another girl makes me sick.

Th: But what does he feel about the other girl?

Pt: Nothing.

Th: You mean a picture in the papers or something?

Pt: Yes, anything.

Th: And you've got the feeling that she is more attractive than you? Is that right? And that he would prefer her to you, and then this sets you off?

Pt: Oh, yes. Definitely. I know this may sound stupid to you, but especially in the last couple of months he's tried to tell me very honestly, and he's trying so hard to tell me that it's all in my mind and I have nothing to worry about. But I just can't accept it.

Th: Is it that kind of thing that has set off what you refer to as your tantrums?

Pt: Yes, a lot.

Th: Can you talk about the things that set them off, or can you perhaps give me a recent example of how it happens?

Pt: If I didn't think it was so stupid, I could talk.

Th: It isn't stupid. It's obviously a very deep feeling inside you, isn't it? There is nothing stupid about it. What is it that upsets you?

Pt: Trying to talk about it, I guess.

Th: Can you try just the same? This is obviously the center of your recent problems, isn't it, and I must know about it.

Pt: I feel very inferior. Even if I can't do something that he can do, like ski or something, it could ruin my whole day. I could be in the greatest mood, and it ruins my whole day because I expect too much of myself. I'm trying to be perfect, and I know that's impossible. I always think negatively. I think if I can't do something then it's going to be the end for me, only bad is going to become of it, and as for the other things I guess you could always call it the sexual things. I just feel so bad, like a mess. If he just looks at another girl or anything, I know I can't stop him from using his eyes. I know what I am doing is completely out of this world, but I can't help it. That's how I feel. I can't control it.

Th: So can you try and give an actual concrete example of how this situation developed between the two of you? A recent one. I want a situation where you were feeling all right, then something happened. I want to know the sequence of events that led finally to your starting to throw things. Can you tell me about them? Perhaps the best example would be to take—I expect there was something definite that made you go to the hospital, wasn't there? Can you tell me about that?

Pt: Yes. Well, this has been going on for a couple of days. It started on a Friday.

Th: You went to the hospital on which day?

Pt: Sunday morning.

Th: So it started on a Friday. Let's go back to then.

Pt: Something started the whole thing, but it's a sequence. Friday I went to the department store, and I was standing there, and this girl works there. My boyfriend was looking at her. With my head, I could make anything worse than it is. Sometimes I might even be imagining things, and I won't even know it. So this really made me angry. I was just standing there, and I felt so much anger and bitterness, and he went to use the telephone there. When I spotted that, I could have yelled at him in the store, and I wouldn't have cared about who was there, but I guess I did control myself a little bit. I was sitting there hard as a statue, if you know what I mean, and as soon as he walked out, well, that was it. I just started yelling and this and that.

Th: In the street?

Pt: In the car, and anybody could have heard. I wanted to get violent in the car, and I started ordering him around, and I got really superior from all this inferiority. I feel like a tower of power or something.

Th: Did you say you feel like a man?
Pt: No. I feel really superior, like I'm running the whole show. Nobody is going to say anything to me. Nobody is going to get in my way. So he just looks like "this big" when I'm like this, and he's right at my mercy practically, and I'll keep going until I want to stop. We went upstairs, and as soon as we got into the house he got a phone call from a friend, you see, and I had spoken to him earlier in the week that some friends of mine had invited us over there to spend the evening on Saturday night, but he got a phone call to go to a movie, a movie out of town, which we are both crazy about, and while he was on the phone he asked me if I wanted to go, and I felt very, very put on the spot. Immediately I remembered my friends who we were supposed to go and see, and that made me very upset.
Th: Had he forgotten about them, do you think?
Pt: He just kept saying that he didn't know what his plans were going to be, and the thing was, I think, that he told me later that he didn't feel like going to my friends', which he had told me about earlier, but he never really said no. He just said, "I don't really feel like sitting at your friends'. I feel like going out and doing something." So I said, "Maybe you're right." This was earlier, maybe a couple of days before. So when this came up, right away I felt the lower one of the two. I gave him such a dirty look while he was on the phone, as if to say, "How dare you ask me while your friend is still on the phone." I made it clear to him that he was to hang up, discuss it with me, and he would call him back. And that's what he did.
Th: You felt the lower one. Why?
Pt: I always feel that. I never can put myself on a par with him or above him. I always feel that he's trying to get me in some way, but I know that it's not true, but at the time...
Th: So you're trying to get him. This is the trouble, and you feel that he feels the same, is that right?
Pt: I don't understand what you mean by that.
Th: Well, you said that you felt that he was trying to get you, but the truth of it is that a lot of the time you're trying to get him. You're trying to make him feel inferior, isn't that right? So that when you feel that he's trying to make you feel inferior, you are really reading into him the same feelings that you've got yourself. Isn't that right?
Pt: I think so, but he never really tries to make me feel inferior.

He may talk like that, but that's just his way, and I can't change that. Like if he says, "Wow, you're really stupid," well, that can just ruin me, ruin my whole mood for that day. But I know that that has a lot to do with when I was younger. My father was like this all the time with me, and I could never do anything good enough. I always felt very, very inferior to my father, very much—really a lot. I always had to be pulling myself all the time.

Th: So you're obviously quite aware that some of the things you do with your boyfriend really belong to the relation with your father.

Pt: Yes. I hope I'm not fooling myself. I just think this has a lot to do with the way you're brought up. These things don't just happen, I don't think.

Th: All right now, can we leave that on one side for a moment? I shall want to come back to that, but I would still like to know what led up to Sunday.

Pt: I went back to the car, and finally I got over it, but that night with all those things happening, I didn't get over it. We stayed in the car talking all night. I drove home with a friend, and I didn't want to go home, and I felt troubled like always. I'm putting him in jeopardy because I'm making him suffer just as much, if not more. He loses practically as much sleep as I do.

Th: So you were talking about what?

Pt: Well, all those things.

Th: Yes, but were you talking in a helpful way or were you going on at each other?

Pt: No. Most of the time it was very helpful. It was very constructive.

Th: And how was it that you went to the hospital on Sunday morning?

Pt: Well, because I've been saying for a long time that I have to see somebody because I could actually feel myself going, losing all sense. I said it can only be so long that this can keep happening and I can get away with it, but I'm afraid that eventually I'm going to do something or I'm going to not come back.

Th: I see. So nothing more dramatic happened on Sunday morning that took you to the hospital. It was just the continuation of what was happening.

Pt: Yes. I just realized that I had to go now, and I didn't want to go back home. I had to go see somebody. In the morning, he drove me to the hospital, and he stayed with me the whole time until the afternoon.

Th: So that makes that clear. Now then, let's go back to what you were talking about earlier. You're obviously quite aware that a lot of this seems to come from your relation to your father. Is this right?

Pt: As long as I know I'm not fooling myself.

Th: I don't think you're fooling yourself. Anyhow, let's see. Will you tell me something about the relation with your father? You've already told me that this was giving you trouble at the age of fifteen, which made you seek help then.

Pt: Yes. It started even earlier than that.

Th: Yes, I'm sure it did. Let's go back to the beginning of your relation with your father. When you were really small, what do you remember?

Pt: When I was really small, I was very, very close to my father, his pride and joy. He was very proud of me, and everything.

Th: Now, can I just get this clear? You've got an older brother, three years older, and you have two brothers younger than you.

Pt: And my other sister is six.

Th: So in the early stages it was just your older brother and you?

Pt: Yes, and we were "black" and "white," you see? My older brother probably didn't agree with my father any more than I did, only he was the kind—"Yes, Dad. Yes, Dad, I'll do that." And he was exactly like my father would have liked to see everybody. But me, the old thing about the "black sheep in the family"— that's the way I was.

Th: But I think you're jumping ahead to your teenage time now.

Pt: When I was little, there was no problem.

Th: Will you tell me something about when you were little, and your relation with him then?

Pt: I remember being very close to him, and everything was fine. I don't remember any problems and that kind of thing. I'm talking about when I was very little.

Th: When you say "close," what do you mean by that word? What would you do together? What would he do with you?

Pt: Well, he used to take me out, and I used to go out a lot with him and my mother. I remember a lot of baby-sitters. I remember that. We would go skating. I was studying dancing right after school. I don't remember school days or that. It seemed all right.

Th: What about your mother at that time?

"THE CASE OF THE SECRETARY WITH TEMPER TANTRUMS"

Pt: I've always loved my mother. Not that I don't love my father; I do. But I just went through too much with my father. My mother was always the one to help me. If it wouldn't have been for her, God knows what would have happened.

Th: I'm still trying to talk about the early days.

Pt: I don't really remember that much about them. I remember weird things, like the layout of the house and that sort of thing. Details. I can't say to you right now all these things. I just remember things being nice when I was a little girl.

Th: And your parents were affectionate with you, were they?

Pt: Sort of. They're not the type that are all over you. They are warm in a very strange way.

Th: Strange how?

Pt: They don't really say their feelings.

Th: What about physically?

Pt: No.

Th: Do you remember being cuddled?

Pt: Not very much.

Th: Sitting on your father's knee?

Pt: A little.

Th: "A little" doesn't sound like very much.

(The patient starts to cry).

Th: Can you tell me what upset you then?

Pt: I don't know. I'm not sure.

Th: Well, it could be two things, you see. It could be that you do remember physical closeness and you've lost it, or it could be that you don't feel you ever had it and you're upset because you never did have it.

Pt: I'm not sure which one it is.

Th: It could be something else.

Pt: I think I had it sometimes. I don't remember it being all the time. Like I said, I don't really remember that much.

Th: You see, you were saying that you remember it as always being nice, but when I ask you questions about it, then you become upset. Now, this could be because it really was nice and what you're sad about is what you lost. But it could be because when I question you about it it wasn't quite as nice as you would like to feel.

Pt: I took my father's word a lot for it, too. He always said to me, "When you were little, you were this, and you were that."

Th: What is "this" and "that"?

Pt: All the trouble started when I grew up, and that kind of thing. I think maybe that's where that knowledge comes from, is his word. I'm not sure.

Th: Do you think that you don't remember much about it yourself?

Pt: Yeah, I don't.

Th: Can you cast your mind back and think what your earliest memories are?

(*Exploration into this area indicates*: *One of the patient's earliest memories was that she was very little in a crib and wearing diapers. Her older brother's bed was next to her crib. "I could remember my diaper was very wet, and I was crying and crying and crying, and they wouldn't hear me." She used to bang herself against the crib until it moved out into the hall so she could see if someone was coming to her. Then the therapist explores her relationship with her father to see when it started to go wrong. She says her father was overprotective and strict, and in that respect was "unbelievable." This was when she started to grow up and wanted to go out with friends. " 'Don't let me catch you doing this' and 'Don't let me catch you doing that.'" She "despised" it. She felt like yelling at him and talks with bitterness about this. He talked of "prostitution." The patient says, "I never did drugs, never became a whore." Then she says her father never gave her a chance to prove that she wasn't going to do that. She says her mother was afraid of her father. Her father is an artist, a painter. He used to go out a lot with his wife, and the patient was left to baby-sit. She felt lonely and used to make a lot of telephone calls to talk with friends. Her mother warned her that her father would be furious. There was an episode when there was a big hassle over a long-distance call she had made.*)

Pt: He came home and started yelling at me, and I said, "I didn't know that to dial 1 meant it was long-distance." He didn't believe me, started banging the plates on the table. It ended up with him cutting the phone wires. He said he was going to put an end to this phone once and for all. He went and got a pair of scissors and cut the phone wires, and he said, "I know you." And this is what did it. He said, "Lately you've been getting phone calls." My father lies, you see. I knew he lies when he's upset. He has to blame somebody. He's the type of person

that to prove his point, he'll lie black to make me feel worse. He said to me, "I think that explains all the strange phone bills we've been getting." I knew that I did not make any more phone calls. If anything, it was this time with the one phone call, but that was it. "So now that explains it," he said. "So you're the culprit for that, too. It's you." And I said, "No, its not me." He said, "Yes, you have. I know you have." It just got to the point where I started yelling and said, "It's not me." Most of the time I used to keep it all in. I never used to say anything. I would take it. If he hit me, I would take it. If he said stop crying, I would stop crying. If he said cry, I would cry.
I was like a machine. Go to your room; I had to go to my room. Come back; I would come back. It was always like this, and there wasn't a week that went by that something didn't happen. Not one week. This particular time I remember I felt I was completely going out of my head with his accusations.
I was going to the police station.

Th: In order to do what?

Pt: To go and get some help, I guess. I never got there. My mother came after me. My mother felt very bad about it. I said, "Oh, please." I was shaking like a leaf, you know? I went back to the house. I went into my room. He didn't come and talk to me or anything.

Th: Was that one of the first times that you ever answered him back?

Pt: Yes, that was one of the times, and one time I hit him back.

Th: Did you?

Pt: Yes.

Th: What happened?

Pt: Well, he was leading me around. He used to not just slap me, he used to knock me on the floor. I used to hit my head. I was surprised I never ended up in the hospital. It was very weird, because I used to get hurt. My head used to fall on corners of the tables and things like that, very dangerous.

Th: Did he slap you or did he punch you?

Pt: Well, he used to slap me, but hard. It was slapping and throwing and knocking me down, not punching.

Th: You said you hit him back?

Pt: Oh, yes. I hit him back. I'll never forget that. I hit him right back in the stomach, but he didn't even budge because he's very big and I'm not. He's quite a big man, quite overweight.

I just didn't care. I punched him back, but I know it didn't do anything.

Th: What's the position between you now?

Pt: Well, it was like this until I was nineteen. Then I moved out, and that wasn't too nice. I was very scared of that, because I thought he was going to kill me, but he didn't. He lectured me, but he was actually quite nice about it. He said, "Now, I want you to feel welcome here, no matter what," but he said, "I know you hate me."

(*The patient again begins to cry.*)

Th: So, the trouble is that you don't really hate him, is that right?

Pt: Yes, I hate him.

Th: Why do you hate him?

Pt: I was always too sensitive for my own good.

Th: So can you tell me again? Whenever I ask you what it is that makes you cry, you can never answer. What made you cry here?

Pt: I'll always remember that thing in particular. I was very proud of him, even after all the damage that he had done, for coming across. It was very strange, because he was lecturing me before I left. The same day I left, I was sitting in the kitchen, and he walked around the kitchen for two hours telling me this and that, that he'll kill my boyfriend because it was his fault. It wasn't my boyfriend's fault, but he always had to blame somebody. He said, "I know you hate me, but we'll see how much you love your mother because I bet you won't call." He was very wrong, because from that day on I used to call my mother every day, and I used to visit once a week and sleep over. I don't think too many people do that. I also felt guilty if I didn't do it, you see? Once it started, I couldn't not do it any more.

Th: You said, though, that you were proud of him. It wasn"t clear to me what you were proud of him about.

Pt: I was proud of him for being different. I never expected him to come and say to me, "No matter what, you're still my daughter and the door is open." I never expected that. I knew he felt very, very hurt because, unfortunately, my father has very many problems, too. He can't think like another person and say, "It's for her own good. She should go." Right away he feels hurt.

Then I'm sorry that he feels hurt. It's too bad that he feels hurt. I wish he didn't feel hurt. I always feel so sorry for him.

Th: How do you get on with him now? Is the situation a bit better or is it as bad as ever?

Pt: Well, it was marvelous. After moving out, I moved back with them when they went to Halifax. He was in heaven. He was so happy to have me there, and he was taking me all over the place. It was very beautiful for my father, and it was the first time in all those years that we felt close. As soon as I came back here and started going out with my boyfriend again and coming home late, that was finished.

Th: He was furious about your relationship with your boyfriend, was he?

Pt: Because of the way it is, but the trouble is that we just can't get married right now.

Th: What happens sexually?

Pt: What do you mean?

Th: Well, let's start with your boyfriend. What's your sexual relation like?

Pt: Very good. Very, very good.

Th: And it's good even when you're fighting?

Pt: What do you mean?

Th: There are some people who can fight all day and have sex at night and it's still okay. Is this the trend with you?

Pt: Yes.

Th: So you don't feel that you have any difficulties sexually?

Pt: No, except for the fact that I'm always aware of my physical appearance. I seem to overcome that in the act. If I don't expect anything to happen to me, well, that's it, I'm leaving. I don't get to that point, but it's on my mind.

Th: Now, how does he make love to you? Does he make love to you forcefully? Gently?

Pt: Gently.

Th: And do you like that?

Pt: Yes. I have not one complaint. Not one.

Th: Do you like it if he is forceful?

Pt: Sometimes, a little bit, I do. But I wouldn't want that all the time.

Th: Do you like to be hurt?

Pt: No.

Th: Some women do, you know.
Pt: I know. I don't like to be hurt. I'm sensitive. I wouldn't like that.
Th: Do you have fears in certain situations?
Pt: Do I have fears? Like, do I have certain fears?
Th: Yes.
Pt: One very big fear I have is snakes.
Th: How badly does it affect you?
Pt: To the point where I dream about it. I have nightmares about it, that I can't get out of bed because they're all over the floor.
Th: Does this prevent you from going places where you might find snakes?
Pt: Yes. I'm terrible with that. I'll give you an example. I remember going about five years ago to a lake with my parents, and it was like a safari-type thing there. I made my parents check every closed cage that was there before I went because I just don't want to see them.
Th: Does it prevent you from walking in the country because there might be snakes around?
Pt: I'd go, but the whole time I would think about it. And when it rains you should see me with the worms. I get paranoid when it's dark out. I strain my eyes so I don't step on one.
Th: Are you even afraid that you might see them where you couldn't possibly see them—for instance, in the snow in wintertime?
Pt: Yes, I think of it. In fact, I thought about it just the other day. If I look at a book, I throw it down if I see snakes. Before, I couldn't even see the word on a page. I can do it now, but I still can't look at a picture of one. The damage that it did to me was the fact that, unfortunately, all these kinds of things affect my eating, and stupidly enough I used to have periods where I would be starving and I would sit at the table and as soon as I would go to eat I would think about it. But it's me.
Th: You would think of snakes?
Pt: Yes, and I couldn't eat any more.
Th: All right. I'd better ask you about eating. Have you ever been through a long period where you ate hardly anything at all and lost a lot of weight?

(*The therapist explores the patient's weight, eating habits and menstrual history to rule out anorexia. He further explores her self-defeating pattern of interpersonal relationships, and more specifically the neurotic pattern of her relationship with her boyfriend.*)

Dr. Brown:

Even though we saw forty-five minutes of video material, I believe all that we saw was not all that occurred in the actual interview. What we heard about the boyfriend in this tape was that he always felt put down by his mother. It seems her boyfriend must also perceive the patient as a very up-and-down kind of person, so the irony of self-defeating repetition in human relationships is replayed in the last moment of the tape. It brings me back to my own preoccupation with how important it is to see people together in order to help them recognize how they may be repeating their own individual past through their current relationship with each other. This can be a first step in crystallizing motivation for therapy. It need not substitute for individual therapy. Once again, back to comments about the patient who appears so well motivated, as in "The Case of the College Student" or this young lady today. It might seem there is no particular need for action on our clinical part to increase motivation in such cases. But I nevertheless find myself thinking that to see this young woman with her boyfriend would clarify for them what each of them might hope to gain from her therapy. Again, I apologize for bringing in another set of concepts from those that are the major intention in this presentation, but I can't help but do so. Especially upon hearing that last little remark about her boyfriend and realizing how that relationship reenforces her neurosis.

As a general comment, I would like to say that the impact of this interview is different for me from "The Case of the College Student." What I experienced then was the very structuring style used by Dr. Sifneos with the associated tendency toward early categorizations of the patient's experiences and points of view. In the present interview there seemed to be more exploration of certain experiences that the patient recounted. Perhaps this difference was simply a function of the length of the interview. As Dr. Malan said, it went on for ninety minutes. In ninety minutes one can dip into actual experiences and not just stay at the level of categorizations, as we perceived in the shorter interview by Dr. Sifneos. The question then arises as to which approach is more valuable for defining the basis for brief psychodynamic therapy. Is it more valuable to start the process off with this longer preliminary interview in which a considerable amount of content of past experience is reviewed or is it better to use the briefer interview in which cognitive categorizations are made and regressive emotions avoided?

What I thought I understood from this videotape today was that the patient lost self-control in the department store and that once she and her boyfriend got out into the car she then began to scream. It was because she saw her boyfriend look at another girl in the department store that she became so distressed. This was consistent with the point she had been making about her inordinate jealousy and her tendency to experience enormous inner disruption the moment she saw her boyfriend look at another girl or a picture of another girl or anything like that. When that first emerged in the beginning of the interview, it alerted me to the possibility that she is a person with very diffuse ego boundaries who can't tell at a given moment whether a projection is occurring. In other words, if her boyfriend looks at a picture of another woman, does that mean she herself simply dissolves in her own separate existence? Is she only an extension of him and subject to sudden erasure? Does she lose the boundaries of herself so easily? It appeared that way at the beginning of the interview. As the interview progressed, however, it seemed less like a problem of ego boundaries and much more a problem of what causes her to lose inner control. The loss of control within herself is of crucial importance for brief psychotherapy.

A little bit further into the session came a question which was a first tentative interpretation by Dr. Malan. The question was, Who's out to get whom? When she said she feels at times that her boyfriend is trying to put her down or get at her or do something to her, Dr. Malan suggested that maybe it's she who wants to do that to him. So Dr. Malan picked up a projective dynamism at that moment, and she seemed to be able to accept that.

I noticed that she was leaning forward in a kind of mutuality with Dr. Malan, and it was a little after this that he raised the question of affection early in life. She was somewhat resistant to pursuing this, couldn't quite get into her early life, and it took a certain amount of energy from Dr. Malan to move in that direction. Then came the memory of her being in her bed and crying but getting no response from her parents. I thought that was a very important piece of information. More material and then came the question of her father being "overprotective" of her. She said he had his "eyes down" all the time, meaning he was always looking at the sexual and the dark and the bad in her. He "never gave me a chance," she said. Following, then, was her very vivid description of how incapable her mother was of buffering between her and her father. Her mother entered into a regressive state with her, became a little girl with her and in effect said, "Oh, my goodness, my goodness! What will we do? What about the telephone? He will be angry at us." So the father became a frightening ogre. The mother became a child along with the patient and in that way the patient lost her mother. In effect, she lost a parental mother and gained a frightened sister.

This brings us back to the discussion about what is oedipal and what is pre-oedipal in the origins of a patient's problems. We can see that in this instance the patient lost her mother as a parenting person. Thus the oedipal triangle became distorted in that degree—but it does not necessarily mean she was deprived of pre-oedipal affection or nurturing. I would like to by-pass the either/or speculation about what is oedipal and what is pre-oedipal and instead explore an area of interest regarding clinical technique. While observing the interview, I found myself preoccupied with the realization that this young woman who talks about feeling inferior and has outbursts in order to get attention and has to disrupt situations in order to feel noticed lives in a world of psychic fantasy in which she believes that she makes no impact on those who are of central importance to her. In order to make an impact she feels compelled to create an enormous scene. The datum in support of that is her idea that her father never knew who she was.

Her father imposed upon her his own fixed ideas about her sexuality, about her "badness," her potential for becoming a "whore," a "drug addict," etc. She did not exist in his mind as an independent and real person. Her screen memory of herself is of a little girl crying out and not being heard, calling to her mother for protection only to find her mother doesn't protect, reaching to her father but finding that the only way to reach him is through combat, and then being with a boyfriend who at any moment might not keep her in mind and might look at other people or women. Thus she feels no control over what goes on between her and others and specifically no impact on their thinking about her. I believe that if I were to undertake therapy with her I would want to attempt to show her early on that this is a central preoccupation and anxiety of hers and that it affects her behavioral adaptations to others and would inevitably affect her relationship with me. It is this theme that might be addressed productively rather than focusing upon pre-oedipal deprivations of affection from her mother or her father which can only be speculative.

Dr. Moll:

I was particularly struck at a certain point during the session by the flow of communication coming from the patient to Dr. Malan and from Dr. Malan to the patient. Now, I thought that was quite remarkable. We're talking about transference, and then, of course, we also have to talk about countertransference. This took place just about one-third of the time in the interview; then somehow it disappeared. I told myself I would have to study the tape again because I can't answer the question as to why it did disappear. I think it was largely due to the fact that the motivation in seeing this patient on the part of Dr. Malan was really to determine whether the patient was suitable for short-term dynamic psychotherapy, and I think we must not forget whether the first initial interview is one of evaluation or one of therapy. Well, obviously therapy takes place even in the first interview, and this was very well shown in this one.

The other problem that emerges is to what extent is the therapist influenced by the time element? In other words, if he decides that he's going to see the patient for forty-five minutes, will that to some extent affect his interview, the questioning ability, the interpretation ability, and so on, as opposed to the individual who gives himself one hundred minutes?

In fact, I would think that even though the aim was to determine whether the patient was suitable for short-term psychotherapy, the approach was quite different, though somehow "The Case of the Italian Housewife" and this patient became somewhat similar, which is rather interesting. Thus it is the focusing on the oedipal situation that brings out similarities between the two patients, even though the two patients are quite different—and I would suggest just as different as the two therapists. In "The Case of the Italian Housewife," the focus was on the oedipal situation in spite of the fact that the patient right in the beginning of the interview demonstrated some very clear-cut oral tendencies and oral pathology, a love for food, and said, "I was a very demanding child." Then we come to this patient today, and again at a certain juncture we have what appear to be certain oral aspects. I'm just wondering whether in this structure of constantly focusing on the oedipal situation we are not running the risk of missing a lot of other pathological findings that we perhaps ought to bear in mind in dealing with a patient.

I can't help, as an analyst, being perhaps much more passive in allowing things to grow and perhaps allowing the patient to take the lead, in order to attempt to get a feeling with the patient. I become somewhat concerned when a patient is approached with a predetermined oedipal focus which at times appears to be somewhat rigid in the sense of omitting all sorts of other things—at what might appear on the surface as a bit of oversimplification. It's so easy to give interpretations according to a certain set of tenets if we firmly believe in them, and it's so easy to jump to conclusions. Even the question of the patient's crying and the parents' not listening. Was she not telling the same thing to the therapist? There was a time in the session when she wanted, in all her low self-esteem, to tell the therapist that she wasn't so bad.

In terms of her suitability for short-term dynamic psychotherapy, she might be suitable for short-term dynamic psychotherapy of the longer form, perhaps the upper limit of forty sessions. Indeed, I go all out and say that she's not suitable for the briefer form of short-term dynamic psychotherapy.

Question from the floor:

What did Dr. Malan think of the possibility of anorexia nervosa? If anorexia nervosa is a part of the dynamic picture, what are the indications of short-term versus long-term psychotherapy in such a case?

Dr. Malan:

I questioned her: "What about your periods?" The answer was that she had never missed her period for any length of time. She might have missed a month here and there, but that was all, and I didn't inquire further because I felt that was sufficient evidence. Obviously, she is somewhere in the direction of an anorexia nervosa, but I felt that it wasn't sufficiently serious to consider her as a potential case of anorexia nervosa. At the same time, her starving herself has to be taken into account in the overall picture. I would like to say this patient was not presented because she's obviously suitable for short-term psychotherapy; she was selected because she was likely to lead to an interesting discussion. But back to the question about anorexia nervosa, it's a very controversial subject, isn't it, and there are degrees of severity, from the patient who really starves herself to the point where she is in danger of dying to the patient who just diets a bit but happens to lose her periods.

We recently took on a patient who seemed to have a very clear-cut oedipal problem. Because of the clear-cut oedipal pathology we thought she would do well. There was a history of having dieted and having got down to a low weight and never having a period for the last three years. This patient, in fact, had a very lively therapy, but it was a failure and she is now in long-term therapy. I give you that as a piece of experience.

Question from the floor:

How does the severity of negative self-esteem affect the decision for suitability for short-term dynamic psychotherapy?

Dr. Malan:

I wouldn't worry about it specifically. I would take that into account in conjunction with all the other phenomena she showed. If her depressive attacks had been worse than they were, then I would have felt very chary about selecting her for brief therapy. I'm not saying I don't feel chary about this patient as she is. I wouldn't worry specifically about the negative self-esteem. What one needs is to understand the patient's pathology, and then the next question is, Do you think you can deal with this in short-term therapy?

Dr. Moll:

There is a lot of lack of self-esteem; she considers herself stupid and so on. This became very apparent, and I think this is the only way we can prove the existence of certain things—if they become apparent in the transference relationship. In her relationship with her boyfriend, at a certain point she felt she was stupid, and then she asked for a cigarette and so on. There is no doubt in my mind that this patient really has a low self-esteem, yet I agree that this is not a contraindication to short-term psychotherapy since if you consider the case, the reversal, the turning of hostility onto herself has never been complete. There is a certain amount of hostility toward herself, but there has been no real suicidal attempt, and, if anything, there is still all this aggression directed outwardly. She punched the car or wall with her fist, and that sort of thing. Nevertheless, the whole picture to me is still one of an individual who is able to externalize her aggression and not internalize it entirely.

Dr. Davanloo:

It seems to me that there has been a great deal of preoccupation with this patient's self-esteem. Dr. Brown mentioned her jealousy re her boyfriend and raised the question of disturbances of the ego boundary. In my opinion, the ego boundary inadequacy—or, for that matter, ego boundary pathology—of this patient is more of a neurotic type, and we have no data to indicate that she is suffering from a borderline personality. About the problem of self-esteem, it would be of crucial importance that we differentiate between the genital and the pregenital kind of problem, keeping in mind that they overlap a great deal. If the self-esteem of this patient is related to disturbances at the pregenital level and we say that there is some developmental failure, then obviously this patient is not a candidate for short-term therapy. But if this patient's self-esteem—"I am inadequate; I am inferior"—is related to problems at the triangular oedipal level, then we are dealing with a different clinical entity.

It would appear from the clinical data that Dr. Malan showed us that the problem of the self-esteem of this girl is not related to the pregenital, and I see it more at the oedipal level. While I watched the interview, something that passed through my mind was: Could this problem of self-esteem, feelings of inferiority and inadequacy in relation to men, have a defensive function in relation to oedipal problems?

From the interview I gathered that she had quite a good early relationship with her father, which is basically something in her favor. We have an indication of her father's jealousy about his daughter's relations with other men. She said she had a close relation with her father, but when she reached puberty major problems with her father started. In spite of the pathology, there are a lot of healthy aspects in this patient. Does she fulfill the criteria for short-term dynamic psychotherapy? In my opinion, she fulfills some of them. I don't consider her a candidate for the briefer form of short-term dynamic psychotherapy, but she might very likely respond well to a longer form of short-term dynamic psychotherapy of about thirty-five to forty sessions. Her current problem in her relationship with men might well be a defense against oedipal problems. She responded to Dr. Malan's interpretation, and she also made a link between her father and her boyfriend, who becomes so preoccupied with her feelings of insufficiency and inadequacy that she plays with it and sexualizes it and monkeys around with it, and it becomes a very impenetrable fantasy system in which she clings to the idea "I am of no value."

The issue of self-esteem puzzles me often. Could one use the term "erotization" of lowered self-esteem? I refer to the kind of person who becomes so preoccupied with feelings of insufficiency and inadequacy that he or she plays with it, sexualizes it, obsesses about it and structures a relatively inpenetrable fantasy system which elaborates the motive "I am of no value."

In this case of short-term dynamic psychotherapy, how can the patient's feeling of low self-esteem be raised to an operational level of exchange between her and the therapist, essentially within the transference? When this woman enters into a relationship and says, "I feel inferior; I feel inadequate," what is she really saying at a transactional level? I think she is saying, "I feel I am not heard; I feel that I make no impact; I feel that I am the child crying across the hall and not responded to; I feel that I cannot make a substantial impact on another person." Then out of this comes the sense of lowered self-esteem. Therefore, I am less concerned with the lowered self-esteem and more concerned with the process that goes on between her and others. In this process she ends up feeling that she cannot make a sufficient impact on the other person and that she can be disregarded or discarded. The very interaction between her and the therapist should awaken in her the realization that she does indeed have an impact. It is this process of interaction that is therapeutic, I believe.

Dr. Nemiah:

It seems to me that the crucial question that was asked was what is the pathology and what is the root of the lower self-esteem? I would be inclined to see it in the same way as discussed by Dr. Davanloo; namely, the distinction between oedipal and pre-oedipal becomes very important. I would say that perhaps it is not possible from what we have seen so far to be absolutely certain, although my hunch is that this woman's problem of self-esteem falls into the category of being much more oedipal, particularly with her history of having been so close to her father as a little child that she blocks out when Dr. Malan tries to get her to talk about it. And perhaps the later relationship with the father in pushing him away and feeling inferior is a defense against a basic oedipal attachment to him.

Dr. Sifneos:

It seems to me that the information regarding this patient's relationship to her mother is crucial, which might clarify what Dr. Davanloo and Dr. Nemiah have just said in terms of evaluating whether the basic problem is on the pregenital level or on the oedipal level.

Dr. Malan:

There was a great deal about the mother. There was the early statement by the patient that she did not get any physical affection from her mother and that both her parents were strange in the way they expressed affection. Next there was the statement that her mother was always the one who protected her from her father, and there was the incident of the telephone call in which the mother got into a state of terror in relation to the father and, in fact, totally failed on this occasion—in spite of the patient's earlier statement that her mother protected her—to protect her from her father. There was then the statement that the father said to her, "We'll see how much you love your mother. I bet after you leave home, you'll never get in touch with her again," to which the patient said, "And he was wrong. I phoned my mother every day and I came to visit," and I think she said that lots of people wouldn't do this. She also said: "I felt guilty if I didn't."

Toward the end of the interview I asked her directly about her current relation with her mother. Her answer was somewhat neutral.

I said to her, "Can you talk to your mother? Can you talk to her about your problems?" And the answer to that was, "Yes, sometimes." "Can you talk to her about your boyfriend?" "Yes, sometimes." So that there was, in fact, a great deal of information about the relation with her mother in that interview.

I would like to say categorically that I did not miss anything about pre-oedipal problems in that interview. I was concerned with pre-oedipal problems for a great deal of the time, and this is why I pressed her for her memories of her early childhood. Her first memory was an extremely distressing one, it seems to me. You can interpret this as a three-person problem because the little girl was being neglected since the parents were together in their bedroom, but you know that's part of the truth. I think she had a memory about her mother somehow inadequately mothering her and the fact that she had to baby-sit. Her mother was interested in bingo so that she used to go out with the father and leave the patient to look after her younger siblings. Again that's a three-person situation, but it has two-person implications as well.

In the latter part of the interview I asked her specifically about what her depression was like and how it affected her. The bit about undereating is obviously about pre-oedipal material and I thought it was extremely important to get this information. I was worried that she was potentially anorexic, so it's not that anything pre-oedipal was missed in that interview; the point is that her current complaint is in relation to a man. It's in relation to feeling inferior to a man, and it's in relation to the struggle between her and a man, and she quite spontaneously made the link between the boyfriend and her father in response to the interpretation about projection which I gave her. I felt that that was one of the two most important points in the interview. It did show that in response to interpretation she could quite clearly unconsciously make a link.

Dr. Marmor:

Dr. Malan, would you want to tell us whether you think this patient was suitable for short-term therapy or not?

Dr. Malan:

In the original discussion I said no, but of course there's a focus. You don't want to be disturbed by the fact that she's polysymptomatic. You don't focus on symptoms in brief dynamic psychotherapy. You focus on pathology, and pathology may lead to a number of different symptoms. Or alternatively you can pick out from the pathology some crucial issue which you work through, leaving the others. Obviously, the one which seems to be most amenable to therapy is the link between this exceedingly pathological relation with her boyfriend and her feelings about her father, which I assume Dr. Davanloo would take as the focus.

Or you could take the very beautiful focus that Dr. Brown suggested about not being noticed, which, in fact, brings in the whole of her history. Regarding the question Is she paranoid? my answer is no. I'm extremely sensitive to this. There is nothing paranoid in this patient. She knew that she was overwhelmed by some uncontrollable feeling which she couldn't deal with. It wasn't paranoia in any way.

Chapter 11

"The Case of the Woman in the Tower of London"

P. E. SIFNEOS

The patient is in her early twenties and was initially seen at the psychiatric clinic. She complained of multiple phobias: fear of escalators, of ten years' duration, which started while she was visiting the Tower of London; fear of crowds and stairs, of two to three years' duration; fear of "being pulled down from the top of a flight of stairs." She has problems in the area of interpersonal relationships, especially heterosexual ones. Her present boyfriend is described as an undesirable character. Her parents are of Swedish origin, were brought up in England and then immigrated to Canada.

Th: What is the problem? Maybe we could start with that. What is the one thing that is bothering you the most?

Pt: Recently, in the past two or three months, I've been having this fear of being out on the street, and then it developed into being afraid of being at work—not all the time, just some days. Like, for instance, today and yesterday I haven't felt it at all, but sometimes it's so strong that I can barely stop myself from breaking out and running away.

Th: And did this fear come suddenly out of the blue or was there an episode that preceded it?

Pt: At around the age of eleven, I started to be afraid of escalators, so I avoided them. Then I started to be afraid of stairs about two years ago, so I avoided the stairs. Then, after I started to avoid the stairs, it seemed to get bigger. Then the same feeling I would get from being on top of a flight of stairs or an escalator I began to get from just being on the street.

Th: But there wasn't anything specific that precipitated it? Let's say, that gave you the fear of escalators, then stairs, or from stairs to places in the street, or at work now? Things like that?

Pt: No. It just seemed after a period of waiting one thing would frighten me, then another thing would come up.

Th: Are you worried more about stairs or escalators?

Pt: Oh, yes, of both.

(*The therapist explores the way patient deals with these fears, and the patient says she avoids them and doesn't fear elevators, which makes things possible for her. Then the therapist asks her what thoughts she has about the stairs. The patient expresses the fear of "being pulled down from the top of a flight of stairs" and says she might faint or her knees might buckle and she'd fall and cause a commotion.*)

Th: A commotion? What would happen? What do you see? You see yourself on top of the escalator, then you fall down, then there is a commotion. You may hurt yourself a little bit. Let's put it that way, that situation. What happens in a commotion? You see yourself as lying down on the floor?

Pt: I see myself being out of control, and it's like when you pass somebody who has had something happen to him on the street, and all of a sudden everyone crowds around and sort of seems to derive some sort of satisfaction at seeing someone incapacitated, I guess. That sort of bothers me.

Th: But there is a component of being the center of attention?

Pt: Yes.

Th: Incapacitated, surrounded by crowds and so forth, but let's come to that a little later on. For instance, is the same fear associated with work, the same thing might happen, which is no longer associated with the stairs?

Pt: Yes.

Th: And that has been going on for four or five months, you say?

Pt: No, two or three months since this feeling when I've been outside.

Th: Two or three months?

Pt: I used to get it before in a movie house or in a room with a large number of people, but never just on a continuing basis. Like, no matter where I was, even if I was eating my lunch alone in an office, I'd feel it. And I'd never had it that way before.

Th: Does this thing worry you? Do you feel you're going to get even more phobias?

Pt: It almost seems to me as if there is something trying to come out that I can't ignore. Something that is frightening me. No matter how much I avoid what it puts itself into, it only grows into something else. Like for the past couple of months, I didn't consider going to have any kind of help about it. I sort of thought that maybe in the long run, if things didn't get any better, I might want help, but I found myself under such a constant worry about it—to be sitting eight hours in a place where you're afraid to be, three days out of five. It just got to be a bit too pressing. That worries me.

Th: I understand. Let's hear something about your own background. How old are you?

(*During the data gathering, it emerges that the patient and her parents live in the same city. She has one sister, six or seven years older. Her earliest memory is of standing in a crib with her mother there, which is a pleasant memory. It becomes evident that the patient was close to her mother until grade school. Then this changed, and the patient said her mother always felt closer to very young children than to older children. Her brothers are older and married.*)

Th: Were you closer to your mother when you were quite young than to your father?

Pt: Yes.

Th: And what was your relationship to your father at that time?

Pt: I couldn't say that he was a distant person. It's just that when I was young he would be working and I'd go to bed quite early, And naturally I would see my mother more because she didn't work. He really started to take an interest in me when I was around ten and I was out of the house more, you know?

Th: So there was a kind of a change of the interaction with your parents in the beginning up until the age of around six or seven, when you were closer to your mother. And your father was not very much in the picture?

Pt: Not really.
Th: Then your mother was more interested in babies so was not as close to you as before.
Pt: No.
Th: But your father became interested in you.
Pt: Yes.
Th: And what about your sister, who is older than you?
Pt: I don't know. I'm very fond of my sister, but she doesn't reciprocate. I think that it took a lot off her when I was born in terms of attention and what have you. And it seems that even now when things seem to be on a pleasant level she'll twist things around.
Th: Are you saying that she might have been a bit jealous of you?
Pt: Oh, definitely.
Th: Then you're putting it in a kind of roundabout way?
Pt: Yes.
Th: Would we say, then, that what we said a minute ago is that you were your mother's favorite, clearly so?
Pt: Oh, definitely. Yes.
Th: And then you were your father's favorite?
Pt: No. My father never played favorites. He's always been very fair to both of us. He was equal in his treatment.
Th: But you would say that your mother was clearly—you were her favorite?
Pt: Oh, definitely.
Th: I see. How were you doing at school?

(*The therapist explores the patient's early schooling. She says she was smart but not necessarily a good student. She couldn't keep her attention on the class, looked out the window and was a bit of a daydreamer, which is gone into by the therapist. Then he explores to see if she had any close friends, and she says not when she was very young. She says her mother was overprotective with her, that when she was teased or criticized by other children she'd run home and her mother would go out and tell them off.*)

Th: She protected you?
Pt: Yes. She sort of alienated me from the other kids.
Th: Did you feel good about that?

Pt: Yes. I would have to say that probably I did.
Th: So you did not have many friends? Now, what about, let's say around the age of twelve, thirteen? How old were you when you had your first period?
Pt: That didn't happen until I was around fourteen.
Th: Fourteen? Were you prepared for that or not?
Pt: I wasn't prepared at all. I was afraid to tell my mother about it.
Th: Afraid? Why? You told me you had such a good relationship.
Pt: But not by then.
Th: I see!
Pt: I'd have to explain to you what happened in the two years I spent in England to understand what happened later.
Th: When you were ten you went to England, right?
Pt: Yes. We went there for two years. Now, originally my mother wanted to go back to England because she remembered it after the war, and she had enjoyed it there. So my father tried to get transferred back to England and he did. We went back there and my sister stayed here to continue her college. My mother had a nervous breakdown; it must have been that. I didn't know what it was then, but looking back on it now I think it must have been a nervous breakdown. She was terribly unhappy there and she went into this period of decay, where she sort of gave up doing anything. We would be sitting in the den and she'd be in tears, and she'd be hanging on to me and she'd be saying, "I'm going to leave your father. Go and tell him that I'm leaving him. Tell him that I'm going to divorce him." So my father would be in the kitchen and I would say to him, "Dad, Mommy said to tell you that she's leaving you," and he would ignore me, ignore what had been said and just continue. I'd go back and she'd say, "What did he say?" and I'd say that he didn't say anything at all, so she would get more and more upset. It was really an awful time for me because I had been put in a very strict school and I was very unhappy there. It was so highly competitive an atmosphere that I just couldn't cope. I'm not a competitive person. I'm more inclined—instead of wanting to be up there at the front, I'm more inclined to sink back in the face of any competition. That was the worst period of my childhood. After that, I'd never remembered my parents fighting before, although my sister has told me since that that my mother would sort of pull the same thing on her. My sister would be going out at night when she was a teenager, and

my mother would say, "Don't leave me alone with your father," which to us was kind of awful because he's such a calm and gentle individual. So it made us really resent her. The fact that she was singling us out like that and the fact that she was just clinging to us, to use us—it was like we were her tools for manipulating. That's when I got closer to my father, because my dad wanted to get me out of that atmosphere. On Sundays he'd take me off and we used to make things together, and we'd go and play with them. He sort of kept me, when he could, out of the house, because it was very, very depressing.

Th: Now, then you came back here?
Pt: Yes.
Th: And you were how old?
Pt: Twelve or thirteen.
Th: How were your high school years?
Pt: You see, there's always been something bothering me, and I think they were very much like I am now. In other words, I can remember having to leave class or lectures because of a feeling of acute nausea, and having to leave the room or put up my hand and say, "Could I leave?" So I think things that happen now that I think of—even since, say, the past ten years—have only been results of something that I felt uncomfortable about for ten years, like in various situations, which is something I never felt before that episode in England, and things after that would only intensify it. My mother became very critical of me when I was a teenager, and I don't know, even now when I go to visit—I don't live with them now—she'll say to my father, "Look at her. Wasn't she lovely when she was a little girl? Isn't it a shame that she had to grow up?" I get that at least twice when I visit them.
Th: Obviously this must be very difficult for you. But there must be something in you that indeed agrees with your mother, isn't there?
Pt: I guess so. I have very little confidence in myself.
Th: Well, can we then possibly say that your symptoms may have something to do with that? You see, the picture you described to me before was a child that is shy surrounded by children, the accent of your parents and so forth, and your mother protecting you. And I wonder, when your mother came to protect you, if the two of you had a very good relationship.

Pt: Oh, yes, definitely.
Th: We know that you became a more and more grown-up girl. Your mother later on makes the statement that you were so lovely when you were a little girl. Obviously, this being lovely, being a little girl, meant something—was communicating to you. And if you could remain a little girl and be protected in that particular way, then you would have this maternal love and affection. But what happened was that you grew up like everybody else, and then pretty soon the episode in England, which was a very difficult situation where the person, the blissful protector of yours, was now very upset and used you in a way and depended on you for her own health rather than you being able to depend on her. So you became closer to your father. Now, the question is, when was the first time that you remember being afraid of escalators and stairs?
Pt: It was in London when we had some friends to visit us, and we were going down into the tube and—no, wait a minute. Something just occurred to me just before I was afraid to go into the tube because of the escalators. We went to the Tower of London, and I remember I've always been a bit afraid of the macabre and that kind of thing, and it struck me as a very gloomy place and we had this other family with us. My mother wanted to show them the Tower.
Th: But you smiled when you thought of the Tower. Why?
Pt: Because something just connected with me. I'd forgotten this incident until now, and I remember I didn't want to go up the stairs, not because of the stairs, but because it was a great big place. I remember her getting furious with me and saying that if I didn't go I would be taking the enjoyment from the other people, and it was after that that I was afraid to go down into the tube.
Th: I see. So we have really now connected intimately your symptoms with your mother.
Pt: Yeah.
Th: Okay, let's leave it at that for just a minute. Did you have any close friends in high school?
Pt: Yes. When I came back from England. I've never really had crowds of friends, just mostly acquaintances. I've always had one or two very close friends.
Th: Do you still have them?
Pt: Oh, yes.

Th: Did you have any boyfriends at that time?
Pt: No, not until I was about fifteen or sixteen.
Th: Was there any boy that you were particularly close to?
Pt: Not really. Not in a very heavy way. Just a couple of months dating one particular person, but nothing that lasted more than, say, two or three months.
Th: I see. And you were quite a good student?
Pt: Oh, yes. I was above average.
Th: And what have you done since graduation?
Pt: I graduated from high school and I went to college. That was a very unhappy time for me. I guess being away from home. I guess you've pointed out being away from the protection. Then the year that I was there my father lost his job as a result of an accident, so I forgot about it for another year. I went to work in a drugstore and saved up some money, and then with that money I took a course and went to work in a bank. Then I left home, and that's what I've been doing for two years.
Th: Are you happy?
Pt: Yes.
Th: The symptoms are there. Now, let's try and get back to see whether these symptoms, peculiar as it may be and unpleasant as they might be, serve a purpose to you. Do they?
Pt: I've been thinking about that myself very recently because I've been trying to analyze my own situation, naturally. And it has occurred to me that it's a dandy way of getting attention. I hate to think of myself as being so weak.
Th: All right. Let's not judge yourself too harshly. Let's say that maybe the reason that would be the case is that there are certain things in a psychological life that follow this thing functioning on two levels: (1) certain things that take value, and (2) certain things that are somewhat hidden. But is it more attention-getting, like you said? When you described to me the possibility of what might happen, you talked about the crowds that would gather around you if you fell from the stairs.
Pt: That's not the part that I'm worried about, my wanting to get attention. The part I was worried about is wanting to get attention from those who are close to me. I guess I feel that I would have to rely on—say, if I was afraid to be in the street— people that would know that I was afraid to be in the street

and therefore maybe protect me. But I certainly don't want the kind of attention that I would get if something happened to me, if I fell down the stairs or collapsed on the street or something.
Th: Who are these people who might give you that attention?
Pt: My close friends, I guess.
Th: Close friends?
Pt: My boyfriend.
Th: You have a boyfriend?
Pt: Yes.
Th: Now, has that been a problem?
Pt: Having a boyfriend?
Th: No. No, his response to your symptoms.
Pt: Sometimes I feel as if I'm hemming him too close here.
Th: What about your own parents?
Pt: My parents know nothing of this at all.
Th: Not at all?
Pt: Nothing.
Th: That's interesting. Why?
Pt: I've always been in the habit of not telling them anything that went wrong in my life.
Th: Now, you say ever since you were a little girl and you had problems with the other children you would go to your mother, but since your mother's illness this has not been the case?
Ph: Yes. I've kept everything to myself since then.
Th: But why do you include your father in this?
Pt: Him? Primarily because I don't want to hurt him.
Th: That's interesting. It would hurt your father if he knew that his daughter had some problems, such as some fears or something like that?
Pt: I think so, yes.
Th: Why? Is he so intolerant?
Pt: No, it's not that he's intolerant. You see, what happened is that when we were in England my sister had a boyfriend and she ended up getting pregnant by him and she had to marry him and she had a child. This fellow that she married turned out to be the worst example of a good husband and father that you could ever meet. He never gave her money; he spent his money downtown; he was never home; he had other women, etc.

So my parents, ever since this happened to her, have been in a continual state of supporting her, giving her some kind of consolation. Even now that she's divorced, she'll run home when she has a problem with her boyfriend, and she'll appear at my mother's doorstep in tears, and they'll have to sit her down and she'll cough out all her problems to them. I feel what their reaction was when this happened to her back then, and I saw how, over the years, it kind of drained a lot from them, because she's an extremely attractive girl and I think they had a lot of hopes for a good life for her. So then it transferred a bit of a load on me because, for instance, my mother has said things to me like "If that ever happened to you it would kill your father." My mother sort of hammers it into me not to make a mess of my life. My dad's never insinuated that he would in any way be mad at me. I feel that's he had enough.

Th: But for all intents and purposes it keeps you away from your father, to whom you are very close?

Pt: Yes, but haven't you ever tried to keep things from a person that might upset him?

Th: Yes, indeed. But the fact is that there might be a part of you that does this because it is the appropriate thing to do, and therefore your not wanting to communicate some of your troubles to your father, on the one hand, makes very good sense. On the other hand, however, there might be another point of view, and that is that you do want to have a closeness with your father and this would be a way of having someone to turn to at a time of difficulty. After all, look at the attention that your sister gets. Negative attention, but she gets plenty of attention, doesn't she?

Pt: Yes.

Th: And you, being such a good girl, are isolated from your parents completely, particularly from your father.

Pt: I know that. But you see I just don't want to put my dad through anything more.

Th: I understand, and I'm not saying what you should or shouldn't do. What I'm saying is that on another level maybe these symptoms serve this kind of purpose.

Pt: You mean as an outlet? In other words, using this as an outlet for everything that I've kept to myself?

Th: If you were to be completely unconscious surrounded by the crowd, it might be that somebody would pick you up and take you to your father. Where does this girl live? Who are her parents? Let's take her there. Now, you're completely unconscious, you've fallen off the escalator or stairs. It isn't anything conscious that you're doing. You have not violated your mother's advice about being at home and being taken care of. You are thereby getting attention, and by somehow or other having your father worry about you. So you say to your mother, "I didn't do it on purpose. I fainted."

Pt: But why would I be so terrified of it, then?

Th: Because I think part of you is terrified that you might do this, and it would be completely in conflict with this notion that you just told me about being the good girl and being kept apart and having a good life and having your parents be proud of you, etc.

Pt: Only if this happened, then he would have to find out that there is something wrong?

Th: I'm not saying that this is what it is, you see, but what we are trying to do here, on the basis of what you are saying, is to try to disentangle a problem which obviously to you is difficult. But this problem is now interfering with your life.

Pt: Yes.

Th: And you are away from home. Where are your parents? Where are they living now?

Pt: They live out in the suburbs.

Th: So it's not very far away?

Pt: No.

Th: But your work is keeping you independent, right? Yet the symptoms are interfering with your independence?

Pt: Yes. It's interfering with what I consider to be a normal life, of being able to go out whenever I want to go out and so forth.

Th: I can see that, and it could be very unpleasant if you have to think all the time about what you're going to climb on or what street you may cross, and all these fears. Now, does your boyfriend understand this problem? What is his attitude about it?

(The therapist explores the patient's relationship with her boyfriend. He is unemployed. The patient prefers not to discuss him, but it is clear that he has many similarities to her sister's ex-husband. Then the therapist indicates that her sister, by virtue of her difficulties, has become the center of her parents' attention.)

Th: You see, psychologically speaking, we also know that on the basis of your past history you've been a shy girl who enjoyed very much being taken care of by your mother when you were a little girl—by your mother, who regrets your not being a little girl any more—and later on by your father when there was quite a rapprochement between the two of you because of the difficulty of your mother's illness in England. Now, the fact is that you've been isolated from your father by being a good girl, and by following your mother's advice.

Pt: Definitely. Because obviously the squeaky wheel gets the grease, and when my sister and I are in the same room it's my sister primarily who will have more to talk about since she is talking about her problems.

Th: If you could talk about your problems, and your problem now is the fear of stairs, escalators, open spaces, going to work, then you would get some attention. But you cannot do that because if you were to do that then you would be causing additional pain to your father. So your symptoms in a sense would be a way for you to get the attention that realistically you feel you shouldn't because you don't want to impose on your parents who already have enough problems with your sister.

Pt: But then would I not make my phobias known to my parents?

Th: Why would you?

Pt: If that was my way of seeking attention.

Th: The first thing that your mother would say is, "We have enough trouble with your sister and you are not going to worry your father with all this foolishness about your being afraid of stairs when he is already worried." Now, what does that mean?
It means that you are a bad girl. You see, first of all, your mother would be disapproving of you, and furthermore she would be cutting you off from your father. So, you are an exemplary person and I'm sure in the eyes of your parents you are doing fine. You have a job; you're doing well in contrast to your sister. You have no problems, and you are giving them no problems. So, in one sense, it satisfies your requirements on one level. On another level, it keeps you isolated from your parents.

Pt: Yes, definitely.

Th: Do you think there is something there? I'm intrigued that we were able to find one thing: that your symptoms about the stairs were intimately connected with your mother. This we have tied together. You remembered this a minute ago when you thought of the interesting episode at the Tower of London. Now, do you want to work on this as well as some of the other issues we discussed?

Do you want to pursue this work that we did here together, with a therapist from the clinic?
Pt: Yes, definitely.

Dr. Marmor:

I think this young lady will benefit from any dynamic psychotherapy she gets. If I were seeing this patient today based on the diagnosis of phobia, the first thing I would want to help her do is get over her symptoms as rapidly as possible. I don't think that insight-oriented therapy, on the basis of years of analytic experience, is the way we would do it, and I would recommend that this young lady be sent for behavior therapy first. Then if she wanted insight-oriented therapy, fine. That is just a comment, and it might be a very unfair one, but I want to address the overall concepts about the specific indications for short-term dynamic psychotherapy. If we review those patients whom we have seen so far, we see that by and large they fall into a common category. They are all young, attractive, verbal, intelligent and strong. We know from experience that these are the patients who respond most favorably, generally speaking, diagnosis apart, to almost any kind of psychotherapy. For years they were considered the most favorable patients for analytic therapy until we learned that they also respond equally well to short-term therapy and to behavior therapy and to a wide variety of other therapies. In general, then what are we saying?

If we look at Dr. Davanloo's concept of ego strengths, or, as I would prefer to call them, "ego adaptive capacities," we find that overall the healthier the patient is to begin with, the better the prognosis is going to be for short-term dynamic psychotherapy and probably for almost any other kind of psychotherapy. There is another criterion, however, that I would like to introduce in weighing the choice of short-term therapy versus long-term therapy. That is the reciprocal relationship between the ego adaptive capacities and life stresses. In general, the greater the life stress, the precipitating factor that has brought the patient to your office, the more favorable the prognosis and the more likely the patient is to respond to some kind of brief intervention—even, as G. Bibring indicated many years ago, to some form of environmental manipulation to reduce the external life stress.

On the other hand, where you have indications from your initial evaluative history that you are dealing with an individual whose ego adaptive capacities have been inadequate through most of his life and, who then decompensates with relatively little life stress, then you know you are in for a much more complicated long-term approach. We have been hearing generally about individuals who have had fairly adequate life-coping mechanisms and have been subjected to a significant precipitating life stress situation, and these individuals are going to respond to dynamic short-term interventions.

One of the other basic premises of this symposium is that by and large what's helping these patients is the insights that are being given to them, the interpretive comments. Now, I don't in any way minimize the value of these insights. I think they are helpful and clarifying. I only want to point out that there is a great deal more going on in the interpersonal relationship between the therapist and the patient besides a cognitive insight that the patient is getting. There is a warm interpersonal supportive relationship. The patient is releasing tension by being able to confide her story to a trusting and sympthetic person. There is a corrective emotional experience that the patient is getting, the way the therapist is responding not only verbally, but, as one patient very intelligently pointed out, even nonverbally. The expression in Dr. Davanloo's eyes every time she said something that didn't make sense—she was being guided by that. This is a kind of conditioning that is taking place, a kind of operant conditioning that tells the patient, that guides the patient, as to whether she is going too far off the beam. There are elements of identification with the therapist that are taking place with the therapist's values. There is persuasion and suggestion, a great deal of it in this last interview, even though it's been given under the guise of cognitive insight. And over a period of time, in the process of therapy, there is a good deal of rehearsal, testing oneself in a life situation.

In the context of the continuing emotional support of the therapist, I think it is well to remember that this is an important aspect of the total therapeutic situation and not get too caught up on the assumption that it is only our interpretive, cognitive insights that we're giving the patient that are curing him. After all, we do know that patients—this kind of patient particularly—will often respond equally quickly to emotive therapies and behavior therapies. We come back to another very basic principle in all of this.

By and large, one of the basic premises of the psychoanalytic orientation was that we should not focus on symptom relief. In terms of the closed system concept of the original psychoanalytic concepts, it was believed that if you merely removed the symptom without altering the internal dynamic balance that was going on within the personality, the disordered balance would simply shift to another system. But in terms of theory we know that you can remove a symptom and that the mere removal of that symptom will so alter the patient's feedback, both internally and externally, that basic character change can take place. This is one of the reasons short-term therapy works. I think that in Dr. Davanloo's dramatic "Case of the Teeth-Grinding Woman," even though people on the panel thought she was a candidate for long-term therapy, what he did fundamentally was enable her to assert herself more directly and more effectively. He dealt with a primary symptom that she had, which was an inability to assert herself. Changing that symptom brought about a change in the entire dynamic framework of her life situation and she began to think better of herself. She began to get more positive feedback from her environment and the result was—*presto*—a new and happier human being.

Dr. Nemiah:

I'd like to make one or two comments focused on the patient and one or two focused on Dr. Marmor. As far as the patient is concerned, whether she is a good candidate for the kind of therapy we are talking about here, I am a little worried that she is not. In the words of her teacher, it seems to me that the patient was just a visitor in the consulting room. Now, I'll clarify that in a moment, but one of the most striking things to me in watching her was how constricted and restricted this woman seemed to be emotionally. Toward the end she did begin to warm up a little bit with Dr. Sifneos, but he had a hard time accomplishing this, so it seemed to me that she didn't think terribly well of herself. It was hard to find a good immediate perceptive for the working of the symptom, although we did find that at the age of twelve it seemed to be quite closely directed toward the mother. But there again, it looks as though a basic issue has to do with her relationship with her mother, and although Dr. Sifneos seemed at the end to be very seriously trying to involve the father more in an oedipal way, I don't think as yet we have convincing evidence one way or another how important that is. It may be important. The one thing that did strike me very positively about her was that she is a reflective woman, that she certainly is concerned about her symptoms, that she is thoughtful about herself. And I was very much impressed with the way she responded to Dr. Sifneos' interviewing, which, at one point, brought back a memory she hadn't thought of for some eight to ten years. This seemed to strike a very responsive kind of note in her that made her liven up. From that point on, there was a little more fluidity in the interview situation. I would consider this hopeful. So I think, on balance, I would want to at least attempt to begin work with this woman in terms of insight psychotherapy and not at this point decide whether it is going to be short or long.

The word "insight" brings me to Dr. Marmor. I just want to say I wouldn't think of insight as being only a cognitive kind of thing. Granted, there is information of a cognitive sort that we give to the patient. That's one kind of insight. But if it's real insight and if the patient accepts it, the experience of insight is, I think, a very profoundly moving kind of inner experience. So I think insight in the basic, deepest sense is not entirely cognitive. If it's purely cognitive, it's like all of us who are obsessionals. We know all about ourselves and we tell our analyst about it for years and then suddenly one day we say, "My God! That's true." Now, that's a totally different experience; that's insight. Finally, as to the use of behavior therapy, I don't think I'd jump into that with this woman. Not that behavior therapy isn't tremendously useful, specifically with phobias, but it seems to me that one area where it is useful is if you have a phobia of long standing in which, so to speak, the fire has gone out. It started for psychodynamic reasons. There have been underlying changes, but the learned pattern remains even though it no longer functions in an economic way to solve problems and therefore, after you have worked through the problems, you still are left with this skeleton of something that comes from the past. Behavior therapy may be very necessary to undo that kind of learning. It seems to me that in this woman the volcano is still active, that it began at twelve but more recently has spread. There is still some kind of dynamic force behind it, and I think I would rather try to get at that first and see whether working with the problems underneath—if one could get at them—would help to remove the symptom. Then, if one couldn't, if although she was better in her relationships and in other ways she still had the phobic symptoms, I would think of turning to behavioral technique to get rid of the symptoms.

Question from the floor:

I would start with the statement the girl made when she repeated what her mother said to her, that it was so much better when she was little. Certainly, to my thinking, she expressed indirectly a lot of hate toward her mother and was keeping her in very closed-in line, in a very phobic way. I would think the mother is a kind of phobic person as well. But, Dr. Sifneos, you didn't mention anything about this angle toward the mother. You were trying to connect the symptom with this demand to be protected. If you were choosing her for short-term treatment, would you think that with all the rage this girl has she would certainly try to put this into the transference, and that one way to do it would be to do everything to make this therapy a failure?

Dr. Sifneos:

I could comment very quickly on this very interesting question. I would certainly say this would be the case if the transference were a maternal transference for this particular patient. Certainly for short-term anxiety-provoking psychotherapy one would not get into that particular problem, which would involve, of course, transference neurosis, and one of the advantages of terminating fairly quickly is to avoid such a situation. But, in my opinion, this lady fulfills all the criteria for short-term anxiety-provoking psychotherapy as I have enumerated them, and although I would agree with Dr. Nemiah's partial doubts about a specific focus, I was satisfied at the end of the interview that this was an oedipal issue; it involved her feelings for her father. Her mental symptoms in many ways were some attempt to replace her mother and get her father's attention, and on that basis I would treat her for not more than sixteen interviews and I think I would get good results.

Question from the floor:

I was concerned about a number of things. I very much share Dr. Nemiah's observations about her being an observer during the consultation, and, although she was clearly intelligent and psychologically-minded and so on, I had a lot of doubts as to whether this woman was motivated toward either short-term or long-term psychotherapy at this time. Although she complained about how her symptoms were bothering her, there didn't seem to be much response to interpretations. Most of the interpretations seemed to go in one ear and out the other. That was the impression that I got despite the fact that she was clearly an introspective woman. The other thing that I was struck by, particularly in comparison to the other videotapes we've seen, is how quickly Dr. Sifneos seemed to go almost into a lecturing style to the patient about the focal conflict after a very short period of time, and after she seemed to resist or not resonate much—continued to pound it, in a sense, to drive the point home. I'm wondering how, that being the case, Dr. Sifneos can predict that this woman would do excellently. Perhaps she might, but I just don't see it that way.

Dr. Sifneos:

It's on the basis of my experience that pounding patients with a truth produces good results.

Question from the floor:

My comment will be related to the key issue of selection of patients and criteria for selection. I've been quite amazed by the rapidity of therapeutic interventions in most of these interviews, maybe less so on the part of Dr. Malan, but clearly shown by Dr. Sifneos and Dr. Davanloo. The question I want to raise is this: Are we witnessing a therapeutic responsiveness in these assessments of criteria, rather than an evaluation of the structure and dynamics of the patient? It seems to me that we are already witnessing a molding of something about five or ten minutes after the interview has started.

Dr. Sifneos:

I think the distinction is a difficult one. Much of what one is doing might be viewed as therapeutic or evaluative. It seems to me that constantly in the mind of the evaluator there is a psychodynamic formulation that is being developed on the basis of the information that is given by the patient. Now, whenever one feels that he is in a position, even in the ten minutes, to test that hypothesis by getting further information, one should try to do that. If the response of the patient is with a fantasy or a dream or a sudden memory, such as this young woman produced about the Tower of London then I view this as being therapeutically promising. So I think keeping those two things together probably facilitates both the evaluation of the psychodynamics and the potential therapeutic prognosis.

Question from the floor:

I would like to bring up something I thought was missed in this interview, which is that Dr. Sifneos was focusing on the regressive longings that he felt the patient had, whereas it seemed to me that somehow it was more her aspirations for growth and the forces that were pulling her back. She was being pulled down the stairs. When she first went to school, she knew she could already read, and she was ahead and being pulled back. I think that's a very important theme of this person that hasn't been given due attention.

Question from the floor:

I'd like to ask one question of Dr. Sifneos. It was, in my opinion, an excellent first interview, and also I find the patient to be ideal for short-term anxiety-provoking psychotherapy. But my question is: If this patient is frigid, for example, and the phobia is related to this frigidity, will it be possible to deal with this problem in fourteen, fifteen or less than fifteen interviews? I base my idea about the phobia on the first words that the patient said about being afraid to escalate. These fears of escalating are particularly sustained by her sentence "I can't go on the top." This makes me wonder about the impossibility, perhaps, of her having a climax. And I go back to another part, which is very short, when she was in England with her mother. The mother was depressed. The patient was assuming the role of the mother and dealing with the mother and the father, arranging a divorce. Then, at that moment, she was probably very much afraid of her own fantasies, relating her own fantasies with the father. I see that as a possible interference in her own sexual life. And then, her interaction with boyfriends never lasted more than two or three months. This can increase the dependency and make the patient break down again or have more phobias. The question in that case is exactly the same. Do you think you can deal with this kind of problem in fifteen sessions or not?

Dr. Sifneos:

Well, I stuck my neck out. I would say yes with this particular patient and with patients with similar kinds of problems. As to the point of frigidity, it's hard to answer. With some patients, frigidity disappears. With others, if it involves something more pregenital, then I think it is less likely. But, if I'm not mistaken, and I cannot be 100 percent sure, this woman had very good sexual relationships with her boyfriend and she was not frigid.

Dr. Malan:

I want to do something which I'm always warning trainees not to do, which is to bring my own fantasy to a case and then attribute it to the patient. But I do think it's worthwhile saying this. It's by no means certain that it was the patient's fantasy. The thing about the Tower of London which she described very graphically was a macabre phase. Now, what are the macabre things that went on in the Tower of London? Dr. Sifneos is a good historian, and of course will know the answer to this, but what the Tower is associated with above all is Henry VIII and his wives. Each time he wanted to have a new wife he incarcerated his present wife, particularly Anne Boleyn, in the Tower of London. Then he had her head chopped off. Then he was free to marry a new one. Now, the situation described by the patient when she was in England, at eleven, was a highly oedipal one in the sense that the mother was saying she was going to leave the father and sent her daughter to tell this to the father, which, as has been pointed out, would be likely to arouse anxiety. I rather suspect that's why she had this anxiety attack in the Tower.

Dr. Kravitz:

I had a similar fantasy about the Tower of London that validates yours. I think perhaps one of the things which has been left unmentioned in all the attempts to establish criteria for evaluation and selection, except in passing, is the kind of developmental model that the evaluator brings to the session. There are probably variations on that theme, even if we stick to the model of psychic functioning as developed by psychoanalytic theory. At present, there are significant developmental models, each of which has its own important watershed or way station which separates those who are on the way to making it or have made it and dropped back, and those who have never made it. To a large extent, of course, evaluation and selection probably falls on those who have passed the watershed, whatever developmental model one brings to the evaluation, and it also seems to me that the way one conducts the interview will probably be pretty much determined by that frame of reference.

Question from the floor:

Dr. Sifneos, I was going over your list of criteria. You stated that she met all five, and I wonder about this. I mean, she does have a circumscribed chief complaint. Her chief complaint is phobia, as I understand it, and she did demonstrate the ability to have one meaningful relationship in her early life. However, when you come down to the other criteria, such as her ability to interact with the evaluator, both with the motivation of affect and flexibility of defensive styles, I felt she was extremely rigid, with not much affect, and I'd agree with the other observation that she seemed to be a visitor in the office. She did have above-average intelligence and some psychological sophistication. But as far as motivation for change is concerned, considering the rigidity of her defensive patterns I question how much this was influenced by her environment and by her boyfriend saying, "Gee, you've got to do something about this." Maybe the boyfriend wouldn't come home, stay with her. How much did that secondary gain enter into it? Can we call this true motivation? Thus I give her about three out of five, and I'm wondering how we can explain the difference.

Dr. Sifneos:

That's an interesting question, since it also came from other sources. People felt that she was quite rigid in her interaction with me. I have called the videotape the microscope for psychiatry that we never had before, and it really gives us a great deal of information. But, of course, it can never give us the complete live aspect of the interaction between the patient and the evaluator. At no time throughout that interview did I feel that this young woman was rigid. She was cautious, she was withdrawn, but at the end when she came in with this spontaneous association about the Tower of London, she said, "I'm analyzing myself recently; I'm looking into myself. I have been thinking about this, whatever it is." Finally, although granted she may have been motivated to come by her boyfriend, at the end of the hour she felt completely interested in pursuing the kind of work that she and I had done during that particular interview. I certainly rate her motivation as being very high. And the third criterion, the interaction with the evaluator, also is a positive one. So I would disagree about your assessment on those criteria. That's why I would accept her for brief psychotherapy.

Dr. Nemiah:

Just two comments—one in passing about training residents. I think Dr. Eisenstein is quite right that for people like himself and myself and Dr. Sifneos, in that generation, it has taken us a long time to learn short-term psychotherapy simply because we were brought up in long-term psychotherapy, and brief psychotherapy didn't exist until people like Drs. Sifneos and Davanloo developed it. I think we can teach our experiences to our residents at the same time that we're teaching them long-term psychotherapy if we can show them which kinds of patients need what. They're just different modalities. I would like to ask Dr. Sifneos one question, or at least say what I think may be happening á propos this woman and her affective response in the interview. A number of us felt that, compared to the other patients we've seen, she was guarded, restricted and distant. When you talked about her response to your interpretation, you were emphasizing psychological-mindedness as opposed to the availability of affect, and I wonder if what's happening is that you are in transition and beginning to lay more stress on the importance of motivation as an indicator for success in this kind of therapy as being even more significant than the immediate availability of affect, which was one of your earlier criteria?

Dr. Sifneos:

Yes. Motivation for change is terribly important, but perhaps the difference is that her feelings might not be as available, immediately, but that they exist nevertheless. She showed a great deal of positive feeling at the end of the interview.

Chapter 12

"The Case of the Angry, Childlike Woman"

H. DAVANLOO

The patient is a thirty-eight-year-old divorcee, mother of three children, who works as a receptionist. She was seen at the psychiatric clinic. She complained of depression, problems in interpersonal relationships characterized by passivity, dependency, wanting men to tell her what to do and resenting it. She has had a longstanding conflict with her parents, both of them of Dutch origin. Presently, she lives with a man of English origin and is very dependent on him, as well as resentful; she herself labels it a father-child relationship, in which she acts like an angry child.

Pt: I feel lost; I feel like I don't have a center. I feel out of touch with myself.
Th: Could you describe what it's like when you say you're out of touch with yourself?
Pt: I do things often that I don't like. I do things that often I'm not sure they're the right thing to do.
Th: You said you feel out of touch with yourself. So, by being out of touch with yourself you mean that you do things and you don't know why you do them?

Pt: It's often that I don't like what I'm doing, and it makes me feel like I'm not a good person. I have that sense that I'm not a good person, that I'm bad.

Th: So then, you feel that you're not a good person. You were telling me that you feel out of touch with yourself. Now you're telling me that you feel that you're not a good person. By "out of touch" do you mean this? Do you see what I mean—you said you're out of touch with yourself and now you're saying that means this?

Pt: It partially means that. That's part of it. Part of it is feeling I do things and I don't know why I'm doing them.

Th: Could we look now at the things that you do and you don't know why you do them? Give a few examples of the things that you do and you don't know why you do them.

Pt: I do things, like being angry a lot, being irritable.

Th: You feel angry or irritable?

Pt: Yes, or instead of thinking of others I think of myself, for a start.

Th: You're saying that you feel angry and irritable. Then you want to say to me what?

Pt: Well, that's one thing.

Th: Okay. Now, you feel angry and irritable. With whom do you feel angry and irritable?

Pt: With people I live with, any one of them; the man I live with and my kids.

Th: So you get angry and irritable with the man you live with and your children, and then you question yourself why you should be angry with them, as if in a way you're saying that for no external reason you get angry with them?

Pt: I'd say that's where my doubts come in; I'm never sure.

Th: So could we make it easier by having you look at it, giving a specific example of a situation with the man you live with and when you get angry with him?

Pt: I know I'm vague, but it's like a generalized feeling very often.

Th: Don't you think in a way that you prefer to talk in general terms, rather than in specific terms, and that we have to see why it is that you prefer to talk in general, vague terms rather than to be specific? Are you always like that, preferring to be general and vague rather than specific?

Pt: I often am.

Th: You're often vague?

Pt: It's hard for me to focus. I mean, that's part of the symptom, not knowing what I'm doing. I mean, I know it's like a defensive thing.
Th: What do you mean by "a defensive thing"?
Pt: I suppose it's a way of not dealing with the problem.
Th: Then the immediate question we have to raise for ourselves here is that you say being vague and talking in a general way is a way of avoiding dealing with the core of the problem. Now, if we continue in this session to deal with it in a vague and general way, then we have defeated the purpose of the interview. So why, then, should we defeat it from the beginning, since obviously you must have difficulties for which you want to get help but then you set it up in such a way that it is going to be defeated from the very beginning—do you see what I mean, since you said to be general and to be vague means not to get to the core of the problem? Are you also vague with the man you live with?
Pt: Sometimes, yes.
Th: But sometimes you are not?
Pt: I am when we're dealing with a problem.
Th: When you're dealing with a problem, then you become vague and general. Otherwise you are not?
Pt: I am with him a lot, and I'm not in every situation in life. I'm not always like that with everyone, but with him I often am, and I feel very defensive. It's like I'm looking to him to tell me what I am or to give approval, or if he disapproves then I feel like I'm nothing.
Th: So you look for approval and disapproval in your relationship with him?
Pt: Yes. I guess being vague is also like not taking a stand. I feel like I don't know what I think; I don't know what I am. If I'm not taking a stand, then he can't attack me or disapprove of me.
Th: In other words, then, what you're saying is that being vague and being general is a way of dealing with that in relation with the man you live with?
Pt: Yes.
Th: But then you also say that you want him to take care of things; to tell you whether you're right or wrong. In everything?
Pt: Yes, pretty much.
Th: Could you give me examples of a few areas in your relationship

Pt: with him where you would like him to guide you and lead you?
Pt: It sounds vague again, but to sort of tell me what I am and whether I'm a good or bad person or if what I've done is right; reassurance that it's okay.
Th: You might not know it exactly, but you might have some sort of ideation about it. For example, are there any other life experiences in which you want to be treated like a child?
Pt: I think in any intimacy I am.
Th: In any relationship?
Pt: With a man particularly; maybe with women friends, too, to a certain extent. Not always.
Th: Okay, so then this is the pattern or style of your relationships with men, that you let them run your life and treat you like a child; with women to a lesser extent, but it's a similar pattern.
Pt: Yes, it's . . .
Th: Could we look at your relationship with other men?
Pt: There was another relationship when I was younger. I was about seventeen.
Th: Seventeen? How old are you now?
Pt: Thirty-eight. It really was exactly the same. The man was different. He wasn't the same. He didn't have the same sort of nature, but it was the same, and I can see the same in my relationship with my father.
Th: What was it like with that man when you were seventeen?
Pt: It was a terrible experience because I became totally dependent on him and I had no identity. It was like I couldn't—you know, if I was someone, myself, whatever that is, it would risk—it would be a threat to him or I would risk losing him or something. I became totally passive. At the same time I was very aware that I hated him and was terribly resentful of him.
Th: What were the things that he was getting you to do, treating you, as you say, like a child?
Pt: I utterly depended on him. He decided everything, like when he would see me, under what circumstances, and I was always very unsure of whether I had him, and that was always a problem. I played games.
Th: What do you mean by "games"?
Pt: I would pretend that all of this didn't exist.
Th: All of what?

Pt: That I wasn't feeling so dependent and passive. You know, I had to hide my hatred, or I wouldn't call him; I'd wait for him to call me, and it would be kind of a victory if he came to see me. Sexually, I totally withheld myself.
Th: What do you mean when you say sexually with him you totally withheld?
Pt: I didn't enjoy sex with him. I had sex with him, but I didn't enjoy it at all. So our sexual life was very bad.
Th: What was it like when you say you didn't enjoy it?
Pt: I was frigid and passive, so the result was I felt used.
Th: You say you felt used?
Pt: Yes.
Th: Are you indicating that you wanted to be used? This is one of the issues that we have to clarify. Is it you or is it the other person?
Pt: Well, it was me, but I felt it was him.
Th: But when you look at it you were the architect; you were the one setting it up.
Pt: Yes, but at the same time I still feel, when I see him, angry with him, although it's so long ago. I'm much better, but I still can't get rid of my resentment. It's still there.
Th: So then, with this person you went through a similar kind of relationship. You would say that your relationship with the man you live with is similar to that relationship?
Pt: Yes. The difference is that they are very, very different people. He doesn't want me to be like that. I mean, he **doesn't enjoy that.**
Th: How about sexually with him?
Pt: It's very good. It's really my first good sexual relationship.
Th: So you enjoy sex and you are pleased with it. That is a difference, then? You were going to tell me that you went through a similar relationship with your father.
Pt: It's still there in my relationship with my father.
Th: How old is your father?
Pt: He's seventy-eight.
Th: What is the relationship with him like now, and what was it like before?
Pt: I'm not sure it's so different. He's very protective. He doesn't like the way I live. He would like me to marry again, and marry a man of our religion. He doesn't exactly approve of my life, and he lets

me know it. It's very dissatisfying. I think I have some love for him, but I'm terribly resentful when he gets bossy.

Th: In what way is he bossy?

Pt: You know, he'll tell me to do things or insinuate he doesn't like things.

Th: I was wondering if you notice that when you discuss things with me, you often use the words "things," "this," or "that," rather than being specific. Do you notice that?

Pt: Yes.

Th: When you look at it, what does it mean?

Pt: It's again being vague.

Th: And you notice it?

Pt: Well, now that you point it out I notice it.

Th: You mean you were not aware of it before?

Pt: Not now, no. I mean, I realize that sometimes I wasn't. For instance, he would like me to be more involved in the religious community so I can meet someone to marry; I'd give my children more of a religious background. If I'm going on a trip, he'll say: "Be careful," or "Maybe you shouldn't do it"—or, you know, he'll put a damper on it. That's something I've always felt, that he wants me to stay put where he can control me. That's what I always felt when I was young: "Don't go out. Stay home and rest."

(*The therapist explores the patient's history. She stayed home until age seventeen, went away to boarding school for a few years, then returned and stayed with her family for two years. She was not happy at home and so moved into an apartment; she says it was an attempt at independence. Her relationship with her father has been disturbed since she was thirteen; he wanted her to get married, and they were critical of each other. Around age twelve or thirteen she was overweight, not sociable, withdrawn, and felt very alone. She felt shy with most people, and she read a lot.*)

Th: One thing I was wondering if you see is that you say in relationship with everybody you have discussed so far you take a very passive role; you are vague, you generalize, and you are not specific. They take a leading role; they guide you; they lead you. This is the way it is with people, especially men. I was wondering how you see your relationship with me. Is it similar or is it different?

Pt: I'd say it's similar to an extent.

Th: Because the question is this: If I don't question you and if I don't guide you to be specific, I wonder what would happen here. Repeatedly, I have to guide you, question you, so do you think you are doing the same thing here?
Pt: I am to an extent. I'm trying not to.
Th: The question is, why is it that you end up being like that? I'm talking about here. Why do you think it is that in a way—and this is very obvious—you want me to guide you?
Pt: I feel I need it.
Th: Are you saying that you are not able yourself to take the lead?
Pt: I feel I don't know how.
Th: Okay. You said that, say, with the man you are living with, you get him to guide you and then you resent him for doing that. How about here with me? You get me to guide you, but then I wonder how you feel here then. With him you feel resentful. How about here?
Pt: Sometimes I feel resentful; sometimes I don't.
Th: But how about here?
Pt: I don't feel resentful.
Th: So you don't feel resentful. So it is different here. Why do you think it is different here?
Pt: I'm not sure; maybe I'm not involved enough with you.
Th: Are you indicating that if this continues further, say, in the process of future sessions for the sake of discussion, then you would start to resent it?
Pt: I probably will; maybe not.
Th: You were saying that all of your life with your father, as far as you can remember, he was critical with you and you were a shy person, or a withdrawn person, and you were mostly with yourself and reading.
Pt: Yes, but I was very rebellious of him. I wanted to do what I wanted to do, like I dressed the way I wanted to dress.
Th: What was the way you wanted to dress?
Pt: I dressed in jeans and men's shirts, and he looked at me like I'm not a woman; I'm a slob, and no one will like me.
Th: So he wanted you to dress up differently.
Pt: Yes. He wanted me to dress like a woman—to wear nice clothes, to wear women's clothes, and to look presentable—and I was messy and I wore pants.
Th: Aren't you then saying that your father was interested in you and

wanted you to dress up like a woman and somehow you didn't like this? From what age were you rebelling against your father about the issue of dress?
Pt: Well, I think as soon as I became an adolescent.
Th: What age would you say?
Pt: I'd say thirteen.
Th: So from around the age of thirteen or fourteen, you became rebellious with your father and this is the time you are not a little girl anymore. How about prior to thirteen? Do you have any memories of early years?
Pt: Yes. Then I felt in conflict with my mother. I felt like I hated her and she didn't love me, and I was very resentful; I felt deprived. She was a very sort of silent, sullen person, and my conflict was with her. I felt she didn't love me, she didn't understand me, and I remember at an early age feeling very alienated.
Th: So you had problems with your mother?
Pt: Yes. I'm not exactly sure of the age. I changed, but then there was a point where my fight was then with my father.
Th: So up to a certain age it was with your mother, and then at about thirteen or fourteen it started with your father and this is the time your body is changing and your father wants you to dress up like a woman.
Pt: Yes.
Th: Okay. Let's look at your earliest memories.
Pt: I admired my father because I thought he was a very active, energetic sort of person. The contrast with my mother was so great, seemingly the opposite.
Th: In what way opposite? You say your father was active.
Pt: Yes, and she was passive and never smiled, barely talked. So I admired him and hated her.
Th: What was the way your father was then? Because what you describe is that your mother was a very withdrawn, detached, cold person, and your father was the opposite to this. What was the relationship between your father and mother like? I'm talking about when you were six or seven years old.
Pt: She was very childlike, and he was very protective, oppressive in a way, like his favorite expression—whenever she talked, he'd say, "Shut up, little mums," which he meant as a joke. She had all kinds of aches and pains and complaints, and really indulged herself in pity.

Th: What were you like at age six or seven?
Pt: I was passive some, but it was like I always had my secret life, my secret thoughts, that they couldn't get at.
Th: What was your secret life and your secret thoughts?
Pt: Part of it was like feeling superior. I don't know if I felt it around six or seven, but it was like I was very secretive and I was superior. I became very critical of their values. I can remember going with them at a really early age and feeling so alienated and depressed, like I was almost physically sick.
Th: Do you have any pleasant memories of your father when you were six or seven?
Pt: No, not really. I don't have pleasant memories at all from my childhood.

(*The therapist further explores the early triangle, and it becomes more evident that the patient was the favorite of her father and that this relationship deteriorated. She describes her mother as exactly the way she herself is. Then she remembers being punished by her father when she was about seven, and she says she always had a secret life, secret thoughts, and felt she didn't belong there: "I was not a part of it." Her memories of those years are unpleasant. Then the therapist points out to the patient that in the very early phase she admired her father and felt close to him, but that somehow that deteriorated and she became very much like her mother. He presents the idea that perhaps she wanted to be like her mother, namely, passive, noninvolved, dependent, so that she would be loved by her father. "The woman my father loves is a passive, dependent, childlike woman."*)

Th: You never did things together, or share?
Pt: Well, the one thing I can think of is going out with him for walks on the mountain every Sunday morning. He was very hearty; he enjoyed the outdoors. I didn't enjoy it. I felt sort of pushed around by him.
Th: So then your problem really goes a long way back to the early phase. You had a phase when you were rebelling about the system, and then at age seventeen you moved to boarding school, and then you went back. The conflict continued with your father when you finished boarding school and came back, and then you finally ended up going on your own. How many children do you have?
Pt: Three.
Th: And how old are they?

Pt: Twelve, eight and six. The oldest is a boy and the two others are girls.

Th: Do you have any problems with them?

Pt: I have a problem with my oldest. I have a lot of guilt toward him; I see in him the things I don't like in myself.

Th: When you say guilt, what do you mean by that?

Pt: Well, I feel that I have made him to be certain ways that I don't like, like passive, withdrawn and detached. It makes me angry, and it makes me feel helpless and depressed that I can't correct that, that he's doing it like I was. Then I get into a state where I punish myself, even though I say I'm not really interested in his welfare, but I just don't want to feel guilty.

Th: Do you see something in them that you dislike in yourself?

Pt: It's in him particularly.

Th: Particularly in him? What are the things that you see in him that you dislike?

Pt: The detachment, and my daughter is very different. She's very vivacious and outgoing. She's fearless about things.

Th: I see. Do you get depressed?

Pt: Yes.

Th: Is there any time that you get so depressed that you get fed up with life?

Pt: Yes, I do.

Th: Is there any time that you felt so depressed that you wanted to do away with yourself, that you felt there was no sense in living and wanted to terminate your life?

Pt: No. At times I feel doomed. Sometimes I think I want to kill myself, but I think about my children and how horrible it would be for them.

Th: You feel you want to do away with yourself, but then you think about the children?

Pt: Yes.

Th: Right now, how do you feel?

Pt: I feel sad.

Th: Do you feel like crying?

Pt: Yes.

Th: I question that because I felt a few times you wanted to cry here.

Pt: Yes.

Th: But then somehow you went dry, let's say.

Pt: It's sort of a waste of time to cry. I'd rather talk.
Th: In other words, you feel talking is more important than your feelings?
Pt: Yes.
Th: And this is a problem, isn't it, that you give priority to talking rather than to the way you feel?
Pt: Yes.
Th: Has it always been like this?
Pt: Yes.
Th: Do you feel lonely in life?
Pt: Often I do, yes.
Th: As if in a way you don't really belong?
Pt: Yes, that's very much so.
Th: And this is the way you've felt all your life, in a sense, because also when you were a child at home you had a feeling of not belonging, and this feeling is there, isn't it?
Pt: Yes, always of being an outsider; very often.
Th: Generally, are you happy with life or unhappy with life?
Pt: No, generally I'm unhappy.
Th: You've had this difficulty for quite some time, but what I'm looking at is this: What is it this time that made you decide that you wanted to get help for yourself?

(*The exploration at this point brings into focus that the patient has had previous treatment: psychoanalytic treatment, three to four sessions per week for a period of five years—three years with one analyst and two with another. This was when she was in her twenties.*)

Th: Three to four times a week. Did it help?
Pt: I don't know. I was very resistant.
Th: So that was the factor. When you say resistant, in what way?
Pt: I refused to really get into it. I couldn't do it, lying on the couch. I was fighting it. I'm a very stubborn person.
Th: And that makes it very difficult, doesn't it, that on one hand you want help but at the same time there's something in you that's going to fight it?
Pt: Yes.
Th: Okay. In what way would a psychiatrist be able to help you now?

Pt: I feel much more motivated to change now. I feel desperate, like if I don't do it now, then all my habits and being will become...

Th: You mean you're not going to fight it any more because you said with Dr. ——— you were fighting it. You went but you were fighting it, isn't that right?

Pt: I can't say that I'm not going to fight it. I think I *will* fight it.

Th: Fight it—to fail, you mean?

Pt: I don't know—resist you and fail. I don't know. I can't imagine being different, for one thing.

Th: But then let's look at it. With Dr. ——— you were in a painful state. You were seeking help, obviously. You saw him three or four times a week. Who paid for it?

(*The father was paying for the treatment with the hope that she might change and marry a man of her own faith. It also came out that the patient had had group psychotherapy for some years but could not get involved enough; she indicated she could help others in a group but was not involved herself and was passive.*)

Th: Now, these forces within you, namely, to resist and fight, what you aim at—this is what we can say is a self-defeating pattern.
A self-defeating pattern is when you want to get help, you want to get out of the state of misery you have, but at the same time there's a force within you that wants to fight and defeat it. Do you think this might become an obstacle in treatment here as well—you know, this self-defeating pattern?

Pt: Well, I'd like to try very hard so it wouldn't become that.

Th: So do you anticipate that it would become a problem?

Pt: I think if it does I would be much more conscious of it.

Th: Obviously, when you say you have difficulty with people, you have difficulty here also because it cannot be different from outside.

Dr. Naiman:

I call upon the chairman of each workshop to tell us briefly if he considers this patient a candidate for short-term dynamic psychotherapy.

Dr. Mann:

There was quite a bit of difficulty in determining whether she fulfills the criteria. It seemed to us that this patient would not be suitable for this type of psychotherapy.

Dr. Kravitz:

It seemed to us, also, that this patient is not acceptable according to the criteria. Yet there seemed to be a pervasive desire among a significant number of the members of the workshop to work with this patient with a time-limited approach, offering her a specific number of sessions within which to work out some of her presenting problems.

Dr. Savitz:

There was much disagreement whether she could be a good candidate for short-term psychotherapy.

Dr. Moll:

Most of the participants were catalyzed into a great deal of discussion, but the majority felt that this patient is not a suitable candidate for short-term psychotherapy.

Dr. Strupp:

There was a great deal of discussion, and the general view was that this patient is fairly unsuitable for short-term dynamic psychotherapy.

Dr. Straker:

In this interview it was evident that Dr. Davanloo interprets transference very early in dealing with the patient. There was general agreement that a countertransference problem with this patient should be anticipated. The consensus was that this patient is not a suitable candidate for short-term dynamic psychotherapy.

Dr. Smith:

In our workshop the general feeling was that the patient is unsuitable for a briefer form of short-term dynamic psychotherapy, but she may possibly be dealt with in a longer type of brief psychotherapy. The feeling was that an oedipal conflict could possibly be carved up, but that there were perhaps many pre-oedipal problems.

Dr. Zaiden:

On the basis of the interaction with Dr. Davanloo I would take her into short-term dynamic psychotherapy, and this is only on that basis. It was the view of our workshop that she had really whipped the therapist and had defeated the previous therapies. It is my feeling that this would be a most difficult patient, and that Dr. Davanloo's technique was the only way in which one could mobilize her. This becomes evident if one compares the first five minutes with the last five minutes—in the last part of the vignette this patient mobilizes herself.

Dr. Davanloo:

This patient was presented to me at an intake conference. The picture was so vague that it was very difficult to decide upon the nature of the patient's presenting problems. It was on that basis that I interviewed her.

In terms of the patient's life problems, as we saw during the early part of the interview, she was vague and the evaluator had to make a confrontation about this and interpret it in terms of the patient's need to make the session useless. The patient said her inability to focus was a "defensive thing." The therapist made an interpretation of the resistance and went on to find out if this is so with the man with whom she lives. Then the patient indicated that she had a poor opinion of herself and is unable to maintain her own ego boundaries, and that the man with whom she lives is the one who guides and leads her. The evaluator went into the patient's contemporary pattern of behavior and explored it to see if there were other human relationships where she set up the situation so as to be treated like a child. It became evident that the patient has had disturbances in interpersonal relationships with both men and women, particularly in close personal relationships. Then I learned about her first relationship at age seventeen. She said she utterly depended on the man and was very passive and dependent.

During the interview, after I had determined both her contemporary pattern and her vertical pattern of behavior in human relationships, I linked the two with her transference pattern of behavior, to which the patient responded positively. Then, in the last part of the session, the patient was more active and some latent affect was mobilized.

In terms of our criteria, would I accept this patient for short-term dynamic psychotherapy? Now, I am talking only on the basis of my interview. Some of her symptoms obviously are circumscribed; others obviously fall into the category of lifelong characterological problems, and we don't have from the tape any evidence of a meaningful relationship. But I was very touched by and felt positive toward her, and as the interview progressed I found her more involved. When I assessed her, I scored her nonacceptable for the briefer form of short-term dynamic psychotherapy, which in our unit means anywhere from two to fifteen sessions. In terms of the longer form, I thought her total score would be "fair," and it was my opinion that in the hands of an experienced therapist she would do well in from twenty-five to thirty sessions, or perhaps the upper limit of forty. But one feature in our project is that we accept both those who score high and those who score low, which we call "rejected."

I was struck by a number of issues in my evaluation which very positively motivated me to give her a try in short-term dynamic psychotherapy. One had to do with the fact that I was able to break through her resistances, which I considered very strong. This interpretation of her resistance, and a number of other interventions along a similar line, I felt mobilized the patient.

The second issue was that I found her very honest. She honestly admitted that she got her father to pay and that she had been all set to defeat her previous treatment. To me, this is the type of patient who would not respond well to a nonstructured, free-associative type of interview.

Dr. Malan:

I am very interested in the marked polarity in response to this patient. I had a most intensely positive reaction to her. I thought she was basically one of the most sincere people I have ever seen. My reaction to her was like Dr. Davanloo's; the degree of polarity is most extraordinary.

Dr. Davanloo (*in answer to a question concerning the outcome of treatment*):

This patient was assigned to one of the therapists in our short-term psychotherapy unit, and I supervised. There were nineteen sessions. There was a tremendous amount of countertransference reaction, and there was a struggle to keep the process in focus.

I asked Dr. Sifneos to evaluate this patient independently, according to his outcome criteria, and I hope he will give us his views. But at this time it would be relevant to hear from Mrs. Benoit, who treated the patient.

Mrs. Benoit:

As was indicated, there was difficult psychotherapeutic work, the main difficulty lying in keeping the therapy in focus. The predominant aim was the treatment of the disturbances in human relationships. The patient was quite in rivalry with me as a therapist, and basically the technique was of a confrontative type with repeated interpretation of resistance and the self-punishing, self-defeating pattern of behavior. From the beginning, our aim in regard to a successful outcome was the development of a feeling of positive self-esteem in the patient, an improved relationship with her son, a global improvement in her interpersonal relationships, autonomy, self-reliance, and to the giving up of the passive, dependent, childlike relationship, etc.

Dr. Sifneos:

I saw this patient a few days ago, and the tone of her initial opening remarks sounded exactly like that in her remarks to Dr. Davanloo. She was withdrawn, somewhat quiet, and took long pauses. We have ten outcome criteria, and I shan't go into detail now but they involve the assessment of the changes in the symptoms, in interpersonal relationships, in new attitudes, self-esteem, new learning, problem-solving, expectations of the result of the outcome, feeling for the therapist, a psychodynamic resolution of the conflict, etc. What she told me was that she came into psychotherapy because she had this negative attitude about herself, that this was of long duration, and she repeated the fact that she had been in psychoanalysis and group psychotherapy for some years. She told me that she felt much better. When I asked her about her relationship with people, she told me that one of the things that had bothered her a great deal was her relationship with her children before she started treatment, that it was bad and she felt guilty about it. Now her relationship with her children has changed dramatically. Her relationship with her boyfriend has also improved.

As far as her general feeling of well-being is concerned, she felt much better. Her self-esteem is indeed greatly improved. When I asked her about her feeling for the therapist, she said that she disliked Mrs. Benoit because she was somebody who had a Freudian mind and was constantly focusing on that issue. She felt that she could not communicate with the therapist. She would have liked to be allowed to have her own way, but her therapist would not allow it, and because of this she decided on her own to end the therapy. I said that I was surprised because it was quite clear that she had presented me with a whole spectrum of improvements and it was the therapy that was responsible. She said: "Well, maybe. Doesn't everybody change in life?" And I said: "Well, why does one not change for twenty years and then decide to change in the last six months?" She smiled and said: "You've got a point there." Realistically, she wanted very much to attribute the changes that she herself had enumerated to something else rather than the therapy, because she did not like the therapist, but the fact was that indeed she couldn't. She was honest enough to admit that her improvement actually had something to do with the therapy.

So, I think we have here evidence of negative transference. I don't know, but I might predict that we may have almost a negative countertransference and a very positive result. Now, this is a very interesting scientific finding.

Dr. Moll:

I wonder if the negative transference is not in this particular patient an indication of improvement since in her past therapy she blamed herself for the failure of the treatment. My only question in listening to this is, whatever might be the reality of what transpired in the treatment, the tendency to self-blame was in fact one of her symptoms, and if she is now able to verbalize anger toward the therapist I would regard that as an improvement in the patient.

Dr. Kravitz:

I would like to offer this explanation for the negative versus negative adding up to positive. It seems to me that one of the issues, at least as I saw them unfolding, was the possibility that the negative or hostile aspects in her relationships were really boundary-setting for her and were one way for her to create a degree of individuality for herself which she felt she couldn't have if she was positively involved; and it seems to me that this negative stance of improving and yet being distant from the giver is a very important issue for her.

Question from the floor:

I would like to ask Dr. Sifneos if he could comment on this patient whom Dr. Davanloo interviewed and accepted for treatment. In view of the criteria that you use, would you have accepted this patient for short-term anxiety-provoking psychotherapy?

Dr. Sifneos:

I feel I am not objective enough now, since I have seen this patient in outcome, to try to change my mind and say that she was a good candidate. I did not think she was suitable, but I certainly think Dr. Davanloo's statement about her honesty, which Dr. Malan also pointed out, and the way in which she responded positively to Dr. Davanloo's interventions are things which one cannot disregard.

Dr. Rosenberg:

I also assessed this patient with psychological tests, and she showed very dramatic improvement on the MMPI with regard to symptomatic relief—certainly marked relief of depression, which seemed almost at suicidal level from the first test and was down in a normal range on the second. Indeed, Dr. Kravitz's idea was very much correct in terms of boundary setting for this patient. It seemed that she, for whatever reason, was unable to really credit the therapist for having helped her and needed very much to take the credit upon herself, which perhaps was an indication of a healthier self-esteem. What was striking was her decision that she had to take much more responsibility for her life, that she could not remain in a helpless dependent position, and that further therapy wouldn't be helpful for her any longer. She had come to terms with her own difficulties and managed them.

The question I would like to raise is related to balancing research issues and clinical responsibility. Are we justified in randomly assigning patients when for some patients a male or a female therapist might be much better for the treatment? The other question is related to multiple interviews. Would it be better for patients to have only one intake interview and for the intake interviewer to be the same person as the therapist?

Dr. Malan:

We have very extensive experience in both situations, that is, the one in which the interviewer is the same person as the therapist and the one in which he isn't. Our data indicate that it does not seem to make the slightest difference, provided the therapist is competent.

Dr. Kravitz:

I'd like to comment on Dr. Rosenberg's point. I think if we had enough information, iron-clad information, telling us that in one case a male therapist and in another case a female therapist is definitely superior, then we could make these decisions. Furthermore, I believe that the male-female dimension is a lot less important than particular characteristics of the therapist. If we knew more about them, what the particular effect of a set of therapist's variables in interaction with a set of patient variables is going to be, I think we would be able to answer the questions. As stated, however, I think male-female is unduly simplified.

Dr. Zaiden:

I wonder if there was not truly a therapeutic alliance that this patient made with the therapist and that this should have been evaluated further. Of course, the issues have been clearly stated about the negative transference and the countertransference, and my feeling is that this is, as was said earlier, the only way that this patient could make a therapeutic alliance at this point in her life, if you look at it from the point of view that in essence she was unable to establish a therapeutic alliance with the previous therapists. This therapist, given the guidelines and the supervision, was very conscious of her countertransference to this patient. Now, I would suggest the possibility that in her previous treatment the therapists were not sufficiently aware of their own countertransference, which resulted in therapeutic failure.

Dr. Sifneos:

I would like to comment on what Dr. Rosenberg said because in our studies in Boston we have extensive experience on the issue of multiple interviews as well as the sex of the therapist. We have found no detrimental effect attached to having quite a number of interviews since we use independent evaluators to assess the patients before and after treatment. We have also found no evidence whatsoever of any differences as far as the sex of the therapist is concerned. As we had expected, by selecting patients who are quite well-put-together individuals the sex of the therapist makes no difference with the single exception that the sequence of material is very different during the psychotherapy. Certain aspects of the triangular situation that a patient has with his father, say, is much easier to talk about to a female therapist, and then certain issues that he has with his mother are much more difficult and are likely to come up in the end of the therapy. It's the other way around if the therapist is male.

Question from the floor:

Regarding "meaningful relationship"—and this is an issue that has come up throughout the symposium—I was wondering from Dr. Sifneos' point of view whether he considers such a relationship one that had been established after adolescence or during adolescence.

Dr. Sifneos:

Certainly this is a very important point. I would view a meaningful relationship with a person later on in life as being a repetition of a meaningful relationship which had occurred earlier in life. For example, I might interview a patient in whom I cannot find a meaningful relationship, but in interaction with me there might be a great deal of it. Then, going back, I would search for a meaningful relation which I may have missed in order to assess correctly. Usually one succeeds in discovering it during the second interview.

Of all the variables that have been mentioned, there is one that I would like to add because I have seen it in my own practice. One has to consider the time in a patient's life at which he is ready for some kind of therapeutic intervention, whether it's an hour of brief psychotherapy or what have you. On the basis of my own experience, I think this is a fairly important variable in dealing with patients.

Part III

THE BORDERLINE BETWEEN EVALUATION AND THERAPY

This section contains presentations from the First International Symposium. In Chapter 13, C. Golden discusses two vignettes: one from an interview by H. Davanloo ("The Case of the Submissive Woman") and one from an interview conducted by himself ("The Case of the Man with a Headache"). Chapter 14 also comprises two vignettes, discussed by C. Yung: one from an interview by H. Davanloo ("The Case of the Man with an Impulse to Murder His Stepfather") and one from an interview conducted by himself ("The Case of the Masochistic Statistician").
In Chapter 14, Dr. Davanloo discusses an interview by P.E. Sifneos ("The Case of the Woman with the Fear of Losing Her Husband"). Each chapter ends with a general discussion of the interviews.

Chapter 13
Implications of the Interviewer's Technique on Selection Criteria

C. GOLDEN

Dr. Golden:

My topic examines the influence of the initial interviewer's technique on the criteria for selection.

There is increasing confidence that short-term dynamic psychotherapy has become established as a successful therapeutic modality in a specific patient population, achieving results previously ascribed to longer forms of therapy. I omit the descriptive term, intensive, since there is no question in my mind that the shorter variety bears, as one of its outstanding characteristics, a high degree of intensity.

As we learned earlier in this Symposium, the basis for selection rests, not with clinical entities but, generally speaking, with the patient's ego functions. For the sake of brevity I would like to specify these as representing the mode of ego function emphasizing, in particular, the conflict-free sphere of the ego, its defensive make-up, including its ability to tolerate reasonable levels of anxiety, and its capacity for establishing significant relationships.

In short-term psychotherapy very much the same techniques are utilized as in longer forms, though in a modified form. However, certain paradoxes exist. In my short experience with the Short-Term Psychotherapy Unit at The Montreal General Hospital, I have become impressed by the very close relationship that exists between the establishment of the criteria for selection with a degree of certainty and the style and related techniques of the interviewer. While we have noticed a very close parallel in the ratings of the observers experienced in the short-term modality, a rather marked discrepancy has occurred between their ratings and the ratings of those who, while being experienced therapists, have not familiarized themselves with the nature of the short-term process.

The use of the descriptive title "Short-Term" implies a need for a rapid acquisition, through validated data or inference, of the unconscious meanings of the patient's communication, experiences and behaviour. Here, the basis is the psychoanalytic theory of neurosis formation and development, and psychoanalytic techique is the methodology. The goal of the psychodiagnostic interview is to obtain an overview of a human being's general lifestyle—a thorough grasp of the current reality situation—and, secondly, to penetrate as quickly as possible and as can be tolerated to major traumatic influences and their effects, in particular to the central forces that need correction or modification. From this we establish a glimpse of the central dynamic structure of the problem. During the process we explore the person's psychopathology and evaluate his strengths and weaknesses. We do this to provide the third goal, namely, a full and accurate understanding of a significant circumscribed conflict or focus that accounts for that person's pain and suffering.

In obtaining these goals it is my feeling that the style and techniques utilized by the interviewer impose a significant influence on the evaluation process. Simply stated, it is the experienced short-term psychotherapist who will most likely actively pursue and delimit a workable focus, if one is present, during the initial interview. This has been my experience in Montreal, an experience now duplicated by the events of the Symposium to date accentuated, in particular, by the queries and comments of those members of the panel and audience whose experience and skills are obviously more related to the longer forms of psychotherapy.

The initial psychiatric interview, by no means a random or arbitrary meeting until recently at least, has received little attention as a procedure occupying a particular phase in the therapeutic process, one warranting a specificity of approach and technical application. As a potentially fruitful area of research it is evident that it has not been adequately subjected to exploitation by dynamically oriented psychotherapists. In the psychoanalytic frame of reference, for example, controversy continues as to the appropriateness of the direct request for specific information versus that which is spontaneously volunteered. Freud, in commenting on the beginning of treatment stated "on the whole one lets the patient talk and explains nothing more than is absolutely necessary to keep him talking." He continues with the admonition that "lengthy preliminary discussions before the beginning of treatment... have certain disadvantageous consequences for which one must be prepared" and "what as subject matter the treatment begins with is on the whole immaterial, whether with the patient's life-story, with a history of the illness or with recollections of childhood." Some four years earlier however, he wrote "I have formed the practice of first undertaking—"the treatment"—only provisionally for one or two weeks... it was only 'taking a sounding' in order to learn more about the case and to decide whether it was a suitable one for psycho-analysis." The initial interview, conducted with the intent of determining an individual's candidacy for short-term psychotherapy, leans more to this latter observation. In essence the interviewer is determining the patient's potential for treatment by conducting treatment during the evaluation. This is more evident when one observes the styles of Doctors Sifneos and Davanloo. Dr. Malan seems to use a more classical psychodiagnostic approach.

In many respects considerable modifications of the free association type of interview have been introduced and the earlier implied interdictions further elaborated upon within the more adequately understood context of the widening scope of today's dynamic psychotherapies. The need for detailed histories and observations of the prospective patient's cognitive and psychic processes is essential to the understanding of the personality structure that underlies and accounts for the maladaptive experiences that have led to the quest for treatment.

Amongst others, Gill, Newman, and Redlich, in their excellent study, "The Initial Interview in Psychiatric Practice" pointed out the "wide range of relevant content in initial interviews" dependent, in part, on the psychiatric purpose for which it was performed. Certainly, despite one's psychotherapeutic frame of reference, there can be little argument with the three aims ascribed to the first interview, namely, to establish rapport, to appraise the patient's psychological status and to reinforce the patient's wish for therapy. It is during the initial interview that one seeks insight into the central dynamics, and presents it constructively and meaningfully to the patient. This process in itself, offers no better impetus to motivation. It is inherent and essential in the case of the patient selected for short-term psychotherapy. Furthermore, these authors indicate an appropriate aversion to the "syllabus" type of evaluative interview. Elaborating further they explain four variables, the personality structures of the participants, their particular perception of their respective roles, the purposes that each is pursuing and, lastly, and in my opinion of greatest significance, the technique employed by the interviewer. In one respect, therefore, one might say that the content is, to a large extent, determined by the interviewer whose "reality situation may force him to direct the interview into certain channels." It is my proposition that the evaluation of an individual as a candidate for short-term dynamic psychotherapy represents a highly specific channel which influences the interviewer both consciously and unconsciously. In this vein we have noticed the frequency with which questions to the panel members and their responses have, implicitly and explicitly, made reference to the issue of countertransference. There are features in the style of the interviewer which are provocative but purposefully geared to the establishment of a therapeutic focus. By and large the initial interview elicits data about the prospective patient that is no different from that compiled by any dynamically oriented therapist. There is however, one significant difference, and, one on which the end result is most dependent. I am referring, again, to the establishment of a psychodynamically functional focus. In achieving this goal the styles of all three major proponents in this Symposium share an enthusiasm, a zealous curiosity maintained by an above-average level of activity. In so doing they adhere to the three aims previously mentioned. In each instance the approach is one which achieves a fine balance of directiveness and non-directiveness permitting the patient to be spontaneous while at the same time (and this is no paradox), defining and re-defining the developing focus. With the possible exception of Dr. Malan, we have not observed the so-called traditional diagnostic interview. Rather, greater emphasis has been placed on a skillfully guided "spontaneous" interchange. In a sense I suggest that what is being accomplished is a condensation of Freud's earlier recommendation for a "trial sounding" during which the interviewer is able to elicit signs of the patient's therapeutic potential, the psychotherapeutic diagnosis. I suggest that for the purpose of short-term psychotherapy more weight must be assigned to this factor than to clinical, genetic or dynamic features, though these cannot be ignored. During these evaluations we have become aware of the interviewer's intuitiveness in his "zeroing-in" on the core of the therapeutic focus, ignoring or interpreting away, on one hand, the patient's natural tendencies to resist and, on the other, the inhibiting characterological features designed to perpetuate the conflict. Traditionally, the analytic interview is designed to permit the emergence of all conflicting data. The short-term psychotherapist must, in a short period of time, select that focal conflict which, if resolved, will bring about the most significant modification of an inhibited lifestyle in a short period of time. To accomplish this, of course, the selection criteria, already described in previous chapters, must be in evidence.

At this point, a note of caution must be introduced. There is no question that the patients presented here could benefit from other psychotherapeutic modalities, in particular, those of longer duration. It is this controversial issue that is recurrently presented as criticism of the short-term process. Only continued research will establish the merits and demerits of the various modalities. I mention this only to elaborate on my contention that the short-term dynamic psychotherapist is unique amongst psychotherapists. His style is unique and he utilizes techniques in a most active fashion to deal with the initial resistances that operate to lengthen the evaluation process as well as treatment. I cannot agree with Rogers' statement "the therapist cannot speed the process by a prior discernment of the problem ... to do so may make the therapist feel good but it cannot make the client feel better." The short-term psychotherapist does discern the problem (focus) and, as we have observed, presents it back to the patient who, quite obviously, does indeed feel better. Some of the critics of this approach have suggested that it is too intellectual. We may, at times, rely on a more cognitive approach but I suggest that the critic look again. The affect is more often than not, right there.

Generally speaking, as is true of all dynamic psychotherapies with the possible exception, at times, of analysis, the short-term psychotherapist must firstly, elicit the central dynamic problem via the route of a rapidly established but comprehensive picture of the patient's life with an even greater necessity than that characteristic of the longer types of therapy. Secondly, the therapist's activity hovers around and is conditioned by a central focus. Thirdly, considerable emphasis is placed on reality events in the patient's life, focusing, in particular, on contemporary relationships. Fourthly, spontaneity, while encouraged, is by no means uninfluenced by active intervention. Fifthly, fantasy is utilized only insofar as it relates to the dynamic focus and the current realities. Lastly, past-present links are repeatedly sought, clarified and interpreted, particularly so in the context of. transference distortions. For the present I would have to concur that this represents a somewhat oversimplified outline of the interviewer-patient interaction. The short-term psychotherapist must maintain an awareness of the functional balance between a more directive style and that which allows for the patient's spontaneous unfolding of his situation with perhaps less obvious, but no less skilled, guidance and prompting.

In my experience in Montreal I have been witness to a somewhat disturbing variability in the diagnostic and prognostic usefulness of the interview in different hands. In this respect audio-visual recording has exerted a major influence in both the execution and study of the short-term process. It has enabled us to closely scrutinize, perhaps with an intensity that may be described as being obsessive, the many phases of the patient-therapist interaction from its inception to its termination. In particular we have become sensitized to those lengthening factors described by Dr. Malan in his first book. The question has often been asked, and I ask it myself at this point, as to whether the outcome of an initial evaluation conducted on the same patient by Dr. Malan and Dr. Sifneos, would have been similar.

Shortly there will be presented segments of two initial interviews—both provocative—each demonstrating a style particular to each interviewer. Observe that I mention style rather than technique for, in my view, techniques remain constant while styles vary. Drs. Davanloo, Malan and Sifneos manifest quite different styles. They do, however, utilize the same psychoanalytic techniques, differing only in the persistence and insistence with which they are applied. One is "gentle" in his pursuit, another more "relentless." Dr. Malan's style, more classical in its form elicits a more comprehensive body of data from which he isolates a focus. In the others it appears that the issue of focality is established in a more obvious manner and, in a manner of speaking the interviewer "locks-in" the patient. I propose that this "technique" pertains to a style of functioning, a style born out of clinical experience, intuition and confidence. The patient's ability to deal with that style is a measure of his or her strength and potential for short-term dynamic—provocative—psychotherapy. I do not believe that every therapist, no matter how skilled, can adapt to this approach without considerable effort and self-scrutiny, particularly, if his basic training has been that of long-term psychotherapy. This has been my own personal experience and I doubt that it represents something unique. Dr. Malan, in his aforementioned text, describes similar difficulties experienced by his initial group of competent analysts.

I apologize for not being more specific in elaborating my belief that the interviewer himself is a significant criterion in the selection of candidates for short-term psychotherapy. One factor does emerge. From the outset of our involvement with our prospective patients we tend not to underestimate their potential strengths. Our approach is described as being more aggressive but it is a functional aggressivity based on confidence and purposeful enthusiasm as well as a keen awareness of our patients' tolerance. The approach is anxiety provoking. Our patients will inform us, if we care to observe, how much anxiety they can handle for the purpose of attaining a meaningful therapeutic goal.

There now follow portions of initial interviews conducted by Dr. Davanloo and myself. The patient interviewed by Dr. Davanloo is a married woman in her early thirties, who was seen with the symptoms of depression, suicidal ideation, obsessional ideations regarding her husband's health, and disturbances in interpersonal relationships. She had a masochistic pattern of relating with her husband, adopting a self-punitive, compliant, submissive pattern. During the early part of the interview it becomes evident that this behavioural style with significant people has been one of long-standing. Her mother was described as being domineering, possessive and masochistic; her father as aggressive, domineering and demanding. During the interview she was depressed and cried frequently. It will be observed that the transference pattern of her behaviour with the therapist is quite similar. In the initial part of the interview Dr. Davanloo is more supportive, but he soon becomes more confronting.

"The Case of the Submissive Woman"

Th: But how did you feel toward your husband when he decided this was the best and you had to go along with it?

Pt: Well, I don't resent that. I mean, he is trying to the best of his capabilities to take care of his family, and I'm his family and he wants to take care of me, and he does take care of me, and I know that he loves me. I don't feel he's doing anything.

Th: I feel in a way that you are very much threatened with the idea of resentment toward your husband, because, you see, when I was asking you how you felt, you had to really reassure me that you don't have resentment.

Pt: Yes, I probably do because I don't want to be here, and I feel that I wouldn't have to be here if it wasn't for him. Obviously, if I wasn't married to him I wouldn't be here. That's right. But I am.

Th: Because also in the back of your mind is that for four years you have been sacrificing because he goes to school, and you have been in a way struggling all along during that time.

Pt: Yes, but it was as much my idea as his, and I don't think I resent that. I don't think I do. I don't know; I don't really know what I think any more.

Th: But do you usually find it difficult to admit to yourself that you might resent things?

Pt: Yes, I think I probably do, because all my life I have been told

276   GOLDEN

>
> that I have certain duties toward certain people and I don't have any choice.

Th: All your life you have been told this?
Pt: Yes.
Th: Would you like to tell me about it?

Here is another vignette with the same patient. The evaluator is questioning her as to whether there is some similarity between her pattern of relationship with her mother and that with her husband. This is a linking between the genetic pattern and the contemporary pattern of her behavior.

Th: If we go back to your relationship with your mother, there you had to comply to what she thought was best for you.
Pt: Yes.
Th: Do you feel some parallel between the two, namely, the relationship with your mother and the one with your husband?
Pt: Yes. I told him that. I told him that I felt I'm just another child, that I don't have any personality, that really what I want and think and feel is never considered. And he said, "That's true, and what do you want me to do? Do you want me to quit my job and go back? We'll have no income again, and you won't be happier anywhere else because it's all just within yourself," and I know that's true.
Th: Could you tell me about the areas of your life where you have had to give up your ideas in relationship with your husband? You know, where you have had to mold yourself to his way of doing things and thinking?
Pt: Sometimes I think it's in every way.
Th: Could you talk about it?

Another vignette of the same patient. Here the evaluator explores her feelings about her husband. She is crying, blowing her nose frequently. The evaluator indicates that her helplessness might be her way of dealing with her rage.

Th: But I'm talking about your feelings at this point.
Pt: I don't know. You mean do I get angry or something?
Th: What do you think?

Pt: Well, I feel hopeless.
Th: But do you think this hopelessness is a way of dealing with your anger? Because somehow any person in your position in most of these situations would have been angry. You see, this is what you described all along, the way it was with your mother. Yes?
Pt: Yes.
Th: You say that you were molded, that you were pushed under the name that this is best for you, but then you find it difficult to announce to yourself that you feel resentment and you feel angry.
Pt: Yes, I do.

Dr. Golden:

Here we have the transcript of a portion of my first interview with a male patient. He had an initial interview with Dr. ——— two weeks prior to this one.

"The Case of the Man With a Headache"

The patient is in his early thirties, married. He was referred with the chief complaints of headaches, "pain in the head," various sensations in his head. He had had these difficulties for a few months. His father had died two years before "of a blood clot in his brain." He and his father used to spend a lot of time together in the basement, where his father had a sizeable workshop with many tools. Early-life memories had to do with working there together while his father taught him skills.

A few months prior to his first visit the patient had a friend and his wife over to his home. He and his friend were working together in the patient's workshop, instructing his friend re the tools, etc. Later that night the patient awoke with a severe headache, and in a panic state, he was rushed to a nearby hospital where he was kept for a complete medical investigation. This was negative and he was placed on a minor tranquilizer. He had a few follow-ups with a psychiatrist there. He was dissatisfied.

Th: It looks like you're not quite sure where to start.
Pt: I don't suppose I ever am. The only thing that bothers me is that

Pt: I've always got headaches and pains in my head. What's causing it, I don't know.
Th: Well, have you given any thought to what might be causing it?
Pt: Like I say, I don't know what's bothering me; that's the problem. It all happened all of a sudden. I had like a little blackout, you know. I was rushed to the hospital. They kept me and they gave me blood tests and cardiograms because I was all excited and nervous.
Th: But you say this thing started suddenly and you went to the hospital?
Pt: I've never had any problems. I'll start from the beginning. I was at home; I had some visitors. This fellow wanted to use my workshop.
Th: You were working with a friend?
Pt: Yeah, I was working with a friend. So, after we worked about an hour, an hour and a half, we went up—
Th: You were building something and he was helping you?
Pt: A machine, yes. Both of us were working on it together.
Th: On something you wanted to build for yourself?
Pt: No, for him. He was using my tools, you see. He had the equipment to make a machine but he needed a cabinet; I've got all the power tools—table saw, etc.—and I had some scrap pieces of lumber, so he wanted to use them. So we were working down in the basement and—
Th: So you're good at that type of thing? I know a bit about you, that you're proficient with tools and things like that.
Pt: Yes.
Th: You have been interviewed previously?
Pt: Yes. I saw a psychologist and also Dr. ———.
Th: Did you get anything out of the previous interview? Did you come away with anything?
Pt: No. They pinpointed—they say it could be a connection—what was bothering me was the way my father died. He had a blood clot in the brain. They think there could be a connection with that. Dr. ——— thought there would maybe be a connection.
Th: Oh? Have you been thinking about that possibility?
Pt: No. I don't think about it. That's the whole main problem.
Th: Dr. ——— suggested that there might be a connection. Between what and what, actually?
Pt: First of all, I've always got pains in the head here, and they travel,

and I get a headache—you know, from the eyeballs and the back of the head, etc. Like I say, my father died with a blood clot in the brain. He thinks there could be a connection there.
Th: What kind of connection?
Pt: Probably because I don't want it to happen to me, and he figures maybe I've been thinking about it or something.
Th: Have you thought yourself that both you and your father had symptoms related to the head, the brain?
Pt: No. I've never thought about that.
Th: How come?
Pt: First of all, maybe it's because I didn't want it to ever happen to me.
Th: At the time that your father was struck down?
Pt: That's possible. It could have been possible, yes.
Th: Had the thought ever occurred to you?
Pt: I thought of it being hereditary.
Th: So when your father was ill you thought that perhaps, being his son, you might possibly have the same thing?
Pt: Yes, right.
Th: When you used to think like that, how did it affect you?
Pt: When I used to think like that? Well, this is it. I don't remember ever thinking about it because I was pretty active around the house, and my life, let's say—
Th: You mean your activity keeps you from thinking about certain things?
Pt: Yes. I keep on the go all the time, and I'm a great thinker. I'm always thinking. My head's always going.
Th: Thinking about what?
Pt: Many things. Things I do in life. My job, let's say, my home life. I've got this to do, not this to do.
Th: But something like your father; that you don't think about?
Pt: That I don't think about.
Th: Do you think it's possible that perhaps you keep your mind active so you don't have to think about certain things?
Pt: No. By nature I'm a nervous guy, to a certain extent, and then I'm the type of guy that's always on the go.
Th: You mean you're more nervous about your work and things you have to do than you are about yourself and your health?
Pt: No. What I mean to say—just in case I contradict myself—I've always been a nervous type of fellow.

Th: Yes, but your own health, your father's death—this doesn't make you nervous?

Pt: Well, no. It didn't exactly make me nervous, but I didn't like the idea. It was too bad he had to die; like there's nothing we can do. The doctor said he had about two years to live, and he was right—dead on.

Th: How was that two years for you, as you were waiting for your father to die?

Pt: A lot of times he was sick. I didn't let it bother me, but I didn't want him to die either, you know.

Th: What do you mean you didn't let it bother you?

Pt: Well, I tried not to think about it, so maybe I put it in the back of my mind.

Th: You try not to think about things that bother you, or that might bother you. How do you do that?

Pt: Well, let's say something bothers me. I'll say to hell with it, and think of something else and go on.

Th: So there are a lot of things that have bothered you that are stored up somewhere?

Pt: It's possible, yes. But I don't realize it's bothering me. This is the problem, you see. Maybe there's a connection there.

Th: You saw Dr. ——— when?

Pt: It was two weeks ago.

Th: Have you noticed any change in your thinking since that time?

Pt: No. I'm the same as I was.

Th: You said that he thought perhaps there might be a connection.

Pt: As he was questioning me, he asked, "How was your father?" He was a handyman, too. I was brought up—he taught me how to do a lot of things, etc. So he related a lot of things—

Th: Your father taught you?

Pt: Yes.

Th: Were you teaching or helping this friend of yours?

Pt: No. I can just do it.

Th: Does he sort of depend on you?

Pt: Well, we worked together. He knows a little bit, too.

Th: Who knows more?

Pt: Who would know more? I would say I would. I would say, yes.

Th: So you were in a sense helping him?

Pt: Yeah, but I wasn't saying so much. As we were working, I was just doing it. I'd say, "Let's do it this way."
Th: How did your father teach you? What was his style?
Pt: Well, with my father, instead of us horsing around, playing around, and running in the streets and that, we used to—
Th: But you and he. Let's say when he was trying to acquaint you with or teach you about a piece of equipment.
Pt: More or less, I used to watch him all the time. If I see somebody doing it once, well, the next time I can pretty well do it.
Th: Would you and he work together?
Pt: Yes. I would say we worked together, yeah.
Th: And how did he tell you to do things when you worked together?
Pt: Going back so far. He would say just do it this way here.
Th: You mean like you told your friend, "Let's do it this way"?
Pt: Let's do it this way, right.
Th: You mean you're like your father?
Pt: I would say in a way I am. A lot of people say, "Your character, too, you take after your father." What they mean by that, I don't know.
Th: But you smiled when you said what do they mean by that.
Pt: My father was—he could do anything; anything he touched or this or that. He did anything and everything. He was good at electronics, anything you can imagine.
Th: How would that have been to you in your younger days, to have a father who could do everything?
Pt: I liked that, sure.
Th: Did you ever wish you could be like him, do everything?
Pt: Well, I pretty well can do pretty well everything.
Th: But what happened, let's say when there were things you couldn't do and he had to say, "Now, look. You do it this way"?
Pt: It didn't bother me. He was right when it happened.
Th: I didn't say anything about bother.
Pt: I would do it when he said it.
Th: But you said it didn't bother you. You didn't say, "I liked it." "I didn't like it." You said, "It didn't bother me," as if to say, "Look. I don't want to think that things bother me." But I wonder, do things bother you?
Pt: I would say yes, but, like I say, I don't want to think about it, you know what I mean? That's my problem.

Th: Let's try for a moment to think about things that bother you. That's what you're here for.

Pt: Right. That's what I'm here for. We used to own property in town, apartments and that. Actually, I used to get fed up. I never did like to go there and help out. I knew how to do all the jobs, but I got fed up. I didn't want to go, and the same at home. And he bought another house where we used to live, and I never used to like to go there and to work. My brother bought it off of him, and when my brother would see me he asked me to give him a hand. It was like an effort. I just didn't like that type of work.

Th: You mean there was a time you didn't like working for your father or with your father?

Pt: I didn't like to work for my father. Sometimes he used to take a drink; he used to drink pretty heavily. We used to take a drink and I used to try to dodge out of helping him; I'd be yelling and—

Th: You didn't like to work with him when he was drinking?

Pt: No. I didn't like that.

Th: What bothered you about that?

Pt: What bothered me? I would say in a way it would get me nervous. He used to yell, and I'd start to run at him. I never did like it. As I got older—

Th: What was it you didn't like? He used to yell. How did his yelling affect you?

Pt: How did his yelling affect me? Let's say in a way it hurt my feelings.

Th: It made you feel what?

Pt: Feel bad, I'd say.

Th: What does that mean?

Pt: Put it this way. When he didn't drink and that, he was okay. He was a nice guy to get along with. But when he drank he was nasty—moody, let's say.

Th: He was a bastard?

Pt: Bastard, if you want to say that.

Th: What do you mean if I want to say that? Am I right? He was a bastard?

Pt: Yeah, I would say so. I've said it many times.

Th: You mean it's easier for me to say than it is for you to say?

Pt: It's not the idea of saying it. I just don't say it—swear. I was brought up right, but—

THE INTERVIEWER, A FACTOR IN PATIENT SELECTION

Th: Brought up not to express anything?
Pt: Yeah, you know.
Th: When you're angry, you don't express anger. When you're sad, you don't express that?
Pt: Right. Many times I used to swear and curse. Let's say I used to take this truck, and then I'd be saying you son of a bitch or bastard, etc., etc.
Th: So this man was perfect at doing many things, but sometimes he was a bastard?
Pt: Oh, yes.
Th: And you would get angry at him?
Pt: Exactly.
Th: How did you let him know you were angry?
Pt: I guess he knew by my character.
Th: How would he know?
Pt: Well, sometimes—let's say there was a piece of equipment and I'd be rough in doing it.
Th: You mean when you're angry you work hard and you're rough with the equipment?
Pt: Let's say if I was making a piece of furniture.
Th: Does that mean that when you're upset you work harder, or when you're angry you throw yourself into work?
Pt: No.
Th: What do you do when you're angry?
Pt: If I'm angry, let's say it pertains to my work even today—the type of job I've got, this or that, the authority that I have, instead of holding everything in I would yell at the guy or give him shit.
Th: You mean like your father?
Pt: I would say, yes.
Th: Do you drink?
Pt: I never drank in my life; I never smoked in my life. I've been drinking in about the last year and a half, I would say.
Th: When did your father die?
Pt: It's two years now, going on three years, that he's dead. It was 1972 he died, I believe.
Th: I see. So in a sense there may be a connection there, too. You didn't like when he drank. He used to get uptight. He'd be tough to work with.
Pt: Well, no. The only reason that made me drink—I work, for

instance, and the job I've got, the guys are always complaining about this and that.

Th: You said Dr. ——— had mentioned something about a possible connection between your symptoms and your father's, and now you talk about drinking and your feet are shuffling. Does the thought make you uncomfortable that there's something—

Pt: No. I'm always like this.

Th: But this idea that people say there's something about your character that's very similar to your father?

Pt: Well, let's say if I get mad or moody or yell, they say I take after my father. "You're like your father," they'd say.

Th: You mean his not-so-good points?

Pt: Well, just like my father, they'd say, good or bad, I guess. I'm like my father.

Th: You have his good points, and you have some of his not-so-good points?

Pt: Yeah, I would say. Yes. Sometimes he would be mean; sometimes I'm mean and that.

Th: Do you want to be sort of known as your father's son?

Pt: No. It doesn't really bother me that way.

Th: You accept it?

Pt: I accept it.

Th: It doesn't bother you a bit?

Pt: No.

Th: Even when you're the angry, moody type?

Pt: No. Whether I liked it or not, let's say it grew on me.

Th: That sounds like a cop-out.

Pt: No.

Th: "It grew on me. That's the way I am. People stay away. Don't try to change it. Don't look into it. That's me." In other words, you sort of put up a little wall now between us.

Pt: Well, I do that all the time. I don't like anybody to ever get near to me or close to me. I don't know for what reason.

Th: You don't want people around?

Pt: Yeah, I love people, like that. I just don't like to get too close or too friendly. You know, underneath there's always a gap.

Th: Is it the same thing with me now?

Pt: No. I can't leave a gap because I want to find out what my problem is.

Th: That sort of makes me different from people in some sense. You mean you're going to let me get close, but you don't let anybody else get close?
Pt: No. I'm here to help myself.
Th: But it must be tough for you to even think about letting me get too close?
Pt: No. It's not. I don't look at it that way at all.

Dr. Sifneos:

I am glad to comment briefly on several aspects that have been brought up. One has to do with Dr. Golden's question, namely, whether if it had been me interviewing Dr. Malan's patient would I have acted in a different way. I do agree with Dr. Davanloo that one does change his technique depending on the patient. Someone mentioned that I was going for the "jugular vein." Well, sometimes I do, but not all the time. As I commented before, the gentleness that Dr. Malan showed in interviewing "The Secretary with the Violent Father" (Chapter 7) was indeed the most appropriate way of approaching this particular patient. Maybe I cannot be as gentle as he, but nevertheless I also have some element of gentleness.

In terms of evaluation, in my opinion the real task of the evaluator is twofold:

One has to deal with the gathering of information in order to establish a focus, as was pointed out by Dr. Golden. The second task has to do with the establishment of a rapport with the patient. Obviously, one does not go into one without the other.

There are cerain technical issues that I think one has to use as a part of the interviewing technique that would be different for the information gathering and for the establishment of rapport. As far as I am concerned, I would divide the nature of the questions that the evaluator has to pose into two kinds: First, there are the "open-ended" type: "Tell me something more about what is bothering you," for example. One expects the patient to associate fairly freely to such a statement. On the other hand, we have questions that are "forced choice," such as "How old are you?" "When did you move from that house?" These questions require only a yes or no.

A judicious use of a balance between these two types of questions is of importance. For the information gathering and the focusing, forced-choice questions in my opinion should be used more often. This may be what some of you might call the pounding of the patient, or going after the "jugular vein." But one has at times to test and to push in order to see how much information he can get. I think both Dr. Davanloo and Dr. Golden have demonstrated this type of approach beautifully in these two interviews.

Dr. Golden went after the patient, kept on asking him anxiety-provoking questions. The patient tried to get away from it, but Dr. Golden insisted and came right back to it, and I think he was able to arrive at a specific focus very quickly and very well.

Dr. Davanloo did it in a very interesting way by changing his technique. In the beginning he was somewhat more open-ended, and in spite of the barrage in the form of blowing her nose, which the patient used to thwart him, he was able to get exactly what he wanted. His timely interpretation changed the course of the interview. I would certainly agree with Dr. Davanloo that our interviewing technique should be changeable in order to establish rapport.

Dr. Malan:

I think these cases that we have been shown so far illustrate very pointedly one of the basic aspects of the initial interview, and that is that you conduct your initial interview according to what the patient is like. There is a constant interaction between your perception of the patient and how he is reacting to what you say, and the degree and depth of your interpretation, and the degree of forcefulness with which you put them.

One of the things that is very difficult for us as dynamically oriented interviewers is to make quite sure that it isn't going to be dangerous to make deep contact with a particular patient. When I teach residents about the initial interview, I tell them that they really ought to do the psychiatric history first, before they start making any interpretation to the patient at all. After all, if you don't know that a patient heard voices for a week after she had a baby, you don't know whether it is wise or not to make any interpretation to this patient. One of the things that I always say about the initial interview is that you should make interpretations to the patient. They should be no deeper, no more forceful, than needed to get the information that you want. It may be necessary to make them forcefully or deeply, or it may not.

It is quite clear with these two patients that we have just been shown that both of the interviewers summed up these patients very quickly as people with whom it would be perfectly safe to make interpretations and to bring out the basic conflict. It is also quite clear that the distinction between the initial interview and the beginning of the therapy is totally blurred. There is no question that these two interviews were therapeutic interviews. With some patients it is absolutely right to do this, and I am quite sure that with these two patients it was right.

I am most struck by the interaction between these patients and the interviewers, and the degree of sensitivity shown. I want to say that I am sure that the technique was absolutely appropriate here. It was the beginning of the therapy, and I would think both of these patients were highly suitable for the kind of psychotherapy we are talking about in this symposium.

However, one should not feel that this should be done with every patient. I can think of two patients that I interviewed. One was a man who remained silent for the first half-hour of the interview. I eventually got him to talk to me by one means or another. In the next interview he told me he had dreams of people being wrapped like a cut of meat and being eaten by a computer. He admitted to hearing voices, and he had ideas of reference. It was necessary to make contact to get this information, but at the same time one does not want to start making unguarded interpretations.

Another patient was a woman who very clearly showed the pattern in her life. At the end of the interview I said to her, "Well, look. What you are telling me is so and so, and this is really the pattern of your life, isn't it?" to which she responded dramatically. She fell in love with me and she was still writing poems to me two years later. You run this sort of risk when you do interviews of this kind, so that it is terribly important to recognize both the power of this technique and its danger. It has to be done with the right patient. And, again, these two patients were the right patients.

Dr. Sifneos

Dr. Sifneos (in response to a question regarding the classification of psychotherapies): I have divided psychotherapies into two categories, long-term and short-term. Supportive psychotherapies use supportive techniques of all kinds, including drugs. Psychoanalysis and psychoanalytic psychotherapies do not. They use, as Dr. Davanloo pointed out so nicely, much more interpretation, and these interpretations, as I have already said, are anxiety-provoking.

Short-term psychotherapy of the kind that we are talking about in Boston, the kind Dr. Malan is using at the Tavistock Clinic, and the kind Dr. Davanloo is using here at The Montreal General are all anxiety-provoking techniques.

Finally, crisis intervention is a very short dynamic intervention, and, as Dr. Malan pointed out, sometimes one can have only one interview and obtain very impressive results.

One also can use a crisis supportive technique. One can see the patient once or twice, very supportively help him overcome a realistic problem that brings him to seek help, and eventually assist him in returning as quickly as possible to his previous state of emotional equilibrium.

Question from the floor:

I would like to hear from some of the panelists to what extent countertransference feeling plays a part in selection criteria.

Dr. Davanloo:

Definitely, countertransference is one of the major variables which is continuously being fed into the evaluation process, and it obviously affects the criteria for selection. In our study we have been very much interested in the relationship between the therapeutic focus, the patient's motivation, and the countertransference.

Dr. Malan:

Of course, this is one of the variables which is continuously being fed into the computer, which ends up with a decision as to whether or not the patient is going to be accepted, whether or not one has a positive feeling toward the patient.

Question from the floor:

It seems to me that there are two types of relatively hard data one can get out of the assessment interview. One is the historical facts; the other, an assessment of the affective state of the patient. I was concerned especially with the two interviews that we have just seen. Dr. Golden, in the process of the interview, very often seemed to stifle affective expression in the patient and to replace it with cognitive interpretation; he did not seem to be mobilizing the affect that was clearly latent under the surface. And I would like to ask the panelists their thoughts about this, attempting to mobilize affect or assess the patient's ability to respond affectively to get a better reading of what the affect is.

Dr. Malan:

I don't agree with you. Concerning Dr. Davanloo's interview, I cannot see that there is any question of his suppressing affect. He made an interpretation on the subject of aggression; she responded to this with highly charged material about what her dentist said, and she ended up by saying she was a "heaving mass of anger." Now, what on earth does that have to do with suppressing affect? I cannot understand.

Dr. Sifneos:

As regards Dr. Davanloo's interview, in my view what he didn't want was her depressive tears. I am identifying with Dr. Davanloo here; what he wanted to get out was what lay beneath the depressive tears, so he cut her short in an attempt to get at the angry feeling. And this was achieved with total success as far as I am concerned.

Dr. Rosenberg:

I have had some contact with Dr. Golden's patient. It is important to clarify that this was the second interview with this patient, but it was Dr. Golden's initial interview. The patient had been seen once before. At that first interview the patient was terribly resistant to any interpretation. I was one of the people who thought at that point his motivation was extremely low. In cases such as this, where there is a very clearly focalized complaint but motivation is very low, and we have a serious doubt, we refer the patient for a second interview.

Dr. Golden went into the second interview with some knowledge of this patient's psychodynamics. He had some definite ideas about the psychodynamics which we thought were quite clear. His father died of a blood clot on the brain; he had a close relationship with his father, and he spent a lot of time working in the shop with his father. The onset of his symptoms began when a friend of his was over at the house, part of which was explained in the interview. He was working with the friend, showing him some techniques of working with carpentry very much as his father used to work with him. Toward the end of the evening he developed an intense panic attack that he was going to die, was afraid he was going to have a blood clot and went to the hospital. We felt after watching the initial interview that his symptoms were clearly an aspect of identification with his father. He resisted this highly throughout the first interview. All of us were certain about it.

Dr. Golden was going after a specific focus in this interview. He was making interpretation specifically designed to elucidate that primary area of conflict and to determine how deep the patient's resistance was. It was less in Dr. Golden's interview than in the first interview. I think something therapeutic happened in the first interview, and the patient was more able to entertain certain psychodynamically oriented concepts.

Question from the floor:

From what I can gather, it seems difficult to make an evaluation for this kind of therapy in one interview. Dr. Malan said that sometimes he goes on for two hours. Well, that is two interviews, maybe, and we are not in the kind of setting where we can do this. So I wonder if the panel will make some comments about the relative advantage of going on for two or three interviews, or maybe even four, before making a decision. Regarding Dr. Malan's patient, I can very well see that some of those things that look like they couldn't be reached, like the great denial, may have fallen away to some extent in the second session. You may have had something else that you felt you could deal with. The one possible disadvantage I see is—and I would like to hear from the panel about this—the development of a strong transference and then the difficulty of transferring the patient on to another therapist.

Dr. Davanloo:

In my research in 1963 I originally set up three diagnostic interviews, but then I changed to two diagnostic interviews and finally became selective and decided upon one to three. A large percentage of the patients in that series fell into the category requiring one or two interviews. For example, with "The Secretary with the Violent Father," whom Dr. Malan interviewed, I would do two diagnostic interviews. Definitely I agree that with some patients there develops a strong transference, but usually we have not been faced with problems. There is the advantage, as we have seen in our first series, that in certain patients in the first interview the motivation is low, but by the third interview the patients are highly motivated.

One might say that in my series most of the patients whose problems were related to the triangular oedipal type had only one initial interview with me. One-third of the patients in our series were treated successfully in from ten to fifteen sessions, and the majority of them fall into the category of one initial evaluating interview.

Chapter 14

Where Does Evaluation End and Therapy Begin?

C. YUNG

H. DAVANLOO

Dr. Yung:

The tasks and goals of a psychiatric evaluation vary with the milieu and the philosophy of the clinical setting; with the orientation, personality and experience of the evaluator; with the nature, urgency and severity of the presenting problem; with the expectations and motivations of the patient; and ultimately with the ability of the patient to benefit from such an evaluation.

The goals and tasks of an initial interview for short-term dynamic psychotherapy are similar to a formal psychiatric evaluation—with one important, additional and specific task, however. The task is the assessment of the patient's ability and potential to withstand or benefit from this form of treatment; in other words, to delineate or elicit those patient variables which have been regarded, either by clinical experience or research findings, as the best possible predications of a successful outcome. This has already been dealt with previously. Now I would like to focus on one of the controversial issues brought forth in the discussion, namely, the early use of confrontation and interpretation in the initial interview, which appears at times to be a therapeutic session rather than a diagnostic or evaluative process. In this sense, treatment appears to begin before evaluation ends. It seems that the rationale for the use of this intervention is twofold: first to test out the tentative psychodynamic hypothesis in relation to the patient's conflict, and second to test the receptivity of the patient to short-term dynamic psychotherapy by obtaining the responses to interpretation. The important question that we are faced with is this: Is it at all possible to answer these two important questions without the early use of confrontation and interpretation in the evaluation? Thus what appears to be "treatment begins before evaluation ends" is in actuality an application of treatment technique to evaluation.

If one reviews the literature on short-term psychoanalytic psychotherapy, one finds essentially two main categories of writing which may throw light on the subject that we are discussing. The first category of these writings suggests the early use of interpretation in the form of either partial or trial interpretation. For example, Franz Alexander used trial interpretation very early to test patients' reactions. He also indicated the possibility that a drastic interpretation given in the first two interviews may fail or even precipitate a psychotic episode. There are those workers who advocate the use of transference interpretation in the initial interview and stress appraising such manifestations rapidly. Other groups, such as Michael Balint and Tarachow, have suggested some psychogenic references to the patient to provoke thinking in the first session about why he is sick.

There are other workers who indicate that the line between evaluation and treatment is not a clear-cut one, and that therapy starts immediately when the therapist and the patient face each other. Some workers regard trial interpretation as one of the major criteria for selection.

In brief, all these statements support the fact that treatment can and does begin in the initial interview. The question is how to identify those patients who can respond to and benefit from these interventions without the risk of psychological decompensation. Obviously, the clinical skill and experience of the evaluator is of major importance.

The second category of literature consists of case reports of patients with one or a few sessions with remarkable outcome. A review of these cases indicates that the early use of interpretation is present in the first or second interview of most of these patients. For example, we know that Freud's treatment of Bruno Walter, who had a fear of paralysis of his right arm, was completed in six sessions in 1906. He utilized the strong positive transference he had with the patient.

Another patient was the case of the famous composer Gustav Mahler, who suffered from a "folie à deux." Freud treated this case of obsessional neurosis in 1908 in one session which lasted four hours. He brought to the patient's awareness the significance and relationship of marrying his wife, Alma Maria, and the fact that his mother's name was Maria.

Another example is Franz Alexander's treatment of a scientist who suffered from a severe depression which prevented him from completing his work to be presented at a national meeting. He treated this patient in two sessions; he made an interpretation that the patient's depression was an alibi to deal with his destructive competitiveness toward his colleagues, which created guilt.

I would like to point out that abstract versions of such do not do justice to these therapists. The full meaning and understanding of the psychodynamic forces in these therapeutic interactions, the intuitive powers of the therapist and the enormous capacity for insight and introspection of these patients can only be appreciated in reviewing the original texts.

Now I would like to present two clinical vignettes which will perhaps illustrate the point that sometimes treatment appears to begin before evaluation ends. The first is from an interview conducted by Dr. Davanloo.

The patient is a twenty-year-old man who came with the chief complaint of being very depressed with disturbances in interpersonal relationships, particularly in the area of heterosexual relationships, who had suffered from anxiety for many years, as far back as he could remember, and who as well had had a persistently hostile relationship with his mother. His mother was described as a person whose "emotions are exaggerated, and her behavior is a great source of anger," to the level that at times he felt "like attacking her." His mother divorced his biological father when the patient was one year old, and he has never seen him. He knows his father was an alcoholic. His mother then remarried. There was constant violent behavior between his parents; his stepfather was violent, had many affairs, and the patient feared him and experienced a great deal of anxiety. During his adolescent years he felt like physically attacking his stepfather and, during the interview, said "murdering him." The way he dealt with his rage was by going to his room.

"The Case of the Man with an Impulse to Murder His Stepfather"

Th: Did your mother used to talk to you about your father when he was not home?
Pt: Lately, yes. Let's say the past five or six years that I remember distinctly. When I was younger, I can't remember.

Th: You can't remember, but what has she talked about in the past five years?
Pt: Just that he's an animal or whatever.
Th: In what way do you mean?
Pt: Just the things he was doing. She didn't really even have to talk to me about it because I saw it.
Th: How about their sexual life?
Pt: Nothing.
Th: You don't know anything about it?
Pt: I once barged in on them when I was younger.
Th: How old were you?
Pt: Five or six.
Th: What do you remember?
Pt: I just remember them getting very upset.
Th: What was the situation in which you barged in on them?
Pt: I usually was supposed to knock on the door, and I didn't. I don't know why; the phone was ringing or whatever; I don't know. They weren't in any sexual act, but she got very upset and told me to close the door.
Th: When you were talking about this, you smiled. I was wondering why.
Pt: I don't know. Just a reaction when I look back on it; it's something kind of humorous.
Th: What do you think is humorous?
Pt: Them getting upset.
Th: You mentioned that your mother is an irritating person in relationship with you.
Pt: Yes. This irritation has been built up over many, many years.
Th: How many years would you say?
Pt: I can trace it back to her arguments with my father.
Th: Are you saying that all along the way there was a problem between your father and your mother as well as between you and your mother?
Pt: Maybe I didn't realize it at the time, but when I got older and started to understand why it was still going on, and why should it be. I was questioning why does she still keep him here. I was getting angry at her; I was beginning to hate her because of it, because I felt it was enough. I finally got up at one point and said, "Either he goes or I do."

Th: Oh! You told your mother this?
Pt: I told her once.
Th: How old were you then?
Pt: Fifteen, maybe.
Th: In other words, you gave an ultimatum to your mother?
Pt: I gave her an ultimatum, yes.
Th: That she choose either you or him.
Pt: If you want to put it that way.
Th: How would you put it yourself?
Pt: Myself, it would be either that she gets him out of the house, which is causing enough pain for everybody else, or I leave.
Th: When I said it that way, you said right away to me, "If you want to put it that way." You must have some ideation about it. What was the idea you had in mind?
Pt: In many respects she had told me that the reason why she kept him here was because she loved him, and I really couldn't understand because it didn't make much sense, because she destroyed me in a certain way. Let's say not destroyed, but caused enough pain in me in a certain way, for my brother and my sister, and the excuse she gave me was because she loved him.
I know the real excuse; that she'd been through one marriage and she wanted a house where she could furnish it and still get money, and she had told me many times, "What if we had to live on alimony; we'd have to go into an apartment." I told her when I was older, I said, "I don't give a damn!
I really don't give a damn!"
Th: So then you must have been very angry with your mother?
Pt: Oh, yes! That's why I hate her so much now. At this point, I should explain it's very difficult for me to live there, at my house, because she can see the hate in my eyes, and I try not to talk to her, and when she does start screaming I get feelings of physically beating her up, which disturbs me.
Th: Do you think there are some similarities here? Your stepfather had a disturbed relationship with your mother, and then you gave an ultimatum, and finally your mother left him. Then as soon as he left, from what I can understand, your relationship with your mother rapidly deteriorated to a level that is more or less similar to your mother's relationship with your stepfather. You find yourself in a similar dilemma, and you experience a great deal of rage toward her.

Pt: Yes. I don't show it. I suppress it internally.
Th: What else do you do?
Pt: I lock myself up in my room.
Th: So you do the same thing still; the same technique that you used with your father?
Pt: Yes.
Th: When you talk about this rage inside, do you feel like attacking her?
Pt: Yes.
Th: Is there any time that you have the ideation that you would actually do something physically?
Pt: The idea is in my head.
Th: With what?
Pt: Just with my fists.
Th: With your fists. Do you feel like doing that? Did you at any time do that?
Pt: Oh, yeah. There were times when I felt like doing that.
Th: But did you?
Pt: Oh, no. Only one time I pushed her on the ground and that was because she was abusing my brother.
Th: Then your relationship with your mother has become much worse since your father left?
Pt: Yes, because in a sense I've realized certain things about her.
Th: What are the things you've realized about her?
Pt: Let's say it came to a point where this hate of her still keeping him in the house, which I still feel for her—I felt that hate even after he had left because I felt it was too late, let's say. Look, you're affected after a certain many years. Could you repeat your question?
Th: What do you think happened that you forgot my question?
Pt: What do you mean?
Th: I was wondering what happened. Do you usually forget?
Pt: No.
Th: What do you think happened here?
Pt: I don't know. I was just thinking of something and all of a sudden it blanked out.
Th: Does it usually happen that way to you?
Pt: No, not usually.

WHERE DOES EVALUATION END AND THERAPY BEGIN?

Th: How do you feel about me questioning you?
Pt: I feel you're very aggressive with your questions.
Th: And how do you feel?
Pt: A little bit on edge.
Th: Do you feel irritated?
Pt: Yes.
Th: Do you think the forgetfulness had to do with that?
Pt: In what respect do you mean?
Th: Because, in a way, what you are saying is this: that I was in a way repeatedly facing you with the problem, and you have a tendency to run away from the problem. Do you see what I mean?
Pt: I know.
Th: Obviously, here I am confronting you with certain issues, and insisting that you look at them, and I didn't let you run away from them. Then you got irritated. Okay?
Pt: Yes.
Th: Now, let's look at your irritation. What was it that you were experiencing inside?
Pt: I just felt I was trying to explain something and it wasn't coming through to you, and you would pound on me with more questions.
Th: And that reminds you of what? Is there any other person with whom you have had an experience like this?
Pt: Yes.
Th: Who?
Pt: My mother.
Th: She pounds on you?
Pt: Let's say there are certain times when I get aggravated at her, and I try to explain, and it's impossible because she's kind of out of touch with what's going on. She has her own problems; she's seeing a psychiatrist, and she'll avoid the questions and avoid my talking and switch from that automatically to something else, or start hurting me by saying certain things. So it's impossible to have any kind of argument with her on a rational basis. I can't, so that frustrates me more, and I hide myself in my room because I can't take it.
Th: So one thing that came out was that here with me you felt irritated; do you think your forgetfulness had to do with that?
Pt: Maybe.
Th: Why do you say "maybe"?

Dr. Yung:

As we see from this vignette of the initial interview, Dr. Davanloo, in the process of evaluating this patient, is using interpretation as well as actively working on the transference axis.

Now I would like to present a clinical case of my own: a patient evaluated, treated and terminated in one session.

The patient is a thirty-year old, married statistician, who came thirty minutes early for his appointment. He was seen at the scheduled hour. An appointment was given to him two months prior to this visit, as a referral from a gynecologist who attended his wife. The patient missed the initial appointment and called back one week later. In the interim, my secretary had gathered information that perhaps he had a drinking problem since he had attended the Alcoholism Unit recently. He was told to return to the Clinic. Two weeks later he called, stating that he was not an alcoholic. At that point I talked to him on the phone with the intention of explaining to him that he should follow through with the Alcoholism Unit, at which point he hung up the phone, apparently in anger. Three weeks later he called again and stated that he needed to see me very badly as his wife had left him. An appointment was then given.

The patient was tense and anxious, which apparently accounted for his slight pressure of speech. He initiated the interview, and was eager to convey to me that it was his wife who kept convincing everyone that he was an alcoholic. He then defended himself in a way by saying that his wife left him two months ago he had not had a drink for the past four weeks.

He continued to enumerate his difficulties with his wife, such as her calling the police many times and claiming that he threatened her and beat her up. He reassured me that these were false accusations. Once his wife used a knife on him and he got ten stitches in his left hand. Since his wife had left him, he had the fear of being alone in his apartment and a feeling of "emptiness." There were recurring thoughts of "the way it was" with his wife, especially when his wife phoned him occasionally. He had no idea of his wife's whereabouts. This had happened to him many times during the past five years. They have been legally married for three years and had marital counseling recently with no improvement.

I inquired further into his recollections of "the way it was" with his wife. He responded, "It still reminds me of the times together, but there was never anything pleasant." His wife was married twice before and both her husbands left her. She had a history of a "nervous breakdown."

At this point I attempted to find out what was so different in this particular crisis situation that led him to seek help, as he had experienced similar situations before. He stated that he lost his job for having taken too many days' leave of absence; he felt empty, feared being alone, couldn't eat, broke things at home, and punched holes in the walls with his fists.

He elaborated further about his job pattern. He had changed jobs frequently: "I change jobs for more money. I gave in to my wife. She kept pushing me for more money." He went on to describe his wife's resistance to seek help, and failing in her duties as a housewife, e.g., she never cooked for him.

He became more anxious and was considerably distressed, asking, "Should I look for another woman now? I want to throw her out, yet I cannot. I need another woman; this fear of emptiness. I swore to myself that I will never divorce in my life." I explored this promise he made to himself.

His associations were abstracted as follows. His parents were divorced when he was six or seven years old, having been separated for one year prior to the divorce. His mother took off with her children (the patient and his one-year-old sister) to England without her husband's knowledge. The patient recalled that his mother told him that they were having a vacation for several weeks in England. Later on, he begged his mother to return to Canada and got a spanking once, and was told not to make similar requests any more. He described his mother as one who was obsessed with getting money and who saw a psychiatrist before leaving Canada. It took approximately two years for his father, with a detective, to track them down. Then, at age fourteen, he returned to Canada.

He reported that while he was in England he had poor school performance, gastrointestinal upsets, and episodes of truancy to look for his father with dreams of returning to Canada. He received beatings from his mother with a belt, which he cut into pieces. Then his mother switched to a wooden salad spoon. He broke it as well. His mother remarried, and he disliked his mother's second husband.

"The Case of the Masochistic Statistician"

Th: When you were young and got punished by your mother, you dealt with it by cutting the belt and breaking the spoon, i.e., the instruments that punished you, and now in your current life you also resort to breaking things at home as a way to deal with your feelings. I wonder if you have any thoughts as to how these two are related.

Pt: You mean I am still angry at my mother?

Th: One can understand how a nine-year-old boy reacted to physical punishment at that time. That was the way you dealt with your feelings toward her then. Your mother was obsessed with money, and your wife happened to be constantly pushing you to bring in more money, and you took this as a reason for your changing to jobs which pay more. What do you think about these similarities?

(*The patient looks somewhat amazed.*)

Pt. Oh ... to think of it, my mother never did any cooking for us. It is fascinating, as if I keep repeating my past, like doing everything twice.

Th: Have you ever thought of the possibility that somehow you got involved with a woman, your wife, who in many ways resembled the way your mother treated you. Perhaps some of the feelings that you now have toward your wife's leaving you have some basis in the feelings you have toward your mother. You are now in a conflicting situation. Your wife left you; you experienced emptiness, and wished to find another woman as a substitute. You keep asking yourself this question, "Should I look for another woman now?" You need your wife, even though recollections about her are not pleasant since you have known her. On the other hand, you fear losing her. What thoughts do you have about this?

Pt: It upsets me very much each time she calls me.

What followed was further history taking and exploration about his relationship with his father. He got along very well with him, and they had great times together. He also got along very well with his father-in-law.

His mother died ten years ago in a car accident. He said, "It didn't bother me that much. It took me one week and it was over. My father asked me how I could be so heartless."

He went on remembering his boyhood, the respiratory and stomach problems. While so reporting his childhood experiences, he stopped rather abruptly and said, "I don't think I want her back now." I was struck by the state of calmness he was in, and astonished at how he arrived at the decision so suddenly.

Pt: I feel so calm. I'm not trembling any more.

(*The patient stretches out his arms to demonstrate what he said. He appears relaxed and at ease.*)

Th: It does happen to many people that once a decision is made while in a crisis situation, one can have a new perspective toward life and things in general.
Pt: I should go celebrate and have a beer.

I asked him if he had additional areas of problems he would like to bring up. He replied in the negative and appeared to be pleased. I told him that since he had made the decision and felt quite at ease, maybe he could try to deal with this crisis on his own. I supported him to alert his feelings appropriately toward the right person instead of letting the past interfere with the present. As I reviewed my notes, I asked:

Th: Earlier you mentioned having fear or a phobia; would you like to elaborate more on this?
Pt: Oh, it isn't a fear of being alone. I've come to understand now that it's the fear of my wife returning home.
Th: You mean, before you made the decision of not wanting her back, you were faced with the dilemma of either throwing her out or taking her back again. Once you made the decision, the fear went away?
Pt: Yes. I have to see Dr. ——— and tell him that I'm fit for service now; also for my stomach.

I recall debating at this point whether treatment would be necessary or not, since he had made the decision regarding his marriage. I gave him a follow-up appointment in three weeks, and also suggested he contact me in the interim if he felt it was necessary. He did not come for the follow-up, and the further information that I have is that he left his wife and moved to another part of the country. After some months his wife was seen in a psychiatric clinic for treatment.

In summary, the successful outcomes of one or two interviews are serendipitous occurrences. Most of us have had similar experiences. It is doubtful that these occurrences could have taken place had it not been for these early interventions such as trial, partial and even total interpretation. In Dr. Davanloo's interview there were a number of interventions. We saw the transference situation; there was the mobilization of anger as a result of confrontation; then came the moment when the patient lost his train of thought. And we saw the triangle of impulse, anxiety and defense which was interpreted. We saw then immediately that there was a corrective emotional experience and the facilitation of rapport. In the case that I presented no transference interpretation was attempted. A trial interpretation was made to test out the dynamic hypothesis that the patient's current conflict over the separation from his wife had a genetic basis related to his conflict and ambivalent relationship with his mother and separation from his father. Needless to say, a long-term follow-up is mandatory for confirmation of outcome and the validity as well as the efficacy. However, the drastic improvement and self-insight which were quite evident can be attributed to intervention in the initial interview. One may argue that these are spontaneous remissions, transference cures and flights into health.

Dr. Malan studied the outcomes of forty-five patients who were seen for only one visit in consultation at the Tavistock Clinic. These patients never received treatment. Eleven of those forty-five patients had improved according to their psychodynamic criteria. There was evidence of therapeutic factors in a significant proportion of those single interviews. The therapeutic factors consisted of evidence of interpretation at the diagnostic interview and the patients' comments that the diagnostic interview had been helpful. He concluded that what appears to be "spontaneous remission" may in fact be the outcome of one session of psychotherapy, and the psychiatrist should be aware of the possibility that a single dynamic interview may be all that is needed for some patients.

Similarly, in respect to Dr. Davanloo's series of 115 patients, within a period of twelve years, with successful outcome, he has twelve patients who were treated in from one to two sessions. He has a five-year follow-up on six of them. He considers interpretation, especially total interpretation (P.P.T. Link) at the diagnostic interview to be one of the most important therapeutic factors.

Finally, early intervention, the use of therapeutic techniques such as confrontation and interpretation, has been recommended by a number of workers in this field. Such intervention might be a part of the process of evaluation of patients for dynamic psychotherapy, and specifically for short-term dynamic psychotherapy, provided the evaluator has enough clinical skill to use it judiciously and cautiously.

Dr. Sifneos:

I think Dr. Yung has summarized very well both the theoretical aspects and the practical considerations for these patients. We also have been very much interested in this area, and we have case examples of these types of interventions. Usually one is unaware of the impact that one may have produced by the end of the first interview. If one has a second interview, however, one can become convinced that a therapeutic intervention has taken place which may be lasting, and that the patient's problem has been solved. We have tried to outline criteria for selecting those patients. I cannot give them to you because they are quite vague at the present time. We have decided to use the term "ripe" to describe such patients. The analogy that one would draw, for those of you who remember qualitative analysis in chemistry, is that the patient is at the point where just one drop of acid changes the solution from a colorless one to a pink one. Now, this drop of acid is obviously something that takes place in that interaction during the evaluation interview. It suddenly becomes a therapeutic one. A process of resolution begins at this point of the whole psychodynamic problem. I think Dr. Malan would have a lot to say about this particular matter because he has important findings in this area.

Dr. Eisenstein:

The question is, Where does evaluation end and therapy begin? I think there are really no boundaries between the two. Whether it is for brief psychotherapy or for prolonged therapy, sometimes we start making interpretations on the phone when the patient first calls for an appointment. I'm sure you are all familiar with the fact that you can detect resistance on the phone and, if not interpreted, you never see that patient. I remember a woman calling me for an appointment. I offered an hour, and she couldn't take it. She had something else to do. I offered the second hour, and she couldn't take that either. Then I ran out of hours, so I mentioned to her, "Maybe you have some reluctance to come and see me," and she said yes, she was a little reluctant. I don't know why, then, I took a stab in the dark and said, "Is it possibly my voice?" She said, "Yes. My father had an accent, too." So there you have it—on the phone. Thus you can't make a sharp distinction as to where you start interpreting. This happens all the time.

If we consider the long-term form of therapy, we may abstain before we start making interpretations, although I am quite convinced that we cannot always do it. I think, whether we like it or not, we do make interpretations from the beginning. Now I want to address myself very briefly to Dr. Yung's case. I was very much impressed with what happened in one hour: a very disturbed man, from the history, and the way he refused to come in. First he comes too early. Then he doesn't answer the phone. Then he finally comes in, and he sits down and tells horrible stories. Actually, if I remember correctly, he had the fantasy to kill the wife also. I think he did, and he gives a story of deprivation and rejection that goes back to age five when the parents separated. A cruel and sadistic mother; a cruel and sadistic, also quite disturbed wife who cuts his arm so that he needs ten stitches to get it fixed. And there is a history of drinking. You have cases where you hear about patients like this; you say, "No. I have no time." Well, Dr. Yung was patient. He put up with all these things. He accepted them. He never mentioned to the patient why he didn't show up. He talked to him; he listened to him and he gave him an interpretation, and there was improvement. The man saw, recognized, during the hour, certain dynamic problems that for the first time were brought to his attention. Is this the only thing that helped this man? I suspect other things took place, too. For such a deprived and buffeted man, for the first time a kind, gentle person doesn't reproach him. He tested the therapist. He is not reproached; he is accepted; he is listened to; he is counselled; he is given an interpretation; he is told to return if he wants to, or to call whenever he wishes. That is unusual treatment for a man like this. I think the man went through a strong corrective emotional experience with Dr. Yung, and I don't think the interpretation alone was the cause. Several factors played a part in the fact that this man improved so dramatically. I'm sure there are many, many other examples in literature.

I will conclude by reminding you that Freud's book *The Study in Hysteria* includes five or six cases that he treated with brief psychotherapy, including one case, Katarina. He treated her for one hour on top of a mountain during his vaction in the Austrian Alps; it's a beautiful vignette of one encounter in 1896 or 1895, before his psychoanalytic period. So there are precedents going way back to Freud, and sometimes we are even forced to treat patients for only one hour.

Dr. Malan:

I think that there is a terrible danger that, in talking about these highly successful cases, we forget about the cases where disasters may have ensued. I am sure this is not because the speakers are not aware of this possibility. When I teach trainees to do a consultation with a patient, what I always say to them is that they must make sure what kind of a patient he is before they start making interpretations to him. In my evaluation I might spend a quarter of an hour exploring whether the patient is suicidal, whether he has done any damage to anybody or to himself. In one of the cases I presented, you saw that I questioned if she used razor blades on herself. This is designed precisely to prevent me from getting into the situation of starting the therapeutic process with someone to whom this treatment would do harm. So I am quite sure that this word of caution is necessary. The thing to be said on the other side is that with experienced clinicians one can often go through that process very quickly and be reasonably sure.

Question from the floor:

From what I can gather, at the very beginning of the evaluation one would like to make a formulation of what the outcome will be; what the change will be, and how this change is going to be expressed.

Question from the floor:

There are a few viewpoints I would like to put forward as to the distinction between the evaluation and the therapy. Dr. Yung—very precisely, I think—quoted two points which gave good reason why we should make interpretation also during the evaluation. Now, I would add one which I also think is very important. These patients come to us of their own free will. They don't know actually what they are asking for except that they ask for help for some things that are troubling them. The reason it is important to do interpretations during the evaluation period is that it gives the patient a chance to see the techniques so that he will have a fair idea about what he is in for if he goes into therapy.

Dr. Sifneos:

We do teach evaluation very extensively, and we emphasize what has already been said, that after the contract has been established the therapy begins. I think what Dr. Yung was saying today was that, although we may try to be as systematic as we can, sometimes we fail. We should never give the impression that our evaluation criteria for our patients are not important.

Dr. Yung:

I assessed this patient with the background criteria in mind for the possibility of short-term dynamic psychotherapy. I think the important thing that we are perhaps missing is that these criteria are used essentially as a guideline. It doesn't mean they are absolute. They are a frame of reference to help us sort out what kind of patient is suitable for short-term dynamic therapy, and I think the findings relevant to this patient are a result of my attempt to sort out whether indeed this patient can respond to some interpretation. So I do not intend to treat every patient in my office with one interview. No. Indeed, I think the patient's ability to take this kind of intervention is also required. That is why in the final analysis, if the therapist and patient variables are at the optimum, then you get results.

Dr. Eisenstein:

I am quite convinced that a therapist would deal differently with a patient that presents serious pathology. For example, for a patient who is severely depressed, more is necessary than one interview or one or two interpretations. I am sure that the therapist is responsible enough to take measures, and to see that the patient is handled differently.

Dr. Marmor:

I just want to make the comment that the issue of the borderline between evaluation and therapy depends in part on how you define therapy. If you define it as the point at which the therapist begins to make certain kinds of interpretation designed to give insight to the patient, then it's a meaningful question. However, if you define therapy as I do, as the total transactional process that goes on between a patient and a therapist, then therapy begins the moment a patient walks into your office. It begins with the look on your face, with the warmth with which you greet him, or the coldness, or the impersonality or whatever. That is why so often, even when you have made no interpretations, patients will walk out of your office with a therapeutic response. However, if you want to define treatment just in terms of the point at which you feel ready to make certain kinds of interpretive comments, then obviously you have to have some evaluative material first.

Chapter 15

Short-Term Dynamic Psychotherapy of One to Two Sessions' Duration

H. DAVANLOO

Dr. Davanloo:

Dr. Eisenstein has indicated that Freud, before his psychoanalytic period in 1895, treated the case of Katarina in one hour while he was vacationing in the Austrian Alps. There are a number of other cases that Freud treated in one or two sessions. Of all such cases reported in literature, by Freud or other workers, content analysis indicates that there are active therapeutic interventions during the evaluation process and that interpretation is used at the initial diagnostic interview.

We also have been very much interested in the nature of the psychotherapeutic factors and processes of those patients who do well in one or two sessions. We successfully treated 115 patients in short-term dynamic psychotherapy from 1963 to 1974. In this study, twelve patients were treated in one to two sessions. The content analysis of these twelve patients indicates that, in the majority of them, the nature of their conflict was a genuine oedipal triangular conflict. In terms of therapeutic factors, interpretation, especially interpretation of the P-P-T Link type, is used in the diagnostic interview.

Here we will present the treatment of a patient in two interviews conducted by Dr. Sifneos. A brief summary of the first interview will be followed by an edited transcript of the second interview.

Due to technical difficulties, the initial interview of this patient was not recorded. The clinical data from that interview indicated that the patient was twenty years old, recently married. Her husband is a thirty-three-year-old computer analyst. Her chief complaints were her feeling of inferiority and irrational concern that her husband might leave her. Her second problem was her fear of sex, of recent onset. This was precipitated by a group sex event involving four men and two women, in which both the patient and her husband participated. She went into panic when another man approached her. She got dressed and left with her husband.

The patient's parents were divorced when she was six years old. There had been constant arguments and fights between her parents. She was the favorite of her father, and she very much idolized him. The father is now married, and the patient's stepmother is the same age as the patient.

One of the patient's earliest memories, around the age of six, is related to her father kissing another woman in front of the patient and her mother.

At age three, the patient had asthma and has a memory of her father taking care of her. She was four years old when her brother was born. Her mother was a strict woman who disliked sex and had wanted to become a nun.

We felt that the patient fulfilled the criteria for short-term dynamic psychotherapy with an "excellent" score. Also, we felt that one more interview would perhaps be sufficient to resolve the nuclear conflict of this patient, and here we present an edited transcript of the audio-visually recorded interview conducted the next day.

"The Case of the Woman with the Fear of Losing Her Husband"

Th: Well, we had to finish yesterday because of the time, and I thought we were in the midst of some very interesting things that we had been discussing. So it was thought that if you were kind enough to come again, we might pursue a little bit more these issues that we were talking about. I'm glad to see you. Tell me, what did you think about yesterday's interview?

Pt: I've been thinking a lot about it. I didn't sleep very well. I was really nervous. The main thing is that I'm looking for answers and you're asking me questions, and I'm trying to find answers for you. Do you know what I mean? And I've been thinking of that thing when you said my father could be my husband or something, and I wrote some notes, you see...

Th: Just tell me what you think.

Pt: Well, remember what we had talked about together, and one thing that I don't understand is that if you think that my husband could be my father—let's say I could say my husband is my father today—but my father left me, you see, and I tied myself more or less to my mother, and I cannot be after my father any more. You see what I mean?

Th: Yes. Let me clarify one thing first. That is, really it isn't that you have to answer my questions, because it really is of no importance. What is of importance is whether my questions happen to strike something in you that is meaningful, because really the important thing is for you to answer your own questions. You know the answers, but they might be somehow or other hidden. They might be pushed aside, a little bit forgotten, something that comes up. Sometimes you don't like the implications and so forth. Therefore, by my asking you some questions, coming from the outside, you see, it may help you look at problems that you have in your life in a different light. So I don't want to give you the picture that somehow or other you have to please me, or that you have to give me the right answers. What is much more important really is for you to decide whether some of these issues are important or not. Now, let's take this question of yours. There might be a connection between your husband and your father. As a matter of fact, you told me that your husband, even himself, mentioned this at times. Now, let's look at it. What did he mean by that? How did he say such a thing? I happen to have raised this question too. What was it that your husband saw in you that made him think there was something like it?

Pt: Because I never do anything by myself. I depend on him. I always go to him, ask him questions, ask him what I should do. Should I do this? Should I do that? And he gives answers. At these times he says to me that he feels in a way that he's my father or something. You see what I mean? Because I cannot make any decisions for myself. I'm always afraid if it's right or wrong.

Th: Now, are you doing the same thing with me here, expecting me to give you answers?

Pt: Well, we have been talking, let's say yesterday, about when I was a child, when my problems today are my husband and myself, and I'm not expecting that right now, but maybe later. You know what I mean?

Th: Right. So let's try, then, instead of my answering your questions or your answering my questions, to look at this thing together. Now, what is possible then? We know that you as a little girl of four years old were very much attached to your father. You used the phrase "idolized" your father. You waited for him, and he was there in his uniform and coming and so forth. There was obviously a feeling that you had for him that was of great importance. This feeling, however, was lost when he left. Now, you obviously felt something when he left, but we saw that in your boyfriend—the first boyfriend, do you remember? The one that at seventeen you had the sexual relationship with—that particular boyfriend, you did something to please him because you were afraid he might leave you, so I then thought that there was a connection between that and keeping somebody from not going away. The question then is, Is it possible that this same thing is happening with your husband?

Pt: Not sexually.

Th: Not sexually, but the fear that your husband is going to leave you because you told me that this is so. You told me that if you're going to work at the university or take certain courses, you're afraid you may find that he's not there, or you're afraid he may go out with some of his friends, or he may leave you. So there's a pattern, right, of your being afraid that the man who happens to be, at the time, of importance to you will leave you. In the first situation it was your father. Then we have the example of your first boyfriend at seventeen, and now your husband. Possibly there are others You respond, then, to these situations by going out of your way to keep these people to yourself. With the boy at seventeen you had intercourse even though at that time you were not particularly ready, or whatever it was. With your husband you have this kind of need to be there to keep him. So there is a parallel. That's what we have established. What else do you want to know?

Pt: Well, what I think is, with my husband my sexual relationship is fantastic. I never had, let's say, so many sensations or feelings before that I have with my husband now. The thing is, I ask myself that maybe if I would go to study at the university or something like that—to become, I don't know; let's say a teacher or another profession; not just a job—I will maybe feel secure because if one day he does go away, well, I just don't know, you see? And this is in a way a very big problem for me.

Th: Why is it a problem? Why is it that by your becoming more secure, more independent, a person with a degree, in any way this is going to interfere with your relationship with your husband, or is going to interfere with your sexual relationship?

Pt: What?

Th: Becoming self-sufficient. As a matter of fact it might even improve your relationships, which are already good, even more so. Why? Why would you feel that this...

Pt: Because I wouldn't feel a failure.

Th: Exactly, but why are you worried, then, about the university?

Pt: Because I never tried it.

Th: All right. It's a new situation, fine.

Pt: But I want to know why I'm so afraid of facing things.

Th: You know the answer somewhere. Why are you afraid of things? In what way are you afraid of facing things? You came yesterday, for instance, to face me, who you knew nothing about and under somewhat difficult circumstances. You faced the situation, and you came in today for more. Obviously, you are perfectly capable of facing the situation. What is the difference here between another situation when you say you are afraid of facing it?

Pt: Because I know you are with me, and the other situations are only against me.

Th: In what way?

Pt: Well, let's say if I start something it might not work. In a way I have to fight against it, but you aren't fighting against me; you're helping me. That's why I'm not afraid.

Th: What, for instance, are the other situations? Taking courses, or improving yourself, or getting your degree, being self-sufficient; in what way would that be fighting? That also would be something that is going to make you feel better in the same way you view me trying to help you feel better. In what way is that other situation different? What are your thoughts about it?

Pt: Let's say when I went to college for the first time, it was in January, to choose my courses for this session, okay? I really got upset about it because in a way I was going to be four nights away and he might do something else, you see? In a way I'm really possessive, I think, or maybe jealous, I don't know, and I was afraid to face that. Maybe I don't know if it's going to be good or wrong for me.

Th: Then let's leave the issue of your being able to study and improve yourself because there is no problem there; you can. The problem that you are having, that you are telling me now, is that you are afraid that if you are away from your husband he might prefer someone else to you.

Pt: Yeah, that's right.

Th: Now, let's look at this. Is it possible that this is so, or is it possible that you think it is so because of the past? Do you see what I mean? What comes to mind?

Pt: When I was with my first boyfriend, I had really been afraid of losing him, and I was making love to him, in a way, to keep him; a kind of security or something. After that another guy came into the picture; another guy, twenty-nine years old, but the other guy was in a way lower than me. Then in a way I didn't have to improve myself, you see? But now I have to open myself to another world because I'm completely free. My husband lets me be free. He's really independent himself. He's not jealous at all. I can do what I want with him, and he opens to me, and I'm afraid to take one of these doors.

Th: But partly this may be so because you haven't been used to that, and it's a new experience. All right, that I think you can adjust to without doubt. What we are interested in is if this person is something that you are accustomed to from the past. This is what I'm interested in, in a sense that we should be interested in, if indeed you are afraid because of these things that happened to you in the past—you see what I mean—that happened to you with your father, that happened to you with your mother, that happened to you as you were growing up, and that is the reason you're afraid of these golden new opportunities that your husband has given you, because of these past things. If it is so, these past things are interfering with your ability to move and be free. This is why it might be helpful to, by seeing somebody and examining these past situations, be able to feel secure enough that you could carry on with your education, with whatever it is that you would like, without this fear. Because realistically speaking there is no evidence, at least from what you told me yesterday, that your husband would ever leave you. Why should he leave you? You are his wife whom he loves, to whom he has given the freedom. That means that he trusts you, that he is not suspicious of you. You have a very good sexual adjustment. What is the matter? Everything is fine. You, on the other hand, are worried. So it is more your problem than it is his.

Pt: That's right.
Th: That's right, and if you are worried it may be because of things you have experienced in the past rather than the present situation with your husband, which is a very good one. Now, let's see what we touched on here today. How much these earlier situations in some way affect you so that you cannot be happy now, so that you cannot take your courses and relax, so you don't have to worry every five minutes that you may come back and your husband might not be there. He might not be there because he went to a movie or whatever it is. It doesn't have to be that you have to be constantly there. Now let's get back to your father, since that was originally one of the problems. Do you remember, for instance, waiting for your father and not finding him?
Pt: I knew I loved him, and I know he was something for me because I know when, let's say just before I met my first boyfriend—it might sound silly to you—but anyhow I was going to bed and I was thinking to myself how it could be if I was, let's say to be in a picture house with him and my mother, my sister, my brother and me, and leading a normal life. And I used to fall asleep with that. Every night I used to do that. I wanted to have my father. I wanted to have a man around, you see?
Th: Tell me about this dream, that is, not really a dream.
Pt: No, because it was reality.
Th: It is what you call fantasy, right? That which was so pleasant that it put you to sleep. Tell me a little more about it; what it was like, for instance.

(The therapist at this point explores the patient's fantasy about her father, the fantasy she had when she went to bed. It also comes out that her sister left home at age thirteen to go with a boyfriend and the patient was jealous. In addition to her father there were other men in her fantasy, especially an actor—"somebody big." The therapist explores what this man did in her fantasy. The patient says, "Protect me."

Th: Protect you only?
Pt: Help me maybe, tell me what to do or something.
Th: Anything else? You wouldn't be kind of attracted to him?
Pt: Yeah, of course, if he was good-looking.
Th: That's what I thought.
Ph: My father was good-looking, anyhow.

Th: Yes, I got the picture. Would you even think of anything more intimate with that actor?

Pt: I don't know any more.

Th: That is a difficult thing to push? Why?

Pt: But you see in that thing, when I was thinking of that, I was always talking about myself. You know what I mean? I was not giving a role to my sister or my brother.

Th: But this person that you are in this family, or with this actor, it is you as a grown-up girl, isn't it, or is it as a little girl?

Pt: A little girl.

Th: How little?

Pt: Little; six or something like that; eight.

Th: Are you saying that a girl of six or seven or eight could be attracted to a movie actor? What do you think?

Pt: Well, you see, when I was dreaming of the house I was about fifteen or sixteen.

Th: I know that. That's what my question is. Is it possible that you were thinking of yourself also at fifteen or sixteen? That would be very different.

Pt: It could be.

Th: It could be? But if you were fifteen or sixteen, then you were a more grown-up woman, and a more grown-up woman can do different things than a girl of six or seven, right? When you say, "Oh, yeah," what do you mean?

Pt: Well, you know, for example I used to see myself little, then like this, and another day I was tall, I was big.

Th: Now did you ever have any sexual fantasies?

Pt: No, not in that situation.

Th: In any other situation?

Pt: When I was thinking of that? No, never.

Th: So it was clear that the sexual thoughts were out?

Pt: Out because I wasn't thinking of that when I was fifteen or sixteen. That's why I'm amazed to see that girls today go to bed when they're fourteen or fifteen, because at home it was so bad; it was such a bad thing.

Th: So then, what is quite clear is that you would push the thought. Let's get back to what the fantasy was. It was that there was a house, that there was your mother, your father, your sister, your brother and yourself. Sometimes you were a little girl.

Sometimes, however, it wasn't your father; it was another man who was attractive and you might have been even a bigger girl, but never thought of possibly having some sexual contact with that actor?

Pt: No.

Th: Never? So that is clearly out? Is it possible that this was clearly out because you connected in your mind that the actor was your father, and that sexual thought would be a terrible thought?

Pt: I cannot associate that actor with my father, or let's say when I was thinking of that at fifteen years old, and thinking sexually about my father.

Th: Can you tell me about that?

Pt: Yes, because I didn't know he was staying with that girl until just before the wedding, and I know he was living with that girl.

Th: Excuse me, which wedding?

Pt: My own wedding. I was with my husband-to-be, but I didn't really see my father any more because when he came home when I was eighteen, and I was mad at him, and telling him all bad things because of revenge or something, I never went to see him. You see, I was more close to my mother. Then finally what happened was that my mother got mad at me and she threw me out of the house.

Th: Why?

Pt: Because of that guy who was twenty-nine years old. I was always staying at his place, to sleep there and things like that, and I enjoyed it. It wasn't just only sexual, but I liked to stay there. Finally, one day I came home and she was tired of that because she thought I could never go to bed until I got married or something. She thought I was somebody like that, you know? Then finally she said to me, "You just give me twenty dollars a week, which is not enough; go live in an apartment and find out things by yourself, and you'll see what it is to pay; not to have money." Then I said, "Okay, that's fine." I looked around, then I went to my aunt's, my mother's sister, and she took me in. I had a room there. I wasn't paying anything. I had a TV; I had everything. I lived like a princess. Then after that I met my future husband, and I moved in with him.

Th: But the notion, then, of doing sexual things came from your mother, and it was taboo, right? It was bad?

Pt: Oh, yeah.

Th: Because your mother said that that's not for you, and your mother felt herself as being a nun; she had talked about her own sexual life as being nonexistent, and so forth. So the notion that sex is bad or that girls at fourteen or sixteen, as you said now, should not be thinking about sex, comes straight from your mother.

Pt: That's right.

Th: Now, what if your mother felt that her own little girl, you now, had sexual thoughts?

Pt: If she would have found that out? Oh, my God! I know that when I was seventeen—when things are forbidden, we always do them. Finally I went to bed with my first boyfriend, and of course I didn't tell her, and she found out. Not then. But it was when I moved in with my future husband, just before I got married. Then she didn't come to my wedding. She was still mad at me, and she said she couldn't believe that "you would do a thing like that to me."

Th: So your mother was very punitive, wasn't she? She actually threw you out of her house because of sex, so you went to your aunt's?

Pt: Because I was not at home with her any more. I was more out of the house.

Th: You were not only not at home with her, but also you were out of the house for sexual reasons which she did not approve of.

Pt: Because my mother might have thought I was having sexual relations, but she had no proof.

Th: So then we can clearly say your mother disapproved of sex, and there is a part of you that learned that sex is bad from your mother, but then there is another part of you that sees that sex is fine, that you enjoy it, and that you are perfectly at ease with it. Now, these two things might be in conflict with each other.

Pt: That's true, yes.

Th: Now, the question is—I am still interested really in coming back now to your father—what about your feelings for your father? You know you were telling me, and you have to finish now; when did you find out about your father and the girl?

Pt: That was just before I got married, before the wedding. I knew he was staying with a girl because I used to phone for the money at home, and a girl used to answer, but I didn't know she was so young, and finally it was in a restaurant, and I gave my father a picture of me, a big picture.

Th: You saw your father often at that time?

Pt: The thing is, when I moved in with my husband-to-be I said to him, "It's funny, but I've always been bad to him, and I feel guilty about it. I think I'm going to give him a call," you see, and finally I gave him a call and I saw him, and I gave him a picture of me and he put it in his room. Then that girl saw me, and she could recognize me anywhere, and I went to the restaurant and she was working there. I knew her name, but I didn't know anything about her. She said to me, "You're ———, and I said Yes. She said, "You don't know me." I said, "No, I don't think so; maybe at school." She's my age. She told me who she was, and my reaction was—really, I just said to myself that I could not believe it, even though I had nothing against it, believe me. But when I go to my father's place with her there, I cannot imagine it; an old man—well, he's not old, but for her he's old— making love to her or something.

Th: Oh, you thought of that?

Pt: Oh, yeah.

Th: What do you think?

Pt: Well, I had pity for her or something, because she shouldn't be with that man.

Th: Why?

Pt: Because she's too young. For herself it's just not good.

Th: Why? Who says that?

Pt: Me. I wouldn't be with a man like that.

Th: Why?

Pt: He's my father.

Th: So you had thoughts specifically about your father and sexual relations with her? But who is this person that says, "No! I can't believe it." Is it you or is it your mother?

Pt: My mother. That's pretty good.

Th: Do you understand? What are you thinking of?

Pt: That's pretty good, because I have some prejudices or principles that she has, you know. But if I'm involved, it's not that bad, you see. Then I said, "Dad, I cannot believe it," but after that I said, Well, you know, that's their life and I accept it. But I want to know something. If I had my future husband, I think I wouldn't feel so bad because I have him. So I could be jealous of her if I didn't have my future husband, or if I didn't have a lover or something. Like maybe I would accept it because I'm in the same situation.

Th: Oh, yes?

Pt: Because I'm with my husband and I make love to him, and we're very much in love, so if I do it, why not them?

Th: Yes, but what is so difficult there to conceive; what is so unbelievable? You even used the word "funny." You said "the funny thing is that I have been so guilty and so mad at my father, yet I wanted to give him a present." It means that there is a part of you that comes from your past that we know loves your father, that is very much attached to your father. But you find out that your father does certain things that you don't like, that the emphasis that you put is on the girl. It is not good for her to have sex with your father. You don't say anything about your father. So it is perfectly all right for your father to have sex with her, but the girl should not have sex with your father. Why?

Pt: Because she could have a younger person.

Th: Why would that make any difference? She could, yes. What is it that would stop the girl?

Pt: Her prejudices or principles.

Th: Well, we know that. That comes from your mother as we have just said a minute ago. But what else? Is there something else that stops the girl, that particular young girl, from having sex with your father?

Pt: Well, I don't know her feelings about him.

Th: No. I'm interested in you. What is going through your head at that time?

Pt: I just cannot find an exact answer.

Th: That's all right. Try.

Pt: But...

Th: Why would that be the case? Why is it that you say the girl should have relations with a younger person? Oh yes, but why shouldn't she have relations with an older person?

Pt: Because it doesn't work that way.

Th: But you are having relations with an older person.

Pt: Yes, but just thirteen years older, not thirty years older.

Th: So?

Pt: This could be my prejudice or principles.

Th: Where do these principles come from?

Pt: My education before.

Th: No, there is something else...

Pt: You know what? Maybe if I would do it, it wouldn't be so bad. If I would be involved in it with, let's say, a person fifty-four years old.
Th: Yes. Have you thought of that? Think of it right this minute.
Pt: I could do it. If I loved him, I could do it.
Th: So you see, there is nothing wrong.
Pt: No, that's true.
Th: Only one thing.
Pt: Maybe with him or something.
Th: Would you do it with anybody? But what if this anybody was your father?
Pt: I wouldn't do it with him.
Th: There is the problem, isn't it?
Pt: I wouldn't do it with him.
Th: If the girl is your age and she is doing it with your father, then it is possible that you also could, and that is a terrible thought, isn't it?
Pt: Because he's my father.
Th: It depends on you, or is it because your mother is going to say, "How could you?"
Pt: Yeah, because things like—because I'm probably not made that way and I would say maybe you could find girls who could make love to their fathers, and me—maybe I could do it in five years' time when I am more open to sex or something; when I can find in a way that there's nothing bad in it, but now I couldn't.
Th: And what is stopping you?
Pt: My prejudices and my principles.
Th: Which come from where?
Pt: My mother.
Th: I think that is the problem. There is a part of you that says, "If I were to find a handsome fifty-four-year-old, I wouldn't mind at all, and she has found one, but my mother says that this is bad, and my mother says that girls like that should not have any sex at all, but if they do have sex maybe they should have it with people their own age." So, you see, you are caught here between two sides. There is one side of you that might consider that, whether it is a movie star or some other attractive man or whoever it is, that would be perfectly all right and you wouldn't mind at all. But then the other side says, "No. This is terrible," and that is what you show me here, or you showed to yourself

here, right in this hour, that there are two sides to this. In the beginning you said, "No. No, she shouldn't." You acted like a mother until I pointed it out to you, and then you said, "Yes, that's interesting." Your whole face lit up, and it was a very great discovery. Now, what happens indeed with your mother is a big problem because we know that your mother disapproves of sex; she has brought you up that way. She never told you about sexual things. You had to find them in a book. You then started your own life, and she disapproved of that, and finally she is pushing you out of her own house. Now, what you have demonstrated to me better than anything is how capable you are of being, of standing on your own two feet. Another girl who was so scared or frightened that somebody is going to drop her would have said, "No. No, Mother. I will give up sex; I will give up everything. Keep me in the house." But what did you do? You said okay. You went around, looked at the situation, found your aunt, talked to your aunt, found a lovely room with TV, and you lived like a princess. You have all the ability to do things perfectly well in your own hands if you want to. I think what is keeping you down in these kinds of issues are these problems that come from the past.

Pt: But how can I get rid of them?

Th: But you have already made a lot of progress yesterday and today in the way of getting rid of these kinds of things.

Pt: But when you're made a certain way, do you always stay that way?

Th: No. You're asking me questions. Why are you made that way? Who made you that way?

Pt: Her.

Th: But you changed very much from what she said. Now you answer your own question. You told me that yesterday after the hour you were thinking a lot about it and you couldn't sleep very well. What were you thinking about in particular? What did you think of our relationship here?

(The therapist explores how she felt about the session the day before, and the decision was to terminate therapy and have a follow-up with her in six months' time.)

Dr. Davanloo:

Dr. Sifneos very skillfully dealt with many areas of this patient's conflict with life, linking her fear of losing her husband with the close relationship that she had had with her father in the very early years, followed by his leaving her. Then also another link was established with her fear of losing her first boyfriend with whom she had sexual relations in order to keep him. I was very impressed by the way Dr. Sifneos explored the triangle—the father, the young wife and the patient. This interview is an excellent example and contains both evaluation and the psychotherapeutic process.

As far as our criteria are concerned, the patient is an excellent candidate, and I would score her very high. Her motivation is very high, and in my opinion there was a great increase in the patient's motivation between the first and second interviews. We have an indication of that early in the second interview when she said she had difficulty sleeping, thinking over what Dr. Sifneos had told her and what unfolded during the first interview. Another element was making notes of things she wanted to ask the therapist, and she raises all sorts of questions which had come to her mind as a result of the first interview. These are all indications that this patient's motivation is high.

Her responses to interpretation, and especially transference interpretation, should also be scored high. Here again, Dr. Sifneos beautifully demonstrated the use of transference interpretation in the very early phase of short-term dynamic psychotherapy. My own experience indicates that when the patient responds to transference interpretation in this kind of psychotherapy, there is a high correlation between this and the therapeutic outcome.

We saw that Dr. Sifneos very nicely clarified with the patient that she always wants men to make decisions for her. Then it was also clarified that this was the same pattern that she had in relationship with her father. We then saw that she was very passively asking Dr. Sifneos questions about how she should think and how she should do things. Then we saw Dr. Sifneos' intervention.

Dr. Malan:

I cannot really add much to what has already been said. I am very interested in one particular side of the triangle of insight, and that is the base of the triangle of transference from the past. Some of our research seems to have shown that it is this kind of interpretation that has the most therapeutic effect. I agree with Dr. Davanloo that this is a marvelous example of how the transference is brought immediately into the second session. I would like to further add that if you do not interpret this transference, then you are waiting until it has become a resistance.

In spite of the fact that I have not seen the first interview, I have no hesitation in saying that the patient has good motivation. What Dr. Sifneos also did was to manage the left-hand side of the triangle of insight. He repeatedly said to her, "The reason you have these hang-ups about your husband in the present is because you are bringing in situations from the past." This again is thought to be one of the important therapeutic factors in psychoanalytic technique.

I want to add simply how pleased I am about the fact that they suggested stopping the therapy when they did, because I felt that this girl could grow from that point as she really had received insight.

Dr. Warnes:

I think it was a masterful session, and I would only like to point out a couple of things on the technique, such as the handling of the massive oedipal material there. For example, Dr. Sifneos pointed out, "Is it because of you or because of your mother that you abhor going to bed with a fifty-year-old man?" This is a technical point, to let the girl see that she was controlled by her mother's morals and superego rather than by her own. I noticed that she also had a tremendous desire to please the therapist, and he used strong emphasis components throughout the interview. I think the therapist did not pick up a lot of the things she said about revenge against her father, anger against her mother for throwing her out of the house, her feeling of being afraid of what was wrong, as if she was wondering whether she would become the "whore," the "slut," she believed her mother thought her to be. I think she had a tremendous competitiveness against women that wasn't brought to the surface, and only the aspect that she would always fail pointed out so clearly her competition with women.

There was another aspect which I think it was right to leave untouched, and that was when she said she was afraid of her freedom. One can go further into this fantasy, which is not unusual in this kind of girl, and especially in the fantasy world in which she was divorcing herself as a woman growing up, instead seeing herself as a little child. The fantasy happened at the age of fifteen, and I think it is a very important one. I believe Dr. Sifneos tried to understand why she repressed all sexual feelings in this fantasy and at fifteen saw herself as a little girl of six having the idea of a home life with her father home instead of leaving. She was also afraid she would find out she didn't love her husband. I think this was why she brought that up, and Dr. Sifneos was extremely supportive and reassuring to the point that he almost idealized the husband. I believe he went a bit too far, in that I don't believe her husband could be that wonderful.

Question from the floor:

My question regards whether Dr. Sifneos is usually this active in therapy, or is it because this was a demonstration interview or what? I thought he was talking more than the patient at times, which often interfered with the patient's free association about the specific area. Another area I was thinking about has to do with what Dr. Warnes touched upon, that is, that the conflict was presented to the patient in an almost predictive sense.

Question from the floor:

I find Dr. Sifneos' interview very instructive, but it struck me at one point, when she was talking about her initial reaction to the girl her father was living with by negation, that she brought up some of her feelings of envy, and possibly also jealousy and anger at both the father for deserting her and her perpetual rival. Was there a particular reason why, Dr. Sifneos, you did not follow up on that? Was it because it was just the second interview? If you had seen her for a longer period of time, would you have gone after that more? The reason I ask is that even in short-term psychotherapy what one would want to deal with in some way is these kinds of affects, as well as with the formulation of the genetic diagnosis.

Question from the floor:

It would appear that, in using this method of psychotherapy, the patient is plied with a framework with which to understand his conflict, his focal problems, and it seems to me there is a danger of overapplication of the framework. The patient touched on this when she questioned her relationship with her husband, and Dr. Sifneos reassured her that that relationship could be understood in terms of the present, that she loves him and he loves her. Again, I wonder if there is not an overapplication of this kind of framework.

Question from the floor:

My question is related to the triangle. The patient mentioned a lot of anxiety about this freedom that her husband is giving her, and her first thought was that he might leave her because of that freedom. I wonder whether her defense was one of projection, and whether it could have been her wish to leave him the way her father left her.

Question from the floor:

Dr. Hans Strupp wrote in one of his books that it is hard to learn to play the violin if you have never heard one played, but this symposium is giving us a chance to see how it is really done. If someone had referred this patient to me and had told me it is a good long-term case, I would have been very cautious and would not have made these interpretations. Perhaps I would have ended up spending a year doing what I could have done in two sessions if I would have been as bold as Dr. Sifneos.

Question from the floor:

There are a number of questions that come to mind. I wonder what the real purpose is of getting at the oedipal core. The actual oedipal fantasy as related to this patient's presenting complaint had something to do with her fear of going out and getting a job or going to school. Now, you can say that might be related to the fact that her father left her or something like that, so that there is a connection between the husband and the father, but what is the real need to get down to the actual oedipal fantasy? The other question I have in mind is that the girl was afraid of her freedom, and it might have to do with her—the idea of her husband leaving her may be a projection of her own feeling that once she is free she will be like her father. The third comment I have has to do with the effect of noninterpretative factors in what we see as cure or improvement, which I think was highly operative in Dr. Sifneos' interview. There was a high degree of suggestion and persuasion—the therapist says, "The husband is a good husband. You can do things on your own,"—and I think some of this may flow into the category of in-act interpretation. In other words, she may be afraid of her own acting out, but you may tell her, "You can do things on your own," and it may have a kind of positive effect on her. Indeed, you might be a believing superego figure of some sort.

Question from the floor:

My question is, What is the curative experience that these people are undergoing? I would agree with the panel that it is not within the scope of this symposium to look at other modalities, but I think we owe it to ourselves to look at the process that is going on and not present a specifically oedipal-genital framework. In Dr. Sifneos' interview, what effect did the interaction have on the patient? It is interesting, the number of people who have taken up the issue of your supporting her relationship with her husband. This lady was spending all night ruminating about your words, and I think one of the things you were doing was diffusing this highly intensified relationship between you and her, but I think you do have to examine the process. Dr. Strupp, whose name was mentioned a while back, recently wrote up a case that was recorded by Dr. Balint a couple of years ago. That case was originally examined, I think, from a similar viewpoint, namely, from an oedipal viewpoint. I would have hoped during this conference to hear another way of looking at these cases and the process that is going on.

Question from the floor:

I was fascinated with Dr. Sifneos' interview. It seemed to be an excellent interview, an excellent example—I would say a rather authoritarian kind of psychotherpy. I am a gynecologist, and in Montreal a gynecologist is in many cases the woman's family physician. Recently, Eisenberg wrote an article on the future of psychiatry in which he pointed out that psychiatry should really stand back and allow the family physician to do most of what I might term bread-and-butter psychiatry. I was wondering if in instructing family physicians whether this would be the kind of approach you would teach them and the way of doing it with such excellent immediate interaction.

Question from the floor:

I felt the interview was technically brilliant, sensitive and artistic, and no problem from a technical point of view. Dr. Sifneos, I believe, uses what in my training was an id-analytic theoretical approach, and he does it beautifully. I don't think he was using a psychoanalytic developmental ego psychological approach. The patient at the end of the interview said, "You can tell me I am strong; I feel weak." The conception of a sense of personal identity in our culture is such that this woman could only begin to relate from a negative sexual point of view to a positive heterosexual point of view, and that the feeling of weakness that she still described is her still-present inability to separate herself from attachment to men.

Question from the floor:

I thought that in the transference that came up at the end, when the patient asked, "Are you going to tell me that I don't love my husband?" Dr. Sifneos was the father figure, and there was an erotic component in it. I thought this was a good opportunity not to reassure her, to show her that she was where she was by her own choice, and that she did not have to wait for her father to call her and give her the cue.

Dr. Sifneos:

It is hard to answer most of the questions that have been raised, because indeed many of them are technical and many of them are right. For example, concentrating on a particular moment of the interview—on issues about anger, or about competitiveness with other women—and choose not to pursue those issues is something that technically another interviewer may have pursued with some very interesting material as a result. It is therefore difficult, I think, to deal with some of these questions as they were presented. One of the special technical parts of our short-term anxiety-provoking psychotherapy has to do with by-passing characterological issues that appear to be there but that one feels are not necessary to go into because the therapy is short-term, and because indeed one does not think they are going to interfere in the long run in the patient's function. Thus, our emphasis is on focus or the framework, whether the framework is right or not. I am perfectly willing to agree with anybody who wants to establish a different framework if he can work with the patient in that framework and produce meaningful follow-up findings. This is perfectly all right. This is exactly what we are here for. Our framework is to establish a focus which in most of our patients—and I am talking about the Boston group—is a triangular oedipal focus. This is where we stand, and this is where we fall.

I appreciate the gentleman who said he had to focus on what he saw. You can decide among yourselves whether this is right or wrong. What is important is whether this patient, seen after some time, as Dr. Davanloo's Unit plans to do, is going to be able to be free of the problem that brought her into the clinic and continue in what appears to be a meaningful marriage that she has now. Now, as Dr. Davanloo pointed out, indeed she withstood a great deal in the first interview, discussing her relationships with men as well as with her father. This was not out of the blue.

As far as the question of why I talk too much, why shouldn't I? Now, what is there that tells us that there is such a thing as a technique that one does one thing and one does not do another. This is my style. You may not like it or you may like it. Possibly the reason for my style has to do with my own training at the Massachusetts General Hospital. I was a serious student interested in psychiatry. I was supervised by a supervisor who believed in the principle of minimal activity. That means that you occasionally make appropriate noises if the material is of interest, and if indeed the patient has said something so significant, you say, "Tell me all about it." Well, I was not going to play roles. I thought that psychiatry has something to do with a certain individuation also in therapy. If I wanted to play roles I would have gone to Hollywood, not to Harvard Medical School. Therefore, I thought it was of some importance to develop a technique, and this is what I have shown you.

Part IV

TECHNIQUES OF SHORT-TERM DYNAMIC PSYCHOTHERAPY

Chapter 16

Principles of Technique in Short-Term Anxiety-Provoking Psychotherapy

P. E. SIFNEOS

A twenty-eight-year-old single male patient came to the clinic complaining of the acute onset of nervousness and phobias, and requested treatment over a period of two months so that he could get married. Since he was our prototype, our first patient to receive short-term psychotherapy, I shall briefly describe what we did for him over that two-month period. This was twenty years ago.

His past history revealed that he had good relationships with both his father and his mother. He was the youngest of two boys, and his father who suffered from emphysema was remembered as a kindly person. The patient remembered witnessing his father's difficulty in breathing and his death due to pulmonary edema and respiratory distress. Then his mother took the two boys and went to New York by train and he remembered that he was frightened of the train engine.

He remembered that at times, particularly when he had a cold and he had difficulty in breathing, he would become apprehensive and call his mother, who would eventually calm him down by putting him in his father's bed next to her. Then he would ask himself such questions as "Am I breathing? Will I die?" He was an excellent student in high school. While in the service, he had an episode when he was impotent with a prostitute.

Then he returned to Boston. He had a relationship with a young woman that was very satisfactory. When he met his present girl friend, he established a good relationship sexually and otherwise. They decided to get married, whereupon he promptly developed his difficulties that brought him to the clinic. He was again very anxious, came early for his interviews and related this nervousness to having gone to the movies with his financée the night before. The picture was about a murderer who was electrocuted. He later asked his therapist whether he would "cut the interview short." He also talked at length about his fear of knives and razors, and this led to his remembering his stepfather's departure for the war and his being told that he should be "the man of the house." He again associated to being in his father's bed with his mother.

The next two hours, he felt better. He talked about his trip to New York with his mother and remembered the fear of the train engine. He also recalled an episode when he was caught by his father, playing "doctor" with a little girl inside a closet, but did not remember being punished for it. These various episodes were connected, and anxiety-provoking confrontations and interpretations produced resistance but brought about more meaningful associations.

The fears of castration were clearly seen in reference to his stepfather and his father, and were also transferred to the therapist.

The therapy was terminated soon thereafter. He went through his wedding ceremony with flying colors. His phobias and nervousness had disappeared.

It was quite clear that we had a triangular focus. There were certain emotional conflicts behind his phobia, and these in turn were connected with his feeling for his father, with people in authority like his commanding officer, with his stepfather, his brother, as well as with the therapist. The triangular situations were clear. There was always a woman and two men. At times he was regressing and was not allowed to do so. He wanted pills, which were denied him. I got him right back to the specific focus. After a certain degree of understanding took place, the therapy was terminated and indeed the problem had been resolved. It was fairly certain that this particular patient had passed the problem-solving test in psychodynamic terms. A characterological dynamic change had taken place. This was our first case.

Let me summarize very briefly what we learned from this patient who as mentioned already was our prototype. He received short-term dynamic psychotherapy, which we call "anxiety-provoking." It is therefore more limited than the kind of brief psychotherapy that Dr. Malan, Dr. Davanloo and others are offering. It usually lasts anywhere from twelve to sixteen interviews. It is open-ended. We differ from Dr. James

Mann, who sets a limit of twelve interviews. What we say to the patient who has fulfilled our selection criteria is as follows: "We found you eligible for short-term psychotherapy, and if you are willing to proceed with it, we will make the appropriate arrangements. It is going to be of short duration. It is going to be focused in the area of the problems that you and your evaluator have established." The patient usually inquires as to what is short: "What is meant by the word 'short-term'?" And the answer is, "It's going to be up to you to solve your problem in whatever time limit you want, but it will be for a few months only. It will not be expected to go on for a long time." Thus we leave it open-ended, as I said. I think in about 10 percent of our patients we have gone anywhere from sixteen to twenty sessions. Twenty is the upper limit. We have had only three patients who had twenty interviews.

To summarize very briefly what the technical requirements for short-term anxiety-provoking psychotherapy are:

1. We establish the focus and we stay within the focus. The focus in these particular patients is an oedipal one.
2. We use the transference openly, explicitly, and as early as it appears, to make links between the experiences that the patient had in the past and the feelings that he has for the therapist; to establish quickly what Dr. Malan calls the most important aspect of short-term psychotherapy, namely, the patient transference link.
3. On the basis of our extensive evaluation we think that the patient who fulfills our criteria is capable of withstanding a great deal of anxiety, and this is the reason we call this treatment anxiety-provoking. We do not decrease the anxiety. We do not give pills. We do not support the patient, and we do not tell him what to do. We simply maintain that the patient is able to look into the areas of his resistance and into the dynamic conflict that underlies his difficulties.
4. We avoid anything that comes in the way of interfering with the focus, such as characterological pregenital issues.
5. Technically speaking, the patients are seen face-to-face once a week for forty-five minutes, and the therapy ends when the problem which has been outlined and the focus that has been established have been resolved.

Although one does not have the evidence all the time, for the greatest number of patients there is actual, tangible evidence that a different attitude has developed, i.e., in the form of new relationships. For example, if a patient had a pattern of domination in his relationships with women and then we have the appearance of a new girl friend with whom he relates in a very different way, a new and dramatic change has taken place. This is important because it shows that things are shifting dynamically and that it is time to stop.

Now, with 50 percent of our patients, it is they who bring up the issues of termination. The patient says, "I seem to have an understanding of what we have set out to do. Where do we go from here?" It is crucial at this point that the therapist not prolong the therapy if he agrees with the patient. He must therefore set a termination date. The other 50 percent of patients expect the therapist to specify when the treatment should end.

I have a tape of one of our patients who came in on the twelfth interview and said, "I've been feeling much better." He gave a list of all his improvements in the areas that had caused him trouble and had brought him into therapy, and related how much he had changed. I interrupted him and said, "Now, when do you want to stop?" and he smiled and said, "Stop what?" And I smiled and said, "Stop treatment." "Stop treatment! Oh, no!" he said. For twenty minutes he went on arguing that we should not stop, trying to find out ways to convince me. By the end of the hour he said, "Well, you know I really was trying to find out something that bothered me so as to pursue our treatment because I like it so much, but really I don't think there's very much more that we can do." And indeed this was the case.

Principles of Technique in Short-Term Dynamic Psychotherapy

D. H. MALAN

I want to begin by speaking about the basic principles of all kinds of psychoanalytic psychotherapy that can be formulated. This applies to psychoanalysis as much as it does to any form of short-term dynamic psychotherapy. In the short-term method one uses these techniques in a rather more active fashion.

The classic thing we have all heard in supervision is that in analysis you must interpret the defense before you interpret the impulse, and you must interpret the anxiety with the impulse. If you interpret the impulse before you interpret the anxiety or the defense, you are likely to raise the patient's anxiety level to the point in which the defenses are increased and the resistance is increased. This does not have to be taken as an absolute statement, and it is obviously true that, particularly with the kinds of patients we work with, one can often interpret the impulse directly because it is so close to the surface. It is often anxiety-relieving rather than anxiety-provoking. It may also be anxiety-provoking but in a constructive way. Here we see the first triangle in which there is the defense, the anxiety and the impulse. This is the triangle we are always dealing with in any form of psychodynamic psychotherapy.

There is another triangle, which Karl Menninger in his book *The Technique of Psychoanalysis* calls the "triangle of insight." I don't like that term, and I would prefer to use the "triangle of person." In this triangle it really doesn't matter in which order one interprets. It is according to what the patient is bringing. The triangle of insight is between current relationships, past relationships and the relationship with the therapist. It is the task of the analyst, just as it is for the brief therapist, to establish a link between the three. He needs to show the patient that his current relationship is in some way repeating something that derived from the past.

Now, in terms of short-term psychotherapy, if transference develops it is important to show the patient that this is also likely to be a derivation from the past, and one equally needs to make the link between the relationship and patterns in the patient's current relationships.

In the triangle of insight one angle has to do with transference, which I call "T." This is usually related to the parents, although obviously it may be also related to others. It can certainly be siblings or parent substitutes. I represent this by "P," because parents are likely to be the most important category of such people.

When one works in any form of dynamic psychotherapy, one has to consider the particular end at any one point in this therapy, and the extraordinary thing is that, although obviously this isn't rigidly true, it is possible to classify the kind of interpretation that one gives at any given moment in terms of those two triangles. If the patient can't speak to you freely, you interpret that he is feeling inhibited. That is the defense. He may be anxious and he might express hostile feelings. That is the impulse. Finally, you are completing that triangle in the transference. Obviously, you may also give partial interpretations. You can say to the patient, "You are afraid of something." That is an interpretation of the anxiety. Or you may say, "I think you are feeling very inhibited today, and obviously you know this is causing your problems," which is just pointing out the defense. You have then clarified it in relation to the transference. When you have clarified it, you may well want to say, "I think this is exactly the same pattern as you show in your relationship with others," whoever they may be. When that is clarified, you can say, "I think this really derives from your relationship with your father." You have then completed the triangle. Almost everything you say to the patient can be put down as an example of one apex or one side of these two triangles.

The therapist's skill is largely concerned with his intuitive understanding. He does not formulate it in those formal ways, and I think it would be very inhibiting if he did. The most disturbing type of interpretation will be about impulse and quite likely the impulses relating to parents. You have to be very careful with such interpretations. You have to sense all this as the therapy proceeds.

One of the questions that is often asked is, "How on earth do you keep your technique focal?" The answer can be very simple. If you select a focal point in the first place, your technique will be focal. This is one example in which you cannot disentangle selection from technique. A patient comes to you, and you can identify a current conflict and a symptom which is precipitated by an identifiable precipitating factor. Obviously, "The Man with the Headaches," who had anxiety symptoms and chest pains precipitated by the cardiac illness of his father is an example of that. Then, if you look back into the past, you can identify something that many a research project refers to as the core of the conflict, which either Franz Alexander or French—I have forgotten who—speaks of as a "nuclear conflict." Going back into the patient's history, you can discover other precipitating events or other traumatic experiences or other family constellations which give you a clue as to what the patient's nuclear conflict or conflicts are all about.

The third thing you want to look for and discover is that the current conflict and the nuclear conflict are the same. If you find such a patient, then the therapy will sort of roll out in front of you automatically. There is no problem about keeping interpretation focal because the patient will always be talking about aspects of his core conflict and you will always be making interpretations about them.

Using these principles as a guide, I will bring up a patient who was an Indian, who lived in England for a few years and who came to the Tavistock Clinic complaining about anxiety over premature ejaculation.

Since age twenty-three, he had started sexual relationships with girls, and as far as he knew there were no problems. In fact, he did frequently suffer from premature ejaculation but none of the girls complained about it. One day he met a girl who pointed out to him that there was something seriously wrong with him and that he ought to see a doctor. This produced considerable anxiety. Actually, he seemed to have functioned pretty adequately most of the time. He only seemed to suffer from this symptom when conditions weren't quite right—if he was in a hurry, if they were afraid to be discovered, or something of this kind. He had other problems as well, which I won't bother going into.

I saw him in consultation and started listening to the facts of his story. He came from a Hindu family. His father was a lawyer. The patient was the eldest in the family. He had tried to form relationships with Indian girls in England, but because they were rather few and far between, he said the competition was much too strong, and so he switched his interest to European girls, though not English girls. These European girls were also sort of displaced persons in a situation somewhat similar to his own. When it came out that there didn't seem to be much wrong with his potency and that I was not sure that he really needed treatment, I said, "Look, I think your potency is adversely affected by external conditions. I think if the conditions were right you could function with no problem. I really don't think there is anything wrong with you." This was perhaps unconsciously a therapeutic experiment as well. The patient turned to me and said, "Yes, but I want you to know what is wrong."

Suddenly the whole atmosphere of the interview changed. He launched into a series of free associations. He said that up to age seventeen he was very pugnacious and used to get into fights with other boys. One day, however, he challenged another boy in the street. This boy was considerably better than the patient at boxing and laid him flat and beat him up. From that time on, since age seventeen, he never got into a fight again. Making use of the previous information about difficulties over competition which I felt were there, I said to him that I thought he was afraid of competing with other men. I was pointing out the anxiety. I was not saying what the anxiety was about. I brought in the word "compete," which the patient had not mentioned in connection with these fights with boys, and thus I was pointing out the anxiety and an interpretation of the impulse. The patient agreed with this, and, encouraged, I made one of these links with the triangles. I said, "I think the person you are afraid of competing with is your father." I knew nothing whatsoever about his father. I just made a guess.

As it turned out, the father was an extremely successful man and a very pugnacious man. He had won a lot of medals for boxing and used to get into many fights as well. I then interpreted the impulse in relation to his father once more and also made the link between his current relationships and his father. I said to him, using analytic theory, "I think that in order to become a man you have got to fight your father. On the occasion that you fought the man in the street and he beat you, you felt that you had been punished and that you never wanted to try again." This interpretation brought out an impulse, namely, that the patient often felt he wanted to rebel against authority.

Another situation related to his father was that the father had often thrashed him when he was a boy and the patient was determined not to cry. He had, therefore, expressed to me some sort of open challenging of the father. There was absolutely no indication from his history that he was deeply disturbed in any way and there was no suspicion that he had borderline personality or anything like that. He had clearly had a good relationship with his mother. I don't think there were problems in relationship with the mother, only in relation to the mother and the father. He had done well academically until age seventeen, when he cracked up academically. He certainly did not currently work up to his potential. There was not the slightest difficulty in making a therapeutic plan. In this case, it was important that he have a male therapist because it was very clear that the main issue was with his father. You most likely will get transference manifestations in terms of rebellion against authority leading to anxiety and inhibition. These you will interpret in terms of underlying impulses and anxieties. You will repeatedly make the link with the father and you will hope that by working on this you can help him over his problems of potency. Actually, the therapeutic plan was never formulated in so many words.

Now I would like to move straight to the climax of the therapy. The patient spoke of how he sometimes thought his father might die but he was afraid of taking over the responsibility of becoming the head of the family. He had borrowed money from his father to come to England, but something in him refused to pay the money back to his father, with the result that the father had to pay bills for him. I said to him that this really seemed to me like he was stealing something from his father. I suspected that what he wanted to steal from his father was his power and that his father's power certainly included his father's power as a sexual man. Therefore, any form of achievement, either in work or in trying to form a relationship with a woman, became forbidden and he became guilty about it.

In response to this, the patient spoke of an anxiety attack which he had had the other day—and, in fact, he had had these regularly—in which he went around all day with a lump in his throat and he eventually traced this to guilt about something he had done that day. I said simply to him that it looked as though guilt was at the center of his problem and it sounded as if it had something to do with his father. I didn't say anything more than that. Suddenly he said, "Yes. You know, once I read my father's love letters to my mother." This was something that he felt terribly guilty about and which he confessed with great relief. Such a confession obviously has all sorts of implications. There seems to be some kind of symbolic interfering between the father and the mother, or trying to identify with his father's feelings about the mother. There is no particular reason why it should make him feel guilty if there weren't such a thing as a need or a complex; one shouldn't read somebody else's letters, but this obviously shouldn't give one anxiety attacks. He went on and spoke of his great love for his mother but that somehow his love for his mother seemed to be blunted recently.

I just simply suggested that father and son could be rivals for the mother's love. In the next session he said that he had experienced an extraordinary feeling of relief after the previous session. He felt he wanted to leap about in the street.

Within the next two sessions he reported that the anxiety attacks which occurred regularly had disappeared. He was no longer worried that there was anything physically wrong with him. He then said openly that he was surprised that I hadn't come to represent an authority for him, toward whom he felt hostile. Moreover, he had had a passion of being deliberately uncooperative with men, and much to his surprise the other day he found himself quite spontaneously cooperating with a man who was asking him to help him out with something at work. In fact, transference was little used in this therapy.

We have a seven year follow-up on this patient. I received a letter from him, which is one of the most touching I have ever received, in which he states in a sense that all aspects of disturbances in his life have been cleared up and that he suffers in no way from premature ejaculation. He has now become a leader in the field in which he works and he is happy. His letter was full of a sense of humor.

Dr. Lowy:

For years I have been a great admirer of Dr. Sifneos, and I think it is probably his work in short-term therapy that gave me the courage to move in that direction. I find him a most compelling and persuasive speaker. What is more, his results speak for themselves. They are good. So, how can I come before a group like this and say that on a number of important points I really don't agree with Dr. Sifneos? Of course, if we are really going to share experiences, we also have to share disagreements as well as agreements. People always ask nowadays, where has the Oedipus complex gone? If you look at psychiatric and certain psychoanalytic literature, you find that in contrast to twenty and certainly thirty years ago the term "Oedipus complex" is rarely seen in titles. Well, where has it gone? It has obviously gone to short-term psychotherapy literature, because here it is. There has been so much focus on oedipal problems, on the triangularities and so on, that one might be led to believe that only patients with clear oedipal conflicts are amenable to short-term psychotherapy, and furthermore I imagine that there is a degree of discouragement when people think they have to find such classical oedipal problems where the evidence is so unmistakable that otherwise, in a sense, their hands are tied.

Personally, I find that patients of the kind that Dr. Sifneos described are indeed suitable for short-term psychotherapy, and in fact probably very little else should be attempted to begin with. There are a great many patients exemplified by the case example that we have heard who really do benefit and who, in fact, should also be offered short-term psychotherapy. There is something else, though, and that has to do with the nature of evidence in psychotherapy. How do we know what we are seeing is what it is? Clearly, experience and intuition are important variables here, but unless we are going to be put in the position of saying that psychotherapists are made, or in a sense born not made, or unless we take the position that only intuitive experts who are certain of what they are seeing are in a position to foresee, we have to devise some method of checking hypotheses. And it seems to me that particularly for people who are starting in this field, and for a great many others who have been going on for quite a long time, there is some advantage in being able to make a hypothesis on the basis of what the patient says—sometimes in the first five or ten minutes as we have seen here.

But then it seems to me that there is an obligation on the part of the therapist to check his hypotheses and not to immediately jump in as though the hypotheses are confirmed simply because one has drawn them. Now, here again it's a difficult thing. It is clear that Dr. Sifneos knows what he is doing and gets good results. Yet sometimes a star athlete, baseball or hockey player, for whom it all comes easy, says, "Look, we just do this, that, and the other thing," but what about the people who need more guidelines?

It appears that there is some merit to perhaps a bit more science and a little less art, because art is such a subjective thing. Now, the science part of it, to the extent that science is possible in psychotherapy, seems to me to involve establishing a hypothesis; take, for example, a triangular situation, as was described in several of the cases already discussed. You have a hypothesis. Then you test it by advancing tentatively, I would hope, an interpretation or a comment and waiting to see what the patient makes of it or what the subsequent material reveals. But if there is very quick confirmation for the therapist that he is right, and if he then proceeds vigorously on that assumption, it would seem that a lot of other factors come into play which may indeed be helpful and therapeutic, but which might conceivably lead a too hasty therapist along the wrong path.

We all know how important it is for many patients to please their therapist. They invest the therapist—for their own needs, of course—with a great many qualities, and the need to come up with what the therapist wants can sometimes, I think, obscure other areas that need to be looked at.

Within the last year I had as a patient, a man of thirty-two who was referred by a G.P. This man had, at least on the surface, a happy marriage with an attractive, vivacious, sexually satisfying partner, but he had recently become depressed. He hadn't told his family doctor, but he very quickly told me that he was depressed because of the loss of a girl friend. Well, to make a long story short, despite his sexually satisfying and—in many respects—happy marriage, he had a girl friend who happened to be older, not nearly so attractive, certainly not so vivacious, certainly not so well educated, etc. The girl friend provided for him essentially a maternal figure with whom he was exceedingly close, and it was the girl friend's move to another city which essentially produced the depression. As one might expect, this turned out very clearly to be an example of separation, and it went back to his mother. I felt this to be essential work that had been done with relation to that particular problem. Now, it is true enough that there were oedipal features in it.

There was, in fact, a triangular situation. But in this particular case, I feel this was really a mask or perhaps the tip of the iceberg, and the bulk of the iceberg and the part that really needed attention I felt was of a totally different order. Now, I suspect that there are many such cases, and if we exclude them from treatment I think those patients are missing out, or if we take them into treatment but focus only on the oedipal aspects I think again there is a possibility of not doing our best. With respect to the steps, I basically agree with what Dr. Sifneos does. There is a need to focus yet not necessarily on the oedipal problems, but on, in French's terms, "the focal conflict," and hopefully "the nuclear conflict" (ideally these are related), or, for example, in Balint's terms, on "identifying the basic fault as it is reflected in the current problem." If it is possible to do this, the likelihood of success of short-term psychotherapy is greatly enhanced. A contract needs to be set, and I personally have found it helpful to set closing deadlines. I try not to do it rigidly. For me, the tentative setting of the deadline has been helpful.

With respect to activity, I think it is implicit that in this kind of treatment there is no place whatsoever for a passive-contemplative therapist who is going to wait for the material to bubble up. You have to go after it. But I'd like to distinguish between being active and being directive. It seems to me one can be exceedingly active and yet remain nondirective, and I think it's a distinction that needs to be made. I think there is an important need to encourage the patient, either subtly or sometimes more overtly, to rehearse what's been learned in therapy. People tend to do this spontaneously, in any event, but where a patient doesn't it tends to slow up therapy. Then it's important, in my view, to pay some attention to the consequences of the conflict as well as the conflict itself. I am reminded here of the analogy that Freud made. I think it was in *Analysis—Terminable and Interminable*—where incidentally he was rather pessimistic about shortening the length—that he commented on Rank's attempts to resolve the birth trauma very quickly and therefore solve all the problems, and he drew the analogy of a fire set by an oil lamp which was knocked over. He felt that if the fireman came in the midst of all this conflagration and simply took the lamp away, it wouldn't be of any great help. You've got to put out the rest of the fire, too. In addition to going after the initial problem, you have also got to deal with the current manifestation of the consequences of the problem.

Dr. Nemiah:

It seems we are starting to develop some nice polarities here for discussion and for debate. I think we might ask ourselves as we reflect upon this, "Do the techniques determine the approach or does the approach determine the techniques?" And how do these interrelate?

Dr. Davanloo:

What I would like to point out is that really there is no polarity of views. Dr. Lowy's point that we should use short-term dynamic psychotherapy for a larger number of patients is true. In my view, there is a spectrum of short-term dynamic psychotherapies, and my years of research data point to this conclusion. If, for the sake of simplicity, we place the short-term dynamic psychotherapies on a continuum, at one end one finds the cases in which the central structure of the patient's conflict is basically oedipal. These are the cases that we treat in from two to fifteen sessions. At the other end of this continuum we see cases where the problems are deeper, and one might produce excellent results within twenty-five, thirty-five or an upper limit of forty sessions. Less than one-third, probably between 25 and 30 percent of the patients we treated successfully, fell into this somewhat sicker category. Somewhere between the two ends of this continuum are cases about which one might say that the nuclear conflict is "oedipal-plus," and that the length of therapy would be somewhere in between the two.

I should add that this categorization is in no way absolute, and, as Dr. Malan points out, there are patients who might respond well in a much shorter period of time. At the same time, I should add that it is not basically the nuclear conflict that determines the length of the therapy. There are many variables that come into play—the patient's ego strength, the therapist's variables (clinical skill), and many other factors.

Comment from the floor:

I would like to ask about what I think is a crucial point raised by Dr. Sifneos, namely, sticking strictly to the transference. I wonder if he will compare and contrast what he meant by that, since I gather he feels that the transference neurosis is something to be clearly avoided. How does he distinguish between the use of the transference and avoid getting entangled in the transference neurosis?

Dr. Sifneos:

This is a complex question, but it is precisely why I think that short-term psychotherapy should remain short-term and that the possibility of getting involved in more characterological issues tends to prolong the therapy. The therapies described by Drs. Malan and Lowy have the potential complication of creating a transference neurosis which cannot easily be analyzed. At best, it would take a long period of time, using a psychoanalytic free-associative technique. I also want to make one other point very clear. I have not said that short-term psychotherapy of the oedipal kind, as we use it in Boston, is the only kind of short-term psychotherapy. I do agree completely with the comments made by Dr. Davanloo. What we are here for in Montreal is to develop a variety of therapeutic techniques of short duration. I wrote a paper in 1967 which described several kinds of short-term psychotherapy. Each one was based on different selection criteria, utilized different techniques and produced a different outcome. So, although I am complimented to be called an artist, I thoroughly believe that I am committed to being a scientist.

Dr. Malan:

I think there is a misconception about concentrating entirely on the transference. Indeed, I am quite sure of this. I would say that the transference should be interpreted from the way it arises. Many of the therapies conducted under my supervision or by me deal with extra-transference issues all the time. When the extra-transference issue becomes relevant in the transference, then we interpret that as well. The issue of the transference neurosis, again, is a very complex one. There has always been a great fear of the transference neurosis on the part of people who have been trained in analysis. It's very difficult to draw any clear-cut distinction between the patient who develops an intense transference earlier and a transference neurosis.

Chapter 17

Basic Methodology and Technique of Short-Term Dynamic Psychotherapy

H. DAVANLOO

Dr. Davanloo:

In our unit, as I have said before, we have a spectrum of short-term dynamic psychotherapies. We accept not only patients whose history and psychiatric symptomatology give us clear evidence that the roots of their problems lie in a genuine triangular oedipal problem, but also patients who have much deeper problems. It is on this basis that we use the term "broad-focused short-term dynamic psychotherapy." Briefly, we use special focus interviews with exploration of the genetic material, with the techniques of confrontation, clarification, and exploration into the conscious, preconscious and derivatives of unconscious material.

The major task of the therapist is to understand as quickly as possible the essential problems and make them understandable to the patient. The therapist is much more active than in classical psychoanalysis, and I very much agree with the statement of Dr. Lowy that there is no place for a passive therapist in this kind of treatment. He very nicely indicated that "we cannot wait for the material to bubble up."

In terms of therapeutic focus one should pay attention very early to the central structure of the patient's conflict. I very much agree with Dr. Lowy, who said that we should pay attention to the present manifestations of the consequences of the conflict. In my experience this is very true, as this reinforces a positive transference climate, which is highly desirable.

Psychoanalytic technique is used, which consists of analysis of defense and transference reaction and resistances, and exploration into the part of the libido structure which is involved in the patient's conflict. I will enumerate below some of the basic dimensions of the technique.

THERAPEUTIC ALLIANCE

The establishment of a working relationship is a prime objective and should be established in the very early phase of the treatment. The therapist and patient together are then able to concentrate on the focus during the entire course of the therapy. The therapist should increase the patient's motivation, obtain his confidence and utilize his positive transference feelings.

TRANSFERENCE

One should utilize the positive transference feelings. Transference reactions are frequently interpreted. Transference clarification and confrontation are used extensively with the interpretation of the past-present transference link, which Alexander calls "total interpretation." We make great use of this type of interpretation in our work from the very first interview, that is, setting up a link between the contemporary pattern of the patient's behavior with significant people in his present life with the vertical, the genetic pattern of the patient's behavior with parents or parent-substitutes, and further linking it with the transference pattern.

An example is the patient I will now speak about. In the first interview he was very passive and nonproductive, and his resistance was high. His relationship with his father was one in which he was passive and submissive, and the father was described as "authoritarian," and the patient was not able to verbalize and communicate his thoughts, ideas, and feelings. We also learned in that session that the patient is dominated by his wife, and especially by his in-laws, who, he said, "are walking all over me." The way he handles himself is to hold on to his irritation, taking a passive, withdrawn stand. I made a link between these two, and then a further link with his behavior with me. I indicated the self-defeating pattern of his behavior, namely, that he is obviously suffering, he comes on his own for help, and at the same time he finds it difficult to talk about his thoughts and ideas.

Interpretation of negative transference is highly essential. I would also emphasize the importance of early and repeated interpretation of resistance, ambivalence and negative transference, which are of great importance in the maintenance of the therapeutic alliance. Parenthetically, I would also indicate what I think Dr. Marmor has already elaborated on: that one should take into consideration some of the realities to which the patient is reacting. The patient's negative reaction to the therapist, the patient's dislike of the therapist, might be related to a negative transference, but it can also be a reaction to certain real deficiencies in the therapist's personality. Similarly, the patient's liking for the therapist might be the result of a positive transference, but it might be a reaction to the realistic attributes of the therapist's personality.

In talking about transference, I would also briefly mention countertransference, which might become a major vehicle in the development of misalliance with the patient. We see this over and over in the supervision of trainees, and I often see it in a situation where the therapist and the patient share an alliance the result of which is not toward insight but toward some form of shared defensiveness.

The process of identification as a therapeutic dimension is in operation from the beginning. Dr. Sifneos has discussed "a new learning experience." This is well demonstrated in "The Case of the Teeth-Grinding Woman" [Chapter 9], and the term "learning experience" is often used by the patient in the evaluation of the outcome.

Now we are going to see two videotapes which I am sure will stir up a great deal of controversy and will provide a background for the discussion of technique, the psychotherapeutic process, and specific and nonspecific therapeutic factors.

"The Case of the Cement-Mixer Man"

The patient is in his early thirties, was born in Winnipeg and has lived in Montreal for the past ten years. He was self-referred and came with symptoms of anxiety and depression and obsessional thoughts. His marriage was breaking down subsequent to a trisomy experience which both he and his wife had willingly entered into about eight months prior to his coming for treatment. Many months prior to the first interview he and his wife, after reading a *Penthouse* magazine, decided to experiment trisomy with a girl friend of his wife whom we will call Miss L. The patient described her as very attractive, like his wife, but one of the major features that had attracted him was her large breasts. The first encounter took place on a weekend. The patient's wife decided to sleep in their bedroom upstairs and the patient slept with Miss L. downstairs. He made a number of sexual attempts. He got an erection but lost it as soon as he attempted sexual intercourse. His mind was not free; it was with his wife upstairs. The next day the wife accepted the role of an active partner, and the setting was that while he had sexual intercourse the wife would observe it and also caress Miss L.'s body. The whole experience was enjoyable to all of them, and he had no further problem with his potency. This continued for a few times, then started to disturb the wife. She felt disturbed as he became more and more attached to Miss L. This ended in constant arguments, but the patient could not break away from Miss L. Then there was discussion of separation, but the patient couldn't give up his wife either. Finally, they decided to separate on a trial basis, and the patient rented an apartment elsewhere.

He stayed a week with Miss L. but his mind was constantly on his wife and his marriage, and he was constantly preoccupied with his wife. This had an obsessional quality. Then he went back to his wife, but then he was constantly preoccupied with Miss L. This preoccupation again had an obsessional quality which interfered with his concentration and his work. For two or three months he went back and forth between his wife and Miss L., and this again began to affect his other functioning, particularly his work. He was in this situation when he sought psychiatric help.

During the first interview it became evident that this patient had a great deal of difficulty in the area of interpersonal relationships, difficulty in asserting himself, especially in personal relationships, and experienced a great deal of anxiety in his relationship with his in-laws. This is his second marriage. His wife is described as an attractive but flat-chested woman, well-educated. The sexual relationship is very satisfactory, but there was a great deal of conflict with his wife in other areas. His character structure could be described as obsessive-compulsive; he cannot stand it if things are not in their place and wants the house to be spotless, and this is a chronic source of bitterness and conflict between him and his wife. The wife is described as a pleasure-seeking type who prefers things to be done whenever she is in the mood. The patient experiences a great deal of irritation about this, bottles up his feelings and takes over the functions of his wife. For example, if the bathroom is not spotless, he takes everything out of it, cleans it and makes it spotless, and is thoroughly irritated the whole time. Whenever they have a party, he spends a great deal of time making sure everything is in its place and prepared on time. After the party he expects everything to be washed and put in its place. His wife doesn't want to do it, and he gets irritated and finally ends up staying awake until one or two o'clock in the morning to clean up. He has no boundaries with his in-laws, and they actually make decisions about the patient's home life. He gets extremely irritated about this, and his way of handling it is to withdraw. He has the fear that if he asserts himself his father-in-law might get violent.

The patient's father is described as an obsessive-compulsive person, highly authoritarian, demanding, and his mother as a "doormat" to his father. He has two sisters and a brother. He described his relationship with his father as being passive; he was fearful of him and at age nineteen finally broke away. As far back as he can remember he worked for his father, feared him, gave up all his activities and chose his career as was dictated by his father, which was in contrast to his brother. His earliest memory of his mother is of her large breasts, which fascinated him. When she was breast-feeding his sister, he would ask his mother to allow him to sit and watch the feeding; he said what he was interested in was not the feeding but her breasts. Another memory that emerged later on was the genitals and large breasts of a woman, with no face or other part of her body, which he would put into a cement mixer. He remembers that he used to lie in bed about age six with this fantasy frequently in his mind. Another early memory relates to sucking his fingers and his father bandaging them to prevent him from sucking them. This was back in his crib. Another very early memory is that his mother held him and showed his penis to his father; it was raw, and his father examined it and put some powder on it.

After he broke away from his father, he married. His wife was already pregnant. She is also described as a very attractive, small-breasted woman. There were sexual problems, as she had frequent vaginal infections.

Then he got involved with a newly married woman whom we will call Mrs. S., who is described as very attractive and large-breasted. After some time Mrs. S. broke her relationship with him and returned to her husband.

The patient's first marriage ended in divorce, and while he was having the affair with Mrs. S. he met his present wife.

My initial evaluation of this patient took three interviews, each of one hour's duration, as I found him to be a rather rigid, passive, ruminative person. He did not fulfill our criteria for selection, and I asked for a comprehensive battery of psychological tests, including projective techniques. A brief summary of the psychological testing reads: "The picture is one of a highly rigid young man who takes the position of coolness, detachment, and intellectualization. He functions in such a way as to experience as little anxiety as possible. An obsessionally inclined person, seeking solutions in the external world..." Then it reads: "In conclusion, I would expect to see a very passive-aggressive personality.... Major change would require long-term intensive psychoanalytic treatment."

Following is an edited transcript of twenty-five minutes of the sixth psychotherapy session and twenty-five minutes of the ninth.

"THE CASE OF THE CEMENT-MIXER MAN"
(6TH PSYCHOTHERAPY SESSION)

Pt: It seems our last meeting triggered a lot of memories.

Th: There was something about the last meeting that...

Pt: Yeah. You remember I said I'd had a hard time remembering my youth unless we went backwards; but associations have taken place, and I've remembered certain things that I didn't remember last meeting. We talked about my father being away and coming home and being scared of him and all that. I seem to remember at some particular time feeling—I felt like I must have said to myself: "Thank God I don't have to be scared of him." I have that memory at some point when I was young—of feeling relieved that something had made me stop fearing my father.

Th: You said that last time you talked about the fear of your father, but what else did you talk about last time?

Pt: About my mother, about wanting to see her body and her breasts and so forth.

Th: Your intense interest in the breasts and body of your mother?

Pt: Yes.

Th: Now what happened when your father was away? He was away for twenty to thirty days at a time. What happened then to you, with all your interest in and fascination with the breasts of your mother and her body? Is there a relationship between that and your fear, since you had eyes, and you discussed also that when he was in bed with your mother, then the idea was that those breasts and that body were in the hands of your father?

Pt: I don't remember feeling that. I remember—like I said, as we talk these things come back, such as the fact of the door being closed. In my mind all I see is a white door, and for that door to stick in my mind it must be what's on the other side of it that made me see the door; and on the other side of it was my mother, and I was not allowed to go in.

Th: What were your fantasies?
Pt: I don't know what they were then. I really don't, because this was when I was five years old.
Th: But you had the memory about the breasts, didn't you?
Pt: Yes, seeing her breasts feeding my sister.
Th: You also said that your interest was not in the feeding; that it was the breasts.
Pt: Right.
Th: And you remember the white door?
Pt: Yes.
Th: But you cannot remember anything in any fantasy about what was behind the door, yet also you remember your fear of your father. Do you see any connection between your fear of your father and your feelings about your mother? Was there a connection between the two? You were alone with your mother, and you were sneaking around to see her body when your father was not around. What sort of thoughts do you have about this?

(*At this point the patient's feelings about his father, which were very ambivalent, were explored.*)

Pt: Yes, and that's the thing that triggered another memory about being very upset with my father. He came home from one of his trips and was to leave within a week or so, again to go away on business. Now, on this particular trip—I presume it was during the summer because he said he was going to take my brother away with him, and I remember very well trying to get in and say: "Can I go, too?" He promised he would take me, and I kept asking him because I guess I detected that his promise didn't seem to be very firm, and I kept asking him and he kept saying yes. So the morning of the departure, they didn't wake me up, but I was awake because I remember pulling the covers over my head and uttering obscenities, saying that it was a dirty trick and "How could you do this?" but I was talking to myself.
Th: But you were awake and you were pretending to be asleep?
Pt: Yes, because I slept in a passageway where they had to pass back and forth as they were getting ready and eating breakfast. This is all going on very early in the morning, about 6:00 A.M., and he and my brother just went away and I was very upset. I remember that episode of pulling the covers over my head

and swearing at my father, but I don't remember the week after when he was away. I don't remember that. That sticks in my mind.

Th: Are you saying that you really wanted to go with him?

Pt: Yes.

Th: You say that you were awake and he had promised you, but you didn't announce that you were awake. You see, you were in bed and you pulled the sheet over your head so this brings the question really of whether you wanted to go away, or whether you were playing a trick with your father in your own mind, because if you wanted to go then you would get out of bed.

Pt: I would think so now, but . . .

Th: So let's look at it. You said your father was playing a trick on you, but the question is really whether you were playing a game. Perhaps you wanted to go with your father, and perhaps also you were jealous of the close relationship between your father and your brother. At the same time, as we have seen, you wanted to be around the house with your mother; but finally the way you handled this conflict was to pull the blanket over your head and utter silent obscenities at your father.

Pt: Could one come to this conclusion from one episode?

Th: Let us look at that episode, and then we will see. There you were, playing a game with your father in dealing with your dilemma. If you had really wanted to go, you would have gotten out of bed and said so.

Pt: But I was scared of my father, too, at that time. If I had gotten out of bed, I don't know what he would have done.

Th: So we can look into that also. Let us go back to that because this is linked with other memories you have, namely, when your father was away, then you could be exclusively with your mother, and at the same time you have brought up fantasies of death wishes toward your father. Then there you were, wanting to be close to your father, and there are negative feelings you had toward your father, and you wanted to be around the house with your mother, her body, her breasts, and all of it. What thoughts do you have about this?

Pt: Yes. Well, talking about the death wish is what made me think about that episode because that had been completely out of my mind for many years, although I can sort of recall having recalled it several times when I was younger. As the years went on I would say: "Gee, last year my father did that to me," or "Two years ago," you know, as I got older, but then there was a time when I didn't think of it any more. Another memory that came back when we were talking about breasts was a fantasy I used to have. I know I used to have it in that same bed that I was in when my father went away without waking me.

(*The patient is silent and appears very uncomfortable.*)

Pt: It's a weird fantasy.

(*He is again silent.*)

Th: You don't feel like talking about it?
Pt: It's just so wild. I feel embarrassed about it, and yet I know I was five or six at the time.
Th: And what was it? It was about the genitals of a woman?
Pt: Yeah, and I used to take them off the women.
Th: Take what off?
Pt: The breasts and the—you see, the breasts I had seen. I knew what they looked like, and I could just imagine what the rest of the genital area looked like, but I used to take them off the woman and put them in a container which...
Th: In your mind?
Pt: In my mind, yes, and I don't know what I did with them. The container was like a big vat.
Th: It was round, you mean?
Pt: Yes. You know, like when you mix cement. They've got a little round thing that they mix cement in, not the trucks, but on site, a thing like that. I used to put them in there and then that would just mix them up. I used to like that.
Th: You would lay down in that bed and then you would have this fantasy?
Pt: I would think of that.
Th: And who was the woman whose breasts and genitals were taken off and put into this thing?
Pt: I think it was a lot of people, different women, because I can't remember that there was any specific face or person. What I remember now is that it was just the genitals and the breasts.
Th: And what sort of idea comes to your mind about this fantasy?

Pt: I find it very hard to tell you. I have no idea about what the fantasy could mean.
Th: This started when you were about six, you said?
Pt: I would think so.
Th: And then it went on?
Pt: I don't seem to remember that it went on very long. It's hard to remember what is a year and what is a month when you're thinking back.
Th: Let's look at it. Here is a fantasy that goes on for some time, the breasts and genitals of a woman with no face or other parts. Who is this woman?
Pt: It could be any woman.
Th: Were there other women you had contact with at that age?
Pt: No. The only woman I knew was my mother.
Th: What do you think now?
Pt: Are you saying that these were the genitals and breasts of my mother?
Th: Tell me what you think yourself.
Pt: Obviously, it must have been my mother, but I had never seen her genitals.
Th: Do you notice that in talking about fantasies and many other memories somehow you prefer not to volunteer information and you put me in a position of questioning you?
Pt: I just want to get to one point. You said I force you to draw things out of me and this is exactly what was in my mind a moment ago.

(*In this part of the interview the patient expresses the idea that some of these things are very difficult to talk about, and this is followed by some transferential material. The therapist finally points out to the patient that he somehow finds it difficult to expose his intimate thoughts and ideas. Then the patient says there are things he wants to talk about, but that the therapist might say he is changing the subject.*)

Th: There is a fear that I might cut you off?
Pt: Yes. A fear that I am not proceeding in the way you think best.
Th: Do you think this might be somewhat similar to your relationship with your father, the idea that I be the one to direct you? Many times you indicated that you wanted to please him, and

everything you did was directed to please your father. You even chose your career to please him. Now, you were talking about your earliest memories.

Pt: The earliest memory—I think it's my earliest memory—is my father inspecting my penis because I was not circumcised, and he was forcing the skin back so that it wouldn't get too tight. And I remember my mother bringing me in to my father and asking him to look at it, and do whatever was required. I just stood there and he did it.

Th: How old were you then?

Pt: I remember that I was about the height of the bed, or maybe a little taller than the bed; I don't remember how old I was.

Th: Your father was inspecting your penis?

Pt: Yes, and he put some powder on it because it was bleeding or something like that. I remember him doing that once. I tell you that's my earliest memory, but now I think it's not because now I remember being in my crib. I probably slept in my crib until I was older than most children; the house wasn't that big so I was in my mother's room. I used to suck my thumb. My mother still bugs me today about how long I sucked my thumb, and if I were to listen to her in college I was still sucking my thumb. She said I sucked it until I was over a year, anyway. The event that I remember was that I went to bed with my thumb normal, and during the night I went to put it in my mouth and it had been bandaged, so while I was asleep my father bandaged my thumb to try to break me of the habit of sucking my thumb.
I remember that night because it was in the crib in my mother's room. I think that that would be my earliest memory. I remember not wanting to go to school. I remember putting up a big fuss the first day of school.

Th: In what way?

Pt: I was scared. I just didn't want to go and be alone.

Th: What happened?

Pt: My brother was going to the same school. He had already been there four years or three years or whatever, so I think that—I don't remember this, but I would think that the fact that my brother was going meant that I had somebody to depend on at school, He took me to school and brought me home. That's pre-school. Now, from school on it's pretty blank. I remember being in school. I remember certain events happening in my first year and my second year of school, my third year of school. Each year, like I can picture the teacher, and from there I can associate certain events during the day, but when I went home at night I don't remember what used to take place. Then I was in fifth grade when my father bought the tavern—fifth, maybe even fourth.

(The therapist says to the patient that in the early part of the session they explored very important material regarding his mother, inspection of his penis by his father, and the thumb-sucking, but that he is now focusing on the area of school and talking about some of the things that we already know, indicating to the patient that perhaps this might be a way of avoiding focusing on his relationship with his mother and father, and what the implications of these memories and fantasies in his early relationship with his parents might be. The therapist attempts to maintain the focus, which is one of the triangular foci.)

Pt: Well, you see, there is a method in what I am doing, and the method is that I was going to go from...

Th: Yes, I noticed that, but it is very important for us to understand this method because there are areas which we have to understand since they are related to your problem. Somehow you prefer to avoid these areas. We discussed two sessions ago your extreme submission in your relationship with your father, and you indicated that for twenty years of your life you have been sentenced to prison, and that you had committed a crime and that you were paying the penalty. You gave up your freedom and didn't have time to play with other children and were frightened to go out with girls. And somehow or other in your present life we see you experience anxiety in relationship with your in-laws, you take a passive, compliant role in relationship with others, and your self-punishing and self-defeating pattern continues. It is our job to understand these things.

(The rest of this session focuses on his relationship with his mother, the positive and the negative aspects, and it also comes to focus that he didn't have the fantasy of breasts and genitals when his father was around the house. The therapist indicates the hostile aspect in his relationship with his mother and with other women. The therapist brings into focus the other triangle, namely, his mother breast-feeding his sister.)

(9TH PSYCHOTHERAPY SESSION)

Pt: In the last session we were talking about the type of woman I am attracted to. The precise thing was that I am attracted to large-breasted women, but I'm married to a small-breasted woman. That was the point.

Th: Did this apply to your first marriage?

Pt: Yes. But then Mrs. S. was different in that respect.

Th: Mrs. S. was different in what way? She was different physically compared to your first wife and also compared with your second wife.

Pt: She was very large-breasted, and she had a nice figure, a nice face.

Th: But if you compare her with, say, your first wife?

Pt: I don't know if I'm looking through sunglasses or what, but I thought she was better all around physically. She had better physical attributes. She was quite attractive. At the time that was very important to me, to be with somebody attractive.

Th: But you said that her breasts were one of the major issues for you?

Pt: Yes.

Th: How would you compare the sexual aspect of that relationship compared with your wife?

Pt: My wife is much more satisfying to me than Mrs. S. was.

Th: Your first or second wife?

Pt: Well, my first wife—we had a lot of trouble sexually because of the baby we had. She was pregnant when we got married. At the beginning it was painful for her. She had a vaginal infection all through her pregnancy. Soon after the baby was born I started to go with Mrs. S. Once I became involved with her, there wasn't much interest in my first wife sexually.

Th: So you lost sexual interest in your wife, and this was after the baby was born?

Pt: Yes, about eight months after, I became involved with Mrs. S.

(*At this point, the therapist prefers not to focus on the patient's wife and newborn baby, and his moving shortly to another woman.*)

Th: Do you remember how you got together?

Pt: How I met Mrs. S.? Yes. It was her breasts that first attracted me.

	I worked with her; and besides her breasts, she was very attractive.
Th:	How did the relationship start?
Pt:	We used to go to lunch together. She didn't want to at first, but I coaxed her along.
Th:	How was your sexual relationship at first?
Pt:	With her, it was good. It was good, but you see with my first wife it wasn't always bad. She was able to reach orgasm, and she was the first woman I had ever been with, my first wife, and I expected that to reach an orgasm was not a problem with a woman. I found out later that it was, and Mrs. S. had a problem with it. She could never reach orgasm. At first I thought it was just in the beginning, but we were together four years and she never did.
Th:	When you met her, you knew that she was married?
Pt:	Yes. She was getting married the next week, but nothing happened until after she was married for six months.
Th:	What was your relationship with her like in that month when she was going through the marriage?
Pt:	I used to look at her and desire her and all that, but the fact that she just got married...
Th:	But you had it in mind to have an affair with her?
Pt:	Well, I didn't know it would come to be, but I thought about it.
Th:	You were talking about your sexual fantasies toward women, and you had sexual fantasies for her; and then after six months these fantasies became reality. Did you know her husband?
Pt:	Yes, I think the first time I met him was at a Christmas party. He was with his wife, and I was with mine.
Th:	This was after you had a relationship with her?
Pt:	Yes, it was a very deceiving-type of relationship. We used to get together, the four of us would get together, so that Mrs. S. and I could be together.
Th:	How did you feel toward her husband?
Pt:	After I got to know him, I didn't think much of him. I thought he was like a big kid. Gee, it's hard to remember. It's not hard to remember him. It's hard to remember my feelings about him. He used to kid me about funny things, like about being Spanish and all that. He was kidding me, but I always felt that I had the last laugh. He didn't know what was happening. When I think about it, it's pretty obvious. I didn't like him.

Th: What was it about him you didn't like?
Pt: Just his manner. He always struck me as somebody who wanted to remain a child. This came through especially in the playing of sports. We used to play sports together, and the way he would take the game was very serious as opposed to being fun. He'd get all excited about it as if it was a big deal, and it wasn't. It was just a pickup team, a bunch of guys together to spend some time.
Th: Did you feel that you were better than him?
Pt: Yes. I remember at the beginning I was very reluctant to meet him. I was sort of afraid to meet him because of what was going on.
Th: You mean your having an affair with his wife?
Pt: Yes.
Th: How did you feel about this toward him? In a way there was also the idea that you were better than him, and his wife preferred you to him, and you had taken over his wife.
Pt: It's funny. I never felt any remorse.
Th: When you look at it, what do you think is there that you say you don't have any feeling about that? Because, you see, this is a paradox. On one hand, you say you are a sensitive person. You react to things, you are a reactor to feelings of others. But then here you are saying that you felt you were better than he was, you had taken over his wife; yet then you say you don't have any feelings toward him. Then he was the beaten man in relationship with you, but you say you don't have any feelings.
Pt: Well, I think what happened was that all through the relationship both Mrs. S. and I felt guilt for both spouses about carrying on, but we always found some way to justify it.
Th: Let's see what were the guilt feelings you felt, because, you see, here you were, you felt you were better than he was, you had taken over his wife, you saw him as a defeated man in relationship to you, but then you say you didn't have any feelings. Yet now you say you had a feeling and that was guilt. Now, let's see what it was.
Pt: The guilt came from the deception. I felt more guilty about all of the deceiving I had to do than I did about being with his wife.

(*Now the therapist confronts the patient with this triangular situation and explores further; was it the body of Mrs. S. that interested him? He also further explores re Mrs. S.'s husband. He suggests that the patient doesn't want to admit that there was hostility toward both Mrs. S. and her husband. The patient denies this, saying: "I don't know what you mean by being hostile." Then the therapist makes a link.*)

Th: Do you think there is some similarity between this and your relationship with your mother and father?

Pt: I had a very intense relationship with my mother, but it was different than with my father. I was very fearful of my father until I was ten years old, different than the fear I had of him later on. The fear I had after ten was the fear that he would strike me, or verbally abuse me. But prior to that it was just a fear of the unknown because I never saw my father that much before I was ten. He was always away, so whenever he came home my mother said: "Daddy is home; be quiet, because you never know what is going to happen."

Th: Why should you have been so frightened of your father in your very early years? From the memories you recounted in previous sessions there is indication that he was interested in you, and he had also promised to take you with him on a trip. You were the one really who pulled the blanket over your head and did not announce that you wanted to go. Your father had a good relationship with your brother, didn't he? And your brother, unlike you, chose his own profession, and from what you told me was not submissive with your father. Do you think there might be a connection between this tremendous fear and your submissiveness and your relationship with your mother and father, and the intimate relationship that you had with your mother, and the fact that you had also talked about the memory of death wishes and you saw him as an intruder into your heavenly relationship with your mother?

(*The session focuses on this triangle and finally is linked with the triangle of himself, Mrs. S. and her husband.*)

Pt: The problem of seeing each other and maintaining the charade, the two lives, became very difficult for both of us, and I told Mrs. S. that we should tell our spouses that we wanted to be with each other and not with them.

Th: What was your plan? Were you thinking of marrying Mrs. S.?

Pt: Yes, in the future, but first to get together and not to have to do it by tricks and slyness and all that. So I told my wife. She was very upset, and Mrs. S. told her husband and he was very upset. Mrs. S. finally did leave her husband, but I'm trying to think of those few months between the time we told them and—I left in July, so it was all of June and some of July I stayed at home with my wife while this thing hung over us. I had decided to stay, too, but my decision was not very firm. I really wanted to be with Mrs. S., so after several weeks of this kind of indecision I started to phone Mrs. S. again and ask her if she would reconsider, and all that. I told her I was going to leave my wife in any case, so I left my wife while Mrs. S. was still with her husband. What I had in mind was that if I was free then she would be more agreeable to come with me, whereas if the two of us were tied up, how do you do it? Whereas if I am free, then she could make her choice.

Th: Did you want to leave your wife even before you met Mrs. S.?

Pt: I don't know if I wanted to leave her. I wanted to experiment. I wanted to be sexually free at that time, because even before Mrs. S. I used to flirt with the girls where I was working, and one of those girls is now my present wife. She was very young at that time, and that is really where I met my present wife, while I was still married to my first wife, but before Mrs. S. But I just met her and we talked and there was nothing sexual. I recall having the desire at the time, and then what happened was that Mrs. S. fulfilled it. It wasn't that I had no desire and then Mrs. S. came along and then I had the desire. That is not the way it happened. I actually was looking, and I didn't have to look further than the end of my nose, because it was right where I was working.

Th: You said you used to flirt with the girls. How is it now?

Pt: It is still there. I have a constant preoccupation with a woman's body. You see, when I see a woman in my mind I want to undress her.

Th: Is it with all types of women? Are they mostly large-breasted women?

Pt: I don't know. Perhaps, mostly.

Th: Why perhaps? Is it or isn't it?

Pt: Yes, it is.

Th: What do you think about this? The first woman in your life was your mother. The next one was your sister, and from what you have told me you used to pretend to be asleep and look at her body while she undressed. Then comes your first marriage to a flat-chested woman. Then while with her Mrs. S. comes along, who is large-breasted. Then you marry for the second time, again with a flat-chested woman. Then Miss L. enters the picture with large breasts. And all along you have had a preoccupation with women who have large breasts. Do you think this might have something to do with your early relationship with your mother and father?

Pt: As far as the breasts go, yes. But that is all I know about my mother.

Th: Let's see what you remember as a child about your mother.

Pt: Only her breasts.

Th: How about her body? Her face and other things?

Pt: I don't remember.

Th: Isn't it interesting that you don't want to look at all those fantasies, lying in bed, breasts and genitals?

Pt: Yes, but I don't know if that was my mother.

Th: Isn't it interesting that you talked about this in detail a few sessions ago, and admitted that it could not have been anyone but your mother, and you said that you were quite young, you had not seen any other woman around except your mother, and then you used to lie in bed and have fantasies when your father was not at home, so where does that come from then? The only woman that you knew so far as you have told me was your mother, and now you again say "if it was my mother."

Pt: I know I've told you that, but I can only deduce that it was my mother.

Th: Let's look at it. There must have been another woman, then, if it was not your mother.

Pt: I was young at that time, about five or six.

Th: And you were constantly exposed to your mother?

Pt: Yes. Then maybe the fantasy had to do with her.

Th: But did it or didn't it?

Pt: Obviously it did. I didn't see any other woman.

Th: What happened? You laughed when you said, "Obviously it did."

Pt: You are asking me to be firm...

(The session explores further and indicates that the patient never found his mother attractive, that she was overweight when he was young, and that when his mother slimmed down he lost interest in her and started thinking about other women. The session again moves toward this

repetition compulsion in his life, and comes to the issue that as much as he is interested, to the point of being obsessed, in large-breasted women, he has never dared to get into a permanent relationship with a large-breasted woman, and also goes back to Mrs. S. and her husband, that finally Mrs. S. left her husband. Then there is exploration into his feelings about Mrs. S.'s husband.)

Pt: I guess the fact that I had no feeling about it is a feeling.
Th: Maybe it is a fear of knowing how you feel.
Pt: I was caught up with what I was feeling at the time.
Th: What were your feelings?
Pt: About Mrs. S., about my wife, about the whole thing, how do you make it work? Will it work? Is it right? Is it wrong? And all these things concerned me, and I did not occupy myself about my feelings about him.

(Now the session moves toward Mrs. S.'s husband, and then toward the transference relationship with the therapist, and the therapist makes a confrontation that for two sessions he was quite late for the session, but the patient did not express any feeling about it, but that when his wife is a few minutes late he becomes greatly irritated, and this is the same with other relationships. The patient denies ever having had any negative feelings toward the therapist and uses intellectualization, and then the session has a climax and mobilizes a lot of resistances.)

Pt: I want to say that I find all the similarities coincidental. In other words, had Mrs. S. been a small-breasted woman, what would have happened? That is a concept that is hard to grasp.
Th: Rationalization is one way to deal with a problem. If all these things were coincidental, you wouldn't be here.

Dr. Sifneos:

This was a fascinating interview, and I will make only three comments. First, one is left speechless after this particular tape. It is short-term dynamic psychotherapy in all its glory. Dr. Lowy said, "What happened to the Oedipus complex?" It is right here, staring us in the face. The fact about the Oedipus complex is that it has produced a tremendous and profound reaction in both men and women from time immemorial. We see this man struggling and trying to solve his basic problem of having to choose between two people, both of whom he loves. As was shown in the tape, he tries to go on a trip with his father but then covers himself up and tries to deceive his father in order to stay with his mother. He wanted to go with his father and expressed anger that his father didn't take him along, but Dr. Davanloo confronted him with this and he finally admitted that indeed he wanted to stay around the house. Another way in which he tries to deal with the situation is by removing his mother's breasts and genitals in this fascinating fantasy of his, but unfortunately for him somehow or other it doesn't work. He tries different ways of dealing with his problem, and eventually he comes out with a neurotic compromise which serves him for twenty years. He puts himself in a prison. He becomes a slave, doing exactly what his father wants him to do. The unconscious dynamic aspects of his unresolved Oedipus complex still persist. He tries to marry someone with small breasts, with no sexual interest, in a defensive pseudo-homosexual reaction to his father. Then Mrs. S. with the big breasts comes along, and the problem starts all over again, and then what? He deceives Mr. S. in the same way in which he deceived his father. Then he divorces his wife, only soon after to marry another woman with small breasts, and then he becomes very interested in Miss L. with her large breasts.

Now, the dynamics are all there; the interaction with the therapist, the transference, Dr. Davanloo's confronting, anxiety-provoking technique is perfect.

Dr. Malan:

I was taken by the intense interaction between these two people. Some very intensive transference work must have been done by the therapist to change a patient who was so exceedingly passive and compliant into the patient we saw in this interview. The patient was being confronted with a great deal, and there were fascinating things coming out.

Dr. Brown:

I, too, was impressed by the intensity of the emotional exchange, the transference exchange, between Dr. Davanloo and the patient. I saw it as a replication of a very profound puzzlement which existed in this man from the time he was a child and which he so clearly revealed to us. That puzzlement had to do with how you connect with an elusive but also phallic father. This same puzzlement returns in the transference with Dr. Davanloo, who is a very phallic interpreter. I think the phallic style of the interpretation must rearouse right there in the consultation room some of those old desires to hide and to be rediscovered by his father.

I would like to extend this notion a little. The Oedipus complex has been talked about as a "triadic" involvement, and that suits me better because it includes both the positive oedipal and the negative or inverted oedipal situations. Each of those occurs and we know from analytic work that each can be a defense against the other at certain times. The positive oedipal activity or fantasy can at times be a defensive behavior to avoid experiencing the fantasies of the inverted oedipal longing toward the parent of the same sex. Now, I would see this man as having an intense inverted oedipal longing. He was deeply wishing for a gratifying connection with his father; I perceive this in his fantasy of his father doing things to his penis, and particularly the bandaging of his fingers while he was asleep. So the castration anxiety related to the positive oedipal striving toward the mother interlaces with the inverted oedipal longings toward the father who cares for his injured finger.

Now, regarding the attraction and fascination to breasts: I think he is fascinated by large breasts but I don't know if he is attracted to them in the erotic sense. He may be, and you might have more material about that, but what I see is that as a very young child he became profoundly fascinated by his mother's breasts. Why did they become such a powerful concern for him? Because he was trying to understand how he could get close to his father. One way is by having breasts like his mother. If he could have had those awesome and marvelous breasts, then he could have had some special connection with his father. It seemed he could never solve that problem of connecting to his father except by a submissive attitude toward him.

Dr. Davanloo showed him in the therapeutic relationship that he doesn't have to be submissive. He found that there is a new way to relate to a father person. But the question of the breasts remains unanswered. More data will help understand his obsession.

Question from the floor:

I agree. The patient has an oedipal problem. Dr. Sifneos seems to feel it has to do with the father, and we haven't really heard enough about the mother. His fantasy about his mother's breasts and genitals and grinding them in a cement mixer gives us a lot of other information. I wonder what Melanie Klein would have to say about that. If the emphasis is to be on the father, then we are missing an important point that is related to his hostility toward women and might really miss the dynamic focus.

Dr. Davanloo:

Regarding his attraction to and fascination for large breasts, the patient used the term in one session that he was "fascinated" by the breasts of his mother. But regarding the comment re the structure of the oedipal conflict, and that if he could have had the marvelous breasts of his mother then he could have had a marvelous relationship with his father, I would suggest that we can look into this after we have observed more clinical data.

It is very obvious that there is a great deal of hostility in this man toward women, and we have explored to a great extent his relationship with his mother, and definitely there are many aspects of the oedipal conflict of this man that I hope we will have an opportunity to look at and discuss. He referred to his mother as a doormat to his father, and there was anger and hostility toward his mother for being attached to his father and not to him.

In this type of patient one can place the oedipal problem at many different levels. The positive component of the oedipal issue is easier to deal with than the negative aspects of disappointment and anger. Psychodynamically speaking, there is a double element to it. If the heterosexual relationship is positive, there is a problem about guilt in terms of the father, but if the heterosexual relationship with the mother is ambivalent, as it is with this man, then the problem becomes much more complex. We can go into these things as we further unfold the psychotherapeutic process of this patient.

(10TH PSYCHOTHERAPY SESSION)

Th: In any other relationship you experience resentment, except here.

Pt: But the thing is that I'm coming here because I want to be helped.

Th: That is the intellectual aspect of it, but I'm saying that in any other relationship you resent to be told, yet here you invite me to tell you what to do, and then you say that if I tell you what to do you don't have any feelings about it.

Pt: Okay, so why is that? Why is it that you can separate the intellectual part from the emotional, and I can't? I don't see the difference. I'm going to react according to the way it strikes me intellectually.

Th: Let's look at this morning. You came to the session as if nothing happened, even though I was late.

Pt: But, you see, I know the problems of getting into town at 8:00 in the morning. I come in every morning.

Th: So then, what you are talking about again is the intellectual, but what I'm looking at is, what did you feel while you were waiting for quite some time until I got here?
Pt: For the most part I didn't feel anything. I was reading; the time went by fast.
Th: Let's look at this. If things are not precise in moments at home with your wife, you get irritated; you are restless; you are angry. Either you withdraw, don't talk with your wife, or you rave around. But then you are here at 8:00 A.M., and I am fifteen to twenty minutes late, and it is an entirely different reaction. If you take the intellectual aspect of it, you could say the same thing about your wife. Here you say that the traffic is heavy or all sorts of ideas.
Pt: Yes, but I wouldn't get mad at my wife for that, either.
Th: But you have repeatedly told me that.
Pt: Not for that type of thing.
Th: That if things are not done on time; even at a party, if things were to be ready at 5:00 and it is 5:30, during the time from 5:00 to 5:30 you are completely disorganized, irritated, and you take over the activities of your wife. Didn't you tell me this?
Pt: Yes, I did. You say 5:30. We're supposed to be ready at 5:00 and it's 5:30 and nothing is done. If I don't begin, it could very easily be 6:30.
Th: But I'm talking right now about here. Again you are moving away from this issue of your reaction in relationship with me and your reaction with your wife or others.
Pt: I don't know why I don't feel—first of all, I don't see the similarity between waiting fifteen minutes and having a disagreement with my wife over something that reoccurs; it constantly reoccurs, the things that I argue over with my wife.
Th: In a way, what you are saying is this, that when you waited there fifteen minutes you didn't have any ideas or any feelings about it.
Pt: Not feelings. I had some ideas.
Th: What sort of ideas?
Pt: Well, maybe that the technician didn't make it, or you didn't make it. You've made appointments for 8:15 and not 8:00, so I feel that any time between 8:00 and 8:15 I can expect to begin. I feel even if I arrive . . .
Th: Then here in a sense all your thoughts have to do with a protective

pattern in relationship with me. In other words, I made an appointment at 8:15, and you were the one who made a mistake and came at 8:00.

Pt: No, not today. I knew you said 8:00 today.

Th: And I'm talking about today.

Pt: Actually, I think that's a poor example. I think a better example would be how I don't argue with you when you present a point that I feel I disagree with. I used to sit there and say yes.

Th: You did?

Pt: Yeah.

Th: So let's look at that.

Pt: I guess it has to do with authority—my father, I guess, He knows best, you know best. Once I have your approval I can proceed without any guilt, I suppose.

Th: So in a way you are saying that if you disagree or you initiate things, you feel guilty?

Pt: Yes.

Th: This is very important if this is so. In a way what you are saying is this, that if you disagree with me or put out ideas that are different from mine, or you assert your views or initiate, then you feel guilty. Is that it?

Pt: I don't know. I would think it's more the fear of doing something wrong, for which I'll be guilty later. It's a guilt-fear thing.

Th: Because these things are connected with each other, in a sense.

Pt: Like with my wife, I feel I need to tell her everything I do, because if I don't tell her I do feel guilty. I feel that I've betrayed her. If I don't tell her, I feel guilty.

Th: Yes, but it has to do with this. All of them in a sense are similar, that you have to get another person to okay what you do. You have to get your wife to agree that the front door is all right. You want to take it off and then she agrees with it. But any other activity, somebody has to okay it, and this was one of the areas of conflict that you also had with your in-laws, that in a sense you have overcome some of these things, but you would invite them to give their opinion. You wanted them to okay things, and you do the same thing here. This is similar also to the issues of the disagreement because it's the idea of asserting your views and putting out your views. In a way what you say is that you feel guilty if you're spontaneous or initiative or if you're active. Remember the first few sessions with me, we worked with this issue, that you constantly wanted me to be questioning you, leading you, and directing you, as if in a way there is something about this; that in all of them a thread goes in all of these areas, namely, you cannot assert your views and you cannot be autonomous in terms of your own actions.

Pt: I would imagine that guilt and fear must be close together, because in some areas I know it's guilt that motivates me, and in other areas I know it's fear that motivates me—fear of doing the wrong thing.

Th: The idea, then, is the fear of doing the wrong things?

Pt: And then I'll feel guilty of having done the wrong thing later.

Th: You are referring also to the issue related to the door?

Pt: Yes.

Th: That if you take off the door...

Pt: And it's the wrong thing.

Th: What sort of idea comes to your mind about this door?

(*The patient wants to paint the house. The way he wants to do it is to take off the front door and paint it. His wife is very angry about this and demands that the door should not be taken off.*)

Pt: I was very upset because I felt that it was my area, first of all. Then I thought to myself that if it was my area why did I even bring it up; why didn't I just wait until the day I start and do it that way and whatever happens...

Th: What does this taking off the door bring to your mind? We have talked about doors here.

Pt: Yes, but it has nothing to do with that door.

Th: What door?

Pt: With my mother? No.

Th: Right away you said it has nothing to do with it, even without thinking.

Pt: Well, because you brought it to my attention. There's no connection.

Th: There was also the door and your father and mother in the bedroom, and you were standing behind the door and listening, and you were curious about what was going on behind that door.

Pt: Yes, but there's no connection between that door and this door. I can be sure about that.

Th: But there is another area that right now comes to my mind. You have expressed an intense desire for other women.

Pt: Yeah. I think they're connected.

Th: You have a lot of sexual fantasies for other women. Do you think there is a connection between many of these arguments or difficulties with your wife and the fact that you have all sorts of intense desires for other women?

Pt: Yes, but I think my seeking approval from my wife or telling her what I'm doing or what I plan to do has a connection with my desire for other women, in that if I begin to not tell her these things, then I feel that it's just a short step . . .

Th: But do you think this is a way of revenge? In other words, all your preoccupation about these issues, how the glass is put there, all these sorts of issues that preoccupy you intensely; constantly you are preoccupied if the kitchen is straight or if the bathroom is in shape, you know, all these sorts of things. I wonder if the source of it has to do with your sexual desire for other women, that in a way you see your wife in your way. In other words, "If I was not married, then I could have a ball with all these women." Okay?

Pt: Yes.

Th: Now, "Here is this woman who prevents me from having all these things," and in a way one wonders if the revenge is not taking the form of a displaced reaction. In other words, you don't talk about the fact that the source of your irritation is all these girls around you that you can't get to bed with. You take it on your wife in terms of the glasses or in terms of the door. Do you see what I mean?

Pt: Yes. I think it's true, too, because if you remember—I remember anyway—when Miss L. was around all these things didn't occupy my mind. I didn't care.

Th: Could we look into that?

Pt: Yes. It's something I want to look into because I feel that, like I said, there's a connection between my desire for other women and my telling my wife everything or needing her approval. Because I feel that if I start doing things without telling her, then I will begin to—how can I say it? Take nonsexual things that I do, and if I don't tell her I feel guilty for it because I'm afraid that it will become sexual things. It's a sort of a way of keeping myself from fooling around with other women. If I get in the habit of telling my wife everything, then I will have a very hard time not telling her about another woman, or feeling guilty about another woman, so I just don't see another woman. Am I making sense?

Th: Supposedly, one thing that you experienced with your father was that you were intensely interested in many girls around, right?

Pt: Yes. I still am.

Th: And then you saw him as the person whom you felt didn't want you to get out. Of course, it was a mutual sort of thing as we look at it. If we look at the relationship with your mother and all the fantasies and wishes around it, and at the same time you took a passive compliant pattern of behavior toward your father, opposite to your brother; then later on you wanted to get out and go with women, and still you complied with your father, and then the desire and actual relationship with women only moved in the field of fantasy. In other words, then you had a life of fantasy with women, never in action. It even went up to age eighteen or nineteen. Then one wonders if you don't see your wife in the same pattern. In other words, if she wasn't there, then you would have all these women around. In all of them, we can see a situation of three. First it is you, your father, your mother; you want to have your mother, but then you have a block. He is there. Then you want to have relationships with other girls, and he is there still. You see him as an obstacle. In your relationship with Mrs. S., she belonged to another man. You were with your first wife, so then you established a relationship with Mrs. S. Then we go on; you were with Mrs. S., then you met your wife. Then you got married and there were other women. In a way the idea is really that if your wife was not there, then you could have all these women.

Pt: Yes. I know that that's true.

Th: So what the idea is, then, is that with all these reactions you have about the nonsexual issues, one wonders if it is not again a displacement. In other words, you don't announce to yourself that it is related to the sexual or your feelings toward other women; rather than that, it is the glasses that are not washed in time that irritates you, or this and that. You see this is displacing it from one thing to another thing.

Pt: Yes. That I've thought about, but I didn't see the relationship between my wanting other women and my getting upset with my wife. I would see it the other way. I would see that because I'm upset with my wife I seek other women.

Th: What do you think about it now that we see it in this light?

Pt: I see it, but I don't know what to do about it.

Th: What to do about it is the second issue. First we have to look at it to see what is there.

Pt: The only way I can validate that idea is to think about how I felt when I was with another woman, either when I was married to my present wife or to my first wife, or when Mrs. S. was on the scene, or when I was going out with Mrs. S. and seeing other women. Whenever those things occurred, I became less rigid about the things around the house, and I remember that very well. The most recent one I remember extremely well, and it didn't bother me at all. I was happy.

Th: When you had the affair with Miss L., then...

Pt: It didn't matter.

Th: If the kitchen was clean or not, it didn't bother you?

Pt: It wasn't an issue, and if I remember back with my first wife, it was the same thing. Prior to getting involved with Mrs. S., we used to fight over the same things I fight with my wife about, and then it just stopped, so it would come first.

Th: So what do you think? Historically, in all of these relationships, when you had another woman then you were not obsessed with the cleanliness of the kitchen or the spotlessness?

Pt: No.

Th: Are you saying that in a sense you have become aware of some sort of connection between the sexual fantasies with other women and the issue that we discussed, your obsession with the cleanliness and spotlessness?

Pt: Yes.

Th: We have also seen the connection between these issues and your relationship with your father and your mother. Really what we also have to look at is your relationship with Miss L., when we look at it now. Was this an acting out of what happened between you and your father and your mother? In other words, then it was your father and your mother in that room, and you were going behind the door repeatedly to see what was going on. So you were witnessing something that went on there. When you had Miss L., then your wife was witnessing it. Do you see what I mean?

Pt: Yes.

Th: When you had Mrs. S., who was married to another person, then there was another man and then he witnessed—I don't mean with his eyes—you having a relationship with his wife, as if in a way you acted out and you repeated it.

Pt: I'm sure that that's not the purpose of my being involved with her.

Th: Let's look at what the similarities are in these areas. There are all the same things, except there is your father there and then you are witnessing, and then you get another man to witness you having intercourse with his wife.
Pt: But for over four years we took great pains to not let him witness it. He didn't know for over four years.
Th: I know, but witness does not mean in the sense of the eyes.
Pt: No, but he didn't even know.
Th: He didn't know?
Pt: He didn't know for four years.
Th: And your father didn't know that you were behind the door.
Pt: But I knew. That's what you're saying. I knew. Okay. In other words, I had this secret pleasure of fooling around with his wife, regardless of whether he knew or not. The important thing is that I knew.

(14TH PSYCHOTHERAPY SESSION)

Pt: I've been trying very hard not to think of these meetings before I get here. I think I succeeded today. A few times I started to think about what we had talked about last time in order to determine what I want to talk about this time, but I changed my mind. I sort of forced myself to think of something else so that when I got here I would be...
Th: But in a way what you are saying is that you forced yourself as if you wanted to think about something?
Pt: As if my mind wanted to think about it.
Th: What?
Pt: I guess there were two parts to me; one part wanted to think about it, and the other part said, "Let it be; forget it."
Th: You are talking about thoughts that get into your head about the session?
Pt: Yes.
Th: What came to your mind about the session?
Pt: Where we were the last time; what we were talking about.
Th: Where were we?
Pt: Where were we? Now I have to think about it. I didn't let myself think about it.
Th: You mean when you left here, you didn't let yourself think about it?

Pt: Not much.

Th: Why do you think that is so?

Pt: I let myself think of it when I left here, but after a couple of days I stopped thinking about it. I think of it after I leave, and then there's a build-up until I get here again. That was the part I didn't allow to take place, the projecting of the next session. I didn't do that. But I always think about what we talk about here, even to the point where I program the next session, whereas this time I didn't do that.

Th: The programming is the thing that you didn't do?

Pt: Yes, that I wanted to stop. I'm going away on Friday, and usually before I go away on holidays I get very anxious about my work, and preparing myself, and all that.

Th: When you go away, you become anxious?

Pt: Yes. The few days before I go, in order to put everything in order so that when I go everything will function properly, whereas this time I said to myself, "Well, every week you do these things and they come out all right. Why not treat this week the same as every other week, and then just go away?" And I plan to do it that way to see if I can lower the . . .

Th: Are you saying that this week you don't feel anxious like in the past?

Pt: I feel anxious, but I feel I'm fighting it; I'm not succumbing to it . . .

(Here the therapist explores and it becomes evident that there was a substantial decrease in his obsessionality and compulsive pattern of behavior. Then the session moves toward the triangle of the patient, his wife and Miss L., and the patient indicates he is searching for something he refers to as "seducing.")

Th: After Miss L., then you lost that feeling? There is the loss of this in relationship with your wife?

Pt: Yeah, I would think since then, and before then, too, because that is one of the things that led me to seek a relationship with Miss L. This part of it I feel very good about when it's there, and I don't know if it's the absence of that that drives me to try to find it.

Th: But you feel that prior to meeting Miss L. it was there with your wife?

Pt: Sometime prior, like at the beginning.

Th: And then, since that time?

Pt: It's reduced. It has to do with availability. It has to do with not having to—it's tied up with seducing. I guess there's great pleasure for me if I can seduce a woman.

Th: And what is it specifically when you say that?

Pt: I don't know. It's hard to separate the seducing from the actual act. They become one.

Th: When you say seducing, what is it like with your wife?

Pt: Well, that's just it; it's not there.

Th: You say this was there up to the time you met Miss L.?

Pt: Up to some months before that.

Th: What do you think happened that this disappeared?

Pt: I don't know. It always disappears. Whenever I become involved with a woman, it disappears.

Th: The same with Mrs. S.?

Pt: Yes.

Th: But what exactly is it? Because it is not clear. Is it part of you or part of the woman or what? What are these qualities or things that you describe?

Pt: When you're just discovering somebody, it's the feelings you get from showing them part of you that they never knew before; finding out some part of them that they never showed you before; not just physical, mental, and their desires. All that stuff becomes very appealing. It's like a constant search.

Th: You just see the body, you mean?

Pt: No, the attitudes and discovering people; discovering them physically and emotionally. That is the thing that I look for. It's like, I guess, a child with a toy.

Th: So, with Mrs. S., you were curious to see what she was like, her attitude, her body?

Pt: Yes. Then when I find it out, I'm not interested; then I look for the same thing in another person.

Th: One issue, then, is that in relationship with a woman first there is the element of being curious, to find out what the body looks like or their attitudes and how they behave. When you come to learn this or get acquainted with this, then you lose interest?

Pt: Yes.

Th: Okay, now what idea comes to your mind about this? Because maybe this is very important in a sense. You see a woman; you are curious to see what her body looks like, what her genitals look like, what her breasts look like, her attitudes. Then you have it; then you lose interest. One wonders what sort of idea you have about this?

Pt: You see, I can look at it from all different points. I can analyze it for you and say that it's like a child that has a toy, plays with it, and then throws it aside.

Th: Then you refer to it as a toy?

Pt: Yes, and I know as a child I didn't have many toys. I can blame it on that. I can say...

Th: But you had another toy as a child.

Pt: My mother? That's a blank area for me.

Th: And that is always something, that as soon as you get there, that is a blank thing.

Pt: Because it's not in my conscious memory.

(The session focuses here on two triangles. One is the patient, his mother and his sister, and his fascination about the breasts of his mother, although he announced he was interested in the feeding. The other is the oedipal triangle of the patient, his father and his mother. Then it moves to the patient's first marriage, and Mrs. S. coming into the picture, and the patient becoming intensely curious about Mrs. S., and giving up his first wife. And then comes the relationship with Mrs. S., and Mr. S. is put out of the picture. Then the therapist confronts the patient with his hostility toward women and brings to his attention that he refers to them as "toys.")

Th: But didn't you say previously that really the motive behind this was not that, but rather Mr. S. chasing Mrs. S. to get her to come back to him? Then you wanted really to pursue the situation in order to keep Mr. S. beaten.

Pt: I didn't say that. I don't remember saying that that was my motive.

Th: Didn't you say that in a way you were pursuing this to keep him beaten, and didn't you say that you got pleasure in beating him in any other situation?

Pt: Yes. I said that.

Th: Because when he found out he started actively getting after his wife to go back to him, and then your excitement here was that—

like a game—you said you are going to win her, as you also did in games that you played with him; you tried to beat him. So here your interest, then, was like in a game, to win.

Pt: So that was the newness. That was the newness there. That's why it was renewed.

Th: First was the curiosity and seeing Mrs. S., but then later on this was replaced by another factor, that you are going to win the game. The gratification was keeping Mr. S. beaten.

Pt: I can say yes to that, but I can't feel it.

Th: I'm sure you would say that.

Pt: You're sure I would say what?

Th: That you would say "I can't feel it," because somehow whenever we come to the issue of your father and mother you always say that.

(*Here the therapist compares the two triangles, the triangle of the patient, Mr. S. and Mrs. S., and the element of hostility, further confronting the patient with his hostile attitude in relationships with women, and brings up again the issue of "toys," as well as the patient's need to have Mr. S. the beaten man. Then the session goes to the oedipal triangle, the negative aspects of his feelings toward his mother, namely, that she preferred his father to him whenever his father was at home, his anger toward his mother that she was a doormat for his father, and the negative aspect of his relationship toward his father, which reminds him of the death fantasies.*)

Pt: As far as my mother goes, I felt guilty about it. It's so hard to put the brain I've got today in the child I was when I was six years old, and it's the same brain as when I was six years old. I like to think of it as a time that I didn't know what I was doing, and if I had the intelligence that I have today, I would not have these feelings for my mother, because you're not supposed to have these feelings for your mother. I guess that's why I want to deny it. I know they were there.

Th: So then it is threatening, but that quality of the desire to undress the woman in your mind has something to do with that. Supposedly you see a woman walking around, then suddenly you have the desire to know how she looks in the nude, how her genitals look or her breasts look. It might happen that this woman is married or it might happen that she is not married, but actively you go through the motions of this. Then we have also seen that there was that white door that you used to sneak in back of to see what went on between your father and your mother, and we have gone through this in one of the sessions; what came to your mind about this white door and your father and mother and so forth, and your fantasies about it. The fact also that in relationship with Miss L., you got your wife to witness you in the sexual act with Miss L. in the same way that there was that strong wish behind that white door.

Pt: You mean that I wanted to see my father?

Th: I don't know. I'm questioning you because you very clearly remember that white door. You had described the bedroom of your parents with a white door.

Pt: I have a hard time connecting feelings with my mother, what I did at that age, with what I do today. The fact that I wanted to undress my mother and see her in the nude and all that, I can see how that would become imprinted on me for later on in my life. Probably my concept of sex was formed then as being to see how a woman looks, and that's what I thought sex was. I don't know, like I'm wondering out loud right now. Is that what happened, that I began to think that that was the way to think that I should pursue sex, and that's why I pursue it that way now?

Th: You talk about one aspect of it, that is your curiosity or seductiveness or secret that was going on between you and your mother. That was a secret, wasn't it?

Pt: Yes.

Th: But then you don't want to bring your father into the picture. In every woman that you take there is another man, either in reality or in fantasy.

Pt: Okay. That's what I'm wondering. Conquering and seducing are very close.

Th: In your mind, then, it is associated that you have mastered the male?

Pt: I'm better than other males. That's what happens.

Th: And the same with your attachment to Miss L.?

Pt: It makes sense because, along with the fact that Miss L. was big-breasted and she was pretty good-looking and all that, aside from that which was of interest to me, another thing that was of interest to me was that a lot of men, and I had heard them, had talked about making it with Miss L., and it became my desire

to be the one to do it, as if, if I do it, then I'm better than you people.
Th: So then there is your father in the picture?
Pt: Yeah, in a roundabout way.

Dr. Straker:

I thought in order to put our present position into some perspective it might be well to refer to the proceedings of the Brief Psychotherapy Council which was held at the Chicago Institute in 1942. Some of the speakers made comments and raised issues which we are still struggling with. Dr. Levine, in talking about the matter of technique, said that flexibility is extremely important in the approach to the patient, and really should be determined by the nature of the patient's problem. Dr. French said that the patient's need really dictates the technique to be utilized. The crucial issue is to foster an increased understanding and use the psychodynamic issues that were presented by the patient. Another participant said that a commonsense approach, as he described it, was really not enough, and that one must uncover the storm centers of the unconscious conflict and interrupt their endless repetition, and in this way foster change. He emphasized that the patient sets the goal and objectives. Dr. Nolan Lewis, in talking about outcome, said something interesting which I would like to repeat, because I think this is one of the issues that we are all struggling with in connection with technique. He said, "The right person with the wrong method will accomplish more than the wrong person with the right method."

Comments have been made about the different styles of intervention. "Pounding the patient" is the term that has been used, and it applies more particularly, perhaps, to the style of Drs. Sifneos and Davanloo than to that of Dr. Malan. I have the feeling that it is pounding the patient for his own good. It is a question that we have to answer and that will be determined when we come to the outcome. But there is sometimes an uneasy feeling within myself as I watch the very skillful interventions that are made and demonstrated by Dr. Davanloo as he carries the patient from the present to the past, from the past into the transference reaction. Wherever the patient is, Dr. Davanloo assists him in making the essential connections in a most skillful way. The uneasy feeling has to do with to what extent there is coercion and persuasion. There are many issues like this which need to be answered.

Perhaps in talking about outcome we may indeed feel that the end justifies the means.

Question from the floor:

My question has to do with this man's need to discard women, which implies a kind of contempt, an aggressive act, suggesting perhaps the nonintegration in the patient of ambivalence toward his mother, and with to what extent the therapy focused on that aspect of his problem.

Dr. Marmor:

I am sure that there are many different ideas about how this material should be interpreted, but that is not the focus here. The focus is on what is happening in the process itself, how is the technique working? I happen to know this patient did very well. Why did he do well? Some therapists would have given alternative interpretations, I have no doubt. But I think one must focus on what makes this process work, and I would like to suggest that there are a number of things that we can abstract here, apart from the content, that are crucial to making short-term dynamic therapy work.

One of the most outstanding things that are sharply focused here is the activity of the therapist. I don't think Dr. Davanloo was in any way coercive. Most of the coercion is in terms of forcing the patient to think about his problem, refusing to let him let go of it, worrying him like a terrier, and not letting him just drop it. Far from being directive, Dr. Davanloo insists that the patient come up with the answer himself, and I think that is a terribly important element of the therapeutic process.

Finally, I would like to emphasize the tremendous element of corrective emotional experience here. Dr. Davanloo is a father authoritative figure with whom the patient argues, with whom he disagrees, and from whom he does not get hostility, and I think this triumph—if you will, an oedipal triumph—in and of itself is the transference process and is a terribly important element of what goes on in this brief encounter.

Dr. Davanloo:

The relationship of this patient with his mother was a very ambivalent one. The hostile aspect of his relationship with women, both actual and in fantasy, was focused on.

My main aim is to maintain the process and not allow it to be derailed and get away from the psychotherapeutic focus. This persistency on the part of the therapist is essential and there is no place for passivity. To keep the process active and have the patient do the unfolding is very essential. For example, when the patient talked about breasts and genitals, I did not make any suggestions; I said to him, "What sort of idea comes to your mind about this fantasy?"

Regarding the questions raised about the patient's response to interpretation and the intellectual understanding of the problem, our research data re patients with this kind of obsessive character structure indicates that there is a phase when the patient understands his problem in terms of intellectual insight followed by a phase when emotional insight comes into the picture, and then comes integration of the two; there is a time lag between emotional and intellectual insight. This happened in relationship with this patient. In many situations he could not experience any feeling in the transference situation. It happened a few times that I was late for a session. Exploration of this brought a lot of intellectualization. I indicated to him that he experienced a great deal of anger and irritation with others and that I was the only exception. The turning point was when on a Sunday afternoon he was at his father's house and they had a barbecue. He lit the charcoal. The smoke went into the bedroom and his father was greatly angered, and this suddenly mobilized a great deal of anger in the patient. Then suddenly his sessions with me came to mind. The next session he told me, "My God! All these months I was relating to you exactly as if you were my father!"

Dr. Naiman:

I have two comments and questions. One is, I think the evidence is that the tying-in with this patient was very good. It started out as a presenting situation in which he had a wife and a mistress, and that his wife had provided him with his mistress, and so on, and we had a repetition of triangles. The question is, was the crucial triangle in fact the oedipal one? Could one consider two other triangles? One is the triangle that he was watching his mother breast-feed his sister, and he was jealous of his sister. The other triangle is when he wanted to go off with his father, and the father went off with his brother instead and left him at home. So I think sibling rivalry is an important component. I think the issue of technique is twofold. One is in terms of focalization. Does one ignore this, and in dealing with the other triangle, which is the oedipal triangle, hope that the oedipal triangle will subsume the triangle which is being ignored? Here I am not saying that the therapist has not worked with the two other triangles that I mentioned, as we are seeing only certain segments of the psychotherapy. One should also take into consideration what Glover said about inexact interpretation and that inexact interpretation can be effective. I would think that perhaps some of what goes on in this form of therapy is what Glover described as a therapeutic response to inexact interpretation.

Dr. Davanloo:

In response to Dr. Naiman's questions, which were extremely important ones, the two triangles mentioned were very well within the focus—the triangle with his sister was very well explored, and he was often present when his mother was breast-feeding his sister. The same with the triangle with his brother; he often talked bitterly about how he made a slave of himself in relation to his father while his brother was able to choose his profession and was not submissive to his father.

Dr. Marmor:

I just want to point out that I think this discussion illustrates one of my favorite theses, that there are many ways to skin the psychotherapeutic cat, and each person has different ways of working which seem to get results. Some people focus on the present, some on the past, some on tying the past to the present; some are concerned with the thoughts of the infant toward the maternal breast. But I think the fact is that results are gotten in a brief encounter in terms of brief dynamic psychotherapy, "dynamic" meaning that some interpretations are given and then efforts are made to clarify what is going on in the patient's life, which must mean that there are common processes going on, and the focus on content, I think, is missing the point. Naturally, some will disagree and others will agree with the content. But if one focuses on technique and what is going on and what is moving this patient, I think one will find perhaps it has less to do with the content, with which one disagrees, and more to do with the aspects of therapist-patient interaction.

Question from the floor:

In the two segments of the interview there appears to be one point where Dr. Davanloo seems to be encouraging the patient to recapitulate what took place in the previous session. I have seen this kind of situation happening with my own patients, where they either spontaneously do that or have been encouraging a kind of summarizing of the progress achieved in the previous session. My question is, is this standard procedure? Does Dr. Davanloo encourage the patient as a rule to recapitulate the progress, the gains, the conclusions of the previous sessions, or is this due more to the obsessionality of this man?

Dr. Davanloo:

During the course of treatment, when there is an opportunity, every fourth or fifth session, I do that. This I see as encouraging the patient, rehearsing what has been learned in the therapy.

The Patient as the Evaluator of the Psychotherapeutic Process and Outcome

A few months after his treatment was terminated, I asked the patient to watch a few of his audiovisually recorded sessions. We will now see transcripts of some vignettes of these sessions and the patient's reactions to them, as well as his evaluation of the outcome of his treatment.

(PLAYBACK OF TREATMENT SESSION)

Th: You are saying that some part of your behavior in relationship to your wife is similar to that of your father. Could we look at it?
Pt: Around the house...
Th: He knows the best.
Pt: Yes.
Th: Now with your wife, you know the best?
Pt: Yes.
Th: What else?
Pt: That covers a lot of area.
Th: Could we look at these areas?
Pt: I mean to say, "You know the best": if you're cooking, it's in cooking; if you're entertaining, it's in entertaining; if it's what time you should leave to go and be at such a place at such a time, I know best. She's so relaxed sometimes that I can't imagine how she can organize herself.

(patient's reactions and evaluation after treatment)

Pt: That's a point now which I've changed on.
Th: In what way?
Pt: I was putting the blame on her—she's so relaxed—as if, if she would only change and be more like me. Now I see my happiness doesn't depend on her, the way she programs herself. I guess it's just more freedom I have within myself. I feel free to let go; there's not this little thing in my mind behind me pushing me to be at such a place at such a time. If we're late, we're late. That's the way I look at it now. What I was talking about then was that I always wanted to be fifteen minutes early in case something happened to delay me so I had fifteen minutes to spare, whereas now when we are ready to leave, we leave. I don't like to show up at a ridiculous time, but there's no longer this little voice inside me telling me to hurry up and be on time. It's disturbing to see myself like that.

(PLAYBACK OF TREATMENT SESSION)

Pt: It irritates me, too, that I—I don't know what irritates me more, what my wife is doing or what I think she's doing, or what I think she's not doing—probably what I think she's not doing. I mean, just to get here today on time; I was very conscious of the time. I was worried about the traffic so I started early programming so that we'd get here on time, and it worried me, but I don't think that worried my wife. She probably gets closer to the problem. I start to worry about it, so my head's full of if's, possibilities. With her it's when the thing arrives, she deals with it then. I sort of envy that type of a person. I wish I could be that type. I try to be like that and I probably talk...

(patient's reactions and evaluation after treatment)

Pt: I'm saying that, but I'm not feeling that. Intellectually I've always thought that way, but it's only in the past six months that I feel it. I even tell my wife now that if a change is going to take place in you, you're going to feel it and you're going to know it. I remember all through our sessions being able to intellectualize about the things that I now feel, and there is a difference. I really see the difference between talking and saying this is what I want to do, and really feeling this is what I want to do.

Th: Now do you feel there is an integration between the two, between the intellectual angle and also the feeling part of it? You feel that there is more integration of the two?

Pt: Right. It's almost impossible to grasp it. It's just there. Intellectually you can grasp it, you can follow the sequence, but when you feel it in your stomach—actually, when you don't feel it in your stomach, that's when you've got it. I find that my stomach can tell me all kinds of things. My stomach, if it's tight, I stop and say, "Why is it tight?" and I can say that I'm rushing about something, I'm worried about something, I'm anxious, and then I can make it go away. I think all through this session, I feel I was saying things that I didn't feel, saying things that I don't even know if I wished if I could feel them. Like about my wife in that she is more relaxed, I don't know if at that time I really wanted to be like her or if I was blaming her for being so relaxed in the face of a problem. That's a very important time when I stopped blaming my wife for my problems. I don't know when it comes but—I don't know whether this is going to be important—it's hard for me to remember what was such a problem. My fear of forgetting the problem, of forgetting how to deal with the problem; I'm losing that fear now because I no longer deal with the problem. I'm into my new phase.

Th: You mean that now that you have mastery over it, it is no longer a problem?

Pt: Yes. Then I look back and say what was the problem? It's so simple. All I've got to do is stop feeling guilty about allowing myself to be me. In essence, that's what it boils down to. I let myself be myself and not feel I have to fit some previously poured mold in which I'm supposed to fit. That's what programmed my actions before, and now I feel that I don't have to.

(PLAYBACK OF TREATMENT SESSION)

Pt: I've been trying very hard not to think of these meetings before I get here. I think I succeeded today. A few times I started to think about what we talked about last time in order to determine what I want to talk about this time, but I changed my mind. I sort of forced myself to think about something else so that when I got here I would be...

Th: But in a way what you are saying is that you forced yourself as if you wanted to think about something?

Pt: As if my mind wanted to think about it... I guess there were two parts to me; one part wanted to think about it, and the other part said, "Let it be; forget it."

Th: You are talking about thoughts getting into your head about the session?... What came to your mind about the session?

Pt: Where we were the last time; what we were talking about.

Th: Where were we?

Pt: Where were we? Now I have to think about it. I didn't let myself think about it.

Th: You mean when you left here, you didn't let yourself think about it?

Pt: Not much.

Th: Why do you think that is so?

Pt: I let myself think of it when I left here, but after a couple of days I stopped thinking about it. I think of it after I leave, and then there's a build-up until I get here again. That was the part I didn't allow to take place, the projecting of the next session. I didn't do that. But I always think about what we talk about here, even to the point where I program the next session, whereas this time I didn't do that.

Th: The programming is the thing that you didn't do?

Pt: Yes, that I wanted to stop. I'm going away on Friday, and usually before I go away on holidays I get very anxious about my work, and preparing myself, and all that.

Th: When you go away, you become anxious?

Pt: Yes. The few days before I go, in order to put everything in order so that when I go everything will function properly, whereas this time I said to myself, "Well, every week you do these things and they come out all right. Why not treat this week the same as every other week, and then just go way?" And I plan to do it that way to see if I can lower the...

Th: Are you saying that this week you don't feel anxious like in the past?

Pt: I feel anxious, but I feel I'm fighting it. I know when I get there, waiting for you, I start to think, "Gee, I could be at work, getting ready, gettings things ready for when I go away," and then I start thinking, "But when I get there I'll get there like I do every other Monday, Tuesday or Wednesday, and things will work out." So, instead of worrying about it today at 8:30, I'll worry about it today at 9:30.

(patient's reactions and evaluation after treatment)

Pt: That reminds me of when I used to think that if we terminated I would forget what I learned and go back to my old ways.
Th: In what way?
Pt: That I don't want to plan any more. I don't want to become programmed. So it sort of emphasizes the fact that I won't forget what I learned, and what I want to do, and I think that's hinged with the fact that I've done the work and not you putting it in my head. I've put it in my head. I've made my mind function in certain paths. It's not as if I was listening to you telling me how to live, and that's why I no longer fear the fact of forgetting what I've learned here. It's there and it can't go away.

(PLAYBACK OF TREATMENT SESSION)

Pt: Why lose interest in Mrs. S.? Why lose interest in my present wife? Why Miss L.?
Th: Now, let's look at Mrs. S. What happened? This is what we really discussed the last time, your feelings toward Mr. S. which you find difficult to declare to yourself, what kind of feelings you have. He was a beaten man. So when you lost interest in Mrs. S., then you returned her back to Mr. S. to repair what you were talking about, the guilt feeling.
Pt: Yes, but I didn't return her. If she had not gone, we would have continued on together.
Th: But didn't you manage it? Your sense of curiosity is there, your seductive qualities and various things; then you lose that.
Pt: I didn't lose that with Mrs. S.
Th: You said a while ago that you did.
Pt: Yeah, okay, but in my mind...
Th: And previously also you have announced that.
Pt: Yeah, but it's at another time.
Th: You said that with Mrs. S. it was so much the center of your mind and then gradually it declined. She sensed that, and she wondered if she left her husband how long it would last with you.
Pt: Yeah, okay. I think maybe she could have sensed that, but just to clarify when this feeling of loss of interest occurred, there are two parts. There's the part when she was with her husband, and

a part after she left him. We had been together secretly for about four years. Oh, no. Three years. Toward the end of the third year, it was then that I started to get interested in other women, but then when I left my wife and Mrs. S. left her husband that interest was renewed. The reason I can say that is that during the third year of us going together I began to be interested in another woman, and when I think back on that, then I can pinpoint the time and say, "Yeah. Why did I do that? Why was I interested in this other woman when I had Mrs. S.?"

Th: There is one thing on which I agree with you. This is definitely there, but you see there is one quality with it, and that is what you call seductive, curious quality. When secretly you are having an affair with Mrs. S., then it has that seductive and curious quality, and that is the quality that keeps you going, and that is the quality that you had exactly with your mother. When you were sneaking around and seeing her, always you anticipated also that you were going to get caught, but then you resort to the idea, "I am interested in the feeding part of it."

(patient's reactions and evaluation after treatment)

Pt: It took a long time for me to admit to myself the feelings I had for my mother. I think the explanation of that fantasy of the genitals separate from the body and all that was very important. I know that was a very strong fantasy when I was young, although I blanked it out. I'd say even by the age of seven or eight I no longer had that fantasy any more, but when I did have it it used to recur and it was very strong. But I never could figure out why I did have it. I thought it was some kind of perverted-type thing. That's why I blanked it out. But when I came to realize that the reason I did it that way was to avoid having to see my mother's face, and to preserve the anonymous part of it, then I was able to accept the fact that it was my mother more readily. Today I can accept it very easily and say, "Yes. I had erotic feelings for my mother, and that's the way it was," and it's not threatening me any more. It all has to do with that not only has my father physically disappeared but he's gone mentally. I don't feel any need to be controlled. I don't feel any pressure to live my life according to a pattern set out by somebody else. I want to live my life according to the way it unfolds. A lot of it has to do with my feelings. Like everything was cerebral with me before. I had to have an explanation for it. If I didn't have an explanation for it, then I shouldn't do it. Today I feel that if I really have a gut feeling for something, then do it.

(PLAYBACK OF TREATMENT SESSION)

Pt: I don't see the connection between that and...
Th: The connection in the sense that you constantly take a submissive attitude. In the interpersonal relationships one of the features of your problem, as we discussed, was taking a passive, submissive role. The connection of this is the same with your father. In other words, you are repeating the same pattern that you had with your father with others, as well as with me.
Pt: I see the same pattern. I can understand the transfer with my mother-in-law more than with my father-in-law, because my mother-in-law is very much like my father.

(patient's reactions and evaluation after treatment)

Pt: You see, it's like a compartment. It's like making compartments. I see it with my mother-in-law, and I'll see it with you. That's what you were asking me there, if I don't see it with you. If I could see that the pattern of paying off to my father is similar to the way I treat my mother-in-law, why can't I see it with you? In my mind, my mother-in-law, I see her in her house and that's a little part of my mind. Here is another part, but not understanding that it's all one, that it's interwoven.
Th: So at this point you don't see it.
Pt: I don't see it.

Psychodynamic Criteria For Evaluation of Treatment Outcome of This Patient

Dr. Sifneos:

We have looked into outcome criteria the same way that we looked into evaluation criteria for selection of patients. We have several criteria for the evaluation of the outcome which I would like to mention very briefly. One is improvement changes in symptoms, physical or psychological. The second is improvement in interpersonal relationships, and of course with the whole set of key people with whom the patient may have been in conflict. The third, changes in self-esteem, evidence of self-understanding, evidence of new learning having taken place as a result of the therapy; evidence of problem-solving as having taken place as a result of the therapy; evidence of utilization of new learning and problem-solving in situations after the therapy has terminated; evidence of new attitudes having been established as a result of the therapy; specific feelings that the patient has for the therapist and evidence of the psychodynamic changes as a result of therapy.

Now, as we watched this vignette we could see beautiful examples of evidence of a new attitude, as the patient himself says. He said that he used to prepare and program himself in advance. Now he says, "I don't have to do this anymore." He gave us clear evidence that his obsessive ways of handling things has disappeared. There is the notion of his freedom in terms of a new attitude about his feelings. He said, "I used to be all cerebral." He says now, "Feeling is what counts," and he very beautifully talks about the integration of intellectual and emotional insight. He also said, "The problem that I used to have was keeping things all in this kind of intellectualized way; now this is different." In terms of his expectations of the results of the therapy, here again we have a beautiful example when he said, "I have done the work myself; it wasn't you. I listened to you, but it was I who decided to learn how to live with myself."

Now, let's look at what he is telling us. We have heard that we tell the patient what to do. Some had an uneasy feeling about the badgering or the pounding that Dr. Davanloo may have done. But right there on the screen the patient said that this was not at all so. It was *his* decision to change, and it was *his* decision to look at things, and Dr. Davanloo was only his guide. Then he talks about having learned to do things. The learning by which we have been very impressed also in our series is the way in which patients are able to utilize problem-solving learning, particularly if they utilize it after psychotherapy. In terms of his relationship with his father, I think he has been freed from his need to be dominated by his father. He has no compulsion now to live his life according to his father's expectations, and he is free to live his life for himself. We hear him also say, "I no longer deal with the problem; I am into my new phase."

Chapter 18

Techniques of Short-Term Anxiety-Provoking Psychotherapy (I)

P. E. SIFNEOS

The patient is a twenty-seven-year-old male, a graduate student, who was a good candidate for short-term anxiety-provoking psychotherapy, fulfilling all our selection criteria. He complained of difficulties in relationships to men and women in the form of always wearing a "facade," always playing a "role," trying to impress the other person with whom he is dealing, feeling dissatisfied by this, realizing that there is something phony about this attitude but finding himself unable to change it. He is compulsive in the way he is putting on these airs or this mask. Why does he do this? He does not know, but he volunteers that it may have something to do with his earlier relationships at home. He is the oldest of two, and has always been very much attached to his mother. She also considered him to be her pet. The father is a businessman who traveled a lot, and particularly when this patient was a young boy his father was out of the house most of the time.

The patient said that from a very young stage, about the age of six, his mother would confide in him and later on would complain about her difficulties with her husband. She had strong religious beliefs. He remembered vividly his mother breast-feeding his sister and her actually having him touch her breasts to see what they felt like. He was very excited. This was followed by an episode when he went into the woods with a little girl and another boy and they exposed themselves. Apparently, the parents of the little girl found out what happened and they were horrified. They called the patient's mother, and she was horrified in turn. He described vividly how she was pleading and crying and telling him never to do such terrible things again. The next day she called him back and asked him to touch her while she was breast-feeding his little sister.

Another episode occurred at the age of eleven, again in the woods, and this involved considerably more sexual activity. It was an attempt at some sex play with a neighbor, the same girl that he was involved with when he was six years old. This again was discovered by his mother. She was once again horrified and proceeded to plead with him, to cry, and ask him never to think of sex. From then on he kept his sexual interests to himself—"I wore a façade with my mother." His father was away a lot, but he was very close to him. His cousin was like a brother to him, but they fought with each other over a young girl who seemed to have liked his cousin better.

He remembered that at age seven, when his father was away, he would have terrible nightmares and invariably would wake up and cry. At such times, he would scream and call his mother until finally she would take him in bed with her. He would fall asleep very quickly and remembered feeling happy.

We soon established that there was a pattern of triangular relations. There was always the girl and the boy, whom he would want to beat up. He was particularly interested in situations when he was attracted to women who belonged to other men. This happened repeatedly with two of his best friends. He felt unusually attracted to their spouses or girlfriends. Having established that there was a clear-cut competition with men over women, I raised the question whether we should examine these triangular relationships and make it the main focus of the therapy. He readily agreed.

"The Case of the Man with the Facade"

(5TH PSYCHOTHERAPY SESSION)

Pt: It's like a contest between us—not between us but inside me, anyway—about who would talk first. I came in and wanted to be able to eye-contest you. The whole hour last Monday really plagued me very much, made me very anxious, because I thought I was being very circuitous, running around things. I covered so many subjects. It was good because we covered many subjects, but it was also very frustrating because we didn't seem to pinpoint anything.

Th: So what you are saying is that if we were to review what happened last week we would find a repetitive pattern of your relationship with men right here in reference to me?

Pt: Yes. I was contesting you. When I was in my late teens, I sort of worked on developing an ability to contest people, direct eye-to-eye contact. Its very hard sometimes to look a person right in the eye and not look away. It's even harder to remain silent. It probably is a contest of your authority.

Th: Authority? Why would I have any authority?

Pt: It's very apparent. You are a professional in the field. Your professional expertise make you an authority. I come in here, and you apparently know what I'm supposed to be driving at and I'm looking for.

Th: But you see, this is a wrong assumption on your part. As a professional person, as a psychiatrist, I know certain things about people. I have some clinical experience. But if there is any authority on you, it is you, because you know more about yourself. You lived twenty-seven years with yourself. Now you expect me to tell you how you are—

Pt: But I disagree a little bit. I think that why I am here is because I have a tremendous ability to camouflage what I really think about myself. I think you have the ability to perceive where I am camouflaging.

Th: All right, but that is a different matter. My statement still holds that you are the best authority on yourself. Now, that you may have certain areas or may have certain ways of avoiding or putting on a façade or contesting is indeed true. If you put me, however, in a position of authority, which we have already seen in the last three or four sessions by asking me questions and so forth, then you are making me something that I am not. So what counts is that that's the way you perceive me, and if you do it's very interesting. Now, let's hear more about the way you perceive me and what you viewed as a contest between us last week.

Pt: I didn't know it was so apparent what I was doing. Maybe I shouldn't ask—I don't know, but I know I was sitting here—I wouldn't say on the defensive, but with that tone, just waiting for you to initiate the conversation. It sort of came down to a contest between us as to who would initiate the first statement. That's what I'm saying, that people do become very uneasy sitting in a position where nothing is said, where no words are flowing. It almost becomes a pleasure—I don't know—maybe a sadistic pleasure to put people in that position, sitting there remaining totally silent. It's a very effective way, many times, to put people on the defensive. So, it would be putting you, an authority person, on the defensive so you would lack your authority; you'd lose your real authority. I think later how silly it is to do things like that.

Th: Can you tell me how that makes you feel at the time? What about this sadistic pleasure of yours?

Pt: It just seems somewhat superior. I could start on a plane somewhat lower than you. If we take a specific instance: you are somewhat elevated; I am somewhat lower than you. As the contest continues, it's like a thermometer. You may remain stationary but I just start moving a little higher. It's a silly contest.

Th: Don't call it derogatory names, such as "silly," and so on. Let's look at it.

Pt: All right. Then it's a contest.

Th: If it is a contest, that is what it is. Whether it is silly or not is another matter. Now, you feel in a special way, rising slowly and eventually being higher than the person who was in authority over you in the first place. If so, what association does that feeling bring up?

Pt: What I was associating with is that it was a disappointing victory because I got out of the circumstances that I was in at the time. Many times I'll contest people on an intellectual level, like once in a while throwing in a multisyllable word; it could be a technical word or something like that, a word that most people are not used to.

Th: You mean like the word "infamous"?

Pt: Well, okay. "Infamous."

Th: You remember we talked about it. That was the time when you told your father off; you put your father down when you elevated yourself above him, showed off to your mother how knowledgeable you were. Are you saying that this is what is happening between us? So are you viewing me as your father?
(The therapist makes a parent-transference link here).

Pt: I think it's apparent that I do.

Th: Can you tell me more about it?

Pt: What do you mean?

Th: What kind of thoughts or feelings do you have about all this?

Pt: Sometimes I can't really get into what it is that may be the cause. I'm not used to thinking that deeply about myself. I'm trying to endear myself to you or make you like me more. The whole gig of my being here in these four sessions has been one of trying not to keep it on a professional level, a professional-client level, but on a sort of more friendly relationship level; and this is why, as I said, a few sessions ago, I felt very anxious about you saying that if I couldn't benefit from your help, I might as well leave. I felt even strongly then that I wanted to establish a friendship because a friendship is much more long-term than a professional relationship; because you can't just cut off a friend. You can't just say goodbye to a friend. There is a certain personal attachment on your part there. It's not easily terminated.

Th: So you are saying that the reason for the friendship is that it cannot be terminated, and the idea of termination is frightening?

Pt: Oh, yes! Very frightening.

Th: Then the question would be, "Is a professional relationship that turns into a friendship of any use at all?"

Pt: No. I've already established that it wouldn't be. Maybe it's significant why I think it wouldn't be. I thought that I could meet you also on a friendly basis, but what I think would happen would be that you, as a professional, would be at a tremendous disadvantage. You couldn't be able to relate objectively to me any more. I would be constantly looking at how you behave so that we would always be contesting each other's roles or whatever. You wouldn't be able to correlate what I do, what I say and my past experiences. You'd become much more personally involved and too many barriers would get in the way of your observations.

Th: So I'd be defeated! Now, let's get back to the contest. If the contest is one in which the person who is in authority is either slowly pushed down or stays on the same level and you get higher up and win, then what happens to this friendship relationship if you have to turn it into a contest and always win?

Pt: Do you remember about the girl who I let go in front of me in line? I think this is directly analogous to what we're talking about. I let the girl in line, and she let my friend in front of her. I was thinking about her. By the seventh grade she wasn't in our school any more. I don't know what ever became of her. Anyway, I became more physically abusive with this guy, pushing him around. The thing was that I liked this guy and I don't know why I did that. I wished I wasn't as sadistic in a way; putting him in situations publicly that would humiliate him. That's why I think that this was very analogous to this situation.

Th: So the notion, then, of putting me down which gives you a sadistic feeling is similar to the sadistic feeling you had before?

Pt: Yes.

Th: So the conflict is between two men over a woman. Now, who is the woman between us?

Pt: If I see you as a father image, then it must be my mother.

Th: That's one aspect, but could it be that there is a woman here between us, any particular woman around here? Has there been any thought about some woman, especially one where there might be some actual conflict between us? Don't dismiss it, now. Is there any woman that you've seen here?

Pt: There is Miss D. I talk to her when I come in.

Th: So, Miss D. is somebody who might be known by you and by me.

Pt: I don't think she knows you, does she?

Th: She is the secretary of the clinic. Why do you think that she doesn't know me?

Pt: Because I came up earlier and asked her for a note for you to sign, and she said she really didn't know you that well.

Th: Maybe she doesn't know me very well, but she knows who I am.

Pt: Yes.

Th: What thoughts do you have about her?

Pt: Well, she's a relatively attractive, nice girl. She's very nice and pleasant.

Th: Then we have someone here who is nice and attractive Now, what interested me was the fact that you say that she didn't know me, when in fact she may indeed know me very well.

Pt: She probably does. I never thought about it.

Th: It's time to think about it right now.

Pt: I saw her one day near my apartment after a session, and I think the only thing we have in common is the clinic. So we talked about that, and we talked about your professional status.

Th: What professional status?

Pt: You, as a good psychiatrist. It was very small talk.

Th: Now, wait a minute. If you talked about my professional status, then she must know something about me.

Pt: She knows your reputation.

Th: But you said before that she doesn't know me. I think you're caught.
Pt: Yes, I'm caught.
Th: Tell me, how do you feel now? How does it feel for your "father" —who is me today—to catch you as I did?
Pt: It's kind of funny. I suppose it might be a need of escape.
Th: How do you feel? Right now.
Pt: It's a very humorous situation. I hadn't thought about it. I feel a little bit uneasy about it.
Th: You see, this is an excellent example to think about. If indeed in the future there is the notion of this contest which comes up and gets stirred up in you, if the feelings you described of a sadistic pleasure of rising above people is present, then I think you should always look around to find out where is the woman for whom the two of you are contesting. This association about the boy and girl in line is precious. You asked me if I remembered it. Why should I have forgotten it? Maybe you wished me to forget it, but I haven't.
Pt: Another association is with my friend, John, whose apartment I'm subletting now. He's probably my best friend. He has a very attractive girl friend. He's a very perceptive fellow and extremely bright and is a professional. I think I also contest him for his level of professionalism, too. If you say I should think about a woman, it would probably be his girl friend, Betsy.
Th: Can you tell me a little more about the nature of this contest?
Pt: Sometimes he gets very adamant with me to straighten out and stop playing the games I'm using, especially with him. He says he sees what I'm doing and he doesn't like it. We should have a more honest relationship.
Th: Can you give me an example of what he views as being a game that you play?
Pt: Trying to contest him on his feeling of authority. I never viewed it as that. I always viewed it as trying to talk to him on some subject that he would be interested in. It may, actually, now that I look at it, have been a contest, but I never viewed it as one. We talked on subjects like history and drama. He's into history now. He considers himself quite an authority on the subject, and he probably is. But I really think I could contest him.
Th: Have you?

Pt: No, I haven't; not directly, because I think that might be a too blatant contest, too apparent; one that I might be shown up in.
Th: This, then, would be another area in which you would want to contest him, and which he perceived to be a game that you were playing with him. Is this why you put on a façade?
Pt: He called it pseudo-philosophical conversations.
Th: You mean the kind of thing you were doing at the beginning of the hour with me—"intellectualizing"?
Pt: Yes, highly intellectualizing; metaphysical type of conversation, bringing all the mysteries of the world into one. It's kind of funny.
Th: So we have to be alerted to that kind of game, too. A red flag should appear before your eyes saying "Contest." Now, can you tell me a little bit about Betsy and your feelings for her?
Pt: Betsy is an older girl. She's five years older than I am. She's physically very attractive She has an outstandingly nice body. She keeps herself in very good shape. She is considered very attractive. She's a girl who I would not in the least bit mind being physically intimate with. In other words, there are fantasies built up around Betsy. She's a nice dream girl. She appears much more real than some women I've been with.
Th: What is her relationship with John?
Pt: As close to marriage as you can get with a girl. They're living together to see if they'll get married. They're extremely intimate; about as intimate as you can get, I suppose. That seems kind of funny.
Th: Why is it funny?
Pt: Intimate is intimate.
Th: Many things are "funny" today.
Pt: I didn't mean hilarious or hysterical, just funny.
Th: What are these thoughts you had in reference to Betsy? Was it that you would then be in a contest about with John? Would you win the contest with John?
Pt: No. I never thought I'd win the contest.
Th: You may not have really thought you'd win in reality, but I'm asking you about your fantasies.
Pt: I had never fantasized winning the contest with John. I had never fantasized John in the contest. It was never a three-way thing. It was always just Betsy and me.
Th: What are your fantasies?

Pt: They were nothing, really. They were never very elaborate.

Th: Let's look at them so we can learn something from them. Don't run away.

Pt: There's really nothing. Okay, let's bring Clark Gable back into it again. He was a very debonaire-type individual. It was sort of this fantasy again. I think that's the way Betsy would have been with someone like Clark Gable, very awe-struck. This is the feeling I get; the totally perfect man sort of fantasy.

Th: And you would be Clark Gable.

Pt: Yes.

Th: What would be the outcome of the Clark Gable fantasy?

Pt: Intercourse and then "au revoir."

Pt: Intercourse and then "au revoir."

Pt: Yes. That's very important. I'd hate to ever dismiss a woman carelessly, sort of "slam, bam, thank you, ma'am," but I'd like the relationship to be terminated as quickly as possible, say, after intercourse in a fantasy or even in real life. It seems that when I become physically intimate with a woman—well no, it doesn't even have to be intimate with intercourse or anything like that—but even after a psychic climax in a relationship I'd like to terminate the relationship as abruptly as possible to be removed from it without hurting the woman involved. Without this quick crash of emotion.

Th: There are some things that don't fit. If the fantasy is that you are an irresistible Clark Gable type, Betsy and yourself alone, then there is the intercourse, why would you say "au revoir"? "Au revoir" means I'll see you again, so it doesn't end the relationship at all.

Pt: No, but it does end the situation.

Th: It doesn't, because it means at another time the same thing would happen again. I think you said that you would like to end the relationship.

Pt: Not the relationship. I didn't mean that.

Th: That's what you said, and if you want to terminate the relationship, it means you were in conflict, and we have to understand why. On the other hand, what spontaneously comes out of you is "au revoir," meaning I'll see you again. The relationship continues versus a conscious awareness that you want to terminate the relationship. Now, there are reasons for this. I think the reasons have to do with your relationship with

Betsy and your relationship with John. Do you see what I mean?
Pt: I see what you're saying.
Th: Now carry on. What do you think I mean? What about these conflicting feelings?
Pt: It's like a constant tranquilizing effect in front of John.
Th: So the need to terminate the relationship has to do with John?
Pt: To reestablish contact with John.
Th: Precisely. So then, what we are saying is this. If in this conflict situation, which you described so nicely in terms of a thermometer—I am going up and you are going up; eventually you are higher and I am lower than you—you have succeeded, you won. Now if you succeeded with Betsy, let's say, as soon as this happens, although you want to continue the relationship with Betsy, John comes back into your mind, or I or your father comes into your mind. You want to reestablish relationship with three people whom you like. We know you like your father, and we know you said you like me, and you like John because he is your best friend. Do you see?
Pt: Yes.
Th: But you also want Betsy. There is a conflict there.
Pt: As with many things we've said here, I see them on an intellectual plane. I just don't feel—I mean, I see what you're saying.
Th: Can you tell me what you think I'm saying?
Pt: Yes. For me the contest is important just to the point where I become superior or remain above the individual. Maybe I'm on a superior level, but it seems I always have to recontest that person. It's almost like the teeter-totter effect. As soon as the contest is over, I no longer have to contest anyone.
Th: What would be the reason you have to reestablish the relationship?
Pt: I would say it's probably very much from the three, my father, you and John. I can learn a lot from all of you, if that helps at all. John is extremely intelligent.
Th: I have no doubt that you like John and I have no doubt that you love your father very much. The need to reestablish the relationship without any doubt has something to do with liking these people, but you have in your fantasy performed an act that they would not like.
Pt: Oh, yes; which would promptly terminate the relationship.
Th: Which would terminate the relationship on their part, right?

Pt: Yes.
Th: Or possibly?
Pt: On mine?
Th: No. You want to terminate the relationship with the girl. What I'm trying to find out is, what is the reason for that? One is because you like these men. Is that the only reason? Now, what would John do if you had intercourse with Betsy and he found out?
Pt: He would probably do the same thing I would do. Probably say, "Goodbye. Thanks. It's been very hot and heated." John would get very angry. He's very emotional.
Th: He would be angry? What would he do?
Pt: I wouldn't have any fear of a physical contest because of my size.
Th: So there is something that comes to your mind again along physical lines; that he gets very mad. You may assure yourself that physically you are bigger than he is, but sometimes these things are not settled physically. He may use a gun!
Pt: Hmmm! I know. It would probably be much more of a psychic conflict. It would abruptly end whatever we had.
Th: So there is a fear, then, in addition to the liking of the person, as to what they would do as a result of your action? Fear of retaliation.
Pt: Yes. The same thing that came through, as I've told you before and I told John, is that they would end immediately and very abruptly the relationship which we had established. In other words, I'm in constant anxiety—not so much with you because I've put a little in resolve that this is a professional level, but still not totally. But with John it is that he might at one point become so tired of the game that I play that he might say, "It's too much trouble to be friends with you. You're not honest with me, and it's too much work on my part to be your friend."
Th: So then, in addition to his being mad and having a temper tantrum, you have a fear of the end of the relationship. This also may motivate you to terminate the relationship with the girl immediately.
Pt: I suppose it could.
Th: When you say the need to terminate the relationship with the girl, what did you mean?
Pt: It's a strange feeling of having been that physically close that

	you also have to be tremendously psychically close. I just don't think this is one of those callous encounters with a woman.
Th:	Now you're becoming intellectual again.
Pt:	No, I'm not.
Th:	By becoming intellectual, you want to run away from the issue we are talking about. Let's recapitulate. The fantasy is as follows...
Pt:	I just don't want to continue with the woman herself.
Th:	Your unconscious says that you *do* want to continue with the woman because you say to her "au revoir," which means "I'll see you again." So the need to terminate the relationship with the woman has nothing to do with the woman if you say to her "au revoir."
Pt:	Okay.
Th:	So, it really means that you have to terminate the relationship for another reason and the other reason is your relationship to a man. Now, the relationship with a man is (1) you like the man, John, or whoever he may be; he's a friend of yours; (2) you're afraid that they may retaliate one way or the other, but the ultimate retaliation would be that they will terminate the relationship. So really, then, there are some specific issues here in your contest with men that shape your relationship with women. Why are you looking kind of vague?
Pt:	The feeling is vague. A lot of times when you relate these things, the same as when John related things to me, I feel extremely vague.
Th:	You feel vague because you don't want to see it.
Pt:	I don't understand how to coerce myself into wanting to see it.
Th:	You don't have to.
Pt:	What do I do?
Th:	What to do is simply to look at the facts. The way you view the facts of this fantasy that you have about Betsy and your being Clark Gable can be understood in a different way. Maybe there is a way. I don't know. It is possible but you show me how.
Pt:	I don't think there is any different way. I think Betsy is attractive and I like her, but other than that, if I met her on the street I'd be friendly with her. So I think overplay of relations would bring in offensiveness in my relationship to John, but I had never thought of it that way. That's why it's vague.

Th: Are you saying, then, that the only reason you would be interested in Betsy is because she goes out with John?
Pt: Well, yeah; that's right.
Th: That's interesting. If Betsy was available, if there was no John in the picture, what would happen?
Pt: If Betsy was available and I thought I had the opportunity to go out with her, I might.
Th: So then, you have a clear-cut desire for Betsy as a person?
Pt: Yes.
Th: Now that is established. However, there is something special about Betsy because she is John's girl friend. There is a fantasy that you have sometimes that you and Betsy would have intercourse and that you would be the seductive movie star, who after the intercourse ends—
Pt: Also wouldn't that seductive movie actor be the one who is never really emotionally involved in a relationship?
Th: Now we have someone who is not emotionally involved with Betsy but has a sexual attraction for her. After the end of intercourse, he wants to end the relationship, but suddenly from within him the words "au revoir" pop up, which means "I will see you again, Betsy." Now, on the basis of this fantasy, you told me that the wish to terminate the relationship is something that you feel. Is that correct?
Pt: Yes.
Th: So then, we must try and understand why you would on the one hand say that you would see Betsy again, and then on the other hand want to terminate the relationship. That's a paradox. It doesn't make sense.
Pt: Yes, it is a paradox. That's why I feel that my relationship to my parents is a paradox also. It's a confront.
Th: Precisely. It involves your parents. That's where it started from. Now, what is it that you didn't understand when we went over that?
Pt: I understand, but it's just that there are different levels of understanding. One is a very cerebral level of understanding, the other one is like an internal kind of understanding.
Th: Now, how do you feel about what we have just said?
Pt: Very cerebral. I know what you said. I think I understand what you said.

Th: But does it ring any bells?

Pt: Well, yeah. I don't have any personal references to it or any past experiences, but it does seem to become a little clearer. I understand that it is a possibility. I just don't attach myself to that possibility. That's what I'm saying.

Th: If you view that as a possibility, we have to see how you would view this situation in a more meaningful way. How can you solve this paradox?

Pt: I don't think I could. That's another quality that I have of being able to detach myself from what I'm involved in. You probably noticed it in the conversation that I can, let's say, intellectualize, which allows me to elevate myself out of the conversation. It's no longer me that's involved in it. It may be my brain that's involved, but that's it. I'm no longer involved.

Th: These are ways out of situations that you claim, at least, that you are not able to explain in a different way than I did. Is this correct?

Pt: Yes, I don't see any other way.

Th: All right, then; there must be some element of truth in it.

Pt: Yes. I think there is, because I was going to relate something else. I very rarely remember dreams, but last night I did recall one. I wrote it down to remember. My cousin, Danny, as we'll discuss later, is getting married this month, and I had this very strange dream. Well, I guess I shouldn't call it strange, but I had this dream that I was lying in bed with Jean, and Danny was at the side sort of looking on.

Th: Jean is the girl he's going to marry?

Pt: Yes. It wasn't just a flash dream, but that's all that I can remember. I only recall the three of us there. That's what I wanted to tell you before. Also, what came to mind there was being able to contest Danny, to show some superiority on my part.

Th: What about this being in bed?

Pt: The exact position was that Jean was lying—sort of not head to head—she was somewhat below so the possibility of physical intercourse was not available. It was just a physical intimacy, a closeness. That was it. There was nothing about lying there in bed together. She was lying on top of me, sort of down. This is the extent that I remember.

Th: Yes, then we have to add this dream to what we have just been talking about.

Pt: Which I think is very similar.

Th: Yes, it is very similar and very important!

Pt: I do realize how much I envy my cousin, Danny, for a lot of reasons, and how much I really like Danny. In fact, Danny is the closest person in the world to me, and I think I don't really like any other person, male or female, as much as I like Danny, or as much as I love Danny.

Th: So, I think really what we can say about today is that one thing seems to be clear—at least even intellectually, but that's more than intellectual. That dream of yours is very important. In situations where there is a triangle, two men and a woman, even if the woman seems to be absent at face value like Miss D., we have to look for two things. One is that this happens at the time when you feel close to the man. You always win in these situations. In the Clark Gable fantasy with Betsy, you win. You have intercourse. In the bed dream fantasy with Jean, you win; he's left out.

Pt: Right. He's standing by the bed.

Th: Secondly, it is quite clear that during these times certain feelings are stirred up. What these feelings are we don't know yet, because you block them; you avoid them, you try to get rid of them, but we know that they exist.

Pt: I think I realize they're true, but I try to avoid them.

Th: I think the pattern is very clear. You avoid them because here we have really the crux of your problem.

Pt: Right. That I can feel, and I can't avoid that.

Th: Okay, then; you are honest. It was a very good dream. It was the perfect crowning to a perfect hour. I want you to think about it, and I'll see you next week.

Dr. Naiman:

I would first like to comment on the consummate skill with which Dr. Sifneos conducted the session. I would also like to underline the dream which the patient presents at the end in relation to something which Dr. Nemiah had said earlier, namely, that a patient's yes or no in relation to an interpretation is really relatively meaningless. Dr. Nemiah, by the way, was quoting Freud. What matters is really the material which comes afterwards, whether it is or is not confirmatory, and I would think that the dream which the patient presented at the very end of the session is confirmatory of the interpretations which Dr. Sifneos was giving during the session.

There was a very skillful moving from the transference to the reference to the father, then a reference to the competition when he was in school, and eventually it went over to his friend and Dr. Sifneos picked the relationship with the friend as the one on which to focus most of the work in the session because, I think, it was the one which was most accessible to the patient. Unless I repressed the word, I don't think the word "mother" appeared in the session. In other words, the issue of the competition with the father was mentioned, but there was no direct reference to the mother, and therefore the issue of competing—the competition between the two men for the woman instead of the mother, so to speak, being forcibly dragged in—what Dr. Sifneos did was to shift to the transference, to there being a woman somehow connected with him that the patient may have some contact with. Then it shifts to the friend, and lastly to the cousin in the dream. Now, there are a good many similarities actually between Freud's case history of Little Hans; there is a fair bit of similarity between the dynamics which Dr. Sifneos discussed with this patient and the treatment of Little Hans, which, by the way, was a case of brief psychoanalysis performed by the patient's own father. Freud never saw the patient.

I think the content of what one interprets is extremely important. I had the feeling in this particular session that the evidence for the conflict was that he did not want to give up the friendship with the man for the relationship with the woman. In other words, the ambivalance was that if he gets more involved with the woman, he loses the friendship of the man. It seemed to me that the evidence of that was greater than the evidence of his fear of punishment by the other male. I'm not saying the fear of punishment wasn't there. There was some evidence when he responded that if he was in that position he would get angry, but it seemed to me on the whole that the evidence was perhaps better that the conflict was really between the friendly relationship to the male and the competition of the male over the girl, and that he would give up the girl as part of his wish of friendship with the male rather than because he was afraid of punishment. Overall, I think this was a masterful interview.

Dr. Strupp:

I would certainly agree that this is a masterful interview, beautifully done, and I think we can learn a lot from it. I would like to confine myself to raising some questions and making a couple of points. I think it is to be noted here that again we are dealing with a patient who has considerable ego strength. The opening statement that

Dr. Sifneos made, which I think is very important in all kinds of therapy, that "You are responsible for yourself," I think is an important goal in short-term therapy as well as in long-term therapy. The other thing to be noted is, of course, Dr. Sifneos' style. The therapist is very active. He is very active in placing things in focus. He is very active in interpreting. He is very active in assembling the pieces of the puzzle for the patient and driving his point home. The question that arises in my mind as to what extent are the patient's feelings at this point, at this hour, in focus? To what extent is the conflict that Dr. Sifneos is working on, the oedipal situation, in focus? I want to call attention here to several times when the patient says, "I understand it intellectually. I can see it intellectually, but I don't feel it." And here is a patient who obviously very much enjoys the therapeutic game, if you want to call it that. He is fascinated by it. He is interested in it. The question, however, that remains, and I would like to focus attention on it, is, "To what extent are the patient's feelings in focus?" and the question arises, "Can you do without the patient's feelings?" Another approach might be to wait more expectantly until the things come into focus. Of course, this is the fifth hour. We haven't seen the preceeding ones; at least, I haven't. So I don't know to what extent it had been possible earlier to define what the nature of the problem is that Dr. Sifneos and the patient had agreed they would be working on. What is the nature of the corrected emotional experience that the patient is undergoing at this time? How is the therapist experienced by the patient? I think this is very important.

In effect, Dr. Sifneos says to the patient that he is not threatened by him. He says it is okay to compete with men, and the patient will not lose his friendship, at least, if he does so. This is perfectly all right, and in the same sense the therapist, by his nonverbal communication that it is all right to compete, encourages the patient in that sense to go ahead, to sally forth and to conquer his fears, and communicates in fact that the threat of incurring another man's wrath or retaliation is less than perhaps the patient's fears. So, in that sense the interview may reduce the patient's anxiety, and it may lay the groundwork for the patient to work on these problems during the interval and to set a train in motion, that is, a train of thought and feelings and associations that may summate into a corrective experience, and may enable the patient to master the problem that indeed he is struggling with.

Dr. Sifneos:

I would agree with Dr. Strupp's point that the intellectual component in this patient and a certain absence of feelings was prevalent even in the previous hours. I would give, I think, what Dr. Naiman gave as an argument, that really the evidence about the feelings comes up through the dream and that there is something being mobilized in an unconscious way that produces the dream, which is in a sense the evidence that we have been talking about.

Actually, what happened with this patient is that the feelings came up around the seventh interview. When they came out, they came in a very explosive way, and they were all related to fears of castration in terms of his father. There were feelings of fear and anger about his father's retaliation, although realistically it is again very true that the fear of the man seems to be avoided at this interview; it's more the relationship with the man that is being emphasized in both. I decided not to give any information up to now so that this interview could be seen cold.

Now, what has happened with this patient is that he came with a chief complaint of wanting to get rid of a façade that he wore in his relationship with both men and women. Pseudo-philosophy is what he talked about. He doesn't like that. He wants to get rid of it. He wants to be honest and spontaneous. His friend has criticized this, and many others have done so before. He doesn't know why he wears a façade, but he wants to find out.

In the second interview, he gives enough evidence on an historical basis that the triangular situations appear at the very start. There is the episode about the little boy at school. It is a very clear-cut one. He picks up a young girl in the sixth grade and asks her to come and stay with him in line, but she invites another boy to come up and stay with her, whereupon the patient became furious and wanted to beat him up. This leads to associations about his relation with his mother, the breast-feeding and all the sexual feelings which he had for her.

He had very competitive feelings for his father. He described his father as being a genius and a magnificent person with artistic talents. He describes him as being fifty feet tall. The father was always big but the patient was able to defeat him by using bigger words when his mother was around. There is where the competition got started.

Dr. Dongier:

How many of your patients are as healthy as this one?

Dr. Sifneos:

In 1970-1971, at the Beth Israel Hospital, we had 25 percent. Since 1974-1975, this number has dropped down to 12 percent because most of the college health services have discovered them and they kept them for themselves.

Dr. Malan:

I want to say something which I think is extremely important. Something just occurred to me about the difference between Dr. Sifneos' technique and mine. I was very impressed at the end of this interview by the sudden emergence of this dream after what I thought was a session which consisted largely of intellectualizing. I have been very troubled in watching Dr. Sifneos' technique, but I have felt that he was somehow either not aware or deliberately ignoring the fact that he and the patient weren't really in true contact at all. I felt this particularly about "The Case of the Woman with a Prostitution Fantasy," (Chap. 19) who seemed to me to have a complacent smile on her face throughout the entire interview, and I wanted to smack it, and I couldn't understand why Dr. Sifneos didn't seem to feel the same. Now then, I think this interview in fact answers my question. This is one of the major differences between Dr. Sifneos and me.

What I would do with these patients would be to interpret defenses. That is, with the woman I just mentioned I would simply have pointed out to her that she seemed to be treating these issues which are very important in an extraordinarily light way. Dr. Sifneos says something about "You know, you might go to bed with your father," and she says something like, "You're a card to suggest this stuff to me," and the hammering that I would have done would have been on the patient's defenses. I wouldn't have paid any attention to the content. No doubt this technique would reach the same end in time also. It's quite clear to me now that what Dr. Sifneos does in fact is to ignore this resistance and to employ a technique which he has obviously correctly labeled "short-term anxiety-provoking psychotherapy," namely, hammering away at the anxiety-provoking content of what the patient says until the defenses break. Obviously, this is a perfectly legitimate way of dealing with the same situation. He just told us that the defenses of this patient broke finally in an explosive way in the seventh session. This was only the fifth. That dream of course was quite possibly the first moment of true contact between the therapist and patient, and so it foreshadowed the breaking of the defenses two sessions later. This now solves for me the difference between Dr. Sifneos and me. We have the same end; we go there by different routes.

Question from the floor:

Dr. Malan has spoken on a lot of the issues that I wanted to raise, and I think it is a very striking difference in technique. I was very impressed with Dr. Sifneos' interview but couldn't help thinking that

I would have gone about it differently. In particular, I was thinking that there seems to be so much very blatant, overt competition right within the interview that it was hard for me to conceive of not going after that and linking it up with the obvious situation that had gone on with the father and with other significant people in the past. It seemed to be kind of a golden opportunity, and that would probably be the kind of tack that I would take. The other thing that I was wondering about was labeling the conflict. To me the conflict that seemed most apparent—in the session, at least—was something along the lines of "How can I beat a man and at the same time remain close to him?", I was also wondering about more or less labeling that to some extent to the patient and tying that in to what was going on right in the therapy; paying attention to that process could have been facilitative.

Comment from the floor:

I'd like to try and put a particular element into perspective. That element is rather a revolutionary one in terms of the whole therapeutic process: the use of audiovisual techniques. I think most of us realize that the part of these interviews that is most stimulating and provoking, thought-provoking and provoking of feelings, is the audiovisual part. Without it, the therapeutic process would be essentially invisible and we would not have the feelings stirred up as we do. I think an important way that this technique is already revolutionizing the therapeutic process is that it breaks down certain defenses which the medical profession as a whole, of which psychiatry is a part, have had.

I would just comment on one aspect of this, and that is the fact that somebody said recently that 92 percent of all physicians in this country are male, and at a recent symposium on sex, culture and illness at McGill and the University of Montreal, a joint conference, it was pointed out rather emphatically that male defenses, if you like, tend to be obsessive defenses of which isolation perhaps is an outstanding one. I was just going through the program here and noticing the words that were used to characterize what was going on. There were words and phrases like "technique," "criteria for selection," "evaluation," "concepts," "therapy"—objectifying, isolating words, if you like, which describe from a very specific standpoint what is going on between people. Words like "emotion," or words of emotional content, connected with the word "therapist," were not particularly introduced in the terminology. I think this is where audiovisual techniques have really had their greatest impact; these defenses, although we may use them when we discuss what is going on, no longer have the same validity because we are seeing the process, and more particularly we are seeing the therapist, that previously unknown quantity who took part in the therapy but then could construct his image of what went on afterwards because no one else was there. I think this again relates to the question of outcome. And from now on I would presume we will be introducing into the equation therapist plus patient, if you like, that equals outcome. We will be recognizing more and more the therapist in his proper role. I think many people have hinted at the fact that some therapists today have widely differing stances in the way they contribute to and take part in the therapeutic process, and we can see this now, and it can now be evaluated directly rather than indirectly.

Dr. Strupp:

I would like to compliment the speaker for calling attention to the tremendous importance of the audiovisual media. I wonder sometimes what the history of psychoanalysis would have been if, instead of Freud's condensed writings, he had a videotape series of his interviews. The story is told, maybe apocryphally, that Freud didn't do psychoanalysis the way he said psychoanalysis should be done in his writings. That, as a matter of fact, while he placed major emphasis on the curative factors of interpretation, a lot of other things were going on in the therapy that weren't conceptualized in his writings, so that while the patient was lying on the couch he would never give advice, but between the time the patient got up from the couch and went out the door he gave all sorts of advice on how the patient might conduct his life. The comment about the therapist's role and function and the nature of his influence, I think, is tremendously important, and I am not sure whether even in these interviews here we capture everything that goes on between the patient and the therapist. What we see on videotape is perhaps not the entirety of the interaction, but certainly we have gained a much clearer picture and will gain a clearer picture of what the nature of the therapist's influence is through the audiovisual method. Freud said cryptically in his writings that psychoanalysis is a private affair and tolerates no third party. I think Rogers needs to be credited with having thrown open the therapy consulting room to earlier tape recordings, and now we have video recordings. I think the breakthrough is very important.

Question from the floor:

I would like to comment on the use of audiovisual media because it happens to be an area of special interest to me. I believe there is a great deal that we can learn from anthropology in producing simple, straightforward behavior records. The other thing that I think is important, as emphasized by the previous speaker, is that perhaps this might help us to question in essence what psychotherapy is about. It's the patient's learning, as Franz Alexander pointed out, enlarging the focus through the social contacts, and in this last interview I was very impressed by the formulations that the patient made in terms of conceptual learning and experiencing himself with the therapist. Perhaps these are some of the issues that could be clarified and documented. There was a great deal going on in terms of psychomotor activity at several points when the female relationship was mentioned, a number of changes in his vocal output, but we could not comment on them because we were concerned with the intellectual insight. I would like Dr. Sifneos to respond to the importance in balancing the reconceptualization or reexperiencing of oneself in this particular patient in this interview.

Dr. Sifneos:

There are so many factors that are going through the head of the therapist in doing this kind of psychotherapy that it is sometimes very difficult to keep on top of everything. It is most helpful for me to go back and look at some of these videotapes and observe my mistakes. The degree of activity, for example, and various other things that one observes in a more detached way when we look at a videotape are very instructive. Maybe what you have seen is something which I failed to see when I was sitting in the "hot (therapeutic) seat." The issue, for example, of the transference and my secretary, I would have dealt with it in a much more forceful way than I did in this hour if I had the opportunity to deal with it once more. One always learns something new and this is what counts.

Comment from the floor:

There has been some mention made today of the process of psychotherapy, but most of the time we seem to have concentrated on single points in the movement through time in therapy. Few people have said that technique and process are wedded together and that psychotherapy can be seen like a chess game with a beginning and a middle and an end. The stages of psychotherapy have been described by some other therapists. K. Rogers described two forms, one client-centered and one more structurally oriented from the therapist's point of view. Sullivan has a four-stage notion of the process of psychotherapy and Dr. Sifneos in his book has five stages. I wonder if the panelists would have a comment on how they would process and stage conception to their technique.

Dr. Eisenstein:

I will try my hand at your question and I will give you my whole idiosyncratic perception of this. I'm not sure that the other panelists agree or disagree. In actual fact, in the literature—analytic literature in particular—a fair bit has been written comparing the initial stages of therapy to the mother-child relationship. There has been a stress on the anaclytic aspect of the beginning, the diatrophic position of the therapist, etc. There has been relatively little written about the termination and conceptualizing it in theoretical terms. My own sort of very rough image is that termination is somewhat similar to what happens to children when they grow up and become adults and leave home and no longer need their parents. And I think that in a sense what one tries to do in the therapeutic process is to enable the patient to utilize, himself, what he has learned without needing the therapist any more.

(9TH PSYCHOTHERAPY SESSION)
with the same male patient

Pt: I sort of get into a contest about a day or a day and a half before I come here. I'm trying to recollect the last session. There are two areas to work on. One I can remember and the other one I don't. One area is availability; available women. The other area is a little hazy. There were some thoughts that came to my mind in conjunction with that; two specific ones. I have the feeling that I demand an awful lot from people that I meet. Both explicitly and implicitly, in a meaningless sort of way I demand a response from people. I ask myself, "What do you want?" When I meet somebody I demand something from them because I want something. It's like a transference thing. I was told quite a few months ago that I judge people too superficially, too fast. The pieces just seem to rebound off from one another. It's a good defense not getting to know someone when I think it might be a threat at the time. This is what occurred to me as a result of the last session.

Th: You mentioned "contest" at the beginning of the hour. Why did you use that word? In what sense is it a contest?

Pt: I don't know. I forgot. Did I use the word?

Th: You said it was a contest within a day or so before you come here. What is the contest about? Is it that you work on trying to remember certain things that have come up here and that you have remembered only one out of two? Contest is an interesting word. Combat between us? We discussed that some time ago, you know.

Pt: I think this is more a contest in myself, or maybe between us; I don't know.

Th: But you see you forgot, you said, that you used the word.

Pt: Well, it was just a word that I used, that I didn't attach very much significance to.

Th: But you know that words are very important. Let's look at it.

Pt: Well, it's a feeling of contest within myself not to come in here and be dumb. I don't want to sit here with nothing to say.

Th: Can you try to understand what this contest is all about? Is it a contest between us?

Pt: Yeah—well, I suppose so because what I assume...

Th: This complicates things. Let's hear about it.

Pt: I don't want to come in here and again disappoint you by sitting totally silent for fifteen minutes. I do have a feeling sometimes of lack of thought or lack of work or something like that, and I don't want to come in here like that. Sometimes I wish you'd be more directive in your questions because it would be easier for me to form some answers. You may disagree with that tack; I wish you would keep asking me questions.

Th: So you wish that I ask more directive questions!

Pt: I don't really know what to say, but that's one thing that came into my mind. In fact, a lot of this week I was wondering what kind of therapist you were.

Th: These are very good things to talk about.

Pt: These are good things to talk about?

Th: Yes, fine. Why don't you talk about them? Let's talk about my therapeutic abilities.

Pt: Abilities? I don't have any question about your abilities. I'm pretty sure that you are quite a capable therapist.

Th: Let's not go too fast. There are some therapists that ask questions to make things easier for their patients. Now, I don't. Why shouldn't you wish for a therapist who asks questions?

Pt: Oh, I do have a wish for that, but I also realize that it is counterbalanced by the fact that if you asked a lot of questions I might come up with a lot of facile answers, a lot of thoughtless answers. I know that, too. I was discussing with a friend last Tuesday or Wednesday evening—I think it was Wednesday—about a film about a girl. I can't remember the name of the girl.

The film was entitled by the girl's name. It occurred to me that every therapist thought this girl would fit into his mold of therapy. Yours is almost a "push," "push," "push" type of therapy.

Th: Tell me what thoughts you have about my therapy, my questioning, my not questioning, and so on.

Pt: I don't question your ability, but I know that there are always other avenues involved in therapy. Other therapists have different opinions, and as I said, it would be very much easier for me to come in here some morning—as last week when I sat around, feeling very ill at ease for about five or ten minutes trying to formulate some thoughts. They just weren't coming up very well, and it would have been easier if you had said, "Well, let's discuss this point," or something like that. Then I can also realize that, as I said a few minutes ago, this is a route for some very facile answers on my part. So I'm stuck between the two alternatives: some easy answers or doing a lot of thinking all by myself.

Th: You have mixed feelings at this point?

Pt: Yes, of course I do. That's what I'm saying.

Th: Which ones predominate right now?

Pt: Well, when I first came to the clinic it was the Tuesday afternoon group meeting. I felt at ease there because I thought my interviewer was a novice. I didn't feel insecure because I didn't feel he had the professional grasp. I think because he was young, not too many years older than I, I felt very comfortable with him, and I thought I could play some games because this was only an evaluation. I also assumed coming to therapy that I would have to like my therapist. I do like you and sometimes I feel comfortable here, but other times I feel very ill at ease when I have to do all the thinking. You said last time, which was very reinforcing, that you thought that there had been some subtle changes, and I agree with you, but I am very impatient. I think it should be very fast.

Th: You shouldn't need me to tell you if there are subtle changes or not. You are the only one who knows if there are any changes.

Pt: Granted. I know that, but what I'm saying is that as an objective observer it's good to hear that there is a change, or that I am behaving differently.

Th: But the question is well taken. What is this work of ours doing for you?

Pt: It's causing a tremendous amount of anxiety. That's what it's doing right now.

Th: Maybe that is bad. What do you think?

Pt: Well, I think it's only positive right now. Just last Saturday, if I can, you know, speak of that day, it was a day of tremendous anxiety. I went skiing with my cousin and his wife and my sister and my sister's boyfriend. It was a very nice day. All during the day I had been very content, but when I got back to Boston and Danny and his wife and my sister and Joe—Joe is my sister's boyfriend— were ready to go, I felt like I was totally void again. I felt very anxious, and that's what I feel this therapy has done for me or to me. It has created this thing where, you know, I can't run away; I can't go into my apartment like I used to when I was in college and be very content sitting there watching television or doing some other idiot thing. Basically, the only thing I see right now as the direct result of therapy is that I'm tremendously anxious, which I think is good because I've never felt it before.

Th: If that's the case, which is an interesting way of putting it—because one would assume that if one is more anxious than he was before the therapy, the therapy might be considered to have been a failure rather than a success—then we must examine this attitude of yours. Let's look at it this way. If you feel that this experience is something which is worthwhile despite the anxiety, let me hear more about it. What does this anxiety do for you?

Pt: You're taking the wrong point. I think that anxiety is a natural product of therapy. I assumed that that would be my reaction, but I didn't know what it would feel like. Now I know what it feels like, and I don't like it now that I feel it, but, you know, this is the definite price that I have to pay because I know that I'm not going to learn anything without having a tremendous amount of conflict.

Th: How can you then use this anxiety if you feel that it is worthwhile?

Pt: How can I use it? Well, I think the direct product of the anxiety is to bring in a lot of alternatives, and to try to examine them.

Th: All right, then. What about your anxiety while skiing last Saturday?

Pt: Well, the initial thought was, "Why am I anxious? Why am I so discontent?" and I thought primarily it's because it's a very easy role for me to relate to my cousin and sister, who both pretty much revere me. Then I have to get into a society where I have to meet people who are taking me on a one-to-one basis, and I have to cope with them, and I have to learn to relate in a very different way. Well, that's the primary thought as it appeared to me on Saturday. There are two alternatives. I can either grow, or I can remain secure. And again that brings up the question of my anxiety. Remaining secure, I would be very content. Anxiety, on the other hand, I had never experienced before. I probably should have experienced some anxiety in adolescence or maybe even preadolescence, but I never did. It seems that at least when I was a teenager I should have started questioning a lot of where I was, what I was doing, rather than being so content. That's what I think this anxiety has done for me. It has created a wish within me to become an active participant in what I'm doing rather than have my role pretty well determined for me by others, and be contented.

Th: And what is your answer to all this? You are saying, if I can put it differently, that you see this anxiety as something that makes you raise questions about yourself. They are painful questions, but you feel that these questions should have been raised, and at least now that you raise them you feel better about them. This is true, and it is an important dimension of our work. Now, there is a very specific situation, however, about skiing on Saturday and feeling anxious after your sister, cousin and his wife left. What do you think about it? Why were you anxious last Saturday?

Pt: Why specifically I was anxious?

Th: Yes. Let's look at it. We discussed your cousin and his wife before. Let's see whether there is anything here. Do you remember that you had a dream and you have taken Danny's wife away from him?

Pt: Yes. As I said last time, I have been thinking very consciously about my role with Danny and his wife, and I feel that I sometimes threaten him. The marriage union is pretty strong in their case, and so I relate to both of them almost as a unit. They function together continually, and it's no longer the same way I used to relate to Danny when he was unmarried. Now he isn't totally independent to do things on his own. He was a guy who I could pretty well rely on in moments of anxiety, you know, just to do something together, and now he has the responsibility of a wife.

Th: Now, are you saying that if on Saturday when you were anxious Danny had been with you and if Danny were not married, then you two would have done something together, gone out or watched TV or something like that? In that situation Danny would have been one of these anxiety-suppressing tools you used to like, but you say now that you don't like these very much any more, like the television set.

Pt: It's not that I don't like them, but I think I realize that they're very negative.

Th: Are these the thoughts that occurred to you after they left, that you would have wished that Danny had not been married, that you would have wished that Danny could have stayed with you? Is that the thought that occurred to you last Saturday?

Pt: Something like that, yes.

Th: Was this the thought or could it be that you had another thought? Now, tell me what thoughts *you* had. I'm really interested in *your* thoughts, not in mine.

Pt: There was another thought. Danny used to do things on the spur of the moment. We used to do anything we wanted. There was another thought. I wished I could have been in my parents' home for a couple of days. It's very strange how the old relationship, the old role, hasn't been very much changed. It's a very secure one, almost like a child again, sitting back, knowing how to relate to my parents, knowing what they want at any given moment. That would be the only other thought that occurred to me.

Th: Let's go back and see exactly what happened. Now, you were skiing with your sister, your sister's boyfriend, Danny and Jean. It was a nice day and you had a good time. Now, when did you notice a change in the way you felt? Was it when they were ready to go, when they were saying goodbye?

Pt: No. It was at my apartment with Danny and Jean, my sister and her boyfriend.

Th: Oh. They all came to your apartment?

Pt: Yes. Danny and his wife and my sister with Joe came to my apartment because I had a television of Danny's that he wanted to pick up. He was just moving it to his apartment.

Th: So they took the TV. You don't have a TV?

Pt: No.

Th: We are equating the TV and Danny as being anxiety-suppressive tools, right?

Pt: Okay, right. That's why I brought that in, because I just realized what it means.

Th: So, they came to take the television set away. Did they stay?

Pt: Oh, just a few minutes.

Th: And?
Pt: And then they left.
Th: And what thoughts occurred to you? When did you start feeling anxious?
Pt: When they were just about ready to leave.
Th: Yes. Go on.
Pt: As they were walking out of the apartment, I thought it would really be nice to be entertained for a little while by Danny and his wife, just sit there and talk for a while. But they had to get back, and that's why I felt pretty anxious. I was outside of their car when they were ready to go. That's just when I started feeling anxious. I just got an overwhelming feeling of sadness. I thought maybe I should ride back with them. Oh yes, because Danny did say, "Are you coming back or are you coming back tomorrow morning?" This was Saturday afternoon, and I had thought that I would come back Sunday morning.
Th: And going back meant going where?
Pt: Oh, I have to work on Sundays and I didn't have a car, so I hitched a ride back yesterday morning, and that's when he asked if I was going back with them. I said, "No. I'll stay here in my apartment."
Th: Now, why did you choose to stay?
Pt: Well...
Th: Because if you went with them things would have been fine. You wouldn't have been anxious.
Pt: Yes, that point crossed my mind. I thought of going out with them and being very secure, but it would have been a very regressive situation. I wouldn't have to think or be alone. I knew how to do it by rote. On the other hand, I knew that night that I would be very anxious because sometimes I get a feeling that I don't know how to relate to new people. Do you understand what I'm saying? It was some sort of fear that was hitting me about the time when they all said goodbye, and I had to decide either to go back with them or to sit there. I decided to stay in the city and try to grow into my own life, but it bothered me to think that maybe I would have a very rough time doing it. There are a lot of reasons why. There are a lot of lonely people in this city, and I'm afraid of being one of them. That was one point that made me very anxious. That's one of the primary thoughts that went through my mind.
Th: Anything else?

Pt: Not a hell of a lot. That evening I just went to visit a friend of mine down the hall, and we spoke a lot.
Th: No. I meant at the moment of separation. Didn't your cousin's wife enter your thoughts at all?
Pt: Well, in a queer sort of way. I kissed her goodbye, and a strange feeling did occur that, well, I hoped I didn't upset Danny by kissing Jean goodbye. I didn't think that it would, but sometimes I fear that I might make him anxious. I don't know where the deception comes from.
Th: A strange feeling; a queer sort of way. Let's hear about it.

(*The patient indicates at length that there is a conflicting feeling inside him. He doesn't want his cousin and his wife to be anxious. He wants to react to Jean very objectively. He expresses the fear, however, that his thoughts might be perceived by his cousin.*)

Pt: Yeah, a lot of times when I'm with Jean I think about Danny perceiving it. That's why I'm consciously thinking a lot about my new role in reference to Jean.
Th: But why does this thought get left out completely from what we're talking about?
Pt: I forget about it.
Th: Oh, come on now! How can you forget about it when we talked about it at length before. Do you really want to find out why you were feeling anxious?
Pt: Yes.
Th: Okay. There's a lovely day and lovely skiing, and everybody is having a good time.
Pt: Yes. Everybody is content.
Th: Danny and Jean, you, your sister and Joe are all happy. They all come to your aprtment to pick up the television set. You are feeling fine up to that moment. Danny says, "Why don't you come with us?" the indication being that you would go with them and that everything would be again secure and peaceful and so forth. As you said a few minutes ago at the beginning of the interview, you have been doing a lot of self-questioning about life, and have arrived at the conclusion that it was best for you to face things as they really are. Okay?
Pt: Yes.
Th: At that time you kissed your sister and Jean, but you had the

"queer" feeling in a "strange sort of way" that Danny might perceive that thought, which was that you might be making advances to his wife, which you did not want him to perceive, yet you felt that sometimes people do. We know that you have had some very strong feelings for Jean in the past and we talked about them. That's perfectly honest and straightforward. We talked about these feelings, and we have seen how they came up in that interesting dream of yours. Now, what were these thoughts about Jean that you forgot completely to mention up to now?

Pt: Any time that I come into any physical contact with her—not any time, but enough times to make it significant—I have—as I said, Jean and I talked on the phone once before she knew she was going to marry Danny.

Th: We talked about all this last time, right?

Pt: And that thought entered my mind, thinking that I hope Jean doesn't still feel that I'm going to make a play for her.

Th: You also don't want Danny to assume that, and you don't want Jean to assume it. If there's going to be someone who is going to make a play at Jean it's you. So, what were your wishes?

Pt. What were my wishes?

Th: At the precise moment of physical contact with Jean. Was it at the time you were giving Jean a kiss?

Pt: Probably.

Th: Not probably.

Pt: I would say yes.

Th: Don't say anything. What I want to know is what happened to you. I mean what *you* want to know is what happened to you. What we both of us want is for you to understand what was happening inside so that we can explain why you felt anxious.

Pt: Okay. When I anticipated saying goodbye to Jean, I felt a little uneasy. So, what I'm saying is that I don't want her to assume that our old relationship is still going on, because I think that it might make her anxious, too.

Th: I understand. Now, what was your reaction at that moment on Saturday?

Pt: That's initially when I started becoming anxious; questioning whether I should go back or not.

Th: So, going back would have had a secondary aspect to it also. First, it would be the security of continuing that lovely day.

The second would be that you might have had the possibility of seeing more of Jean. Was that what convinced you not to go?

Pt: Primarily, I suppose, because of that. My feeling right now is that my family—I'm very uneasy with my family so the only one who I'm really content with right now and still communicate with, as I did with my family at one point, is with Danny and his wife. The thought which occurred to me was, "I know he loves her and if I went home with Danny and Jean it would be like the old triangular relationship, the same one that I had with my family at first."

Th: That's fine. I agree. The triangular situation with your mother and your father would be similar to the one with Jean and Danny. Now, tell me if this is the *real* reason why you decided not to go back with them and not so much the security. If the real reason was that you felt that if you went along, this might have given some ideas to Jean and to Danny of your old relationship with Jean. Then you decided, maybe for the sake of your new relationship with them, that it might be better not to go with them. You said to yourself, "I'm going to stay in the city and be lonely even if I don't like it." That decision took courage. Now, what I'm interested in really is the moment when you decided to kiss Jean. You said something about physical contact. What about that?

Pt: Well, I just thought physical contact leads up to a lot of thoughts about, you know ...

Th: What were your thoughts on Saturday when you had physical contact with Jean?

Pt: As previously. Engineering some way of getting together with her.

Th: The thought occurred to you at that time?

Pt: Yes.

Th: It did, really? You're not just saying that because you think that this is what I want to hear?

Pt: No. This is what I'm saying. Danny could have perceived this thought.

Th: Now, you see, that's what you did not allow yourself to think right in here a minute ago. Tell me, was that the same thought as the one you had when you were kissing your sister?

Pt: No. She is my sister.

Th: Of course! So if the thought was not there as far as your sister was concerned, and it was present about Jean, then this is the precise point, namely, that you had different physical feelings for these two women. You were not kissing both of them in the same way. One was Jean and the other your real sister, but a kiss for one was of a very different kind than it was for the other. Now, if this was the case at that time, the immediate thought which followed it was that Danny might perceive it.

Pt: Well, during, you know, even before that moment, I thought of it.
Th: When did you start being anxious?
Pt: When they both were going to leave.
Th: Before or after the kiss?
Pt: A little before.
Th: A little before?
Pt: Yeah.
Th: Do you remember when?
Pt: Well, I think it was specifically at the point before Jean was getting into the car and I was going to walk around and say goodbye to Danny. It was then that I kissed Jean. The whole thought preceding my kissing Jean was of seeing her again. It was at the point when she was getting in the car. So, when I kissed her goodbye the thought was, "Boy! Maybe I would really like to go out with her again." So that was the specific point when I got anxious.
Th: So the specifice point was that you wanted to go with her. Now we know why you wanted to go with her, not because of the security of old times, but precisely because of your physical attraction for her. This thought, of course, stopped you cold, and you decided not to go. It was then that you decided maybe instead a kiss will do. Is that true or not?
Pt: I don't know. Of course, when you bring up the thought of kissing my sister and Jean as being different, it's a new avenue of thought. Of course they're most different. My whole feeling is that I don't want either my cousin or Jean to infer that I want a physical relationship with Jean. Jean is a very attractive girl. She's very pleasant.
Th: I understand very well. This is why it is important to examine these feelings right in here, rather than to avoid looking at these feelings and to act them out in all kinds of roundabout ways. Now, what we are interested in here is to explain or to understand your anxiety. Let me recapitulate. I suspect that you were anxious the other day *primarily*, as we have traced it out now it is quite

clear, at the moment when you had a desire to go along with them. That meant that you would have been with Danny and Jean, and that meant the continuation of your physical attraction for Jean, who is a very attractive woman and so forth. At that moment you started being anxious. That anxiety stopped you. It was utilized by you in a meaningful way. It stopped you because if you had gone along with them the old relationship would have been reduplicated. This relationship was similar to the triangular one which you had with your parents, as you told me a minute ago, and that you are really afraid but would also try to change. But you had the courage to say no, so something from within you said no. But it didn't say no 100 percent. It said no 99 percent.

Pt: No, about 80 percent.

(Both patient and therapist laugh.)

Th: Eighty percent. Okay, so that 20 percent was the kiss to Jean which was different than the kiss to your sister. Then they left, is that it? And then you felt what?

Pt: Lonely.

Th: Lonely because you were not with Jean?

Pt: Yes. Well, I would say Jean and Danny.

Th: No! No! No! Because you were not with *Jean.* Now we can understand it in a completely different way. If you can be straight and honest with yourself, and if you really see what your thoughts are, all will be all right. Do you remember your dream? In that dream you and Jean were in bed together, and Danny was on the side. It does not mean that you don't love your cousin. It is precisely because you love your cousin that you have these problems. You remember our session two weeks ago. The whole issue at that time was your love for your cousin. I know that indeed you would like to have a new relationship with your cousin and Jean. But the fact is that you are honest enough to admit to yourself that you have also some sexual feelings for Jean, which existed before she was married and which still exist. If they had vanished into thin air I would have been surprised, and so would you. It doesn't mean that you couldn't have a relationship with them in a meaningful way, exactly the way you have described, but my feeling is, and what I was saying last time, is that you have a tendency to be attracted to women who are unavailable, and

there is a whole world of beautiful, available women for you to choose from.
Pt: It is very hard for me to communicate with available women.
Th: I think you enjoy being in that other triangular situation, and we know what happens to you because it has something to do with your earliest relationships at home with your mother and father. Now, this is still something that persists and it is why you're here trying to figure it out. We can't expect it to change overnight. I do think, however, that we have a much better understanding of your anxiety about this episode on Saturday. Okay. See you next week.

Dr. Malan:

This is really a most fascinating interview. If one wants to use the word "focal," that is, it sticks to one theme, it could not be more focal than it is. I am fascinated by this patient. We did not see his initial interview. We did not see how he was in the initial stages of therapy, but it seems to me that if one wants to judge his motivation at this stage, obviously it is ambivalent. There are things he doesn't want to look at, but I was very impressed with the sincere attempt to understand himself, he has the sincere wish not only not to fall back on a dependen relationship with his parents, but to break free from it, which he expresses time and time again in the initial part of the interview. I was very interested how in the early part of the interview Dr. Sifneos was very much less active and thoughtful than he was in other interviews that we saw. If everybody was criticizing him previously for not allowing the patient time to think or to express his feelings, then this criticism certainly doesn't apply to the initial part of this interview.

I have an uneasiness about the latter part of the interview, where Dr. Sifneos became more active again. I think there has been some reaction against this style of his. I react against it a bit myself in the sense that the patient is chased around and pinned down to the point where he is forced to agree with what Dr. Sifneos says. I'm damned sure what Dr. Sifneos says is right, but at the same time my style wouldn't be like his. I would try somehow, by rather more indirect methods, to get the patient to express his feelings himself, but I really think that's a minor criticism because I feel sure that what came out of this interview was essentially correct. Dr. Sifneos saw it from the beginning of the interview and he had to make the patient see it.

There was this crucial point at which he chose the direction of the interview. The incident of the Saturday skiing had been spoken of and there was a lot of talk about could he or couldn't he make friends easily. There was also this questionnaire at school that he filled out in order to try and imply that he could when he knew that he couldn't. He then ended up saying that there were a lot of lonely people in the city, and he was afraid of ending up being one of them. This was sort of getting away from the focus somehow and Dr. Sifneos then made a plunge.

This is part of the difference in styles and it is not my style. I would have done the same in analysis, but I think that perhaps I would have let the patient go on at this point. I would have done, if I had been clever enough, exactly the same as Dr. Sifneos in trying to bring him back forcibly to the central issue. Dr. Sifneos says to him at the moment of separation, "Did Jean enter into your mind?" The patient hadn't mentioned Jean as an important part of this situation at all. It was just that his cousin was there and Jean was there and his sister and Joe were there. You know, she wasn't really an issue and Peter sees this as an issue and focuses on that point in the whole interview of his relationship with Jean. There's an immediate response to this. At the moment of separation, Dr. Sifneos say, "Didn't Jean enter into your mind?" and he responds that "a strange feeling occurred to me that I musn't upset my cousin." At the moment he gives that response, we know that the question is relevant. When the patient starts talking about the fact that it gave him a strange feeling, one knows he is with you, his unconscious is with you; his conscious may not be. This is typical of this kind of active technique, which would be exactly the same as I would use. I feel that I am no longer in any danger of being a sort of "yes man" to Dr. Sifneos' technique.

He uses this phrase "strange feeling." What does one do with that? Again, you just have to wait and see what he says next. I'm interested in Felix Deutsch—I hope it was he—who coined the phrase "the associative anamnesis," in which he repeats significant words as used by the patient or directive associations. Dr. Davanloo's technique is very much along similar lines. I don't do it in the way Felix does it, that is to just say "strange feeling." I would say, "What do you mean 'strange feeling'?" or something like that. What Dr. Sifneos says is "Strange feeling? Can you say more?" This produces even further information: "I don't want my cousin to infer that I'm making a play for his wife." This is an illustration of the effect of the active technique. The patient is threatening to run away and to associate with other things, such as getting lonely in the city which, although these are important issues, are not the central issues in the session. The central issue is the situation of the skiing day and it's fascinating the way the patient gets ahead of one, in a sense. He doesn't really get ahead because one knows where it should be, but he gets ahead of one's last remark. One's last remark is simply, "Strange feeling." The patient says, "I don't want my cousin to infer that I'm making a play for his wife." We know he's not making a play for his wife, so what does that have to do with it? The patient's unconscious or not very conscious produces this, and then, impressed by the patient again, by his thoughtfulness, the next remark that he made was, "I don't know where deceptions come from." It's most fascinating that he is aware or half-consciously aware of the phenomena of suggestion in the sense that he's almost saying, "I know my cousin doesn't really see this. I know it's really just in my mind, but just the same I feel that he sees this." You know, it's a marvelous patient that can say that sort of thing, and it's this kind of indication that you get that a patient is a good candidate for this kind of abbreviated psychotherapy. You know he's going to work and be thoughtful about his problems.

This is a highly skillful interview. It's fascinating to watch these interviews in which what the patient says goes into the computer of one's own mind, and one associates to what one would say oneself, and, lo and behold, the therapist settles one problem before one would have had a chance to process it oneself.

Dr. Warnes:

I have very little to add except a few questions. At the beginning of the interview the patient said he was very comfortable with you, and obviously he wanted to say the opposite. After a while he said you were causing him too much anxiety, and by this he felt he profited because prior to that he explained the feeling of strangeness to the point of depersonalization as a defense against feeling, the kind of thing we are talking about. This came very clearly, and the second aspect was the feeling that others might perceive his fear. He wasn't sure whether his cousin perceived his wishes for Jean or whether she, herself, had forgotten the fact that they were close before marriage, and he might perceive these feelings. He was a bit confused regarding where to place his feelings.

This goes together with an expressed fear of being misjudged. He said, "I fear people will misjudge me," and the judgment comes from the therapist, and the therapist was in fact very supportive. There was a displacement from the parental relationship to his cousin and Jean, but I would work more with the guilt over his relationship with Danny, his father, the hostile competitiveness, and the self-punishment as a result of his guilt. He is staying alone. He suffers alone. He must go for therapy. He must beat his head, and this came out also throughout the interview in trying to outdo, to outsmart the therapist. I wonder why Dr. Sifneos did not welcome this transference aspect. I know it was an excellent interview. I don't think there was time to do more, but maybe later on he would have taken this up.

Question from the floor:

My question has to do with Dr. Malan's comment that Dr. Sifneos was either too bold or too anxious, and his indication that he wouldn't proceed the same way. I wonder if Dr. Malan's different technique has a lengthening effect on the course of the therapy in spite of the fact that he treats a different kind of patient.

Dr. Naiman:

I would just like to comment on what I believe to be the specific nature of Dr. Sifneos' interpretation. It seems to me that the patient indicated in effect that there were, or one can conceptualize the patient as having, four possibilities in terms of where his life is going to go. One is that he can be alone. Another is that he can be like a child with Danny and Jean, both of them replacing the parents and he being in a dependent, childlike relationship with them. The third position he can be in is to compete with his cousin for Jean, and the fourth position is to progress and get a woman of his own, leaving Jean to his cousin.

It seems to me that what Dr. Sifneos did at the end is really very specifically to encourage the fourth alternative; he clarified the distinction between the women who are in fact forbidden and the women who are in fact permitted. I think this was a very specific interpretation, and I think it is the sort of interpretation which would be applicable not only in brief psychotherapy, but also in psychoanalysis.

Dr. Davanloo:

In my view, this specific type of interpretation was really a genetic interpretation given the patient by Dr. Sifneos.

Dr. Moll:

I am impressed, and it is a magnificent and skillful session. With reference specifically to the patient, I am just wondering whether he was able to communicate or whether any one of us could see a certain element of depression in the sense that in order for him to get well it involved giving up his therapist. The focus was on anxiety at the time of the session, but I thought I could detect, in the way he described his anxiety when he came to the decision he would not go home with his cousin, that there was an element of depression. He had to give up both Danny and Jean, which means that in order to get well there must be a certain working through or giving up love objects. I would like to ask whether there was a feeling about the patient, besides being anxious, having a certain depressive feature which would have to be dealt with in therapy?

Question from the floor:

In the first part of this interview the patient talked about a contest, and I noticed that Dr. Sifneos was aware of this, interested in it, he pursued it for a while, and then shifted to the oedipal situation and pursued this to its fruitful conclusion. I wonder why Dr. Sifneos decided to drop the issue of the contest, and I don't know how he made this perception and made the shift.

Question from the floor:

I would like to know how one would handle slips of the tongue in short-term therapy.

Question from the floor:

Should one wait until the transference appears as a resistance?

Question from the floor:

I wonder if Dr. Sifneose could say something about residents in the first three or four years of their training program using this type of technique. You, yourself, sound pretty sure about yourself and about what you are doing. Would you want residents to be doing something like that?

Dr. Sifneos:

I am much more sure of myself now than I was six years ago. Residents also develop self-confidence, but we must supervise them and teach them systematically. Yes, we do analyze slips of the tongue. We do not wait until the transference appears as a resistance.

Question from the floor:

I would like to raise the question of timing and the number of sessions in short-term psychotherapy. Dr. James Mann, in his book, makes a big point of being very definitive about the number of sessions the patient is going to have, even to the extent of looking at the calendar and giving the patient the date when his therapy will be terminated. I heard Dr. Davanloo comment that he is more flexible with regard to the timing of the therapy. Now, it seems to me also that both Dr. Sifneos and Dr. Malan are a bit more flexible. I would like to know why, and I would also like to know about termination.

Question from the floor:

My question regards criteria in relation to this last interview. One of the criteria emphasized is that the patient should have at least one meaningful relationship. I thought that this patient's previous relationship was with his mother and a competitive relationship with his father. With which of these persons did he have a meaningful relationship?

Dr. Davanloo:

I could make some comments regarding the timing of the therapy and the number of sessions. Dr. James Mann, in his book, does not really give any explanations how he decides so definitely on the number of sessions. Since 1963, in a large series of patients that we have worked with using this technique, I have found it very difficult to determine the number of sessions for a large number of patients, except in a few patients whom we treated in from between two and five sessions.

In 1965, after having worked with our first series of patients, we decided in our evaluation sheet to ask the evaluator how many sessions he estimates the therapy would take. All these evaluations, for some years, were done by me exclusively. I would say that we were correct in approximately 5 percent, because there were so many variables entering into the therapeutic work which affect the length of therapy one way or another. For example, we can take one variable as a therapeutic focus versus patient's motivation. Now, if the therapeutic focus is not properly picked up by the therapist, you might have a situation in which five or six sessions have passed until the therapist and patient have arrived at the proper therapeutic focus. Such a variable which involves the therapist and the patient is very difficult to evaluate fully in a clinical situation.

In a practical sense I always tell the patient that the therapy will be of short-term duration and might take somewhere around, for example, fifteen to 20 sessions. As far as termination is concerned, when I have come to the conclusion that the patient has worked through some of his major areas of conflict and is applying his new self-awareness in dealing with his life, I review this with the patient, then set a definite date for termination. I would say I leave on the average three to five sessions for ending.

Dr. Sifneos:

I appreciate very much the discussion as well as the questions from the floor. I think they are very productive questions, although I may not be able to answer all of them.

In terms of Dr. Warnes's question as to why I did not pursue the competition with his cousin and with his father and the transference issue rather than go into this specific case of anxiety, it is difficult to be sure. There was a kind of uneasiness that I felt about a certain degree of intellectualization going on in the first part of the hour, although realistically speaking he was very sincere in the issues that he spoke about, such as anxiety being constructive and making him willing to change. We had never dealt with anxiety in the previous sessions in those terms. I feel that in this type of psychotherapy it is very important to be very systematic, almost dissecting the piece of work which has to be done, and to do it clearly. If this can be done successfully, one could keep on returning to it and referring to it over and over. It is like a jigsaw puzzle. Every piece must fit into a whole. You may start working in one specific area until, finally, a pattern emerges, and when that pattern emerges it very quickly gives you a picture, more or less, of what the rest of the jigsaw puzzle picture is going to be like. The best way to do this is to analyze a specific episode. In this hour the skiing episode and what followed gave me this opportunity.

I thought the issue of the skiing episode was of great importance, and that it was connected in some way to the triangular situation which I have already mentioned was our focus. During the first eight interviews we went into it in great detail. I was not sure about this episode at first. It was he, however, who brought it up spontaneously. It was he who brought up, also spontaneously, the dream about when he was in bed with Jean, during the earlier interview. When he brought up this example about anxiety, which was very specific and which did not seem to be related to our general discussion about anxiety, I thought there might be something important hidden in it, and so I was determined to pursue it. So this is why I decided not to deal with the issue of transference, Dr. Warnes. The transference, by the way, as I have already mentioned, had come up and was dealt with repeatedly before. For example, competitive feelings with me in reference to my secretary had come up during the fifth interview and were interpreted appropriately.

With reference to the question about transference, what I am saying is that we don't have to wait for it to appear as a resistance. During the early part of the interview the transference is indeed a resistance, but at other times the transference is not a resistance. The patient may bring up very positive feelings about the therapist, and one must pursue them extensively in order to find out what his thoughts are about these positive feelings. This patient, during the second interview for example, inquired about my qualifications and various other things, and he spoke quite openly and quite positively. The therapeutic alliance had clearly been established by the second interview at the latest.

Regarding Dr. Naiman's point about the fourth solution, I am completely in agreement with his idea. Indeed, I am supporting him in order to help him learn to choose. The other three solutions appear to be neurotic solutions, and these are the ones that he had been using up to then. He has been unhappy, however, and these feelings were instrumental in bringing him to therapy.

With reference to Dr. Moll's point about his experiencing mild depression, I also agree that there was a depressive component in this patient when he thought of losing his cousin and Jean.

Regarding the question related to our criterion of the "meaningful relationship," I say categorically that I think that he had a meaningful relationship with his mother. It was a very sexualized kind of relationship in which he got a great deal out of it, but also he gave a great deal to her. He had also an excellent relationship with his father despite their competition. He described in great detail his father taking him traveling and the fun they had together. His relationship with Danny is also a good one despite their competition. He had a very good friend with whom he worked for quite a period of time. His relationship with his sister is also good. I certainly think, therefore, that he passed this particular criterion triumphantly.

As far as his competitiveness is concerned, we went into it in great detail. He had competitive feelings for his father as well as for me, and we had a very interesting hour in which this came out into the open. He was challenging me, and at the same time he was quite aware of the positive aspects of our relationship and the work we have done together.

With reference to the question which was raised about the teaching of residents, it is of great interest to me. We used to have residents spend the third year or the fourth year with us at Beth Israel Hospital, who came from other psychiatric centers. I found it difficult to supervise them. All in all I discovered quickly that the first-year residents are fresh, open-minded, interested people who like to do things in a different way. I prefer to take first-year residents and supervise them than I do the older ones. This does not mean that all are narrow-minded; far from it. But there is a kind of brainwashing about the advantages of long-term psychotherapy which is emphasized in some psychiatric centers, and which is difficult to change.

With reference to the question of the number of sessions and termination, I agree with Dr. Davanloo's comments. In this patient the issue of termination clearly came up in the eleventh interview. He opened that interview saying that things were going very much better, and that he felt fine. He worked up to the last minute of the last hour without having to deal with the problems of separation. He said that the therapy has helped him. That was it.

Chapter 19

Techniques of Short-Term Anxiety-Provoking Psychotherapy (II)

P. E. SIFNEOS

"The Case of the Woman with a Prostitution Fantasy"

The patient is a young female who came to the clinic after she had an abortion, with the complaint of being "tired of her relationships with sick men." It was one of these "sick men" who made her pregnant. She claimed that she wanted to free herself from this particular pattern because she wanted to get married and have a family. She fulfilled all the criteria for short-term anxiety-provoking psychotherapy, and she was accepted as a candidate in our research study. She was seen by two independent evaluators before and after the therapy, respectively. The patient was the youngest of four girls. She came from a very close-knit family. She was very attached to her mother and to her father. But when her mother became sick and was in a hospital on and off during her childhood, she replaced her mother and became her father's "little wife." She talked about having strong sexual feelings for her father, but as she grew older these subsided and her feelings and her attachment for her mother increased. From then on, she started to have a pattern of relationships with the so-called "sick men," who took advantage of her and yet whom she dominated.

Pt: Last week when I got out of here I was just drained, such frustration.
Th: It was a difficult hour, don't you think?

Pt: It must have been, going into all those dreams; that was difficult. Remember Phil? Well, I have always been haunted by him ever since I kicked him out. Oh, when I was in Florida waiting to get this operation, the phone rang at 10:00 and I knew it was him calling. It wasn't, but I just felt as if it were him: "Oh, here he is in Miami." Then this happened many times. This fantasy is what it is. I met a man who has the same coloring as Phil, same build, everything, but it wasn't Phil. I looked at him, and it's so freaky because for a minute I really believed that he was Phil in another person, and I had this fantasy that Phil was spying on me. Like this man is dumb and everything and Phil is not, but I thought that Phil was this man. This fantasy stayed with me during the night. It wasn't a brief fantasy that just lasted on and on. I went over it back and forward in my mind. "How nutty Phil is, how crazy. He is the craziest person I have ever met.

Th: Now, what is the exact fantasy? Can you tell me about it?

Pt: That he's nuts. That Phil could do anything he wanted. He could find me wherever I went if he wanted to. He is a magician, that's what he is. A ghost, a witch or whatever is the name for a man witch.

Th: So you're saying that you have a view of Phil as a magical person?

Pt: Yes, not human.

Th: A magical person? One has thoughts of this kind when one is a child. It's at that time that we believe in magic and we have certain kinds of fears and notions of this kind. Does that remind you of the time when you were a child?

Pt: I can't remember having any fantasies like this, about witches when I was a child. I've always been interested in witchcraft. I've read a couple of books on it, but I can remember having this type of fantasy and relating it to another human.

Th: But when you say you are interested in witchcraft, when did it start? When you were quite young?

Pt: No, when I was an adult. It was after I left home.

Th: After you left home?

Pt: Yes.

Th: Was that in any way connected? I mean, did this notion of magic follow your being alone, after being away from home?

Pt: I don't think so.

Th: Does this subject make you tense?

Pt: What we're discussing now?
Th: The subject of Phil.
Pt: No. I'll let you know at the end of the session.
Th: Why don't you tell me right now?
Pt: No, it doesn't make me tense. I'm in a good mood today, a very good mood. This happened two nights ago, this fantasy.
Th: Can you give me the details of what happened? Did you wake up, for instance, with this fantasy?
Pt: No, I was at a bar and I saw this guy. I took a double-take. I looked again and I said, "Who are you?" He said he was working close by. I looked at him: I talked to him and told him that he reminded me of an old boyfriend, and that was it. But then this thought, "Wow, that could be Phil. Really, it could be Phil." That thought stayed with me. I thought about it. I didn't dispense with it. "How could Phil change his appearance to that extent? Why would he pull a trick like that?"
Th: Were you attracted to this person?
Pt: No.
Th: No sexual attraction?
Pt: No sexual, nothing. He was a dummy. His teeth were all messed up. No sexual attraction whatsoever.
Th: What are your feelings about Phil right now?
Pt: I'm afraid he's going to show up one day.
Th: Are you afraid of him or are you angry at him?
Pt: I'm afraid of him. I don't like Phil. I have no sexual feelings for him any more, and I know I'm convinced now that if he ever does show up I will tell him to get out. I will never go through what happened last time, because there's nothing that Phil could do that would make me go back to him or start liking him again. Nothing. He frightens me now. It's the dangerous type of thing. Like he told me on several occasions that if he wanted me to be one of his girls, or one of his prostitutes, would I? I said, "No, I wouldn't."
Th: Prostitutes?
Pt: Yes. He told me he could manipulate me to where I would go out and be a prostitute. Now, this is what he told me, and I disagreed. I said, "I wouldn't do this for any man, or me, or anybody." Then I asked, "Well, why aren't you manipulating me to do this?" He said, "Because I like you." He did like me. I think Phil did have a fondness for me that he didn't have for too many other

women. He did like me, but this is what he had told me once, and though I realize I would never become a prostitute for him or anybody else, the fact that he had the gall to tell me this meant something.

Th: Yes, indeed. We know something special about prostitutes, don't we?

Pt: You mean about my father and the prostitute in Texas?

Th: Yes, now what about that? What comes to mind?

Pt: I don't hate prostitutes. I don't feel sorry for prostitutes. In fact, they fascinate me, as we discussed before. What comes to mind? You mean Phil's relation—Phil and me—and my father and his prostitute?

Th: Yes, what about them?

Pt: I don't see any relation there. When Phil said this to me, I didn't think of my dad.

Th: I know that. I wonder, could it be that you didn't think of it because it was a loaded subject?

Pt: But if it's so loaded—like my friends and I would drive around where they have the prostitutes. This was after I knew about my dad. We used to drive around and look at the prostitutes and all the other degenerate things happening. If it's so loaded—I mean, why do I keep going back to it?

Th: Well, that's a good question. Why do you keep going back to it?

Pt: I don't know. Maybe because my father could have a fascination, could be attracted to a prostitute.

Th: *And what would happen if you were one of Phil's?*

Pt: Oh, no! No. *Never!* Well, I mean, Phil is in Texas.

Th: Go on. I'm not talking about reality. What I am talking about is what may be in the back of your mind in some of these associations.

Pt: I would never be a prostitute, not one of Phil's or anybody's.

Th: I know that, but could it be that there is a part of you that might wish just that?

Pt: In a way. Well, they're so well-dressed. They have so much money. I could have anything I wanted if I was a prostitute, money-wise. They're very well-dresed, most of them.

Th: And we know that you like clothes?

Pt: Oh, I love clothes.

Th: Now, what else comes to mind about prostitutes?

Pt: Nothing. I don't consider them to have a personality. I don't consider in a way that they are human. They have no brains, no mind. They're just a good-looking human walking around in very nice clothes. I've thought of what goes on with a prostitute. In fact, I've asked my boyfriend. When he was in the service, he had prostitutes, and I asked him what he thought of prostitutes when he had a prostitute in Europe, when he was overseas. And I have also asked Bob what it was like to sleep with a prostitute.

Th: What did they say?

Pt: Bob said he would not come in a girl unless she is on pills or they are using something else or he knows her well. He got one girl pregnant and he doesn't want to do that again. I asked him, What did he do with a prostitute? Did he come in the prostitute? He said yes. Now, I didn't like that. I don't think that was very nice. If he'd come in a prostitute and he didn't care if she got pregnant, I guess I *do* consider them human.

Th: What you just told me emphasizes that you do consider them human.

Pt: Yes, oh ...

Th: Were you going to say something else?

Pt: This is sort of like me in a way. Now, he didn't come in me unless I was on my pills or I was over my fertility period, but John didn't care. He didn't even ask me, and I could have become pregnant.

Th: So John treated you like a prostitute?

Pt: Yes.

Th: What about Phil?

Pt: Phil? Well, I think Phil knew I was on pills. I had been on pills for two years, so I think I had told him. Yes, I had told him I was on pills. He treated me very nicely. Well, no, he didn't. No. He didn't treat me very nicely. It was he who got me pregnant when I was off my pills.

Th: You have, up to now, I think, as we have viewed it, presented Phil and John always together, and it was your boyfriend and Bob who were also associated together, because they were the nice ones. The others were not nice. Now, if John didn't care and treated you like a prostitute, why is it that you seem to have a fascination for him?

Pt: Not any more.

Th: But you had, and you have a fascination about Phil even in terms of your fantasy. Then there is something about your being treated like a prostitute by a man that has a fascination above and beyond the problems that it may create. Is that correct?

Pt: Possibly.

Th: Now, the question is: What is the fascination?

Pt: I don't know.

Th: Come, now. Look, you remember the subject that we were talking about last week that you didn't like at all. Jeff and your interest in him.

Pt: About the rapes?

Th: Yes. Well, let's stick to that man Jeff. What did you say about him? You said that you were afraid but you told him that he could rape you—and then we talked about rape and rape we defined as sexual intercourse when the person has no way to defend herself. It is imposed upon her. Now, isn't that what you described here about Jeff and John last week? What did these men do to the prostitutes? Isn't that the same thing? It wasn't rape because the prostitutes agreed with them, but in a sense it was the same attitude of not considering them of any importance, of doing something to them for their own satisfaction and not to consider them as a human being.

Pt: Yes, like pregnancy could be imposed. It seems that there *is* a relation. I don't know. I don't know how to answer that.

Th: It is not a question. I'm not asking you to answer yes or no. What I'm saying is, let's try to look at all this and try to understand what may be happening in you during these situations. These situations, as you know, touch on every single thing that is going on at the present time. What brought you here was your relationship with men, particularly this unpleasant relationship with men that led to your difficulties. So, we are right in the midst of this difficulty. We must try to disentangle this problem and we must try to solve it.

Pt: What time is it? I don't like all this.

(*The patient appears quite anxious.*)

Th: Now, what is it that you don't like?

Pt: I don't like to think of myself as a prostitute, or that I enjoy being treated like a prostitute.

Th: You see, what is of importance is this: if you do, or if there is a part of you that does, it's much better to know about it, talk about it, to see what it's all about, rather than to keep on doing it and hoping against hope that it isn't so.

Pt: I understand that.

Th: You see, it would be easy for us to say, "Well, you know, all these unpleasant things are in the past. Let's forget about them," but that's not what you came here for. You came here because you told me that you want to change all this. Isn't that true?

Pt: I know. I don't know how to answer that. I don't know how to start thinking about it.

Th: Let's go back to this episode in Texas.

Pt: What? You mean the episode with my father and the prostitute? All right. Dad and Mom had gone there. I can't remember the event, but Jane was still married to her first husband, Dick, who drank a lot, so Dad and Dick went out drinking. Now, I didn't hear about this until Dad had gone back home, but Dad had a black eye the next day when I saw him. He told Mom he had fallen down the stairs or something like that, but Dick had told Jane what happened and she relayed the message to me. Dad had tried to pick up a prostitute, and when he and the prostitute left the bar two guys mugged Dad. The prostitute and the two guys were working together. When I heard about this, *I was sick to my stomach.* I mean I was *really sick*, and I pitied my dad. I said, "What a fool." Here he was, maybe sixty-eight years old, I'm not sure, who couldn't . . .

Th: Let's look at it this way. You told me exactly the same story before, with the same details. But what is quite striking is how upset you are. You were *"sick to your stomach."* Now, what were you sick to your stomach about? What were your thoughts at this time?

Pt: I didn't really feel sorry for Mom. I really think I felt sorry for me.

Th: For you? About what?

Pt: I don't know. It was sort of similar to the dream about the rape. The same sick feeling, you know. It was like *he* cheated *me*, instead of thinking about my mother. *He* cheated *me*, and again maybe if he could sleep with a prostitute he would probably sleep with me. Oh, that's awful . . . ech . . .

Th: Do you remember that thought?

Pt: No, I don't think I remember that thought.

(*The patient looks very tired and anxious.*)

Th: How did that thought come to your mind?
Pt: I had the same sick feeling about the dream that I do with this thing that happened to Dad, and I felt cheated, or that Dad is so corrupt that he could even have incest with his own daughter. Shortly after this, there was this little old guy that my friend and I met on the street one night where we live and we started talking to him. He was a real cute little guy about Dad's age. One morning I was waiting for the bus to go to work, and this guy came up to me and said that maybe I could go over some night when his wife was gone. He said he didn't get along with his wife. I got the same *sick feeling* again, but this made me *sick*, because I thought, How degenerate of this man wanting to sleep with me; I could be his daughter.
Th: Can we tie all this together?
Pt: I'm sure we can one way or another. They were in the same age group, my dad and this little old man. And the thought that this little old man would sleep with me and the thought that my father would want to sleep with a prostitute, you know? (*sighs*)
Th: You sigh. What about?
Pt: I don't know. (*her voice becomes tremulous*)
Th: I know this is very difficult.

(*The patient starts to cry.*)

Pt: I'm trying. I want to think about these things, but it's hard.
Th: I know. You know again I couldn't say more than to encourage you. I know that it is difficult, but all these things have been with you for a long time, and they have led to some very painful situations for you.

(*Now the patient is sobbing.*)

Pt: He's my dad. I hate him and I hate me, too.
Th: Now, come on, let us hear about how you feel.

(*The patient continues to cry.*)

Pt: Why do I hate my father?
Th: Yes.

Pt: I think I started hating my father the day the thing with the prostitute happened, because if he could do that to a prostitute, then he could maybe do that to me, and I don't think I've ever liked the thought of that.

Th: Tell me, is it since then that your feelings for your father have changed?

Pt: I think that put the clincher on it. I think my feelings for my father changed as I was getting prepared to leave home. I think that's when it really happened, but the prostitute thing just put the clincher on it, you know, put the lid on real tight.

Th: Now, when you went back looking for the prostitutes, what happened then?

Pt: I was with my girlfriend, and with her brother, and the three of us would drive around and he would say there's a prostitute, and I'd look at her and her clothing and I think I wondered, What is she thinking? I felt embarrassed to be going around looking at these prostitutes like they were showpieces, and my girlfriend kept saying, "I feel so sorry for them." I got angry with her and said, "You know this is what they want to do. They're making good money, and it's not so horrible for them."

Th: So the one thing that invariably seems to come to mind out of all this has to do with the clothes. This was the one thing that you saw about them that was quite characteristic.

Pt: Yes.

Th: Can you tell me more about clothes?

Pt: I love clothes. I would love—I envy women, especially in this city. I never saw so many well-dressed women that have outfits from head to toe that match, and beautiful clothes. They look suave and straight out of *Vogue* magazine. I never bought clothes. Most of my better clothes are gifts or hand-me-downs. I don't buy expensive clothes, and I sort of don't like to spend my money on clothes.

Th: Is that a way of denying your wishes to be a prostitute? Do you see what I mean?

Pt: Possibly, though I never liked to look cheap. I've always liked to look nice. I've always tried to put my make-up on subtly, and my hair today is curly but it's not all ratted.

Th: I noticed that you have changed in your appearance here. The first time you came here, you were wearing your blue jeans. Today you're all dressed up.

Pt: Because I'm not going to work.
Th: Even last week, you were dressed up.
Pt: I had a crummy outfit on, didn't I?
Th: I don't think so.
Pt: Well, it was a pair of pants. Today I felt so good in my clothes. This is a hand-me-down, but a very nice, expensive suit. It's my sister's.
Th: It seems to be matching with your blouse.
Pt: It's nice, you know.
Th: What about your appearance today?
Pt: I look very nice today. When I set my hair and put on my make-up very nicely, and when I stepped out the door, I felt that everybody was looking at me, watching me because I looked so good.
Th: What are your plans? What are you going to do?
Pt: Well, I'm going to parade around the city.
Th: Are you going out with your boyfriend?
Pt: From here back to my house I'm going to be alone, and then my boyfriend is picking me up at 4:00 and I'm going to spend the weekend with him.
Th: So in a sense you are dressed up for him?
Pt: No. I intend to put on a nicer dress for him. Now I'm just parading around the city on my own.
Th: I see. So are we included in this parade? Are you dressed up for coming here?
Pt: Yes, I think so. At first I have to take the bus from my house to here and there are a lot of men on the bus and on the trolley, and then once I get here I do look nice for anybody who is walking by. I felt good today, yet it's only Friday.
Th: What made you feel good?
Pt: I don't have to go to work because I called in sick. I did it because I just didn't want to go to work tonight. I set my hair last night. What else made me feel so good this morning? Well, I'm seeing Robert, that's my boyfriend's name. I'm going to his house, cooking and doing nice things. Usually, on days like today, I'm not happy, but today I was happy. I don't know why.
Th: There must be something special about today to make you feel happy?
Pt: Maybe it's because I have a plan tonight with a man, with Robert, that I enjoy being with him. Oh, by the way, I do enjoy coming here. I forgot to tell you that!

(*The patient smiles.*)

Th: Oh, you do. Well, tell me about it, then.
Pt: I'm very anxious to get here. I'm anxious from Monday on. I'm anxious to get here. I try to remember everything I can and do as much thinking as I can. I get angry with myself when I can't remember something. Like I had a dream last week, and I got up and I remembered it the whole day, then I forgot it. I don't think it was a bad one or anything, but I was mad at myself for that. Then I wanted to tell you very much about this fantasy with Phil because I think this sort of points out a couple of things. I wanted to tell you that I feel anxious to have my sessions. I sometimes feel good when I get out of here. Like last week I was sweating and everything. Robert was waiting for me. I sort of love myself because I'm trying. Last week's session wasn't as bad as that, after all.
Th: I understand what you're saying, and I think its important to talk about your feelings for here as well as anywhere else. Because, after all, here we can see and examine what is happening, and even when, a few minutes ago, you were sad and crying, it was important. I also know that you are working very hard and that you are trying. I think this is fifty percent of the battle, but I think it is important even if sometimes it's a bit embarrassing. You may have a fantasy or a thought about me. These also we should examine, just as we do anything else, because that's the only way in which we can solve your problem, and I think we have already gone fast. This is the fourth session. I think it's quite impressive, but we have to try over and over to see all the connections, all the associations with things that happened in the past to things that happen now. We've looked at a few already.
Pt: My roommate, she's also seeing a psychiatrist, and she complains of this, too, but I am trying to please you also. (*smiling*)
Th: You are? Tell me about it.

(*The therapist smiles.*)

Pt: I don't want you to get angry with me for dismissing thoughts. I want to be a good patient. I want to think of all the bad things that I don't like thinking of, and I want to go in depth into everything, and I feel that I am afraid that you are going to get angry with me.
Th: Why?

Pt: Because possibly I'm not trying hard enough. I remember the first day I saw you. I was frightened. In that interview with you and Dr. L., you said something to the effect, "Well, you are going to try very hard," something like that, and I think I retorted with "It's painful, this therapy stuff, but I want to try," and I felt a little threatened by you when you said that I was expected to try real hard, painful or not. But I'm going to try.

Th: I felt that you would, and I think you are trying.

Pt: I thought I would. I'm disappointed. Like there are statements, questions you ask me, and it goes right over my head. I know that you're putting it in simple English, but I know that I don't want to think about it or I want to dismiss the question.

Th: Let's put it this way. Maybe there is a part of your feeling good and looking well that has something to do with me.

Pt: Maybe.

Th: Some part?

Pt: I think so. Well, I feel good today, and I look good and everything. I even love myself today, while I was on the trolley.

Th: Now, you said a few minutes ago that you hated yourself. You said just now, "I *even* love myself." Why is this? You don't like yourself? That's not true at all.

Pt: No.

Th: Maybe you don't like yourself sometimes.

Pt: Oh, yes. There are days when I think I'm the best thing that ever happened. I really do. I think I'm unique and quite a person and quite a woman and everything. But the trouble is that it isn't a permanent feeling. I don't think it can be, but I wish it could be.

Th: Well, you know, it may not be completely permanent, but it would be one of the things that may have something to do with what you're doing here. The times that you don't like yourself are because of some of these other unpleasant things that have been left out, have been avoided or have been pushed out of your mind. Now, in a sense, coming and having a look at these issues may be difficult, may be unpleasant, but at least they are out in the open, in the fresh air, to be looked at. There really isn't anything so bad if one can try to understand what it's all about.

Pt: No. I don't feel so bad about the discussion about prostitution.

It's just that I'm anxious to get this cleared up. I don't want to think of myself as a prostitute, and then I get anxious. Like 1 wish it was six months later, six months from now.

Th: O.K. It is time to stop now.

Dr. Nemiah:

I think the jist and the essence of this was quite clear to everyone. To borrow a phrase from Dr. Sifneos, I would say that this is a short-term psychotherapy in "all its glory." Actually, I think it is one of the earlier cases that Dr. Sifneos taped. It's hard at this point in the conference to say very much that is new about technique, and maybe what I shall do is just reemphasize a few relative points and perhaps bring in a bit of what Dr. Davanloo was doing this morning. I do find that over the past two or three days I have had a thought that has been intruding itself upon me with increasing insistency, and that is the rather dismaying thought that I wish I had had short-term anxiety-provoking psychotherapy rather than my long and expensive five-year analysis. I don't mean to be heretical about it, but let's just stop for a moment and contrast what this is with analysis.

Certainly in analysis the free-floating attention that the analyst gives is in a way a kind of self-contained thing. The analyst drifts along until suddenly, as he's thinking, he gets a notion of what is going on and then makes his interpretation. But I would suggest that for those of you who may get to be analysts, if we think about ourselves honestly we find that at times there is a certain laziness involved in analysis—and I use that word advisedly, in an extreme sense—since for many patients obviously there has to be a long period of drift because of their personality structures and so forth for the thing to work. But when one sees a patient like this, one wonders is it perhaps really the appropriate technique or is it better to try something different, the sort of thing that we are seeing here.

Now, what is the essence of what we are looking at today? It has been said that the essence is activity and focus and that the therapist is really working. He is working hard; he is with the patient, he is having to get material, he is taking advantage of everything that comes along at every point in time rather than letting it drift. This was certainly characteristic of what both Drs. Sifneos and Davanloo did. I think perhaps Dr. Malan, in one tape that we have seen, is a little less directive in this way, at least verbally, although you'll notice that in a nonverbal way all of them are very active with their expressions, with their encouragements, really with their demand for the patient to work. What struck me about watching the present tape—and I have seen this before in the past—Dr. Sifneos focused much more on the wish, on the drive, on the impulse, constantly focusing and asking for fantasy, for feeling, and trying to get the patient to come through with what she obviously is struggling against, the sexual preoccupation with the father.

Now, in order to do that there has to be a focus, and the focus here has to be put on the oedipal situation, which very clearly is what Dr. Sifneos was doing. This leads then to one last comment. In response to the feeling of many people that this is beating or hammering on patients, molding them, shaping them, guiding them, suggesting, etc., I really think this is unfair. It certainly is being hard on patients and it certainly is putting a lot of pressure on them, but it's doing it for a very specific reason and with a very specific theoretical set in mind. In the first place, remember, at least with this kind of therapy, these patients are chosen because it looks from the initial assessment as though the basic and essential problem and hang-up of the patient is in the oedipal area. Now, this does not mean there aren't many other kinds of conflicts, pre-oedipal, of all sorts, going on inside the patient, just as there are in all of us here. We have all been through a developmental period of our lives, and we have all picked up certain kinds of hang-ups all along the way. The point is that the focus has to be on the oedipal—that this seems to be what the patient has the most conflict over, and is perhaps the most defensive about, and the patient may indeed use some of the more regressive pre-oedipal kind of material as a defensive way of avoiding the most anxiety-provoking factors. This can be very seductive to the therapist who follows the patient's leads into all kinds of pre-oedipal sorts of material. Unless the therapist has in mind the conviction that the oedipal is central, that any dodging of this has to be avoided, pressure has to be applied even when the conflict is not clearly in the patient's mind. It may be almost like using a cutting knife, going in and making suggestions of an oedipal sort before the patient has introduced them directly.

I don't think this is entirely suggestion. If one says to a patient, "You are feeling such-and-such" or "You have such-and-such a thought," granted that is imposed by the therapist. If the patient simply says yes, and that's all that happens, then one would have to call this at best "not proven." But when you elicit a response, as we have seen in some of these cases, and the patient suddenly stops and thinks, and you can hear it in the tone of voice, see it in the expression of the face, and he suddenly says, "Oh, yes, I never thought of it that way before" and comes forward with new material then you really have opened up the nuclear conflict, so to speak, so that more material comes out. That, it seems to me, is good operational evidence for the fact that what you are saying has hit home. I think at that point, what comes out of the patient from then on, which is new and not simply parading back to what the therapist has done, is not the result of suggestion but is really the opening up of new material. And I think as we watch Dr. Sifneos do this kind of thing we see a person who is a master at it.

Dr. Straker:

I shall try to make some comments about technique and limit my comments on content. As we go through Dr. Sifneos' interview with his patient, it seems that, as has been stated before, the emphasis is on activity and focus. It would also seem that it doesn't really matter very much what the focus is and that Dr. Sifneos' focus seems to have shifted through the interview, even though he seems to have been working with a formulation in mind. A number of concepts haven't been mentioned yet. We have talked about reinforcements, we have talked about conditioning in relation to the technique. There is also perhaps a process of desensitization going on. Dr. Sifneos, in this interview, seemed to make comments which would elicit anxieties from the patient and then subsequently follow up by saying something that would be supportive. He commented, for example, on her clothes and how well-coordinated she was during the session, reinforcing the self-esteem which she was feeling. For every dose of anxiety she seemed to be getting a dose of support.

It seemed to me that another aspect of the technique, regardless of whether one is using confrontation or interpretation or clarification, was letting the patient know that we are with them, that we are attempting to understand them. I am reminded of a phrase that to understand means to stand under, which means to look up, and when one looks up, one prizes the other individual. I think this would be one aspect of the therapeutic relationship.

We talked about the relationship regardless of technique sometimes as being a very important aspect of therapy. Dr. Sifneos seems to home in on specific issues. He is very sensitive to cues both verbal and nonverbal. The word "even," for example, is picked up, and he asks for greater specificity and does not allow the patient to become very diffused. It seems also that he is rather selective in what he chooses to have the patient be specific about. It's almost as though there is a play going on in Dr. Sifneos' mind. There is a script and he seems to be directing the patient but it's directing rather than telling the patient where to go. He is guiding, and the patient is self-discovering.

This self-exploration is a notion in patient-centered therapy. Dr. Sifneos leads the patient to explore himself by being respectful, and we see this in the way he looks at the patient, in the way he gives the patient his total and undivided attention, showing the patient that he is with her. There is also the idea of self-concurrence—that Dr. Sifneos is open to himself, aware of his reactions and comfortable with his reactions. I think that right toward the end of the session he puts it extremely well when he says there really isn't anything so bad, that he is willing to confront and deal with any material which the patient is willing to bring, that he is comfortable with it, that he is not afraid. This is transmitted to the patient and provides a safe setting. He does this in a very active way. Perhaps in long-term therapy we tend to be more passive. I am not sure really that there is all that much difference between long-term therapy and short-term therapy in terms of the conditions that we provide. The main differences seem to be in the degree of activity, or the amount of activity and the amount of focusing, the amount of directing that is done by the therapist. This seems to be critical and if the therapist has a specific focus one can constantly work with that focus. It seems that one carves out an area in which to work in short-term therapy and then concentrates on that. There may be other issues which come up at another time, yet there may not be. That's the way I see the technique as demonstrated in this videotape.

Dr. Naiman:

My feeling was that the interpretations given by the therapist flowed very directly from the material provided by the patient in this interview and from his knowledge of this patient in the past. I did not have the feeling of coercion. This was in many respects, not all that different from an analytic session, except perhaps for a certain amount of reassurance which was provided here. I would be interested in the outcome with patients like this where the situation appears somewhat different. I think the patient did most of the talking. It would be an interesting research question as to whether the outcome in patients like this is better than in the other group. I would rather suspect it would be.

Question from the floor:

I was very inspired by Dr. Sifneos' interview. I felt that you were quite explicit in the initial interpretation to the girl about her desire to sleep with her father. My question is this: Why do you seem to temper your interpretation of the transference at the end of the session?

Dr. Sifneos:

As Dr. Davanloo has pointed out, one is faced in every situation with too many different issues from which one has to choose. I thought the material about her wishes for prostitution and for her father had been adequately discussed, and considerable affect was associated with it. "I hate my father, and I hate myself." She takes the responsibility upon herself for these wishes. The transference was secondary up to that point and not particularly striking. There was obviously some mention by the patient of the previous hour, where she described it as being a difficult one and that she was perspiring when she left. When the issue of her appearance came up, dressing up, mostly for her boyfriend, parading around in the city streets but also partly for me, I thought this material was also adequately dealt with. If you mean that I could have pursued, as some people who have viewed this videotape have suggested, a connection between her boyfriend and myself, I felt that it would have been a bit far-fetched. I thought it was clear to imply that it was important for me to know that she may want to come in order to please me, which is what she described, or to be a good patient. But how much more I should have done that was necessary in this particular session is hard to say. I thought it was adequate. Now, I can see that somebody else may have pursued this much more and obtained more information, but I could also see somebody arguing that one should not deal with the transference at all, since this was only the fourth interview. So it varies.

Question from the floor:

I would like to raise two questions about style and energy. I wonder if there is any research available on comparison of styles irrespective of how successful the technique might be and what effect style and energy have on outcome.

Dr. Sifneos:

I don't have any information of this kind. I think that both are good points. Perhaps some of the others would like to comment.

Dr. Malan:

This is a research question which is incredibly difficult to answer, but we do have some evidence on this. One of the variables which is presumably correlated with the amount of energy that the therapist puts into his therapy is how fully he writes it up. In fact, in our series, when one makes a comparison of the fullness of recording with final outcome, the correlation is slightly positive but not significantly so. In my book, I published a tentative result about therapists' enthusiasm, suggesting that those therapists who were seeing their first case tended to do better with that case than with subsequent cases. This didn't stand up to subsequent examination so that we have ended up with no positive evidence about the amount of energy that the therapist puts into his therapy. Some evidence about style also exists. There is a very little-known and a very fascinating study by Fosberg in Pittsburgh, who used to process notes of the outpatient department of his hospital and correlated—not terribly profoundly, since he didn't use dynamic criteria—final outcome with the style in which the notes were written up. There was, in fact, a very significant correlation between good outcome and the therapist who recorded give-and-take interaction between himself and the patient. The ones whose attitude in the write-up was distant and who made theoretical formulations about the patient tended to get results that were not as good. Still, it's obviously an enormous problem.

Dr. Dongier:

One always wonders whether the notes reflect appropriately what goes on in the interview.

Dr. Malan:

Yes, but the way the therapist writes up the interview obviously reflects something about his attitude toward what is going on. Agreed, there is no one-to-one relationship between the two.

Question from the floor:

I'd like to make a comment pertaining to technique. Something occurred to me while watching the tapes this morning with Dr. Davanloo, and I watched this afternoon's tape a little differently. To use quotes out of this afternoon's tapes, the style of which may be at least one thing I found in terms of similarity in both, I think potentially they may relate to outcome. Dr. Sifneos is describing to the patient, saying, "Now let us try to understand; let us look." At another point he speaks of "a problem that we have to solve." Later on the patient says, "I don't like talking about this." Dr. Sifneos says, "But it's better to know about things," and he continues, and the patient's comment is: "Okay, I'm going to try." I think there were some studies in New Jersey on the level of empathy that therapists have as a variable that hadn't been measured much before an outcome study, and there is a relevant paper by Ralph Greenson on the working alliance which I would like to mention, because one of the things that struck me as a unifying feature of both interviews, though the style was quite different, was that both therapists seemed to have a great deal of respect for their patients. They seemed to indicate that they were going to be with them. I think, in some of Greenson's work about unsuccessful analysis and some of the reasons for it, that the formation of a strong and affective working alliance is one of the common things I have seen here.

Dr. Sifneos:

I think that such an alliance is crucial. It relates to the importance of establishing a therapeutic interaction and a therapeutic contract, and it involves a mutual approaching of the problem, as something which is foreign, to be looked at and understood despite the fact that there might be pain involved. At times the therapist may act as an adversary to the patient because of the resistance, as we saw so nicely this morning in Dr. Davanloo's case. When we succeed in establishing a working alliance with the patient, then the treatment is proceeding on the right course.

Comment from the floor:

I think also that there is a large amount of research which has been reported in this area, which supports the concept that the greater the degree of respect shown to the patient and the higher the degree of empathy given the patient, the more successful the therapeutic outcome.

Comment from the floor:

I would like to emphasize Dr. Sifneos' extraordinarily personal way of empathizing positively with the patient when she has to deal so fast with so deep a significant problem for her as well as his timing, which I feel is perfect. I was finding that the countertransference was in some way helping the positive transference all the time in this case. Also in another part of the session, when she is seducing him, he assures her in a very natural and spontaneous way, showing clearly that he knows this and that it is part of the treatment. Essentially, I want to stress empathy, and the appearance of humor to bring emotion in so natural and spontaneous a way.

Question from the floor:

My question is really a technical one. I would like to ask Dr. Sifneos whether, despite the fact that he is very empathic with this patient, he thinks that the ability to avoid the transference neurosis lies in his keeping a cool atmosphere in the room by using reassurance, by using notes and writing notes. He is very close to her in some ways but still he keeps quite an objectifying distance. Was this done consciously to avoid the development of transference neurosis?

Dr. Sifneos:

The answer is no. I take notes on all of my patients in short-term psychotherapy as well as psychoanalysis. It is of the greatest importance, I feel, for research purposes. I have discussed this while training residents, who never take notes. I disagree with them. I have found that it does not hinder my style or my dealings with the patient. I don't think that it is to avoid the transference neurosis—which should be avoided at all costs, but not by this means. I avoid the transference neurosis by not getting involved in the pregenital characterological issues.

Question from the floor:

Most of the questions have been in reference to outpatient therapy, and I would like to ask a question in reference to in-patient service: Can this kind of short-term dynamic therapy be used in this situation? In the United States, we are finding that inpatient services are having to take on patients for increasingly shorter periods of time because of insurance purposes, and I would like to ask whether this kind of therapy can be used in an inpatient service where the milieu is set up to deal with the patient who cannot tolerate the anxiety which may come to the surface. I am speaking now of patients who have more primitive problems and whose anxiety is suppressed by the milieu.

Dr. Malan:

I don't know anything about this because we are an entirely outpatient clinic, but I believe there is some evidence from Oslo on this. Dr. Heiberg wrote a paper on this subject.

Dr. Dahl:

A study of inpatients at the University Clinic in Oslo found that 8 percent of the inpatients could tolerate this kind of psychotherapy, but I think this figure was too high since when they reproduced it in the outpatient department they came up with only 4 percent.

Dr. Sifneos:

In reference to the questions about inpatients: In my experience, one cannot do short-term dynamic psychotherapy in an inpatient unit. The ward setting is anxiety-suppressive and we want to be anxiety-provoking. The two don't go together. We should not give the patient a double message.

Chapter 20

Techniques of Short-Term Dynamic Psychotherapy (I)

D. H. MALAN

"The Case of the Woman in Mourning"

Pt: I feel better than I did on Friday.

Th: I imagined you might, but it was an important session on Friday. It seemed to indicate that you'd been hiding from yourself—no, to put it another way, that you had been making out to yourself that you were much better than you were.

Pt: I felt I was much better, and I thought, Now I'll start getting better and better. It's the whole business of thinking that it's just time. I seemed to be meeting more people in the last six weeks, but it seems to be so unsatisfying—that's what I felt. And this isn't right. I'm sort of feeling that with the people I thought were beyond superficial, it's not very satisfying with them either. I guess I was struck when you said you thought I hadn't really realized or been sad about leaving America, and I thought about that quite a bit, and I think there's a lot there, but somehow I seem to feel, although I used to get depressed and have bad times—but I didn't think it was like this; this bad.

Th: Before you left America?

Pt: Yes, when I was there. It's hard to say because I was changing all the time. But I couldn't understand it last week when I felt so bad, just as much as, as I've said, after Simon, and after W———, which were hard times, and, you know, I hadn't lost anyone then, last week, so I didn't understand why I felt so bad. I just felt like I'd lost everything. I just didn't care much. I felt bad for the next day or two, and then J——— called me, and I wasn't tearful any more after that, and I haven't been since. I saw him, and it went well.

Th: It sounded to me, thinking about it afterwards, as if you might be using each new relationship, including the one with J——— and with me, and in the sense of putting so much hope in them, you forgot about the past sadness, you see, as if you're using the new relationships as a defense against facing the sadnesses which hadn't yet been dealt with.

Pt: Yes, that's what you said, and I thought a lot about that. I think that might be right. I did notice then that it seems when I talk to people my thoughts always go back to America. I always think of examples of things there as though somehow my center is there and not here. But I guess I distrust that because it's like—I think I felt that about England when I'd been in America about a year or two. That's why I guess I think it's just time that I stopped thinking that way about America after a year or two. At first I always thought of examples of things, how things are in England, everything is better in England, but I stopped. Maybe I will here. I guess I'm afraid I won't somehow. I'm so much more aware now than I was eight years ago. It seems it shouldn't take as long—ever since I've come back, I've known about being sad, about losing life there. I've just been aware of it and I feel it, but it shouldn't be taking this long to feel good about things. I don't feel good about things, really, at all. Work is all right. That's one thing that's all right. It's just that I get so tired, and I feel like I must seem very unenthusiastic because I just don't feel like being bothered with things. Everything is a drag. I'm not sure whether to cool it for a while. I can always go back. I can make myself go back, although I don't usually believe in making myself do things I don't feel like doing. I had kind of a funny dream last night. I haven't dreamed much for a while, and I haven't remembered anything. This one was that I was going to leave home, leave London and my job, and it was obviously a very clear plan that I was going to live in Wales with my brother and share a flat with him. That's my brother G———, who is younger than me. It was all sort of set, and I sort of thought that I'd decided to change my mind and stay where I am, because I thought, Well, I've got so much to leave; I've got a job. My mother said to me that she thought I didn't like it there last year. You kept saying, "You're not happy." And I thought that was true, and I started thinking about it. Should I go or not go? It's a very nice flat, and I'm sure it's very modern and nice. Anyway, in the end, I decided not to go, and my brother was cross with me. He said, "You let me down, it was all set, all planned." And I thought, Who knows, he's got a girl friend now, and she'll probably go and stay with him so it won't be too bad for him. So in a kind of way, that's what happened, and the whole feeling that I've got is very sort of dull and hopeless. Part of me wants to talk about last year, and another part of me is really feeling like sort of self-pity, really. But it's depressing to talk about being depressed.

Th: Can you give any associations to the dream? What about going to join your brother in Wales, for instance? What do you make of that?

Pt: Well, that's where I was in college. I hate Wales; at least, I did then. Perhaps I wouldn't now. I would hate to live with my brother. Sounds horrible. I wasn't excited about it. It was just like something that had been planned, but it didn't feel like me. I was going along with something that didn't really feel like me, I think.

Th: Yes, exactly.

Pt: I'm terribly different from G———. There couldn't be two more different people.

Th: In what sense?

Pt: Well, he's the one, I think I told you about it, he seems kind of rigid to me. He's been much warmer lately. He, for the first time, has a girl friend. Sort of a serious girl friend. He doesn't value the things I value.

Th: The two alternatives in the dream are both bad ones, aren't they? Either you go along with something that somebody else has arranged for you, it seems, which is absolutely the opposite of what you'd like to do. Or alternatively, you stay where you are, in a state of apathy. And neither is a very good alternative.

Pt: That's right.

Th: So the dream is about a feeling of hopelessness, you see? The only alternatives you've got are worthless.

Pt: That's where I am. I don't know. I don't think I'm getting anywhere at all. I feel like I'm going round and round. I guess I feel very lonely. Probably the best time is when I'm working and I can forget about me and get into something else.

Th: Yes, but that's just covering up.

Pt: I think it's a bit like that with J——— because then I forget about me for a while.

Th: I've been having, running through my mind, something you said about ten minutes ago. It looks as if you want to be closer to other people than they want to be to you. As far as Simon was concerned, and probably from what you say about J———, this may well be true, but one must remember that it was you who left Mary, and Mary didn't leave you. I keep thinking of this. It's one of the puzzles of your story. The fact that you left Mary. Mary represents—and she is perhaps the most important person here—she represents the whole life that you built up for yourself there, yet you left. I thought I understood it, but I'm not quite sure now. You see, you—someone to whom closeness means so much, and that's unquestionably true—you threw it all up.

Pt: That hurts.

Th: Well, it wasn't meant to hurt, but if it did, so be it.

Pt: Perhaps I decided to come back for something kind of abstract, which was—but I saw myself settled and near my family, married and with children. As I say, perhaps that's kind of abstract.

Th: No, I don't think it's abstract. I don't think somebody does something like that for any abstract reason.

Pt: I saw that, and I really liked that; and it seemed more important to me than Mary or being there.

Th: All right, I see that. It's not abstract exactly, but I keep thinking of the saying "A bird in the hand is worth two in the bush." It's abstract in the sense that you threw up something you really did have for something which you had no idea whether you could have or not.

Pt: That's true.

Th: But, at the same time, it was important enough for you—and this is the way that it is not abstract—it was important enough for you to give up all that you had built for yourself.

Pt: It is important to me.

Th: I'll tell you: it's suddenly come to me that perhaps the problem is about not being able to fully mourn each thing that you lose. You've sort of given indications to me now of not having properly gotten over—even in well over a year now—not having properly got over the loss of America. And the indication is, from how you gave up America in order to come here, that you somehow haven't been able to get over the loss of the family and needed to return to it. But really, I would guess that the problem is—not really being able to get over these losses, although I have a feeling that the loss of the relation with Simon was something you did mourn and get through—I may be wrong, I don't know about that—but it does seem that the problem is that in certain situations you were not able to mourn and get over them and always wanted to return to them.

Pt: I've been thinking lately that I'm not sure that I got over Simon completely.

Th: You obviously haven't completely, but from what you described about the way you mourned him when you did break up, it seemed to me to be the way everybody mourns.

Pt: It would have been a lot easier if he would have let me go, too, because he never did. I mean it's easier to get over a person than a life. Everything else doesn't shift. That's the thing that kept me going with losing him—sort of nothing is going to change my world. But I don't have a world any more, and I don't seem to be able to make a new one. I don't think I've been able to, and I guess I feel like I never will, which is really frightening. I thought, well, there would be another Mary and another Simon in time. I don't know, maybe when you find something good, you have to not leave, or maybe I just didn't value it enough.

Th: That's rather a strange thing to say. Maybe when you found something good, you have to not leave. I would have thought that that was almost self-evident. It has to be sufficiently good, of course.

Pt: I just never really let myself think that a friendship with a woman could be that important to me. I could only have that kind of relationship with a man. I mean, I went to America to be with Fred, but I couldn't go to America to be with Mary. It's just as though women friends sort of come and go.

Th: I wasn't ever suggesting that it was only Mary. The point is you used the word yourself. It was your life.

Pt: Yes. Ever since you said I was depressed about leaving America, when I first came here, I've remembered how about three weeks before I left one night we had a really good party in the apartment where I lived, and it looked really nice, and it was a good party with people whom I cared about and who cared about me, and the next morning, T———, that was my boyfriend, and I sort of ripped the place apart. That's how it felt to me, because people were coming to pick up things that we were selling, like my desk, bookshelves, and this and that; and I got so upset by the end of the day I was really tearful, and I said to T——— "It just breaks my heart." It was like my actual life was being torn up. I've always hated to move. I remember when we left the East, how sad I felt to leave the place where we lived, even though I had been homesick for a long time; but it was home.

Th: The ripping the place apart was out west, just before you came back to England? You were saying something very evocative there about destroying the place you loved because it's not going to be with you any longer.

Pt: You mean destroying it because I'm angry with it?

Th: Yes, I do mean that.

Pt: I guess the implication is that I can never move because it's like that when you move. I've always disliked it, packing everything up.

Th: Well, no, I think you've suddenly said something very deep that might go to the heart of this whole thing; and that is, when you lose something, even if it is by your own actions, as this was, that you are so angry that you want to destroy it and then you're left empty.

Pt: An alternative being what?

Th: The alternative, just to be very sad about things, and to go through your sadness, and to come out the other side, and to start again somewhere else.

Pt: I thought I could do that. Perhaps there is something in the way. I guess there is such a thing as jumping into something new and not being so ambivalent about it, because when I left the East Coast, there was a loss; but a year after, a little over a year after, I was sort of saying to somebody that I had so much more energy. I guess I was feeling relatively good. That certainly hasn't happened here yet. But I really loved the West Coast as a place, and it was sort of mine. I found it myself and chose it and moved there. You have to work hard to get a job there, and that was my project, and I succeeded. So I guess it made it special. It was the first place I've ever really chosen in my life, whereas coming here I wanted to be near my family. London is the only place where there are a lot of things going on, so therefore it had to be London. The West Coast was really mine in my life, and it was different.

Th: I absolutely agree with that, but the mystery is why you gave it up.

Pt: I feel like saying, "Isn't that obvious?"

Th: It isn't obvious. It's not obvious to me. It's obvious to you, so you tell me.

Pt: I guess, just the belief that family is the most important thing, and nothing else is. But somehow I felt the family was more important than choosing somewhere to live. It meant something to me that was special. I guess that's what I thought, but I've got to think my family is the most important thing somehow. They expect that of me.

Th: Wait a minute. That's something very different, isn't it? That's what is expected of you, but not what you're actually wanting to do within yourself?

Pt: I thought I was, obviously. I never thought that was important before just now. I mean I never saw so clearly the difference. No, I was aware of it, because I had come back to England for three weeks in the spring before I came back here and I had a really great time. It was my sister's wedding, and we were all very close, and it was nice, and I said, "I'm going to move back." At first they didn't believe me, and then I went and looked for a job, so it was settled. I went back to the West Coast, and the plane landed, and I sort of looked at the sea and the city from the plane, and I thought, Well, how can I go away from this place? I was puzzled because I sort of thought that I'd have to try this England business, and if it doesn't work out then I can come back. But I knew that that was a problem. Maybe it was more important than I thought to choose a place.

Th: I'm reminded of what I infer to be one of the major themes of your previous therapy. It's to do with your relation to your father, in particular, rather than your family in general. Something to do with: "Were you allowed to be yourself as opposed to having to be what everybody else expected you to be?" And one of the things that came out—and I'm only making a lot of guesses and inferences from the small amount that you've told me—but one of the things that came out was your anger, or the important thing that emerged first was your anger with your husband, and behind that, presumably your anger with your father about not being allowed to be yourself and having to conform to what they expected. Now, you're telling me, you see, that you chose the West Coast yourself, and this was really one of the big moments of your life in which it was one of the first things that you had really done and chosen for yourself. And yet you're not for certain telling me, but you've almost said it, that the ghost, so to speak, hadn't fully been laid. The ghost of you having to do all that is expected of you, and therefore you have to give up the whole of what you built up and come back and be with your family. Your dream is about—I couldn't get this, though I saw the references—but your dream is about that it's all been arranged for you to go and live with your brother in Wales, which is the last thing you want to do. It seems to me that you're saying you came back to England not in order to please yourself, but to please your family.

Pt: That could be. I have to think about that. A lot of what you're saying has helped me. It's helpful. As much as I felt right being there, I loved it there, I felt when I was with Simon, and I felt after I wasn't with him, isolated. Like I had nowhere to go at times, like Christmas. I felt deprived of warmth.

Th: This is one thing that I've always said that has never been sufficient. You see, I've struggled with this. One of the mysteries of your life is why you came back to England? The thing that I said to you before is that there was unfinished business at home, that somehow you needed to come back and try and get from your family what in fact they had never given you, which is the closeness that you seek in all your relationships. And that you could not let this be, so to speak. And you remember I said to you in the second or third session that you couldn't allow yourself to think that in fact it wasn't there and never would be. Although I've said that to you, it's never been sufficient, it's never really explained why you came back. And now it looks as if there is another root to it, namely, that it is somehow a feeling that you have got to come back to please them, that you've got to do what they expect of you. You've come to the other one, you see, about Christmas. This is why I suddenly reminded you that we talked about this six or seven sessions ago. It wasn't enough, but you are now saying this in the context of the other one as well. Perhaps the two together might explain it.

Pt: I guess I'm sort of still resisting saying I gave that up to be here, being with my family for Christmas, even though it's so, so... It's not really what I need from people. It's hard to imagine being without that. I just don't know. I'm confused, feeling depressed and everything. Yet things like doing things with my goddaughter here give me great satisfaction, and I knew they would, and at times like that I'm glad to be here. Maybe that's not enough for life.

Th: But in comparison to what you had on the West Coast it isn't, is it? I mean, it can't be, but somehow you feel it ought to be.

Pt: I'm confused about places and people. I mean, as we talk, it seems to me that maybe places are more important than I ever thought. Because there are people here. I don't seem to feel good in terms of friendship, but there obviously are people here I could feel very warmly about and close to, but maybe having chosen a place that is sort of yours is much more important than I ever thought it was.

Th: You're referring to the West Coast or are you referring to home? It's not clear.

Pt: I was thinking of the West Coast. I see home as sort of connected with my childhood. I'm flashing back now to the fact that years ago, on the West Coast, I went with a friend to see a medium, and I asked her if I would go back to England, and she said I would go back and visit my family but I would stay in America. So when I came back here I said the medium was wrong, and for some reason I flashed back to that now.

Th: She might still be right. Let's stop here.

Dr. Nemiah:

In our workshop we felt that we could really see a spectrum of approaches; that is to say, Dr. Sifneos was at one end of the spectrum with confrontation, focusing, etc., and at the other end was Dr. Malan, who seemed to many of us far less active than Dr. Sifneos, and in fact some of us wondered how this might be different from long-term analytically oriented psychotherapy. And we felt that Dr. Davanloo fell somewhere in the middle, perhaps closer to Dr. Sifneos, in his approach, and that he combined the best of both possible worlds in some ways.

The question that we could not answer and that was troubling us was this: Here we have three therapists with quite different approaches in some ways, and yet clearly all three of them are very skilled and all three of them we know get very good results with patients. Now, what does that mean?

Dr. Mann:

In watching the first part of the interview, the workshop was impressed by the feeling that was going on between the patient and the therapist, and how much empathy was there. And this was a moving session. Later on, there was a feeling in the group that Dr. Malan was not active enough, did not interpret the transference that was developing, and avoided the issue of anger and talking about it with the patient and interpreting that part to the patient. Some of the members of our workshop raised the question that there was some countertransference, and that Dr. Malan was avoiding that subject.

Dr. Kravitz:

Regarding Dr. Malan's technique with this patient, the workshop felt that there was a kind of sharing in a trial-and-error way of both trying to arrive at the focus and sharpening it—and to a point to arrive at it by mutual agreement. The members of the workshop raised the question, Could one differentiate this session from an analytic session, since there were a lot of silences and allowing the patient to associate?

Dr. Naiman:

Dr. Malan's technique provoked a considerable amount of controversy, and the view was that he wasn't active enough and could have dealt more with the transference. The possibility was raised that the patient's aggression could have been a way of maintaining her separation, individuation. The question was raised that, in view of the patient's problem, just how long would this therapy take and was it a case for brief therapy?

Dr. Moll:

With regard to Dr. Malan's technique, there was a great deal of discussion as to whether he wasn't too much a follower of classical analysis in short-term psychotherapy treatment, and that there was much more scope for free association in his technique. And also there was the question whether he was at all times in charge of the situation or whether the patient was leading. But as the session proceeded, the view changed and the group felt that he was very much in charge, and there was a high admiration for his skill.

Dr. Strupp:

The workshop thought there was not much evidence of anxiety-provoking interpretation. They raised the question whether there was a focal problem. The patient seemed to act out her longing to get from the therapist what she hadn't had from significant figures in her past, and indeed Dr. Malan seemed willing to provide her with some of these narcissistic supplies.

I would like to note that perhaps in terms of long-term perspective or analytic therapy, I think that what we have been viewing here is really a variety of psychoanalytic therapies, the application of psychoanalytic principles and techniques at their best. And I think what we are dealing with is a continuum that extends from perhaps long-term analysis on the one end to short-term on the other; but the techniques, while they are at times adapted, are really the same principles and techniques that should operate at all times.

Dr. Yung:

The question that was raised in our group was, Does Dr. Malan have in mind to focalize the problem of this patient on the process of mourning? If that is the case, then this was a beautiful session. That was the way we perceived the process. For our group, it was impossible to compare the techniques because in our opinion the patients were different.

Regarding the silence, many of us thought that this in itself is far more anxiety-provoking. The general view of our group was that Dr. Malan was, generally speaking, not active.

Dr. Abdelmalek:

Our workshop felt that with this patient Dr. Malan shared the process of mourning, and that he allowed the patient to experience sadness. The general view related to the specificity of Dr. Malan's approach and how his technique is different from a longer-term psychotherapy. Also, it was our view that with this patient he did not deal with the transference situation.

Dr. Smith:

Regarding this psychotherapy session, there was a general question in our workshop—how much does Dr. Malan's technique really differ from a longer-term psychotherapy? And there was also the question of potential suicide in this patient. The general feeling was that Dr. Malan was very supportive of her, and that there were transference issues that came up but were never discussed.

Dr. Malan:

Regarding the question about how my technique in the treatment of this patient differs from psychoanalysis, the answer is that it is very much less passive than it appears. For instance, the silences: you have to watch the patient to know whether the silence is a productive one or a resistant one. It was quite obvious that the silence was a productive one, and I deliberately left her to find her own route toward what she wanted to say. The principle on which I operate with all patients, in fact, is to try to help to guide the patient toward finding what he is feeling most prominently at any given point. I have very clearly in my mind what the basic focus is. Someone asked the question, "Did he really have a focus?" Well, yes. Of course I had a focus. The focus is what it meant to her to leave the United States and to come to England, which had led her to a state of depression. Now, my general formulation was that it was about loss, and that she had experienced a very severe loss in her childhood, namely, of her nurse at the age of five. And my original plan was that I would relate the loss of all that she had built up for herself in the States to the loss of her nurse.

Now, she had painted a far more favorable picture of what her family was like than transpired in the therapy. In fact, it became very clear during the course of the therapy that she had had neither understanding nor acceptance nor care from either her mother or her father, really, at any time in her life, and that the only really good experience had in fact been with the nurse. It was quite clear from the way in which she related to me, and from the progressive emotional growth in her life, that she must somehow have had some very good experience in her life.

As to the question whether this patient is really suitable for short-term dynamic psychotherapy, the answer is, I don't know because the therapy is not finished. All I know is that we are exploring, trying to deal with these severe problems in brief therapy, and we will just have to see what happens.

Now, then, I think the thing I would want to say above all else is that what I am pursuing the whole time is rapport and communication. And if one is sensing the degree of communication that is going on, then one at all times has an indication of whether what the patient says is close to what she is really feeling or not.

The clear-cut example was this: In session twelve, she started with a dream about her grandmother and aunt dying, and we worked on this for ten minutes and got absolutely nowhere. I have no more idea now of what that dream means than I did then, or what one could do with it, and both of us then reached the point at which we realized there was something wrong with that discussion.

Now, that was me being active. I was pursuing her dream and it was obviously wrong; so I therefore made another active step, which was to say to her, "Look here, it doesn't seem to me that what you're talking about is what you really want to talk about, you know, what's happening?" She then says, "Well, I had an experience today which has disturbed me." Now, I didn't know whether that was important or not, but it seemed to me that since the previous discussion had been useless we'd better go into what that experience had been, and I hoped that it would lead to something. Well, in fact, it was an experience, as you know, about anger and separation, and since that was my focus I therefore was able to say to her, "Look here, that was an experience of anger about separation." What this led to was the most important moment of the whole therapy so far: namely, a moment of both tremendous feeling and of new insight to both of us—that, in fact, she had got depressed because of what she hoped for when she arrived in this country and because it wasn't there—and then she brought out with tremendous feeling this dream about her father's rejection. That moment was arrived at by a process of empathy with the patient. You may call it passive, if you wish, but I don't think it's passive.

Now, in regard to a question that has been raised about termination. You could see that with this patient the issue of termination is going to be absolutely crucial. You are seeing what is still the middle game of this therapy, and therefore termination is not yet an issue. I didn't feel that it was an issue in those sessions, and I didn't deal with it. She already had, in fact, actually come and cried in the session about the fact that she was going to miss me for one week over Christmas, so that we know termination is going to be a major issue. What one usually finds over the termination issue is that of course it will not be a separate issue at all, but it will be straight on the focus. There will be an aspect about it which is all about the focus, and in this patient it will be because the focus is about mourning and loss and anger, about those things. So the next ten sessions which I'll have with her will be about termination. Patients can be divided into classes, so to speak, those in which termination is a major issue and those in which it isn't; also, I think techniques can be divided in the same way. It's quite clear that with the kind of technique used by Dr. Sifneos and Dr. Davanloo, the kind of patient they see, termination is not an issue. With the kind of technique I use with this kind of patient, it is a major issue.

Dr. Straker:

There was a related issue that came up in our workshop, and that was the question, How final is the termination? Is it an open or closed issue? That is, after the patient leaves treatment, is there an open door to return, and if so, when?

Dr. Malan:

Yes, this is an important question. We always, nowadays, set a time limit from the beginning, and we prefer to do it as James Mann does it—in terms of a date rather than the number of sessions. It's so much easier to remember. Again, what James Mann says is that this date becomes a crucial issue in therapy. It's denied at first, but then later on it becomes a crucial issue. And with us often our therapies are done by trainees who are at the clinic for only a year and cannot say to the patient, "I will see you again." Now, what I do, in fact, is always say to the patient that the end of regular sessions will not necessarily be the end of your therapy. If you've got further things you want to discuss, you can come back later. But they always perceive the termination of regular sessions as if it were an absolute termination. It doesn't soften it, really, to tell them that.

Dr. Davanloo:

My comment on what Dr. Malan said regarding termination is that I don't agree with James Mann's position in prescribing a definite number of sessions. To me, that is too artificial. But I definitely agree with Dr. Malan that with patients who come with a predominantly oedipal problem, termination is usually not going to be a difficulty. With sicker patients, however, as I have said before, it might. For example, in "The Case of the Cement-Mixer Man" that I presented, when we came to the issue of termination he expressed the fear that all his difficulties might come back; he said, "For thirty years he had lived like this; how could he believe this will not come back?" An exploration into this brought into focus the other triangle, namely, the patient, his father and his brother. A lot of transference feelings came out, which were then linked with his wish—that he had had a closer relationship with his father. So, as you see, during termination there is also an opportunity to work through unresolved problems.

# Chapter 21

Techniques of Short-Term Dynamic Psychotherapy (II)

H. DAVANLOO

"The Case of the Man Obsessed with the Small Size of His Genitals"

The patient is a twenty-nine-year-old male, married for two and a half years. He was seen in a psychiatric emergency service in a state of panic after his wife left him for another man. The psychiatrist who saw him gave him a minor tranquilizer, which he did not take, and he was then referred to the psychiatric clinic.

His marriage was described as a sadomasochistic one in which he humiliated his wife by frequently calling her "frigid" and "lesbian." He was close to his wife, but after marriage he became "animalistic"— he wanted only sex, no emotional involvement, and he forced her into the sex act. Six months prior to the separation, his wife began an affair with another man. At that time the patient and his wife started to see a marriage counselor. The final crisis that brought about the separation took place during the twelfth counselling session. The wife ran out and went to the house of the man she was having an affair with. The patient ran after her through the streets and subsequently was brought to the psychiatric clinic accompanied by the marriage counselor.

There was also a general problem in interpersonal relationships. The patient described it as feeling insecure, and his behavior could be seen as a self-defeating, self-punishing pattern. He would set up a competitive situation and manage to be the loser.

The problem in heterosexual relationships was there all along, prior to marriage as well.

His father was a salesman and was away during the early life of the patient. He described his relationship with his father as "hostile" and indicated that his father saw him as a rival.

The patient's relationship with his mother was described as very close in the early phase, but later on it became ambivalent. He said he resented it when his father was at home because the close relationship with his mother was disturbed.

During the initial interview, a severe triangular oedipal problem was revealed. One of the patient's earliest memories is that when he was five years old he went to the beach with his father, who wanted to teach him to swim. The father pushed the patient's head under the water, and the patient felt very frightened; ever since that time he has had a fear of putting his head under water while swimming. Another memory is related to age five or six. The patient was behind his parents' bedroom door with his sister, who is two years younger than he.

Another memory had to do with a "genital sensation" whenever he was with his mother and she showed some physical expression of affection.

He reported another memory in which his father and uncle were sitting by a hot stove. His father put a dime on it, then put it on the floor, then called the patient into the room to pick it up; the patient burned his hand, and he said his father "got a charge out of it."

Another memory has to do with the large size of his father's genitals. As far back as he can remember, he has compared the size of his own genitals with those of others, and even now in a locker room he looks at the genitals of other men. He admitted that he has been obsessed with the idea of whether his penis is large enough to satisfy a woman, and this was expressed in his behavior with both his wife and the girls with whom he had had sexual relationships prior to his marriage. After intercourse he always questioned his sexual partner as to whether she had enjoyed it and even directly asked if his penis was large enough.

After the initial interview, psychological testing was done consisting of an MMPI and projective techniques, and their view was that the patient was primarily a male hysteric. The psychological test reads: "His reality testing is generally good, although his perception can be quite distorted when sexual issues are involved." "He would become anxious when confronted with his passive-dependent needs, castration anxiety, and repressed homosexual wishes." "Considerable analysis of his defenses against his unconscious conflicts would be necessary."

In terms of the psychodynamics, at the end of the initial interview the problem was considered a triangular oedipal one: the reenactment of the old rage and guilt reaction; his mother as the center of his universe, then suddenly not paying any attention to him and cuddling with his father ("Then she came to me for something, and for something else she went to him. How could she do that to me?"); reference to the larger genitals of his father.

The question was raised, Is one dealing with a purely oedipal problem or is there also a homosexual component? Regarding the latter, if it is simply because of his response to his mother going to bed with his father, perhaps he should be the mother; the mother should be replaced, and he should be the one with his father—a kind of defensive homosexuality. He feels furious toward his mother for going to bed with his father. "I should be there with my father because he is going to give me much more love than she is going to give me."

When he married Miss K., she took his mother's name, and the fury and rage which belonged to the past was now poured onto his wife until finally he pushed her into the arms of another man. Then he has a severe attack of anxiety. I saw him originally for two sessions, for both evaluation and to deal with the crisis: he couldn't sleep at night and had thoughts such as How could she do this to me? and many other ideas and fantasies related to his wife and her lover. He had the recurrent thought that the other man must have larger genitals. Early in therapy the question of homosexuality was brought into focus, and he admitted to having frequent thoughts of whether he is latently homosexual.

I saw his wife separately for two interviews, and it became evident that she also has psychological problems of many years' duration. She spontaneously announced by the second interview that her extramarital affair was not a healthy relationship, and she decided to break away from that relationship, enter therapy and return to her husband on a trial basis. She was assigned to another therapist.

(2ND PSYCHOTHERAPY SESSION)

Pt: That tonight I would become more introspective, and that's what I'm talking about in terms of anticipation.
Th: But when you were talking in the previous session you were trying to move away from the focus of your difficulties, weren't you?
Pt: Right.
Th: And I was trying to bring you into the focus of your difficulties.

Are you saying that in a sense your apprehension has to do with that? That you want to move away from the focus?

Pt: No, I don't think so. I want to get more into it. I want to get more involved. Perhaps I am trying to move away, and it seems that I'm moving away, but I've been thinking about it and trying to relate to particular situations in my past.

Th: Like what? Can we look at those things in the past?

Pt: I was discussing my own personal sexual behavior with my wife and saying that I think my sexual desires or my sexual drives have something to do with what happened in my past, and in addition to having a normal sex drive I feel I have certain abnormal feelings toward sex.

Th: Could we look at this? What do you have in mind about "normal" and "abnormal"?

Pt: For instance, I think I do have a strong sex drive, but in addition I don't feel right about myself physically in terms of my sexual prowess.

Th: Do you want to tell me about it?

Pt: For one thing I think I have a small penis, and for me that's a large concern. In addition, I find myself feeling that gaining satisfaction out of being with somebody else, or getting satisfaction, or getting pleasure from being with someone else, a woman, has to be in the sex act. It always has to be sexual in nature, my relationship with a woman. Otherwise it's not meaningful. I'm concerned. I said something about being a pervert last week, but the more I thought about it the more I sort of said, "That came from me, and there must be some reason why I said it."

Th: But you see you use terms, and then you don't describe them. For instance, a moment ago you said "abnormal sex" but then you started talking about the small penis. Then also you used the word "pervert." But somehow you don't want to elaborate on these issues.

Pt: I would say sex is almost an obsession with me.

Th: This is what you refer to as "abnormal"?

Pt: Abnormal, right.

Th: In what way is sex an obsession with you?

Pt: Being with my wife is—for me, it always reverts to a sexual relationship. It always sort of comes down to sex play. I'm always interested in fondling her breasts and touching her, and basically forcing her to have sex with me, sometimes when she doesn't

want to. Sometimes when she does, but I'm always the aggressor, and really I'm very forceful at times. I force myself upon her as opposed to letting things happen naturally.
Th: Has this been happening all through your marriage?
Pt: Yes, I'd say so.
Th: When you say you force yourself upon her, exactly what do you mean?
Pt: Basically, if she goes along with it, it terminates in the sex act, but if she doesn't, and she gets upset about it, we stop there. I'm constantly trying to make love to her when I have the opportunity, when the opportunity presents itself. I mean, I don't come home from work and try to rape her, but when we go to bed together at night I basically try to rape her. I force myself upon her. I am constantly trying to pull up her nightgown, and things like that. I'm very forceful with her, aggressive with her.
Th: This is at present?
Pt: Yes, and in the past I was, too.
Th: All through your marriage. What was it like before?
Pt: The same thing. I was forceful with sex, very demanding, always, about sex. It seemed to me to be the only expression of love.
Th: But from what you have told me, prior to marriage you also had an emotional involvement with your wife. There was a lot of foreplay, and you also spent a lot of time together. But somehow after marriage this pattern changed. Am I right?
Pt: Yes, it's not there.
Th: Do you see a difference in the pattern of your sexual relationship with your wife? When you compare it with that prior to marriage?
Pt: We saw each other on weekends and sometimes during the week, and when we did, a lot of the time we would make love, but there was never a day-to-day relationship with each other. We didn't live with each other before we were married. She lived out in the suburbs, and I lived in town, so we sort of traveled back and forth to see each other, and in doing so we didn't see that much of each other during the week. It was primarily on the weekends, and at that point in time we'd spend weekends together. Then it was very gratifying. It was satisfying in every way.
Th: Yes, but what was it that was very gratifying for you then and is not there now? As far as your wife is concerned, one thing is that there was more affection and a lot of emotional expression

on your part, from what we know from previous sessions, that disappeared after the marriage.

Pt: Yes.

Th: So that is one change. Now, sex. You say now that you might have a pattern like rape, that you force your wife. What was it like, then, before your marriage?

Pt: I think in terms of my pattern of foreplay and sex, my approach toward her was about the same. I think perhaps there was more foreplay. There wasn't the forceful demand to get her clothes off and make love. There was more foreplay.

Th: So it was not a rape type of behavior?

Pt: No, but now it isn't, either. Now I'm more conscious of trying to make it comfortable for her.

Th: Okay. So prior to marriage there was a lot of emotional involvement. There was an expression of affection on your part. Then ultimately it ended up as a sexual relationship, and there was no pattern of rape. But when you got married, then the affection and the emotional involvement decreased and moved to a pattern which is more similar to—you used the term "animalistic," and you also refer to it now as a sort of rape pattern, that you force her. Then gradually the pattern moved more and more toward rape because she became more disinterested. Now, let's see what sort of idea you have in mind about this, because there is quite a change in this pattern. Prior to marriage there is a lot of expression of affection, a lot of involvement, and there was no rapelike pattern, but then after marriage that aspect of it declines and moves to a rapelike pattern. Something suddenly was lost in you, and it is important that we look at this.

Pt: Okay, looking into that, does that go back into my past, or does that happen...

Th: What sort of idea do you have yourself?

Pt: I would say it was something that did happen in my past, and I can relate what happens presently to me, but I still can't bring it back into the past.

Th: Do you mean some idea has popped into your head?

Pt: I asked my wife the other night whether it would be the fact that I was breast-fed. I'm very conscious of my wife's breasts, and I'm wondering if it might have something to do with that.

Th: But if you say you have interest in the breasts of your wife, how do you explain that? Because we are talking in terms of you

losing your emotional involvement with your wife, you were demonstrating love in terms of affection, you were emotionally involved prior to marriage. How would the interest in the breasts of your mother affect that?
Pt: Relating it back to my mother, if I were preoccupied with my mother's breasts, would that pattern...
Th: But so far your memories about your mother...
Pt: Are very vague or nonexistent.
Th: Supposedly today you're talking about your small penis, and you are concerned about your small penis, but what have you told me about your penis and your mother? At the age of six, what were your memories then?
Pt: That I had feelings that related, in addition to other people, to my mother in terms of feelings in bed, that I had a feeling in my penis.
Th: You had it at the age of six?
Pt: I can't pin it down to that age, but I would say that at a very young age I had those feelings. It could have been a little later on. I related this feeling in my penis to my mother.
Th: What was the idea in your head in terms of fantasies?
Pt: Lying beside her, lying next to her, the desire to be with her.
Th: Then this was a fantasy that you had?
Pt: In addition to other women. I spoke about movie stars, feeling it that way. I think it must have been later on. I must have been nine or ten, because I don't think it would have been that early. I'm quite sure it would have been a little later.
Th: You mean when you had fantasies about the movie stars?
Pt: Yes.
Th: What happened to your fantasy about your mother, then, when you started to have fantasies about movie stars?
Pt: I think it diminished somewhat. It moved away. It could have transposed itself to other women, but in reality it still existed, that I wanted my mother physically, but merely I transposed it to other things, to other females, and in doing so I guess erased my mother from the picture and transposed other females. Almost every other female I had a relationship with I had to be involved with sexually almost immediately.
Th: How old were you then?
Pt: Fifteen or sixteen.
Th: At age fifteen or sixteen. Was this your first sexual experience?

Pt: I was trying to think about that, when exactly my first sexual experience was. I think it was about fifteen or sixteen.

Th: What do you remember about that relationship?

Pt: It was at summer camp, and it was an older girl.

Th: How old?

Pt: She was one of the counselors. I think she was about eighteen or nineteen.

Th: And you were then what age?

Pt: I think I was about fifteen. I can't remember the actual date, fifteen or sixteen.

Th: What are your memories about it?

Pt: It wasn't very... you know.

Th: This was your first time?

Pt: Yes. All I can recall is her being upset because I just ejaculated right away and that was it. There was no sex play whatsoever. There was no real intercourse. It was just, almost immediately I ejaculated. It only happened once, and then after that I didn't have another experience for about a year, a year and a half. Then it was with a girl who was about the same age as I was. She was my girl friend for a while, and we started having sex, and initially it wasn't very satisfying. She was very scared. She was a virgin, and she was very frightened, but afterwards it was a bit more satisfying.

Th: When did you start to be conscious about your penis?

Pt: At about—I think I was always conscious about my penis. I'm sure from the age of eight or nine I was.

Th: But now you said you had become conscious of the size.

Pt: Oh, the size. When I was involved in athletics. I was showering with other guys, and I got to looking around and checking out other fellows.

Th: You were comparing yourself?

Pt: Yeah, right, comparing myself with others. I felt that physically I seemed to compare all right with most fellows. I'm fairly healthy physically, but in terms of penis size I seemed smaller.

Th: How old were you when you started to become concerned about the size of your penis?

Pt: About thirteen or fourteen.

Th: Why should you have started to become concerned about the size of your penis then?

TECHNIQUES OF SHORT-TERM DYNAMIC PSYCHOTHERAPY (II)   477

Pt: Maybe it was older.
Th: Why? Can you think about it? Why suddenly you became concerned about the size of your penis?
Pt: Because I felt inadequate in some way.
Th: But still you hadn't had a sexual relationship at that age.

(*The patient then related this to the size of his father's genitals.*)

Pt: His was the first penis I saw. I remember thinking about that, and saying that I should mention that. Yes. I was aware that he had a large penis, but it would have been natural. He was a grown man. I was quite young, because I would say that my father's penis would have been at eye level to me, so I would have been maybe five or six.
Th: So then you were conscious of this.
Pt: Yes.
Th: What happened?
Pt: I was curious. I never asked any questions, but I looked, and maybe just looking at him and looking at myself I was very conscious of the fact that I was different from him. If I compared, I must have felt some reason for doing so.
Th: But you talk about it in terms of "If I compared," and a moment ago I asked you about your father, and then you told me that you had this in mind to talk about. We can see that somehow here with me you prefer that I be the one who actively searches into your past experiences rather than you being the one to search. Let's look at that. Why do you think this is?
Pt: Because there's something there that I either don't want to discuss or is maybe too painful for me to discuss.

(*A transference confrontation is made, and the patient is faced with his lack of spontaneity. Then the session moves into the understanding that the period when he had genital sensations was at the time when he had his eyes on the larger genitals of his father, and also the idea that his father wanted to do away with him at the beach,. Then came the idea that his mother to some extent gave him up and preferred his father. The patient then talks about the bedroom of his parents, and*) *that he lost his mother because his father had larger genitals. The therapist makes an interpretation that his mother preferred his father to him and reminds the patient of the times he stood behind the bedroom door.)*

Pt: I have had thoughts of asking my wife whether the man she was going out with had a larger penis.

Th: Did you ask?

Pt: Yes, I did. As a matter of fact, I always asked her about what happened, what went on sexually between them. I constantly ask her about that since we've been back together.

Th: What are your ideas?

Pt: Just that we were having trouble with sex, and how could she go away and have sex with another man? She says it didn't happen for a long time, it didn't happen overnight, but she didn't go into detail. But I want to hear it; I want to hear something I know would hurt me.

Th: Something that would hurt you?

Pt: Yes, her sleeping with another man, and the idea about the penis of the other man. You know, I questioned her whether or not he has a larger penis than I have. The idea pops into my head when we have sexual relations, but she doesn't want to talk about it, and she's having difficulty feeling comfortable about having sex. She's always said that she's had a difficult time with it. I'm very demanding, and she on the other hand doesn't want to have anything to do with it. I try to get things out of her about this fellow.

Th: But this has to do predominantly with his larger genitals?

Pt: Yeah, that's the main idea.

Th: And you have also said that in a sense you had a tremendous rage toward this man, and you wanted to send some of your friends to beat him up, and then you told yourself that this wasn't rational.

(The session moves into more exploration and clarification and brings into focus the patient's fury and hostility toward his mother, which is then poured onto his wife. The therapist indicates that when Miss K. becomes Mrs X. [name of mother] the patient becomes "animalistic" and the wife takes what belongs in the past.)

(3RD PSYCHOTHERAPY SESSION)

Pt: I'd like to discuss a few things that I experienced this week. In one situation I find myself constantly calling my wife "Mom." Now, it's an expression which is perhaps significant. I don't refer to her by name. I call her "Mom" and I'm wondering whether or not this is much more significant than I make it out to be.
Th: This has always been in your marriage?
Pt: Always. It hasn't been in my mind as much.
Th: I know, but this has been the way you call your wife?
Pt: Always.
Th: How about before marriage? What did you call her?
Pt: No, not before marriage.
Th: What did you used to call her then?
Pt: By her name, but after we were married I made perhaps a transformation in my mind. I preferred to call her "Mom."

(*At this point, exploration is made into the significance of the patient calling his wife "Mom." He is now conscious about this, and his wife doesn't like it. Exploration is made into his obsession with sex, the orgasm of his wife; and it is linked with his concern about the size of his genitals. "Am I homosexual?" Also it is brought into focus that when he receives positive feedback he thinks less of the woman. The therapist explores the sex life with his wife, and when the changes took place; comparison of his genitals with others; athletic situation. There is some exploration into transference relationship, and the patient expresses that he feels inadequate with the therapist.*)

Th: Now, let's look at that. You refer to this as wasting my time.
Pt: Our time. My time. In terms of consulting, you'd get paid more than I would, but our time is still valuable.
Th: What do you have in your mind, that I get paid more than you?
Pt: Another insecurity, I suppose, in my mind.
Th: You said, "You would get paid more than I would".
Pt: An insecurity on my own part. I look to you as a highly skilled professional, and I would say in terms of being rewarded or remunerated for our work—I would say that you would get paid more than I would because of your skill. Again, that's an insecurity

on my part because perhaps I say to myself, "I'm not esteemed by society as high as you."

Th: Let's look at this part of it, because in a sense we have seen similar patterns that you have in other relationships. Is that not so?

Pt: Yes, that's right.

Th: In relationships with people you have a certain way of looking at yourself. Isn't that so?

Pt: Yes.

Th: Could we look at that also? What you describe in one aspect of your problem in relationship with women spreads into your relationships with other human beings as well. I remember vaguely you talking about a situation in the athletic field, that you might get very angry at the deficiency of another person. Am I right?

Pt: Yes, that's correct.

Th: Could we look into that?

Pt: Being very aggressive toward an individual who I felt wasn't doing his best, or perhaps wasn't doing what I thought was correct.

Th: Wasn't as good as you, you mean?

Pt: Yes, wasn't as good as me. At the same time, I can recall almost consciously making mistakes as an athlete to seek out some sort of revenge upon myself—not revenge, but to seek out some sort of expression of guilt on my own part.

Th: You mean that in one situation you would get to beat other persons, beating in that sense, and then you would set up a situation where you would be beaten?

Pt: Not that I would be beaten.

Th: A loser, then?

Pt: Yes. In a sort of team-involvement situation, I would be the one who would let the person down or let the team down. It's a way of managing to be the loser.

Th: And a while ago also you were putting yourself into a competitive situation with me, and the idea that you presented was that I am more skillful and have a better deal in this situation.

Pt: I always compare myself with others.

Th: What does this bring to your mind? You say managing to be a loser, and you also referred to it as a way of paying off the guilt. What does this bring to your mind?

Pt: Acting out the guilt that I feel about another situation, and sort of acting it out in that situation. In other words, heaping shit upon myself.

Th: But what happened in the recent part of your life that you managed to be the loser?

Pt: With my wife?

Th: Could we look at that and at this? Definitely, it is like a thread in your life that you manage to be the loser.

Pt: Right.

Th: And this relationship with your wife and this man was the climax of this. In a way, in previous relationships you set up the stage to be the loser, but in that one, really, it was a dramatic acting out of that. Isn't that so?

Pt: Yes. It was the height of loss in my mind, because I threw away from myself the thing that was most important to me. I didn't realize it at the time, but I do now .

Th: What do you see in it now?

Pt: That in throwing away my wife, in losing her to another man, I acted out something that has been on my mind since I was young, and in doing so I also came to the realization that that's in fact what I've been doing all the time and making myself feel guilty on an almost daily basis about the way I communicate with people, the way I communicate with my wife, the way I act with my wife, the way I feel about my wife. In addition to that, to throwing her away, the night I sort of beat her up and pushed her around, I don't think I was doing harm to her as much as I was doing it to myself, and finally coming to the realization that what I had been doing was wrong, and I had to move away from that and do something better with my life. This is perhaps the most conscious part of it now that is coming out, that I can move away from that and do more to feel good about myself and less insecure. That's why I'm here.

Th: So, in other words, this punitive behavior that you started to take in relationship with your wife obviously alienated your wife and set up the stage for her to run to this other man. How do you explain that to yourself?

Pt: Maybe I was setting up a crisis situation in my own way. That's pretty frightening. I don't know how I could actually say that. In other words, setting up a situation whereby I would throw away my wife to improve my own situation because she had said to me; "You've got to see a psychiatrist. You've got problems."

Th: When was that?

Pt: A couple of years ago. After about a year of marriage, she felt that I was pretty sick at times, disturbed, mentally disturbed.

Th: In what way do you mean mentally disturbed?

Pt: The way I treated her at times. I was so brutal to her and used her inadequacies to vent my frustrations.

Th: Do you think there is a link between this and the way you felt about your mother? Because in a sense you saw a split situation; you felt that for something she came to you and for something else she went to your father, and you refer to larger genitals and all the fantasies like behind the bedroom door that you have talked about. Then there was the positive and close intimate relationship, and at the same time you were furious.

Pt: With my mother, yes.

Th: And isn't it now with your wife?

Pt: I'm getting my revenge on my mother, but using my wife. I took one woman and replaced her with another. I could look at my wife as being a female and associate her with my mother.

Th: But we have discussed this, and in previous sessions it became clear that when your wife was Miss K. you had a lot of affection for her, there was a lot of emotional involvement and investment, but when Miss K. became Mrs. X., then the whole picture changes and she becomes the target of your anger and hostility. And as we discussed, you very beautifully managed that she get involved with another man, and then you can't sleep and your whole preoccupation is that this man has a larger penis than yours and that this is what attracted your wife. Now suddenly we see a new triangle—you, your wife and the other man—and the idea of the larger penis. Your mind is in their bedroom. And "How could she do that to me?" Isn't there a similarity between this triangle and the triangle of you and your father and your mother?

Pt: The idea is very disturbing, the idea of repeating something that went on between me and my parents.

(*The patient is highly charged emotionally and is close to tears.*)

Pt: Well, I have hurt my wife quite a lot. I mean, she has her own problems, but in addition I have made her life quite miserable for a long time. But now in the past two weeks we are getting to be much happier with each other; even our disagreements are much more amiable.

Th: How do you feel right now?

Pt: I feel bad. I feel upset because I have hurt my wife.

(The patient is now very close to tears but is still controlling himself.)

Th: How do you feel at this moment?
Pt: I want to cry.
Th: You feel that way; what prevents you?

(Patient cries.)

Th: Is it all because you hurt your wife, or is it also partly in relationship with your own self?
Pt: I don't know.
Th: Because, you see, one thing also about your own self in relationship with your own self is that you have a self-denying and self-punishing pattern of behavior. In a sense, you have progressive forces within yourself, positive forces within yourself, but then there is this self-defeating pattern that repeats itself over and over, and that in a sense goes opposite to your potential.
Pt: Yeah, right. One big nagging thought in my mind is that when I finished Arts I went back to college. After a year and a half I quit because I just robbed myself. I said I didn't want to, but I basically just didn't try hard enough. After I graduated from college with a Bachelor of Arts I went back and finished two years but didn't get my degree.
Th: You had two years, and then you gave it up? What do you think happened that you gave up?
Pt: Just another self-denial on my part. I just punished myself really.
Th: A self-denial?
Pt: Yes, because I now compare myself—for instance, this interplay with you about the consulting fee. I compare in a professional vein with friends. I have one in particular who is very successful. I look at him, and I think I'd be more competent than he is. This is a self-denial on my part. As a matter of fact, last year I went to McGill to see if I could get back in, and they said I would have to take an extra year. I've been taking my M.B.A. at night school. They said I would have to go back and complete my M.B.A. first and then maybe they would let me back into school because my marks were not that good, obviously, because I failed. So I went to that extent, and then I thought it over and discussed it with my wife, and she said, "If you want to, we can both work and you can go back to school." I thought about it, and I thought of the

time involved, so I just decided against it. That's been one thing that's been really bothering me.

Th: That you had to give up that idea?

Pt: I didn't have to give it up, I just didn't work hard enough at it. I almost chose to be a failure at it, another situation where I've brought about my own failure. That's another situation that's been very—I can't deny that I wouldn't like to be a professional in terms of the financial aspects of it, but more so perhaps on a day-to-day basis I would want to be a professional.

Th: So this is something that has been on your mind, that this was something that you wanted to achieve in your life and didn't, and you know that you have the potential for it. Do you think that this is also within the same complex of the difficulties?

Pt: Yes, definitely.

Th: That in a way you set up the stage to fail in what you want to do?

Pt: My crying was particularly because I hurt my wife a lot. I mean, I hurt myself a lot, too. I've cheated myself out of a lot, but I've hurt my wife, too. I think she and I are now much happier, and we're going to be much happier. I feel more committed about that now because I want to make her happy, because I think she hasn't had as much happiness in life as she could have. I know I haven't, but I think for my part I want to make her happier. I'm really acting toward that, but I've also cheated myself quite a bit, too. I don't think that's irretrievable. I think I can enjoy my life in the future, and I think what I have achieved for myself is not that negative. I have achieved some things. I think I just have to move beyond that now and be more happy with what I do for a living and more happy about my situation at home, and this is helping a lot.

Dr. Mann:

Our workshop was very impressed with Dr. Davanloo's technique, his ability to get the patient to explore different areas. We felt he had a clear focus.

Dr. Strupp:

The group felt it was an outstanding example of an interpretation at the right time in the context, when the feelings were mobilized. As we saw somewhere toward the end, the conflict came into focus, resulting in the patient crying; and it is at such times that typically in analytic work important structural change occurs and quite clearly in this case did occur.

Dr. Abdelmalek:

Our workshop felt that the technique and total process of the treatment was fabulous. There was the moment when the patient developed deep emotional insight, and there was corrective emotional experience. Also, the question was raised that maybe the patient is subordinating himself to Dr. Davanloo.

Dr. Zaiden:

It was felt that the session was a very moving one; there was a great learning process showing how the oedipal conflict of this man was worked out in a most beautiful way at the end. Around the end of the session there was a moment of emotional insight associated with crying, and the therapist was very sensitive and indicated this to the patient when he said, "But you also have been hurt in the process."

Dr. Sifneos:

I would like to make a comment about Dr. Davanloo's technique in the treatment of this patient, particularly in the third session, because I think it was a splendid example not only of the dynamics but also of the unfolding resolution of his conflict, which was shown beautifully. As soon as he is able, as a result of the second session as well as after the early part of the third session, to see clearly the displacement of anger from his mother and father onto his wife, he is able to develop insight. It is at that precise moment that all the affect comes into the open. He realizes that his anger did not belong to his wife, and this realization produces the tears in a meaningful way. The reason he came for treatment had to do with his marriage falling apart. He is separated. At the end of the third session, he is not only not going to beat his wife but also he is not going to push his wife into another man's arms. Furthermore, he is not going to flunk out of school. The whole hour ends on a positive note, which proves that his problem has been resolved.

Question from the floor:

I would like to ask in reference to termination, and specifically to the technique during termination, how one can use the final termination session to further advance the therapy?

Dr. Davanloo:

We don't set up a definite number of sessions. We never tell the patient, for example, "your treatment will last for ten sessions." We might say to the patient, the treatment will be of short duration, fifteen to twenty sessions, and also at the same time communicate to him that we evaluate as we go along. Then, as we come to see that the patient now has understanding of the central structure of his neurotic pattern of behavior, and is now able to apply this understanding in his daily life and is bringing about changes in his external life, that is when we bring up termination. But the fact is, many of our patients raise the question of termination themselves. I have clinical data regarding this. In one project, in which we treated successfully 115 patients, approximately one-third of these patients were treated in between two and fifteen sessions, and we considered their problem a basically oedipal one. In this group approximately 70 percent brought up the question of termination themselves. One-third of the patients who were treated in from twenty-five to forty sessions, and where the problem was not purely oedipal, the number of patients who brought up the question of termination was much lower, around 20 percent.

I told the patient presented today that we might have anywhere between ten and fifteen sessions.

Dr. Sifneos:

We do not set up a specific time limit, and by virtue of focusing on the oedipal issue it is quite clear that we do not need to deal with more severe characterological problems. As you saw in my treatment with the male patient ("The Case of the Man with the Facade), it is impressive to see how he works up to the last hour, and only in passing says: "Well, I realize that this is the last. I will miss this therapy." As you saw also in Dr. Davanloo's male patient ("The Case of the Cement-Mixer Man"), he says: "I did the hard work myself, and now it is time for me to take charge of my own life, and the fact is that what I learned I will never forget."

Comment from the floor:

In terms of a future conference, I thought it might be useful to consider adding another input to this way of looking at brief dynamic psychotherapy, namely, from the point of view of family therapy. Now, I can't speak for all the schools of practice, but certainly in terms of what I know was being taught here at Jewish General and is being taught at McMaster, the ways in which the technique is being practiced are very similar. The content is obviously much different, but not the technique. First of all, there is very clearly the focusing upon nuclear problems. Family therapy as it is practiced at McMaster is very much centered on the brief aspects of it. The saying is that 80 percent of therapy is achieved between the sixth and tenth sessions. Second is the attention to affect and the transference in this kind of brief therapy in a different kind of setting. Thirdly, contracts again are an essential element. Again, the similarity between Dr. Davanloo and Nathan Epstein is in that sense unbelievable. Let's work for ten sessions, but we'll see how it works and it might terminate in five and it might terminate in fifteen. The use of videotapes and the way they have been used in teaching students is another similarity.

Question from the floor:

I would like to raise a question regarding the focus. Should the therapist choose the focus; should the patient choose the focus; or should the therapist and the patient together choose the focus?

Dr. Straker:

Your question as to who selects the focus—is it by agreement or by the patient or by the therapist—is an extremely important one. This is one of the major problems arising in the use of the problem-oriented medical record and it's application to psychiatry. I think it is obvious that if the therapist decided to work in one direction without the patient going along with him, there would be disaster ahead.

Dr. Davanloo:

In my opinion, psychotherapeutic focus is a function of the evaluation process. That is to say, some agreement should be made between the therapist and the patient on the psychotherapeutic focus, keeping in mind that in the evaluation process obviously the psychotherapeutic focus is formulated in the mind of the evaluator. For example, let's take the problem in the area of interpersonal relationships that you saw in the patient we've been discussing. He managed to lose his wife to another man and to fail at college. When, during the first session, we got a clear picture of his self-defeating, self-punishing pattern of behavior and the fact that this was a translation of a triangular oedipal conflict, then in this way we set up for a goal this specific oedipal psychotherapeutic focus.

Dr. Strupp:

I think the question of psychotherapeutic focus is of utmost importance because it directly relates to the problem of evaluation of outcome. In the past, it has not been done in psychoanalysis and psychotherapy in general, relating outcome to specific problems that were agreed upon at the beginning of treatment, and until that is done we are in quicksand and will never be able to resolve the issue. In the project that we are conducting at Vanderbilt University, which is a short-term psychotherapy study extending over a period of four years, the therapist or the interviewer in conjunction with the patient tries to arrive at a focus at the end of the assessment interview. Very often it comes about that the way the patient formulates the problem that he would like to work on is not what is in fact feasible; it's much too broad and much too general. Then what needs to be done is to have the therapist and the patient agree on some kind of reasonable focus. But again the point I want to emphasize is that the outcome of psychotherapy occurs and should occur on the basis of a relatively specific target or targets that are agreed upon in advance. That's the only way in which I think we ultimately are going to make progress.

Dr. Malan:

The issue about the focus is a very complicated one. I never agree on focus with a patient for the very simple reason that my focus is deep and psychodynamic and the patient is not ready to hear it.

Dr. Sifneos:

I think it is imperative that evaluators keep the focus in mind. This is what we are trained for. We know about the psychodynamics; the patient does not. I do think it is of vital importance that some agreement be reached between the evaluator and the patient on the focus on which they are going to concentrate.

Dr. Naiman:

I would like to draw attention to the patient that Dr. Davanloo presented for the following reason. I don't have Dr. Strupp's research knowledge or sophistication, but I certainly am concerned as to how much we do, and would the patient get better by himself, and so on. Now, the kind of patient that Dr. Davanloo presented, who managed to wreck his marriage and also his professional career, this is the kind of patient that has been known to psychoanalysis for a very long time.

Freud mentions this kind of patient in analysis, terminable and interminable, as being particularly difficult to treat—the patient with a strong unconscious sense of guilt. These are the kinds of patients who will wreck anything, including the therapy, and they don't get better by themselves. In this context, I would say that if brief psychotherapy as done by Dr. Davanloo and his associates can in fact be therapeutically effective with this particular kind of patient, this would be a most impressive achievement.

Dr. Zaiden:

In New York we are training ourselves to establish a criterion for working with families, children and adolescents in short-term. We started a unit less than a year ago, and we are going to work with a low socioeconomic group with not above-average intelligence, and so on, and we are hopeful that something will come out of it. We know that we are up against tremendous odds, but I think that if we do come up with anything it is due in part to what we have learned here.

Part V

Chapter 22
The Teaching and Supervision of STAPP

P. E. SIFNEOS

Short-term anxiety-provoking psychotherapy (STAPP) is a specialized kind of dynamic psychotherapy which is offered to carefully selected patients. Its technique involves the establishment of a therapeutic focus which includes the psychodynamic conflicts underlying the patient's psychological problem. This problem usually involves difficulties occurring as a result of the early preference of one parent at the expense of the other, which is referred to as triangular, oedipal or genital. The therapeutic focus is jointly agreed upon by the therapist and the patient, and it becomes the main area of concentration for this treatment.

Important technical requirements include the establishment of a therapeutic alliance; the utilization of the patient's positive transference feelings, which usually predominate during the early part of the treatment; and the use of confrontation, clarification and anxiety-provoking questions in order to establish the necessary parent-transference links. The avoidance of characterological issues which, if dealt with at length, tend to give rise to an insoluble transference neurosis and finally the early termination of the treatment after the main psychological conflicts underlying the therapeutic focus have been resolved also constitute basic technical requirements for this therapy. These techniques must be learned by the student and in addition must be put into practice while he is treating a suitable patient under individual supervision.

THE TRAINEES

Since the technical requirements must be followed very precisely, it would appear at first glance that STAPP is easy to learn. It should be remembered, however, that these requirements are very different from what usually takes place during other kinds of psychotherapy. The therapist must be active. He must quickly confront the patient with anxiety-provoking questions tending to make him resistant and angry or at times giving rise to regressive tendencies which he must not allow to develop. At the same time, he must deal with transference and countertransference feelings and remain centered within the therapeutic focus which has been defined. Nevertheless, it should be emphasized that these requirements do not constitute a cookbook type of guideline. The variety of ways in which each patient goes about working at solving his problems is so diversified that constant vigilance is required on the part of the therapist. Because of these considerations, it has been said that short-term anxiety-provoking psychotherapy is more difficult to learn than other kinds of therapy, and that it should therefore be offered only to fairly experienced therapists. On the basis of many years of supervising trainees, however, at both the Massachusetts General and Beth Israel hospitals, I am not inclined to agree with this thesis. Of course, as in any other learning experience, a great deal depends on the talents and interests of the students. The trainees whom I have supervised came from four different disciplines: psychiatry, psychology, social work and nursing. They were at various levels of their training, ranging from first-year residents, MSW social work students and psychology Ph.D. candidates, to advanced psychiatric residents and postgraduate Ph.D's in psychology, social work and nursing. Included in this group were also some Harvard medical students who were interested in psychiatry and who had taken their elective courses at these hospitals. All our students shared several common characteristics. They were young. They were volunteers who were interested in learning a technique of psychotherapy of brief duration. They were enthusiastic because they could observe its immediate effects on the patient and its results after a short period of time. In addition, some had also attended our weekly research conference dealing with the evaluation of the outcome of this therapy and were familiar with the problems encountered in psychotherapy research.

Generally speaking, it turned out paradoxically that of these trainees with various backgrounds, the less experienced ones were better therapists and more often obtained successful results than did their more experienced counterparts. A possible explanation for this observation about the younger supervisees has to do with a lack of certain preconceived ideas about psychotherapy in contrast to the older ones who believed in the stereotype that long-term psychotherapy is the treatment of choice and that brief therapy is only a poor substitute. Such attitudes in the older trainees who had several years of previous experience tended to have at times a detrimental effect on the way in which they dealt with their patients and with the overall outcome of treatment. Thus the enthusiasm to learn an innovative treatment such as STAPP, and a lack of preconceived prejudices, proved to be valuable assets for the younger therapists.

In addition to good motivation and an open mind, the only other prerequisites necessary to learn to offer STAPP have to do with a general psychodynamic orientation, an ability to select an appropriate patient according to the specified criteria and a knowledge of the specific technical requirements already enumerated. All this can take place within the context of intensive weekly individual supervision.

SPECIAL ASPECTS OF STAPP SUPERVISION

Since learning the specialized aspects of selection of an appropriate candidate for STAPP is important, I would like again to review the criteria involved in this selection. These are: a circumscribed chief complaint; a history of one meaningful (give and take, altruistic) relationship with another person in early life; an ability to interact with the evaluator flexibly and to have access to one's feelings during the evaluation interview; a certain degree of psychological sophistication and above-average intelligence; and finally a motivation to change.

The first supervisory session should take place before the supervisee has seen the patient so that various aspects of the selection criteria and other technical considerations can be discussed in detail. Before the following session, the supervisor should select a patient suitable for STAPP who is to be treated by the student and he himself should interview that patient. During the subsequent supervisory session, special attention must be paid to the discussion of the therapeutic focus as formulated by the supervisor. Although it should be made clear to the student that he may formulate a different therapeutic focus if he disagrees with the one that has been formulated by his supervisor, he should have enough evidence from the material which has been obtained during his own interview to justify his conclusions. He should be careful, however, not to communicate this to the patient until he has had a chance to discuss the difference of opinion, if any, which may exist with his supervisor. On the other hand, if he does agree with him, he may present their ideas on this issue to the patient and attempt to obtain his agreement. Although on occasion important information has been obtained by the supervisee requiring a modification of the original focus, in most cases the student usually agrees with his supervisor's therapeutic focus, which as mentioned already is an oedipal one.

The basic principles of STAPP supervision have similarities with those prevailing in supervision of patients in other kinds of psychodynamic psychotherapy. As Zetzel has stated, it is important for the supervisor to create "a framework of security in which to develop and learn." (2) It is also obvious that the transference and countertransference feelings of the supervisor and student which will invariably develop must be dealt with if they give rise to difficulties and interfere with the educational process. (3) STAPP patients tend to bring up a great deal of material early during the therapy, and at times it is anxiety-provoking to the therapist as well as to themselves. Occasionally, the student's anxieties may denote a certain degree of his own psychopathology. Usually in such cases the student starts indirectly to hint at psychological difficulties in himself or may even frankly admit his own problems. The supervisor should listen for a while but he should not encourage the student to continue. In the same way as the therapist must avoid getting entangled in certain characterological areas of his STAPP patient, the teacher must not get mixed up in the psychological problems of his supervisee, which would eventually turn supervision into the psychotherapy of the student.

Here is an example: A male patient, while talking about some enjoyable homosexual experience during his adolescence, was interrupted repeatedly by the student-therapist, who tried to make him change the subject. As he was recounting the episode to his supervisor, the student appeared to have been very irritated with the patient, but when the supervisor brought this to his attention he denied it vehemently. Soon afterwards, however, he started to talk about his own early life experiences and his difficulties with his parents. The supervisor interrupted him and suggested gently that they should return to the discussion of the patient's difficulties. The supervisee appeared to become annoyed by this suggestion, but after a while he did admit that he had been irritated with the patient when he talked about his homosexual difficulties.

During the next supervisory session the student started again to talk about his past life experiences, and the supervisor suggested more forcefully this time that they should talk about the patient's homosexual problems and the supervisee's irritation. The student blushed at this point and said that he had become annoyed when the patient insisted that he had enjoyed occasional homosexual experiences during his puberty. When asked directly by the supervisor why this had made such a difference, the student was silent for a while and finally admitted that he had experienced similar episodes during his own adolescence at a time when an uncle of his had masturbated him on several occasions. He emphasized, however, that he in contrast to the patient had felt disgusted by the whole situation and had not enjoyed these episodes in the slightest. The supervisor stopped him and expressed his surprise, but the student continued to emphasize his distaste for the whole situation. The teacher interrupted him again and confronted him with the fact that if indeed he had been so disgusted by the whole situation with his uncle, as he claimed to be, why did he allow his uncle to masturbate him "on several occasions?" The student finally admitted that indeed he had also enjoyed these episodes and since that time had harbored fears that he was a homosexual.

He was reassured that such episodes occur commonly during puberty and that they are perfectly normal. He was therefore urged to pursue the job of treating the patient. From then on, the psychotherapy proceeded uneventfully and ended soon after successfully. It was obvious that neither the patient nor the student had serious psychological difficulties in the sexual area, but their fears and misunderstandings could have complicated and terminated the therapy and these diffculties, although mild, would have persisted. (4)

On rare occasions, however, the supervisor should discuss the student's problems, particularly if they interfere with the patient's treatment, and may refer him for a psychiatric evaluation.

Certain aspects of the technique of STAPP may put pressure on the therapist and give rise to additional complications which will interfere with the process of therapy. One of these technical requirements has to do with the very early appearance and rapid flow of fantasies and dreams similar to those which one encounters during psychoanalysis, all relating to the therapeutic focus. Because the beginning therapist is unfamiliar with such a situation, and because very often such material is anxiety-provoking to the patient and on occasion equally disturbing to the therapist, it is important that the therapist not reassure or support the patient. On the contrary, he must keep him centered on the established therapeutic focus, he should not deviate from it, and above all he should not help him to suppress his anxiety. Rather, he must encourage the patient to continue looking into the conflicts underlying the psychological difficulties and confront him with situations which make him even more anxious. It should be remembered, however, that the patient has been selected because of his strength of character and because he is perfectly capable of withstanding anxiety. It is precisely this element that lends the name "anxiety-provoking" to this kind of short-term psychotherapy.

The early appearance of the patient's transference feelings must also be recognized by the therapist. Since many students have been previously taught not to interfere with the transference until it appears "as a resistance," they usually ignore it and fail to deal with it. The use of the patient's transference feelings in conjunction with material which has been obtained about his early relations with his parents helps establish the crucial "parent-transference link," which Malan has proved to be of vital importance in the successful therapeutic outcome of short-term dynamic psychotherapy. (5)

Here is an example of the difficulties which may arise if transference is avoided during STAPP: A twenty-one-year-old single student who had a very strong attachment for his mother and guilt feelings and antagonism for his father became critical of his therapist during the second month of the therapy and while in the process of investigating his feelings for his parents because of the prospective cancellation of an interview. Up to that time, positive feelings seemed to have predominated. The therapist, who was planning to go skiing, had felt somewhat on the defensive about this cancellation and had tried during the interview to justify it in the best way he could. When the patient started to become sarcastic, the therapist felt more apprehensive and changed the subject. During the supervisory session, the therapist's avoidance of handling the negative transference was brought to his attention, and he was encouraged to deal with it openly if the opportunity arose during the next session.

After his return and during the following two weeks, the patient continued to talk angrily about the cancelled interview, and although the therapist listened for a little while, he again interrupted the patient by emphasizing that more important matters had to be discussed. The supervisor urged the student strongly to deal with the negative transference once and for all. In the subsequent session, however, it became apparent that the patient appeared to have become depressed. After considerable questioning and investigation on the therapist's part, the patient finally mentioned that his mother was sick with cancer and had been operated upon. On further investigation it was discovered that the patient had found out about his mother's condition only two days before the interview during which the therapist had announced the cancellation and during which he had become critical of him. The displacement of angry feelings upon the therapist was obvious, and the prospect of the loss of both his mother and the student at the same time became discernible. Had the therapist dealt with the negative transference at the time it had first appeared, it is possible that he would have helped avert the patient's depression.

Another pitfall to be avoided has to do with the therapist's getting entangled in the patient's early characterological conflicts which, although they may be present, do not require much clarification and, if dealt with during psychotherapy, tend to prolong it.

Here is an example: A young female psychology trainee who discovered after the second interview that her patient had lost her grandmother, to whom she was very much attached, at the age of twelve, proceeded to investigate these feelings of loss. The patient had complained of difficulties with men, and the therapeutic focus which had been agreed upon involved the investigation of conflicts about the patient's attachment to her father and competition with her mother. Despite this, the therapist continued to deal with the feelings of loss while she paid lip service to her awareness of the therapeutic focus, encouraging the patient to talk about her feelings of loss of her grandmother—something which she had discovered, since it had not come up during her supervisor's interview with the patient. She was therefore determined to pursue it. It was clear, however, that both the patient and supervisor were becoming impatient as this investigation went on, while nothing significant was happening otherwise.

It was only after considerable time had elapsed that the therapist finally started to deal with both the therapeutic focus and the patient's negative transference feelings for her which by then had become apparent, and soon significant changes started to take place during the course of the therapy. The patient became interested again in the treatment while she had given clear indication of having been bored. She announced soon after that she had a new boyfriend with whom she had established a good sexual and "give-and-take" relationship. Much progress took place rapidly and the treatment finally ended successfully.

It was of interest, however, that when this patient was seen in a follow-up interview one year later she said: "I am feeling quite well, and I have overcome my difficulties with my parents. I also like Miss M. She was able to help me a great deal, but there is one thing I did not understand. I do not know why she was so much interested in my grandmother's death. Although it was of importance, it had nothing to do with the problems which had brought me to the clinic."

The early termination of STAPP is possibly the most difficult aspect for the therapist to learn. Usually about half of the patients bring up the issue of ending their treatment by themselves after they are satisfied that they have resolved their psychological problem. It is up to the therapist, therefore, if he is in agreement with the patient, to set up a termination date. The other half of the patients, possibly because they enjoy the treatment too much and despite their awareness of the futility of its prolongation, wait until the therapist brings up the issue of termination. Therapists who fail to deal with termination in one way or the other tend to prolong treatment. It is in the final analysis the responsibility of the therapist to judge more objectively whether or not the agreed-upon therapeutic focus has been dealt with adequately, the appropriate parent-transference links have been made, and the underlying psychological conflicts have been resolved. Under those circumstances, it is up to the therapist to initiate the talk about the termination of the treatment.

In my experience during the supervisory sessions, termination has taken more time to discuss than any other of the special aspects of STAPP technique. The biggest resistance arises from the inability of the student to believe that the therapeutic results which he observes taking place in his patient will be maintained. Having heard from so many sources that psychotherapy, in order to be effective, must be long-term, he has difficulty believing that what he has helped to achieve will be lasting. It is very helpful, therefore, if at all possible, to have videotaped follow-up interviews. In this way, it is possible to demonstrate tangibly to the student that the patient's improvement has indeed been maintained.

In reference to videotaped interviews, it should be emphasized that they constitute one of the best ways to demonstrate how to learn to offer short-term dynamic psychotherapy. I have treated several patients with STAPP and videotaped all the interviews. These have then been used for demonstration purposes with the students. On the monitor, for all to see, one can show the technical aspects which have already been discussed. Another advantage of videotape has to do with asking the group, after viewing these tapes, to make predictions about what is likely to take place in the following session. This kind of exercise has been very popular with our students and is highly recommended as a teaching device.

I would like to emphasize that, from the experience of supervising more than forty trainees in STAPP, the one element which was shared by all had to do with their enthusiasm and their motivation to learn. Dr. Malan has commented on this point but more recently has not been able to demonstrate its specific therapeutic effect. Nevertheless, I am convinced that, at least as far as supervision is concerned, the student's enthusiasm has a great deal to do with learning and makes the supervisory session a very pleasant experience for both the student and his teacher.

REFERENCES

1. Sifneos, P.E. *Short-Term Psychotherapy and Emotional Crisis.* Cambridge, Mass.: Harvard University Press, 1972.
2. Zetzel, E.R. The Dynamic Basis of Supervision. *Social Case Work*, April 1953.
3. Sifneos, P.E. Tutorial. A Useful Way to Teach Psychiatry to Senior Medical Students. *Amer. J. Psychiatry*, 118, 9, 1962.
4. Sifneos, P.E. Sex from the Clinician's Point of View. *Acta Neurol. Psychiatr. Hellenica*, 11, 2:1120–30, 1972.
5. Malan, D.H. Personal communication.

Chapter 23

The Challenge of Short-Term Dynamic Psychotherapy*

H. H. STRUPP

The dream of developing a form of treatment that is efficient, effective and preferably inexpensive came into existence almost as soon as Freud had made his revolutionary discoveries almost a hundred years ago. In his early writings he tended to be apologetic that psychoanalysis took as much as nine months to a year, defending his position by stating that therapeutic change could not be hurried. As we know, psychoanalysis for reasons which I will not explore at this time, has tended to occupy increasing periods of time, sometimes unconscionably so. The goal of creating a shorter form of treatment, without abandoning basic psychoanalytic insights, has always remained, however, and various proposals toward this end were made by early workers beginning with Rank and Ferenczi and later by Alexander and French, Balint, and other therapists following in their footsteps. (For an excellent review, see Castelnuovo-Tedesco [2]).

In recent years the search for efficient modes of psychotherapeutic intervention has become intensified. Reasons for this renewed interest are not difficult to find: Increasingly, society demands that the helping

---

*The work reported was supported, in part, by NIMH Research Grant MH-20369.

professions bend their energies to the task of providing services that are effective, practical and inexpensive, and it demands evidence that we can deliver what we promise. This does not mean that we should be able to work miracles, but the challenge to demonstrate that we can do certain things under particular circumstances with particular patients has been made, and we are expected to provide answers that the patient/consumer, legislators, insurance companies and others can understand and accept.

Basically, we are interested in developing and purveying a product—short-term dynamic psychotherapy—and our task is to (a) describe the nature of the product and its active ingredients, (b) stipulate the conditions under which it can optimally be applied, and (c) demonstrate the extent and range of its effectiveness. Conceptually, these tasks are simple; in practice, as we all know, we face tremendous difficulties. Nonetheless, the goal must be clearly kept in mind.

The following questions must be addressed:

I. What is the modus operandi of short-term dynamic psychotherapy?

II. Under what conditions should it be used? Since no therapeutic technique can be applied *in vacuo*, this calls for a discussion of patient, therapist and situational variables.

III. What must be done to evaluate the effectiveness of the product? Under this rubric we must deal with systematic investigations designed to identify and document the kinds of changes that may be expected under particular circumstances.

The questions asked of short-term dynamic psychotherapy are in principle no different from those leveled at all forms of psychotherapy, and the strategies to be employed for evaluating its effectiveness are substantially identical. In a sense, however, the task is easier because our inquiry, like the therapy itself, can be more sharply focused; the answers we might be able to adduce can accordingly be obtained in shorter periods of time, and they can emerge with greater salience.

I. MODUS OPERANDI OF SHORT-TERM DYNAMIC PSYCHOTHERAPY

Despite certain quantitative differences between classical psychoanalysis and other approaches based on dynamic principles, the assumptions are basically identical, and this is true as well of the associated technical operations.* I shall state these assumptions succinctly:

---

*This formulation is in substantial agreement with the point of view advanced by Alexander and French (1946). I believe it is time to take a new look at this truly innovative, forward-looking book, which gains new and even greater significance in light of the developments sketched herein.

(1) The patient always seeks to achieve gratification by means he has learned in the past, and he presents symptoms, problems in living, etc., because learned patterns (including fantasies, fears, misconceptions, etc.) are inappropriate, self-defeating, anachronistic and generally maladaptive in his adult living. In Alexander's (1) words: "Every neurosis and every psychosis represents *a failure of the ego in performing its function of securing adequate gratification for subjective needs under existing conditions*" (p. viii). Thus the task of any form of psychotherapy is to correct failures of adjustment.

(2) Since these learned patterns are rooted in early significant relationships and their vicissitudes (e.g., deprivation, trauma, etc.), they can only be resolved within an interpersonal framework that in some ways resembles the earlier one but which in important respects is different from it. To the extent that the present-day relationship is experienced by the patient as similar to (reminiscent of) the earlier one, it will evoke the conflictual patterns of relatedness; conversely, to the extent that it is experienced by the patient as different, it can serve a corrective (therapeutic) function (Alexander's concept of the "corrective emotional experience"). The more poignant the difference between the two forms of relatedness can be made—here the so-called transference neurosis serves its unique function—the more incisive and radical the therapeutic change can become. Classical analysis differs from short-term dynamic psychotherapy solely in the degree to which the contrast is made vivid and explicit, worked through and assimilated.

The foregoing is the transference paradigm pure and simple. It follows that psychoanalytic psychotherapy, regardless of whether it is termed classical analysis or brief psychotherapy, achieves results to the extent that it uses a "real" relationship between a patient and a therapist for the purpose of correcting patterns of relatedness traceable to the earlier ones which continue to be conflictual and therefore troublesome. Depending on the nature of the earlier difficulties, the extent to which they have interfered with the patient's maturation and a host of other factors which have been extensively discussed in the literature and which represent prognostic indicators, psychotherapy may take varying amounts of time and varying therapeutic efforts, and at times it may be virtually impossible to effect the corrections that are needed and called for. However, no matter how brief or intensive the therapeutic effort may be, the basic formula remains the same: It is the utilization of an interpersonal relationship in the present to correct persistent difficulties created by an interpersonal relationship in the past. Whatever learning can be mediated by the therapeutic relationship—whether it is over a period of three months or three years—represents the therapeutic yield and thus the effectiveness of the psychotherapeutic effort. Difficulties in living that cannot be dealt with in this manner lie outside the province of psychoanalytic psychotherapy and cannot be remedied by its techniques.

Fundamentally, the technique for bringing about the necessary corrections has two major components:

(a) The therapist facilitates and encourages development of a viable interpersonal relationship between the patient and himself. This may lead to the so-called transference neurosis in classical psychoanalysis, or the patient may continue to experience the conflict as existing between himself and other significant people in his life, as is typically the case in brief dynamic psychotherapy.

(b) In both instances the therapist, in addition to providing sympathetic understanding, emotional support, etc., seeks to identify and correct maladaptive patterns of relatedness by helping the patient to appreciate their inutility.

To reiterate, it matters little whether the conflict centers around the patient-therapist relationship or whether the conflict is experienced with other significant figures in the patient's life. In either event, the therapist uses his position as a "good object" to produce corrections in the patient's self-esteem by appropriate therapeutic maneuvers. In analytic terms, he comes to the aid of the patient's beleaguered ego, which means that he is strengthening the patient's adaptive resources. Insight is an appreciation of what one is doing wrong *when* one is doing it in the present (whether with the therapist or other significant persons), and therapy is successful to the extent that the therapist can bring maladapive patterns into focus and that the patient can experience with sufficient vividness their maladaptive character and utilize this appreciation to feel, think and act differently, i.e., in more adaptive ways.*

The fact that classical psychoanalysis encourages the development of a transference neurosis whereas brief dynamic psychotherapy relies heavily on a "real" relationship does not contradict the foregoing assertions. All forms of psychotherapy—not only classical analysis or short-term dynamic psychotherapy—make effective use of a "real" relationship between two adults which is, of course, heavily supported and made meaningful by the degree to which this relationship resembles and makes contact with what the patient has experienced in the way of "good relationships" with significant figures in the past. Classical analysis cannot dispense with this relationship any more than can other forms of

---

*I share the view of most analytic writers that nothing is as convincing as something that is experienced directly with the therapist, but I do not believe that we have the data to show that it is necessarily true. This is merely another challenging question for research.

therapy. Unless, as I shall describe later, the patient can make effective use of a "good relationship," a serious contraindication for short-term dynamic therapy exists.

The difference between psychoanalysis and brief dynamic therapy appears to be quantitative rather than qualitative. Where the classical analyst strives to bring conflicts which the patient is acting out with others into the patient-therapist relationship, which is accomplished by regression, the brief dynamic therapist seeks to utilize the qualities of a "good object" with which the patient invests him by making interpretations of the conflict the patient is experiencing with other significant persons in his present life. In either event, the therapist uses the current relationship that exists between him and the patient to introduce corrections in the patient's maladaptive patterns. He may do so by becoming a good parent figure and thus allowing the patient to identify with his strength, maturity, fearlessness, tolerance, acceptance, respect and other qualities inherent in such a figure. In classical analysis it is frequently necessary to expend considerable time and effort to bring a conflict into focus, whereas for best results the patient coming to brief psychotherapy should experience a focal conflict. In the absence of such a focal conflict, usually characterized by pronounced anxiety, distress and suffering, brief dynamic psychotherapy may have little chance of success. The opposite case consists of more diffuse characterological difficulties, which may indeed dictate long-term intensive work.*

The preceding discussion does not answer the question of how the therapist can most effectively intervene in short-term dynamic psychotherapy, and what technical approaches are most propitious. In general, he will presumably engage in one or more of the following: management of dependency needs, evaluation of emotional reactions with positive focus, objective review of stress situations, emotional decompression (catharsis), reinforcement of ego defenses, educative guidance, effecting changes in the life situation, modification of patient's goals, use of magical omnipotence, and use of the patient-therapist relationship (transference) (Goldman [4], cited by Offenkrantz and Tobin [6]).

Clearly, these are complex operations. It is also apparent that the short-term therapist, like any other, brings to bear a combination of influences which summate into a therapeutic outcome. What needs to be understood and investigated empirically is whether a particular *focus* is more therapeutic than another. Malan (5) has stressed "parent transference links" and Sifneos' (7) interpretations are focused on oedipal conflicts. While there is preliminary evidence that these approaches

---

*I am indebted to Dr. Pietro Castelnuovo-Tedesco for a helpful discussion of this issue, although he disagrees with some aspects of my position.

appear to be effective under certain circumstances, we have as yet no demonstration that they are uniquely effective or more effective than any other combination. In terms of the preceding discussion, it may be hypothesized that interventions creating the sharpest possible contrast between the "good" parent-therapist relationship and the conflictual (transference) aspects of the patient's relationship with others that has given rise to the difficulties he is presenting have the greatest chance of success. Thus Malan's emphasis on "parent transference links" makes good sense, and it is in line with Gill's (3) emphasis on the current patient-therapist interaction in psychoanalysis as well: It is only in and through the *current relationship* between the patient and the therapist that effective therapeutic modifications can be achieved.

I shall next turn to a brief discussion of the conditions that are essential for the success of short-term dynamic psychotherapy, keeping in mind the formulations advanced earlier.

II. CONDITIONS

As usual, distinctions must be made between characteristics of the *patient,* the *therapist* and *situational variables.*

Malan ([5] and in subsequent work) has put forward two major criteria that must be met by a prospective patient for short-term dynamic psychotherapy: He or she must be (a) willing and able to explore feelings, and (b) able to work within a therapeutic relationship based on interpretation.

With respect to *motivation,* Malan, along with others, stresses that the patient must have an intense wish for help through insight. This means in part that he must be suffering from an acute conflict, which provides a strong motivating force and thus creates one of the necessary conditions for short-term intervention.

The wish to be helped, however, is not enough; it must be supported by a "history of real and good relationships." In other words, the patient must have what Freud called a relatively "intact ego"; that is, he must have reached a sufficiently high level of integration, autonomy and capacity for object relationships. Conversely, there must be a notable absence of deep-seated and pervasive characterological distortions, few fixations at early stages of psychosexual development and relatively little regression to earlier modes of adaptation, unlike what is found in markedly obsessional and narcissistic patients. In short, the patient must be significantly mature, and the task of therapy must not be the kind of extensive and large-scale reconstructive work therapists are frequently called upon to do in classical psychoanalysis. By the same token, when the patient suffers from marked ego defects, focal psychotherapy appears to be contraindicated, and when it is applied (as it should not be) it will predictably lead to failure (cf. Waelder [9], quoted by Castelnuovo-Tedesco [2]). In keeping with the earlier formulation, the patient must be capable of entering into and utilizing an adult relationship, as implied by Malan's assertions that he must be capable of becoming "deeply involved" (in a relatively mature, nondefensive and nondependent manner) with the therapist, of "bearing the tension that ensues" and generally being able to appreciate the positive, constructive, curative and pleasurable aspects of a good human relationship.

Several implications of this position should be noted:

(1) A very sizable number of patients who seek psychotherapy or for whom psychotherapy is prescribed do not meet these criteria; hence brief dynamic psychotherapy may be unsuitable for them. Consequently, attempts to achieve therapeutic goals in the absence of these conditions are foolhardy and result predictably in a situation that makes psychotherapy appear to be less effective than it actually is. It also results in diluted outcome statistics that have given psychotherapy the reputation of being able to achieve only "weak" results.

(2) The criterion of capacity for a good relationship highlights the overriding importance of extremely careful assessment, including a fine-grained analysis of what therapy can accomplish for a particular patient under particular circumstances.

(3) The stringency of the foregoing selection criteria invites the oft-repeated allegation that psychotherapy is most successful with patients who need it the least, and that patients who show the most impressive therapeutic gains are the ones who are least disturbed to begin with. This charge is based on a gross misunderstanding of the goals and purposes of analytic psychotherapy, and as such it does irreparable harm to the therapeutic enterprise. It cannot be stressed too much that the success of analytic (or any other form of) psychotherapy is clearly a function of the nature of the patient's disturbance and his capacity to benefit from the kind of relationship sketched earlier. Failure to make a careful analysis of the antecedent conditions, to apply psychotherapy as if these antecedent conditions did not matter, and then to fault therapy for its length is to ignore the reality of powerful psychological factors.

(4) True psychotherapeutic change is not behavioral but intrapsychic, and it consists of structural alterations that are brought about by and within the dynamics of a particular kind of interpersonal relationship. Conversely, as already stated, problems in human living that are not so amenable are not the proper province for analytic psychotherapy. Again, we are forced to give careful consideration to the nature of the problem for which therapeutic help is enlisted, as well as a determination of the extent to which the patient's problem is amenable

to therapeutic intervention via this route. It is undeniably true that a large number of so-called problems in living are not susceptible to this approach and persons in whom they exist are not the kind who are sufficiently differentiated or psychologically mature to make short-term psychotherapy a viable course of action.

Having said this, the question persists: What about the large number of applicants presenting themselves to outpatient clinics and other treatment facilities who do not meet the foregoing criteria? It may be easy for a theoretician or researcher to assert that such patients are simply to be excluded because they are poor prospects, but a clinic administrator is faced with the practical problems of providing services to all applicants regardless of whether they meet strict criteria. These are thorny problems that permit no ready answer. Consider an analogy from the field of medicine: Every suffering person assuredly has a right to treatment, and it is the responsibility of the helping professions to do all they can to provide it. However, having conducted a meticulous diagnostic assessment, the physician may be forced to conclude that because of various complicating factors (e.g., advanced age, concurrent physical or metabolic defects) the "ideal" treatment is not available, or even if it is applied in such a case the prognosis must be guarded. These limitations are readily accepted in medicine, and it is recognized that one must often settle for a less than complete cure. Such cases, however, do not detract from the utility of the "ideal" therapeutic remedy nor are they a threat to its value. All that can be concluded is that the treatment is highly effective when optimal conditions are met, and its effectiveness is lessened when such an optimal state of affairs does not exist. The same criteria should be applied in psychotherapy.

Nor can we any longer assume that psychotherapy achieves more or less *positive* results. There is the distinct possibility—recognized clinically but not as yet very well documented empirically—that patients exposed to forms of psychotherapy that are inappropriate for them may suffer *negative effects* (8). A few examples must suffice: A patient may show improvements in overt behavior but may remain as unhappy and distressed as before; a patient may become disillusioned when therapeutic goals are poorly defined and he retains magical expectations of what the treatment might accomplish, which in turn may discourage him from seeking more appropriate treatment; latent conflicts that had best remain untouched may become stirred up as a result of inept, aggressive or poorly focused interventions. In short, we must face the fact that psychotherapy can be a force for improvement as well as deterioration, and an approach that says "anything goes in short-term psychotherapy" must be vigorously rejected.

With respect to *therapist* variables, Malan (5) mentions the therapist's ability (a) to arrive at an understanding of the patient's problems in dynamic terms and (b) to formulate some kind of circumscribed therapeutic plan (p. 277).

In addition to the therapist's ability to *invest* significantly of himself or herself in the treatment of a particular patient, I would emphasize the ability to *care* deeply about the patient as a person and thus for the outcome of therapy. On the basis of my own work, I have become increasingly impressed by the importance of the therapist's caring, his liking of the patient as a person, and his ability to identify with the patient. I would rate these qualities as among the most crucial factors in the outcome of any therapy, and they may assume even greater importance in short-term dynamic approaches. At the same time, there is increasing reason to believe that the therapist must have a high level of *technical expertise*, which, if properly applied, should result in highly significant and visible therapeutic gains.

I shall dispense with a discussion of *situational variables* except to note that their careful assessment must lead to the judgment that short-term dynamic psychotherapy has a reasonable chance of success. Such an assessment clearly must take account the patient's total life situation, including the determination that external circumstances are fairly propitious for intrapsychic change in the patient to make a significant difference. To say more on this subject would merely be traversing well-known territory.

III. EVALUATION OF THE PRODUCT

As indicated earlier, short-term dynamic psychotherapy, like any other form of psychotherapy, proceeds on a relatively broad front and makes use of numerous technical interventions, of which interpretative operations are only one. Nevertheless, it is possible—indeed, essential—to investigate under controlled conditions the differential effectiveness of different emphases, e.g., whether focus on transference interpretations linked to the early parent-child relationship is significantly more effective than other technical procedures or a general atmosphere of understanding, respect and support. These recommended steps will also serve to rule out alternative hypotheses, which must be retained as viable contenders—at least until such time as the appropriate research has been carried out.

While it is relatively easy to outline an ideal study, it is a different matter to implement it. To illustrate the problem, I shall refer to a long-term psychotherapy study currently in progress at Vanderbilt

University, which qualifies as short-term psychotherapy (up to twenty-five hours over a three-to-four month period). Part of the initial assessment included the delineation of "targets" set by the patient in consultation with the clinician-interviewer. Therapists to whom the patients were assigned were given the opportunity to accept or reformulate these targets. Typically, they accepted the patient's goals.

A male college student, age twenty, stated the following targets:

"1. I want to learn to meet people, interact with them and be more comfortable in doing so. I want to stop avoiding people and 'freezing up' when I meet them.

"2. I want to work especially in dealing with the opposite sex; what to say and do; how to make things happen.

"3. I want to learn more about me; get self-confidence, more of an ability to find some enjoyment in life."

The therapist accepted these formulations and proceeded to engage in psychoanalytically oriented therapy, which turned out to be quite successful in terms of the outcome criteria employed in this study. The gains were maintained over the follow-up period of about eight months.

Is it possible to focus therapy in this particular way or some other way? Can one identify specific "problems" or difficulties which, if dealt with decisively in therapy, will result in significant change? Or, must one employ an open-ended approach, comparable to long-term psychoanalysis, and deal with whatever problems emerge focally in the early hours? If one or more problems emerge, is it possible to direct the therapeutic effort toward their resolution in the available time?

In terms of the preceding discussion, the problems stated by the patient are not amenable to therapeutic attack in short-term dynamic psychotherapy; rather, they seem to point to more pervasive characterological difficulties that might call for intensive analytic psychotherapy. Parenthetically, it should be noted that at least some of the therapists in our study tended to proceed as if they were engaged in open-ended long-term analytic therapy, which may have resulted in the relative absence of decisive successes suggested by preliminary analyses of the data.

But let us assume that the therapist provisionally accepts the patient's formulations and proceeds in an effort to discern whether in early interviews there might emerge "foci" that might lend themselves to short-term dynamic psychotherapy. If and when they do, he would have to make a judgment, such as: "If I focus on Issue A, I will be of greatest help to the patient; conversely, I must ignore Issues K, L, M . . . Z because they are too deep-seated, too well-defended, and thus beyond time-limited therapy. And once having decided to deal with Issue A (and possibly B and C) I must remain focused on them, not get sidetracked by other material that may emerge in later sessions." In short, what is called for is a functional therapeutic diagnosis of what is most central in the patient's current problem, most amenable to therapeutic attack and most promising in terms of a significant positive outcome.

All analytic therapists (including proponents of brief dynamic therapy) look for "core conflictual themes" that may provide points of entry. Luborsky, for example, in viewing an early session with a patient, called attention to the patient's struggle with the therapist over passivity, negativism and the attendant anger at being coerced by the therapist into accepting the "basic rules" of therapy. Other therapists may have formulated different "Core Conflictual Themes," and in each case the interpretive interventions based on these hypotheses might be different. It is a moot question whether the pursuit of one "Core Conflictual Theme" is more propitious than that of another, whether the same theme must be dealt with in highly specific ways if one wishes to obtain a given therapeutic result, etc. These are ultimately empirical questions susceptible to controlled investigation. While it is apparent that differential outcomes based on alternative courses of action are exceedingly difficult to investigate, this is precisely what is needed.

Having reached this juncture, we are again brought back to the necessity of investigating the relative effectiveness of different therapeutic approaches to the problem. In such an endeavor we must also make certain that whatever changes occur in the patient cannot be attributed to "spontaneous remission"—the fact that since the patient possessed adequate ego resources, any form of benign attention and interest would have been beneficial, perhaps no more or no less than other technical procedures. In brief, we must measure outcomes in highly specific, meaningful and precise ways, and we must increasingly gear the treatment to the patient's problem, however we choose to define it. This should become standard practice in all forms of psychotherapy, but it is crucial in short-term approaches. It will not do simply to judge the patient as having generally "improved"; we must adduce appropriate evidence to convince other clinicians, the scientific community and the public that the preferred technique is indeed superior.

As in any therapy outcome study, we must define criteria and stay with them. If we decide that *dynamic change* is what we are looking for, we must be able to document the change that has occurred; if we elect to focus on the patient's *feeling state*, we must make certain that we measure it in a meaningful way; if we are looking for *behavioral change*, we must specify what kinds of behavioral changes we shall accept as evidence for the efficacy of the interventions. It has become increasingly clear that we must oppose the traditional practice of mixing criteria; we must agree in advance on the *value* to be placed on the changes our measurement techniques may identify, and in general we must strive for a kind of specificity that has hitherto been lacking in therapy outcome research. As developed at some length in another context (8), we have come to believe that any therapy outcome must be judged from the perspectives of (a) *society*, (b) the *individual patient*, and (3) the *mental health professional*. Conversely, if these perspectives are not kept separate and if change is not judged in relation to specific antecedent assessments, we shall never be able to adduce the kind of hard-core empirical evidence that is needed.

The foregoing stipulations are no longer niceties propounded by methodological purists whose concerns might be an unwelcome intrusion into clinical practice. Far from it. What we are facing today is a powerful challenge by society (whose spokesmen are legislators, insurance companies and the consumers) to demonstrate what psychotherapy of whatever variety can deliver, what it cannot do and under what conditions it can achieve maximal productivity. We are being pressed to provide solid evidence in favor of our product or alternatively face the prospect of being disbarred from the marketplace. We are being asked to show that our "drug" is effective, what precautions must be taken and what risks are incurred.

Psychotherapy has always had its critics. Professional therapists have attempted to answer them, but the public remains unconvinced, and the evidence we have been able to marshal has been less than impressive. Society demands that we do better. The only course of action open to us is to engage in the arduous pursuit of spelling out the conditions and the circumstances under which particular techniques will achieve particular results. These results may not be judged highly worthwhile by those agents of society whose opinions carry weight. But at least we will have given them a choice. This is the least but also the most we can and should do.

REFERENCES

1. Alexander, F. and T.M. French. *Psychoanalytic Therapy.* New York: Ronald Press, 1946.
2. Castelnuovo-Tedesco, P. Brief Psychotherapy. In *American Handbook of Psychiatry,* Second Edition, Vol. 5. New York: Basic Books, 1975, pp. 254–268.
3. Gill, M.M.

4. Goldman, G. Reparative Psychotherapy. In S. Rado and G. Daniels (eds.), *Changing Concepts of Psychoanalytic Medicine*. New York: Grune & Stratton, 1956, pp. 101–113.
5. Malan, D.H. *A Study of Brief Psychotherapy* (1963). New York: Plenum, 1975.
6. Offenkrantz, W. and A. Tobin. Psychoanalytic Psychotherapy. *Archives Gen. Psychiatry*, 30: 593–606, 1974.
7. Sifneos, P. *Short-Term Psychotherapy and Emotional Crisis*. Cambridge: Harvard University Press, 1972.
8. Strupp, H.H., S.W. Hadley, and B. Gomes-Schwartz. *Psychotherapy for Better or Worse: The Problem of Negative Effects*. New York: Jason Aronson, 1977.
   Negative Effects in Psychotherapy (tentative title; in press).
9. Waelder, R. The Goal of Psychotherapy. *Amer. J. Orthopsychiatry*, 10: 704–06, 1940.

Chapter 24

Short-Term Dynamic Psychotherapy: A Retrospective and Perspective View

M. STRAKER

Along with pharmacotherapy, short-term psychotherapy has become the dominant psychiatric intervention of the past twenty-five years. In looking back, one can identify major signposts marking its growth and development. The view of the future is far less clear, as psychiatric prediction is hardly infallible. Indeed, it may be little better than chance.. However, I venture that the further evolution of short-term psychotherapy is closely linked with the future of clinical psychiatry itself.

THE RETROSPECTIVE VIEW

Freud at first practiced brief treatment when he believed that to know the cause of a neurosis would quickly lead to its resolution. In the next half-century, psychoanalysis had so expanded its theory, goals and time frame that by 1946 Alexander was experimenting with briefer psychotherapy. (1) He wrote that primarily supportive measures are indicated whenever the functional impairment of the ego is of a temporary nature caused by acute emotional stress. "The successful basis of brief therapy then is to apply techniques which aid in the resolution of the temporary crisis, and permit further independence and ego growth to continue unaided." (2)

Military psychiatry (W.W. II) firmly established the value of brief psychotherapy when applied promptly and skillfully. Demobilized psychiatrists were joined by a stream of graduates from expanded psychiatric training programs. They returned to the community and moved into new professional territory and expanded roles. Many entered private practice. Others joined general hospitals and provided new services in consultation and direct patient care on the wards, in the emergency room and in outpatient clinics. These activities fused with awakened community needs to fuel the development of community and social psychiatry. As a result of the greater acceptance of psychiatry, an increased range of emotional crises presented for treatment. Some of these yielded quickly to short-term therapy. During the 1950's the antipsychotic and antidepressant drugs greatly enlarged the pool of patients who could be treated on an ambulatory basis. The pressing needs of many for psychological treatment provided further impetus for brief methods of various kinds. (3) Fenichel succinctly described brief psychotherapy as "the child of bitter practical necessity." (4) Congested clinics with long waiting lists provided added social pressures. (5)

The gradual emergence of a theoretical understructure for short-term psychotherapy added new roots to nourish its growth. Contributions were derived from the growing preoccupation with ego psychology, from the neoanalytic offshoots and from increased boldness in flexible applications of psychoanalytic insights. (6) The development of "crisis intervention" concepts served as an important stimulus (1), as did Lindemann's description of acute grief, and its management and resolution. (8)

Indications

Short-term psychotherapy has been recommended as a preventive technique in high-risk groups (9) and to reduce the need for rehospitalization. (10) It is proposed as the most appropriate, applicable and practical psychotherapy for the poor. (11), (12), (13) It has its greatest success when applied in situations of crisis and acute stress, (14), (15), (16) especially meeting patient needs of the emergency room (17) and the brief hospitalization unit. (18) It is indicated on the consultation-liaison service to meet the treatment needs of patients with psychiatric reactions to physical illness. (19) It can be effective as intervention for the behavioral problems of the child or to meet the situational anxiety of the adult or the family group. The more specific indications for anxiety-provoking dynamic short-term psychotherapy include defining a focal problem in a well-motivated patient who has good ego resources and the capacity to relate in a meaningful way.

Short-Term Techniques

The major varieties include:

(1) *The crisis intervention model.* The intervention aims to resolve the crisis through a number of stages. Rapport is established and is utilized to review the development of the crisis, the precipitating events and the previous coping attempts. The exploration is cathartic, providing opportunity for crisis resolution and fostering recompensation and opportunity for prevention of future episodes.

(2) *Enhancement of coping responses.* Effective problem-solving is achieved through ego support, clarification of the conflict issues, identification with the therapist and encouragement of new learning. (3), (5), (16), (20)

(3) *Emphasis is placed on existing ego strengths,* utilizing the positive resources and environmental manipulations to foster stabilization. (5), (21)

(4) *The search for new insights and further maturation* is an important therapeutic objective.

Wolberg states that the psychodynamic interpretation of operational dynamics, using history, symptoms, observed patient behavior, is "like a biopsy of the total psychodynamic picture." (22). The goal is not simply the resolution of the presenting crisis, but capitalizing on the fluid ego state to facilitate further maturation.

Enthusiasts insist that short-term psychotherapy is a valuable technique to avert or reverse emotional decompensation, and is not, by default, a second-rate psychoanalysis. (16) However, the effective application of psychoanalytic insights is invaluable, (2), (6), (23), (24) and such insights are relevant to the tasks of evaluating complaints, assessing defenses, transference and resistance, and selecting the specific kind of intervention and its timing. (6) It is this specific professional competence and its appropriate exercise that differentiate the soundly based use of dynamic short-term psychotherapy from the simple overinclusive common-sense platitudes that are offered by empathic and supportive others.

It is a time-limited approach which does not aim for basic personality reconstruction, but whose goals are symptom reduction, relief of suffering, improved coping and restoration of homeostasis. Beyond these modest objectives, a continuing further improvement may be possible. (4), (13), (23), (24), (25)

This is more likely if the conflict resolution arrived at is "true" psychodynamically, rather than a "false solution." (26) Acute crisis increases patient susceptibility to therapeutic intervention, and this enhances outcome. (27)

The Patient-Doctor Relationship

The patient with the best prospects is one who demonstrates a strong positive motivation to accept the therapeutic alliance and the associated work tasks. Addicts, the markedly narcissistic or the excessively dependent patient may pose special hazards. (28) However, even these may respond to brief therapy with benefit, provided the transference reactions are correctly dealt with. (6)

In the presence of a therapeutically accessible patient, the therapist must approach actively, with whatever style will help to facilitate and firmly establish the patient-doctor relationship. The contractual boundaries and the individual responsibilities must be quickly defined, and focusing on selected tasks becomes a major commitment. Quick rapport (25) and empathic qualities are important. (29) The therapy is focused toward the major problem (15), (30) and is goal-oriented, avoiding or ignoring diversions. (20) The therapist throughout is actively helpful. (31) The therapist who remains distant, detached and withdrawn will not find short-term psychotherapy a rewarding technique.

Most therapists agree that a positive transference creates a desirable therapeutic climate and that this should be fostered and utilized. Alexander supported the principle of flexibility. "We have sought to learn how to control and manipulate the transference relationship, so as to achieve the specific goal and fit the particular psychodynamics of each case." (1) Strupp states that the patient-therapist relationship creates the therapeutic vehicle which permits the therapeutic tasks to go forward. (32)

There are varied opinions regarding transference interpretations. The view expressed by some clinicians suggests that the therapist accept the role of transference object without interpretation but utilize it to move toward the treatment goal. (20), (23) When insight is a major objective, transference interpretation becomes an important activity. Whatever the theoretical orientation, the effective clinician will inervene with transference interpretation when necessary to achieve momentum in the therapy. Indeed, Offenkrantz and Tobin state, "every competent psychiatrist regardless of discipline must be able to recognize

(a) the occurrence of a transference reaction, (b) the criteria for deciding when to interpret its presence, and (c) how to make a transference interpretation." (6)

Results of Short-Term Psychotherapy

It is not unreasonable to raise the question whether a good outcome represents spontaneous symptom remission or is a placebo response resulting from the charged interaction between an enthusiastic therapist and a susceptible and willing patient. Certainly, shared hopeful expectations do constitute an extremely potent force. (31), (33), (34), (35), (36) This area needs further study in spite of the difficulty in designing and carrying out comparison clinical studies with acceptable controls. (30)

Aynet (37) reported that of 1,115 patients treated for a maximum of fifteen visits by participating psychiatrists, approximately 80 percent reported improvement after treatment. The survey was done two or three years later. Another study (38) approaches treatment outcome with collection of multiple data from nearly 1,000 patients who received brief psychotherapy (five visits or less). The data considered epidemiological factors, outcome ratings, as determined by both treating professionals and self-rating symptom check list, and an intensive process study. The latter involved short-term prediction and a review of the therapeutic interpretations. This intensive survey concluded that "brief, well-conceptualized psychoanalytically-oriented psychotherapy has a demonstrable rationale and success."

A more recent study from a university psychiatric outpatient clinic compared patients treated by short-term analytically oriented psychotherapy with those receiving behavioral therapy. At four months, behavior therapy produced significantly more overall improvement. However, at two years, all groups showed improvement to an approximately equal extent. This included an untreated group placed on the waiting list. (39)

A Tavistock Clinic report on "untreated" cases followed up forty-five patients who were examined and assessed but not treated two to eight years earlier. It was found that 51 percent showed symptomatic improvement but only twenty-four percent demonstrated psychodynamic change. The authors had at the start expected to demonstrate the role of spontaneous remission but found strong evidence that "powerful therapeutic effects may follow from a single interview." (40) They concluded that a single psychiatric contact may initiate emotional maturation or may facilitate further improvement even if this has spontaneously begun.

THE PROSPECTIVE VIEW

Glimpses into the future are provided by projecting present trends beyond the immediate time horizon. Prediction might be more reliable if psychiatry were unified around an accepted theory and were in a more stable state. In my view there appears to be a fusion between the future of short-term psychotherapies, including the dynamic anxiety-provoking type, and further developments in clinical psychiatry.

Our professional future is undoubtedly being shaped by some of the present-day issues in psychiatry. The shift of some of the burdens of patient care from institution to therapeutic and support programs at the community level is one such element. Another is the impact of third-party payment and the related pressures to develop cost-efficient procedures. Ongoing developments in psychopharmacology and in computer technology are bound to have important repercussions. Professional activities are increasingly being influenced by consumer demands for increased participation, informed consent and a clear accountability. The future role of the psychiatrist and boundary issues relating to paraprofessionals need consideration. Recent applications of Weed's problem-oriented medical record and the pressures for evaluation of both process and outcome will also have their effects upon the future of psychiatry.

Community Change Factors

Societal changes have influenced the demand for mental health services at the community level. Changes in modes with respect to individual freedom no longer sanction the past practices for isolation and confinement for those who demonstrate deviant behaviors. Antipsychotic medication has also brought preventive and after-care treatment in the community closer to reality. This results in a declining institutional population and a shift of the burdens of patient care to other resources. The developments in ambulatory care provide new responsibilities, as well as new opportunities for therapist and patient to work together within the community setting.

Third-party payment inevitably increases demands for service at the community level, creating pressures and opportunities for the increased application of short-term methods. More and more frequently one also hears the term "cost efficiency." This is an obvious early warning for the time when treatment choices will be determined by national budget considerations, when health-care dollars will compete with other items for national priority.

There is also a progressive sophistication in the patient consumers. They increasingly demand a freedom to choose, based on a truly informed consent. In my view this represents a push to renegotiate the traditional nature of the patient-therapist relationship. (41) It is entirely possible that the choice for brief treatment in the future may be determined not alone by the professional's opinion that the patient meets prescribed clinical selection criteria. It may be increasingly necessary to acknowledge the patient's own perceptions, the patient's treatment goals and the patient's wishes in choosing the therapeutic tactics.

Clinical Change Factors

Ongoing psychopharmacology research will shortly enable us to predict the therapeutic response to a psychotropic drug from a test-dose response. This will provide guidance and direction for more sophisticated biochemical interventions. Even when this millennium has arrived, it will still require more than medication alone to help patients who have a serious emotional disorder. It remains a challenge to select patients not only for specific pharmacologic interventions, but also for specific psychotherapeutic approaches. Our past clumsy clinical trial methods need to be refined and shaped by more sophisticated predictors. The ongoing work in selecting and following up patients treated with dynamic short-term anxiety-producing psychotherapy is an encouraging start in that direction. Careful process and outcome evaluations need to be made for other treatment modalities as well.

Computer technology has been moving slowly but steadily into psychiatry. It seems likely that in the near future computer-assisted technicians will play a much larger role. If computer supremacy ultimately emerges with unchallenged authority, the following speculation seems reasonable.

Questionnaires, both self-completed or staff-assisted, will collect historical and current data, while paraprofessionals complete behavioral observation check lists. These data will be keypunched for computer diagnosis and treatment recommendations. The computer may also be able to identify special problem areas for focused interventions. Within such a system the present clinical psychiatric role is replaced by "the mental health engineer." The retreat from direct patient care will be covered by functions as consultant, educator, adviser to computer programmers, participant in community health planning. The clinical intervention may be preserved for computer treatment failures or for consultation liaison work. West has predicted that the major role of the future psychiatrist will be as a superconsultant. It will require that special skills be developed in order to integrate and synthesize data from the psychosocial and biomedical bodies of knowledge. (41)

Professional role problems and conflicts of authority are already evident in many treatment settings. Paraprofessionals are often cast in the role of "primary therapists." Their response may be warm, supportive and intuitively correct but unrefined by training or a capacity for insight into behavioral complexity. In the Aynet study, (37) there was little difference in the results obtained from brief treatment by psychiatrist, social worker or psychologist.

Role and boundary realignments are both appropriate and inevitable. The important question is whether this can be rationally determined by matching patient needs with professional training and competence. Research is required in a number of areas. It is not clearly understood what makes an effective therapist. Another problem lies in the limitations of our diagnostic classification system. Patients to whom the same diagnosis may be assigned may have significantly different functional deficits and have different requirements for specific psychotherapeutic interventions. Those patients who will improve with the help of a supportive human contact can surely do well with paraprofessional assistance. On the other hand, other patients may require interventions which incorporate a high degree of integrative skills, to identify and formulate hypotheses about complex problems. Particularly when the integration of biological and psychosocial data is essential, the intervention of the psychiatrist is of critical importance. At times, professional teamwork involves some inevitable overlap of function. However, such teamwork is most effective when each member contributes special skills toward the shared common goal.

The application of dynamic short-term psychotherapy requires that the patient's major problems and conflicts be defined and that the therapeutic tasks are focused upon these issues. These goals seem congruent with Weed's problem-oriented medical record. (43) This collects basic patient data from which is formulated a list of problems for further investigation, treatment, patient education and outcome evaluation. The application of this different medical record philosophy to the field of psychiatry holds considerable promise that it may change our traditional habits of perception. While similar to target symptom definition, it goes much beyond that narrow field. As this different form of data collection and synthesis becomes more sophisticated, it may emerge as a significant force in the future of psychiatry. This can be of benefit if the focusing on patient problems does not preclude the continuing need to retain the view of the patient as a whole.

The increasing pressures for evaluation of both process and outcome represent a significant shaping force for the future. The difficulties of evaluation in psychiatry are obvious, but external demands are now adding a new dimension to establish and meet predicted criteria regarding outcome. Anecdotal accounts are less and less acceptable even at this time. The continuing review of therapeutic practices is now more urgent than ever, and this will inevitably bring changes in the future.

Treatment Considerations

Effective treatment depends upon the collection of data which are correlated and psychodynamically synthesized into a diagnostic formulation. This permits the development of hypotheses, possibilities, priorities and a treatment plan. The data include social, cultural, individual and family material. They include psychosocial and biological events, and identify both assets and pathology. They include the present, the past and the transference responses in the therapeutic interactions.

A large reservoir of psychiatric patients exists who are still deprived of any significant psychotherapy.. This group is already defined as, or represents, the high-risk population. Psychiatry is thus confronted with responsibility and an opportunity. Continuing work is required to develop criteria for optimal selection and appropriate application of method and procedure for the patient's needs. The questions that need investigation include who should be treated, by whom, when best applied, and in what settings. The successful use of short-term psychotherapy in a general hospital outpatient setting is no longer new. (44) The answers to these questions will tell us much not only about the future of short-term psychotherapy, but about the future of clinical psychiatry as well. An increased use of short-term psychotherapy, together with increased risk-taking in its application to wider patient populations, provides a broad avenue, rich with opportunities, which leads from the clinical psychiatry of the past into the psychiatry of the future.

REFERENCES

1. Alexander, F. and T.M. French. *Psychoanalytic Therapy.* New York: Ronald Press, 1946.
2. Alexander, F. Current Views on Psychotherapy in the Scope of Psychoanalysis. New York: Basic Books, 1961, pp. 276–89, 1953.
3. Frank, J.D. The Role of Hope in Psychotherapy. *Internat. J. Psychiat.,* 5:383–95, 1968.
4. Fenichel, O. Brief Psychotherapy. In H. Fenichel and D. Rapaport (eds.), *The Collected Papers of Otto Fenichel.* New York: Norton, 1954.

5. Straker, M. Brief Psychotherapy: A Technique for General Hospital Out-Patient Psychiatry. *Compr. Psychiat.*, 7, 41:39–45, 1966.
6. Offenkrantz, W. and A. Tobin. Psychoanalytic Psychotherapy. *Archives Gen. Psychiat.*, 30, 5:593–609, 1974.
7. Caplan, G. *Principles of Preventive Psychiatry.* New York: Basic Books, 1964.
8. Lindemann, E. Symptomatology and Management of Acute Grief. *Am. J. Psychiat.*, 101:141–48, 1944.
9. Klein, D. and E. Lindemann. Preventive Intervention in Individual and Family Crisis Situations. In G. Caplan (ed.), *Prevention of Mental Disorders in Children.* New York: Basic Books, 1961.
10. Coleman, M.D. Methods of Psychotherapy: Emergency Psychotherapy. In J.H. Masserman, and J.L. Moreno (eds.), *Progress in Psychotherapy.* New York: Grune & Stratton, 1960.
11. Normand, W., and H. Fonsterheim, et al. The Acceptance of the Psychiatric Walk-In Clinic in a Highly Deprived Community. *Amer. J. Psychiat.*, 120, 6:533–39, 1963.
12. Barten, H. The Expanding Spectrum of the Brief Therapies. In H. Barten (ed.), *Brief Therapies.* New York: Behavioral Publications, 1971.
13. Wolberg, L.R. *Short-Term Psychotherapy.* New York: Grune & Stratton, 1965.
14. Bellak, L. The Emergency Psychotherapy of Depression. In G. Bychowski and J.L. Despert (eds.), *Specialized Techniques in Psychotherapy.* New York: Basic Books, 1952.
15. Harris, M.R., B.L. Kalis, and E.H. Freeman. Precipitating Stress: An Approach to Brief Therapy. *Amer. J. Psychother.*, 17:465–571, 1963.
16. Jacobson, G.F., D.M. Wilner, W.E. Morley, et al. The Scope and Practice of an Early-Access Brief Treatment Psychiatric Centre. *Amer. J. Psychiat.*, 121:1176–82, 1965.
17. Hayworth, R.M. Positive Outcome in Psychiatric Crisis: Evaluation of Thioridazine Concentrate in an Intensive Short-Term Psychiatric Program. *Psychosomatics*, 14, 1:42–45, 1973.
18. Straker, M., C. Yung, and L. Weiss. A Comprehensive Emergency Psychiatric Service in a General Hospital. *Can. Psychiat. Assoc. J.*, 16:137–39, 1971.
19. Stein, F.H.. J. Murdaugh, and J.A. Macleod. Brief Psychotherapy of Psychiatric Reactions to Physical Illness. *Amer. J. Psychiat.*, 125:1040–47, 1969.
20. Sifneos, P. Two Different Kinds of Psychotherapy of Short Duration. *Amer. J. Psychiat.*, 123:1069–74, 1967.
21. Wayne, G. How Long? An Approach to Reducing Duration of In-Patient Treatment. In G. Wayne and R. Koegler (eds.), *Emergency Psychiatry and Brief Therapy. Internat. Psychiat. Clinics*, Vol. 3, 1966, pp. 107–17.
22. Wolberg, L. Methodology in Short-Term Therapy. *Amer. J. Psychiat.*, 122:135–40, 1965.

23. Sarvis, M., S. Dewees, and R.F. Johnson. A Concept of Ego-Oriented Psychotherapy. *Psychiatry*, 22:277–87, 1958.
24. Bellak, L. and L. Small. *Emergency Psychotherapy and Brief Psychotherapy*. New York: Grune & Stratton, 1965.
25. Wolberg, L. *"Brief" or "Short-Term" Psychotherapy*. New York: Grune & Stratton, 1954, pp. 103–05.
26. Malan, D.: On Assessing the Results of Psychotherapy. *Br. J. Med. Psychology*, 32: 86–105, 1959.
27. Sterlin, H.: Short-Term vs. Long-Term Psychotherapy in the Light of a General Theory of Human Relationships. *Br. J. Med. Psychology*, 41:357, 1968
28. Swartz. J.: Time Limited Brief Psychotherapy. *Seminars in Psychiatry*, 1:380–88, 1969.
29. Chessick, R.D.: *How Psychotherapy Heals*. New York:: Science House, 1969, pp. 107–122.
30. Cawley, R., J. Candy, D. Malan, and I. Marks. Dynamic Psychotherapy: Can it be Evaluated? *Proc. Royal Soc. of Med.*, 66, 9, 1973.
31. Baum, O.E. and S.B. Felzer. Activity in Initial Interviews with Lower Class Patients. *Arch. Gen. Psychiat.*, 10:345–53, 1964.
32. Strupp, H.H. Psychoanalysis, "Focal Psychotherapy," and the Nature of the Therapeutic Influence. *Arch. Gen. Psychiat.*, 32:127–35, 1975.
33. Rosenbaum. C.P. Events of Early Therapy and Brief Therapy. *Arch. Gen. Psychiat.*, 10:506–12, 1964.
34. Stotland, E. *The Psychology of Hope*. San Francisco: Jossey-Bass Inc., 1969.
35. Sloane, B.: The Converging Paths of Behavior Therapy and Psychotherapy. *Internat. J. Psychiat.*, 8, 1, 1969.
36. Marmor, J. Neurosis and the Psychotherapeutic Process: Similarities and Differences in the Behavioural and Psychodynamic Conceptions. *Internat. J. Psychiat*, 8, 1, 1969.
37. Aynet, H. How Effective Is Short-Term Psychotherapy. In L. Wolberg (ed.), *Short-Term Psychotherapy*. New York: Grune & Stratton, 1965.
38. Appendix A: Multiple Level Study of Brief Psychotherapy in a Trouble Shooting Clinic. In L. Ballak, and L. Small. *Emergency Psychotherapy and Brief Psychotherapy*. New York: Grune & Stratton, 1965, pp. 141–63.
39. Sloane, B., F.R. Staples, A.H. Cristol, N.J. Yorkston, and K. Whipple. Short-Term Analytically-Oriented Psychotherapy Versus Behavior Therapy. *Am. J. Psychiat.* 132, No. 4, pp. 373–77, April 1975.
40. Malan, D., E.S. Heath, H.A. Bacal, and F.H.G. Balfour. Psychodynamic Changes in Untreated Neurotic Patients. *Arch. Gen. Psychiat.*, 32:110–26, 1975.
41. Straker, M. Current Medico-Legal Issues—A Psychiatrist's View. Dis. of Nerv. Systems (in press).
42. West, L.J. The Future of Psychiatric Education. *Amer. J. Psychiat.*, 130, 5:521–28, 1973.
43. Weed, L. *Medical Records, Medical Education, and Patient Care*.

Chicago: Western Reserve University Press. Distributed by Yearbook Medical Publishers, 1971.
44. Straker, M. Institutional Psychiatry Revisited. *Dis. of Nerv. Systems,* 35:123–27, 1974.

Chapter 25

Research Strategies in Short-Term Dynamic Psychotherapy

C. YUNG

This chapter deals with two major issues of research strategies in short-term dynamic psychotherapy (STDP) which form the basic orientation and methodology for one of the projects currently in progress at the Short-Term Psychotherapy Teaching and Research Unit of The Montreal General Hospital.

These are the selection of suitable candidates for STDP and the classification of psychotherapeutic outcomes. Other important issues, such as content analysis, inter-rater reliability and validity of measurement scales, methods of data collection and outcome evaluations will be dealt with in subsequent publications.

The reader is referred to sections of this volume on the historical antecedents of psychoanalysis, past attempts of psychotherapy research and brief therapy in reference to STDP and criteria for selection of patients by various proponents of short-term dynamic psychotherapists for a better perspective and understanding of the issues and problems existing in STDP research.

Only those clinical investigations with research planning, methodology and documentation of using principles in therapy will be reviewed here. Special emphasis is put on issues relating to motivation and response to partial or total interpretation in the diagnostic interview.

I. REVIEW OF STUDIES

There are essentially three major approaches to STDP research: naturalistic-observational, correlational and comparative.

Naturalistic-Observational Approaches

Seitz's study of 1953 can be regarded as a pioneer attempt to study systematically the outcome of STDP in a group of twenty-five patients with psychocutaneous excoriation syndromes with one year follow-up (33). He used four scales on motivation: poor, fair, good and excellent. A psychodynamic hypothesis and criteria of outcome were postulated for each patient prior to treatment. Seitz concluded that patients who discontinued treatment were significantly less well-motivated for psychotherapy than were the patients who completed treatment.

Schoenberg and Carr used similar methodology on a group of twenty-six patients with neurodermatitis (34). Motivation was rated as slight, moderate and marked. It was not related to outcome.

Stewart reported his own observation and experience with twenty patients treated with a six-month fixed-term once-weekly psychotherapy and follow-up of outcome. He confirmed the efficacy of the method but there were no definitive findings on selection of patients (40).

Bellak and Small's study of 1,414 patients seeking emergency help concluded the following: 70 percent of these patients were given a full course of five interviews, and approximately 82 percent of the treated group improved significantly (7).

Correlational Approaches

These consist essentially of attempts to identify either patient or treatment variables to therapeutic outcomes.

Gottschalk et al. reported "Good Responders" as having the following characteristics: a positive interest in interpersonal object relationship, acutely distressing and disabling psychological symptoms and a lower socioeconomic background (23).

Although most studies suggest that motivation, as has been outlined by Drs. Sifneos, Malan and Davanloo, is an important variable for successful outcome in STDP, there are studies failing to support this, namely, the study by Schoenberg and the Menninger Research Project Report. The latter states, "Motivation and psychological mindedness are *not* necessary prerequisites to enter psychoanalytic-oriented treatment modalities. There is a lack of prognostic significance of initial motivation for patients undergoing psychotherapy." (11)

Luborsky et al.'s review on "Factors Influencing the Outcome of Psychotherapy" concluded as follows on motivation (27): "Although amount of motivation and/or expectation tends to be positively related to outcome, type of motivation is not predictive." Surprisingly, patients with congruent motivation for treatment do not fare better than those with noncongruent motives.

It is difficult to compare meaningfully the results of long-term psychotherapy to those of STDP, notwithstanding that there are no standard operational definitions or reliable and valid methods of assessment for these psychological concepts. Be that as it may, the basis of controversy may arise from the fact that different workers may have different meanings on just one concept, or different terms meaning similar concepts and observations. For example, the Menninger Research Project separated motivation from psychological-mindedness, as does Dr. Davanloo, whereas Dr. Sifneos subsumes psychological-mindedness as one of the seven subcriteria of motivation. Dr. Malan's criterion of patient's responses to interpretation may be viewed as one of the dimensions of psychological-mindedness.

Comparative Approaches

These consist of studies comparing the treatment outcomes of behavior therapy to those of STDP. The studies of Gelder (22) and Patterson (29) gave behavior therapy a more favorable status.

However, a recent well-designed and well-controlled study by Sloane et al. comparing the outcome of short-term psychoanalytically oriented psychotherapy vs. behavior therapy of neurotic or personality disorder outpatients concluded that there is no clear evidence for the superiority of behavior therapy over psychotherapy (37).

In view of the aforementioned divergence of findings, I feel it necessary to study these variables in question through a naturalistic-observational approach in order to identify their phenomenological manifestations, as well as attempt to set up operational definitions of these variables through content analysis of initial assessment interviews and therapeutic sessions.

II. OUTLINE OF A RESEARCH STUDY

At the Montreal General Hospital, STDP has been applied in various forms to a variety of outpatient populations, ranging from supportive short-term interventions based on psychodynamic principles to a highly interpretative type of psychotherapeutic intervention.

These activities have been formulated into a number of systematic research projects. Dr. Davanloo has reported on one of these systematic researches over a period of ten years: the treatment of 115 patients in STDP with two- to seven-year follow-up. Outlined below are some of the basic guidelines and assumptions which form the basis of the research methodology and orientation, with particular reference to studying the correlation of patient variables to STDP therapeutic outcomes and classification of therapeutic outcomes.

The Basic Guidelines and Operational Definitions

(1) The therapeutic principles of STDP adhere to the basic tenets of psychoanalysis, which postulate that the curative process is a result of the analysis of the transference and interpretations of unconscious psychodynamic forces. If there is no evidence of these variables in the content analysis of the psychotherapeutic sessions, it is presumed that STDP has not been applied.

(2) There are two basic components of a psychotherapeutic intervention—the nonspecific and the specific. The former consists of those variables which are (a) closely related to the therapist, i.e., the therapist factor (personality, attitudes, empathy, experience, etc.), (b) present in almost all forms of a helping relationship (listening, understanding, empathizing, etc.), and (c) are *not* implicated as the primary factor to account for successful outcome and to induce change.

The specific components are those specific measures claimed to be the curative forces by a specific type of treatment. They are unique to the particular theory and are not implicated as important or as the curative force by other types of treatment.

For example, the process of systematic desensitization and the analysis of transference and resistance are regarded as the specific components of behavior therapy and psychoanalytically oriented psychotherapy, respectively. The specific components of STDP as proposed here are defined as follows: (a) psychotherapeutic intervention, namely, interpretation, (b) unconscious material made conscious for patient, and (c) evidence of a corrective emotional experience for the patient, either in or outside the session.

(3) Some basic aspects of the General Systems Theory in conceptualizing the interrelationship between the patient and the therapist are adopted. Thus the entire dyadic psychotherapeutic process can be conceptualized as consisting of two major subsystems, (a) the patient and (b) the therapist, which together form a new system: (c) the psychotherapeutic process. (These are defined in detail later in this

chapter.) However, only selected elements of these subsystems will be investigated in the research project. These selected elements are those variables which have been implicated as essential for a successful outcome of STDP by various research studies in the past as well as those variables which have been postulated to be essential. These have been reviewed earlier.

Assumptions

Assumption I. Since this is a correlational study (i.e., correlating patient variables to psychotherapeutic outcomes), all therapy variables will be studied and correlated for significance of each. In other words, one cannot study the effect of a subsystem A on subsystem B at the exclusion of either the effect of subsystem B on A or the sum total of these two subsystems.

Assumption II. There are a number of essential patient variables which are necessary conditions for a successful outcome of STDP. These variables can be objectively and operationally defined and quantified.

Assumption III. The methods of evaluation and implementation of such a research study are clinically relevant, practical and feasible. It is easily replicable and without undue burden on organization, testing procedures and training of personnel.

Assumption IV. A number of variables are excluded from data analysis, e.g., personality of the therapist and nonverbal communication. This is due to the complex task involved in data collection, the assessment and lack of a unified system of evaluation. One may infer that these variables will definitely play a major role if there is no evidence of a therapeutic specific component through the therapeutic process, e.g., in cases of spontaneous remission and transference cure.

Assumption V. Therapeutic outcomes can be classified and operationally defined. (See later in this chapter.)

Hypothesis Testing

Hypothesis I. All variables under investigation in the project (patient, therapist and the therapeutic process) can be operationally defined and rated quantitatively as scale items. Each variable has seven scale positions (from 1–7) in ascending order of increasing degree of dimension. (See appendices to this chapter for scales of these variables). Tentatively a total of twenty-seven variables are being explored. It should be mentioned that there is overlapping of some of the variables as different forms of manifestations of the same phenomenon. This overlapping may serve as a test for reliability and validity of the scale. For example:

(1) Psychological-mindedness, associations to dreams and receptivity to interpretation.
(2) Verbal articulation, interaction with the interviewer and activity of the interviewer.
(3) Level of psychosexual conflict, defense mechanisms and object relationship.

Hypothesis II. The "Substrate Factor" is a necessary condition for STDP. This factor may be a far more significant criterion for a good potential candidate for STDP and correlation with successful outcome than patient variables such as motivation and psychological-mindedness. (See the following section.)

Hypothesis III. The earlier the therapist initiates the specific therapeutic components, the shorter the duration of treatment and the greater the likelihood of a successful outcome.

Hypothesis IV. The specific therapeutic components are *not* necessary conditions for certain categories of therapeutic outcomes, such as Category II. They are, however, necessary conditions for Category I outcomes.

Hypothesis V. All therapeutic outcomes can be evaluated with reference to the classification system proposed.

Hypothesis VI. The skill and technique of STDP can be delineated objectively by process analysis of therapeutic sessions.

Hypothesis VII. Interpretation and transference interpretations, especially total interpretation, correlates with successful outcome; i.e., the higher the number of interpretations, the better the outcome.

Hypothesis VIII. Specific therapeutic components used by the therapist should be followed in temporal sequence by patient's responses, which are defined as retrieval of repressed material, corrective emotional experiences in or outside the session, and evidence of symptom and behavior change.

III. PROPOSALS OF POSTULATED SIGNIFICANT VARIABLES FOR INVESTIGATION

Patient Variables

The patient subsystem consists of patient variables which are further divided into two parts: (a) the capacity factors, and (b) the substrate factor.

The capacity factors are as follows: (a) intelligence, (b) range and expression of emotions, (c) psychological-mindedness, (d) motivation. (For detailed subcategorization and operational definitions of these variables, see appendices).

The substrate factor is defined as all those verbal productions from the patient as elicited during the interview assessment session which can be formulated into a psychodynamic formulation as a guideline for therapy. They are (a) focality of symptom, (b) precipitating events, (c) psychosexual conflict level, (d) defense mechanism, (e) object relationship, (f) preconscious and unconscious materials, and (g) environmental factors. The substrate factor serves as a substrate for the patient and therapist to interact. In other words, it serves as the medium for the "specific therapeutic component" to take place. Therefore, one can justifiably presume that it would not be possible to have a psychodynamic formulation if there is a total lack of this factor. As a matter of fact, in clinical practice we often regard patients who provide us with dreams, clear-cut dynamic conflicts, as good candidates for therapy. It is interesting to note that no studies have ever put emphasis on the importance of this "substrate factor" as one of the significant criteria for successful outcome.

The therapist subsystem consists of variables which have been described above as the nonspecific and specific therapeutic components.

The psychotherapeutic process system, which is the sum total of the two subsystems previously described, consist of the verbal contents of the session and various aspects of the nonverbal communication. One can assume that if the system psychotherapeutic process is present, as evidenced by "specific components," the elements of both the therapist and patient subsystems are also present.

Classification of Therapeutic Outcomes

First, one of the rationales of psychoanalytic therapy is based on the assumption that "A neurotic behavior or symptom can be resolved by way of making the unconscious conflict to consciousness through the therapeutic process of interpretation and transference." Putting this statement in a simplified form, the above statement becomes: "Therapy given, symptoms disappear or behavior changes occur." Using the symbol Condition A to denote therapy (i.e., specific components described earlier) and Condition B as a symptom or behavior change, there are four probabilities of occurrences, as shown in Table I. Condition B is defined operationally as (a) disappearance or elimination of symptom/behavior, (b) improvement in interpersonal relationships, and (c) intrapsychic conflict resolution. Thus there are four major categories of outcomes, as shown in Table III. The studies of Drs. Malan and Sifneos have emphasized the importance of finding evidence of psychodynamic changes in follow-up studies of outcome evaluation as valid evidence of successful outcome. Incorporating this criterion in the system of categories in Table II, one obtains these probabilities of occurrences:

Table III is further elaborated into Table IV, which consists of four major categories, each category having three subcategories of outcomes. It is assumed that all these categories do exist in clinical situations. "The Case of the Cement-Mixer Man" presented in Chapter 17 is a clinical example of psychodynamic change, where we see changes in the nature of the defense mechanism; the patient had insight into the nature of his unconscious conflict; he understood his symptoms in dynamic terms. Further documentation with clinical examples for each of these categories will be the topic of a separate paper (46).

This classification system is then compared with the existing criteria on terminology of outcomes as used in various research studies. One can put into order no less than fifteen terms used as outcome categories, to the four major categories of outcomes proposed here (See Table V).

This can eliminate the confusion of terms such as Recovered, Improved, Cured, Successful resolution, etc., which may or may not mean similar phenomena by various workers. With this classification system most of the controversial issues in comparing findings of different studies may be avoided, and questions such as the following can be answered quite readily: "How many behavior therapy patients have psychodynamic changes?" "How many patients receiving psychodynamic therapy are actual spontaneous remissions?" "Can the outcomes of behavior therapy and psychodynamic therapy be compared?"

REFERENCES

1. Alexander, F. and T.M. French. *Psychoanalytic Theory*. New York: Ronald Press, 1946.

Table I

	A	B
Category I	+	+
Category II	−	+
Category III	+	−
Category IV	−	−

Table II

Category I:	Successful outcome with evidence of therapeutic intervention
Category II:	Successful outcome without evidence of or incorrect therapeutic intervention
Category III:	Unsuccessful outcome with evidence of therapeutic intervention
Category IV:	Unsuccessful outcome without evidence of or incorrect therapeutic intervention

Table III

	Conditions A	B	C
Category I	+	+	+
	+	−	+
Category II	−	+	+
	−	+	−
Category III	+	−	+
	+	−	−
Category IV	−	−	+
	−	−	−

Condition C: Psychodynamic changes defined as (a) changes in nature of defense mechanisms (i.e. mature defenses replace immature defenses); (b) achieving insight into the unconscious conflict with evidence that this understanding has been applied to resolve successfully a similar conflict which was dealt with unsatisfactorily; (c) meaning of symptom understood in dynamic terms.

Table IV
Categories of Outcomes

Category I: Successful Outcome with Evidence of Therapeutic Intervention
  Subcategory A: Absence of symptom + psychodynamic change + gain
  Subcategory B: Absence of symptom + psychodynamic change
  Subcategory C: Absence of symptom + no psychodynamic change (i.e., original status)
Category II: Successful Outcome without Evidence of or Incorrect Therapeutic Intervention
  Subcategory A: Absence of symptoms + psychodynamic change + gain
  Subcategory B: Absence of symptoms + psychodynamic change
  Subcategory C: Absence of symptoms + no psychodynamic change
Category III: Unsuccessful Outcome with Evidence of Therapeutic Intervention
  Subcategory A: Symptom remains or modified + psychodynamic change
  Subcategory B: Symptom remains or modified + no psychodynamic change
  Subcategory C: Deterioration + no psychodynamic change
Category IV: Unsuccessful Outcome without Evidence of or Incorrect, Therapeutic Intervention
  Subcategory A: Symptom remains or modified + psychodynamic change
  Subcategory B: Symptom remains or modified + no psychodynamic change
  Subcategory C: Deterioration + no psychodynamic change

Table V
Proposed Categories of Therapeutic Outcome as Compared to Criteria of Others

Condition	A	B	Terms used by Researchers
Category I	(+)	(+)	Recovered; Improved; Successful Resolution; Cured
Category II	(−)	(+)	Spontaneous remission; Transference cure; Flight into health
Category III	(+)	(−)	Failure; Unsuccessful; Not improved; No change; Deterioration; Adverse effects; Worse
Category IV	(−)	(−)	No change; Deterioration

2. Alexander, F. Principles and Techniques of Brief Psychotherapeutic Procedures. *Proc. Assoc. Res. Nerv. & Ment. Dis.*, 31:16, 1951.
3. Balint, M. *The Doctor, His Patient and the Illness.* London: Pittman, 1957.
4. Balint, M., et al. *Focal Psychotherapy: An Example of Applied Psychoanalysis.* London: Tavistock, 1972.
5. Barten, H.H. The Coming of Age of the Brief Psychotherapies. In L. Bellak & H.H. Barton (eds.), *Progress in Community Mental Health*, Vol. 1. New York: Grune & Stratton, 1969.
6. Barten, H.H. *Brief Therapies.* New York: Behavioural Publications, 1971.
7. Bellak, L. and L. Small. *Emergency Psychotherapy and Brief Psychotherapy.* New York: Grune & Stratton, 1965.
8. Bergin, A.E. and H. Strupp. *Changing Frontiers in the Science of Psychotherapy.* Atherton, N.Y.: Aldine, 1972.
9. Berliner, B. Short-Psychoanalytic Psychotherapy: Its Possibilities and Its Limitations. *Bull. Menninger Clinic*, 5:204, 1941.
10. Breuer, J. and Freud, S. (1895). *Studies on Hysteria*, J. Strachey (ed.), Standard Edition, London: Hogarth, 1955, pp. 1–305.
11. *Bulletin of the Menninger Clinic.* Final Report of the Menninger Foundations Psychotherapy Research Project, Vol. 36, No. 1/2, 1972.
12. Burdon, A.P. Principles of Brief Psychotherapy. *J. Louisiana Med. Soc.*, 115:374–78, 1963.
13. Caplan, G. *Principles of Preventive Psychiatry.* New York: Basic Books, 1964.
14. Davanloo, H. Personal Communication.
15. Eysenck, H.J. The Effects of Psychotherapy: An Evaluation. *J. Cons. Psychol.*, 16:319–24, 1952.
16. Eysenck, H.J. The Effects of Psychotherapy. *Intl. J. of Psychiatry*, 1:97–178, 1965.
17. Ferenzi. S. (1920). *The Further Development of an Active Therapy in Psychoanalysis:* In *Further Contribution to the Therapy and Technique of Psychoanalysis.* New York: Basic Books, 1951.
18. Ferenzi, S. and O. Rank (1925). Development of Psychoanalysis, Trans. C. Newton. Nervous and Mental Disease Monographs, No. 40.
19. Freud, S. (1901). Fragment of an Analysis of a Case of Hysteria. In J. Strachey, ed., Standard Edition, Vol. 7. London: Hogarth, 1953.
20. Freud, S. (1909). Notes upon a Case of Obsessional Neurosis. In *The Complete Psychological Works of S. Freud*, Vol. 10. London: Hogarth. 1955.
21. Freud, S. (1918). From the History of an Infantile Neurosis. In J. Strachey, ed., Standard Edition, Vol. 17. London: Hogarth, 1955.
22. Gelder, M.G., I.M. Marks, and H.H. Wolff. Desensitization and Psychotherapy in the Treatment of Phobic States: A Controlled Inquiry. *Br. J. Psychiatry*, 113:53–73, 1967.
23. Gottschalk, L.A., P. Mayerson and A.A. Gottlieb. Prediction and Evaluation of Outcome in an Emergency Brief Psychotherapy Clinic. *J. Nerv. & Ment. Dis.*, 144:77–90, 1967.

24. Jones, E. *The Life & Work of Sigmund Freud*, Vol. 1. New York: Basic Books, 1955, p. 88.
25. Kellner, R. Discussion on Eysenck's Paper—"The Effects of Psychotherapy." *Intl. J. Psychiatry*, 2:322–27, 1965.
26. Lewin, K.K. *Brief Encounters: Brief Psychotherapy*. St. Louis: Warren H. Green, 1970.
27. Luborsky, L., M. Chandler, A.H. Auerbach, and J. Cohen. Factors Influencing the Outcome of Psychotherapy: A Review of Quantitative Research. *Psycholog. Bull.*, 75,3:145-85, 1971.
28. Malan, D.H. (1963). *A Study of Brief Psychotherapy*. New York: Plenum/Rosetta Edition, 1975.
29. Paul, G.L. Insight vs. Desensitization in Psychotherapy Two Years after Termination. *J. Consul. Psychol.*, 31:333–48, 1967.
30. Patterson, V., H. Levene, and L. Breger. Treatment and Training Outcomes with Two Time-Limited Therapies. *Arch. Gen. Psychiat.*, 25:161–67, 1971.
31. Proceedings of the Brief Psychotherapy Council. Chicago Institute for Psychoanalysis, 1942, 1948, and 1946.
32. Rosensweig, S. A Transevaluation of Psychotherapy: A Reply to H. Eysenck. *J. Abn. Soc. Psychol.*, 49:298–304, 1954.
33. Seitz, P.E.D. Dynamically-Oriented Brief Psychotherapy: Psychocutaneous Excoriation Syndrome. *Psychosomatic Med.*, 9,3:200–42, 1953.
34. Schoenberg, B. and A.C. Carr. An Investigation of Criteria for Brief Psychotherapy of Neurodermatitis. *Psychosomatic Med.*, 25:253–63, 1963.
35. Sifneos, P.E. The "Motivational Process": A Selection and Prognostic Criterion for Psychotherapy of Short-Duration. *Psychiatry Q.*, 42:271–80, 1968.
36. Sifneos, P.E. *Short-Term Psychotherapy and Emotional Crisis*. Cambridge, Mass: Harvard University Press, 1972.
37. Sloane, R.B., F.R. Staples, A.H. Cristol, N.J. Yorkston, and K. Whipple. Short-Term Analytically-Oriented Psychotherapy vs. Behavior Therapy. *Am. J. Psychiatry*, 132:4,373 or 384, 1975.
38. Small, L. *The Briefer Psychotherapies*. New York: Brunner/Mazel, 1971.
39. Sterba, R. A Case of Brief Psychotherapy by S. Freud. *Psychoanal. Rev.*, 35:75–89, 1951.
40. Stewart, H. Six Months Fixed Term, Once-Weekly Psychotherapy: A Report of 20 Cases with Follow-Up. *Br. J. Psychiat.*, 121:425–35, 1972.
41. Straker, M. Brief Psychotherapy: A Technique for General Hospital Out-Patient Psychiatry. *Compr. Psych.*, 7:39–45, 1966.
42. Straker, M. Brief Psychotherapy in an Out-Patient Clinic: Evaluation and Evolution. *Am. J. Psychiat.*, 124:1219–25, 1968.
43. Strupp, H. In Critical Review: The Effects of Psychotherapy. *Intl. J. Psychiatry*, 1:165–69, 1965.

44. Walter, B. *Theme and Variation.* New York: Knopf, 1946, pp. 164–69.
45. Wolberg, L.R. *Short-Term Psychotherapy.* New York: Grune & Stratton, 1965.
46. Yung, C. Research Strategies in Short-Term Dynamic Psychotherapy: III. Criteria and Categories of Psychotherapeutic Outcomes: Further Considerations, Methods of Evaluation and Supporting Evidences (in preparation).

APPENDICES

Appendix I: Potential Criteria for Exclusion

1. Past history of psychiatric hospitalization   Yes _____   No _____
2. Potential of a psychotic process   Yes _____   No _____
3. Suicide, homicide and acting-out behaviors   Yes _____   No _____
4. Severe personality disorder   Yes _____   No _____
5. Drug dependence and abuses   Yes _____   No _____
6. Other forms of intervention more preferable   Yes _____   No _____
7. Unable to wait six months   Yes _____   No _____
8. Rejects videotaping and research follow-up   Yes _____   No _____

Appendix II: Potential Criteria for Admission to STDP

A. Patient Variables

   1. Capacity Factor

      (a) Schooling

College, 1 year and above	_____ 7
High school diploma	_____ 5
8th grade and below with repeat of grade	_____ 3
No formal schooling	_____ 1

      (b) Verbal Ability

Highly articulate and expressive, with excellent vocabulary	_____ 7
Average articulation, with good to average vocabulary	_____ 5
Difficulties in articulation, and misuses words and concepts	_____ 3
Inability to use words appropriately for expression of thought	_____ 1

   2. Range and Expression of Emotion

      (a) Expression of Affect Variable

Appropriate fluctuations of emotion (depression, anxiety, anger, guilt, etc.)	_____ 7
Limited range of fluctuation yet one type of emotion is expressed or predominant	_____ 5
Inhibition of emotions yet with help can still be brought to awareness	_____ 3
No awareness of an inability to describe feeling states in spite of interviewer's bringing into awareness	_____ 1

      (b) Anxiety Variable

Anxiety predominant with good tolerance level	_____ 7
Moderate degree and marginal tolerance of anxiety	_____ 5
No anxiety expressed (especially in reference to stressful events and situations)	_____ 3

No anxiety in the interview and evidence that
patient can't tolerate slightest anxiety ———1

3. Psychological-Mindedness Variable

Spontaneously giving relevant historical data or current events and attempting to work out on his own same form of explanation of the conflict or symptom, or making connection with past and present thoughts, feelings, and behavior. ———7

Shows ability to do above but in a lesser degree and spontaneity; may require interviewer's intervention. ———5

Some ability to do above after intervention but still externalizes problems. ———3

Denies any connections and meaning in thoughts, feeling and behavior; externalizes problems. ———1

(a) Motivation to Seek Treatment

Seeks treatment out of own initiative. ———7

Suggested by others but accepts readily without reluctance. ———5

Has doubts of seeking help or psychotherapy will help. Much ambivalence. ———3

Forced into treatment out of necessity, or came to treatment in order to mobilize help for the other significant person. ———1

(b) Unconscious Motivation Variable

No evidence from patient's behavior or verbal communication to contradict patient's wish to seek help. ———7

Behavior contradicts the wish but has been dealt with in the interview and presumably will not interfere with therapy. Secondary gain is minimal. ———5

Present and dealt with and patient shows no signs of changing. Secondary gain is too great (i.e. behavior becomes egosyntonic and environment accepts this behavior). ———3

Interested in symptom relief only. Has magic craving and expectation from the treatment ———1

4. Substrate Factor
   (a) Focality of Symptom/Complaint

   Focalized to an interpersonal relationship difficulty by patient as the *only* area of conflict. _____7

   Focalized as somatic symptomatologies which is clearly related to an interpersonal relationship difficulty. The patient accepts this interpersonal relationship conflict as focus of treatment. _____5

   Great difficulties to focalize patient's conflict but an interpersonal relationship conflict may be the chief complaint. _____3

   Complaints cannot be focalized (e.g. somatic symptoms, behavior disturbances, intrapsychic and interpersonal conflicts all present). _____1

   (b) Precipitating Factors

   A clear-cut precipitating event identified within the past six months, with direct relationship to focal conflict (give data). _____7

   Not as a clear-cut event in direct relationship to focal conflict. _____5

   Probable but not definitive that it is the only or major factor. _____3

   None identified. _____1

5. Psychosexual Conflict Level:

   Predominantly triangular conflict with no pre-genital conflict. _____7

   Predominantly triangular conflict with minimal pre-genital conflict. _____6

   Predominantly triangular conflict with moderate pre-genital conflict. (Give evidence.) _____5

   Triangular & pre-genital conflicts both equally dominant. _____3

   Predominantly pre-genital conflict with minimal to no triangular conflict. _____1

6. Defense Mechanism Variable:

   Mature defenses are essentially intact with sublimation. ———7

   Multiplicity of defenses with mostly neurotic ones: If immature defenses are present, they are only transitory. ———5

   Rigid & severe defenses. ———3

   Immature defenses predominant and lacking any mature defenses. ———1

7. Object Relationship Variable:

   (a) Parent-Child Relationship:

   Very satisfactory parental relationship. ———7

   Reasonably satisfactory or other significant person available. ———5

   No satisfactory relationship. ———3

   Deprivation and neglect. ———1

   (b) Current Object Relationship:

   Give and take. ———7

   Giving is neurotically based with ability to take. ———5

   Great difficulty in giving and taking. ———3

   Taking in only; No giving. ———1

8. Preconscious and Unconscious Conflict Variable

   (a) Childhood Recollections and Fantasy:

   Abundant and can be understood in line with current focal conflict. ———7

   Some recollections which may be of dynamic significance. ———5

   Minimal and can't be understood. ———3

   No significant childhood events reported. ———1

   (b) Dream Recall (Childhood):

   Recurrent dreams support dynamic formulation. ———7

       Dream reported. May be of dynamic significance. _____ 5

       Dream sketchy and fragmented, can't be interpreted. _____ 3

       No dreams.

  (c) Dream Recall (Current):

       Dream reported, related to current conflict. _____ 7

       Dream reported; can't be understood definitely for dynamic formulation. _____ 5

       Dreamt, but no recall. _____ 3

       No dreams. _____ 1

  (d) Association to Dream Contents:
       (Check this item only when (b) or (c) is present.)

       Interest in reporting dream. Associates content readily with further significant historical data. _____ 7

       Needs instruction to associate for further data. _____ 5

       Needs assistance, further data can't be understood. _____ 3

       Gives no effort, interest, and further data. _____ 1

9. Environmental Variables:

    No environmental variable impedes the patient's potential for change (i.e. no significant person or reality factor to sabotage the therapy. _____ 7

    Present but can be overcome or manipulated. _____ 5

    Present and will be less likely not to interfere. _____ 3

    Current situational variable will interfere with patient's growth and change. _____ 1

B. *Interacting Variables:*

1. Receptivity to Interpretation:

    Interpretation (total, partial or trial) given, patient gives further supporting data (give verbatim statement). _____ 7

    Accepts readily with only minimal further supporting data. _____ 5

Rejects interpretation, or shows no signs or attempts to comprehend further.	_____ 3
Does not understand at all. Shows no interest, in spite of further attempts to clarify this for the patient.	_____ 1

2. Interaction with the Interviewer:

Patient challenges therapist appropriately and constructively; highly inquisitive; and simultaneously gives relevant historical data.	_____ 7
Occasionally need guidance; once asked to think, patient can freely produce pertinent data.	_____ 5
Moderately passive, compliant, dependent and lacking interaction.	_____ 3
Totally lacking spontaneity. Interviewer senses constant need to ask patient questions.	_____ 1

C. *Interviewer Variable:*

1. Experience Variable:
   (counting from date of first contact in treating patient)

More than 10 years	_____ 7
9-10	_____ 6
7-8	_____ 5
5-6	_____ 4
3-4	_____ 3
1-2	_____ 2
Less than 1 year	_____ 1

2. Activity of Interviewer:

Extremely active with the patient	_____ 7
Moderately active	_____ 5
Less active	_____ 3
No activity	_____ 1

3. Empathic Responses:

Felt greatly for the patient	_____ 7
Felt moderately for the patient	_____ 5

No particular feeling for or against the patient ____3

Can't feel with the patient's feeling at all; or felt opposite to patient's feeling. ____1

4. Psychodynamic Formulation Variable:

Symptom and conflict can be understood with a clear-cut psychodynamic formulation (give formulation) which will guide the therapy. ____7

Psychodynamics can be formulated with certain aspects to be understood. ____5

Tentatively formulated and mostly speculative. ____3

No formulation can be established. ____1

5. Number of Sessions Projected:

Less than 12 ____7

    12-20 ____6

    20-30 ____5

    30-40 ____4

    40-50 ____3

    50-60 ____2

More than 60 ____1

6. Prediction of Therapeutic Outcome:

Successful with psychodynamic change and gain. ____7

Successful with psychodynamic change and return to initial level of function. ____6

Successful, with doubts of psychodynamic change. ____5

Spontaneous remission most likely. ____4

Symptomatic relief at best. ____3

Remain status quo. ____2

No change, probably deteriorate. ____1

7. Confidence Variable:

Great confidence in treating this patient. ____7

Very good confidence. ____6

Good confidence. ____5

Fairly confident. ____4

Doubtful. ____3

No confidence.	_____ 2
Absolutely no confidence.	_____ 1

8. Likability of Patient:

Very pleasant & likable.	_____ 7
Moderately likable and pleasant.	_____ 5
Neutral toward patient.	_____ 3
Unlikable person, irritates and annoys interviewer, has feeling to terminate interview early.	_____ 1

APPENDIX III. SHORT-TERM PSYCHOTHERAPY PATIENT PROFILE

		1	2	3	4	5	6	7
1	Level of Education							
2	Verbal Ability							
3	Expression of Affect							
4	Anxiety Variable							
5	Psychological Mindedness							
6	Motivation to Seek Treatment							
7	Unconscious Motivation							
8	Focality							
9	Precipitating Events							
10	Level of Psychosexual Conflict							
11	Defense Mechanism Variable							
12	Object Relationship							
13	Childhood Recollection & Fantasy							
14	Dreams (Childhood)							
15	Dreams (Current)							
16	Association to Dreams							
17	Environmental Factors							
18	Receptivity to Interpretation							
19	Interaction with the Therapist							
20	Experience Level							
21	Activity of Intervention							
22	Empathic Responses							
23	Psychodynamic Formulation							
24	Number of Sessions Projected							
25	Prediction of Outcome							
26	Confidence Level							
27	Likability of Patient							

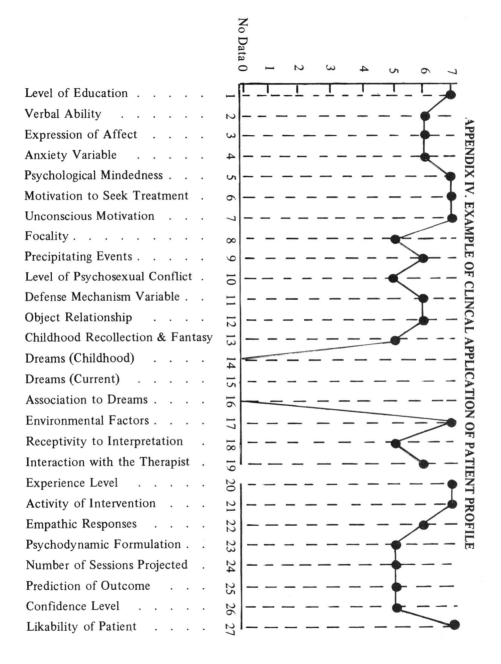

Index

Abraham, C., 15
Affect, 15-17, 28, 74, 144, 260, 288, 540
Alexander, F., 2, 25, 45, 52, 74, 81, 83 86, 292-293, 410, 501-503, 515, 518
Anorexia Nervosa, 219
Anxiety, 16, 25, 120, 188, 336, 363, 505, 540
   Anxiety Attack, 336
   Castration Anxiety, 363, 406
   Oedipal Anxiety, 188
   Primary Traumatic Anxiety, 16
   Separation Anxiety, 16, 188
   Signal Anxiety, 16
Audiovisual, 171-200, 343-388, 408-409, 498

Balint, M., 52-53, 85, 501
Behavior Therapy, 1, 3, 75, 76, 240, 519, 529-530
Bibring, E., 17, 78
Brown, S., 161, 215, 362

Characteriological Issues, 11-13, 50, 189-190, 192-193, 238-239, 326, 331, 343-388, 452, 497, 505-506, 510
Client-Centered Therapy, 75-76
Conflict, 11-12, 19-20, 37, 43, 80, 339, 504, 532, 542
   "Core Conflictual Themes," 511
   Current Conflict, 43, 58
   Interpersonal Conflict, 11-13
   Intrapsychic Conflict and Anxiety, 11-12
   Nuclear Conflict, Focal Conflict, 20, 58, 60, 165, 334, 339, 505
   Psychodynamic Resolution of the Conflict, 262, 485
Conjoint Marital Therapy, 4
Contraindications, 52, 58-59, 87, 97, 304, 465, 504
Corrective Emotional Experience, 45, 238, 302, 304, 378, 405, 485, 503-504, 530, 532
Countertransference, 3, 11, 22-23, 217, 259, 261, 345, 451, 464
   Countertransference in Broad-Focused Short-Term Dynamic Psychotherapy 345
   Countertransference and the Therapeutic Focus, 288
   Negative Countertransference, 263, 265
   Negative Countertransference and the Initial Interview, 288
Crisis and Crisis Intervention, 2, 13-14, 27, 44-45, 90, 95, 146, 287, 469, 515-517
Criteria for Selection, chapters 2, 3, 4, 5, 6, 7, 8, 9, 10, 11, 12, pp. 10, 31, 36, 45, 58-60, 74, 85, 274, 290, 387, 506-508, 516, 523, 527
   for Broad-Focused Short-Term Dynamic Psychotherapy, chapters 2, 5, 9, 12, p. 144
   for Short-Term Anxiety-Provoking Psychotherapy, chapters 3, 6, 8, 11, pp. 81-84, 143
   for Short-Term Dynamic Psychotherapy, chapters 2, 3, 5, 7, 9, 10, 12, pp. 85-91, 167

INDEX

Davanloo, H., chapters 2, 5, 9, 12, 14, 17, 21, pp. 63, 74, 85, 88, 89, 90, 91, 93, 94, 97, 144, 167, 190, 192-193, 197, 220, 260-261, 320, 364, 378, 468, 486-487, 528-529, 530
Defense Mechanisms, 10, 15, 18, 41, 96, 188, 193, 216, 221, 333, 505, 532-533, 543
   Ego Defense, 15
   Male Defense Mechanisms, 408
Dependence, 61, 66, 87, 505
Depression, 16-17, 142-146, 169, 171, 187
Desensitization, 3
Diagnosis,
   Clinical Diagnosis, chapter 2, pp. 11-12, 27, 75
   Computor Diagnosis, chapter 2, p. 521
   Dynamic Diagnosis, chapter 2, pp. 11-13, 39, 75, 96, 125
   Functional Therapeutic Diagnosis, chapter 2, p. 510
   Genetic Diagnosis, chapter 2, pp. 13-14, 23, 75
   Psychotherapeutic Diagnosis, chapter 2, pp. 14, 23, 75, 272
Dongier, M., 406, 450
Dream Interpretation, 25, 46, 94, 404, 406-407, 429, 466-467, 533, 543
Dynamic, *see* Psychodynamic

Ego, 10, 15-16, 18, 503-504, 506, 511, 517
   Affective Function of the Ego, 15-16
   Ego-Adaptive Capacities, 12, 237
   Ego and Object Cathexis, 15
   Ego and Symptom Formation, 12
   Ego and the Id, 10-11
   Ego Boundary, 216, 260
   Ego Defect, 500
   Ego Identification, 15
   Ego Psychology, 10-11
   Evaluation of Ego Function, 14-15
   Fluid Ego State, 517
   Functional Impairment of Ego, 515, *see also* Defense Mechanism
   Psychoanalytic Ego Psychology, 10-11, 516
Eisenstein, S., 165, 198, 303, 306, 411
Empathy, 22, 451-452
Epstein, N., 487
Erikson, E., 10
Evaluation, *see* Criteria for Selection

Family Therapy, 4, 487
Federn, 74
Fenichel, 516
Ferenczi, S., 2, 501
Fixation, 14, 19, 506
Focus, Psychotherapeutic, 14, 20-21, 27, 37-38, 58-60, 120, 272, 331, 379, 484, 487-488, 505, 510-511
Frank, J., 2
French, T., 2, 20, 502
Freud, A., 10
Freud, S., 2, 9-10, 13, 16, 74, 118, 270, 292, 307, 340, 506

Golden, C., 269-290
Group therapy, 1, 4
   Analytically Oriented Group Therapy, 4

Hartmann, H., 10
Homosexual, 495
   Pseudohomosexual Reaction, 362
Human Relationship, 14-15, 27, 36, 37, 83, 266, 507, 532-533, 543

Id, Structure and Function, chapter 2, pp. 14, 19
   Id-Oriented Psychology, 10-11
Identification, 15, 124, 238, 289, 345, 517
   Ego Identification, 15
Insight,
   Cognitive Insight/Emotional Insight, 240, 279, 388, 410, 467, 485
   Insight in Psychoanalytic Treatment, 13, 293, 501, 506, 518,
   Insight through Interpretation, 79, 97
Intelligence, 15, 18, 25, 74, 143, 533
   Intelligence as a Criteria for Selection, 10, 28, 36-37
Interpretation, 9, 15, 18, 25, 29-31, 45-50, 53, 55-56, 59-60, 77-80, 92, 94, 126, 163, 167-168, 241, 259-262, 286-288, 291-292, 298, 302, 307, 333-334, 339, 344-345, 379, 404, 409, 426, 449, 464, 484, 506, 509, 511, 517, 519, 527, 530, 532, 534
   Cognitive Interpretation, 288
   Interpretation in Classical Psychoanalysis, 80
   Interpretation of Defenses, 407
   Interpretation of Resistance, 60, 260, 262, 345

Parent Transference Link, 496, *see also* chapter 4
Partial Interpretation, 333
Past-Present Transference Link in the Psychodiagnostic Interview, 25, 30-31, 260-261, 302, 307, 344
Past-Present Transference Link (P-P-T Link), 77-78, 196-198, 260, 273, *see also* chapter 2
Response to Interpretation, 15, 18, 29, 77, 544
Response to Interpretation and Motivation, 31, 59
Response to Interpretation in the Initial Interview, 95, 286, 291-292, 307
Total Interpretation, 30
Transference Interpretation, 39-40, 53, 168, 259
Transference Interpretation in the Initial Interview, 92, 286, 298, 302
Triange of Insight, 333
Intuition, 334, 451

Jones, E., 86

Kaplan, G., 13
Knight, R., 43-44
Kravitz, H., 145-146, 244, 259, 264, 464
Kris, E., 13

Learning, 13, 40
Evidence of New Learning, 388, 485
Levine, M., 11
Lindemann, E., 13, 516
Lowy, F., 92-94, 168, 337

Malan, D., chapters 4, 7, 10, 20, pp. 23, 85, 91, 121, 146, 166, 219, 222, 243, 261, 264, 304, 321, 362, 423, 468, 505, 528-529
Mann, A.M. 71-72, 258, 463, 484
Mann, J., 468
Marmor, J., chapter 1, pp. 74, 92, 96, 187, 190, 196, 198, 237, 306, 378
Menninger, K., 333
Moll, A.E., 122-123, 217, 220, 259, 464
Motivation, 15, 17, 21-23, 28, 31, 36, 38, 59, 84, 88, 94, 143, 244-245, 271, 506, 518, 527-529, 533, 541, *see also* Ego, and chapter 3

and Psychotherapeutic Focus, 21-22
and Response to Interpretation, 95
Mourning and Grief, 39, 146, 465, 516

Naiman, J., 123-124, 141-142, 144, 258, 379, 403, 426, 464, 488
Nemiah, J., 187, 190, 192, 222, 239, 245, 463
Neurosis,
Narcissistic Neurosis, 10, 506, 518
Neurotic Compromise, 362
Obsessive-Compulsive Neurosis, 52
Transference Neurosis, 10, 45, 80, *see also* Transference
Traumatic Neurosis, 79
Nunberg, 74

Oedipal, 19, 39, 49, 63, 117-119, 121, 124-125, 141, 163, 165-166, 190, 193, 216, 218, 222, 239, 241, 243, 259, 322, 326, 331, 338-339, 362-363, 378, 470, 505, 542
Inverted Oedipal Longing, 363
Oedipal Core, 324
Oedipal Depression, 169
Oedipal Focus, 326
Oedipal Pathology, 219
Oedipal Triumph, 378
Outcome,
Outcome Criteria, 25, 262, 510, 523
Outcome Evaluation, 387, 502, 503, 509, 511, 519, 521
Patient as the Evaluator of the Psychotherapeutic Process and Outcome, 381, chapters 9, 17
Psychodynamic Changes, 388, 511, 521, *see also* chapters 4, 23, 25
Psychotherapeutic Outcome, 41, 62, 64-65, 451, 509, 511, 512, 527, 528, 531, 533, 534
Past-Present Transference Link (P-P-T Link), *see* Interpretation
Placebo Response, 519
Pregenital, 19, 122, 125, 193, 217
Pregenital Characteriological Issue, 125, *see also* Characteriological Issues
Psychoanalysis, 2, 9-10, 12-13, 45, 74, 77, 79-80, 94, 238, 270, 287, 341, 344, 409, 488, 501, 515
Id-Analytic Theoretical Approach, 325

Psychodynamic, 9-13, 119, 141, 364, 388
  Psychodynamic Formulation, 21, 23, 27
  Psychodynamic Understanding, 7
Psychological-Mindedness, 15, 17, 28, 527, 529, 532-533, 541, *see also* Ego
Psychological Tests, 54, 87, 264, 470
Psychotherapeutic Alliance, 15, 39, 265, 344, 430, 451, 518
Psychotherapeutic Factors, 196-197, 345, *see also* chapter 23
Psychotherapeutic Process, 10, 198, 321, 507, 530
  in Broad-Focused Short-Term Dynamic Psychotherapy, 364-387, 410
Psychotherapy,
  Long-Term Psychotherapy, 509-510
  Negative Effect of Psychotherapy, 508, 511
  Psychoanalytic Psychotherapy, 9-10
  Supportive Psychotherapy, 75-77, 97, 287
Rank, O., 2, 340, 501
Rado, 10
Regression, 13-15, 19, 39, 162
  Ego Regression, 15
  Instinctual Regression, 13
  Regression and Symptom Formation, 14
  Regression in Psychoanalytic Treatment, 13
Research, 25, 502, 504, chapter 25
Resistance, 18, 31, 80, 261, 273, 303, 407, 466, 517, 530, 533

Self-Esteem, 41, 219-220, 262, 504
  Disturbances of Self-Esteem, 220
  Negative Self-Esteem and Short-Term Dynamic Psychotherapy, 219
  Postitive Self-Esteem, 262
Sifneos, P.E., chapters 3, 6, 8, 11, 16, 18, 19, 22, pp. 15, 17, 23, 31, 88, 91, 118, 126, 142-143, 169, 187, 222, 245, 361, 452, 485, 528-529
Slip-of-the-Tongue in Short-Term Dynamic Psychotherapy, 427
"Spontaneous Remission," 511, 519, 531
Straker, M., chapter 24, pp. 95, 126, 259, 467, 487
Strupp, H., chapter 23, pp, 259, 404, 409, 418, 464, 484
Superego, 12, 14, 20
  Structure and Function of the Superego, 14, 20, *see also* chapter 2

Teaching and Supervision, chapter 22, pp. 199, 245, 430
Transference, Countertransference in Supervisory Process, 494
Technique,
  Abreactive Technique, 78-79, 517
  Basic Psychotherapeutic Technique, 60, 71-98
  Broad-Focused Short-Term Dynamic Psychotherapy Technique, chapters 17, 21, pp. 23, 191
  Confrontation, 23, 40, 80, 262, 291, 302, 343, 463
  Manipulative Technique, 78-79
  Short-Term Anxiety-Provoking Psychotherapy Technique (S.T.A.P.P.), chapters 3, 16, 18, 19, p. 17
  Short-Term Dynamic Psychotherapy Technique, chapters 16, 20, p. 7
  Suggestive Technique, 78, 121, 324
  Technique of Broad-Focused Short-Term Dynamic Psychotherapy, chapters 5, 17, pp. 23, 25, 343-344
  Technique of Clarification, 23, 40, 78-80, 343, 517
  Technique of Interpretation, 9, 78-79
  Technique of Short-Term Anxiety-Provoking Psychotherapy, chapters 15, 16, 18, 19, pp. 39-41, 162
  Technique of Short-Term Dynamic Psychotherapy, chapters 15, 16, 17, 20, 21, pp. 60-62, 505, 509
  Technique of the Initial Interview, 120-121, 187, 192, 215, 270, 285
  Technique of the Initial Interview and Short-Term Dynamic Psychotherapy, 285, 291
Termination, 40, 61-62, 66, 332, 428, 467-468, 485-486, 497-498
  Analysis, Terminable and Interminable, 340
Transference, 2, 11, 16, 22, 25, 30, 37, 39-40, 43, 45, 50-51, 53, 57, 60, 62, 77, 80, 161-162, 168, 217, 221, 240, 275, 290, 331, 336, 341-342, 344-345, 362, 404, 427, 452, 465, 496, 503, 506, 517-519, 530, 534
  Intensive Transference Work, 362
  Maternal Transference, 241
  Multiple Transference, 4
  Negative Transference, 263, 265, 344-345, 496
  Parent-Transference Link, 60, 496, 505, 509

Positive Transference, 452
"Transference Cure," 82, 531
Transference Distortion, 273
Transference in Broad-Focused Short-Term Dynamic Psychotherapy, 344,
Transference Interpretation, 92, 94, 197, 321, 509, 518-519, 532
Transference Neurosis, 9-10, 16, 25, 51, 74, 77, 80-81, 241, 341-342, 452, 503-504
Transference Resistance, 427

Unconscious Dynamic, 96, 362
Unconscious Sense of Guilt, 489

Warnes, H., 425
Wolberg, L., 517

Yung, C., chapters 14, 25, pp. 305, 465

Zaiden, J., 259, 265; 485, 489
Zitzel, E., 16-17, 83, 124-125, 494